AN INDEX TO

THE WILLS PROVED IN THE

PREROGATIVE COURT OF CANTERBURY

1750 - 1800

Vol. I

A - Bh

edited by

ANTHONY J. CAMP, B.A. Hons.
Director of Research, Society of Genealogists

LONDON
The Society of Genealogists
1976

Published by

The Society of Genealogists,

37 Harrington Gardens,

London SW7 4JX

(c) Society of Genealogists, 1976

ISBN 0 901878 18 9

PREFACE

Indexes to the Wills proved in the Prerogative Court of Canterbury and now preserved in the Public Record Office, London, have been printed from their commencement in 1383 to 1700, mainly by the British Record Society in the series known as the Index Library. That Society does not intend to continue the work beyond 1700 until similar indexes to the Wills proved in the local English and Welsh courts, of which there are about three hundred, have been published to a similar date. At the present rate of progress this will take many years.

A manuscript index on cards covering the first half of the eighteenth century exists in private possession and although it is at present inaccessible and is thought to be incomplete I decided to concentrate on the later period 1750–1800 and attempt to compile an index to the Wills proved and Administrations granted in that time. By 1750 the Prerogative Court of Canterbury was proving Wills and granting Administrations at a rate of about 7,000 a year, and this number had grown to about 12,000 a year by 1800. It was the supreme court in the British Isles for the probate of wills, and because of the great prestige of its acts and the greater safety of its records it had attracted the probate of wills of men of substance at least since the Reformation. The Bank of England acknowledged no probate other than of this court, and the wills of persons who died abroad possessing property in this country were almost invariably proved there. Because of this there survives amongst its records copies of the wills of numerous Irish and colonial persons which had a second probate there and which have not survived in their own countries, and particularly in the period under consideration, of thousands of bi-national Hollanders and other Europeans who had invested money in the British funds (and again whose wills may not have survived or be easily accessible in their own countries). It was of course also the 'local court' for those possessing property in more than two dioceses in the Province of Canterbury and thus contains the wills of a great number of people in the south of England and particularly in the Home Counties (excepting Kent where the Archbishop's powers had been delegated to his commissary general), as also for those who had property in both the provinces of Canterbury and York.

The only means of reference to these records was the series of contemporary manuscript calendars arranged in chronological order and subdivided by the first letter of the surname only. Towards the end of the eighteenth century fifteen or twenty minutes might be needed to search through a year's entries in these calendars for a single surname and a search over several years when the exact date of death was not known could sometimes be a very lengthy task. There are three or four sets of these calendars, one set having been used in the Literary Department at the Principal Probate Registry and another in the Public Search Room there, and individual volumes having been copied again as they became faint and worn. One of these sets was borrowed by the Society of Genealogists and between 1968 and 1973 volunteers were organised to write slips for the half million entries they contained. These were then sorted into strict alphabetical order, no attempt being made to sort variants of surnames together or to cross-reference them, the will references (about 330,000) being kept separate from the administrations (about 170,000). It is from this slip index that the present index is being typed.

It has long been recognised that the calendars from which this index is compiled are not complete. From the work done on the late seventeenth century calendars it has been calculated that references to about a tenth of the filed original and register copy wills were accidentally omitted. There is no reason to expect that the compilers of the later calendars were any more careful. However, the immense labour of checking the calendars against the Act Books, the Original Wills and the Register Copy Wills was clearly impossible in this case with the resources available and in any case beyond my intention of providing an interim index in a relatively short period. However, it is important that users of this index should realise its limitations. In

3

the first place it remains almost impossible without such a check to detect errors in the calenders carried from one to another or created in their recopying over the years. Some may be guessed at as when an I has been crossed in error to produce a t, thus accounting for the name Donatty, or left uncrossed to produce such names as Palrick. A misplaced dot converted Donoghue to Donogline. In the second place there are undoubtedly a large number of errors resulting from the peculiar handwriting of the manuscript calendars. The uprights and adjoining lines are identical in and between i, m, n and u, so that Cumming has eleven identical strokes, relieved only by the dot over the i. The commonest errors therefore result from the confusion of n and u, of m, in, ui and ni, and particularly of the pairs im, mi, nn, nu and un, due in part to over-looking the dot on the i. Thus such names as Dunsey, De Luna, Druig and Dunns, appear instead of Dimsey, De Lima, Dring and Dinnis. The capitals I and J being formed in the same way produced names like Juge and Juman instead of Inge and Inman. The letters c, r and t, which are very similarly written are another cause of confusion (producing names like Jonachan) and z was often copies as r. The long s used in the calendar as the first of a pair of ss, was often copied as f or I, as in Belse for Besse. The double FF in capitals has been eliminated as far as possible. The second loop of the letter w, mistaken for o, caused such errors as Dekroer and De Leemo for Dekewer and De Leeuw, and Andrevo for Andrew. The confusion of g and y led to such oddities as Curlucy for Curling, and q was sometimes copied as g. Again in the indexing h and li were also confused; and e was very frequently copied as o, as in Ponelope.

Great care has been taken to discover and correct as many of these errors as possible. Thousands of doubtful entries spotted in the sorting and typing have been checked against the calendars now in use at the Public Record Office which are clearer and probably more accurate than those used by the indexers. Nevertheless, many errors have almost certainly gone undetected, especially where the incorrect name produced by an indexer is also a known surname (e.g. Baron for Bacon). This is also so where a letter has been omitted, converting for example Davies into Davis or Woods into Wood. There may be other errors or omissions due either to the fading of the parchment or to carelessness, but I hope that these have been reduced to a minimum by the checking which has taken place. However, if all the above possible variations are taken into account and an entry is not found in this index which might with good cause be expected to be there I can only suggest that the Probate Act Books at the Public Record Office be searched. The folio numbers given in the calendars are not infrequently found to be incorrect, but if a will is not found registered in the folio indicated those on either side should be searched. For names with two or more variants the folio number is often found entered under only one of the names. All such aliases are cross referenced in this index. It will be noted that many only appear at the time of second or subsequent grants.

It only remains to add that the only other published index to any part of the probate records of the Prerogative Court of Canterbury which relates to this period covers the Inventories from 1750 to 1782 (List and Index Society, vol. 86, 1973) but as there is only about one inventory filed for each eight hundred grants and two-thirds of these relate to administrations and not to wills they are little help as a check in this instance.

Anthony J. Camp
January, 1976.

Society of Genealogists,
37 Harrington Gardens,
London SW7 4JX.

4

ACKNOWLEDGEMENTS

The duplicate series of calendars then at the Principal Probate Registry from which this index was compiled were most kindly made available to us by the Senior Registrar, Sir John Compton Miller, and by the Record Keeper, their existence having first been pointed out to me by Miss Alice Stanley then Superintendent of the Literary Department. She and her assistant, the late W.E.H. Cheape, were particularly helpful in all the subsequent arrangements. I am grateful to the Principal Registry and to the Public Record Office which now has the care of all the records mentioned for permission to publish this index.

Those who wrote index slips for individual volumes were M.A. Byrne (1761 A-B), Anthony J. Camp (1770, 1776 U-Z), Mrs J. Crawley (1796), I.E. Dickens (1779), A.R. Dickins (1759), Philip Dyke (1781, 1799 F-Z, 1800 B-Z), K.J. Dyer (1762), G.K.S. Hamilton-Edwards (1794), V.P. Elliott (1787), W.S. Field (1789), Mrs M.J. Hadaway (1792, 1798), Mrs Joyce Hanson (1769), A.S. Harcourt (1784), David Hawkings (1771), Mrs E.B. Hilken (1765), Miss Mary Hollingsworth (1773, 1774), Col and Mrs H.S.P. Hopkinson (1768 A-G), P. Horsley (1783), A.J. Howard (1791), S.H. Jollye (1799 A-E), Edward Legg (1777), Miss J.M. Masters (1750, 1752, 1755, 1758, 1763, 1766, 1768 H-Z, 1772,1785 Administrations, 1795), Dr W.E.D. Moore (1788), Miss J. Mount (1757), Mrs R.A. Newland (1767), W.B. Pearman (1778), J.L. Rayment (1753, 1786), G.M. Smart (1760), Miss A. Stanley (1754), Mrs Brenda Swain (1790), the late Commander P.C. Patten-Thomas (1776 A-T), F.J. Thomason (1751, 1756, 1780), Mrs M. Tisdall (1761 C-Z, 1775), Clifford Towse (1800 A), J.A.S. Trydell (1793), Michael L. Walker (1764), Mrs Margaret Whicher (1797), Mrs F.B.L. Wood (1785 Wills), and M.J. Wood (1782), the cost of the slips themselves being generously borne by Dr John E. Frost of New York. The sorting of the will slips was completed by Miss J.M. Masters, M.J. Wood and myself with the assistance of Dr Joseph Druse. Miss Masters and Mr Wood checked the many hundreds of doubtful entries marked by the slip writers and others which were noted during the sorting. Miss Masters who had already written slips for ten volumes also completely checked the entries in eight others where the slip writers appeared to have had difficulties. Without her enormous energy and patience this project would probably never have been completed. Mr Wood has been responsible for all the work so far done in the sorting and checking of the administration slips and I am indebted to him for the notes on the difficulties encountered by the slip writers which I have incorporated in the Preface.

J.A.S. Trydell and G.K.S. Hamilton-Edwards generously paid for the typing and checking of letter A, the typing being the work of Mrs Doreen Cowan. The typing of letter B, the work of the West One Secretarial Services, was paid for partly by Dr Frost and partly from search fees and funds provided by the Society of Genealogists. S.C.G. Bach, J.S.W. Gibson, G.K.S. Hamilton-Edwards and R.W. Massey checked B-BAR, and I completed the ramainder.

The considerable labour of compiling indexes of this kind is rarely recognised by their users and because of this I have recorded here the part played by some who would not have wished for any particular credit but to whom generations of users will have cause to be indebted for their patience and care.

A.J.C.

ABBREVIATIONS

A	Administration	Gt	Grant
Aberd	Aberdeen	Guery	Guernsey
Angly	Anglesey	G.V.	Gun Vessel
Anor	Another	Hants	Hampshire
Apr	April	Haver	Haverfordwest
Archbp	Archbishop	Herfd	Herefordshire
Aug	August	Herts	Hertfordshire
A with W (or AwW)	Administration with Will annexed	Hon	Honourable
Beds	Bedfordshire	Hull	Kingston upon Hull
Berks	Berkshire	Hunts	Huntingdonshire
Bp	Bishop	Int	Interlocutory
Brcon	Brecon	Int Dec(r)	Interlocutory Decree
Brstl	Bristol	IOW	Isle of Wight
Bucks	Buckinghamshire	Irel	Ireland
Bwick	Berwick on Tweed	Jan	January
By dec(r)	By decree	Jersy	Jersey
By int dec(r)	By interlocutory decree	Jly	July
By sen(t)	By sentence	Jne	June
Camb	Cambridgeshire	Jny	January
Cardn	Cardiganshire	Jul	July
Carmn	Carmarthenshire	Jun	June
Carvn	Caernarvonshire	Kt	Knight
Chesr	Cheshire	Lancr	Lancaster
Chest	Chester	Lancs	Lancashire
Chich	Chichester	Ld	Lord
Cntby	Canterbury	Leics	Leicestershire
Cod	Codicil	Lichd	Lichfield
Corn	Cornwall	Lieut	Lieutenant
Coven	Coventry	Lincs	Lincolnshire
Ct	Court	Lond	London
Cumb	Cumberland	Ltd	Limited
Dbl(e) Pr(ob)	Double Probate	Ly	Lady
Dec	December	Mar	March
Dec(r)	Decree	Mch	March
Denbh	Denbighshire	Middx	Middlesex
Dorst	Dorset	Mgomy	Montgomery
Dr	Doctor	Mon	Monmouthshire
Dr Dy	Doctor of Divinity	Mrion	Merionethshire
Dubln	Dublin	M.S.	Merchant Ship
Durhm	Durham	Mth	Month
Edin	Edinburgh	Mt.S.	Merchant Ship
E.I.	East India	NBrit(ain)	North Britain
E.I.C.	East India Company	Newcl	Newcastle upon Tyne
E.I.C.S.	East India Company Service	Nhant	Northamptonshire
E.I.Mt.S.	East India Merchant Ship	Nland	Northumberland
E.I.S.	East India Service or Ship	Norf	Norfolk
Exter	Exeter	Notts	Nottinghamshire
Feb	February	Nov	November
Gds	Goods	NSarm	New Sarum (Salisbury)
Glam	Glamorgan	Nunc	Nuncupative
Glos	Gloucestershire	Nwich	Norwich

Oct	October		
Oxon	Oxfordshire		
Pemb	Pembrokeshire		
Phys	Physic		
Prev	Previous		
Pr(ob)	Probate		
Proc Gen	Procurator General		
Pts	Foreign Parts (may apply to any place outside the British Isles)		
Rad	Radnorshire		
Regd	Registered		
Regt	Regiment		
Rev	Reverend		
Rgd	Registered		
Rt	Right		
Roch	Rochester		
Roy	Royal		
Rutld	Rutland		
Salop	Shropshire		
Sched	Schedule		
Sen(t)	Sentence		
Sep	September		
Ser(v)	Service (i.e. other ranks in the Army and ratings in the Royal Navy; not officers; with seamen the name(s) of the ship(s) on which they have recently served is often given, shown in inverted commas)		
Sfolk	Suffolk		
SHant	Southampton		
Som	Somerset		
Sp(ec) Pr(ob)	Special Probate		
Staff	Staffordshire		
Sthl	Southall		
Strat	Stratford		
Surry	Surrey		
Sussex	Sussex		
Tble	Treble		
Test(y)	Testamentary		
Unad(m)	Unadministered		
W	Will		
Wark	Warwickshire		
Wilts	Wiltshire		
W.I.S.	West India Ship		
Winch	Winchester		
Wmord	Westmorland		
Worcs	Worcestershire		
Yorks	Yorkshire		

Note: Since the transfer of the records of the Prerogative Court of Canterbury to the Public Record Office a system of numerical identification has been adopted in place of the personal names whereby each year of registered wills was formerly known. However, the names for the years 1700-1800 are given below as a guide to those references in the index which have not been converted into years:

Abbott, 1729	Caesar, 1763	Henchman, 1739	Price, 1733
Adderley, 1800	Calvert, 1788	Heme, 1702	Richmond, 1723
Alexander, 1775	Cheslyn, 1761	Herring, 1757	Rockingham, 1784
Anstis, 1744	Collier, 1777	Holman, 1794	Romney, 1725
Arran, 1759	Collins, 1780	Howe, 1799	Rushworth, 1765
Ash, 1704	Cornwallis, 1783	Hutton, 1758	St Eloy, 1762
Aston, 1714	Degg, 1703	Isham, 1731	Searle, 1753
Auber, 1730	Derby, 1736	Jenner, 1770	Secker, 1768
Bargrave, 1774	Dodwell, 1793	Lane, 1709	Seymer, 1745
Barnes, 1712	Ducarel, 1785	Leeds, 1713	Shaller, 1720
Barrett, 1708	Ducie, 1735	Legard, 1767	Simpson, 1764
Bedford, 1732	Dyer, 1701	Lisle, 1749	Smith, 1710
Bellas, 1776	Edmunds, 1746	Lynch, 1760	Spurway, 1741
Bettesworth, 1752	Eedes, 1706	Macham, 1789	Stevens, 1773
Bevor, 1791	Exeter, 1797	Major, 1787	Strahan, 1748
Bishop, 1790	Fagg, 1715	Marlbro, 1722	Taverner, 1772
Bogg, 1769	Farrant, 1727	Newcastle, 1795	Tenison, 1718
Bolton, 1724	Fountain, 1792	Noel, 1700	Trenley, 1742
Boycott, 1743	Fox, 1716	Norfolk, 1786	Trevor, 1771
Brodrepp, 1738	Gee, 1705	Ockham, 1734	Tyndall, 1766
Brook, 1728	Glazier, 1756	Paul, 1755	Wake, 1737
Browne, 1740	Gostling, 1782	Pinfold, 1754	Walpole, 1798
Browning, 1719	Greenly, 1750	Plymouth, 1726	Warburton, 1779
Buckingham, 1721	Harris, 1796	Poley, 1702	Webster, 1781
Busby, 1751	Hay, 1778	Potter, 1747	Whitfield, 1717
			Young, 1711

1762	AA, Clara Rebecca VAN DER	Pts	Feb	84
1768	AA, Cornelis VAN DER (Ltd Pr)	Pts	Jne	260
1778	AA, Josua VAN DER (Ltd Pr)	Pts	Nov	470
1772	AA, Pedro, otherwise Pierre VAN DER AwW	Pts	Dec	--
1798	AALST, Andries VAN	Pts	Aug	570
1756	AALST, Cornelius VAN, Lord of Soetermeer (Ltd Pr)	Pts	Oct	266
1774	AALST, Rt Noble & Awful Hendrik Balthazar VAN	Pts	Jne	248
1789	AARDENSTOFF, Daniel VAN (Ltd Pr)	Pts	Jne	337
1755	AARDENSTOFF, Pieter VAN (Ltd Pr)	Pts	Jne	177
1769	AARON, Frances (sent)	Worcs	Jne	193
1752	AARON, George	Surry	Jly	176
1795	AARON, Isaac	Lond	Apr	232
1769	AARON, John	Worcs	Nov	363
1755	AARON, Richard	Berks	Jne	153
1764	AARON, William	Worcs	Aug	295
1781	AARONSON, otherwise ARONSON, Aaron	Pts	Nov	510
1781	AARSEN, Rt Hon Ly Maria Cornelia, Baroness of Wassenaen, Ly Ruyven VAN	Pts	Jly	272
1760	AARTSEN, otherwise AARTSAI, Cornelia (Ltd Pr)	Pts	Jny	1
1789	AARTSEN, Jacobus	Pts	Jny	1
1760	AARTZAI, otherwise AARTSEN, Cornelia (Ltd Pr)	Pts	Jny	1
1755	AARTZEN, Elisabeth	Pts	Jne	153
1778	ABADHAM, John	Essex	Oct	385
1750	ABADHAM, Josiah (AwW rgd Dec last)	Pts	Apr	--
1759	ABARBANEL, Abigail	Lond	Oct	316
1777	ABARBANEL, David	Lond	Feb	50
1777	ABARBANEL, Hannah	Lond	Mar	93
1790	ABARBANEL, Jael	Lond	Sep	409
1788	ABARBANEL, Rachel	Lond	Nov	518
1759	ABBADIE, Francis D' AwW	Middx	Apr	117
1793	ABBADIE, Jane D' AwW	Middx	Apr	197
1799	ABEE, Pierre L' AwW	Middx	Apr	288
1771	ABBEMA, Catherina Abbema VAN KINSCHOT, formerly (Ltd Pr)	Pts	Sep	391
1760	ABBEMA, Jacoba Agnes (Ltd Pr)	Pts	Apr	134
1791	ABBEMA, Jacoba Mathia (Ltd Pr)	Pts	Sep	414
1795	ABBETT, Daniel	Kent	Feb	61
1764	ABBETT, George	Dorst	Apr	128
1750	ABBETT, Mary	Middx	Apr	101
1763	ABBETT, Robert	Pts	Sep	415
1760	ABBETT, otherwise ABBITT, otherwise ABBOTT, Samuel	Som	Sep	346
1785	ABBEY, John	Rutld	Apr	168
1782	ABBEY, Jonathan	Middx	Dec	569
1783	ABBEY, otherwise ABBY, Joseph	Yorks	May	210
1758	ABBEY, Marmaduke	Devon	Apr	99
1760	ABBEY, Mary	Devon	May	180
1757	ABBEY, Robert	Devon	Jny	1

1762	ABBEY, Robert AwW of Gds unadm W rgd 1757, 1	Devon	Feb	--
1777	ABBEY, Robert	Nhant	Jne	251
1768	ABBEY, Thomas	Lond	Feb	41
1768	ABBEY, Thomas Dble Pr, W rgd Feb last	Lond	Apr	--
1788	ABBEY, Thomison	Midlx	Jne	281
1786	ABBEY, William	Rutld	Mch	133
1781	ABBIS, Thomas, The Hon.	Middx	Jny	1
1794	ABBIS, William	Lond	Nov	535
1779	ABBISS, Elizabeth	Surry	May	185
1758	ABBISS, James	Surry	Jly	207
1770	ABBISS, John	Surry	Sep	319
1760	ABBITT, otherwise ABBETT, otherwise ABBOTT, Samuel	Som	Sep	346
1758	ABBON, Robert, Esq.	Norf	Oct	283
1761	ABBOT, Alexander	Middx	Jly	239
1789	ABBOT, Alice	Middx	Jny	1
1779	ABBOT, Catherine	Kent	Jne	230
1787	ABBOT, Eleanor HUGHES, formerly	Middx	May	217
1800	ABBOT, Elizabeth	Dorst	Jly	499
1799	ABBOT, Frances	Cntby	Nov	756
1756	ABBOT, John	Pts	Oct	266
1760	ABBOT, Dr John (Dr Dy)	Essex	May	180
1764	ABBOT, John	Nhant	Oct	376
1766	ABBOT, John	Middx	Apr	125
1766	ABBOT, John Dble Pr, W rgd this month	Middx	Apr	--
1794	ABBOT, John Farr	Middx	Oct	485
1790	ABBOT, otherwise ABBOTT, Joseph	Sussx	Jny	1
1798	ABBOT, Lœtitia	Kent	Jne	377
1779	ABBOT, Leonard	Yorks	Nov	440
1787	ABBOT, Mary	Lond	Jne	251
1751	ABBOT, Thomas	Kent	Mch	70
1762	ABBOT, Thomas	Pts	Nov	444
1768	ABBOT, William (late one of Proc Gen of Arches Ct of Cntby)	Lond	Sep	336
1796	ABBOT, William (late one of Proc Gen of Arches Ct of Cntby)	Kent	Sep	439
1760	ABBOT, Walter	Devon	Dec	449
1770	ABBOTT, Abraham	Middx	Dec	420
1765	ABBOTT, Ann OSBALDISTON, formerly	Lond	Feb	71
1780	ABBOTT, Ann	Essex	Jne	299
1790	ABBOTT, Ann	Sthl	Jny	1
1795	ABBOTT, Anthony	Lond	Jne	360
1760	ABBOTT, Bartholomew AwW	Pts	Jny	227
1780	ABBOTT, Benjamin	Lond	Mch	117
1793	ABBOTT, Charles	Kent	Aug	397
1770	ABBOTT, Christopher	Middx	Nov	387
1758	ABBOTT, Daniel	Pts	Apr	100
1795	ABBOTT, Daniel	Middx	Jny	2
1752	ABBOTT, David	Pts	Dec	292
1781	ABBOTT, Elizabeth	Middx	Oct	459
1791	ABBOTT, Elizabeth	Kent	Aug	368
1795	ABBOTT, Elizabeth	Sfolk	Jny	2

1751	ABBOTT, Ester	Lond	Mch	70
1783	ABBOTT, Francis	Essex	Jne	277
1792	ABBOTT, Ffrancis AwW of Gds unadm			
	W rgd 1783, 277	Essex	Apr	--
1756	ABBOTT, George AwW	Pts	Nov	286
1756	ABBOTT, George	Middx	Nov	286
1783	ABBOTT, George Ser	Pts	Aug	397
1790	ABBOTT, Henry	Dorst	Jny	1
1791	ABBOTT, James (by int decree)	Middx	Jny	314
1794	ABBOTT, James AwW	Kent	Apr	181
1797	ABBOTT, James	Middx	Mch	126
1798	ABBOTT, James	Middx	Aug	523
1798	ABBOTT, James	Surry	Dec	755
1776	ABBOTT, Jane	Lond	Jne	253
1782	ABBOTT, Jeremiah	Kent	Apr	161
1753	ABBOTT, John	Lond	Dec	307
1756	ABBOTT, John	Essex	Mch	58
1760	ABBOTT, John	Lond	Feb	45
1767	ABBOTT, John	Middx	Nov	399
1768	ABBOTT, John	Dorst	Jly	265
1782	ABBOTT, John	Lond	Oct	478
1785	ABBOTT, John	Cntby	Jly	350
1787	ABBOTT, John	Middx	Jly	308
1787	ABBOTT, John	Middx	Nov	479
1796	ABBOTT, John	Essex	Aug	393
1796	ABBOTT, John	Camb	Sep	439
1797	ABBOTT, John	Som	Oct	624
1772	ABBOTT, Jonathan	Bucks	Jny	1
1793	ABBOTT, Jonathan	Bucks	Apr	179
1790	ABBOTT, otherwise ABBOT, Joseph	Sussx	Jny	1
1790	ABBOTT, Joseph	Essex	Jne	275
1800	ABBOTT, Joseph Samuel	Middx	Mch	171
1785	ABBOTT, Leonard AwW of Gds unadm			
	W rgd Nov 1779	Yorks	May	--
1793	ABBOTT, Leonard	Yorks	Dec	578
1766	ABBOTT, Mark	Lond	Feb	45
1765	ABBOTT, Mary	Dorst	Jne	205
1770	ABBOTT, Mary	Herts	Mch	84
1780	ABBOTT, Mary	Lond	Mch	118
1800	ABBOTT, Mercy	Middx	Mch	171
1750	ABBOTT, Michael	Lond	Oct	313
1791	ABBOTT, Philip	Middx	Feb	52
1757	ABBOTT, Richard	Middx	Feb	37
1777	ABBOTT, Richard	Herts	May	195
1784	ABBOTT, Richard Ser. "Assurance"	Pts	Nov	583
1755	ABBOTT, Robert, Esq.	Midlx	Jly	180
1760	ABBOTT, otherwise ABBITT, otherwise			
	ABBETT, Samuel	Som	Sep	346
1762	ABBOTT, Samuel AwW	Pts	Oct	408
1783	ABBOTT, Samuel	Hunts	Sep	441
1796	ABBOTT, Samuel	Essex	Aug	393
1770	ABBOTT, formerly WILTON, Sarah (Ltd Pr)	Middx	Jly	251
1787	ABBOTT, Sarah	Middx	Sep	395

1763	ABBOTT, Septimus		Kent	Jly	320
1764	ABBOTT, Sparrow		Kent	Oct	376
1766	ABBOTT, Stephen		Pts	Jly	255
1782	ABBOTT, Stephen		Lond	Apr	161
1787	ABBOTT, Stephen		Surry	Dec	528
1783	ABBOTT, Susanna		Middx	Sep	442
1766	ABBOTT, Susannah		Wark	Apr	125
1754	ABBOTT, Thomas		Surry	May	123
1762	ABBOTT, Thomas		Berks	Sep	365
1762	ABBOTT, Thomas		Bucks	Oct	408
1765	ABBOTT, Thomas		Bucks	Dec	438
1780	ABBOTT, Thomas		Kent	Jny	1
1797	ABBOTT, Thomas		Surry	Apr	221
1753	ABBOTT, William AwW		Lond	Jny	1
1755	ABBOTT, William		Oxon	Jny	1
1755	ABBOTT, William		Kent	May	121
1759	ABBOTT, William		Devon	Sep	287
1760	ABBOTT, William		Exter	Oct	378
1762	ABBOTT, William		Lond	Jny	1
1763	ABBOTT, William	Pts -	Middx	Mch	103
1795	ABBOTT, William		Middx	Feb	61
1797	ABBOTT, William AwW		Middx	Apr	220
1800	ABBOTT, William		Berks	Sep	641
1800	ABBS, Cooper, Rev. AwW		Durhm	Oct	697
1785	ABBS, otherwise APPS, John, "Sultan"		Pts	Jne	288
1759	ABBUTT, Ann		Essex	Dec	381
1751	ABBUTT, Henry Ltd AwW of Gds unadm				
	W rgd 1701, 14 Last Grant Feb 1739/40		Essex	Jan	--
1772	ABBY, Daniel		Middx	Dec	429
1783	ABBY, otherwise ABBEY, Joseph		Yorks	May	210
1781	ABBY, Robert		Middx	Jny	2
1782	ABCHURCH, John		Middx	May	211
1775	ABDY, Anthony Thomas, Sir		Essex	Apr	126
1760	ABDY. Elizabeth		Essex	Jly	271
1800	ABDY. Esther		Lond	Sep	639
1792	ABDY, Harriot		Essex	Mch	124
1767	ABDY, Joanna		Middx	Apr	120
1759	ABDY, John, Sir		Essex	Apr	115
1780	ABDY, Martha		Middx	Feb	53
1792	ABDY, Dame Katherine		Middx	Oct	495
1773	ABDY, Rev. Stotherd, Archdeacon of Essex		Essex	May	190
1790	ABDY, William		Lond	Sep	409
1795	ABEAR, Alice		Oxon	May	294
1771	ABEAR, John		Berks	Nov	428
1795	ABEAR, John		Berks	Oct	578
1776	ABEARN, William		Hunts	May	209
1763	ABEDWARD, Edward	Pts -	Rad	Oct	457
1759	ABEL, Ann		Middx	Jne	191
1773	ABEL, Elizabeth		Middx	Apr	144
1775	ABEL, Ester		Middx	Apr	126
1772	ABEL, Francis		Middx	Mch	81
1796	ABEL, Henry		Kent	Jly	343
1767	ABEL, John		Surry	Dec	435
1771	ABEL, Margaret		Surry	Jly	283

1772	ABEL, Robert	Middx	Jne	202
1766	ABEL, William	Middx	Jne	210
1771	ABELEVEN, Gertruida Jacoba (Ltd Pr)	Pts	Oct	395
1760	ABELEVEP, Johannes	Pts	Nov	412
1770	ABELL, Ann	Middx	Jny	1
1759	ABELL, Anne	Middx	Nov	346
1792	ABELL, Anthony AwW	Derby	Jne	313
1784	ABELL, Bartholomew	Middx	May	243
1777	ABELL, Elizabeth AwW of Gds unadm W rgd 1731, 54	Surry	Jny	--
1784	ABELL, Elizabeth	Bucks	May	244
1750	ABELL, James	Pts	Feb	35
1757	ABELL, John	Middx	Sep	265
1768	ABELL, John	Lond	Aug	305
1777	ABELL, John W rgd 1737, 216	Lond	Jny	--
1783	ABELL, otherwise ABLE, John Ser.	Pts	Jly	332
1754	ABELL, Richard	Middx	Jny	1
1759	ABELL, Richard, Esq.	Surry	Mch	80
1760	ABEN, otherwise EBIN, Jacob	Pts	Mch	85
1759	ABENATAR, Abraham	Pts	Apr	115
1782	ABENATAR, David, otherwise ABENATAR, David Haim, otherwise VAN DER CROON, David	Pts	Apr	163
1776	ABENATAR, Jacob the Younger, otherwise ABENATAR, Jacob, otherwise Francisco de MELO, the Younger		Aug	343
1760	ABENCAR, Vega Moses	Pts	Mch	85
1756	ABENDANA MENDES, Judica (Ltd Pr)	Pts	Jly	186
1760	ABENDANA DE BRITTO, Haim Isaac	Pts	Jne	242
1766	ABENSUR, Reina	Lond	Feb	45
1776	ABERCORN, Rt Hon Ly Ann, Countess Dowager of	Middx	Aug	343
1754	ABERCORN, Rt Hon Elizabeth, late Countess Dowager of	Middx	Mch	66
1789	ABERCORN, Rt Hon James, Earl of	Yorks	Oct	481
1761	ABERCROMBIE, James AwW	Pts	Jly	239
1771	ABERCROMBIE, James	Pts - Kent	Aug	328
1775	ABERCROMBIE, James, Esq AwW	Pts	Oct	365
1791	ABERCROMBIE, Joanna	Kent	Nov	492
1757	ABERCROMBIE, John Ltd AwW	NBrit	Jly	211
1760	ABERCROMBIE, Mungo	Pts	Aug	312
1799	ABERCROMBIE, Sarah	Yorks	Mch	161
1778	ABERCROMBIE, Thomas	Pts	Mch	94
1761	ABERCROMBIE, William AwW	Pts	Oct	335
1791	ABERCROMBIE, William	Yorks	Sep	414
1791	ABERCROMBIE, Dr William (Dr of Phys) W rgd Sep last	Yorks	Nov	--
1792	ABERCROMBY, Burnet, Esq.	Middx	Apr	189
1767	ABERCROMBY, Francis	Middx	Sep	331
1772	ABERCROMBY, Francis AwW unadm W rgd 1767, 331	Middx	Apr	--
1775	ABERCROMBY, James, Esq	NBrit	Dec	454
1782	ABERCROMBY, James, Esq	NBrit	Nov	526
1780	ABERCROMBY, John	Pts	Jny	1

1799	ABERCROMBY, John	Surry	Apr 239
1767	ABERCROMBY, Robert	Middx	Sep 330
1774	ABERCROMBY, Robert W rgd 1767, 330	Middx	Aug --
1798	ABERDEEN, otherwise ABERDEIN, John E.I.S. "Alfred"	Pts	Jne 377
1778	ABERDEIN, Ann AwW	Middx	Mch 93
1798	ABERDEIN, otherwise ABERDEEN, John E.I.S. "Alfred"	Pts	Jne 377
1778	ABERDEIN, William	Middx	Jny 1
1778	ABERDORE, Thomas	Middx	Oct 385
1770	ABERG, otherwise OBERG, otherwise OBERY, Jonas AwW	Pts	Nov 387
1778	ABERGAVENNY, otherwise PINCKE, otherwise PINKE, Elizabeth, commonly called Ly	Kent	Mch 127
1785	ABERGAVENNY, Rt Hon George, Earl of	Middx	Sep 452
1758	ABERGAVENNY, Rt Hon Rebecca, Ly Dowager	Herts	Nov 318
1762	ABERLE, otherwise ABERLEY, John	Pts	Jny 1
1762	ABERLEY, otherwise ABERLE, John	Pts	Jny 1
1765	ABERN, Francis	Oxon	Feb 40
1785	ABERNATHY, James E.I.S."London"	Dubln	Jly 350
1767	ABERNETHIE, George, Esq	Pts	Feb 33
1799	ABERRY, George "La Virginie"	Pts	Nov 757
1791	ABERRY, William	Surry	Dec 553
1793	ABERRY, William AwW of Gds unadm W rgd Dec 1791	Surry	Sep --
1785	ABERY, Anna Maria	Berks	Apr 168
1773	ABERY, Ann	Middx	Jly 276
1795	ABERY, Jane	Surry	Feb 61
1773	ABERY, Richard	Middx	Jny 1
1761	ABERY, Sarah	Berks	Dec 416
1789	ABERY, William	Berks	Jny 1
1764	ABINGDON, Anna Maria, Countess Dowager of	Middx	Mch 78
1757	ABINGDON, Rt Hon Mary, Countess Dowager of AwW	-	Jne 179
1763	ABINGDON, Rt Hon Mary, late Countess Dowager AwW of Gds unadm W rgd 1757, 179	Dorst	Feb --
1773	ABINGDON, Rt Hon Mary, late Countess Dowager of AwW of Gds twice unadm W rgd 1757, 179 Last grant Feb 1763	Dorst	Apr --
1760	ABINGDON, Rt Hon Willoughby, Earl of	Oxon	Jly 271
1800	ABINGDON, Rt Hon Willoughby Bertie, Earl of	Middx	May 336
1770	ABINGTON, Catherine	Middx	Jne 218
1786	ABINGTON, Jane	Middx	Mch 134
1761	ABINGTON, John, Esq	Lond	Oct 335
1764	ABINGTON, John	Middx	Mch 78
1770	ABINGTON, John Dble Pr W rgd 1762, 78	Middx	Aug --
1775	ABINGTON, Joseph AwW (by int decree)	Middx	Feb 37
1770	ABINGTON, Keziah	Middx	Sep 319
1774	ABINGTON, Sarah	Middx	Dec 418
1760	ABINGTON, Thomas	Middx	Apr 134

Year	Name	County	Month	Page
1789	ABLAINEY, Cornelia Charlotte Willemina, Baroness D' (Ltd Pr)	Pts	May	--
1768	ABLAING VAN GIESSENBURG, Philippina Susanna Elizabeth COTTRELL, formerly Baroness D' AwW	Middx	Sep	340
1751	ABLARD, Christopher	Lincs	Apr	101
1759	ABLE, John	Midlx	May	155
1783	ABLE, otherwise ABELL, John Ser	Pts	Jly	332
1781	ABLE, Thomas	Pts	Apr	179
1767	ABLESON, John	Lond	May	162
1800	ABLETT, Anthony "Kangaroo"	Pts	Mch	171
1760	ABLETT, Elizabeth	Middx	Feb	45
1767	ABLETT, Robert	Lond	Apr	122
1776	ABLETT, Sarah	Lond	Oct	410
1767	ABLETT, Thomas	Lond	Nov	399
1754	ABLETT, William	Lond	Nov	292
1751	ABLEY, Weaver	Nhant	May	130
1757	ABLIN, George	Middx	Aug	238
1769	ABLITT, Diana	Sfolk	Aug	271
1759	ABLITT, Edward	Sfolk	Jne	191
1799	ABLITT, John	Sfolk	Oct	694
1760	ABLITT, Joshua	Sfolk	Nov	412
1764	ABLITT, Thomas	Sfolk	Jne	210
1782	ABNEY, Elizabeth	Middx	Aug	390
1761	ABNEY, Dame Frances AwW	Leics	May	158
1790	ABNEY, George Frederick	Worcs	Feb	55
1750	ABNEY, Dame Mary	Middx	Feb	35
1798	ABNEY, Parnel	Leics	Jne	377
1750	ABNEY, Hon Sir Thomas, Knight, late one of Justices of H.M.'s Ct of Common Pleas A granted July last		Sep	285
1783	ABNEY, Thomas AwW	Wark	Dec	596
1791	ABNEY, Thomas, Esq	Derby	Nov	492
1800	ABNEY, William, Esq	Derby	Sep	640
1775	ABOAB OSORIO, otherwise OSORIO, Benjamin	Pts	Dec	452
1786	ABOAB, Isaac	Lond	Oct	500
1779	ABOLL, Elizabeth, formerly BOWMAN (Ltd Pr)	Essex	Nov	440
1786	ABORN, Thomas	Middx	Feb	60
1784	ABOROUGH, Yough, otherwise ALBERTS, Joachim, otherwise ALBRIGHT, Joshim, otherwise ALBOROUGH, Jochin E.I.S. "Major" "Superb" & "Monmouth"	Pts	Aug	425
1761	ABOTT, Margaret	Middx	Oct	335
1771	ABOURN, George	Middx	Jly	282
1773	ABOURN, George (Dble Pr) W rgd Jly 1771	Middx	Aug	--
1773	ABOURN, Mary	Middx	Oct	379
1760	ABRABANEL, Dame Ester, otherwise PINTO	Pts	Feb	46
1750	ABRABANEL DAVIDS, Isaac	Pts	Jny	1
1765	ABRABANEL SOUZA, Judith	Pts	Apr	127
1787	ABRAHALL, Frances	Worcs	Oct	436
1766	ABRAHALL, Rev John	Herfd	Feb	45

1773	ABRAHALL, John	Herfd	Dec	456
1794	ABRAHALL, Lettice	Herfd	Jny	1
1781	ABRAHAM, Alice	Kent	Sep	417
1758	ABRAHAM, Carsten, otherwise OBERAM, Carsen	Pts	Jne	194
1774	ABRAHAM, Charles	Middx	Mch	76
1790	ABRAHAM, Ebenezer	Bucks	Nov	491
1800	ABRAHAM, Edward	Bucks	Jne	430
1790	ABRAHAM, Elias	Middx	Apr	168
1766	ABRAHAM, Esther	Lond	Aug	290
1792	ABRAHAM, Esther	Shant	Jne	313
1789	ABRAHAM, George	Lond	Dec	571
1793	ABRAHAM, George	Lond	May	238
1751	ABRAHAM, otherwise METCALFE, Henry	Oxon	Jny	1
1770	ABRAHAM, Humphry Nendick	Shant	Mch	85
1764	ABRAHAM, James	Pts	Oct	376
1781	ABRAHAM, James	Pts	Aug	374
1752	ABRAHAM, John	Middx	Apr	82
1767	ABRAHAM, John	Middx	Jne	204
1752	ABRAHAM, Lawrence AwW	Pts	Jne	145
1756	ABRAHAM, Margaret	Lond	Aug	215
1760	ABRAHAM, Martha	Middx	Dec	449
1760	ABRAHAM, Moses AwW	Middx	Feb	45
1751	ABRAHAM, Richard	Middx	Mch	70
1778	ABRAHAM, otherwise ABRAM, Richard Ser	Pts	Jne	229
1798	ABRAHAM, Richard	Som	Jne	376
1791	ABRAHAM, Samuel (by int decree) A.granted this month	Lond	Apr	164
1774	ABRAHAM, Thomas	Shant	Dec	419
1784	ABRAHAM, Thomas AwW unadm W rgd 1774, 419	Shant	Mch	--
1794	ABRAHAM, Thomas	Bucks	Aug	402
1790	ABRAHAM, Thomas	Middx	Nov	491
1750	ABRAHAM, William	Surry	May	135
1774	ABRAHAM, William	Shant	Oct	357
1794	ABRAHAMS, Abran otherwise Abraham E.I.S."Hindostan"	Pts	Sep	443
1776	ABRAHAMS, Dorothy	Essex	Jny	1
1767	ABRAHAMS, Edward	Lond	Oct	360
1800	ABRAHAMS, Easter	Cambs	Aug	574
1756	ABRAHAMS, Hanna	Pts	Sep	236
1779	ABRAHAMS, Henry	Middx	Oct	401
1782	ABRAHAMS, Mary	Surry	Nov	526
1769	ABRAHAMS, Jan BRUYN (Ltd Pr)	Pts	Sep	301
1784	ABRAHAMS, Peter "Orpheus"	Pts	Oct	534
1759	ABRAHAMS, Robert	Pts	Jny	1
1779	ABRAHAMS, otherwise ABRAMS, Sipora	Pts	Jny	1
1754	ABRAHAMS, Thomas	Middx	Jly	187
1750	ABRAHAMS, Timothy	Worcs	Sep	285
1757	ABRAHAMSON, Errick, otherwise ABR ANSON, Erick	Pts	Sep	265
1767	ABRAHAMSZ, Daniel	Pts	Apr	145
1775	ABRAHAMSZ, Herman VAN LOON	Pts	Mch	120

1779	ABRAHAMSZ, Janvan Jarelink	Pts	Aug	333
1761	ABRAM, Francis	Essex	Apr	116
1778	ABRAM, otherwise ABRAHAM, Richard Ser	Pts	Jne	229
1780	ABRAM, Robert	Cambs	Apr	169
1760	ABRAM, William	Brstl	Mch	85
1787	ABRAM, William	Middx	Jny	1
1794	ABRAMS, John	Middx	Mch	119
1779	ABRAMS, otherwise ABRAHAMS, Sipora	Pts	Jny	1
1792	A'BRANDIS, Coenraad BRENDER (Ltd Pr)	Pts	Jny	1
1757	ABR ANSON, Erick, otherwise ABRAHAMSON, Errick	Pts	Sep	265
1783	ABRATHAT, Daniel	Shant	Apr	158
1756	ABRATHAT, William	Pts	May	128
1761	ABRATHAT, William	Pts	Dec	416
1763	ABRATHAT, William W rgd Dec 1761	Pts	May	--
1796	ABRAY, Robert AwW	Middx	Apr	159
1760	ABREE, William AwW	Shant	Jny	1
1782	ABRESCH, Frederik Lodewyk, otherwise Lord Frederik Lodewyk, Lord of Amerengen (Ltd Pr)	Pts	Nov	527
1787	ABREY, Daniel	Essex	Sep	395
1800	ABREY, Elicia	Essex	Jny	3
1751	ABREY, James	Berks	Jne	164
1779	ABREY, Samuel	Essex	Feb	37
1798	ABREY, Samuel	Essex	Aug	523
1774	ABREY, Thomas	Essex	Jly	253
1777	ABSALOM, Humphry	Surry	Jne	251
1779	ABSALOM, Mary	Surry	Dec	482
1777	ABSOLAM, Robert	Pts	Jly	296
1795	ABSOLON, Charles	Essex	May	294
1755	ABSOLON, Humphry	Berks	Aug	209
1756	ABSOLON, John	Berks	Apr	93
1761	ABSOLON, Mary	Middx	Dec	416
1777	ABSOLON, Mary	Berks	Aug	339
1773	ABSOLON, otherwise ASPLOM, Richard	Berks	Oct	379
1793	ABSOLON, William	Surry	Oct	487
1777	ABSOLUN, John	Berks	Jly	296
1799	ABSON, George, Esq.	Devon	Nov	757
1770	ABSON, Thomas	Pts	Jly	251
1779	ABUD, Richard	Middx	May	186
1774	ABUEARY, otherwise AWBERY, otherwise AUBERY, Elizabeth	Berks	Jly	252
1798	ABURN, John	Nwich	Jny	1
1777	ABURROW, John	Shant	Sep	374
1800	ABURROW, Mary	Shant	Sep	641
1771	ABURROW, Thomas	Shant	Sep	364
1778	ABURROW, William	Shant	Feb	45
1797	ABURROW, William AwW	Surry	Feb	66
1798	AB UTRECHT, Arent	Pts	Jne	376
1795	ACCAR, John	Kent	Jny	2
1754	ACERS, William	Oxon	Jne	157
1782	ACHARD, Antoine	Pts	Sep	437
1770	ACHARD, John	Middx	Oct	348

17

1777	ACHERY, Nicholas Claude Ambroise D', otherwise Nicholas D'	Middx	Mch	107
1788	ACHISON, Ellen, otherwise Elin	Staff	Nov	518
1764	ACHISON, otherwise ATKINSON, John	Pts	Aug	295
1762	ACHISON, otherwise ATKINSON, Poorteen	Pts	May	182
1768	ACHLEY, Elizabeth	Lond	Sep	336
1759	ACHONRY, Rt Rev Mordecai, Lord Bishop of KILLALLA and	Irel	Jly	238
1791	ACKERMAN, Abraham	Dorst	Apr	165
1757	ACKERMAN, John	Pts	Sep	265
1773	ACKERMANS, formerly SMITMAN, Cornelia Johanna (Ltd Pr)	Pts	Jly	277
1786	ACKERMANS, Pieternella (Ltd Pr)	Pts	Jny	1
1759	ACKERS, Charles, Esq.	Middx	Jne	191
1780	ACKERS, otherwise AKERS, otherwise ACRES, Edward AwW	Kent	Jny	1
1779	ACKERS, Elizabeth	Cntby	Jny	1
1759	ACKERS, Isaac	Pts	Dec	381
1789	ACKERSDYCK, Corridis Lambertus	Pts	Jly	343
1789	ACKERSDYCK, Hendrik Jacob (Ltd Pr)	Pts	Feb	70
1770	ACKERSDYCK, formerly VAN ECK, Maria Adriana (Ltd Pr)	Pts	May	170
1755	ACKERSDYK, Theodorus VAN	Pts	May	149
1800	ACKERVELT, Adriana Susanna	Pts	Aug	573
1764	ACKERVELT, Jan (Spec Pr)	Pts	Apr	129
1800	ACKERY, William Ser."Suffolk"	Pts	Feb	81
1761	ACKIN, James	Pts	Jne	199
1783	ACKLAM, Elizabeth	Middx	Aug	397
1800	ACKLAND, Charles	Lond	Jny	1
1795	ACKLAND, Dudley, Esq.	Kent	Nov	620
1779	ACKLAND, Margaret	Salop	Jly	283
1786	ACKLAND, Maria	Devon	Feb	60
1799	ACKLAND, Richard	Kent	May	331
1793	ACKLAND, Robert, Esq.	Middx	Feb	61
1799	ACKLAND, Robert "Crescent"	Pts	Apr	239
1794	ACKLAND, Sir Thomas Dyke, Bart.	Kent	Jne	293
1796	ACKLOM, Ann	Middx	Jny	2
1762	ACKLOW, Richard, Esq.	Notts	Mch	89
1778	ACKMAN, otherwise HICKMAN, Andrew AwW	Pts	Oct	385
1750	ACKRES, George, Esq.	Middx	Apr	101
1760	ACKRILL, William	Pts	Feb	45
1799	ACKROYD, Charles	Middx	Feb	89
1771	ACKROYD, John	Lond	Jne	240
1750	ACKWORTH, Mary	Surry	Apr	101
1771	ACLAND, Ann	Kent	May	191
1771	ACLAND, Arthur, Esq.	Som	Jly	282
1799	ACLAND, Gideon	Devon	Jne	413
1798	ACLAND, Hugh, Esq. AwW	Surry	May	306
1778	ACLAND, John Dyke, Esq.	Som	Dec	474
1793	ACLAND, Price	Kent	Apr	180
1785	ACLAND, Sir Thomas Dyke, Bart.	Devon	Apr	169
1766	ACLON, John	Pts	Sep	327
1792	ACOCK, otherwise TOWNSEND, George	Wark	Jne	356

1761	ACOCK, Henry	Pts	Feb	43
1774	ACOCK, Richard	Wark	Nov	384
1760	ACOCK, otherwise HAYCOCK, Robert	Pts	Aug	312
1792	ACOCKS, Samuel	Middx	Dec	593
1778	ACORST, George	Kent	Nov	427
1760	ACOTT, Catherine AwW	Lond	Apr	134
1754	ACOTT, Edward	Middx	Jly	187
1771	ACOTT, William	Middx	Jne	240
1793	ACOTT, William	Middx	Jly	349
1792	A'COURT, Charles	Dorst	Apr	189
1765	ACOURT, James, Esq.	Middx	Jny	1
1769	A'COURT ASHE, Pierce, Esq. (sent)	Wilts	Feb	32
1781	A'COURT ASHE, William, Esq., General of			
	H.M.Forces	Wilts	Aug	374
1785	ACRE, otherwise ACRES, John "Cumberland"	Pts	Sep	453
1800	ACREMAN, Ann	Som	Sep	639
1772	ACREMAN, Robert	Devon	Aug	282
1780	ACRES, otherwise AKERS, otherwise ACKERS,			
	Edward AwW	Kent	Jny	1
1792	ACRES, Elizabeth	Berks	Dec	593
1776	ACRES, Ezekiel	Surry	Jly	296
1785	ACRES, otherwise ACRE, John "Cumberland"	Pts	Sep	453
1759	ACRES, Joseph	Surry	Jny	1
1780	ACRES, Joseph	Herts	Oct	458
1791	ACRES, Randall	Essex	Jny	1
1764	ACRES, Rebecca	Middx	Jne	209
1788	ACRES, Thomas	Surry	Jne	281
1761	ACTON, Ann	Lond	Jly	239
1775	ACTON, Ann	Kent	Nov	399
1780	ACTON, Anne	Corn	Mch	118
1761	ACTON, Charles	Kent	Apr	115
1758	ACTON, Corbett	Lond	Sep	257
1762	ACTON, Rev Edward	Shant	Apr	136
1769	ACTON, Edward	Surry	Sep	299
1772	ACTON, Edward	Salop	Jly	243
1775	ACTON, Edward, Esq.	Salop	Oct	365
1775	ACTON, Rev Edward	Shant	Nov	400
1791	ACTON, Rev Edward	Middx	Apr	164
1760	ACTON, Elizabeth	Middx	Feb	45
1791	ACTON, Frances	Dorst	Mch	108
1793	ACTON, Hester	Middx	Apr	179
1776	ACTON, Rev James	Dorst	Mch	107
1759	ACTON, Jane	Brstl	Aug	255
1765	ACTON, Jane	Shant	May	166
1783	ACTON, Jane	Worcs	Jly	331
1762	ACTON, John	Pts	Mch	89
1775	ACTON, Rev John	Surry	Jly	259
1759	ACTON, Joseph	Lond	Aug	255
1772	ACTON, Joseph	Middx	Jly	244
1783	ACTON, Joseph Penn	Worcs	Apr	158
1795	ACTON, Nathaniel, Esq.	Sfolk	May	292
1754	ACTON, Oliver	Middx	May	123
1781	ACTON, Philip	Lancs	Jly	326

1782	ACTON, Philip AwW	Middx	Jly	334
1753	ACTON, Richard	Middx	Mch	69
1761	ACTON, Richard Ser	Pts	Dec	416
1792	ACTON, Sir Richard, Bart.	Salop	May	254
1766	ACTON, Sarah	Middx	Dec	439
1800	ACTON, Sarah	Surry	Mch	171
1789	ACTON, Susan AwW of Gds tw. unadm			
	Last grant March 1784	Surry	Nov	--
1784	ACTON, Susan AwW unadm W rgd Feb 1780,			
	53	Surry	Mch	--
1780	ACTON, Susan	Surry	Feb	53
1760	ACTON, Thomas	Lond	Sep	346
1793	ACTON, Thomas	Staff	Mch	124
1757	ACTON, William	Middx	Sep	265
1762	ACTON, William Spec AwW of Gds unadm			
	W rgd 1757, 265	Middx	Jly	--
1774	ACTON, William AwW	Pts	Jny	1
1782	ACTON, William	Lond	Jny	1
1787	ACTON, William	Worcs	Nov	480
1794	ACTON, William, Esq.	Middx	Feb	59
1795	ACTON, William	Middx	Jny	1
1799	ACTON, William	Salop	Aug	560
1781	ACWORTH, Abraham, Esq.	Middx	Apr	179
1768	ACWORTH, Delicia	Middx	Jne	224
1786	ACWORTH, Elizabeth	Kent	Feb	62
1769	ACWORTH, Gabriel, Esq.	Surry	Mch	73
1784	ADAIR, otherwise O'DAIR, Dennis	Pts	Jny	1
1782	ADAIR, James, Esq.	Middx	Jne	262
1798	ADAIR, James, Esq. AwW	Middx	Nov	691
1771	ADAIR, John	Middx	Apr	140
1794	ADAIR, John, Esq.	Middx	Sep	443
1766	ADAIR, Margaret	Berks	Aug	290
1750	ADAIR, Mary	Middx	Sep	285
1764	ADAIR, Patrick	Lond	Mch	79
1790	ADAIR, Robert, Esq., Surgeon Gen of			
	H.M.Forces, AwW	Middx	Apr	169
1798	ADAIR, Robert, Esq.	Glos	Feb	75
1798	ADAIR, Robert "Iphigenia"	Pts	May	306
1764	ADAIR, Thomas	Middx	May	162
1770	ADAIR, Rev. William	Shant	May	169
1781	ADAIR, William Ser.	Middx	Sep	417
1783	ADAIR, William, Esq.	Middx	Jly	331
1796	ADAIR, William	Pts	May	232
1757	ADAM, David AwW	Devon	Jne	179
1764	ADAM, David	Pts	Sep	335
1787	ADAM, Elizabeth	York	Jne	251
1783	ADAM, Helen	Middx	Sep	441
1753	ADAM, Henry AwW of Gds unadm W rgd			
	1742, 206	Surry	May	--
1771	ADAM, Henry	Surry	Aug	328
1771	ADAM, James Mc	Middx	Apr	168
1775	ADAM, James	NBrit	Jne	219
1794	ADAM, James, Esq.	Middx	Oct	484

```
1780  ADAM, John, Esq.                                        Middx  Sep  425
1790  ADAM, John                                              Cumb   Jly  317
1789  ADAM, Mary                                              NBrit  Oct  481
1792  ADAM, Robert, Esq.                                      Middx  Mch  124
1763  ADAM, Thomas                                            Surry  Jly  319
1779  ADAM, William, Esq.                                     Lichd  May  185
1760  ADAMES, William                                         Essex  Aug  312
1761  ADAMS, Abraham                                          Middx  Oct  336
1774  ADAMS, Abraham                                          Lond   Aug  289
1777  ADAMS, Abraham                                          Middx  Sep  374
1799  ADAMS, Abraham                                          Middx  Jly  472
1752  ADAMS, Ann                                              Chich  May  115
1753  ADAMS, Ann                                              Middx  Jne  158
1758  ADAMS, Ann                                              Middx  Jny    1
1762  ADAMS, Ann                                              Middx  Jny    1
1765  ADAMS, Ann                                              Middx  May  166
1767  ADAMS, formerly MORGAN, Ann                             Surry  May  161
1771  ADAMS, Ann                                              Lond   Dec  466
1772  ADAMS, Ann                                              Herts  Nov  390
1774  ADAMS, Ann                                              Lond   Aug  289
1775  ADAMS, Ann                                              Middx  Nov  400
1779  ADAMS, Ann                                              Essex  Jne  230
1780  ADAMS, Ann  AwW                                         Oxon   Jny    1
1784  ADAMS, Ann otherwise Anne                               Devon  May  244
1786  ADAMS, Ann                                              Middx  Jne  319
1791  ADAMS, Ann                                              Lond   Dec  553
1795  ADAMS, Ann                                              Surry  Nov  620
1797  ADAMS, Ann                                              Kent   Feb   67
1797  ADAMS, Ann                                              Som    Jne   --
1797  ADAMS, Ann                                              Essex  Jne  394
1793  ADAMS, Anna Marie                                       Middx  May  239
1757  ADAMS, Anne                                             Surry  Jly  211
1770  ADAMS, Anne                                             Winch  Apr  128
1760  ADAMS, Alexander otherwise Thomas  AwW                  Pts    Jne  227
1792  ADAMS, Alexander   (No ship)                            Pts    Jly  362
1751  ADAMS, Anthony                                          Berks  Sep  250
1785  ADAMS, Anthony                                          Oxon   Nov  536
1787  ADAMS, Anthony                                          Devon  Dec  527
1782  ADAMS, Barbara                                          Lond   Jne  261
1785  ADAMS, Bartholemew                                      Lond   Dec  583
1755  ADAMS, Benjamin                                         Middx  Jly  180
1787  ADAMS, Benjamin                                         Shant  Dec  529
1792  ADAMS, Benjamin, Esq.                                   Middx  Nov  542
1798  ADAMS, Benjamin  AwW  Ser. "Courageux"                  Pts    Dec  754
1781  ADAMS, Bethia  AwW                                      Lond   Apr  179
1788  ADAMS, Cain                                             Middx  Mch  113
1774  ADAMS, Catherine                                        Middx  Oct  357
1782  ADAMS, Charles                                          Pts    Nov  527
1783  ADAMS, Charles, Esq.                                    Worcs  May  210
1783  ADAMS, Charles, Esq.  Dble Pr W. rgd
      last month                                              Worcs  Jne   --
1785  ADAMS, Charles                                          Middx  Aug  400
1789  ADAMS, Charles                                          Cambr  Apr  186
```

```
1800   ADAMS, Charlotte Margaret                              Middx Jne 469
1779   ADAMS, Christopher                                     Middx Nov 440
1776   ADAMS, Clarke, Esq.                                    Nhant Jly 295
1750   ADAMS, Collins  AwW                                    Kent  Jly 220
1777   ADAMS, Daniel                                          Herts Aug 339
1786   ADAMS, Dorcas                                          Oxon  Oct 499
1758   ADAMS, Edward                                          Pts   Mch  61
1760   ADAMS, Edward  AwW                                     Cambr Nov 412
1766   ADAMS, Edward                                          Middx Oct 360
1784   ADAMS, Edward                                          Som   Oct 534
1794   ADAMS, Edward                                          Middx Apr 180
1800   ADAMS, Edward                                          Berks Aug 573
1757   ADAMS, Edmund                                          Som   Oct 293
1758   ADAMS, Edmund                                          Middx Dec 354
1772   ADAMS, Edmund  AwW unadm W rgd 1758,354               Middx Dec  --
1797   ADAMS, Edmund                                          Glos  Jly 468
1778   ADAMS, Eleanor                                         Som   Aug 308
1759   ADAMS, Elizabeth                                       Herts Jne 191
1761   ADAMS, Elizabeth                                       Middx Feb  43
1764   ADAMS, formerly LUNTLEY, Elizabeth
         Ltd AwW                                              Lond  Nov 413
1765   ADAMS, Elizabeth                                       Kent  May 166
1765   ADAMS, Elizabeth                                       Oxon  Sep 319
1769   ADAMS, Elizabeth                                       Lond  Apr 110
1769   ADAMS, Elizabeth, otherwise Elisabeth                 Kent  Jne 193
1770   ADAMS, Elizabeth                                       Middx Aug 283
1771   ADAMS, Elizabeth                                       Middx Jny   2
1776   ADAMS, Elizabeth, otherwise Elisabeth
         Dble Pr W rgd 1769, 193                              Kent  Apr  --
1785   ADAMS, formerly BROOKES, formerly
         BARRATT, Elizabeth (Ltd Pr)                          Bucks Apr  --
1785   ADAMS, Elizabeth                                       Berks Dec 583
1788   ADAMS, Elizabeth                                       Middx Apr 170
1789   ADAMS, Elizabeth  AwW                                  Salop May 232
1793   ADAMS, Elizabeth                                       Herts Feb  62
1793   ADAMS, Elizabeth  Anor Pr W rgd this
         month                                                Herts Feb  62
1798   ADAMS, Elizabeth                                       Middx Feb  75
1798   ADAMS, Elizabeth                                       Kent  Mch 150
1798   ADAMS, Elizabeth                                       Surry Mch 150
1799   ADAMS, Elizabeth                                       Sfolk Jny   1
1762   ADAMS, Fortunatus                                      Pts   Jne 230
1756   ADAMS, Frances                                         Middx May 128
1786   ADAMS, Frances                                         Middx Oct 499
1772   ADAMS, Francis                                         Lond  Jly 243
1799   ADAMS, Francis, Esq.                                   Herts Apr 240
1784   ADAMS, Francis Robert                                  Middx Feb  60
1751   ADAMS, George                                          Sussx Jny   1
1753   ADAMS, George  AwW (sent)                              Brstl Jly 193
1754   ADAMS, George  AwW unadm W rgd Jly 1753               Brstl Jly  --
1760   ADAMS, George                                          Middx Nov 412
1761   ADAMS, George                                          Kent  Feb  43
1761   ADAMS, George                                          Shant Feb  43
```

1769	ADAMS, George	Wilts	Jly	233
1772	ADAMS, George	Lond	Oct	348
1774	ADAMS, George	Middx	Jny	1
1777	ADAMS, George	Essex	May	194
1783	ADAMS, Rev. George	Essex	Jny	1
1783	ADAMS, George	Dorst	Mch	106
1783	ADAMS, George	Herts	Nov	548
1795	ADAMS, George	Lond	Sep	531
1798	ADAMS, George	Som	Dec	755
1799	ADAMS, George	Essex	Apr	241
1783	ADAMS, Grace	Nhant	Jly	332
1763	ADAMS, Hannah	Glos	Oct	457
1750	ADAMS, Hargrave AwW	Pts	Apr	101
1758	ADAMS, Henry	Cambs	Sep	257
1759	ADAMS, Henry	Middx	Oct	316
1774	ADAMS, Henry	Salop	Oct	357
1783	ADAMS, Henry	Pts	Jny	1
1783	ADAMS, Henry	Pts	Nov	548
1793	ADAMS, Henry, Esq.	Lond	Jly	349
1800	ADAMS, Henry	Middx	Aug	574
1795	ADAMS, Hester	Wilts	Nov	621
1762	ADAMS, Hugh AwW	Pts	Aug	330
1761	ADAMS, Humphrey	Herts	Apr	115
1755	ADAMS, Humphry, Esq.	Surry	Dec	303
1776	ADAMS, Humphry, Esq. AwW Feb. unadm			
	W rgd 1755, 303	Surry		
1782	ADAMS, Isaac	Essex	May	210
1788	ADAMS, Isaac	Lond	Jny	1
1758	ADAMS, Jacob	Lond	Apr	100
1783	ADAMS, Jacob AwW	Pts	Feb	56
1751	ADAMS, James	Middx	Jne	164
1753	ADAMS, James AwW of Gds unadm W rgd			
	1729, 218	Leics	Nov	--
1755	ADAMS, James	Middx	Mch	65
1759	ADAMS, James	Middx	Feb	44
1763	ADAMS, James AwW (by int dec)	Pts	Jny	1
1763	ADAMS, James	Pts	Aug	367
1765	ADAMS, James, Esq.	Essex	Oct	359
1765	ADAMS, James Mc	Pts	Dec	458
1768	ADAMS, James	Middx	Aug	305
1775	ADAMS, James, Esq.	Bucks	Dec	452
1779	ADAMS, James	Surry	Aug	333
1781	ADAMS, James	Middx	Jne	281
1781	ADAMS, James	Pts	Dec	569
1783	ADAMS, James AwW,"Centaur"	Pts	May	210
1785	ADAMS, Rev. James	Essex	Apr	168
1788	ADAMS, James, Esq. AwW of Gds unadm			
	W rgd 1775, 452	Bucks	Nov	--
1791	ADAMS, James	Middx	Apr	164
1793	ADAMS, James	Surry	Sep	451
1794	ADAMS, James	Kent	Jny	2
1800	ADAMS, James	Surry	Feb	80
1800	ADAMS, James	Middx	Jne	431

1755	ADAMS, Jane		Middx	Sep	232
1761	ADAMS, Jane		Surry	Apr	116
1779	ADAMS, Jane		Brstl	Dec	483
1788	ADAMS, Jane		Bucks	Nov	518
1797	ADAMS, Jane		Middx	Jny	1
1799	ADAMS, Jane		Surry	Mch	161
1788	ADAMS, Jarvis		Lond	May	224
1751	ADAMS, Joan		Kent	Aug	228
1751	ADAMS, John		Kent	Mch	68
1751	ADAMS, John		Pts	May	130
1750	ADAMS, John		Som	Jny	1
1750	ADAMS, John		Middx	Mch	66
1753	ADAMS, John AwW (by dec)		Surry	May	126
1753	ADAMS, John		Bucks	Aug	222
1754	ADAMS, John	Pts –	Middx	Jny	1
1754	ADAMS, John		Surry	Mch	66
1755	ADAMS, John		Som	Aug	209
1757	ADAMS, John	Pts –	Shant	May	144
1757	ADAMS, John		Pts	Jne	179
1759	ADAMS, John		Surry	Apr	115
1759	ADAMS, John		Devon	May	155
1759	ADAMS, John		Shant	Sep	287
1760	ADAMS, John		Devon	Feb	45
1760	ADAMS, John		Pts	Oct	378
1761	ADAMS, John		Leics	May	157
1763	ADAMS, John		Lond	Sep	415
1764	ADAMS, John		Herts	Apr	129
1764	ADAMS, John AwW		Lond	Aug	295
1767	ADAMS, John		Middx	Apr	121
1769	ADAMS, John		Lond	Feb	32
1772	ADAMS, John, Esq.		Carmn	Aug	282
1772	ADAMS, John		Surry	Sep	316
1773	ADAMS, John		Cntby	Jne	233
1774	ADAMS, John AwW		Herts	Feb	36
1775	ADAMS, John		Middx	Apr	126
1776	ADAMS, John		Bucks	Mch	107
1776	ADAMS, John		Middx	Mch	107
1776	ADAMS, John AwW	Pts –	Kent	Jly	296
1777	ADAMS, John		Salop	Oct	406
1778	ADAMS, Rev. John		Nhant	Jny	1
1779	ADAMS, John Joseph Ser.		Pts	May	185
1781	ADAMS, John		Oxon	Mch	107
1781	ADAMS, John Ser. AwW		Sfolk	Sep	417
1783	ADAMS, John (1st)		Pts	Feb	56
1786	ADAMS, Dr John Till, Dr of Physic		Brstl	Apr	--
1786	ADAMS, John		Middx	Nov	552
1788	ADAMS, John		Berks	Jny	1
1788	ADAMS, John		Nhant	Feb	52
1789	ADAMS, John, Esq.		Glos	Apr	184
1789	ADAMS, John		Middx	Jne	296
1789	ADAMS, John		Middx	Oct	481
1791	ADAMS, John William		Middx	Feb	52
1791	ADAMS, John AwW		Som	Oct	449

24

1793	ADAMS, John			Middx	Dec	578
1794	ADAMS, John Phillipps		Pts -	Pemb	Feb	59
1795	ADAMS, John (poor)			Middx	Feb	61
1796	ADAMS, Rev. John			Devon	Jne	291
1796	ADAMS, John "Intrepid"			Pts	Dec	590
1797	ADAMS, John			Kent	Mch	124
1798	ADAMS, John Ser. "Valiant"			Pts	May	306
1798	ADAMS, John			Middx	Jly	457
1799	ADAMS, John, Esq. AwW of Gds unadm					
	W rgd 1789, 184			Glos	Aug	--
1799	ADAMS, John			Exter	Sep	639
1799	ADAMS, John			Staff	Oct	693
1799	ADAMS, John Ser. "Stately"			Pts	Nov	755
1800	ADAMS, John			Berks	Aug	574
1800	ADAMS, John			Beds	Sep	639
1751	ADAMS, Jonathan			Lond	Nov	298
1786	ADAMS, Jonathan			Middx	Dec	597
1792	ADAMS, Jonathan			Kent	Feb	53
1758	ADAMS, Joseph AwW			Pts	Jne	175
1759	ADAMS, Joseph Ser.			Pts	Oct	316
1761	ADAMS, Joseph			Devon	Mch	80
1764	ADAMS, Joseph			Kent	Sep	335
1765	ADAMS, Joseph		Pts -	Lond	Sep	319
1766	ADAMS, Joseph			Surry	May	166
1774	ADAMS, Joseph			Wark	Dec	418
1781	ADAMS, Joseph			Dorst	Feb	54
1783	ADAMS, Joseph			Lond	Jne	277
1784	ADAMS, Joseph			Herts	Apr	186
1791	ADAMS, Joseph			Devon	Feb	52
1775	ADAMS, Judith			Lond	Oct	365
1769	ADAMS, Rev. Knightley			Nhant	Dec	403
1771	ADAMS, Margaret			Middx	Mch	92
1772	ADAMS, Margaret, otherwise Margarett					
	AwW			Surry	Oct	347
1786	ADAMS, Margaret, otherwise Margarett					
	AwW			Middx	May	258
1788	ADAMS, Margaretta Anna			Middx	Jne	282
1769	ADAMS, Martha			Surry	Dec	403
1768	ADAMS, Martha			Surry	Jly	265
1795	ADAMS, Martha			Middx	Mch	136
1797	ADAMS, Martha			Kent	Apr	220
1798	ADAMS, Martha			Herts	Feb	76
1751	ADAMS, Mary			Middx	Apr	101
1754	ADAMS, Mary			Middx	Jny	2
1755	ADAMS, Mary AwW			Middx	Jne	153
1761	ADAMS, Mary			Herts	Jly	239
1763	ADAMS, Mary AwW			Middx	Aug	366
1765	ADAMS, formerly CROUCH, Mary			Middx	Dec	438
1766	ADAMS, Mary			Lond	Feb	44
1767	ADAMS, Mary AwW			Som	May	161
1769	ADAMS, Mary AwW			Middx	Oct	331
1771	ADAMS, Lady Mary			Middx	Dec	466
1772	ADAMS, Mary			Brstl	Jly	244
1775	ADAMS, Mary			Worcs	May	168

1775	ADAMS, Mary	Kent	Aug	298
1777	ADAMS, Mary	Middx	Apr	144
1778	ADAMS, Mary	Surry	Jly	271
1782	ADAMS, Mary	Surry	Jly	332
1783	ADAMS, Mary	Nhant	Jly	333
1788	ADAMS, otherwise ADDAMS, Mary	Middx	Feb	52
1788	ADAMS, Mary	Middx	Apr	171
1788	ADAMS, Mary	Kent	Jne	282
1789	ADAMS, Mary	Devon	Jny	2
1792	ADAMS, Mary	Surry	Oct	495
1798	ADAMS, Mary	Surry	Jly	456
1799	ADAMS, Mary	Leics	Jly	471
1799	ADAMS, Mary	Beds	Nov	756
1793	ADAMS, Mary	Middx	Jly	349
1787	ADAMS, Matthew	Pts	Jne	251
1800	ADAMS, Messer John, otherwise Mercer John	Oxon	Jly	500
1759	ADAMS, Moses	Berks	Jne	191
1800	ADAMS, Moses	Middx	Apr	250
1753	ADAMS, Nathaniel AwW	Middx	Feb	37
1758	ADAMS, Nathaniel	Pts	Oct	282
1775	ADAMS, Nathaniel	Middx	Nov	399
1778	ADAMS, Nathaniel	Sfolk	Mch	94
1782	ADAMS, Nathaniel AwW	Pts	Apr	162
1780	ADAMS, Nichola	Devon	May	234
1760	ADAMS, Nicholas	Berks	Jne	227
1765	ADAMS, Nicholas AwW	Kent	Dec	439
1778	ADAMS, Nicholas, otherwise Nicolas AwW	Devon	Apr	141
1784	ADAMS, Nicholas	Beds	May	243
1789	ADAMS, Nicolas, otherwise Nicholas AwW of Gds unadm W rgd 1778, 141	Devon	Jly	--
1793	ADAMS, Nicholas (By Sentence regd May 626)	Middx	Jne	296
1783	ADAMS, Noah Ser.	Devon	Dec	596
1768	ADAMS, Patience	Lond	May	184
1793	ADAMS, Patience Thomas, Esq.	Middx	May	238
1776	ADAMS, Paul	Middx	Nov	447
1800	ADAMS, Paul	Surry	Jne	430
1771	ADAMS, Peter, Esq.	Middx	May	191
1783	ADAMS, Peter	Pts	Oct	494
1788	ADAMS, Peter	Kent	Mch	114
1798	ADAMS, Peter AwW	Middx	May	306
1753	ADAMS, Philip	Lond	Oct	262
1764	ADAMS, Rachel	Som	Jny	1
1782	ADAMS, Ralph	Sfolk	Sep	437
1767	ADAMS, Rebecca AwW unadm W rgd 1746, 138	Middx	Mch	--
1770	ADAMS, otherwise ADDAMS, Rebecca	Berks	May	169
1780	ADAMS, Reddevira	Middx	Jny	1
1777	ADAMS, Reynold	Pts	Jly	296
1766	ADAMS, Richard	Surry	Feb	44
1767	ADAMS, Richard	Kent	Sep	331
1769	ADAMS, Richard	Lond	Nov	363

1774	ADAMS, Hon Sir Richard, late one of			
	Barons of H.M. Ct of Exchequer	Middx	Mch	77
1777	ADAMS, Richard	Middx	Sep	374
1780	ADAMS, Richard	Devon	Jne	299
1784	ADAMS, Richard AwW "Cato"	Pts	Oct	534
1788	ADAMS, Richard	Lond	Jne	281
1790	ADAMS, Richard AwW	Middx	Mch	115
1793	ADAMS, Richard	Midlx	Jne	296
1797	ADAMS, Richard	Surry	Feb	66
1797	ADAMS, Richard, Esq.	Middx	Nov	672
1799	ADAMS, Richard	Devon	Oct	693
1800	ADAMS, Richard	Nhant	Sep	640
1752	ADAMS, Robert AwW of Gds unadm W rgd			
	1724, 186	Middx	Jne	--
1754	ADAMS, Sir Robert	Surry	Oct	264
1765	ADAMS, Robert AwW	Middx	Oct	359
1766	ADAMS, Robert	Sfolk	Jny	1
1778	ADAMS, Robert	Surry	Jne	229
1778	ADAMS, Robert	Middx	Nov	427
1784	ADAMS, Robert Pts –	Shant	Jny	1
1788	ADAMS, Robert (Ltd Pr)	Pts	Feb	52
1789	ADAMS, Robert AwW	Pts	Jny	2
1792	ADAMS, Robert AwW W rgd Jny 1789	Pts	Dec	--
1798	ADAMS, Robert	Surry	Nov	692
1800	ADAMS, Robert	Middx	May	335
1750	ADAMS, Roger	Middx	Jny	2
1754	ADAMS, Roger	Middx	Dec	317
1756	ADAMS, Roger	Shant	Oct	266
1771	ADAMS, Rose	Herts	Nov	428
1751	ADAMS, Dr. Samuel, D.D.	Oxon	Mch	68
1755	ADAMS, Samuel	Surry	Oct	252
1767	ADAMS, Samuel AwW unadm W rgd 1738, 54	Middx	Dec	--
1782	ADAMS, Samuel	Lond	Jly	332
1799	ADAMS, Samuel	Middx	Apr	238
1794	ADAMS, Samuell	Worcs	Jne	295
1765	ADAMS, Sanders	Surry	Dec	438
1752	ADAMS, Sarah	Surry	Jly	176
1754	ADAMS, Sarah HARRIS, formerly	Brstl	Jly	200
1761	ADAMS, Sarah	Middx	Apr	115
1774	ADAMS, Sarah	Glos	Feb	36
1776	ADAMS, Sarah AwW	Som	Aug	342
1782	ADAMS, Sarah	Middx	Aug	390
1761	ADAMS, Seth	Middx	Jne	199
1752	ADAMS, Stephen	Lond	Jne	145
1757	ADAMS, Stephen	Pts	Oct	293
1781	ADAMS, Stephen	Pts	Mch	107
1781	ADAMS, Stephen	Sfolk	Jly	326
1784	ADAMS, Stephen	Surry	Feb	60
1796	ADAMS, Stephen	Kent	Aug	394
1760	ADAMS, Susanna PIMM, formerly DAULING,			
	afterwards	Surry	Mch	116
1775	ADAMS, Susanna	Herts	Apr	126

1799	ADAMS, Susanna	Salop	Feb	89
1773	ADAMS, Susannah	Surry	Mch	90
1790	ADAMS, Susannah	Middx	Dec	536
1791	ADAMS, Susannah	Middx	Aug	370
1750	ADAMS, Thomas	Lond	Jny	1
1750	ADAMS, Thomas AwW	Pts	Jne	185
1758	ADAMS, Thomas	SHant	Feb	28
1758	ADAMS, Thomas	Lond	Oct	282
1756	ADAMS, Thomas	Staff	Nov	286
1760	ADAMS, Thomas, otherwise Alexander AwW	Pts	Jne	227
1760	ADAMS, otherwise OAKES, Thomas	Surry	Aug	312
1762	ADAMS, Thomas	Pts	Jny	1
1762	ADAMS, Thomas	Middx	Jne	230
1762	ADAMS, Thomas	Pts	Sep	365
1763	ADAMS, Thomas	Norf	May	211
1764	ADAMS, Thomas	Middx	Feb	36
1765	ADAMS, otherwise ADDAMS, Thomas Pts –	Devon	Aug	282
1766	ADAMS, Thomas AwW	Berks	Aug	290
1767	ADAMS, Thomas	Nhant	Feb	33
1768	ADAMS, Thomas	Middx	Dec	437
1768	ADAMS, Thomas AwW unadm W rgd Feb 1767	Nhant	Jly	--
1770	ADAMS, Sir Thomas, Bart.	Pts	Nov	387
1771	ADAMS, Thomas	Bucks	Sep	364
1776	ADAMS, Thomas	Som	Jly	295
1778	ADAMS, Thomas	Middx	Apr	141
1779	ADAMS, Thomas	Essex	Jly	282
1779	ADAMS, Thomas	Leics	Jly	284
1780	ADAMS, Thomas	Pts	Jne	299
1781	ADAMS, Thomas	Middx	Aug	374
1782	ADAMS, Thomas	Wilts	Feb	59
1782	ADAMS, Thomas	Middx	Jne	261
1783	ADAMS, Thomas	Corn	Jne	278
1783	ADAMS, otherwise ADDAMS, Thomas AwW "Princess Royal", "Lecocadia", "Pomona"	Pts	Jly	331
1783	ADAMS, otherwise ADDAMS, Thomas AwW of former grant dtd July last	Pts	Sep	441
1783	ADAMS, Thomas	Pts	Nov	548
1784	ADAMS, Thomas	Middx	Jny	2
1784	ADAMS, Thomas	Lond	Jne	302
1787	ADAMS, Thomas	Herts	Sep	396
1788	ADAMS, Thomas	Lond	May	224
1790	ADAMS, Thomas AwW of Gds unadm W rgd 1782, 261	Middx	Jne	--
1791	ADAMS, Thomas	Essex	Nov	492
1798	ADAMS, Thomas	Midlx	Aug	522
1799	ADAMS, Thomas	Surry	Oct	693
1759	ADAMS, Timothy AwW of Gds unadm W rgd 1749, 1	Lond	Jly	--
1792	ADAMS, Unity	Bucks	Nov	542
1750	ADAMS, Walter	Herts	Jny	1
1766	ADAMS, Walter	Herts	Jly	255
1783	ADAMS, Walter	Herts	Jne	277

1784	ADAMS, Walter		Kent	Jly	364
1774	ADAMS, Warren		Camb	May	165
1750	ADAMS, William	Pts –	Surry	Jly	220
1757	ADAMS, William		Lond	May	144
1757	ADAMS, William		Notts	Jne	179
1758	ADAMS, William AwW		Som	Dec	354
1761	ADAMS, William		Kent	Apr	115
1764	ADAMS, William, Esq.		Shant	Jny	1
1764	ADAMS, William AwW		Lond	Jne	209
1764	ADAMS, William		Lond	Nov	413
1765	ADAMS, William		Kent	Apr	127
1765	ADAMS, William		Pts	Sep	319
1767	ADAMS, William AwW		Herts	Mch	83
1767	ADAMS, William Dble Pr W rgd Jny 1764		Shant	Nov	--
1768	ADAMS, William		Shant	Feb	41
1768	ADAMS, William Esq.		Surry	Mch	93
1769	ADAMS, William		Middx	Jly	233
1769	ADAMS, William		Middx	Nov	363
1770	ADAMS, William		Cntby	Feb	40
1770	ADAMS, William AwW		Dorst	May	169
1771	ADAMS, William		Essex	Nov	428
1774	ADAMS, William Ltd AwW		Pts	Oct	357
1775	ADAMS, William		Kent	Jne	218
1776	ADAMS, William		Oxon	Jly	295
1777	ADAMS, William		Devon	Aug	339
1777	ADAMS, William		Bath	Oct	406
1781	ADAMS, William		Som	Jny	3
1781	ADAMS, William		Pts	Jly	326
1781	ADAMS, William		Middx	Nov	511
1782	ADAMS, William		Essex	Mch	108
1783	ADAMS, William		Glos	Jne	277
1784	ADAMS, William		Middx	Jly	363
1790	ADAMS, William		Sthl	Mch	114
1790	ADAMS, William		Middx	Dec	535
1792	ADAMS, William		Lond	May	256
1792	ADAMS, William		Middx	May	256
1793	ADAMS, William		Cntby	Jny	1
1794	ADAMS, William		Middx	Jny	1
1794	ADAMS, William		Surry	Apr	180
1795	ADAMS, William		Som	Feb	61
1796	ADAMS, William AwW		Essex	Dec	590
1798	ADAMS, William "Landovery"		Middx	Apr	231
1798	ADAMS, William		Nhant	Sep	581
1798	ADAMS, William		Surry	Dec	755
1800	ADAMS, William		Essex	Jny	1
1750	ADAMS, Windham		Lond	Mch	66
1799	ADAMSON, Alexander "Alexr."&"Spartiate"		NBrit	Dec	820
1783	ADAMSON, Andrew Ser.		Pts	Jny	1
1762	ADAMSON, Ann		Lond	Aug	330
1783	ADAMSON, Benjamin		Bath	Jly	331
1762	ADAMSON, Bridget		Middx	Dec	491
1788	ADAMSON, Caesar		Surry	Sep	423
1772	ADAMSON, Catherine		Middx	Aug	282

```
1772  ADAMSON, Christiana, otherwise Christina Middx Sep 316
1761  ADAMSON, Christopher    AwW              Pts    Aug 275
1762  ADAMSON, Christopher    AwW              Pts    May 182
1786  ADAMSON, Christopher                     Norf   May 257
1763  ADAMSON, Rev. Daniel                     Salop  Apr 163
1782  ADAMSON, David                           Middx  Nov 526
1800  ADAMSON, Donald  Ser.  "Proserpine"      Pts    Mch 172
1765  ADAMSON, Elizabeth                       Middx  Feb  40
1772  ADAMSON, Elizabeth                       Middx  Dec 429
1783  ADAMSON, Elizabeth                       Roch   May 210
1757  ADAMSON, Isabella                        Middx  May 144
1759  ADAMSON, James    AwW                    Pts    Nov 347
1764  ADAMSON, James                           Pts    May 162
1783  ADAMSON, James    Ser.                   Pts    Jny   1
1790  ADAMSON, James                           Middx  Apr 168
1795  ADAMSON, James                           Middx  Dec 666
1797  ADAMSON, James    Ser.  "Albercord"      York   Jly 468
1759  ADAMSON, John, Esq.                      Lond   Dec 381
1780  ADAMSON, John                            Lond   Sep 425
1796  ADAMSON, John                            Kent   Aug 393
1800  ADAMSON, John  Ser.  "Raisonable"        Pts    Apr 250
1773  ADAMSON, Joseph                          Lond   Jne 223
1765  ADAMSON, Laurence  AwW  Ser.             Pts    Sep 319
1771  ADAMSON, Laurence  AwW  W rgd 1765,319   Pts    Nov  --
1765  ADAMSON, Mary  (W nunc)                  Lond   Nov 397
1782  ADAMSON, Mary                            Lond   Sep 437
1760  ADAMSON, Peter                           Pts    Jny   1
1765  ADAMSON, Ralph                           Pts    Feb  41
1800  ADAMSON, Richard, Esq.                   Sfolk  Jly 500
1774  ADAMSON, Robert                          Kent   Feb  36
1779  ADAMSON, Robert                          Pts    Feb  36
1779  ADAMSON, Robert                          Middx  Mch  87
1761  ADAMSON, formerly HAMILTON, Robina  AwW  Edin   May 158
1791  ADAMSON, Sarah                           Norf   May 208
1761  ADAMSON, Thomas    AwW                   Pts    Jny   1
1772  ADAMSON, Thomas                          Lond   Jny   1
1788  ADAMSON, Thomas                          York   Nov 518
1788  ADAMSON, Thomas                          Surry  Dec 573
1794  ADAMSON, Thomas                          Herfd  Jny   2
1752  ADAMSON, William              Pts – Middx Jne 145
1760  ADAMSON, William    AwW                  Pts    May 180
1764  ADAMSON, William    AwW                  Pts    May 162
1770  ADAMSON, William                         Middx  Nov 387
1790  ADAMSON, William                         Middx  Jny   1
1793  ADAMSON, William                         Chest  May 239
1797  ADAMSON, William                         Essex  Aug 538
1784  ADAMSZ, Willem Smits (Ltd Pr)            Pts    Oct 534
1774  ADAR, otherwise ADEARE, Grisel           Middx  Apr 125
1800  ADBRIDGE, John  AwW                      Sfolk  Apr 250
1774  ADCOCK, Abraham                          Middx  Jny   1
1764  ADCOCK, George                           Lond   Mch  78
1753  ADCOCK, John                             Rutld  Jny   1
1757  ADCOCK, John                             Pts    Jny   1
1766  ADCOCK, John                             Wark   Oct 360
```

1774	ADCOCK, John	Middx	Sep 328
1792	ADCOCK, John, Esq. AwW	Middx	May 255
1800	ADCOCK, John	Surry	Nov 760
1779	ADCOCK, Joseph	Rutld	Nov 441
1767	ADCOCK, Mary	Middx	Dec 435
1795	ADCOCK, Mary	Kent	Sep 532
1798	ADCOCK, Mary	Middx	Dec 755
1775	ADCOCK, Rachel	Rutld	Mch 81
1787	ADCOCK, Richard	Lond	Jny 1
1782	ADCOCK, Robert	Nhant	Nov 526
1798	ADCOCK, Robert	Middx	Jny 1
1775	ADCOCK, Samuel	Rutld	Feb 37
1762	ADCOCK, Sarah	Herts	Oct 409
1788	ADCOCK, Sarah Maria, otherwise Sarah	Middx	Mch 113
1759	ADCOCK, Thomas	Middx	Dec 381
1760	ADCOCK, Thomas	Middx	Feb 45
1790	ADCOCK, Thomas	Lond	Apr 168
1785	ADCOCK, William	Oxon	Oct 489
1773	ADCOCKS, Edward	Kent	Jne 233
1762	ADDAMES, William AwW of Gds unadm W rgd Aug 1760	Essex	Sep --
1791	ADDAMS, Ann	Surry	May 208
1774	ADDAMS, Arthur	SHant	Aug 289
1755	ADDAMS, Elizabeth	Middx	Jly 180
1762	ADDAMS, Ellen	Middx	Dec 491
1785	ADDAMS, George Frederick, Esq. AwW	Herts	Jly 349
1772	ADDAMS, Henrietta	Nwich	Feb 36
1752	ADDAMS, James	Pts	Jne 145
1766	ADDAMS, Mary	Surry	Oct 360
1788	ADDAMS, otherwise ADAMS, Mary	Middx	Feb 52
1800	ADDAMS, Mary	Surry	Jny 1
1770	ADDAMS, otherwise ADAMS, Rebecca	Berks	May 169
1790	ADDAMS, Rebecca	Berks	Dec 535
1777	ADDAMS, Stephen	Som	Mch 93
1750	ADDAMS, Thomas	Essex	May 134
1765	ADDAMS, otherwise ADAMS, Thomas Pts - Devon		Aug 282
1783	ADDAMS, otherwise ADAMS, Thomas AwW "Princess Royal", "Lecocadia", "Pomona"	Pts	Jly 331
1783	ADDAMS, otherwise ADAMS, Thomas AwW of a former grant dated July last	Pts	Sep 441
1785	ADDAMS, Thomas, Dr. of Phys.	Berks	May 228
1754	ADDAMS, William	Mon	Dec 317
1793	ADDAMS, William	Kent	Feb 62
1751	ADDEE, Louisa	Middx	May 130
1791	ADDENBROOK, Edward	Herfd	Dec 553
1769	ADDENBROOKE, Ann	Salop	Aug 271
1780	ADDENBROOKE, Elizabeth	Hunts	Apr 169
1776	ADDENBROOKE, Rev. John, D.D.	Derby	Jne 253
1798	ADDENBROOKE, John	Worcs	Jne 377
1780	ADDENBROOKE, Rev. Nicolas AwW	Hunts	May 233
1756	ADDERALL, otherwise HADDERILL, otherwise HADERELL, John "Sartine","Chator" & "Worcester"	Pts	Sep 460

1767	ADDERLEY, Ann		Middx	Apr 120
1772	ADDERLEY, Francis		Middx	Feb 33
1782	ADDERLEY, Frances		Wark	Feb 59
1784	ADDERLEY, Lettice		Middx	Jly 364
1784	ADDERLEY, Lettice W rgd last month		Middx	Aug --
1760	ADDERLEY, John AwW		Pts	Feb 45
1776	ADDERLEY, Mary		Wark	Apr 159
1794	ADDERLEY, Mary W rgd 1776, 159		Wark	May --
1760	ADDERLEY, Samuell		Lond	Oct 378
1758	ADDERLEY, Thomas, Esq.		Wark	Mch 61
1787	ADDERLEY, Thomas, Esq.	Pts — Kent		Mch 101
1800	ADDERLEY, Thomas, Esq. (late one of Proc Gen of Arches Ct of Cntby)		Middx	Sep 639
1788	ADDERLY, Ann (by int decree)		Brstl	Sep 424
1758	ADDERLY, Elizabeth		Herts	Apr 99
1786	ADDERLY, George		Brstl	Mch 133
1756	ADDERLY, John		Middx	Aug 215
1783	ADDERLY, John		Berks	Jly 331
1774	ADDERLY, Thomas, Esq.		Herts	Apr 125
1776	ADDERTON, Hill AwW of Gds unadm W rgd 1746, 343		Salop	May --
1755	ADDESON, John		Sfolk	Apr 92
1773	ADDESON, Rachel, otherwise Rachael		Sfolk	Sep 350
1765	ADDESON, Thomas		Sfolk	Apr 127
1778	ADDEY, Ann		Middx	Nov 427
1760	ADDEY, John AwW		Camb	Aug 312
1797	ADDEY, John, Esq.		Nwich	Aug 538
1761	ADDEY, Mark		Middx	Oct 336
1793	ADDICOTT, Edward AwW		Exter	Aug 397
1757	ADDICOTT, Hugh		Pts	Apr 109
1795	ADDINALL, Mary		Middx	Mch 137
1790	ADDINGTON, Ann AwW		Berks	Jly 317
1790	ADDINGTON, Anthony, Dr of Physic		Berks	Mch 114
1782	ADDINGTON, Rev. Charles		Nhant	May 211
1776	ADDINGTON, Constant Heyne		Middx	Apr 159
1760	ADDINGTON, John		Lond	May 180
1793	ADDINGTON, John, Esq.		Middx	Oct 488
1795	ADDINGTON, Joseph		Middx	Nov 620
1785	ADDINGTON, Samuel Reymes		Lond	Aug 400
1758	ADDINGTON, Thomas		Middx	Oct 282
1760	ADDINGTON, otherwise ADDINTON, Thomas		Pts	Jny 1
1779	ADDINGTON, William		Middx	Jne 230
1760	ADDINTON, otherwise ADDINGTON, Thomas		Pts	Jny 1
1778	ADDIS, Elizabeth		Middx	Nov 427
1785	ADDIS, George		Surry	Jne 288
1798	ADDIS, Luke		Surry	May 306
1786	ADDIS, James		Som	May 257
1758	ADDIS, John		Middx	Oct 282
1798	ADDIS, John		Surry	Feb 75
1758	ADDIS, Joseph	Pts — Surry		Oct 282
1785	ADDIS, William		Lond	Jny 1
1762	ADDISON, Alexander		Pts	Jne 230
1769	ADDISON, Ann		Surry	Mch 73

```
1795  ADDISON, Ann                                      Middx Dec 666
1787  ADDISON, Barbara                                  Middx Nov 479
1787  ADDISON, Barbara   Anor. Pr last month            Middx Dec  --
1798  ADDISON, Charlotte  AwW                           Wark  Aug 522
1800  ADDISON, Charlotte  AwW of Gds unadm
        W rgd Aug 1798                                  Wark  Nov  --
1783  ADDISON, Rev. Daniel                              York  Jly 332
1750  ADDISON, Edward, Esq.  AwW unadm 1729,156 Wark   Oct  --
1787  ADDISON, Eldred, Esq.                             Middx Nov 479
1778  ADDISON, otherwise ADISON, Elizabeth              Middx Jne 229
1763  ADDISON, George                                   SHant Apr 164
1794  ADDISON, Henry                                    Cumb  Mch 120
1762  ADDISON, James                                    Middx Oct 408
1783  ADDISON, James "Arrogant","Glorieaux"
                                         Pts - Middx May 210
1784  ADDISON, otherwise EDDISON, James
        E.I.S. "Lascelles"                              Pts   Jly 380
1756  ADDISON, John                                     Lond  Jne 157
1775  ADDISON, John                                     Middx Mch  81
1777  ADDISON, John                                     Kent  Jny   2
1787  ADDISON, John, Esq.                               York  May 194
1791  ADDISON, John                                     Middx Apr 165
1798  ADDISON, John  AwW                                Lond  Mch 150
1787  ADDISON, Joseph                                   Middx Jly 308
1779  ADDISON, Juliana, alias Jule Ann                 Middx Feb  36
1764  ADDISON, Mary                                     SHant Oct 376
1783  ADDISON, Mary                                     Kent  Dec 596
1771  ADDISON, Richard                           Pts - Kent  Jly 282
1771  ADDISON, Richard  W rgd last month Pts - Kent  Aug  --
1774  ADDISON, Richard                                  Middx Jly 252
1774  ADDISON, Richard  (Dble Pr) W rgd Jly
                                   last  Middx Sep  --
1800  ADDISON, Richard "Bedford" & "Queen
        Charlotte"                                      Pts   Sep 641
1763  ADDISON, Robert                                   Pts   Jly 320
1796  ADDISON, Robert                                   Middx Jny   1
1799  ADDISON, Robert                                   Middx Oct 694
1782  ADDISON, Simon, otherwise Simeon                  Kent  Apr 161
1794  ADDISON, Thomas  "Lion"                           Pts   Dec 593
1762  ADDISON, William                                  Pts   Apr 136
1763  ADDISON, William                                  Kent  Dec 537
1781  ADDISON, William                                  Pts   Jly 326
1798  ADDISON, William                                  Middx Dec 754
1799  ADDISON, William                                  Kent  Dec 819
1800  ADDISON, William                                  Middx Sep 639
1792  ADDISON, Rev. William Thomas                      Cumb  Mch 127
1782  ADDLETON, William                                 Pts   Apr 163
1789  ADDS, William                                     Kent  Jne 297
1783  ADDSON, John  Ser.                                Devon Oct 493
1761  ADDY, Mary                                        Middx Dec 415
1768  ADDY, Richard                                     Durhm Oct 367
1800  ADDY, otherwise EDDY, Thomas                      Kent  Jny  --
1798  ADDY, Wright  Ser. "York"                         Pts   Dec 755
```

1763	ADDYES, John	Wark	Mch	104
1786	ADDYES, Mary	Staff	May	250
1765	ADDYES, Thomas, Esq.	Strat	Oct	351
1775	ADE, Mary	Middx	Nov	400
1766	ADEAN, Elizabeth	Brstl	Dec	440
1772	ADEAN, James, Esq.	Glos	Apr	119
1762	A DEAN, John	Brstl	Jny	1
1750	ADEAN, otherwise DEAN, Thomas	Berks	Mch	66
1789	A'DEANE, Harry	Sussx	Sep	447
1750	ADEANE, John	Middx	Nov	344
1791	A'DEANE, Matthew	Glos	Aug	368
1795	ADEANE, Rebecca	Berks	Dec	666
1764	ADEANE, Richard	Pts	Jly	248
1767	ADEANE, Thomas AwW	Berks	Sep	331
1773	ADEANE, Rev. William	Som	Oct	379
1782	ADEANE, William Whorwood	Oxon	Jne	262
1774	ADEARE, otherwise ADAR, Grisel	Middx	Apr	125
1769	ADEE, John AwW	Middx	Jny	1
1786	ADEE, Dr. Swithin, Dr. of Physic	Oxon	Aug	418
1762	ADELBERG, George Gustavus	Pts	Dec	491
1757	ADELSTONE, otherwise HUDDLESTON, Joseph	Middx	Jny	16
1767	ADEN, Sarah	Middx	Aug	294
1791	ADESSEN, Richard Ser. "Ajax"	Middx	Feb	52
1774	ADEY, Ann	Middx	Sep	328
1777	ADEY, Ann	Glos	Jne	250
1782	ADEY, Ann AwW unadm. W rgd Jne 1777	Glos	Feb	--
1797	ADEY, Charles, Esq.	Glos	May	290
1752	ADEY, Daniel, Esq.	Glos	May	115
1764	ADEY, Daniel	Glos	Oct	376
1771	ADEY, Daniel, Esq.	Glos	Feb	42
1795	ADEY, Elizabeth AwW	Glos	Aug	492
1768	ADEY, Henry	Glos	May	305
1786	ADEY, James	Middx	Nov	551
1792	ADEY, James	Middx	Jne	313
1786	ADEY, Rev. John	Kent	Aug	418
1771	ADEY, Martha	Middx	Dec	467
1786	ADEY, Nathaniel	Worcs	Jne	318
1792	ADEY, Robert	Lond	Jly	362
1794	ADEY, Samuel, Esq.	Glos	May	239
1766	ADEY, William, Esq.	Glos	Mch	88
1796	ADGMAN, Mary	SHant	May	233
1779	ADIE, otherwise EDIE, James Pts –	Newcl	Feb	48
1755	ADIE, William AwW	Lichd	Aug	209
1768	ADIN, Elizabeth	Middx	Jne	224
1790	ADINSTON, James	Bwick	Apr	169
1783	ADISON, Alexander Ser. AwW	Pts	Apr	159
1778	ADISON, otherwise ADDISON, Elizabeth	Middx	Jne	229
1766	ADKESON, otherwise ADKSON, James	Middx	Oct	360
1776	ADKIN, Abigail	Middx	Feb	47
1759	ADKIN, John	Middx	Jne	191
1798	ADKIN, Rev. Robert	Norf	Mch	151
1763	ADKINS, otherwise ATKINS, formerly SHELDON, Elizabeth Ltd AwW	Surry	Aug	366

```
1761  ADKINS,  Henry                                          Pts    Dec 416
1786  ADKINS,  Henry                                          Middx  Feb  62
1783  ADKINS,  otherwise ATKINS, Jeremiah                     Essex  Apr 158
1799  ADKINS,  John                                           Norf   Oct 694
1793  ADKINS,  Joseph                                         Bucks  Aug 397
1788  ADKINS,  Margaret, otherwise Margrat                    Middx  Dec 572
1784  ADKINS,  Ormond                                         Middx  Dec 627
1783  ADKINS,  Richard                                        Wark   Jne 278
1788  ADKINS,  Sarah                                          Herts  Dec 572
1764  ADKINS,  Thomas                                         Surry  Mch  78
1796  ADKINS,  Thomas                                         Bucks  Oct 485
1765  ADKINS,  William                                        Lond   Aug 282
1773  ADKINS,  William                                        Bucks  Apr 144
1781  ADKINS,  William                                        Pts    Nov 510
1773  ADKINSON, James                                         Middx  Jne 233
1766  ADKSON,  otherwise ADKESON, James                       Middx  Oct 360
1775  ADLAM,  Edward                                          Wilts  Nov 399
1796  ADLAM,  John Melville                       Pts  -  SHant  Aug 394
1798  ADLAM,  Samuel                                          Wilts  Feb. 75
1756  ADLAM,  Thomas                                          Pts    Sep 236
1760  ADLAM,  Thomas                                          Wilts  Jly 270
1762  ADLAM,  Thomas                                          Wilts  Jly 282
1792  ADLAM,  Thomas   No ship                                Pts    Dec 593
1750  ADLAM,  William                                         Wilts  Dec 376
1764  ADLAM,  William                                         Pts    Sep 335
1765  ADLAM,  otherwise ADLUM, William                        Pts    Jly 244
1784  ADLARD,  Richard                                        Middx  May 243
1779  ADLARD,  Thomas                                         Middx  Jly 282
1760  ADLER,  Anne                                            Surry  Feb  45
1785  ADLERCRON, John, Esq.                                   Dubln  Jly 350
1797  ADLERCRON, Meliora                                      Irel   Nov 672
1766  ADLEY,  Elizabeth                                       Lond   Nov 395
1762  ADLINGTON,  Edmund                                      Middx  Aug 330
1762  ADLINGTON,  George                                      Middx  Jly 282
1763  ADLINGTON,  Gilbert  AwW                                Pts    Sep 416
1771  ADLINGTON,  Jonas                                       Pts    Dec 467
1764  ADLINGTON,  Leighton                                    Glos   Jne 210
1768  ADLINGTON,  Mary                                        Middx  Mch  93
1772  ADLINGTON,  Mary                                        Middx  Jny   1
1795  ADLINGTON,  Thomas                                      Middx  Jly 426
1785  ADLOR,  Joseph                                          Surry  Dec 583
1765  ADLUM,  otherwise ADLAM, William                        Pts    Jly 244
1770  ADMIRAULD,  Francis                                     Middx  Jny   1
1771  ADNAMS,  William                                        Berks  Jne 240
1760  ADNAY,  otherwise ADNEY, Joseph                         Pts    Jny   1
1786  ADNETT,  Ann                                            Middx  Jne 318
1762  ADNETT,  Joseph                                         Middx  Jly 282
1764  ADNETT,  Joseph, Esq.  AwW                              Pts    Jny   1
1796  ADNETT,  Joseph                                         Lond   Feb  53
1787  ADNETT,  William                                        Middx  Apr 155
1790  ADNETT,  William (Dble Pr) W rgd 1787,155  Middx  Apr  --
1782  ADNEY,  Ann                                             Middx  Nov 526
1785  ADNEY,  Anne                                            Dorst  Nov 536
```

1759	ADNEY, Benjamin		Dorst	Oct	316
1779	ADNEY, Benjamin, Esq.		Devon	Mch	85
1786	ADNEY, Eleanor		Middx	Aug	417
1792	ADNEY, George, Esq.		Dorst	Sep	458
1763	ADNEY, Hugh	Pts	Middx	Jne	263
1760	ADNEY, otherwise ADNAY, Joseph	Pts		Jny	1
1782	ADNEY, Lancelot		Salop	Jne	260
1782	ADNEY, Richard		Lond	Aug	390
1788	ADNEY, Richard (Ltd Pr)	Pts		Sep	424
1798	ADNEY, Sarah		Lond	Apr	231
1777	ADNEY, Thomas		Lond	Apr	143
1791	ADOLPH, Hon. Johan (Ltd Pr)	Pts		Nov	--
1785	ADOLPHUS, Michael, Esq.		Middx	Feb	61
1759	ADOLPHUS, Reuben		Middx	Oct	316
1759	ADOLPHUS, Reuben, Esq. (Dble Pr) W. rgd Oct last		Middx	Nov	--
1768	ADQUIST, Charles		Pts	Apr	138
1776	ADRIAANS ZOON, Isaac Hubert (Ltd Pr)		Pts	Aug	--
1752	ADRIAENSZ, Leeudert DE WITT (Ltd Pr)		Pts	Jly	203
1764	ADRIAN, Aaron		Middx	Feb	36
1769	ADRIAN, Emma		Middx	Dec	402
1770	ADRIAN, formerly CAM, Emma W rgd last month		Middx	Jan	--
1757	ADRIAN, John		Kent	Mch	72
1781	ADRIAN, John		Middx	Nov	510
1784	ADRIAN, Marie, otherwise Mary			Feb	59
1779	ADSHEAD, Joseph		Middx	Nov	440
1772	ADSON, John		Nhant	Jne	203
1794	ADSTEY, William		Middx	Dec	594
1771	ADSTON, James, Esq.		Pts	Oct	395
1768	ADSTON, Mark		Pts	May	184
1772	ADSTON, Mark		Essex	May	155
1798	ADSTON, Sarah Brace		Middx	Jny	2
1785	ADY, Elizabeth		Glos	Nov	537
1766	ADYE, Joseph Ser.		Pts	Oct	361
1767	ADYE, Susanna AwW		Surry	Jly	250
1760	ADYERS, George	Pts	Devon	May	180
1764	AERDEN, formerly PONDERUS, Maria VAN (Ltd Pr)		Pts	Jne	244
1762	AEILKES, Kasper		Pts	Nov	444
1778	AELST, Isabella Clara de Bruyne VAN (Ltd Pr)		Pts	Mch	135
1797	AERSSEN VAN SOMMELSDYK, Rt. Hon. Baron Francois Cornelis VAN Ltd AwW		Pts	May	380
1758	AERTZLAER CLYDAEL ETC., Passchasius Joannes Argustinus Vanden Cruyce, Lord of		Pts	Sep	258
1795	AETH, Dame Ann D'		Middx	Jly	438
1774	AETH, Sir Narborough D' AwW		Kent	Jny	9
1753	AETH, Thomas D'		Pts	Nov	289
1771	AFEREN, Catharina VAN		Pts	Mch	135
1771	AFFLACK, Susannah Catherine		Essex	Dec	467
1771	AFFLACK, William AwW		Essex	Dec	467

1793	AFFLECK, Ann	Sfolk	Feb	62
1788	AFFLECK, Sir Edmund, Baronet	Middx	Nov	518
1788	AFFLECK, Sir Edmund, Bart. (Dble Pr)			
	W rgd last month	Essex	Dec	--
1775	AFFLECK, Elizabeth AwW	Sfolk	Mch	81
1763	AFFLECK, Rev. Gilbert	Sfolk	May	211
1765	AFFLECK, Gilbert, Esq. AwW	Lincs	Apr	127
1779	AFFLECK, James	Middx	May	185
1799	AFFLECK, James (Ltd Pr)	NBrit	Jny	2
1776	AFFLECK, John	Sfolk	Mch	107
1781	AFFLECK, John (Ltd Pr)	Pts	Mch	107
1782	AFFLECK, Rev. John	Corn	Feb	59
1782	AFFLECK, John AwW	NBrit	May	210
1780	AFFLECK, Joseph	Middx	Jne	300
1799	AFFLECK, Margaret, Lady MC KINNON,			
	formerly	Middx	Dec	860
1800	AFFLECK, Philip, Esq.	Middx	Jny	2
1785	AFFLECKE, Rev. James	Nhant	Jny	1
1767	AFTHUR, otherwise ARTHUR, Hannah	Corn	May	161
1780	AGACE, Jane	Essex	Oct	458
1782	AGACE, Jacob	Middx	Mch	108
1786	AGACE, Martha	Middx	Jly	359
1755	AGACE, Obadiah	Middx	Sep	232
1787	AGACE, Obadiah	Essex	Sep	393
1794	AGATTER, Hillersdon	Lond	Oct	484
1794	AGATTER, Hillersdon W rgd Oct last	Lond	Nov	--
1765	AGAN, Brion AwW	Pts	Jne	205
1756	AGAR, Constance Susanna D'	Irel	Aug	215
1781	AGAR, Edward	Middx	Sep	418
1795	AGAR, Edward	Cntby	Feb	60
1780	AGAR, Gertrude AwW	Middx	Aug	383
1783	AGAR, Jacob AwW	Middx	Sep	441
1786	AGAR, Jacob AwW unadm. W rgd Sep 1783	Middx	Mch	--
1750	AGAR, James	Middx	Oct	313
1754	AGAR, John, Esq. AwW	Lond	Mch	66
1759	AGAR, John	Surry	Oct	317
1763	AGAR, Margaret	York	Mch	103
1768	AGAR, Sarah	Middx	Jly	265
1788	AGASSE, Catherine (Ltd Pr)	Pts	Mch	113
1780	AGATE, James	Pts	Feb	54
1795	AGATE, Robert "Asia" & "Retort"	Pts	Jne	360
1754	AGATE, William	Lond	Jny	2
1758	AGATE, Rev. William	Lond	Dec	355
1772	AGATE, William	Sussx	Sep	316
1783	AGATE, William	Sussx	Jne	279
1778	AGATE, Zachariah (by int decree)	Middx	Mch	93
1775	AGERON, Jane	Middx	Dec	452
1772	AGERON, John William	Middx	Dec	429
1774	AGERON, Sara Susanne, otherwise Susanne			
	Sara	Pts	May	166
1793	AGGE, Mary	Glos	Apr	179
1783	AGHIB, Jacob di Salamon (Ltd Pr)	Pts	Sep	442
1760	AGHIB, Solomon	Pts	Jly	270

```
1795   AGHIT,  Peter                                        Middx  Dec  666
1796   AGHIT,  Peter  (Dble Pr) W rgd Dec last              Middx  Mch  --
1791   AGLAND,  Samuel                                      Lond   Jny    1
1793   AGLAND,  Thomas                                      Lond   May  238
1799   AGLIONBY,  Julia                                     Cumb   Aug  561
1783   AGNEW,  Andrew  Ser.                                 Pts    Jne  278
1763   AGNEW,  Archibald  AwW                               Pts    May  210
1767   AGNEW,  Elizabeth                                    Middx  May  161
1785   AGNEW,  Elizabeth                                    Durhm  Sep  451
1778   AGNEW,  James,  Esq.                                 Durhm  Feb   46
1778   AGNEW,  James,  Esq.   Spec. AwW                     Durhm  Mch   93
1788   AGNEW,  James  AwW                                   Irel   Jne  281
1776   AGNEW,  John  Ser.                                   Kent   Jny    1
1754   AGNEW,  Moses                                        Pts    Jne  157
1759   AGNEW,  Patrick,  Esq.                               Yorks  Jly  223
1768   AGNEW,  William  AwW                                 Pts    Mch   94
1785   AGNEW,  William,  Esq.                               Pts    Mch  110
1760   AGRAY,  William  (by int. decree)                   Middx  Nov  412
1794   AGUILAR,  Abraham,  Esq. (Spec. Pr)                 Lond   Jly  343
1774   AGUILAR,  Joseph DE                                  Lond   Aug  289
1787   AGUILAR,  Rachel DE, otherwise PERIERA,
         Rachel Lopes                                       Middx  Oct  465
1796   AGUILAR,  formerly PEREIRA, afterwards
         PEREIRA MENDES, Rebecca D' (Ltd Pr)
         (By Sentence regd 1796 648)                        Middx  Jly  --
1798   AGUILAR,  Theodorus Joannes SANCHEZ DE
         Esq. Spec. AwW                                     Pts    Feb   93
1793   AGUTTER,  Ann                                        Nhant  Jly  350
1795   AGUTTER,  Ann  (Dble Pr) W rgd Jly 1793             Nhant  Jne  --
1754   AGUTTER,  James                                      Nhant  Aug  218
1763   AGUTTER,  James                                      Kent   Feb   41
1762   AGUTTER,  Jonathan                                   Middx  Nov  444
1784   AGUTTER,  Martha                                     Nhant  Apr  186
1785   AGUTTER,  Martha                                     Lond   Apr  169
1763   AGUTTER,  Paul                                       Nhant  Jly  319
1757   AGUTTER,  Thomas                                     Middx  May  144
1764   AGUSCOMBE,  Mary                                     Middx  Nov  413
1778   AHERN,  Philip  AwW                                  Pts    Jne  229
1799   AHIER,  Esther                                       Guery  Oct  694
1784   AHIER,  John  AwW                                    Guery  Jly  363
1794   AHMUTY,  Arthur,  Esq.                               Pts    Oct  484
1794   AHMUTY,  Arthur,  Esq. (Cod) W rgd Oct last         Pts    Nov  536
1797   AHMUTY,  Arthur                                      Middx  Dec  722
1754   AIGNAN,  Mary DE ST.-                                Middx  Aug  226
1792   AIGREMONT,        Paul D' Esq.                       Middx  Jny   13
1783   AIKEN,  otherwise AIKIN, David                       Pts    Aug  397
1778   AIKEN,  Mary                                         SHant  Nov  429
1756   AIKEN,  John                                         Pts    Nov  286
1766   AIKEN,  Peter                                        Pts    Jne  209
1761   AIKEN,  Robert                                       Kent   Feb   44
1768   AIKENHEAD,  James                                    Middx  Feb   41
1765   AIKENHEAD,  Jasper                                   Pts    Feb   40
1763   AIKENHEAD,  John                                     Middx  Mch  105
```

1780	AIKENHEAD, John Lawrence	Middx	Mch	118
1763	AIKER, Charles	Pts	Feb	41
1783	AIKIN, otherwise AIKEN, David	Pts	Aug	397
1795	AIKIN, James David "Lion" & "Dictator"	Pts	Feb	60
1785	AIKIN, Jane	Lancs	Mch	110
1756	AIKIN, John	Leics	Dec	318
1773	AIKIN, Thomas	Kent	Jny	1
1783	AIKINS, John Ser.	Pts	Jne	277
1783	AIKINS, William	Pts	Jny	1
1764	AIKMAN, otherwise YOUNG, Agnes AwW	NBrit	Mch	79
1764	AIKMAN, Alexander AwW	Pts	Jny	1
1799	AIKMAN, James	NBrit	Jne	413
1779	AIKMAN, Mary	Middx	Mch	85
1763	AIKMAN, otherwise AIKMANT, Robert	Pts	Dec	538
1760	AIKMAN, William	Surry	Jne	225
1778	AIKMAN, William	Middx	Oct	385
1785	AIKMAN, William (Ltd Pr)	Pts	Jny	2
1763	AIKMANT, otherwise AIKMAN, Robert	Pts	Dec	538
1767	AILION, Ribra	Lond	Aug	294
1753	AILLCE, Francis	Lond	Feb	37
1792	AILLCE, Gabriel	Middx	Jly	362
1793	AILWAY, John	Herts	May	238
1764	AILWORTH, Bartholomew	Kent	Feb	37
1786	AIMES, otherwise AMES, Samuel Pts -	Worcs	Mch	132
1773	AINELL, Francis	Herts	Sep	350
1796	AINGE, Alexander	Pemb	Nov	538
1770	AINGE, Edward	Middx	Mch	84
1774	AINGE, Edward	Middx	Mch	76
1768	AINGE, Elizabeth	Middx	Oct	367
1771	AINGE, George, Esq.	Middx	Apr	140
1781	AINGE, George AwW	Middx	Sep	417
1771	AINGE, Hannal	Middx	Mch	91
1762	AINGE, Oliver	Lond	Dec	491
1778	AINGE, Richard	Glos	Jne	230
1786	AINGE, Susanna	Middx	May	257
1791	AINGEL, Richard	Worcs	Dec	552
1790	AINGELL, Ann	Salop	Dec	535
1773	AINGELL, Thomas	Salop	Sep	350
1753	AINGER, Elizabeth	Surry	Dec	307
1795	AINGER, Elizabeth	Camb	May	292
1766	AINGWORTH, formerly WEAVER, Mary (Ltd Pr)	Lond	May	166
1764	AINSBY, Ralph	Pts	Sep	336
1756	AINSLEY, George	Middx	Nov	287
1769	AINSLIE, George	Pts	Jne	193
1798	AINSLIE, Rev. Gilbert	Pts	Sep	580
1796	AINSLIE, Harrison Philip AwW	Middx	Dec	590
1757	AINSLIE, William	Middx	Jly	212
1786	AINSLIE, William, Esq.	Bath	May	258
1769	AINSWORTH, Edmund	Surry	Jly	233
1761	AINSWORTH, Francis	SHant	Jne	199
1763	AINSWORTH, John AwW of Gds unadm W rgd 1746, 172	Beds	Jne	--
1787	AINSWORTH, John	Middx	Mch	101

1782	AINSWORTH, Mary AwW	Middx	Jny	1
1782	AINSWORTH, otherwise HAINSWORTH, Mary			
	AwW Anor. grant this month	Middx	Jny	--
1778	AINSWORTH, Nathaniel	Som	Jly	271
1752	AINSWORTH, Samuel	Surry	Mch	56
1797	AINSWORTH, formerly HARRIS, Sarah			
	(Ltd Pr)	Middx	Apr	220
1779	AISHLEY, Richard	Wilts	Aug	333
1789	AISKEW, Rev. John	SHant	Dec	571
1750	AISLABIE, Hon. Elizabeth	Middx	Jne	185
1796	AISLABIE, Samuel	Yorks	Apr	160
1781	AISLABIE, William, Esq.	Yorks	May	222
1763	AISLEY, Robert	Middx	Apr	163
1789	AISHTON, otherwise ASHTON, Joseph	Som	May	232
1775	AISTROP, Henry	Middx	Nov	400
1778	AISTRUP, Samuel	Lincs	Dec	474
1756	AIR, Francis AwW	Pts	Aug	215
1762	AIR, George AwW	Pts	Feb	37
1769	AIRAY, Elizabeth	Middx	May	149
1764	AIRAY, John	Middx	Mch	78
1798	AIRD, James Ltd AwW	Pts	Mch	151
1775	AIRD, John	NBrit	Apr	126
1793	AIRD, John	Worcs	May	238
1784	AIRES, Abraham "Burford" (Ser.)	Middx	Jly	363
1777	AIRES, otherwise AYRES, James	Pts	Nov	445
1799	AIRES, Robert, Esq.	Som	Dec	819
1766	AIREY, George	Middx	Apr	125
1779	AIREY, Katherine	Middx	Apr	138
1776	AIREY, Thomas, Esq.	Newcl	Dec	484
1755	AIRS, William	Pts	Oct	252
1763	AIRS, William AwW	Pts	Nov	493
1784	AITCHISON, Andrew	Middx	Jne	304
1784	AITKAN, otherwise AITKEN, otherwise			
	AITKENS, Robert Ser. "Barfleur" AwW	Pts	Jny	2
1761	AITKEN, Alexander AwW	Pts	Oct	335
1794	AITKEN, George	Cumb	Feb	59
1791	AITKEN, John	Middx	Jly	314
1784	AITKEN, otherwise AITKAN, otherwise			
	AITKENS, Robert Ser. "Barfleur" AwW	Pts	Jny	2
1762	AITKEN, William	Pts	Sep	365
1784	AITKEN, William	Wark	Jny	2
1769	AITKENS, Alexander	Middx	Jny	1
1778	AITKENS, James AwW	Pts	Oct	385
1794	AITKENS, John	Middx	Apr	180
1794	AITKIN, Alexander	Pemb	May	239
1782	AITKIN, George	Pts	Oct	478
1800	AITKINS, Peter (No ship)	Pts - Herfd	Jny	1
1752	AITON, otherwise EATON, John AwW	Pts	Oct	247
1793	AJAX, Thomas	Berks	Mch	124
1760	AKEAN, James AwW	Pts	Aug	312
1790	AKED, Benjamin Spec. AwW	Middx	Apr	168
1789	AKED, Elizabeth	Surry	Apr	180
1799	AKED, Elizabeth	Middx	Feb	89

1785	AKED, Joah	Yorks	Jne	288
1782	AKED, John	Lond	Mch	108
1791	AKED, Margaret	Middx	Nov	493
1784	AKED, Thomas	Lond	Mch	117
1786	AKED, William	Lond	Feb	60
1784	AKEHURST, otherwise AKHURST, Thomas	Sussx	Jne	303
1755	AKEN, Abraham VAN (Ltd Pr)	Pts	Jne	177
1774	AKEN, otherwise VAN DER WELL, otherwise VAN DER WEL, Geertruyda Roelanda, formerly VAN (Ltd Pr)	Pts	Nov	413
1767	AKEN, Hendrik VAN (Ltd Pr)	Pts	Sep	358
1763	AKEN, otherwise AKIN, John	SHant	Jne	263
1768	AKEN, Robert Ser.	Pts	Jny	1
1767	AKEN, Roeland VAN (Ltd Pr)	Pts	Aug	326
1792	AKEN, Roelanda VAN (Ltd Pr)	Pts	Dec	640
1764	AKEN, otherwise AKIN, Thomas AwW	Pts	Feb	36
1782	AKEN, William Cornelis Son VAN (Ltd Pr)	Pts	Nov	--
1758	AKEN, otherwise FRANKEN, Wyntje VAN	Pts	Jly	216
1765	AKENHEAD, James	Middx	Aug	282
1750	AKENN, otherwise AKIN, Robert	Pts	May	134
1770	AKENSIDE, Dr. Mark (Dr. of Physic)	Middx	Jly	251
1797	AKERHOLM, George, otherwise Georg M.S. "Manship" & "Louisa"	Pts	Oct	625
1782	AKERLAKEN, Joan VAN (Ltd Pr)	Pts	Oct	520
1785	AKERLAKEN, Rt. Worshipful Pieter VAN (Ltd Pr)	Pts	Apr	--
1763	AKERMAN, Elizabeth	Surry	May	210
1765	AKERMAN, Francis	Middx	Jny	2
1799	AKERMAN, Harry	Lond	Mch	161
1792	AKERMAN, Isaac, Esq.	Middx	May	253
1757	AKERMAN, John	Surry	Sep	265
1761	AKERMAN, John	Middx	Aug	276
1789	AKERMAN, John	Bucks	Feb	70
1790	AKERMAN, John	Wilts	Jny	1
1761	AKERMAN, Margaret	Middx	Dec	415
1792	AKERMAN, Richard	Lond	Nov	542
1797	AKERMAN, Sarah	Middx	Nov	673
1763	AKERMAN, Thomas	Pts	Dec	538
1785	AKEROYDE, Thomas	Middx	Jny	1
1785	AKERS, Avetas, Esq.	Pts	May	229
1780	AKERS, otherwise ACKERS, otherwise ACRES, Edward AwW	Kent	Jny	1
1799	AKERS, George Alexander, Esq.	Middx	Jny	1
1753	AKERS, John	Herts	Mch	69
1759	AKERS, John	Pts	Dec	381
1760	AKERS, John	Pts	Mch	85
1780	AKERS, John	Kent	Apr	168
1752	AKERS, Mary	Middx	Jne	145
1783	AKERS, Mary	Surry	Jny	1
1768	AKERS, Thomas	Berks	May	184
1783	AKERS, Thomas	Kent	May	211
1781	AKERSLOOT, Jacob, Esq. (Ltd Pr)	Pts	Jny	1
1773	AKERSLOOT, Paulus (Ltd Pr)	Pts	Nov	413

1784	AKHURST, otherwise AKEHURST, Thomas	Sussx	Jne	303
1796	AKHURST, Thomas	Middx	Sep	439
1785	AKHURST, William	Kent	Feb	61
1789	AKHURST, William	Surry	Jly	343
1770	AKID, Michael	Surry	Jny	1
1781	AKID, Samuel	Kent	Aug	374
1769	AKID, William AwW	Kent	Apr	110
1779	AKIN, Alexander Ser.	Pts	Dec	482
1763	AKIN, otherwise AKEN, John	SHant	Jne	263
1750	AKIN, otherwise AKENN, Robert	Pts	May	134
1764	AKIN, otherwise AKEN, Thomas AwW	Pts	Feb	36
1769	AKINE, Robert	Middx	Jne	193
1791	AL, Duyfie Jansz AwW	Pts	Jne	263
1783	ALABASTOR, Henry	Devon	Oct	493
1756	ALANCON, Margurite D', otherwise De BERGIER, Margaret	Pts	Dec	317
1786	ALAND, Isaac	Wilts	Jly	361
1750	ALAND, Jane AwW	Wilts	Apr	101
1782	ALAND, John Fortescue	Middx	Jly	333
1765	ALAND, Richard	Middx	Nov	398
1800	ALAVOINE, Esther	Middx	Feb	80
1777	ALAVOINE, Mary Magdaline	Lond	Nov	445
1785	ALBAN, Jane ST.	Som	Aug	--
1786	ALBANS, Most Noble George, Duke of ST.	Pts	May	303
1787	ALBANS, Most Noble George, Duke of ST.	Middx	Feb	92
1779	ALBANS, Most Noble Ly Jane, Duchess of ST. (Ltd Pr)	Kent	Feb	37
1767	ALBANY, His Royal Highness Prince Edward, late Duke of York and		Oct	398
1774	ALBARES, otherwise ALVARES, Pereira Rachel AwW	Lond	Jne	239
1800	ALBECK, Thomas	SHant	Jly	500
1789	ALBEMARLE, Rt Hon Lady Ann, Countess Dowager of	Middx	Nov	528
1772	ALBEMARLE, Rt Hon George, Knight of Most Noble Order of Garter & Gen. of H.M.Fs., Earl of	Surry	Oct	347
1751	ALBERDINGH, Dr.(in Phys) Adriaan VAN (Ltd Pr)	Pts	May	161
1783	ALBERT, Elizabeth	Middx	Jne	279
1785	ALBERT, Jacob	Middx	Feb	62
1753	ALBERT, John	Pts	Sep	244
1798	ALBERT, Louis	Middx	Aug	522
1754	ALBERT, Marianne	Middx	Dec	317
1765	ALBERT, Mary, otherwise Mary Anne	Middx	Sep	319
1765	ALBERT, Mary Anne, otherwise Mary	Middx	Sep	319
1796	ALBERT, Mary	Glam	Jne	291
1763	ALBERT, Peter AwW	Middx	Apr	163
1763	ALBERT, Richard AwW	Worcs	Jny	1
1766	ALBERT, Thomas	Middx	Sep	327
1789	ALBERTI, Rev. Ericus Fredericus (Ltd Pr)	Pts	Apr	186
1789	ALBERTINI, H.E.Dom Giovanni Battista, Prince of Cimitile	Pts	Jly	344

1784	ALBERTS, Joachim, otherwise ALBRIGHT, Joshim, otherwise ALBOROUGH, Jochin, otherwise ABOROUGH, Yough E.I.S."Major", "Superb", & "Monmouth"		Pts	Aug	425
1773	ALBERTUSZ, formerly LOOTEN, otherwise VERHAMME, otherwise Elizabeth VERHAMME		Pts	Sep	375
1767	ALBERTUSZOON, Abraham VERHAMME AwW		Pts	Dec	467
1775	ALBIN, Ezechiel		Linc	Mch	81
1788	ALBIN, John		Surry	Feb	54
1790	ALBIN, Margaret AwW		Surry	May	221
1789	ALBINUS, Anna Sophia (Ltd Pr)		Pts	Jny	1
1772	ALBINUS, Bernard Siegfried		Pts	Apr	119
1752	ALBINUS, Christian Bernhard (Ltd Pr)		Pts	May	115
1776	ALBINUS, Christiana Elisabeth (Ltd Pr)		Pts	Jly	296
1756	ALBINUS, otherwise de JONG, Hon Lady Cornelia Aletta (Ltd Pr)		Pts	Feb	26
1768	ALBINUS, Dorothea (Ltd Pr)		Pts	Jne	224
1774	ALBINUS, Frederica (Ltd Pr)		Pts	Oct	357
1778	ALBINUS, Fredicus Bernardus (Ltd Pr)		Pts	Aug	309
1781	ALBINUS, Maria Wilhemina (Ltd Pr)		Pts	May	221
1764	ALBIRO, otherwise ALLBOROUGH, Jeremiah		Pts	Apr	128
1765	ALBISTON, John		Lond	Mch	84
1765	ALBISTON, John Dble Pr & W rgd Mch last		Lond	Apr	--
1775	ALBON, Dorcas		Sfolk	Jne	219
1795	ALBON, James		Kent	Jny	2
1797	ALBON, Mary		Middx	Dec	722
1795	ALBON, Richard		Middx	Jly	428
1768	ALBONE, Francis		Middx	Nov	400
1751	ALBORN, Samuel		Wilts	Mch	68
1764	ALBOROUGH, George	Pts -	Essex	Mch	78
1784	ALBOROUGH, Jochin, otherwise ABOROUGH, Yough, otherwise ALBERTS, Joachim, otherwise ALBRIGHT, Joshim E.I.S. "Major", "Superb" & "Monmouth"		Pts	Aug	425
1792	ALBRIGHT, John		Middx	May	124
1779	ALBRIGHT, otherwise ALLBRIGHT, Joseph		Oxon	Dec	482
1784	ALBRIGHT, Joshim, otherwise ALBOROUGH, Jochin, otherwise ABOROUGH, Yough, otherwise ALBERTS, Joachim E.I.S. "Major", "Superb" & "Monmouth"		Pts	Aug	425
1792	ALBRIGHT, Mary		Herts	Feb	53
1754	ALBRIGHT, otherwise ALLBRIGHT, William		Bucks	Oct	264
1779	ALBRIS, otherwise ALEBERS, Richard		Pts	Feb	36
1764	ALBROW, Thomas		Sfolk	Apr	129
1763	ALBSZ MATEN, formerly SPANNYT, Geertruy Susanna (Ltd Pr)		Pts	Apr	189
1794	ALBURN, Robert		Lond	Sep	443
1794	ALBURY, Catherine		Middx	Aug	402
1782	ALBURY, Hester		Middx	Jny	1
1783	ALBURY, John		Surry	Oct	494
1755	ALBURY, William		Middx	Dec	303
1781	ALBYN, Ann ST.		Som	Apr	212
1768	ALBYN, John ST. Esq.		Som	Dec	466
1791	ALBYN, Rev. Lancelot ST.		Bath	Feb	99
1775	ALCE, Elizabeth		Surry	Dec	452

1750	ALCE, James		Surry	Apr	101
1771	ALCE, John		Surry	Jny	2
1792	ALCE, Robert		Sussx	Jne	313
1771	ALCE, Thomas		Middx	Aug	328
1791	ALCE, Thomas		Essex	Dec	552
1774	ALCHIN, Anna		Kent	Feb	36
1778	ALCHIN, Anna Dble Pr W rgd Feb 1774		Kent	Jly	271
1775	ALCHIN, Anthony		Kent	Jly	259
1779	ALCHIN, Amy		Surry	Mch	85
1785	ALCHIN, George		Kent	Mch	110
1777	ALCHIN, Henry		Kent	Nov	445
1769	ALCHIN, Thomas		Kent	Nov	363
1770	ALCHIN, Thomas Dble Pr W rgd Nov last		Kent	Jne	--
1752	ALCHORNE, Elizabeth		Middx	Aug	204
1756	ALCHORNE, Elizabeth		Essex	Jne	156
1771	ALCHORNE, Elizabeth		Middx	Apr	140
1769	ALCHORNE, Mary (Ltd Pr)		Sussx	Jly	233
1795	ALCHORNE, Mary		Sussx	Jly	428
1758	ALCHORNE, Philip		Kent	Sep	257
1760	ALCHORNE, Richard		Kent	Jne	225
1768	ALCHORNE, Robert AwW unadm W rgd Aug 1767		Lond	Jne	--
1800	ALCHORNE, Stanesby, Esq.		Lond	Dec	833
1757	ALCOCK, Ann		Surry	Jny	1
1771	ALCOCK, Daniel		Glos	Apr	142
1754	ALCOCK, Elizabeth		Surry	Jny	1
1757	ALCOCK, Elizabeth		Middx	Sep	265
1786	ALCOCK, Elizabeth		Sussx	Nov	552
1796	ALCOCK, Elizabeth		Surry	Jly	343
1765	ALCOCK, Francis		Worcs	Dec	438
1779	ALCOCK, James, Esq.		Nhant	Sep	364
1752	ALCOCK, John	Pts -	Middx	Jny	1
1753	ALCOCK, John		Lond	Oct	262
1762	ALCOCK, John		Middx	Oct	408
1762	ALCOCK, John		Surry	Oct	409
1772	ALCOCK, Rev. John		Surry	Mch	81
1787	ALCOCK, John		Pemb	Nov	479
1798	ALCOCK, John Dormer AwW	Pts -	Irel	Jny	1
1765	ALCOCK, Lydia		Glos	Nov	397
1786	ALCOCK, Mary (Spec Pr)		SHant	Mch	134
1787	ALCOCK, Mary		Middx	Oct	436
1789	ALCOCK, Mary (Spec Pr) W rgd 1786, 134		SHant	Nov	--
1798	ALCOCK, Mary		Bath	Jly	457
1763	ALCOCK, Matthew		Middx	May	210
1765	ALCOCK, Matthew		Lincs	Aug	283
1758	ALCOCK, Michael, Esq.		Middx	Jne	175
1769	ALCOCK, Rebecca		Oxon	Sep	299
1774	ALCOCK, Richard		Lond	Feb	36
1800	ALCOCK, Robert Ser. "Culloden"		Pts	Dec	833
1755	ALCOCK, Thomas		Surry	Nov	274
1755	ALCOCK, Thomas		Leics	Dec	303
1771	ALCOCK, Thomas		SHant	Jny	1
1792	ALCOCK, Thomas		Middx	Jny	1

```
1798  ALCOCK, Rev. Thomas                                    Chest  Sep 580
1750  ALCOCK, William                                        Pts    Feb  35
1762  ALCOCK, William    AwW                                 Pts    Apr 136
1766  ALCOCK, William                                        Oxon   May 166
1794  ALCOCK, William                                        Middx  Jny   2
1775  ALCOTT, Elizabeth                                      Worcs  Jny   1
1774  ALDAY, John                                            Middx  Dec 419
1776  ALDAY, Sarah  (Ltd Pr)                                 Bucks  May 209
1761  ALDBOROUGH, Jeremiah  Ser.                             Pts    Jny   1
1774  ALDCROFT, Charles                                      Surry  Oct 357
1797  ALDCROFT, Charles                                      Lancr  Sep 583
1797  ALDCROFT, James, Esq.                                  Pts    Nov 673
1760  ALDEN, Ann                                             Pts    Jny   1
1755  ALDEN, Charles                                         Devon  May 121
1756  ALDEN, Charles  AwW unadm  W rgd May 1755              Devon  Jne   --
1750  ALDEN, Elizabeth                                       Sfolk  Jne 185
1765  ALDEN, Joseph                                          Middx  Mch  84
1757  ALDEN, Samuel                                          Brstl  Dec 348
1762  ALDEN, William                                         Middx  May 182
1756  ALDER, Amos                                            Kent   Jly 360
1757  ALDER, Christopher                          Pts -     Devon  Jny   1
1794  ALDER, Elizabeth                                       Middx  Sep 442
1775  ALDER, Henry                                           Middx  Jne 219
1791  ALDER, Isabella                                        Middx  Jne 263
1798  ALDER, Jane                                            Middx  Oct 631
1800  ALDER, Jeremiah                                        Wark   Jne 430
1766  ALDER, John, Esq.                                      Dubln  Feb  45
1774  ALDER, John                                            Berks  Dec 418
1767  ALDER, Margret, otherwise Margaret                     Irel   Mch  82
1752  ALDER, Mary                                            Bath   Nov 267
1773  ALDER, Robert  AwW                                     Middx  Dec 456
1759  ALDER, Thomas  AwW                                     Pts    May 155
1785  ALDER, Thomas                                          Berks  Dec 584
1800  ALDER, William                                         Nland  Sep 639
1766  ALDERIDGE, William                                     Middx  Sep 327
1756  ALDERMAN, George                                       Beds   Feb  26
1784  ALDERMAN, John  AwW                                    Berks  Sep 488
1750  ALDERMAN, Richard                                      Surry  Oct 313
1797  ALDERMAN, Robert                                       Beds   Mch 124
1759  ALDERMAN, Thomas                                       Beds   Aug 255
1783  ALDERMARY, formerly INGLEDEW, Elizabeth
        (Ltd Pr)                                             Kent   Oct 518
1794  ALDERS, James  "Minerva" & "Crown"                    Pts    Jne 294
1763  ALDERSEY, Hugh                                         Kent   Mch 103
1764  ALDERSEY, Joseph                                       Berks  Jly 248
1786  ALDERSEY, Joseph                                       Surry  Mch 132
1796  ALDERSEY, Joseph  AwW of Gds unadm
        W rgd 1786, 132                                      Surry  Mch  --
1792  ALDERSEY, Mary                                         Chest  Aug 413
1775  ALDERSEY, Sarah                                        Middx  Feb  38
1770  ALDERSEY, William                                      Middx  Jly 251
1800  ALDERSEY, William, Esq.                                Surry  Jne 429
1767  ALDERSON, Christopher                                  Norf   Jne 204
```

45

```
1798   ALDERSON, Christopher                              Middx Apr 230
1768   ALDERSON, George                                   Middx Jne 224
1750   ALDERSON, John                                     Pts   Aug 250
1751   ALDERSON, John                                     Pts   Jne 164
1754   ALDERSON, John  AwW                                Pts   Feb  31
1792   ALDERSON, John                                     Middx May 253
1791   ALDERSON, Joseph  (Ltd Pr)                         Pts   Jne 263
1798   ALDERSON, Mary                                     Lond  May 306
1778   ALDERSON, Sarah                                    Sfolk Apr 141
1752   ALDERSON, Thomas                                   Kent  Aug 204
1761   ALDERSON, Thomas                                   Sfolk Feb  44
1792   ALDERSON, Thomas, Esq.                             Norf  Jly 362
1799   ALDERSON, Thomas                                   Durhm Jly 472
1755   ALDERTON, Joel                                     Middx Mch  65
1780   ALDERTON, Mary                                     Middx Feb  53
1786   ALDERTON, Robert                                   Essex Jly 361
1765   ALDERTON, Samuel                                   Middx May 167
1790   ALDERTON, Sarah                                    Surry Mch 114
1764   ALDERTON, Thomas                           Pts - SHant Mch  78
1787   ALDERTON, Thomas                                   Sfolk May 195
1787   ALDERTON, Thomas                                   Sfolk Jly 300
1772   ALDERTON, William, Esq.                            Middx May 155
1779   ALDERTON, William                                  Surry Mch  86
1792   ALDERTON, William                                  Surry Jny   2
1781   ALDERTS, Joost  (Ltd Pr)                           Pts   Jne 280
1791   ALDERWERELT, Rt. Hon. John Carol VAN
         (Ltd Pr)                                         Pts   Oct  --
1789   ALDERWERELT, Susanna Maria VAN  Ltd AwW            Pts   Feb 124
1765   ALDERWICK, Richard                                 Middx Mch  84
1771   ALDERWICK, Richard                                 Lond  Apr 142
1786   ALDERWICK, Richard                                 Middx Jly 361
1754   ALDEY, William, Esq.                               Mon   Jny   1
1771   ALDIN, Catherine, otherwise Katherine              Surry Mch  91
1782   ALDING, Elizabeth                                  Middx Jny   1
1762   ALDING, John                                       Middx Jny   1
1775   ALDREAD, otherwise ALDRED, John                    Pts   Sep 332
1783   ALDRED, George                                     Sfolk Sep 441
1799   ALDRED, James Ser.                         Pts - York  Apr 241
1775   ALDRED, otherwise ALDREAD, John                    Pts   Sep 332
1796   ALDRED, Mary                                       Herts Mch 106
1798   ALDRED, Matthew                                    Essex Jly 456
1788   ALDRED, Obed                                       Sfolk Aug 381
1789   ALDRED, Richard                                    Lancs Nov 520
1792   ALDRED, Samuel Dixon                               Middx Apr 189
1791   ALDRED, Tripheria                                  Sfolk Feb  52
1778   ALDRED, otherwise ALLDRIDGE, William AwW           Middx Apr 141
1770   ALDRICH, Ann                                       Middx Aug 283
1798   ALDRICH, George, Esq. Dr. of Physic                Notts Jny   2
1769   ALDRICH, Rev. Stephen                              Middx Sep 299
1758   ALDRICH, Walter  AwW                               Staff Oct 282
1784   ALDRICH, William May                               Surry Aug 425
1756   ALDRIDG, Martha                                    Lond  Jne 156
1756   ALDRIDG, Martha (Dble Pr) W rgd Jne last Lond      Oct  --
```

46

1758	ALDRIDGE, Abel	Middx	Sep	257
1782	ALDRIDGE, Abel, Esq.	Middx	Dec	569
1769	ALDRIDGE, Ambrose	Essex	Mch	73
1761	ALDRIDGE, Amey	Essex	Apr	115
1769	ALDRIDGE, otherwise ALLDRIDGE, Ann	Lond	Jny	1
1782	ALDRIDGE, Ann	Middx	Dec	569
1783	ALDRIDGE, Ann AwW unadm W rgd Dec last	Middx	Feb	--
1784	ALDRIDGE, Ann	Leics	Feb	59
1763	ALDRIDGE, Charles	Wilts	Dec	537
1799	ALDRIDGE, Charles	Wilts	Nov	756
1779	ALDRIDGE, Christian	Lond	Mch	87
1760	ALDRIDGE, Christopher	Middx	Dec	449
1771	ALDRIDGE, Elizabeth	Lond	Dec	467
1772	ALDRIDGE, Elizabeth	Middx	Dec	429
1790	ALDRIDGE, Elizabeth	Middx	Sep	409
1755	ALDRIDGE, Edward	Middx	Jne	153
1766	ALDRIDGE, Edward	Lond	Jny	1
1787	ALDRIDGE, Edward	Glos	Mch	101
1779	ALDRIDGE, George	Pts	Apr	138
1789	ALDRIDGE, George	Lond	Apr	185
1763	ALDRIDGE, Henry	Berks	Nov	493
1784	ALDRIDGE, Isaac Ser. "Worcester"	Brstl	Jny	1
1760	ALDRIDGE, James	Devon	Nov	412
1762	ALDRIDGE, James AwW	Bucks	Aug	330
1768	ALDRIDGE, James	Pts	Aug	305
1754	ALDRIDGE, John	Pts	Aug	217
1760	ALDRIDGE, John	Middx	Dec	449
1764	ALDRIDGE, John	Brstl	Jny	1
1767	ALDRIDGE, John	Berks	Nov	399
1768	ALDRIDGE, John (late one of Proc Gen of Arches Ct of Cntby) AwW unadm W rgd 1747, 115	Lond	Mch	--
1770	ALDRIDGE, John	Nwich	Mch	84
1772	ALDRIDGE, John	Bucks	Sep	316
1781	ALDRIDGE, John	Pts	Jne	280
1783	ALDRIDGE, John	Berks	Apr	158
1784	ALDRIDGE, John	Middx	Aug	425
1791	ALDRIDGE, John	Berks	Nov	493
1793	ALDRIDGE, John	Herts	Mch	124
1795	ALDRIDGE, John	Sussx	Jne	360
1799	ALDRIDGE, John	Glos	Sep	640
1759	ALDRIDGE, Margaret	Bucks	Nov	347
1756	ALDRIDGE, Mary	Bucks	Feb	40
1778	ALDRIDGE, Mary	Lond	Jne	229
1788	ALDRIDGE, otherwise BARNETT, Molly	Bucks	May	225
1768	ALDRIDGE, Rachel	Middx	Apr	138
1764	ALDRIDGE, Samuel, otherwise ALDRIDGE, Samuel Smith AwW	Pts - SHant	Nov	413
1764	ALDRIDGE, Samuel Smith, otherwise ALDRIDGE, Samuel AwW	Pts - SHant	Nov	413
1752	ALDRIDGE, Thomas	Kent	Feb	27
1783	ALDRIDGE, Thomas	Bucks	May	211
1783	ALDRIDGE, Thomas, Esq.	Bucks	Nov	548

1784	ALDRIDGE, Thomas AwW "Sybil",			
	"Boreas" & "Centaur"	Pts	Jne	302
1786	ALDRIDGE, Thomas	Middx	Oct	499
1794	ALDRIDGE, Thomas	Bucks	Apr	180
1795	ALDRIDGE, Thomas	Surry	Dec	666
1762	ALDRIDGE, otherwise ALLDRIDGE, William	Middx	Aug	331
1764	ALDRIDGE, otherwise HALTRIDGE, William	Pts	Mch	96
1777	ALDRIDGE, William	Middx	Jly	296
1784	ALDRIDGE, William	Notts	Apr	185
1784	ALDRIDGE, otherwise ALLRIDGE, otherwise			
	ALLRIGE, William Anor. grant this			
	month	Notts	Apr	--
1790	ALDRIDGE, William AwW	Middx	May	221
1791	ALDRIDGE, Rev. William	Surry	Apr	164
1794	ALDRIGE, William	Lond	Oct	484
1791	ALDOUS, Robert	Middx	May	208
1791	AL DUYFIE, Jansz AwW	Pts	Jne	263
1765	ALDWELL, Thomas AwW	Middx	Aug	282
1752	ALDWIN, Martha	Middx	Mch	56
1750	ALDWIN, Philip	Middx	Jny	1
1778	ALDWIN, Philip	Middx	Feb	47
1780	ALDWIN, Sarah	Middx	Mch	117
1780	ALDWIN, William	Middx	Mch	117
1793	ALDWINCKLE, Ann	Nhant	Nov	537
1775	ALDWINCKLE, John	Nhant	Jne	217
1777	ALDWINCKLE, Robert	Nhant	Aug	339
1753	ALDWINCKLE, Mary	Dorst	Jne	159
1778	ALDWORTH, Hannah	Berks	Jne	229
1780	ALDWORTH, Joseph	Middx	Aug	383
1783	ALDWORTH, Margaret	Middx	Mch	106
1766	ALDWORTH, Mary	Berks	Mch	88
1765	ALDWORTH, Richard	Berks	Jne	205
1795	ALDWORTH, Richard	Berks	Sep	532
1777	ALDWORTH, Robert	Berks	Feb	49
1760	ALDWORTH, William	Berks	May	180
1769	ALE, Jane	Middx	Dec	402
1799	ALEA, otherwise LEA, otherwise COOK,			
	George	Herfd	Jne	414
1779	ALEBERS, otherwise ALBRIS, Richard	Pts	Feb	36
1765	ALEE, Thomas	Wilts	Jne	205
1763	ALEFOUNDER, John	Essex	Jly	319
1785	ALEFOUNDER, John "La Fortuna" &			
	"Valiant"	Pts — Kent	Aug	400
1795	ALEFOUNDER, John	Pts	Oct	579
1784	ALEFOUNDER, Robert	Kent	Sep	488
1761	ALEGRE, Nicolas	Pts	Oct	335
1789	ALEHOUSE, Robert AwW	Middx	Apr	185
1753	ALEN, Catherine	Middx	May	126
1750	ALENBURGH, Adriana VAN (Ltd Pr)	Pts	Mch	98
1775	ALENSON, otherwise GRONOVIUS, otherwise			
	ALENSOON, Johanna Susanna, formerly			
	(Ltd Pr)	Pts	Feb	52
1775	ALENSOON, otherwise GRONOVIUS, formerly			
	ALENSON, Johanna Susanna (Ltd Pr)	Pts	Feb	52

Year	Name		Month	Page
1798	ALERDINCK, VAN VOORST VAN, otherwise VAN BERGENTHEIM, Dirk Fredrik	Pts	Sep	622
1782	ALESTER, otherwise MC ALLISTER, Charles MC	Pts	Oct	506
1758	ALESTER, John MC AwW	Pts	Nov	311
1767	ALEWYN, The Noble Lord Abraham AwW	–	Aug	294
1768	ALEWYN, otherwise The Lady Agneta Elisabeth VAN SON, formerly (Ltd Pr)	Pts	Feb	81
1780	ALEWYN, Anna (Ltd Pr)	Pts	May	234
1784	ALEWYN, Cornelia Jacoba (Ltd Pr)	Pts	Jne	304
1763	ALEWYN, Duyfie	Pts	Sep	415
1771	ALEWYN, Eva Anna	Pts	Nov	428
1790	ALEWYN, Gillis (Ltd Pr)	Pts	Mch	114
1761	ALEWYN, The Hon. Jacob, Esq., otherwise Sir Jacob	Pts	Sep	307
1789	ALEWYN, Jacob (Ltd Pr)	Pts	Nov	528
1785	ALEWYN, Maria Catherina (Ltd Pr)	Pts	Aug	400
1788	ALEWYN, Dr. Zacharias Henric, (Dr. of Laws) (Ltd Pr)	Pts	Aug	381
1750	ALEWYNSE, Coninck Gerritt (Ltd Pr)	Pts	Nov	344
1784	ALEXANDER, Albina, otherwise Ablina	Glos	Sep	488
1760	ALEXANDER, Alexander	Pts	Jne	227
1765	ALEXANDER, Alexander	Pts	Oct	359
1788	ALEXANDER, Alexander (Dr. of Laws)	Middx	Oct	468
1750	ALEXANDER, Alice	Camb	May	135
1787	ALEXANDER, Andrew	Surry	Feb	51
1798	ALEXANDER, Ann	Middx	Mch	151
1768	ALEXANDER, Dr. Benjamin (Dr of Phys)	Lond	Apr	138
1762	ALEXANDER, Biss (Ltd Act W)	SHant	Jne	230
1784	ALEXANDER, Catherine CLIPPERTON, formerly	Pts	Nov	591
1786	ALEXANDER, Catharine	Glos	Sep	461
1759	ALEXANDER, Charles AwW	Pts	Apr	115
1775	ALEXANDER, Charles, Esq. (late one of Proc Gen of Arches Ct of Cntby)	Essex	Aug	298
1778	ALEXANDER, Charles	Essex	Dec	474
1800	ALEXANDER, Charles	Notts	Mch	172
1798	ALEXANDER, Charlotte	Sfolk	Nov	691
1759	ALEXANDER, Christopher	Lond	Jly	223
1772	ALEXANDER, Cosmus	Edin	Sep	316
1758	ALEXANDER, David	Chest	May	139
1784	ALEXANDER, David E.I.S. "Stafford"	Pts	May	243
1772	ALEXANDER, Deborah	Herts	Oct	347
1786	ALEXANDER, Dykes	Sfolk	Sep	461
1772	ALEXANDER, Edmund	Middx	Feb	35
1752	ALEXANDER, Edward (late one of Proc Gen of Arches Ct of Cntby) AwW	Lond	Dec	292
1759	ALEXANDER, Edward	Glos	Sep	287
1763	ALEXANDER, Edward (Dble Pr) W rgd Sep 1759	Glos	May	—
1775	ALEXANDER, Edward	Lond	Sep	332
1796	ALEXANDER, Edward	Lond	Jne	291
1790	ALEXANDER, Elizabeth	Durhm	Nov	492

1788	ALEXANDER,	Frances		Middx	Jne	281
1756	ALEXANDER,	George	Pts –	Devon	Jne	157
1757	ALEXANDER,	George		Surry	Feb	37
1786	ALEXANDER,	George, Esq.		Cork	Jly	360
1786	ALEXANDER,	George (Ltd Pr)		Pts	Jly	361
1785	ALEXANDER,	Henry		Essex	Sep	453
1752	ALEXANDER,	James AwW		Pts	Sep	227
1756	ALEXANDER,	James		Herts	Feb	26
1763	ALEXANDER,	James		Pts	Mch	104
1763	ALEXANDER,	James	Pts –	Middx	Jly	319
1764	ALEXANDER,	James		Lond	Feb	36
1775	ALEXANDER,	James		Essex	Jly	259
1777	ALEXANDER,	James		Pts	Apr	143
1781	ALEXANDER,	James		Middx	Oct	459
1782	ALEXANDER,	James (by int dec)		Middx	Jly	332
1786	ALEXANDER,	James		Middx	Jny	2
1783	ALEXANDER,	James Ser. "Diamond"		NBrit	Dec	596
1794	ALEXANDER,	James		Berks	Jne	294
1794	ALEXANDER,	James		Middx	Jly	344
1797	ALEXANDER,	James		Kent	Dec	722
1800	ALEXANDER,	James		Essex	Jny	3
1785	ALEXANDER,	Jane		Middx	Apr	168
1753	ALEXANDER,	John		Som	Apr	100
1756	ALEXANDER,	John		Pts	Dec	317
1766	ALEXANDER,	John AwW		Berks	Feb	44
1766	ALEXANDER,	John Ser.		Pts	Aug	290
1767	ALEXANDER,	John		Berks	May	162
1776	ALEXANDER,	John		Lond	Apr	159
1776	ALEXANDER,	John AwW		Middx	May	209
1779	ALEXANDER,	John		Essex	Aug	333
1781	ALEXANDER,	John		Pts	Feb	54
1782	ALEXANDER,	John		Pts	Mch	108
1787	ALEXANDER,	John Ser.		Devon	Sep	395
1795	ALEXANDER,	John		Surry	Aug	492
1796	ALEXANDER,	John		Surry	Feb	52
1798	ALEXANDER,	John		Surry	Oct	631
1799	ALEXANDER,	John "Heroine" & "Carysfort" AwW		Pts	Apr	240
1752	ALEXANDER,	Joshua		Essex	Apr	82
1750	ALEXANDER,	Lewis Ltd AwW unadm W rgd 1732, 1		Middx	Aug	——
1780	ALEXANDER,	Loury		Surry	Apr	168
1798	ALEXANDER,	Lydia		Berks	Mch	150
1783	ALEXANDER,	Margaret AwW		Lond	Nov	548
1786	ALEXANDER,	Margaret AwW & 2 Cods. & a W & 1 Cod. rgd Nov 1703 (by int dec)		Middx	Nov	551
1768	ALEXANDER,	Martha		Middx	Jny	1
1752	ALEXANDER,	Mary		Middx	Jly	176
1754	ALEXANDER,	Mary		Middx	Jny	1
1763	ALEXANDER,	Mary AwW		Middx	May	211
1787	ALEXANDER,	Mary		Surry	Aug	354
1797	ALEXANDER,	Mary		Middx	Oct	625
1776	ALEXANDER,	Nathaniel		Berks	Dec	504

```
1794   ALEXANDER, Nathaniel  (Spec Pr)              Pts    Apr 181
1755   ALEXANDER, Richard                           Surry  Apr  92
1758   ALEXANDER, Richard                           Middx  Jne 175
1794   ALEXANDER, Richard                           Middx  Jny   3
1750   ALEXANDER, Robert                            Pts    Jne 185
1791   ALEXANDER, Robert                            NBrit  Sep 414
1770   ALEXANDER, Samuel                            Sfolk  Dec 420
1797   ALEXANDER, Samuel                            Norf   Dec 722
1800   ALEXANDER, Samuel                            Norf   Dec 833
1773   ALEXANDER, Sarah                             Norf   Jly 277
1777   ALEXANDER, Sarah                             Essex  Aug 339
1781   ALEXANDER, Sarah                             Lond   Mch 109
1778   ALEXANDER, Susannah                          Middx  May 182
1753   ALEXANDER, Thomas                            Surry  Nov 284
1770   ALEXANDER, Thomas                            Middx  Jne 218
1781   ALEXANDER, Thomas AwW                        Surry  Feb  54
1762   ALEXANDER, William, Esq. (late one of
       Aldermen of City of Lond)                    Lond   Oct 408
1767   ALEXANDER, William                           Pts    Mch  82
1768   ALEXANDER, William  AwW                      Surry  Dec 437
1770   ALEXANDER, William                           Surry  Jly 251
1774   ALEXANDER, William                           Lond   Dec 419
1777   ALEXANDER, William                           Lond   Jne 251
1781   ALEXANDER, William   Ser.                    Middx  Sep 417
1782   ALEXANDER, William                           NBrit  Mch 108
1783   ALEXANDER, William                           Salop  Jne 277
1777   ALEXANDRE, Jeanne  (Ltd Pr)                  Pts    Feb  50
1751   ALEXANDRE, Sara                              Pts    Dec 325
1763   ALEYN, Giles, Esq.                           Middx  Dec 538
1750   ALEYN, Mary                                  Berks  May 134
1768   ALEYN, William                               Brstl  Jly 265
1751   ALFEN, otherwise ALFONE, Gregory             Pts    Jne 164
1751   ALFONE, Gregory                              Pts    May 130
1751   ALFONE, otherwise ALFEN, Gregory             Pts    Jne 164
1792   ALFORD, Amelia                               Wilts  Dec 593
1754   ALFORD, Edward                               Middx  Jly 187
1765   ALFORD, Edward                               Irel   Jny   2
1756   ALFORD, Elizabeth                            SHant  Aug 215
1763   ALFORD, James (W nunc)                       Devon  Jne 263
1759   ALFORD, John                                 Devon  Dec 381
1765   ALFORD, John  AwW of Gds unadm W rgd
       1730, 270                                    Dorst  Feb  --
1765   ALFORD, John                                 Middx  May 167
1784   ALFORD, Joseph                               Middx  Oct 534
1785   ALFORD, Joseph  E.I.S. "Hawke"               Pts    Jly 351
1764   ALFORD, Mary                                 Lond   Aug 295
1779   ALFORD, Mary                                 Som    Apr 139
1752   ALFORD, Philip                               Som    Mch  56
1795   ALFORD, Rachel, otherwise Rachael            Kent   Apr 232
1782   ALFORD, Richard                              Exter  Jly 334
1776   ALFORD, Ruth                                 Middx  Jne 253
1799   ALFORD, Rev. Samuel                          Som    Sep 639
1760   ALFORD, Thomas                               Pts    Feb  45
```

1761	ALFORD, otherwise ALFORT, Thomas AwW	Pts	Dec 415
1765	ALFORD, Thomas	SHant	Jny 2
1765	ALFORD, Thomas	Middx	Dec 438
1777	ALFORD, Rev. Thomas	Som	Aug 339
1759	ALFORD, William	Corn	Mch 80
1760	ALFORD, William	Devon	Aug 312
1777	ALFORD, William	Som	Jly 296
1789	ALFORD, William	Denbh	Nov 528
1796	ALFORD, otherwise ALFRED, William Ser. "Victory" AwW	Pts	Sep 440
1761	ALFORT, otherwise ALFORD, Thomas AwW	Pts	Dec 415
1755	ALFOUNDER, Robert	Rutld	Jne 153
1799	ALFRAY, Mary	Middx	May 332
1796	ALFRED, otherwise ALFORD, William Ser. "Victory" AwW	Pts	Sep 440
1794	ALGAR, Ann AwW	Nhant	May 239
1798	ALGAR, otherwise ALGER, Edward	Lond	Feb 75
1794	ALGAR, Elizabeth AwW	Nhant	May 239
1796	ALGAR, Elizabeth AwW of Gds unadm W rgd May 1794	Nhant	Jny —
1782	ALGAR, John	Pts	Dec 569
1791	ALGAR, John AwW	Essex	Nov 492
1795	ALGAR, otherwise ALGER, John Ser. "Dictator"	Pts	Feb 62
1795	ALGAR, otherwise ALGER, John William	Essex	Jne 361
1765	ALGAR, Mary	Lincs	Feb 40
1785	ALGAR, Samuel	Devon	May 228
1791	ALGATE, Sarah	Lincs	Jly 314
1794	ALGEHR, Anne	Essex	Dec 593
1777	ALGEHR, Peter Christopher AwW	Essex	Jny 1
1767	ALGEO, John	Salop	Jly 250
1779	ALGEO, John (Dble Pr) W rgd 1767, 250	Salop	Mch —
1798	ALGER, otherwise ALGAR, Edward	Lond	Feb 75
1795	ALGER, otherwise ALGAR, John Ser. "Dictator"	Pts	Feb 62
1795	ALGER, otherwise ALGAR, John William	Essex	Jne 361
1762	ALICE, otherwise ELLES, Ann	Surry	May 193
1753	ALIE, Lucy	Herts	Sep 333
1771	ALINGHAM, Mary	Lond	Aug 328
1782	ALINGHAM, otherwise ALLINGHAM, Thomas "Terrible" AwW	Pts	Mch 108
1781	ALINGTON, Rev. Henry	Herts	Oct 459
1755	ALINGTON, Hildebrand, Esq.	Surry	Oct 252
1791	ALINS, James	Chich	Jly 314
1754	ALISBURY, Andrew	Lond	Aug 217
1776	ALISON, otherwise ELLISON, Andrew Ser.	Pts	Sep 386
1780	ALISON, David Ser.	Pts	Oct 458
1799	ALISON, Thomas	Lancs	Apr 238
1757	ALISTER, MC, otherwise MC ALLSTER, Archibald	Pts	Sep 281
1798	ALISTER, Colin MC "Vanguard"	Pts	Sep 609
1787	ALKEE, John	Lancs	Oct 436

```
1771   ALKEMADE, Elizabeth Maria CROMHOUT, Lady
         of NIEMOERKERK                                    Pts    Feb   51
1800   ALKEMADE, Jerome Balthazar De Roest D',
         otherwise DE ROEST, Hieronimus
         Balthazar                                         Pts    Feb  100
1769   ALKEN, Oliver                                       Middx  Apr  110
1778   ALKEN, Sefferin   Ser                               Pts    Dec  474
1782   ALKEN, Sefferin                                     Middx  May  210
1765   ALKER, George                                       Glos   Nov  397
1789   ALKIN, Mary                                         Kent   Jne  296
1752   ALKIN, Sarah                                        Cntby  Feb   27
1778   ALKIN, Thomas                                       Cntby  Apr  141
1780   ALKIN, Thomas   AwW  unadm   W rgd Apr 1778 Cntby  Jne   --
1752   ALLABLASTER, Henry                                  Pts    Jne  145
1789   ALLAIN, Francis                                     Middx  Sep  447
1771   ALLAIRE, Esther                                     Lond   Jny    1
1773   ALLAIRE, Esther                                     Surry  Nov  413
1751   ALLALEE, Richard                          Pts - Middx Jny    1
1761   ALLALEY, Isaac   Ser.  AwW                          Pts    Nov  378
1755   ALLALEY, John   AwW  unadm   W rgd 1742, 75 Middx  Dec   --
1779   ALLAM, Aaron                                        Middx  Apr  138
```

(Continued on Page 54)

1798	ALLAM, Ann	Middx	Nov	691
1793	ALLAM, Betty	Middx	Oct	489
1763	ALLAM, Edward	Lond	Oct	457
1752	ALLAM, otherwise ALLOM, Edwin	Surry	Sep	227
1778	ALLAM, Elizabeth	Middx	Jny	1
1789	ALLAM, Francis	Middx	Sep	447
1752	ALLAM, George	Surry	Dec	292
1778	ALLAM, Jane	Oxon	Dec	474
1792	ALLAM, John	Berks	Mch	124
1775	ALLAM, Louisa	Middx	Nov	401
1761	ALLAM, Mary	Surry	Jne	199
1797	ALLAM, John	Middx	Jne	393
1784	ALLAM, Robert	Middx	Jny	1
1775	ALLAM, Thomas	Middx	Dec	453
1795	ALLAM, William	Middx	Feb	61
1787	ALLAMAND, Jean Nicolas Sebastien	Pts	Jly	308
1772	ALLAMAND, Pernette	Pts	Jne	202
1767	ALLAMAND, Peter	Pts	Mch	82
1787	ALLAMBRIDGE, John	Dorst	Jly	308
1757	ALLAMBY, Thomas AwW	SHant	May	144
1751	ALLAME, Susanna	Middx	May	130
1770	ALLAN, Alexander	Middx	Feb	40
1790	ALLAN, Alexander	Middx	Nov	491
1794	ALLAN, Alexander	Devon	May	239
1796	ALLAN, Alexander, Esq. (Ltd Pr)	Pts	Mch	--
1800	ALLAN, Alexander Peter, Esq.	Essex	Nov	760
1782	ALLAN, otherwise ALLEN, Andrew	Pts	Mch	108
1785	ALLAN, Ann	Durhm	Dec	583
1777	ALLAN, Bridget	Lond	Feb	49
1784	ALLAN, Daniel "Prince William"	Pts	Mch	117
1753	ALLAN, David	Middx	May	126
1753	ALLAN, David	Middx	Oct	262
1785	ALLAN, David	Edin	Mch	110
1793	ALLAN, Dorothy	Middx	Aug	397
1789	ALLAN, Elizabeth	Lond	Feb	70
1800	ALLAN, Elizabeth	Glos	Oct	647
1800	ALLAN, Hannah NICHOLS, formerly	Som	May	391
1784	ALLAN, Harry Ser. "Ps Royal"	Pts	Mch	117
1751	ALLAN, James	Pts	Jny	70
1758	ALLAN, James AwW	NBrit	Jly	207
1759	ALLAN, James	Pts	Mch	80
1759	ALLAN, James AwW	Pts	May	155
1768	ALLAN, James	Edin	Jny	1
1782	ALLAN, James, Esq.	Surry	Aug	390
1783	ALLAN, James	Lond	Sep	441
1784	ALLAN, James	Lond	Dec	627
1786	ALLAN, James	Lond	Dec	597
1790	ALLAN, James, Esq.	Durhm	Feb	57
1757	ALLAN, John AwW	Pts	Nov	319
1765	ALLAN, John	Pts	Oct	360
1776	ALLAN, John	Surry	Mch	108
1782	ALLAN, otherwise ALLEN, John "Alcide"AwW	Pts	Apr	161
1787	ALLAN, John	Lond	Nov	479

1751	ALLAN, Mary		Middx	Mch 68
1779	ALLAN, Mary		Middx	Mch 85
1792	ALLAN, Mary		Middx	Sep 458
1784	ALLAN, Patrick "Sceptre"		Pts	Jne 302
1792	ALLAN, Rachel		Kent	May 253
1751	ALLAN, Robert, Esq.		Kent	Jly 197
1754	ALLAN, otherwise ALLEN, Robert		Kent	Dec 317
1766	ALLAN, Robert	Pts —	Middx	Nov 395
1768	ALLAN, Robert AwW		Pts	Jny 1
1781	ALLAN, Susanna		Kent	Sep 417
1754	ALLAN, Thomas		Berks	Aug 217
1756	ALLAN, otherwise ALLEN, Thomas AwW		Pts	Jly 186
1769	ALLAN, Thomas		Middx	Dec 402
1798	ALLAN, Thomas, Esq.		Surry	Jly 456
1780	ALLAN, William		Middx	Mch 117
1785	ALLAN, William		Middx	Sep 451
1779	ALLANBY, Alice		Lond	Oct 402
1793	ALLAND, John Fortescue otherwise Fortesque, Esq.		Middx	May 238
1791	ALLAND, Mary		Wilts	Jny 1
1792	ALLANSON, Bridget		York.	Dec 593
1796	ALLANSON, Bridget		York	Feb 52
1775	ALLANSON, Charles, Esq.		York	Nov 400
1790	ALLANSON, Gawin		Brstl	Dec 535
1788	ALLANSON, John		Middx	Nov 518
1793	ALLANSON, otherwise ALLENSON, Joyce		Middx	May 238
1753	ALLANSON, Michael		York	Oct 262
1785	ALLANSON, Margery		Middx	Mch 110
1767	ALLANSON, Philip		Wells	Mch 82
1756	ALLANSON, Rachell		York	Jly 187
1762	ALLANSON, Susanna		Middx	Dec 491
1758	ALLANSON, Thomas AwW		Middx	Feb 28
1794	ALLANSON, Thomas		Middx	Feb 59
1758	ALLANSON, William, Esq. AwW unadm W rgd 1745, 316		Middx	May ——
1781	ALLARD, Ann		Middx	Oct 459
1775	ALLARD, Henry		Middx	Apr 126
1775	ALLARD, Jeanne		Middx	Apr 127
1792	ALLARD, John		Surry	Aug 413
1767	ALLARD, Margaret		Middx	Feb 33
1762	ALLARD, Thomas		Wark	Jny 1
1771	ALLARD, Thomas		Brstl	Oct 395
1784	ALLARD, William		Middx	Apr 185
1800	ALLARD, William		Surry	Aug 573
1786	ALLARDES, Susanna		Middx	Nov 552
1788	ALLARDICE, John AwW		NBrit	Mch 113
1785	ALLARDICE, otherwise ALLERDICE, Thomas Ser. "Tartar" AwW		Pts	Apr ——
1778	ALLASON, Frances		Worcs	Jny 1
1794	ALLASON, Vinsed		Som	Jne 295
1765	ALLATSON, William		Sussx	Feb 40
1781	ALLATSON, William W rgd 1765, 40		Sussx	Aug 374
1779	ALLATT, John Ser.		Pts	Feb 36

1783	ALLATT, John AwW unadm W rgd Feb 1779	Pts	Aug	--
1787	ALLATT, John	Lincs	Feb	51
1796	ALLATT, John`	Salop	Nov	538
1768	ALLATT, Park	Middx	Mch	93
1793	ALLATT, Thomas	Leics	Dec	578
1797	ALLAWAY, Elizabeth	Oxon	Jne	394
1798	ALLAWAY, John AwW of Gds unadm W rgd			
	Nov last	Surry	Jny	--
1786	ALLAWAY, otherwise ALLEWAY, John	Berks	Mch	133
1797	ALLAWAY, John AwW	Surry	Nov	673
1789	ALLAWAY, Mary (spinster; by Sent. regd 626)	Som	Feb	71
1778	ALLAWAY, otherwise HALLAWAY, Richard	Pts	Oct	385
1752	ALLAWAY, Richard Boake Pts -	Kent	Oct	241
1784	ALLAWAY, Samuel	Middx	Apr	185
1761	ALLAWAY, Thomas	Middx	Apr	115
1774	ALLAWAY, Thomas	Oxon	Aug	289
1777	ALLAY, otherwise COOKE, Thomas	Kent	Dec	495
1752	ALLBEARY, John	Middx	Jny	1
1774	ALLBONE, Mary	Surry	May	165
1779	ALLBRIGHT, otherwise ALBRIGHT, Joseph	Oxon	Dec	482
1754	ALLBRIGHT, otherwise ALBRIGHT, William	Bucks	Oct	264
1770	ALLBRITTON, Joseph	Essex	Mch	84
1764	ALLBOROUGH, otherwise ALBIRO, Jeremiah	Pts	Apr	128
1780	ALLCHIN, John	Kent	Oct	458
1773	ALLCHIN, Nicholas	Kent	Feb	41
1751	ALLCHURCH, Abraham	Kent	Dec	325
1750	ALLCHURCH, Richard	Pts	Jne	185
1765	ALLCOCK, Ann AwW	Middx	May	166
1798	ALLCOCK, Ann	Lond	Feb	76
1762	ALLCOCK, Daniel	Lond	Mch	89
1798	ALLCOCK, Edward (Ltd Pr)	Pts	Oct	631
1794	ALLCOCK, Francis	Surry	Aug	402
1789	ALLCOCK, George, Esq.	Middx	Jny	1
1773	ALLCOCK, Hannah	Essex	Mch	90
1776	ALLCOCK, Hewson	Middx	Jly	295
1756	ALLCOCK, Jane Ltd AwW (by int dec)	Middx	Feb	26
1778	ALLCOCK, John	Middx	Sep	345
1792	ALLCOCK, John	Middx	Aug	414
1800	ALLCOCK, John	Worcs	Feb	80
1756	ALLCOCK, Joseph Ser.	Middx	Jny	1
1767	ALLCOCK, Joseph	Middx	Feb	33
1752	ALLCOCK, Mary	Middx	Feb	27
1765	ALLCOCK, Mary	Wark	May	166
1796	ALLCOCK, Mary	SHant	Nov	538
1764	ALLCOCK, Robert	Pts	Sep	335
1754	ALLCOCK, Sarah	Lond	Jny	1
1752	ALLCOCK, Thomas	Pts	Jne	145
1791	ALLCOCK, Thomas	Cardn	Jly	314
1790	ALLCOCK, William	Worcs	Jny	1
1799	ALLCOCK, William	Surry	Nov	755
1780	ALLCOTT, John AwW	Salop	Apr	169
1776	ALLCOX, Grace	Worcs	Aug	343
1763	ALLCRAFT, Deborah	Lond	May	210

```
1757  ALLCRAFT, Martha                                    Surry  Sep  265
1773  ALLDAY, Thomas                                      Nwich  Mch   89
1795  ALLDEN, Mary                                        Bucks  Jly  428
1791  ALLDEN, Sarah                                       Camb   Jne  263
1780  ALLDEN, otherwise ALLDIN, William                   Middx  Aug  383
1756  ALLDER, Constantia                                  Bucks  Apr  201
1780  ALLDER, John                                        Berks  Jne  299
1791  ALLDER, Sarah                                       Bucks  Mch  108
1796  ALLDER, Thomas                                      SHant  Oct  485
1767  ALLDIN, John                                        Surry  Nov  399
1764  ALLDIN, Joshua                                      Worcs  Oct  376
1780  ALLDIN, otherwise ALLDEN, William                   Middx  Aug  383
1757  ALLDING, Joseph                                     Lond   Jny    1
1781  ALLDIS, Bartholomew                                 Surry  Oct  459
1796  ALLDIS, John                                        Middx  Sep  440
1769  ALLDRIDGE, Ann                                      Lond   Jny    1
1776  ALLDRIDGE, Barbara, formerly GOODWIN AwW            Lond   Aug  342
1751  ALLDRIDGE, Elizabeth                                Middx  Mch   69
1753  ALLDRIDGE, Mary                                     Leics  Jly  193
1787  ALLDRIDGE, Phillippa                                Kent   Jny    1
1765  ALLDRIDGE, Sarah                                    Middx  Oct  359
1752  ALLDRIDGE, Thomas                                   Pts    Aug  204
1785  ALLDRIDGE, Thomas                                   York   Jne  289
1790  ALLDRIDGE, Thomas                                   Kent   Aug  363
1762  ALLDRIDGE, otherwise ALDRIDGE, William              Middx  Aug  331
1778  ALLDRIDGE, otherwise ALDRED, William AwW            Middx  Apr  141
1766  ALLEBONE, Elizabeth                                 Nhant  Sep  327
1785  ALLEE, otherwise ELLEE, David   AwW                 Essex  Apr  168
1750  ALLEE, Elizabeth                                    Devon  May  134
1752  ALLEGREE, James                          Pts -      Middx  Jne  145
1759  ALLEINE, Henry                                      Pts    Sep  287
1760  ALLEINE, John                                       Middx  Aug  312
1767  ALLEINE, Mary                                       Lond   Jly  250
1772  ALLEKER, Daniel   AwW                               Essex  Sep  317
1764  ALLEN, Affabell                                     Lond   Mch   79
1775  ALLEN, Alexander                                    Som    Sep  332
1780  ALLEN, Alexander                                    Corn   Apr  168
1784  ALLEN, Alexander  Ser. "Standard"                   Pts    Nov  583
1797  ALLEN, Alexander                                    Middx  Mch  125
1750  ALLEN, Alice                                        Bucks  Feb   35
1769  ALLEN, Alice                                        Middx  Nov  364
1770  ALLEN, Alice  AwW unadm  W rgd 1750, 35             Bucks  May   --
1771  ALLEN, Alice                                        Surry  Jny    2
1800  ALLEN, Alice                                        SHant  Feb   80
1750  ALLEN, Alles, otherwise Alice                       Middx  Nov  344
1776  ALLEN, Amy                                          Middx  Jly  295
1786  ALLEN, Anderson                                     Norf   Feb   62
1753  ALLEN, Andrew                                       Middx  Oct  262
1782  ALLEN, otherwise ALLAN, Andrew                      Pts    Mch  108
1752  ALLEN, Ann                                          Kent   Oct  241
1772  ALLEN, Ann   AwW                                    Surry  Jne  202
1772  ALLEN, Ann                                          Middx  Oct  347
1764  ALLEN, Ann                                          Kent   Apr  128
1764  ALLEN, Ann                                          Kent   Sep  336
```

1768	ALLEN, Ann		Middx	Feb	41
1784	ALLEN, Ann		Middx	Feb	59
1786	ALLEN, Ann		Surry	May	259
1789	ALLEN, Ann		Middx	Jly	343
1795	ALLEN, Ann		Middx	Jne	361
1796	ALLEN, Ann		Pemb	Oct	485
1798	ALLEN, Ann		Wilts	Nov	692
1800	ALLEN, Ann		Kent	Jny	3
1752	ALLEN, Anne		Middx	Feb	27
1775	ALLEN, Anne		Kent	Nov	400
1782	ALLAN, Anne		Surry	Mch	108
1786	ALLEN, Anne AwW unadm W rgd 1752, 27		Middx	Aug	--
1796	ALLEN, Anne		Middx	May	232
1754	ALLEN, Anthony, Esq.		Middx	Apr	97
1760	ALLEN, Anthony		Pts	Aug	312
1751	ALLEN, Archer (by dec)		Middx	May	130
1772	ALLEN, Audry		Middx	Sep	316
1759	ALLEN, Austin, otherwise Augustine		Lond	Sep	287
1758	ALLEN, Bagge	Pts -	Lond	Jly	207
1750	ALLEN, Bennet, Esq. AwW		Kent	Sep	285
1750	ALLEN, Bennet, Esq. AwW unadm W rgd in Sep last (by int dec)		Kent	Nov	--
1752	ALLEN, Bennett, Esq. AwW of Gds unadm. W rgd Sep 1750, last grant Nov 1750		Kent	Jne	--
1751	ALLEN, Benjamin		Pts	Aug	228
1752	ALLEN, Benjamin		Middx	May	115
1754	ALLEN, Benjamin	Pts -	Middx	Oct	264
1756	ALLEN, Benjamin		Middx	Nov	286
1757	ALLEN, Benjamin		Surry	Feb	37
1797	ALLEN, Caroline		Middx	Jny	1
1750	ALLEN, Catherine		Pts	Apr	102
1782	ALLEN, Catherine		Kent	Jny	2
1787	ALLEN, Catherine		Bath	Sep	395
1763	ALLEN, Charles, Esq.		Middx	Mch	104
1763	ALLEN, Charles		Bath	Nov	493
1758	ALLEN, Charles		Middx	Jny	1
1783	ALLEN, Charles		Bucks	Feb	56
1789	ALLEN, Rev. Charles		Norf	Apr	186
1795	ALLEN, Rev. Charles		Kent	Apr	232
1796	ALLEN, Rev. Charles		Leics	Apr	159
1782	ALLEN, Christopher		Surry	Mch	108
1764	ALLEN, Churchell		Middx	Dec	452
1775	ALLEN, otherwise ALLING, Cyprem, other- wise ELLENS, Sybran		Pts	Apr	137
1776	ALLEN, Daniel		Camb	Jne	253
1783	ALLEN, Daniel AwW		Pts	Nov	548
1756	ALLEN, David, Esq.		Pemb	Jne	319
1765	ALLEN, David, Esq.		Pemb	Oct	360
1798	ALLEN, David "Worcester" & "Dorset"		Pts	Feb	74
1798	ALLEN, David Anor grant June 1797		Haver	Dec	756
1790	ALLEN, Deborah		Middx	Jne	275
1779	ALLEN, Dorothy		SHant	Mch	87
1795	ALLEN, Dorothy		Notts	Mch	136

1770	ALLEN, Edith	Kent	Oct	348
1767	ALLEN, Edith	Glos	Jly	250
1772	ALLEN, Edmund, Esq.	Norf	Dec	429
1750	ALLEN, Edward	Berks	Jny	1
1750	ALLEN, Edward AwW	Middx	Jly	220
1750	ALLEN, Edward	Middx	Sep	285
1751	ALLEN, Edward	Oxon	Dec	325
1751	ALLEN, Edward	Pts	Dec	325
1756	ALLEN, Edward the younger	Berks	May	128
1764	ALLEN, Edward	Pts	Jly	248
1774	ALLEN, Edward, Esq.	Middx	Feb	36
1775	ALLEN, Edward	Middx	Sep	333
1781	ALLEN, Edward	Middx	Feb	54
1788	ALLEN, Edward	Brcon	Jne	282
1793	ALLEN, Edward	Essex	Sep	451
1798	ALLEN, Edward	Herts	Feb	74
1758	ALLEN, Edward William	Pts	Dec	355
1769	ALLEN, Eleanor	Middx	Dec	402
1750	ALLEN, Elizabeth	Lond	Jly	220
1763	ALLEN, Elizabeth	Middx	Jly	319
1764	ALLEN, Elizabeth	Kent	Mch	79
1765	ALLEN, otherwise ALLIN, Elizabeth	Middx	Jny	2
1766	ALLEN, Elizabeth	Som	Nov	395
1768	ALLEN, Elizabeth	Lond	Aug	305
1770	ALLEN, Elizabeth	Lond	Nov	387
1771	ALLEN, Elizabeth	Middx	Jny	2
1771	ALLEN, otherwise BERRYMAN, formerly ALLIN, Elizabeth	Surry	Sep	366
1771	ALLEN, Elizabeth	Middx	Nov	428
1772	ALLEN, Elizabeth	Herts	May	155
1772	ALLEN, Elizabeth	Kent	Dec	429
1773	ALLEN, Elizabeth	Surry	Nov	413
1779	ALLEN, Elizabeth	Yorks	Jny	1
1779	ALLEN, Elizabeth	Middx	Feb	37
1781	ALLEN, Elizabeth	Hants	Jne	280
1783	ALLEN, Elizabeth AwW	Lond	Mch	106
1784	ALLEN, Elizabeth	Kent	Feb	59
1787	ALLEN, Elizabeth	Kent	Feb	51
1787	ALLEN, Elizabeth	Poole	Sep	395
1788	ALLEN, Elizabeth AwW	Surry	Jly	335
1790	ALLEN, Elizabeth	Surry	Apr	169
1792	ALLEN, Elizabeth	Middx	Aug	414
1794	ALLEN, Elizabeth	Kent	Sep	443
1798	ALLEN, Elizabeth	Kent	Dec	754
1756	ALLEN, Ely	Wilts	Nov	286
1788	ALLEN, Emblem	Surry	Mch	113
1778	ALLEN, Ephraim	Surry	Jne	229
1779	ALLEN, Esther	Middx	May	185
1764	ALLEN, Fifield, D.D.	Middx	May	162
1777	ALLEN, Frances	Middx	Jny	1
1784	ALLEN, Frances	Middx	Jne	302
1784	ALLEN, Frances W rgd Jne last	Middx	Aug	--
1787	ALLEN, Frances	Sussx	Dec	527

```
1795   ALLEN, Frances                                    Middx Mch 137
1755   ALLEN, Francis                                    Middx Jny   1
1758   ALLEN, Francis                                    Staff Nov 318
1773   ALLEN, Francis                                    Middx Jny   1
1774   ALLEN, Francis                                    SHant Nov 384
1775   ALLEN, Francis, Esq.                              Essex Dec 453
1785   ALLEN, Francis                                    Middx Nov 536
1792   ALLEN, Francis                                    Lond  May 253
1778   ALLEN, Francklen                                  Kent  Oct 385
1751   ALLEN, George                                     Kent  Jly 197
1752   ALLEN, George                                     Middx Jny   1
1757   ALLEN, George  AwW of Gds unadm  W rgd
          1738, 53                                       Kent  May  --
1758   ALLEN, George                                     Pts   Jly 207
1760   ALLEN, George                                     Middx Jny   1
1761   ALLEN, George  Ser.  AwW                          Pts   Jne 200
1762   ALLEN, George                                     Essex Jne 231
1765   ALLEN, George                                     Middx Feb  41
1769   ALLEN, George                                     Kent  Mch  73
1771   ALLEN, George                                     Middx Dec 466
1771   ALLEN, otherwise ALLEYNE, George  W rgd
          this month                                     Som   Dec  --
1773   ALLEN, George                                     Pts   May 190
1773   ALLEN, George                                     Herts Oct 379
1773   ALLEN, George                                     Lond  Oct 379
1776   ALLEN, George  AwW                                Pts   Jny   1
1778   ALLEN, otherwise DUNCAN, George                   Pts   Sep 352
1781   ALLEN, George  AwW                    Pts - Asia  Oct 460
1782   ALLEN, George                                     Middx Oct 478
1786   ALLEN, George  "Dolphin"                          Pts   Apr 201
1797   ALLEN, George                                     Pts   Aug 538
1800   ALLEN, George                                     Kent  May 336
1784   ALLEN, Rev. Gerveys                               Corn  Apr 186
1767   ALLEN, Giles                                      Camb  Aug 294
1750   ALLEN, Godfrey, otherwise ALYN, Gottfried Pts    May 136
1785   ALLEN, Hannah                                     Lond  Oct 489
1786   ALLEN, Hannah                                     Surry Oct 500
1787   ALLEN, Harriot                                    Surry Mch 101
1764   ALLEN, Henry                                      Oxon  Sep 335
1767   ALLEN, Henry, Esq.                                Bath  Sep 330
1783   ALLEN, Henry  Ser.                                Middx Jny   1
1786   ALLEN, Henry                                      Kent  Oct 499
1791   ALLEN, Rev. Henry, Esq.                           Middx Mch 108
1792   ALLEN, Henry  "Leopard"  AwW                      Pts   Jny   2
1795   ALLEN, Henry                                      Som   Dec 666
1797   ALLEN, Henry                                      Middx Apr 220
1799   ALLEN, Hester                                     Kent  Nov 756
1771   ALLEN, Hugh                                       Lond  Jly 283
1771   ALLEN, Hugh  W rgd Jly last (by int dec) Lond    Aug  --
1775   ALLEN, Hugh  AwW unadm  W rgd 1771, 283  Lond    Jne  --
1791   ALLEN, Isaac                                      Surry Nov 492
1750   ALLEN, James                                      Middx Mch  66
1750   ALLEN, James                                      Middx Nov 344
```

1750	ALLEN,	James	W rgd Mch last		Middx	Jne	--
1751	ALLEN,	James			Surry	Jne	164
1751	ALLEN,	James			Surry	Oct	273
1752	ALLEN,	James	AwW		Lond	Feb	27
1752	ALLEN,	James			Surry	Jly	176
1753	ALLEN,	James			Pts	Jny	1
1754	ALLEN,	James			Pts	Nov	292
1759	ALLEN,	James			Middx	Jly	223
1763	ALLEN,	James			Lond	Jne	263
1765	ALLEN,	James			Middx	Jny	2
1766	ALLEN,	James	AwW		Pts	Apr	125
1767	ALLEN,	James			Middx	May	162
1770	ALLEN,	James			Bath	Jne	218
1771	ALLEN,	James	(By Sentence regd Feb 511)		Pts	Mch	91
1771	ALLEN,	James	AwW		Kent	Mch	92
1772	ALLEN,	James			Surry	Nov	390
1774	ALLEN,	James			Middx	Jny	1
1777	ALLEN,	James			Middx	Feb	50
1781	ALLEN,	James			Kent	Feb	54
1784	ALLEN,	James	E.I.S."Warren Hastings"	Pts-Kent		Nov	584
1785	ALLEN,	James			Essex	Apr	168
1785	ALLEN,	James			Middx	Apr	168
1785	ALLEN,	James	AwW		Lancr	Jly	349
1786	ALLEN,	James			Lond	Nov	552
1799	ALLEN,	James			Wilts	Oct	693
1763	ALLEN,	Jane			Middx	Sep	416
1763	ALLEN,	Jane	W rgd Sept last		Middx	Dec	--
1767	ALLEN,	Jane			Bath	Jne	204
1767	ALLEN,	Jane			Middx	Jly	250
1775	ALLEN,	Jane			Kent	Aug	298
1786	ALLEN,	Jane			Surry	Aug	419
1789	ALLEN,	Jane			Berks	Feb	70
1792	ALLEN,	Jane			Surry	Mch	124
1789	ALLEN,	Jaspear, otherwise Jasper			Kent	Apr	184
1797	ALLEN,	Job			Bucks	Jne	393
1775	ALLEN,	Johanna, otherwise Jhanna			Surry	Apr	126
1751	ALLEN,	John			Pts	Jny	1
1751	ALLEN,	John			Bucks	Aug	228
1751	ALLEN,	John			Kent	Oct	273
1755	ALLEN,	John			Pts	Sep	232
1755	ALLEN,	John			Surry	Nov	274
1755	ALLEN,	John			Middx	Dec	303
1756	ALLEN,	John	AwW		Som	Jne	156
1758	ALLEN,	John			Berks	Mch	61
1760	ALLEN,	John	AwW		Pts	Jny	1
1760	ALLEN,	John			Middx	Sep	346
1761	ALLEN,	John			Pts	Jny	1
1761	ALLEN,	John			Middx	Feb	44
1761	ALLEN,	John			Middx	Jne	199
1761	ALLEN,	John			Pts	Sep	307
1762	ALLEN,	John	AwW		Berks	Jly	282
1762	ALLEN,	John			Pts	Aug	331
1762	ALLEN,	John	AwW		Berks	Dec	491

1763	ALLEN, John AwW	Pts	Apr	163
1764	ALLEN, John	Lond	Jne	209
1764	ALLEN, John	Kent	Jly	248
1765	ALLEN, Rev. John	Herts	Jne	206
1765	ALLEN, John	Middx	Oct	369
1767	ALLEN, John	Bath	Aug	294
1769	ALLEN, Rev. John	Essex	Feb	32
1769	ALLEN, John, Esq. AwW	Pemb	May	149
1769	ALLEN, John	Lond	Jne	193
1771	ALLEN, John	Kent	Aug	328
1773	ALLEN, John	York	Mch	90
1773	ALLEN, John	Surry	Jne	233
1774	ALLEN, John, Esq.	Middx	Mch	77
1775	ALLEN, John	Middx	Jny	1
1775	ALLEN, Dr. John (Dr. of Phys)	Middx	Jny	1
1775	ALLEN, John	Pts	Mch	81
1775	ALLEN, John	Surry	Aug	298
1776	ALLEN, John	Middx	Jly	295
1776	ALLEN, John	Corn	Aug	342
1776	ALLEN, John	Middx	Aug	343
1777	ALLEN, John	Kent	Apr	143
1777	ALLEN, John (Dble Pr) W rgd Aug 1776	Corn	Aug	—
1778	ALLEN, Rev. John	Salop	Apr	141
1778	ALLEN, John	Pts	Jly	271
1779	ALLEN, John Ltd AwW	Pts	Jly	282
1780	ALLEN, John	Pts	Nov	503
1782	ALLEN, John	Pts	Jny	2
1782	ALLEN, John	Essex	Feb	59
1782	ALLEN, John	Dorst	Mch	138
1782	ALLEN, otherwise ALLAN, John "Alcide"AwW	Pts	Apr	161
1782	ALLEN, John	Wilts	May	210
1782	ALLEN, Rev. John AwW unadm. W rgd 1765, 206	Herts	Jly	—
1782	ALLEN, John	Glos	Aug	390
1782	ALLEN, John "Resolution"	Pts	Sep	438
1783	ALLEN, John	Kent	Feb	56
1784	ALLEN, Rev. John	Surry	Oct	534
1785	ALLEN, John	Middx	Jly	349
1785	ALLEN, John Ser. Sloop "Ariel"	Pts	Dec	583
1786	ALLEN, John	Kent	Nov	552
1788	ALLEN, John	Dorst	May	224
1788	ALLEN, John	Essex	May	224
1791	ALLEN, John	Surry	Nov	493
1791	ALLEN, John	Middx	Dec	553
1792	ALLEN, John	Salop	Jny	1
1792	ALLEN, John, Esq.	Middx	Mch	124
1792	ALLEN, John	Corn	Apr	189
1793	ALLEN, John	Herfd	Apr	180
1793	ALLEN, John No ship. AwW Pts -	Irel	Oct	487
1794	ALLEN, John	Middx	Nov	535
1795	ALLEN, John Esq.	Perth	Apr	232
1795	ALLEN, John AwW	Wark	Jne	362
1796	ALLEN, John	Kent	Jny	1
1796	ALLEN, John AwW	Middx	Nov	538

1797	ALLEN, John, Esq.	Worcs	Feb	65
1798	ALLEN, John AwW	Lond	Jny	1
1798	ALLEN, John	Som	Nov	691
1799	ALLEN, John	Wark	Aug	560
1800	ALLEN, John	Middx	Mch	172
1800	ALLEN, John Carter, Esq. Admiral of White Squadn. of H.M. Fleet	Middx	Oct	697
1782	ALLEN, Jolley	Middx	Jly	332
1752	ALLEN, Jonathan	Pts	Jne	145
1751	ALLEN, Joseph	Pts	Mch	70
1753	ALLEN, Joseph AwW unadm. W rgd 1722,109	Pemb	Nov	--
1762	ALLEN, otherwise CUNNINGHAM, Joseph W rgd Sep last	Pts	Apr	--
1766	ALLEN, Joseph AwW	York	May	167
1774	ALLEN, Joseph	Middx	Mch	76
1776	ALLEN, Joseph	Wilts	Oct	410
1781	ALLEN, Joseph	Middx	Jny	1
1781	ALLEN, Joseph	Hants	Jne	280
1783	ALLEN, Joseph	Pts	Jne	278
1784	ALLEN, Joseph (poor) "Rose"	Pts	Jly	363
1786	ALLEN, Joseph AwW	Essex	Mch	133
1788	ALLEN, Joseph	Surry	Aug	381
1791	ALLEN, Joseph		Jny	1
1795	ALLEN, Joseph	Middx	May	292
1796	ALLEN, Dr. Joseph, Dr of Physic	Surry	Jny	1
1759	ALLEN, Joshua	Pts	Aug	255
1765	ALLEN, Rev. Joshua	Pemb	Jne	205
1792	ALLEN, Joshua AwW of Gds unadm. W rgd 1759, 255	Pts	Sep	--
1792	ALLEN, Joshua AwW of Gds unadm. W rgd 1759, 255	Middx	Sep	--
1763	ALLEN, Josiah	Middx	Jne	263
1764	ALLEN, Katherine	Middx	Mch	79
1770	ALLEN, Lewis	Middx	Mch	85
1799	ALLEN, Lucy	Bucks	Jly	471
1753	ALLEN, Luke	Middx	Dec	307
1758	ALLEN, Rt Hon Margaret, Viscountess Dowager	Middx	Nov	318
1790	ALLEN, Margaret	Surry	Oct	450
1790	ALLEN, Margaret W rgd this month	Surry	Oct	--
1752	ALLEN, Marguerite	Middx	Jly	176
1781	ALLEN, Mark	Derby	Sep	417
1758	ALLEN, Martha	Lond	Nov	318
1769	ALLEN, Martha	Bath	Aug	271
1775	ALLEN, otherwise ALLIN, Martha	Middx	Jne	219
1784	ALLEN, Martha	Surry	Jly	364
1795	ALLEN, Martha AwW of Gds unadm. W rgd 1784, 364	Surry	Aug	--
1795	ALLEN, Martha AwW of Gds unadm. W rgd 1784, 364, Anor grant last month	Surry	Sep	--
1797	ALLEN, Martha	Middx	Jne	394
1754	ALLEN, Mary	Brstl	Oct	264
1755	ALLEN, Mary	Middx	Jny	1

1756	ALLEN, Mary		Berks	Feb	26
1757	ALLEN, Mary		Surry	Aug	238
1762	ALLEN, Mary AwW		Kent	Apr	136
1763	ALLEN, Mary		Kent	Jny	1
1763	ALLEN, Mary		Surry	Mch	103
1766	ALLEN, Mary		Middx	Jny	1
1767	ALLEN, Mary		Surry	Jly	250
1774	ALLEN, Mary		Glos	Apr	125
1776	ALLEN, Mary		Norf	Oct	410
1777	ALLEN, Mary		Kent	Jny	1
1781	ALLEN, Mary		Bath	Mch	109
1782	ALLEN, Mary		SHant	Jne	261
1782	ALLEN, Mary		Surry	Jne	261
1783	ALLEN, Mary		Kent	Feb	56
1783	ALLEN, Mary		Herts	Jne	279
1783	ALLEN, Mary		Middx	Jly	331
1784	ALLEN, Mary		Dorst	Oct	535
1788	ALLEN, Mary		Surry	Mch	113
1789	ALLEN, Mary		Kent	Mch	131
1789	ALLEN, Mary		Middx	Aug	417
1798	ALLEN, Mary		Middx	Nov	692
1800	ALLEN, Mary		Exter	Jny	4
1800	ALLEN, Mathew		Kent	May	335
1760	ALLEN, Michael	Pts –	Kent	May	180
1763	ALLEN, Michael AwW		Pts	Jly	320
1784	ALLEN, Michael "Formidable","Superb" & "Burford"		Pts	Jne	302
1799	ALLEN, otherwise ALLIN, Michael Ser. "Ville de Paris"		Pts	Jne	414
1792	ALLEN, Miles Button AwW		Middx	Nov	542
1800	ALLEN, Moses Ser. "Terrible"		Pts	Jne	429
1775	ALLEN, Mundeford		Middx	Jne	219
1771	ALLEN, Nathaniel	Pts –	Nland	Apr	142
1782	ALLEN, Nathaniel		Kent	Nov	527
1796	ALLEN, Nathaniel "Medusa"		Pts	Jly	343
1768	ALLEN, Netter		Kent	Jny	2
1773	ALLEN, Nicholas		Kent	Feb	41
1753	ALLEN, Patrick		Middx	Mch	69
1775	ALLEN, Pannet		Surry	Dec	453
1773	ALLEN, Paul		Middx	Aug	318
1751	ALLEN, Peter		Kent	Dec	325
1758	ALLEN, Peter		Corn	Jny	1
1765	ALLEN, Philip, Esq.		Bath	Nov	397
1786	ALLEN, Phillip, Esq.		Lond	Feb	60
1789	ALLEN, Poulton		Essex	Apr	185
1759	ALLEN, Ralph		SHant	Jne	191
1759	ALLEN, Ralph		Lond	Dec	381
1764	ALLEN, Ralph, Esq.		Som	Aug	294
1777	ALLEN, Ralph		Som	Oct	406
1799	ALLEN, Ralph Spec AwW of Gds unadm. W rgd 1777, 406		Som	May	--
1778	ALLEN, Rebecca		Middx	Aug	309
1785	ALLEN, Rebecca		Surry	Oct	489

```
1751   ALLEN, Richard                                        Kent    Mch   70
1756   ALLEN, otherwise AYLEN, Richard                        Pts     May  141
1756   ALLEN, Richard                                         Berks   Jly  186
1758   ALLEN, Richard  AwW of Gds unadm.
         W rgd 1748, 169                                      Oxon    Sep   --
1760   ALLEN, otherwise ELLEN, Richard                        Norf    May  180
1764   ALLEN, Richard, Esq.                                   Berks   Apr  129
1766   ALLEN, Richard                                         Brstl   Jny    1
1770   ALLEN, Richard                                         Glos    Mch   85
1771   ALLEN, Richard                                         Berks   Jly  283
1775   ALLEN, Richard                                         Surry   May  168
1781   ALLEN, Richard  AwW                      Pts  -  Poole   Mch  107
1785   ALLEN, otherwise COOPER, Richard                       Glos    Feb   70
1786   ALLEN, Richard                                         Staff   Aug  418
1788   ALLEN, Richard   "Elizabeth" "Ganges"                  Pts     Jny    1
1793   ALLEN, Richard                                         Som     Mch  124
1796   ALLEN, Richard                                         Bucks   Jly  342
1800   ALLEN, Richard  "Bristol""Puissant" &
         "Termagant"                                          Pts     Feb   81
1752   ALLEN, Robert, Esq.                                    Kent    Mch   56
1754   ALLEN, Robert                                          Kent    Nov  292
1754   ALLEN, otherwise ALLAN, Robert                         Kent    Dec  317
1757   ALLEN, Robert                                          Pts     Dec  348
1759   ALLEN, Robert, Esq. Cod.(Ltd Pr)                       Middx   May  155
1759   ALLEN, Robert                                          Pts     Jly  223
1760   ALLEN, Robert, Esq. Ltd Pr of W. & Cod.
         Anor Cod. rgd May 1759                               Middx   Feb   46
1761   ALLEN, Robert                                          Kent    Sep  307
1763   ALLEN, Robert                            Pts  -  Devon   Apr  163
1763   ALLEN, Robert                                          Pts     Jly  319
1763   ALLEN, Robert   AwW                                    Oxon    Nov  493
1764   ALLEN, Robert                                          Surry   Apr  129
1765   ALLEN, Robert                                          Middx   Oct  359
1767   ALLEN, Robert                                          Lond    Jny    1
1769   ALLEN, Robert                            Pts  -  Middx   Jne  193
1773   ALLEN, Robert                                          Worcs   May  190
1774   ALLEN, Robert                            Pts  -  Middx   Sep  328
1780   ALLEN, Robert                                          Lond    Nov  502
1783   ALLEN, Robert   AwW                                    Pts     Jne  279
1783   ALLEN, Robert                                          Middx   Aug  397
1783   ALLEN, Robert   "Rippon" & "Brittania"                 Pts     Oct  494
1784   ALLEN, Robert                                          Berks   Dec  627
1785   ALLEN, Robert   "Monarch" (by int dec)                 Pts     Mch  110
1790   ALLEN, Robert                                          Middx   Mch  114
1792   ALLEN, Robert                                          Bucks   Jny    1
1793   ALLEN, Robert                                          Middx   Feb   61
1793   ALLEN, Robert                                          Kent    Jly  349
1793   ALLEN, Robert                                          Surry   Oct  487
1794   ALLEN, Robert                                          Norf    Nov  534
1765   ALLEN, Rowland                                         Middx   Feb   41
1768   ALLEN, Rowland                                         Middx   Nov  400
1777   ALLEN, Ruth  AwW                                       Surry   Jny    2
1760   ALLEN, Sarah                                           Middx   Aug  312
```

1763	ALLEN, Sarah	Lond	Jne	263
1767	ALLEN, Sarah	Lond	Apr	121
1776	ALLEN, Sarah	Lond	Apr	159
1776	ALLEN, Sarah	Yorks	May	209
1782	ALLEN, Sarah	Kent	May	210
1795	ALLEN, Sarah AwW	Lond	Feb	60
1795	ALLEN, Sarah	Middx	Apr	234
1799	ALLEN, Sarah	Herts	Jly	471
1762	ALLEN, Samuel (sent)	Middx	Feb	37
1789	ALLEN, Samuel	Bucks	Feb	70
1795	ALLEN, Samuel	Surry	Jne	361
1782	ALLEN, Sophia AwW	Middx	Jly	334
1751	ALLEN, Stephen	Norf	Sep	250
1763	ALLEN, Stephen	Norf	May	211
1770	ALLEN, Stephen	Middx	Dec	420
1789	ALLEN, Strother	Middx	Jne	297
1790	ALLEN, Suesana	Dorst	Jne	275
1781	ALLEN, formerly CATLING, Susanna	Essex	Dec	568
1787	ALLEN, Susanna	Kent	Jny	2
1791	ALLEN, Susanna	Essex	Dec	553
1800	ALLEN, Susanna, otherwise Susana	Exter	Jly	501
1798	ALLEN, Susannah	Berks	Sep	580
1791	ALLEN, Tamar AwW	Berks	Mch	108
1759	ALLEN, Theodosia	Lond	Aug	255
1762	ALLEN, Theodosiah	Berks	Jly	282
1751	ALLEN, Thomas AwW	Pts	Sep	250
1752	ALLEN, Thomas	Norf	Aug	204
1753	ALLEN, Thomas AwW	Wark	Jly	192
1754	ALLEN, Thomas	Kent	Mch	66
1756	ALLEN, Thomas	Surry	Apr	93
1756	ALLEN, otherwise ALLAN, Thomas AwW	Pts	Jly	186
1757	ALLEN, Thomas	Berks	Jly	211
1757	ALLEN, Thomas	Kent	Aug	238
1759	ALLEN, Thomas	Surry	Feb	44
1759	ALLEN, Thomas	Pts	Aug	255
1759	ALLEN, Thomas	Pts	Oct	316
1760	ALLEN, Thomas	Middx	Sep	346
1761	ALLEN, Thomas	Som	Apr	116
1761	ALLEN, Thomas	Coven	Oct	336
1762	ALLEN, Thomas	Essex	Sep	365
1762	ALLEN, Thomas	Surry	Nov	444
1763	ALLEN, Thomas	Pts	Aug	366
1763	ALLEN, Thomas, Esq.	Middx	Nov	493
1764	ALLEN, Thomas, Esq.	Middx	Apr	128
1765	ALLEN, Thomas	Kent	Feb	40
1767	ALLEN, Thomas	Kent	Mch	82
1767	ALLEN, Thomas	Wark	Mch	83
1767	ALLEN, Thomas	Wark	May	161
1769	ALLEN, Thomas	Pts	May	150
1769	ALLEN, Thomas	Lond	Jne	193
1769	ALLEN, Thomas (Dble Pr) W rgd Jne last	Lond	Aug	--
1770	ALLEN, Thomas	Surry	Feb	39
1771	ALLEN, Thomas	Pts	Oct	395

1772	ALLEN, Thomas		Herts	May	154
1773	ALLEN, Thomas		Middx	Mch	90
1774	ALLEN, Thomas		Bucks	Sep	328
1776	ALLEN, Thomas		Nhant	Feb	47
1779	ALLEN, Thomas		Kent	Mch	85
1780	ALLEN, Thomas, Esq.		Middx	May	233
1781	ALLEN, Thomas		Chich	Feb	54
1781	ALLEN, Thomas		Middx	Jly	326
1782	ALLEN, Thomas		Lond	Sep	437
1783	ALLEN, Thomas		Sussx	Oct	494
1785	ALLEN, Thomas	E.I.S."Alfred" AwW Pts -	Middx	Nov	536
1786	ALLEN, Thomas		Middx	Feb	60
1786	ALLEN, Thomas		Middx	Apr	201
1786	ALLEN, Thomas	E.I.S."Brittain"	Pts	Aug	418
1788	ALLEN, Thomas		Norf	Jne	281
1790	ALLEN, Thomas	AwW	Surry	Apr	169
1790	ALLEN, Thomas		Middx	Nov	491
1791	ALLEN, Thomas		Middx	Jly	313
1791	ALLEN, Thomas		Middx	Dec	553
1792	ALLEN, Thomas		Glos	Jly	362
1792	ALLEN, Thomas, Esq.		Middx	Aug	414
1795	ALLEN, Thomas		Essex	Mch	136
1796	ALLEN, Thomas, Esq.		Worcs	Jny	--
1796	ALLEN, Thomas	Ser. "Belliqueux"	Pts	May	231
1798	ALLEN, Thomas		Essex	Jny	2
1799	ALLEN, Thomas		Berks	May	331
1799	ALLEN, Thomas	E.I.S."Albion" AwW	Lond	Sep	639
1799	ALLEN, Thomas	Ser. "Venerable"	Pts	Dec	820
1800	ALLEN, Thomas	Ser. "La Lutine"	Pts	Jne	429
1785	ALLEN, Titus		NSarm	Aug	400
1790	ALLEN, Ursula		Middx	May	221
1773	ALLEN, Vincent		Pts	Jly	276
1753	ALLEN, Walter		Surry	May	126
1756	ALLEN, Walter		Pts	Feb	26
1773	ALLEN, Walter		Sussx	Apr	144
1750	ALLEN, William		Middx	May	160
1751	ALLEN, William		Pts	Nov	298
1754	ALLEN, William		Dorst	Feb	31
1755	ALLEN, William		Middx	Jay	1
1759	ALLEN, William	Pts -	Surry	Feb	44
1759	ALLEN, William Esq.		Pemb	Mch	80
1759	ALLEN, William		Pts	Nov	346
1763	ALLEN, William	AwW	Pts	May	211
1763	ALLEN, otherwise ALLIN, William		Nhant	Sep	415
1764	ALLEN, William		Kent	Aug	295
1765	ALLEN, William		Middx	Apr	127
1765	ALLEN, William		Herfd	Apr	128
1765	ALLEN, William	Ser.	Pts	Aug	282
1766	ALLEN, William		SHant	Aug	291
1769	ALLEN, William		Kent	Feb	32
1769	ALLEN, William		Middx	Aug	271
1770	ALLEN, William		Pts	May	169
1771	ALLEN, William		Middx	Apr	140

1772	ALLEN, William	Kent	May	155
1773	ALLEN, William AwW	Lond	Jly	276
1777	ALLEN, William	Middx	Apr	143
1778	ALLEN, otherwise ALLIN, William	Wilts	Feb	47
1778	ALLEN, William	Pts	Mch	94
1783	ALLEN, Rev. William (Ltd Pr)	Pts	Apr	159
1783	ALLEN, William Ser. "Triumph" &			
	"Alligator"	Pts	Oct	493
1783	ALLEN, William	Surry	Oct	494
1784	ALLEN, William	Middx	Jne	303
1784	ALLEN, William Master of "Orestes" Pts –	Middx	Aug	425
1785	ALLEN, William	Lond	May	229
1787	ALLEN, William AwW	Middx	Mch	101
1789	ALLEN, William	Middx	Feb	71
1791	ALLEN, William	Surry	Nov	493
1795	ALLEN, William	Middx	Dec	666
1796	ALLEN, William	Essex	Dec	590
1797	ALLEN, William "Agamemnon"	Pts	Mch	124
1798	ALLEN, William, Esq	Kent	Jny	1
1798	ALLEN, William, Esq.	Flint	Mch	151
1798	ALLEN, William	Middx	Nov	692
1799	ALLEN, William	Som	Jne	414
1800	ALLEN, William	Hunts	Aug	573
1779	ALLEN, Willis	Middx	Feb	37
1795	ALLENBY, Thomas, Esq.	Surry	Oct	579
1783	ALLENDER, Edward	Worcs	Nov	548
1779	ALLENDER, John	Pts	Jne	230
1788	ALLENDER, Sarah	Surry	Sep	423
1780	ALLENSON, Allen	Middx	Feb	54
1798	ALLENSON, Ann AwW	Middx	Feb	76
1785	ALLENSON, John AwW	Middx	Mch	110
1793	ALLENSON, otherwise ALLANSON, Joyce	Middx	May	238
1777	ALLEQUE, John	Leics	May	195
1799	ALLER, William	Kent	Mch	161
1756	ALLERDICE, otherwise ELLERDICE, Robert	Pts	Jly	187
1785	ALLERDICE, otherwise ALLARDICE, Thomas			
	Ser. "Tartar" AwW	Pts	Apr	--
1754	ALLERWAY, Martha AwW	Kent	Aug	217
1764	ALLERY, otherwise ALLRY, George	Devon	Jne	209
1800	ALLES, James	Lond	May	335
1788	ALLES, John AwW	Essex	Apr	171
1800	ALLES, Peter "Colussus"&"Carnatic"Pts –	Aberd	Oct	697
1756	ALLESON, John	Kent	Dec	317
1797	ALLESON, otherwise ALLISON, Mary	Middx	Feb	66
1765	ALLESON, William	Lond	Apr	128
1797	ALLESTER, MC, otherwise ALLISTER, MC,			
	Hercules "Caesar" & "P. of Wales"	Pts	Mch	184
1759	ALLESTER, MC, otherwise COLLISTER, MC,			
	Henry	Pts	Feb	64
1783	ALLESTER, MC, John	Pts	Feb	--
1777	ALLESTER, MC, Robert	Pts	Dec	519
1770	ALLESTER, MC, otherwise ALLISTER, MC,			
	Samuel	Pts	Dec	442

1753	ALLESTREE, Thomas	Derby	Jny	1
1798	ALLET, otherwise ALLOTT, Margaret	Yorks	Jne	376
1776	ALLETT, Rev. James	SHant	Oct	410
1795	ALLETT, Mary Priscilla	SHant	Mch	137
1781	ALLEWAY, Catherine	Oxon	Sep	417
1786	ALLEWAY, otherwise ALLAWAY, John	Berks	Mch	133
1754	ALLEWAY, Mary	Middx	Jne	127
1758	ALLEXANDER, Sarah	Lond	Mch	61
1784	ALLEY, Elizabeth	Oxon	Oct	535
1761	ALLEY, Joanna	Lond	Nov	378
1767	ALLEY, Mary	Middx	Jly	250
1751	ALLEYN, Augustus AwW	Pts	Jny	1
1759	ALLEYN, Sir Edmund	Essex	Nov	346
1765	ALLEYN, Mary	Essex	May	166
1755	ALLEYNE, Abraham	Kent	Feb	31
1797	ALLEYNE, Anne AwW	Sussx	May	291
1756	ALLEYNE, Elizabeth	Pts	Nov	287
1784	ALLEYNE, Harry AwW	Kent	Oct	534
1777	ALLEYNE, John	Middx	Sep	374
1792	ALLEYNE, Rev. John	Glos	Dec	593
1794	ALLEYNE, John	Leics	Apr	180
1771	ALLEYNE, George	Som	Dec	466
1771	ALLEYNE, otherwise ALLEN, George W rgd this month	Som	Dec	--
1761	ALLEYNE, Rev. Thomas	Leics	Aug	275
1775	ALLEYNE, Thomas, Esq.	Lond	May	168
1779	ALLEYNE, Thomas	Surry	Nov	441
1793	ALLEYNE, Ursula	Leics	Jny	2
1800	ALLEZ, John Mt. S."Venus"	Pts	Jne	430
1775	ALLFORD, Joane	Berks	Jly	259
1760	ALLFORD, otherwise ORFORD, John AwW	SHant	Jny	29
1783	ALLFORD, John	Middx	May	210
1765	ALLFORD, Richard AwW	Pts	Oct	359
1772	ALLFORD, Sarah	Middx	Dec	429
1759	ALLFORD, William	Pts	Dec	381
1785	ALLFREE, Alexander	Surry	May	228
1764	ALLFREY, George	Sussx	May	162
1794	ALLFREY, George	Sussx	Dec	594
1781	ALLFREY, otherwise ALFREY, Thomas	Middx	Oct	459
1756	ALLGOOD, Barbara	Newcl	May	128
1786	ALLGREEN, Claus "Alfred"	Pts	Nov	551
1770	ALLIBAN, otherwise ALLIBEN, Thomas	Lond	Dec	421
1770	ALLIBEN, otherwise ALLIBAN, Thomas	Lond	Dec	421
1768	ALLIBON, Henry, otherwise ALLIBONN, Hennry	Middx	Apr	138
1755	ALLIBOND, Ann	Bucks	Jny	2
1754	ALLIBOND, Henry	Wark	Mch	66
1751	ALLIBONE, Benjamin	Lond	Sep	250
1773	ALLIBONE, Mary	Lond	Jny	1
1768	ALLIBONN, Hennry, otherwise ALLIBON, Henry	Middx	Apr	138
1762	ALLICANT, John	Pts	Jne	231
1750	ALLIN, formerly WALKER, Anna	Berks	Feb	64

69

1773	ALLIN, Sir Ashurst	Sfolk	Mch	89
1775	ALLIN, Benjamin	Lond	Dec	454
1763	ALLIN, Edward	Rutld	Mch	105
1791	ALLIN, Edward, Esq.	Pemb	May	209
1765	ALLIN, otherwise ALLEN, Elizabeth	Middx	Jny	2
1771	ALLIN, otherwise ALLEN, otherwise			
	BERRYMAN, Elizabeth, formerly	Surry	Sep	366
1758	ALLIN, Jacob, Esq. AwW	Som	Nov	319
1751	ALLIN, John (by int dec)	Pts	Nov	298
1795	ALLIN, John	Kent	Mch	137
1757	ALLIN, Joseph	Staff	Jne	179
1759	ALLIN, Sir Joseph	SHant	Sep	287
1775	ALLIN, otherwise ALLEN, Martha	Middx	Jne	219
1779	ALLIN, Mary	Kent	Jny	1
1799	ALLIN, otherwise ALLEN, Michael Ser.			
	"Ville de Paris"	Pts	Jne	414
1790	ALLIN, Richard	Oxon	Apr	169
1799	ALLIN, Samuel	SHant	Feb	89
1765	ALLIN, Sir Thomas, otherwise ANGUISH,			
	Thomas AwW	Sfolk	Nov	397
1763	ALLIN, otherwise ALLEN, William	Nhant	Sep	415
1778	ALLIN, otherwise ALLEN, William	Wilts	Feb	47
1792	ALLINDAR, Thomas	Middx	Mch	124
1765	ALLINE, Charles	Lond	Mch	83
1777	ALLINE, Rachel	Middx	Nov	445
1775	ALLING, otherwise ALLEN, Cyprem, other-			
	wise ELLENS, Sybran	Pts	Apr	137
1784	ALLINGAM, Thomas "Thetis"	Pts	Apr	186
1764	ALLINGHAM, Ann	Kent	Feb	36
1772	ALLINGHAM, Archibald	Pts	Jny	1
1765	ALLINGHAM, David	Surry	Apr	127
1770	ALLINGHAM, Elizabeth	Lond	May	170
1777	ALLINGHAM, Henry Spec AwW	Sussx	Dec	495
1764	ALLINGHAM, James	Surry	Feb	36
1795	ALLINGHAM, James	Wilts	Mch	138
1759	ALLINGHAM, John	Kent	Jne	191
1774	ALLINGHAM, John	Lond	Feb	36
1775	ALLINGHAM, John	Sussx	May	168
1778	ALLINGHAM, Joseph	Bath	Feb	46
1778	ALLINGHAM, Katherine	Surry	Sep	345
1784	ALLINGHAM, Richard "Renown"	Pts	Sep	488
1768	ALLINGHAM, formerly WHEELER, Sarah			
	Ltd Pr AwW (By Sentence regd Dec 476 1767)	Essex	Mch	94
1798	ALLINGHAM, Sarah	Kent	Jly	457
1782	ALLINGHAM, otherwise ALINGHAM, Thomas			
	"Terrible" AwW	Pts	Mch	108
1765	ALLINGHAM, William	Surry	Oct	360
1766	ALLINGHAM, William	Surry	Apr	125
1751	ALLINGTON, Edward	Middx	Apr	101
1796	ALLINGTON, Hugh	Middx	Apr	160
1795	ALLINGTON, Mary	Sfolk	May	293
1781	ALLINGTON, William	Middx	Dec	568
1777	ALLINSON, Henry	Middx	May	194

1767	ALLINSON, John	Bucks	Nov	399
1763	ALLINSON, Joseph	Pts	Feb	41
1783	ALLINSON, Thomas	Middx	Oct	493
1758	ALLION, Joseph	Pts	Jly	207
1795	ALLIS, Anna	Kent	Feb	61
1772	ALLIS, Elizabeth	Essex	Jly	244
1768	ALLIS, John	Essex	Jne	224
1787	ALLIS, John	Herts	Oct	436
1792	ALLIS, John	Herts	Jne	314
1756	ALLISON, Ann MASON, formerly	Middx	May	145
1760	ALLISON, otherwise OLESON, Benjamin	Pts	May	209
1797	ALLISON, Christian	Devon	May	291
1790	ALLISON, Edward	Derby	Jne	275
1751	ALLISON, Elizabeth	Brstl	Feb	34
1781	ALLISON, George	Pts	Aug	374
1797	ALLISON, George	Beds	Feb	65
1776	ALLISON, Hannah	Middx	Aug	343
1756	ALLISON, Henry AwW	Middx	Dec	318
1750	ALLISON, otherwise OLLESON, James W rgd Nov 1748	Pts	Jly	--
1779	ALLISON, Jane	Lond	Apr	138
1764	ALLISON, John	Middx	Oct	376
1768	ALLISON, John	Middx	Mch	93
1771	ALLISON, John	Middx	Oct	395
1777	ALLISON, John (sent)	Lond	Jly	296
1791	ALLISON, John	Middx	Aug	369
1768	ALLISON, Joseph	Middx	Mch	93
1796	ALLISON, Joseph	Devon	Aug	393
1794	ALLISON, Joshua	Wark	Nov	535
1793	ALLISON, Margaret, otherwise Margrat	Middx	Jny	2
1763	ALLISON, Mary	Middx	Sep	415
1797	ALLISON, otherwise ALLESON, Mary	Middx	Feb	66
1797	ALLISON, Mary	Cumb	Dec	722
1773	ALLISON, Sarah	Lond	Feb	42
1788	ALLISON, Simon	Derby	Feb	52
1780	ALLISON, Susanna	Sthl	Oct	458
1770	ALLISON, Thomas	SHant	May	169
1774	ALLISON, Thomas	Middx	Sep	328
1799	ALLISON, Thomas	Norf	Aug	560
1777	ALLISON, Thomas Pearce	Brstl	Jne	250
1795	ALLISON, Wenman "Agamemnon" Pts -	Norf	Dec	666
1772	ALLISON, William	Middx	Feb	33
1782	ALLISTER, Angus MC AwW	Pts	Dec	569
1786	ALLISTER, Ann	Middx	Oct	500
1782	ALLISTER, MC, otherwise ALESTER, MC, Charles	Pts	Oct	506
1786	ALLISTER, Edward MC "Blandford" "Superbe" "Worcester" Pts -	Kent	Mch	--
1797	ALLISTER, MC, otherwise ALLESTER, MC, Hercules "Caesar" & "P. of Wales"	Pts	Mch	184
1762	ALLISTER, MC, otherwise COLLISTER, MC, Malcolm AwW	Pts	Apr	164
1770	ALLISTER, MC, otherwise ALLESTER, MC, Samuel	Pts	Dec	442

71

```
1759  ALLISTON, John                                    Pts    Dec 381
1757  ALLISTON, Thomas                                  Middx  Nov 319
1765  ALLIX, Andrienne                                  Surry  Jny   2
1795  ALLIX, Charles Esq.                               Camb   Jny   1
1796  ALLIX, Rev. Charles Wager                         Wilts  May 232
1767  ALLIX, Gilbert                                    Surry  Jly 250
1776  ALLIX, Jane                                       Bath   Jne 253
1769  ALLIX, William Esq.                               Middx  Apr 110
1758  ALLKIN, Matthew  Ser.                             Middx  Nov 319
1770  ALLKINS, Thomas                                   Middx  Dec 420
1764  ALLMAN, John                                      Bucks  May 162
1767  ALLMAN, Judith                                    Lond   Jny   1
1762  ALLMAN, otherwise ALMOND, Robert                  Pts    Aug 330
1797  ALLMAN, otherwise MANLEY, Thomas                  Middx  Nov 672
1772  ALLMEY, Elizabeth                                 Kent   Feb  33
1771  ALLMEY, Thomas                                    Kent   Jny   1
1789  ALLMOND, otherwise ALMOND, Elizabeth              Berks  Dec 571
1799  ALLMOND, Mary                                     Lond   Jny   2
1759  ALLMOND, otherwise ALMOND, Sarah                  Middx  Nov 346
1760  ALLMOND, otherwise ALMOND, Thomas                 Middx  Jne 225
1767  ALLMOND, William                                  Oxon   Dec 435
1758  ALLNATT, Edward                                   Berks  Oct 282
1789  ALLNATT, Elizabeth                                Oxon   Feb  71
1784  ALLNATT, William                                  Oxon   Nov 583
1766  ALLNUTT, Alice                                    Middx  Oct 360
1763  ALLNUTT, Ann                                      Herts  Jne 263
1782  ALLNUTT, Ann                                      Bucks  May 210
1770  ALLNUTT, Elizabeth                                Lond   Feb  40
1778  ALLNUTT, Frances                                  Oxon   Jne 229
1787  ALLNUTT, Francis  (by int dec)                    Surry  Jne 251
1795  ALLNUTT, Francis                                  Surry  Apr 232
1768  ALLNUTT, George                                   Middx  Sep 336
1788  ALLNUTT, Henry                                    Berks  May 224
1795  ALLNUTT, Henry                                    Bucks  Feb  60
1778  ALLNUTT, Moses                                    Lond   May 182
1782  ALLNUTT, Moses Esq.                               Middx  Dec 569
1789  ALLNUTT, Richard Esq.                             Kent   Aug 417
1779  ALLNUTT, Thomas Esq.                              Lond   May 185
1764  ALLNUTT, Zachary                                  Herts  Jne 209
1789  ALLNUTT, Zachary                                  Bucks  Aug 471
1752  ALLOM, otherwise ALLAM, Edwin                     Surry  Sep 227
1756  ALLOM, Elizabeth                                  Middx  Jly 186
1750  ALLOM, William                        Pts - Middx  Nov 344
1798  ALLOTT, otherwise ALLET, Margaret                 Yorks  Jne 376
1758  ALLOTT, Robert                                    Essex  Feb  28
1763  ALLOWAY, Elizabeth                                Brstl  Dec 537
1773  ALLOWAY, Elizabeth                                Surry  Jne 233
1796  ALLOWAY, Elizabeth  AwW                           Surry  Mch 106
1794  ALLOWAY, Matthew                                  Pts    Jny   2
1789  ALLOWAY, Morris                                   Middx  Feb  70
1765  ALLOWAY, Nathaniel                                Som    Aug 290
1763  ALLOWAY, Philip                                   Surry  Aug 366
1796  ALLOWAY, Ralph                                    Surry  Aug 393
```

72

1765	ALLOWAY, Sarah	Brstl	May	167
1789	ALLOWAY, Thomas	Berks	Jne	296
1788	ALLPORT, Henry, otherwise ALPORT, Henery "Vestal"	Pts	Nov	518
1784	ALLRIDGE, otherwise ALLRIGE, otherwise ALDRIDGE, William Anor. Grant this month	Notts	Apr	--
1784	ALLRIGE, otherwise ALDRIDGE, otherwise ALLRIDGE, William Anor. Grant this month	Notts	Apr	--
1790	ALLRIGHT, John	Middx	Feb	55
1796	ALLRIGHT, John	Berks	Feb	52
1780	ALLRIGHT, Martha	Berks	May	118
1766	ALLRIGHT, Thomas	Berks	Aug	290
1764	ALLRY, otherwise ALLERY, George	Devon	Jne	209
1798	ALLSOP, George Gould	Middx	Jne	376
1760	ALLSOP, James	Pts	May	180
1791	ALLSOP, James	Middx	Apr	164
1788	ALLSOP, otherwise HALLSOP, Susannah	Roch	Dec	572
1770	ALLSOP, Thomas	Middx	Feb	39
1790	ALLSOP, Thomas	Essex	Mch	115
1798	ALLSOP, Thomas Esq.	Middx	Jly	456
1800	ALLSOP, William Esq.	Herts	Feb	80
1797	ALLSOPP, Mary	Leics	Feb	65
1757	ALLSOPP, Thomas	Leics	Apr	109
1778	ALLSOPP, Thomas	Leics	Feb	46
1784	ALLSOPP, Thomas	Derby	Feb	59
1795	ALLSOPP, William	Notts	Apr	233
1757	ALLSPIKE, Richard	SHant	Dec	348
1757	ALLSTER, MC, otherwise ALISTER, MC, Archibald	Pts	Sep	281
1750	ALLSTER, John MC	SHant	Dec	376
1790	ALLTREE, Ann AwW	Middx	Jly	317
1784	ALLTREE, Mary SHAW formerly AwW	Middx	Dec	665
1761	ALLUM, Ann	Berks	Jly	239
1766	ALLUM, Richard AwW of Gds unadm. W rgd 1733, 192	Berks	Mch	--
1775	ALLUM, Richard	Lond	Nov	399
1786	ALLUM, Richard	Berks	Apr	201
1764	ALLUM, Robert MC	Pts	Nov	435
1786	ALLUM, Saint	Surry	May	257
1767	ALLVEY, Joseph	Middx	Sep	331
1794	ALLWARD, Thomas Ser. "Thetis"	Pts	Nov	535
1763	ALLWAYS, Thomas	Pts	May	210
1798	ALLWOOD, Ann	Middx	Jny	2
1772	ALLWOOD, John	Surry	Oct	347
1796	ALLWOOD, John	Middx	Apr	158
1781	ALLWOOD, Mary AwW	Middx	Dec	568
1797	ALLWOOD, Mary AwW of Gds unadm. W rgd 1781, 568	Middx	Nov	--
1800	ALLWOOD, Philip Esq.	Middx	Oct	697
1782	ALLWOOD, Selina	Middx	Nov	527
1789	ALLWORK, otherwise JAMES, otherwise LIVINGSTON, Elizabeth	Kent	Oct	501

1792	ALLWRIGHT, Aaron		Surry	May	252
1757	ALLWRIGHT, Alice		Berks	Aug	238
1770	ALLWRIGHT, James		Surry	Mch	85
1770	ALLWRIGHT, James		Berks	Dec	420
1750	ALLWRIGHT, Jane		Middx	Aug	250
1779	ALLWRIGHT, Richard Esq		Worcs	Sep	364
1775	ALLWRIGHT, Thomas		Wilts	Aug	298
1794	ALLWRIGHT, formerly HIBBERT, Thomazin,				
	otherwise Thomasin		Berks	Feb	59
1787	ALLWRIGHT, William		Berks	Aug	353
1779	ALLYN, Margrat, otherwise Margaret		Essex	May	185
1782	ALMA, Jacob		Pts	Jne	261
1762	ALMACK, John		Middx	Apr	136
1781	ALMACK, William		Middx	Jny	2
1766	ALMBERG, Jeistaf		Pts	Nov	395
1764	ALMEDO, otherwise DELMEDO, Philip D'		Pts	May	169
1758	ALMERS, Johann, otherwise John		Pts	Aug	236
1767	ALMOND, Ann		Lond	Apr	121
1798	ALMOND, Daniel VAN AwW		Pts	Jne	446
1763	ALMOND, Elizabeth		Middx	May	211
1789	ALMOND, otherwise ALLMOND, Elizabeth		Berks	Dec	571
1756	ALMOND, John		Oxon	Apr	93
1765	ALMOND, Paul		Lond	Apr	128
1762	ALMOND, otherwise ALLMAN, Robert		Pts	Aug	330
1759	ALMOND, otherwise ALLMOND, Sarah		Middx	Nov	346
1760	ALMOND, Thomas		Essex	Jne	225
1760	ALMOND, otherwise ALLMOND, Thomas		Middx	Jne	225
1765	ALMOND, Thomas		Pts	Aug	282
1789	ALMONDE, Elisabeth VAN (Ltd Pr)		Pts	Sep	476
1785	ALMONDE, Johanna VAN (Ltd Pr)		Pts	Jny	——
1764	ALMONDE, Susanna GRAAFMAN ISAACZ VAN		Pts	May	177
1774	ALMONDE, Susanna GRAAFMAN ISAACZ formerly				
	VAN AwW unadm. W rgd 1764, 177		Pts	Jne	——
1777	ALMS, John		SHant	May	194
1771	ALMSWORTHY, Richard		Devon	May	191
1786	ALNER, William AwW		Dorst	Nov	551
1787	ALNER, William		SHant	Dec	527
1798	ALNWICK, Robert		Nland	Jny	1
1797	ALNWICK, William		Nland	May	290
1767	ALPALHAO, James RODRIGUES AwW		Pts	Dec	459
1765	ALPE, Elizabeth		Middx	Mch	83
1760	ALPE, Frederick AwW of Gds unadm. Last				
	Grant May 1727, W rgd 1727,56 & 90		Sfolk	Apr	——
1786	ALPHEN, Abraham VAN (Ltd Pr)		Pts	Feb	——
1777	ALPHEN, Lady Anna Cornelia VAN (Ltd Pr)		Pts	Apr	189
1775	ALPHEN, Rt Hon Anthony VAN, Esq.(Ltd Pr)		Pts	Sep	362
1795	ALPHEN, Gysbert VAN (Ltd Pr)		Pts	Oct	——
1767	ALPHEN, Hermanus VAN (Ltd Pr)		Pts	Sep	357
1758	ALPHEN, Hieronimus VAN (Ltd Pr)		Pts	Oct	315
1788	ALPHEN, Isaac VAN (Ltd Pr)		Pts	Nov	——
1750	ALPHEN, Jan VAN AwW		Pts	May	180
1780	ALPHEN, Jan AwW unadm. W rgd 1750,180		Pts	Mch	——
1796	ALPHEN, Jan VAN (Ltd Pr)		Pts	Jne	335

1789	ALPHEN, Johan VAN (Ltd Pr)	Pts	Oct	521
1784	ALPHEN, Nicolaas VAN (Ltd Pr)	Pts	Mch	--
1773	ALPHEN, Pieter VAN (Ltd Pr)	Pts	Dec	495
1773	ALPHEN & RIETVELD, Lord, Hon Theodorus DE SMETH, Baron of DEURNE & LIESSEL (Ltd Pr)	Pts	Jny	34
1773	ALPHEN, Willem VAN (Ltd Pr)	Pts	Dec	496
1792	ALPHEN, William, otherwise Willem VAN (Ltd Pr)	Pts	May	307
1784	ALPHEY, Albrecht	Surry	Feb	59
1765	ALPHEY, William	Sussx	May	167
1781	ALPIN, Daniel MC, Esq. AwW	Pts	Dec	--
1761	ALPIN, James MC	Middx	Nov	401
1799	ALPIN, John MC Ser. "Lowest","Discovery" & "Caroline"	Pts	Oct	729
1792	ALPORT, Edward	Worcs	Sep	458
1788	ALPORT, otherwise ALLPORT, Henry, otherwise Henery "Vestal"	Pts	Nov	518
1793	ALPORT, otherwise APORT, John	Middx	Dec	578
1797	ALPRESS, Margaret Eleanor	Bath	Apr	220
1781	ALQUIER, Sarah	Hants	May	221
1759	ALQUIST, Matthias Henrickson	Pts	May	155
1799	ALRIC, James Esq.	Nwich	Jny	1
1784	ALRICK, John	Surry	Jne	302
1766	ALRICK, Willim, otherwise William	Surry	Oct	361
1800	ALSAGER, otherwise ALSEAGER, James	Worcs	Mch	171
1795	ALSAGER, Judith	Chest	Jly	426
1795	ALSAGER, Mary	Chest	Jly	427
1791	ALSAGER, Richard	Lond	Oct	449
1790	ALSAGER, Thomas	Surry	Feb	56
1800	ALSEAGER, otherwise ALSAGER, James	Worcs	Mch	171
1797	ALSEPT, Moses	Middx	Nov	672
1786	ALSIEN, Francis	Pts	Dec	597
1760	ALSIOFRACO, Henriques Judica	Pts	Mch	104
1783	ALSLEY, otherwise STUBBS, otherwise STUBS, Jonathan, otherwise STUBBINS, Jonathan Halsey	Pts	Sep	--
1783	ALSON, Richard	Pts	Aug	397
1759	ALSOON, otherwise OLSON, John, otherwise John Seron	Pts	Mch	80
1759	ALSOON, otherwise OLSON, John Seron, otherwise John	Pts	Mch	80
1763	ALSOP, Arabella	Notts	Jne	264
1763	ALSOP, Elizabeth	Berks	Jny	1
1786	ALSOP, otherwise JENKINSON, George	Staff	Aug	417
1769	ALSOP, Henry	Derby	Jny	1
1794	ALSOP, Henry	Lond	Jne	294
1767	ALSOP, John AwW	Pts	Jne	205
1751	ALSOP, Mary	Notts	Oct	273
1759	ALSOP, Mary	Surry	Dec	381
1763	ALSOP, Mary	Middx	Jny	1
1780	ALSOP, Mary	Wilts	Sep	425
1785	ALSOP, Mary	Essex	Dec	584
1798	ALSOP, Peter Esq.	Pts	Aug	522
1753	ALSOP, Robert	Surry	Mch	69

1759	ALSOP, Robert AwW of Gds unadm. W rgd 1750, 69	Surry	Jne	--
1785	ALSOP, Robert, Esq. Late one of Aldermen of City of London	Middx	Jne	288
1792	ALSOP, Susannah Maria	Middx	Jny	2
1785	ALSOP, Thomas	Sfolk	Apr	168
1795	ALSOPP, Andrew	Notts	Sep	533
1778	ALSTON, Dame Catherine Davies	Staff	Jne	230
1775	ALSTON, Elizabeth	Sfolk	Aug	299
1780	ALSTON, Elizabeth	Middx	Apr	169
1781	ALSTON, Elizabeth	Sfolk	Oct	460
1783	ALSTON, Elizabeth	Middx	Sep	441
1783	ALSTON, Sir Evelyn, Bart.	Middx	Mch	106
1755	ALSTON, Hannah	Lond	Sep	232
1760	ALSTON, Jacob	Sfolk	Jly	271
1784	ALSTON, Joseph	Essex	Jne	304
1789	ALSTON, Mary AwW of Gds unadm. W rgd 1741, 26	Sfolk	Jne	--
1759	ALSTON, Sir Rowland	Beds	Jny	1
1766	ALSTON, Sir Rowland AwW unadm. W rgd 1759, 1	Beds	Jly	--
1787	ALSTON, Rowland, Esq.	Beds	May	195
1791	ALSTON, Sir Rowland, Kn.	Beds	Jly	313
1752	ALSTON, Samuel	Sfolk	Nov	267
1781	ALSTON, Samuel	Essex	Jny	2
1796	ALSTON, Samuel	Sfolk	Aug	394
1755	ALSTON, Thomas	Lond	Jny	1
1756	ALSTON, Thomas AwW	Essex	Dec	318
1776	ALSTON, Sir Thomas, Bart. Spec Pr of rest of Gds. Grant in Feb last (Sent.)	Beds	Nov	447
1761	ALSTON, Theodosia	Middx	Jne	199
1780	ALSTON, William	Surry	May	233
1787	ALSTON, William No ship	Pts	Nov	480
1750	ALSWORTH, John	Berks	May	134
1772	ALT, Hannetta	Middx	Oct	347
1753	ALT, John Jacob	Middx	Jny	1
1768	ALT, Just Henry, Esq. AwW	Middx	Dec	437
1782	ALTENA, Jan Leendertse, otherwise Jan Leenderse (Ltd Pr)	Pts	Mch	108
1751	ALTENHAUSEN, Frederica Carolina Wilhelmina D' (Ltd Pr)	Pts	May	130
1757	ALTHAM, Edward Esq.	Essex	Jny	1
1793	ALTHAM, Katharine	Kent	Nov	539
1751	ALTHAM, James	Surry	Feb	34
1779	ALTHAM, Roger Esq.	Middx	Nov	440
1788	ALTHAM, Roger, Esq.	Middx	Oct	468
1775	ALTHAM, Samuel	Surry	Dec	453
1782	ALTHAM, Dr. Thomas Dr. of Laws	Essex	Dec	569
1765	ALTHORN, Elizabeth AwW of Gds unadm. W rgd 1714, 18	Sussx	Apr	--
1767	ALTHORN, Robert	Lond	Aug	294
1761	ALTHROUP, Jane	Middx	Oct	335
1772	ALTING, Rev. Johannes (Ltd Pr)	Pts	Dec	447

```
1755  ALTON, Elias                                        Middx  Jny    2
1751  ALTON, Sarah                                        Derby  Jny    1
1767  ALTRAP, Ann                                         Surry  Sep  332
1758  ALTREE, James                          Pts -  Lond  Nov  318
1755  ALTREE, Dr. John  (Dr. of Physic)                   Middx  Jny    1
1761  ALTREE, Dr. John  (Dr. of Physic)  AwW
         unadm.  W rgd 1755, 1                             Middx  May   --
1767  ALTZENHEIM, Hon Friedrich Philip VON      Pts    Feb   78
1764  ALVARES, Moses Jesurun                              Middx  Mch   78
1791  ALVARENGA, Esther                                   Lond   May  208
1774  ALVARENGA, Judith                                   Lond   Oct  357
1782  ALVARENGA, Sarah, otherwise Sara                    Lond   Jne  261
1761  ALVARES, Corcho Moses                               Middx  Jly  243
1753  ALVARES, Emanuel                                    Lond   Jne  158
1781  ALVARES JESURUN, Ester                              Middx  Jny    3
1773  ALVARES DE PINTO, Moseli, otherwise
         DE PINTO, Moseli de JAHACOB  (Ltd Pr)  Pts    Oct  403
1755  ALVARES, Sarah MENDES DA COSTA                      Lond   Jly  180
1779  ALVARONGA, Moses                                    Lond   Nov  440
1786  ALVAZ, John "Lascelles"                   Pts    Jne  318
1753  ALVES, William                                      Middx  May  126
1754  ALVES, William                            Pts    Oct  264
1761  ALVEY, Henry                              Pts    Nov  378
1765  ALVEY, John                               Pts    Apr  127
1764  ALVIS, Edward                                       Sfolk  Mch   78
1782  ALWAY, Elizabeth                                    Glos   Apr  161
1781  ALWAY, Sarah                                        Herts  Apr  179
1761  ALWEN, John                                         Kent   Dec  416
1778  ALWEN, Thomas                                       Kent   Apr  141
1772  ALWEN, William                                      Kent   May  154
1797  ALWEN, William                                      Surry  Jne  393
1764  ALWIN, John  AwW                                    Kent   Jne  210
1772  ALWIN, John                                         Kent   Jny    1
1776  ALWIN, John  AwW   unadm.  W rgd 1772, 1   Kent   Sep   --
1765  ALWIN, Michael                                      Herts  Mch   84
1769  ALWOOD, Rev. John                                   Salop  Aug  271
1750  ALWYN, Jane                                         Kent . Aug  250
1750  ALYN, Gottfried, otherwise ALLEN, GodfreyPts    May  136
1760  AMAN, otherwise HARMON, otherwise
         HAMMOND, William  W rgd Apr last         Pts    Jne   --
1760  AMAN, William                             Pts    Apr  134
1754  AMAND, James ST., Esq.                              Middx  Sep  243
1782  AMAR, John  AwW                           Pts    Oct  478
1789  AMAS, Francis  AwW                                  Middx  Mch  131
1793  AMAS, John                                          Kent   Jly  350
1779  AMATT, Jennet                                       Middx  Jny    1
1784  AMBER, Elizabeth                                    Middx  Apr  186
1774  AMBER, Norton                                       Middx  Nov  384
1784  AMBEROUS, George  AwW  "Monarca"          Pts    Jly  363
1753  AMBERTON, otherwise HAMBERTON, Benjamin
         AwW                                              SHant  Feb   37
1774  AMBLER, Brian                                       Middx  Jny    1
1794  AMBLER, Charles, Esq.                               Berks  Mch  119
```

```
1783   AMBLER, John                                      Lincs  Jly  333
1756   AMBLER, Phoebe                                    Middx  Mch   58
1798   AMBLER, Richard                                   Yorks  Mch  151
1775   AMBLER, Thomas                                    Middx  Sep  333
1750   AMBLER, William                                   Pts    Jly  220
1781   AMBOY, Pennywell, otherwise Pennel                Pts    Apr  179
1754   AMBRIDGE, James                                   Middx  Mch   66
1769   AMBRIDGE, James                                   Middx  Apr  110
1778   AMBRIDGE, William                                 Middx  Sep  345
1779   AMBROSE, Ann                                      Middx  Jly  283
1779   AMBROSE, Charles, Esq.                            Middx  Feb   36
1779   AMBROSE, Charles  AwW of Gds unadm.
         W rgd Feb last                                  Middx  Mch   --
1760   AMBROSE, Edward                                   Middx  Jny  225
1794   AMBROSE, Eleanor                                  Kent   Aug  402
1769   AMBROSE, Elizabeth COURTNEY, formerly
         Ltd AwW                                         Surry  Feb   40
1778   AMBROSE, George                                   Pts    Jly  271
1788   AMBROSE, Hannah                                   Middx  Jny    1
1768   AMBROSE, Henry                                    Herts  May  184
1755   AMBROSE, John                                     Berks  Nov  274
1771   AMBROSE, John, Esq.  AwW                          SHant  Apr  140
1798   AMBROSE, John                                     Camb   Mch  150
1771   AMBROSE, Lawrence                                 Middx  Aug  328
1750   AMBROSE, Mary                                     Middx  Apr  101
1772   AMBROSE, Mary                                     Middx  Feb   33
1797   AMBROSE, otherwise AMBROSSE, Rachael              Middx  Oct  624
1775   AMBROSE, Richard                                  SHant  Aug  298
1794   AMBROSE, Richard                                  Middx  May  240
1784   AMBROSE, Samuel                                   Kent   Mch  117
1756   AMBROSE, Sarah                                    Kent   Oct  266
1753   AMBROSE, William                                  Lond   May  126
1783   AMBROSE, William                                  Kent   Dec  596
1797   AMBROSSE, otherwise AMBROSE, Rachael              Middx  Oct  624
1779   AMCOTES, John                                     Lond   Jny    1
1790   AMCOTES, Mary SUMMERLING, formerly                Lond   Apr   --
1786   AMELIA, H.R.H. Princess of England                Middx  Nov  550
1767   AMELISWEERT & HEESWYK, Hendrick VAN
         UTENHOVE, Lord of  (Ltd Pr)                     Pts    Sep  357
1774   AMELONSON, Elizabeth VAN                          Pts    Sep  352
1754   AMENT, John                                       Surry  Aug  218
1763   AMENT, John                                       Surry  Jny    1
1773   AMERONGEN, Anna Maria Taets VAN, other-
         wise Lady Anna Maria Baroness Taets
         VAN AMERONGEN  (Ltd Pr)                         Pts    Oct  468
1792   AMERONGEN, Rt Hon Joost, Baron TAETS VAN
         AwW                                             Pts    Feb  117
1771   AMERSON, otherwise EMMERSON, Edward               Kent   Dec  467
1757   AMERSON, William                                  Middx  Apr  109
1758   AMERY, John                                       Middx  Jne  175
1767   AMERY, John                                       Lond   Sep  331
1784   AMERY, John                                       Middx  Feb   60
1799   AMERY, John                                       Middx  Apr  238
```

1755	AMERY, Thomas			Middx	Nov	275
1761	AMERY, Thomas			Pts	Feb	43
1788	AMERY, Thomas			Staff	Dec	572
1792	AMERY, Thomas	AwW		Middx	Sep	458
1796	AMERY, Thomas	AwW of Gds unadm. W rgd				
	1788, 572			Staff	Oct	--
1759	AMERY, William	AwW		Lond	Oct	317
1767	AMERY, William	Ltd AwW unadm. W rgd				
	1759, 317			Lond	Mch	--
1784	AMERY, William			Middx	Jny	2
1785	AMERY, William			Middx	Jny	1
1768	AMES, Elizabeth	AwW (by int dec)		Middx	Jne	224
1796	AMES, Henry	AwW		Middx	Oct	485
1779	AMES, Jeremiah, Esq.			Brstl	Jly	283
1772	AMES, Josiah			Som	Feb	34
1795	AMES, otherwise EMES, Margaret			Kent	Sep	--
1763	AMES, Peter AwW			Som	Mch	105
1787	AMES, Robert			Som	Apr	155
1786	AMES, otherwise AIMES, Samuel		Pts - Worcs	Mch	132
1782	AMES, Thomas			Middx	Sep	438
1785	AMES, William			Surry	May	228
1751	AMESDEN, William			Herts	Oct	273
1784	AMESHOFF, Hermanus			Pts	Mch	117
1756	AMEY, Charles			Camb	Jne	157
1770	AMEY, Charles			Camb	Dec	421
1784	AMEY, John "Carolina"			Pts	Oct	534
1792	AMEY, John			Kent	Aug	415
1799	AMEY, Mary			Kent	Jne	414
1781	A.'MEYNSMA, Fransiscus			Pts	Dec	569
1772	AMHERST, Charles Selby, Esq. AwW unadm.					
	W rgd 1746, 34			Kent	Nov	--
1797	AMHERST, Charles Selby, Esq. AwW of Gds					
	twice unadm. W rgd 1746, 34. Last grant					
	Nov 1772			-	Apr	--
1753	AMHERST, Elizabeth			Kent	Jny	1
1750	AMHERST, Jeffery, Esq.			Kent	Nov	344
1797	AMHERST, Rt Hon Jeffery, Lord			Kent	Aug	538
1778	AMHERST, John Esq. Admiral of the Blue					
	Squadron			SHant	Feb	47
1786	AMHERST, John AwW			Middx	Apr	201
1797	AMHERST, John, Esq.			Kent	Nov	673
1773	AMHERST, Mary			Kent	May	190
1798	AMHERST, William Kerrill			Pts	Dec	754
1795	AMHURST, Ann			Kent	Apr	233
1754	AMHURST, Edward Esq			Pts	Jne	157
1756	AMHURST, Edward			Kent	Nov	287
1753	AMHURST, John			Kent	Sep	244
1762	AMHURST, John			Kent	Aug	330
1788	AMHURST, John Esq.			Roch	Feb	52
1800	AMHURST, Mary			Roch	Aug	573
1756	AMHURST, Nicholas			Pts	Oct	236
1760	AMHURST, Stephen			Kent	Jne	226
1754	AMIAND, John AwW W rgd 1741, 141 (by int decree)			Guery	Aug	--

```
1788  AMICI, Joseph                                          Lond   May 224
1800  AMIES, Richard                                         Middx  Mch 172
1789  AMIOT, Magdalene otherwise Magdalen                    Middx  Jny   1
1786  AMIOT, Stephen                                         Middx  Aug 419
1755  AMIRAN, Christopher                                    Nwich  Nov 274
1781  AMIRANT, Christopher  W rgd Jly 1780                   Bath   Aug  --
1787  AMIRANT, Elizabeth                                     Nwich  Mch 102
1779  AMIS, Elizabeth                                        Beds   Mch  86
1780  AMIS, Elizabeth                                        Beds   Oct 458
1753  AMIS, Mary                                             Essex  Jne 159
1759  AMIS, Sarah                                            Sfolk  Oct 316
1759  AMIS, Rev. Thomas                                      SHant  May 155
1750  AMLER, Ann                                             Middx  May 135
1754  AMLER, George, Esq.                                    Salop  Jny   2
1787  AMLER, John, Esq.                                      Salop  Jny   2
1791  AMLER, John, Esq.                                      Salop  Feb  52
1790  AMLER, Mary                                            Salop  Oct 450
1793  AMLER, Rev. Thomas                                     Salop  May 238
1768  AMMASON, otherwise EMMERSON, John  Ser.                Devon  Jly 265
1795  AMON, Ann COTTON, formerly                             Middx  Jny  11
1777  AMON, Bennet                                           Nhant  May 194
1761  AMON, George                                           Pts    Jny   1
1796  AMOORE, Sarah                                          Sussx  Jny   1
1781  AMOR, John                                             Middx  Aug 374
1782  AMOR, Robert                                           Wilts  Jly 332
1761  AMOR, William                                          Dorst  Nov 378
1780  AMOR, William                                          Wilts  Nov 502
1783  AMOR, William                                          Wilts  Feb  56
1783  AMOR, William  AwW unadm. W rgd Nov 1780 Wilts  Feb  --
1763  AMORE, Thomasin  AwW                                   Wark   Feb  41
1782  AMORIE, Nicolaes DES (Ltd Pr)                          Pts    Sep 447
1787  AMORY, Isaac                                           Middx  Aug 354
1800  AMORY, John                                            SHant  Jly 500
1800  AMORY, Samuel, Esq.                                    Middx  Jny   1
1766  AMORY, Simon  (Ltd Pr)                                 Pts    Nov 395
1774  AMORY, Rev. Dr. Thomas, D.D.                           Lond   Jly 252
1763  AMOS, Francis                                          Lond   Mch 103
1772  AMOS, otherwise THOMPSON, Henry                        Pts    Jly 243
1757  AMOS, John                                             Lond   Apr 109
1765  AMOS, Mary                                             Middx  Nov 397
1765  AMOS, Roger                                            Som    Dec 438
1773  AMOS, William                          Pts - Lond   Dec 456
1785  AMOSON, Knut, otherwise HANMERSON, Newte
         E.I.S."Ponsborne"                                   Pts    Jne  --
1795  AMOTT, James  AwW                                      Mon    Mch 136
1797  AMOUR, Elizabeth                                       Middx  Jny  --
1773  AMOUR, James ST                                        Middx  Mch 129
1774  AMOUR, Mary DE ST                                      Middx  Jne 223
1769  AMOUR, William DE ST, Esq.                             Middx  Oct 331
1781  AMOYL, Owen                                            Pts    May 221
1769  AMPHLET, William, Esq.                                 Worcs  Nov 363
1782  AMPHLETT, Charles                                      Middx  Sep 437
1783  AMPHLETT, Frances                                      Staff  Jly 333
```

80

1790	AMPHLETT, Frances (Dble Pr) W rgd 1783, 333		Staff	May --
1777	AMPHLETT, John		Staff	Sep 374
1780	AMPHLETT, Dr. Joseph (Dr. of Laws)		Oxon	Jly 345
1766	AMPHLETT, Mary		Worcs	Aug 290
1780	AMPHLETT, Mary		Oxon	Apr 168
1789	AMPHLETT, Richard, Esq.		Staff	Oct 481
1764	AMPHLETT, Thomas, Esq.		Pts	Nov 413
1771	AMPROUX, Lucy Elizabeth DE MISSY, formerly D¹ (Ltd Pr)		Middx	Jly 311
1754	AMSBURY, Robert		Wilts	Oct 264
1784	AMSDELL, Francis	Pts -	SHant	Nov 583
1765	AMSINCK, Paul		Lond	Apr 127
1767	AMSINCQ, Ann LUFNEU, formerly (Ltd Pr)		Pts	Jne 273
1752	AMSINCQ, otherwise BASNAGE DE BEAUVAL, Marie (Ltd Pr)		Pts	Jny 2
1764	AMSINK, William		Lond	Jny 1
1789	AMSON, Ann		Middx	Jny 2
1775	AMSON, John		Lond	Feb 37
1766	AMSON, Zacharias AwW		Chest	Aug 291
1774	AMSTEL, Aletta PLOOS VAN (Ltd Pr)		Pts	Mch 110
1758	AMSTEL, Boudewyn PLOOS VAN (Ltd Pr)		Pts	Nov 344
1766	AMSTEL CORNELISZOON, Boudewyn PLOOS VAN (Ltd Pr)		Pts	Apr 125
1764	AMSTEL, Cornelis PLOOS VAN		Pts	Feb 64
1775	AMSTEL JACOBSZ, Cornelis PLOOS VAN (Ltd Pr)		Pts	Dec 490
1776	AMSTEL JACOBSZ, Cornelis PLOOS VAN (Ltd Pr) W rgd Dec last		Pts	Apr --
1763	AMSTEL, PLOOS VAN, otherwise GRUN, Geertruy (Ltd Pr)		Pts	May 249
1760	AMSTEL JACOBSZ, Jacob PLOOS VAN (Ltd Pr)		Pts	Oct 402
1770	AMSTEL, Jan PLOOS VAN (Ltd Pr)		Pts	Aug --
1778	AMSTEL, Johanna Clementia PLOOS VAN (Ltd Pr)		Pts	Nov 469
1763	AMSTEL, Thomas PLOOS VAN (Ltd Pr)		Pts	Apr 193
1770	AMSTERDAM, formerly DE JONGE, otherwise VANDER HIEL, Petronella, formerly (Ltd Pr)		Pts	May --
1755	AMY, Elizabeth		Surry	May 121
1774	AMY, Francis		Jersy	Jly 252
1783	AMY, formerly LE HARDY, Jane		Pts	Dec 596
1757	AMY, John		Bucks	Apr 109
1783	AMY, otherwise HAYMEE, otherwise HAYMY, Philip AwW Ser.		Pts	Jne 278
1778	AMY, Susanna		Jersy	Mch 94
1782	AMY, otherwise OMMY, Thomas AwW		Pts	Jny 1
1767	AMYAND, Dame Anna Maria		Middx	Jly 250
1784	AMYAND, Charlotte AwW		Herts	Feb 59
1774	AMYAND, Claudius, Esq.		Herts	Apr 125
1783	AMYAND DE GRAVE, Daniel		Middx	Apr 158
1799	AMYAND, Frances		Herts	Aug 561
1766	AMYAND, Sir George, Bart.		Lond	Aug 290

1780	AMYAND, John	Lond	Jne 299
1760	AMYAND, Mary	Middx	Mch 85
1762	AMYAND, Thomas	Middx	Jne 230
1778	AMYAS, Alexander	Glam	May 182
1763	AMYAS, John	**Norf**	Aug 366
1761	AMYATT, Ann	Hunts	Oct 335
1752	AMYATT, Elizabeth	Devon	Jny 1
1753	AMYATT, Elizabeth (Dble Pr) W rgd Jny		
	1752	Devon	Nov —
1764	AMYATT, Peter Esq. AwW	Pts	Apr 128
1762	AMYE, John	Essex	Nov 444
1799	AMYOT, Peter	Nwich	Dec 819
1788	AMYOT, Thomas	Middx	Dec 572
1799	ANBUREY, Thomas	Middx	Jny 3
1794	ANCASTER & KESTEVEN, Most Noble Lady Mary,		
	Dowager Duchess of	-	Jny 2
1755	ANCASTER & KESTEVEN, Most Noble Peregrine,		
	late Duke of AwW W rgd 1742, 141	Middx	Sep —
1778	ANCASTER & KESTEVEN, Most Noble Peregrine,		
	Duke of .. & Lord Hered. Gt Chamb. of		
	England	Lincs	Aug 308
1779	ANCASTER & KESTEVEN, Most Noble Robert,		
	Duke of .. Lord Hered. Gt Chamb. of Eng	Middx	Jly 282
1776	ANCELL, Francis	Kent	Dec 484
1770	ANCELL, John	Surry	Oct 348
1780	ANCELL, Katherine	Middx	Mch 118
1768	ANCELL, Stephen	Surry	Feb 41
1794	ANCHANT, otherwise ANCIENT, Daniel		
	"Resolution" & "Terrible"	Pts	May 239
1750	ANCHIE, otherwise ANCHIY, John	Pts	Jne 185
1750	ANCHIY, otherwise ANCHIE, John	Pts	Jne 185
1794	ANCIENT, otherwise ANCHANT, David		
	"Resolution" & "Terrible"	Pts	May 239
1756	ANCIENT, John Ser.	Middx	Apr 93
1795	**ANCONA**, Leon	Middx	Mch 138
1800	ANCONA, Moses D', otherwise ANCONA, Moses		
	Van Jacon D'	Pts	Jne 450
1750	ANCOMB, David	Surry	Jne 185
1762	ANCOR, John	Sfolk	Aug 330
1766	ANCOTT, William	Lond	Jne 210
1795	ANDAS, Margery, otherwise Margary, other-		
	wise Margrary, otherwise Margray	Middx	Mch 184
1786	ANDAS, William	Middx	May 258
1754	ANDEFFRE, Anne	Middx	May 123
1786	ANDER, Marial, otherwise ENDER, Ulrick		
	W rgd May last	Pts	Jne —
1799	ANDERDON, Elizabeth	Som	Jne 414
1750	ANDERDON, Mary	Som	Aug 250
1772	ANDERS, Sarah	Kent	Nov 390
1799	ANDERSON, Aaron AwW	Middx	Jly 472
1759	ANDERSON, Adam AwW	Pts	Apr 115
1765	ANDERSON, Adam	Middx	Jny 2
1766	ANDERSON, Adam AwW	Pts	Apr 125

```
1772  ANDERSON, Agnes                            Middx Feb  33
1761  ANDERSON, Alexander   Ser.                 Pts   Jly 239
1763  ANDERSON, Alexander                        Pts   Dec 537
1764  ANDERSON, Alexander                        Pts   Jly 248
1778  ANDERSON, Alexander                        Middx Jny   1
1781  ANDERSON, Alexander                        Middx Sep 417
1784  ANDERSON, Alexander  "Sultan"              Devon May 244
1784  ANDERSON, Alexander, otherwise Andrew
          AwW "Daphne" & "Essex"                 --    Jly 363
1784  ANDERSON, Alexander                        Lond  Dec 627
1787  ANDERSON, Alexander, Esq.  Spec AwW or
          Testy. Schedules                       NBrit Jny   1
1794  ANDERSON, Alexander  "Terpsichore"         Pts   Sep 443
1796  ANDERSON, Alexander                        Lond  Nov 538
1797  ANDERSON, Alexander (Dble Pr) W rgd Nov
          last                                   Lond  Jny  --
1799  ANDERSON, Alexander                        Middx Apr 241
1800  ANDERSON, Alexander                        Middx Mch 172
1790  ANDERSON, Alice                            Middx Sep 409
1753  ANDERSON, Andrew   AwW                     Berks Dec 287
1758  ANDERSON, Andrew                           Pts   Feb  28
1767  ANDERSON, Andrew                   Pts - Middx Oct 360
1767  ANDERSON, Andrew  Ser                      Kent  Dec 435
1781  ANDERSON, Andrew                           Lond  Sep 417
1782  ANDERSON, Andrew                   Pts - Middx Jly 333
1783  ANDERSON, Andrew  Ser                      NBrit Oct 493
1784  ANDERSON, Andrew, otherwise Alexander
          AwW "Daphne" & "Essex"                 --    Jly 363
1785  ANDERSON, Andrew  AwW of Gds unadm.  W
          rgd Jly 1782                           Middx May  --
1761  ANDERSON, Andrews, otherwise Andrew        Pts   May 157
1769  ANDERSON, Ann                              Mon   May 149
1769  ANDERSON, Ann                              Middx Dec 402
1764  ANDERSON, Ann                              Middx Jny   1
1782  ANDERSON, Ann                              Middx Sep 438
1784  ANDERSON, Ann                              Kent  Nov 584
1788  ANDERSON, Ann                              Middx Apr 171
1791  ANDERSON, otherwise DICKSON, Ann           Nhant Oct 449
1795  ANDERSON, Ann                              Kent  Aug 492
1797  ANDERSON, Ann                              Surry Sep 583
1800  ANDERSON, Annabella                        Middx Jny   1
1790  ANDERSON, Archibald  E.I.S. "Nottingham"   Pts   May 221
1793  ANDERSON, Barnard                          Berks Jly 349
1773  ANDERSON, Bersheba                         Middx Dec 456
1787  ANDERSON, Bersheba  AwW of Gds unadm.
          W rgd 1773,456                         Middx Aug  --
1768  ANDERSON, Burt                             Middx Sep 336
1780  ANDERSON, Charles, Esq.                    Lincs Apr 168
1781  ANDERSON, Charles                          Pts   Jly 327
1783  ANDERSON, Charles             Pts - Kent  Dec 596
1784  ANDERSON, Charles  (Dble Pr)
          W rgd Dec last               Pts - Kent  Jny  --
1759  ANDERSON, Christian            Pts - SHant Nov 347
```

```
1758  ANDERSON, Christopher              Pts - Surry Apr 100
1766  ANDERSON, Christopher                    Middx Apr 125
1762  ANDERSON, otherwise SUDERSTROM, other-
      wise SERESTROM, otherwise SEARSTROM,
      otherwise SUDOSTROM, Cornelius, other-
      wise Nicholas                            Pts   Oct   --
1781  ANDERSON, Daniel                         Middx Mch 107
1750  ANDERSON, David    AwW                    Pts   Feb  35
1750  ANDERSON, David                          Middx Jne 185
1768  ANDERSON, David    Poor                   Pts   May 184
1774  ANDERSON, David                          Middx Apr 125
1779  ANDERSON, David                          Pts   Feb  36
1780  ANDERSON, David                          Pts   Nov 502
1781  ANDERSON, David                          Pts   Jly 326
1783  ANDERSON, David                          Pts   Oct 494
1799  ANDERSON, David   Ser  "Santa Marga"     Middx Aug 560
1767  ANDERSON, Diederich Nicolaus             Middx Sep 331
1765  ANDERSON, Sir Edmund, Bart.              Yorks Oct 359
1766  ANDERSON, Edmund, Esq.  AwW              Kent  Mch  88
1799  ANDERSON, Sir Edmund, Esq.  AwW          Lincs Sep 639
1762  ANDERSON, Edward                         Middx May 183
1765  ANDERSON, Edward                         Middx Mch  83
1785  ANDERSON, Edward                         Middx Jly 349
1770  ANDERSON, Elizabeth WATSON, formerly
      (Ltd Pr.)                                Surry Jny  35
1798  ANDERSON, Elizabeth, formerly SINCLAIR   NBrit Dec 754
1799  ANDERSON, Elizabeth                      Glos  Feb  89
1762  ANDERSON, Erick                          Pts   Feb  37
1774  ANDERSON, Eugin                          Middx Jny   1
1750  ANDERSON, Francis                        SHant Jly 220
1763  ANDERSON, Francis, Esq.                  Lincs Mch 105
1786  ANDERSON, Francis  "Steady"              Pts   Mch 133
1800  ANDERSON, Francis                        Middx Sep 641
1760  ANDERSON, George                         Middx Jny   1
1760  ANDERSON, George  AwW                     Pts   Nov 412
1767  ANDERSON, George, Esq.                   Middx Apr 120
1785  ANDERSON, otherwise ROUGH, George
      "Royal George"  "Sandwich"               Pts   Jne   --
1788  ANDERSON, George  AwW  No ship           Pts   Nov 518
1794  ANDERSON, George, Esq.  AwW              Pts   Jny   1
1797  ANDERSON, George  AwW                     Middx Jny   1
1766  ANDERSON, Gilbert                        Pts   Mch  88
1800  ANDERSON, Gilbert  AwW  Ser "Hermione"   Pts   Aug 574
1799  ANDERSON, otherwise DICK, Helen  AwW     Edin  Mch 163
1785  ANDERSON, Hendrick  "Centaur"            Pts   May 228
1758  ANDERSON, Henry                          Lond  Apr  99
1761  ANDERSON, Henry  Ser                     SHant Aug 275
1764  ANDERSON, Henry (by int dec)             Lond  Feb  37
1766  ANDERSON, Henry                          Middx Oct 360
1783  ANDERSON, Henry  AwW  "Vaughan"          Pts   Feb  56
1780  ANDERSON, Hugh                           Middx Feb  53
1759  ANDERSON, Isaac                          Pts   Jly 223
1759  ANDERSON, otherwise ANDREWS, Isaac W rgd
                       Jly last                Pts   Nov   --
```

1754	ANDERSON,	James		Middx	Nov	292
1756	ANDERSON,	James AwW Ser		Pts	Jly	187
1757	ANDERSON,	James AwW		Surry	May	144
1760	ANDERSON,	James		Pts	Aug	312
1761	ANDERSON,	James		Pts	Jny	1
1762	ANDERSON,	James AwW		Pts	Nov	444
1763	ANDERSON,	otherwise HUETT, James		Middx	Sep	435
1768	ANDERSON,	James		Pts	Sep	336
1770	ANDERSON,	James	Pts —	Middx	Aug	283
1772	ANDERSON,	James		Lond	Mch	81
1778	ANDERSON,	James, Esq.		Surry	Jly	271
1780	ANDERSON,	James		Pts	Dec	550
1781	ANDERSON,	James		Pts	Aug	374
1781	ANDERSON,	James	Pts —	Hants	Aug	374
1783	ANDERSON,	James "Monarch"		Pts	Sep	441
1783	ANDERSON,	James Ser (the 1st)"Monarch"		Pts	Oct	493
1783	ANDERSON,	James Ser "Barfleur"		Pts	Oct	494
1784	ANDERSON,	James AwW "Grosvenor",				
	"Coventry"			Pts	Feb	57
1784	ANDERSON,	James "Swiftsure"		Kent	Sep	488
1785	ANDERSON,	James "Egmont" & "R.Bishop"		Pts	Jne	228
1786	ANDERSON,	James "Alfred" & "Gibraltar"		Pts	Jly	360
1791	ANDERSON,	James		Newcl	Jly	313
1796	ANDERSON,	Dr. James (Dr of Physic)		Middx	Jny	2
1796	ANDERSON,	James		Middx	May	233
1799	ANDERSON,	James		Middx	May	332
1784	ANDERSON,	Jane		Bucks	Nov	584
1750	ANDERSON,	John		Pts	Feb	35
1750	ANDERSON,	John		Pts	May	135
1751	ANDERSON,	John (by int dec)		Pts	Jny	1
1752	ANDERSON,	John		Pts	Aug	204
1753	ANDERSON,	John		Pts	Jny	1
1754	ANDERSON,	John		Pts	Feb	31
1755	ANDERSON,	John		Middx	Jny	1
1758	ANDERSON,	John		Pts	Jne	175
1759	ANDERSON,	John AwW		Pts	Jly	223
1760	ANDERSON,	John alias Jons		Pts	May	180
1760	ANDERSON,	John AwW		Pts	Jne	227
1760	ANDERSON,	John		Pts	Jly	270
1761	ANDERSON,	John		Surry	Sep	307
1762	ANDERSON,	John AwW		Pts	Mch	89
1763	ANDERSON,	John (by int dec)		Pts	Mch	103
1763	ANDERSON,	John		Middx	Apr	163
1764	ANDERSON,	John		Pts	Mch	78
1764	ANDERSON,	John		Pts	Nov	413
1765	ANDERSON,	John		Pts	Jly	244
1772	ANDERSON,	John		Pts	Feb	34
1772	ANDERSON,	John		Middx	Sep	316
1773	ANDERSON,	John		Pts	Sep	350
1773	ANDERSON,	John (Dble Pr) W rgd Sep last	Pts	Oct	——
1773	ANDERSON,	John Ser		SHant	Nov	413
1776	ANDERSON,	John (Tble Pr) W rgd Sep 1773	Pts	Mch	——
1777	ANDERSON,	John		Pts	Mch	94

```
1781  ANDERSON, John                                         Middx  Jly  326
1781  ANDERSON, John                                         Pts    Nov  510
1782  ANDERSON, otherwise HENDERSON, John
         "Triumph", "Andromache"                             Pts    Apr  161
1782  ANDERSON, John                                         Camb   Jly  334
1782  ANDERSON, John  "Repulse"                              Pts    Oct  478
1782  ANDERSON, John  "Worcester                             Pts    Nov  527
1783  ANDERSON, John  AwW                                    NBrit  Feb   56
1783  ANDERSON, otherwise HENDERSON, John  Ser
         "Brilliant"                                         Pts    May  --
1783  ANDERSON, John  Ser                                    Brstl  Jne  277
1783  ANDERSON, John  Ser  AwW  "Russel","Victor",
         "Lion", "Grafton", "Bellona" &
         "Magnificent"                                       Pts    Jly  333
1784  ANDERSON, John                                         Middx  Jny    1
1784  ANDERSON, John                                         Lond   Mch  118
1785  ANDERSON, John                                         Essex  Sep  451
1794  ANDERSON, John  E.I.S."Brunswick"                      Middx  Sep  443
1797  ANDERSON, John, Esq. 56th Regiment                     Pts    Apr  221
1797  ANDERSON, John                                         Brstl  Jne  393
1798  ANDERSON, otherwise MC KENZEY, John
         "Illustrious" & "St. George"                        Pts    Apr  271
1798  ANDERSON, John  "Tickler"                              Pts    May  306
1798  ANDERSON, John                                         Middx  Dec  754
1800  ANDERSON, John  Mt Ship "Seven Sisters"
         Ltd AwW                                             Pts    Apr  250
1800  ANDERSON, John  Ser "Hermione"  AwW                    Pts    Aug  574
1760  ANDERSON, Jons, alias John                             Pts    May  180
1757  ANDERSON, Joseph                                       Middx  Dec  348
1759  ANDERSON, Joseph                                       Pts    Jly  223
1761  ANDERSON, otherwise ANDERTON, Joseph                   Pts    Mch   81
1794  ANDERSON, Joseph                                       Middx  Apr  181
1771  ANDERSON, Katherine                                    Middx  Jny    2
1790  ANDERSON, Katharine                                    Essex  Oct  450
1750  ANDERSON, Larinss, otherwise Lawrence,
         otherwise Lurinss                                   Pts    Jny    1
1781  ANDERSON, Lawrence, otherwise Laurence                 Kent   May  221
1788  ANDERSON, Lucy WHITE, formerly    AwW                  Middx  Dec  --
1751  ANDERSON, Margaret  AwW                                Surry  Jny    1
1750  ANDERSON, Mary                                         Middx  May  134
1763  ANDERSON, Mary                                         Berks  Jly  319
1772  ANDERSON, Mary                                         Middx  Jne  202
1780  ANDERSON, Mary                                         Sfolk  Jny    1
1781  ANDERSON, Mary                                         Herts  Mch  107
1794  ANDERSON, Mary                                         Kent   Jne  295
1799  ANDERSON, Mary                                         Middx  Nov  758
1774  ANDERSON, Mathew    (poor)                             Pts    Aug  289
1776  ANDERSON, Mathew                                       Pts    Jly  295
1778  ANDERSON, Matthew                                      Berks  Nov  427
1798  ANDERSON, Miriam, otherwise Marian                     Middx  Apr  230
1784  ANDERSON, Neal  Ser                                    SHant  Jly  363
1762  ANDERSON, otherwise SUDERSTROM, other-
         wise SERESTROM, otherwise SEARSTROM,
         otherwise SUDOSTROM, Nicholas, other-   Pts    Oct  --
         wise Cornelius
```

```
1785  ANDERSON, Nicholas  "Burford"                    Pts   Aug 400
1795  ANDERSON, Nicholas  "Vengeance" &
         "Alligator"                                   Pts   Jly 428
1766  ANDERSON, Niel                                   Middx Sep 327
1783  ANDERSON, Niell Alexander          Pts - Surry  Apr 158
1782  ANDERSON, otherwise ANDREWS, Oliver             Pts   Nov 527
1784  ANDERSON, Oliver "Culloden"&"Royal Oak"         Pts   Oct 534
1785  ANDERSON, Dr Patrick (Dr of Physick)            Middx Aug 401
1786  ANDERSON, Patrick  AwW  "Eagle"                 Pts   Jne  --
1779  ANDERSON, Penelope                              Middx Jne 230
1757  ANDERSON, Peter                                 Brstl May 144
1763  ANDERSON, Peter                                 Pts   Jly 319
1765  ANDERSON, Peter                                 Lond  Nov 397
1780  ANDERSON, Peter                                 Pts   Oct 458
1783  ANDERSON, Peter                                 Pts   Sep 441
1775  ANDERSON, Rebecca                               Lond  Jny   1
1752  ANDERSON, Richard                      Pts - SHant  May 116
1772  ANDERSON, Richard                               Middx May 155
1779  ANDERSON, Richard                               Middx Feb  36
1779  ANDERSON, Richard                               Lond  Nov 441
1784  ANDERSON, Richard  "Leander"                    Pts   May 244
1800  ANDERSON, Richard  E.I.S."Indostan" AwW         Pts   Oct 697
1751  ANDERSON, Robert                                Middx May 130
1752  ANDERSON, Robert                                Pts   Jne 145
1756  ANDERSON, Robert                                Surry Mch  58
1756  ANDERSON, Robert                                Oxon  Jly 186
1760  ANDERSON, Robert                                Pts   Sep 346
1761  ANDERSON, Robert                                Pts   Nov 378
1769  ANDERSON, Robert                                Glos  Oct 331
1780  ANDERSON, Robert                                Middx Dec 550
1782  ANDERSON, Robert                                Pts   Jny   1
1782  ANDERSON, Robert                                Pts   Sep 437
1784  ANDERSON, Robert                                Kent  Mch 118
1788  ANDERSON, Robert  "Princess Royal"              Pts   Aug 381
1791  ANDERSON, Robert                       Pts - Surry  Aug 368
1794  ANDERSON, Robert                                NBrit Sep 442
1795  ANDERSON, Robert  W rgd Sep last                NBrit Jne  --
1798  ANDERSON, Robert  "Sandwich"                    Pts   Feb  74
1798  ANDERSON, Robert                                Middx Nov 691
1798  ANDERSON, Robert  "Proserpine","Boyne",
         "Comm de Mayeille","Grampus"&"Edgar"         Irel  Dec 754
1800  ANDERSON, Robert                                Middx Jny   2
1758  ANDERSON, Samuel                                Middx Nov 319
1760  ANDERSON, Samuel                                Middx Apr 134
1763  ANDERSON, Samuel                                SHant Mch 103
1765  ANDERSON, Samuel                                Middx Jny   1
1760  ANDERSON, Stephen                               Surry Dec 449
1761  ANDERSON, Stephen  Ser                          Pts   Dec 415
1773  ANDERSON, Sir Stephen                           Beds  Feb  42
1787  ANDERSON, Sir Stephen, Bart.  AwW of Gds
         unadm.  W rgd 1773, 42                       Beds  Jly  --
1784  ANDERSON, Stewart  Ser  "Preston" &
         "Minorca"                                    SHant Jne 302
```

Year	Entry		Month	No.
1758	ANDERSON, otherwise ANDERSSON, Swen, otherwise Swan, otherwise Swaine	Pts	Mch	61
1750	ANDERSON, otherwise HENDERSON, Thomas	Pts	Jny	15
1758	ANDERSON, Thomas AwW	Pts	Jly	207
1759	ANDERSON, Thomas	Pts	May	155
1763	ANDERSON, Thomas	Pts	Apr	163
1763	ANDERSON, Thomas	SHant	May	211
1764	ANDERSON, Thomas	Middx	Dec	452
1765	ANDERSON, Thomas Dble Pr & W rgd Dec last	Middx	Apr	--
1765	ANDERSON, Thomas	SHant	Apr	127
1776	ANDERSON, otherwise ANDERSSON, Thomas	Pts	Oct	410
1778	ANDERSON, Thomas (Ltd Pr)	Pts	Oct	385
1779	ANDERSON, Thomas (Ltd Dble Pr) W rgd Oct last	Pts	Apr	--
1780	ANDERSON, Thomas	Middx	Jny	1
1783	ANDERSON, Thomas "Ville de Paris" Pts -	Devon	May	210
1784	ANDERSON, Thomas	Durhm	Sep	488
1791	ANDERSON, Thomas	Middx	Jny	1
1791	ANDERSON, Thomas AwW	Oxon	Jny	1
1792	ANDERSON, Thomas AwW "Granado"&"Boreas"	Pts	May	256
1793	ANDERSON, Thomas	Middx	Sep	451
1797	ANDERSON, Thomas	Middx	May	291
1766	ANDERSON, Walter Ltd AwW	Pts	Oct	360
1783	ANDERSON, Walter	Salop	Aug	397
1760	ANDERSON, William	Middx	Dec	449
1761	ANDERSON, William	Pts	Feb	44
1763	ANDERSON, William	Sfolk	Mch	104
1763	ANDERSON, William AwW	Pts	May	210
1764	ANDERSON, William	Pts - Brstl	Jly	248
1764	ANDERSON, William AwW	Pts	Aug	295
1764	ANDERSON, William AwW	Pts	Oct	376
1766	ANDERSON, William AwW	Pts	Jne	209
1767	ANDERSON, William	Middx	Sep	331
1768	ANDERSON, William AwW	Middx	Dec	432
1771	ANDERSON, William	Lond	Jny	1
1772	ANDERSON, William	Middx	Jne	202
1774	ANDERSON, William Dble Pr W rgd Jny 1771	Lond	Aug	--
1777	ANDERSON, William	Middx	Mch	93
1777	ANDERSON, William	Pts	Sep	374
1777	ANDERSON, William AwW of Gds unadm. W rgd Jne 1776	Pts	Nov	--
1780	ANDERSON, William	Pts	Nov	502
1781	ANDERSON, William, Esq.	Middx	Jny	2
1782	ANDERSON, William "Grafton"	Pts	Nov	527
1783	ANDERSON, otherwise HOWIE, William	Pts	Sep	441
1786	ANDERSON, William "Duke of Savoy" & "Ann"	Pts	Jny	1
1786	ANDERSON, William "Alfred" Pts -	Surry	May	257
1788	ANDERSON, William	Kent	Nov	519
1790	ANDERSON, William	Edin	Aug	363
1791	ANDERSON, William	Middx	Feb	52
1795	ANDERSON, William	Kent	Sep	532
1795	ANDERSON, William AwW	Kent	Sep	533

1796	ANDERSON, William	Surry	Jny	1
1796	ANDERSON, William	Middx	Feb	52
1799	ANDERSON, William	NBrit	May	332
1800	ANDERSON, William **Henry** (Lt in Marine Forces)	Pts	Aug	574
1758	ANDERSSON, otherwise ANDERSON, Swen, otherwise Swan, otherwise Swaine	Pts	Mch	61
1776	ANDERSSON, otherwise ANDERSON, Thomas	Pts	Oct	410
1751	ANDERTON, Ann AwW	Essex	Jne	164
1756	ANDERTON, Charles	Kent	Aug	215
1774	ANDERTON, Dennis AwW	Pts	Aug	289
1795	ANDERTON, Elizabeth	Surry	Apr	233
1779	ANDERTON, Francis, Esq.	Salop	Oct	401
1755	ANDERTON, James	Pts	Aug	209
1769	ANDERTON, John	Middx	Aug	271
1773	ANDERTON, John	Kent	Jne	233
1790	ANDERTON, John	Middx	May	221
1791	ANDERTON, John	Middx	Jne	263
1794	ANDERTON, John	Middx	Oct	484
1761	ANDERTON, otherwise ANDERSON, Joseph	Pts	Mch	81
1795	ANDERTON, Robert	Middx	Jny	1
1760	ANDERTON, Samuel	Pts	Oct	378
1775	ANDERTON, Sarah	SHant	Sep	332
1792	ANDERTON, Sarah	Kent	Aug	413
1782	ANDERTON, Thomas	Middx	May	211
1783	ANDERTON, William	Pts	Jne	279
1798	ANDERTON, William "Scout" & "Saturn"	Pts	Jny	2
1799	ANDIS, George	Lincs	Dec	819
1797	ANDOE, Hilary	Middx	Sep	583
1757	ANDOVER, Rt Hon Lord William Howard, Esq. commonly called Lord Viscount	Staff	Jne	191
1794	ANDRÉ, Adrien Panchet ST.	Middx	Mch	167
1769	ANDRE, Anthony	Middx	Apr	110
1792	ANDRÉ, David, Esq. (Spec Pr)	Lond	Jny	1
1786	ANDRÉ, Jane Mary	Lond	Nov	551
1779	ANDRÉ, Jeanne Ester, otherwise Jane Esther (Ltd Pr) (by int dec)	Pts	Jny	1
1764	ANDRE, John	Pts	Dec	452
1781	ANDRE, John, Esq.	Pts	Jny	1
1793	ANDRÉ, Louise	Pts	Sep	451
1767	ANDRE, Mary, formerly PRIVAT	Pts	Dec	435
1800	ANDRÉ, Mary Ursule ST., otherwise Ursula ST.	Surry	Jny	64
1776	ANDRE, Nathaniel ST.	SHant	Apr	199
1772	ANDRE, Sarah ST. AwW	Middx	Jne	235
1791	ANDREAS, William	Lond	Sep	414
1784	ANDREE, Susannah	Middx	Sep	488
1781	ANDREW, Abigail	Herts	Mch	107
1765	ANDREW, Agnes	Devon	May	168
1768	ANDREW, Catherine	Middx	Jne	224
1772	ANDREW, Elizabeth	Middx	Jly	243
1797	ANDREW, Elizabeth	Beds	Jly	468
1799	ANDREW, Frances AwW	Nhant	Nov	755
1750	ANDREW, Hester	Middx	Oct	313

1786	ANDREW, James		Sussx	Apr	201
1791	ANDREW, Dr. James, D.D.		Kent	May	208
1796	ANDREW, James, Esq.		Middx	Mch	106
1764	ANDREW, otherwise ANDREWS, Johannah, otherwise Jone		Surry	Mch	78
1766	ANDREW, John, Esq.		Nhant	Feb	44
1772	ANDREW, Dr. John (Dr of Physick)		Exter	May	154
1799	ANDREW, Rev. John		Sussx	Aug	560
1764	ANDREW, otherwise ANDREWS, Jone, otherwise Johanna		Surry	Mch	78
1779	ANDREW, Joseph		Bucks	Dec	482
1776	ANDREW, Julia		Middx	Feb	47
1793	ANDREW, Lois		Middx	Jny	3
1764	ANDREW, Mary		Kent	Dec	452
1797	ANDREW, Patrick		Lond	Nov	673
1769	ANDREW, Phinees		Middx	Jny	1
1794	ANDREW, otherwise ANDREWS, Richard AwW		Yorks	Nov	535
1792	ANDREW, Robert		Lond	Apr	189
1759	ANDREW, Sarah		Lond	Jny	1
1750	ANDREW, Thomasine CARRYER, formerly AwW		Beds	Oct	321
1767	ANDREW, Thomasine		Herts	Jny	1
1773	ANDREW, Thomas		Berks	Dec	456
1789	ANDREW, Thomas		Herts	Apr	185
1750	ANDREW, William		Herts	Oct	313
1775	ANDREW, William	Pts –	SHant	Dec	453
1790	ANDREW, William		Beds	Jne	275
1792	ANDREW, William, Esq. AwW		Middx	May	256
1796	ANDREW, otherwise ANDREWS, William		Carmn	Oct	485
1759	ANDREWES, Barbara AwW		Surry	Jne	191
1764	ANDREWES, Elizabeth		Norf	Jny	1
1786	ANDREWES, Frederick AwW		Middx	Feb	62
1769	ANDREWES, George Ltd AwW		Essex	Mch	73
1791	ANDREWES, George		Essex	Feb	52
1774	ANDREWES, Henrietta		Surry	Jly	252
1774	ANDREWES, Henrietta W rgd Jly last		Surry	Aug	––
1795	ANDREWES, Jesse		Brstl	Jly	426
1761	ANDREWES, John		Essex	Jny	1
1772	ANDREWES, Lancelot, Esq.		Middx	Feb	35
1796	ANDREWES, otherwise ANDREWS, Mary		Som	Sep	440
1787	ANDREWES, Samuel		Som	Feb	51
1753	ANDREWES, Thomas AwW of Gds unad. W rgd 1745, 264		Kent	Mch	––
1756	ANDREWES, Thomas, Esq.		Pts	Oct	266
1800	ANDREWES, Thomas		Som	Jly	499
1760	ANDREWES, William, Esq.		Lond	Oct	378
1762	ANDREWS, Adam		Middx	Oct	408
1754	ANDREWS, Ambrose		Middx	Apr	97
1775	ANDREWS, Amos		Surry	Sep	333
1762	ANDREWS, Ann		Som	Oct	409
1769	ANDREWS, Ann		Middx	May	149
1799	ANDREWS, Ann		Surry	Mch	163
1800	ANDREWS, Ann		Middx	Jly	501
1767	ANDREWS, Anne		Herts	Oct	360

```
1786  ANDREWS, Anthony                                    Lond   May 258
1797  ANDREWS, Arabella                                   Glos   Jne 393
1798  ANDREWS, Arabella  AwW of Gds unadm.W rgd
        Jne 1797                                          Glos   May  --
1798  ANDREWS, Arabella  AwW of Gds unadm. W
        rgd Jne 1797.  Anor grant May 1798                Glos   Oct 632
1753  ANDREWS, Benjamin                                   Middx  Apr 100
1777  ANDREWS, Bridget                                    Kent   Mch  94
1750  ANDREWS, Catharine                                  Surry  Mch  66
1770  ANDREWS, Catherine                                  Surry  Sep 319
1784  ANDREWS, Catherine                                  Bath   Nov 583
1785  ANDREWS, Catherine                                  Wells  Aug 400
1750  ANDREWS, Charles                                    Lond   Jne 185
1780  ANDREWS, Charles                                    Middx  May 233
1800  ANDREWS, Christian                                  Middx  Sep 641
1799  ANDREWS, Deborah                                    SHant  Apr 240
1800  ANDREWS, Diana                                      Middx  May 337
1774  ANDREWS, Dorothy                                    Middx  Apr 125
1791  ANDREWS, Dorothy                        Leics & Derby Mch 108
1761  ANDREWS, Rev. Dummer                                SHant  Jny   1
1783  ANDREWS, Edward                                     SHant  Nov 549
1786  ANDREWS, Edward, Esq.                               Devon  Oct 501
1788  ANDREWS, Edward                                     Bucks  Apr 171
1790  ANDREWS, Edward                                     Wilts  Apr 168
1798  ANDREWS, Edward                                     Kent   Nov 692
1799  ANDREWS, Edward William Roberts                     Surry  May 332
1769  ANDREWS, Eleanor                                    Som    Aug 271
1775  ANDREWS, Eleanor                                    Middx  Feb  37
1790  ANDREWS, Eleanor                                    Lond   Jne 275
1760  ANDREWS, Elizabeth  AwW                             Middx  Oct 378
1761  ANDREWS, Elizabeth                                  Middx  Feb  44
1773  ANDREWS, Elizabeth                                  Kent   Jny   1
1776  ANDREWS, Elizabeth                                  Middx  Mch 107
1785  ANDREWS, Elizabeth  AwW                             Som    Jne 288
1788  ANDREWS, Elizabeth                                  Oxon   Mch 112
1788  ANDREWS, Elizabeth                                  Lond   Jly 335
1789  ANDREWS, Elizabeth                                  Surry  Jly 343
1800  ANDREWS, Elizabeth                                  Lond   Mch 171
1770  ANDREWS, Ester, otherwise Hester                    Herts  Aug 283
1759  ANDREWS, Finch                                      SHant  Oct 316
1798  ANDREWS, Frances                                    Bath   Jne 376
1755  ANDREWS, George  AwW                                Herts  Nov 275
1763  ANDREWS, George                                     Pts    Dec 537
1780  ANDREWS, George, Esq.                               Wells  Dec 550
1782  ANDREWS, George                                     Pts    Nov 526
1796  ANDREWS, George  Anor Grant Apr last
        (by int dec)                                      Middx  Jly 343
1779  ANDREWS, Hannah                                     Som    Jly 283
1760  ANDREWS, Henry                                      Pts    Feb  45
1764  ANDREWS, Henry                                      Middx  Oct 376
1782  ANDREWS, Henry  AwW                                 Pts    Mch 108
1786  ANDREWS, Henry                                      Middx  Mch 134
1770  ANDREWS, Hester, otherwise Ester                    Herts  Aug 283
```

```
1780  ANDREWS, Hugh                                        Staff  Feb   53
1795  ANDREWS, Hugh    81st Regiment                       Pts    Dec  667
1759  ANDREWS, otherwise ANDERSON, Isaac
        W regd Jly last                                    Pts    Nov   --
1799  ANDREWS, Isabel                                      Oxon   Jne  414
1777  ANDREWS, Jacob   AwW                                 Pts    Sep  374
1750  ANDREWS, James                                       Pts    Nov  344
1763  ANDREWS, James                                       Devon  Jne  263
1767  ANDREWS, James                                       Middx  Feb   33
1769  ANDREWS, James                                       Middx  Nov  363
1772  ANDREWS, James   AwW                                 Herts  Oct  347
1777  ANDREWS, James                                       Pts    Mch   93
1779  ANDREWS, James                                       Kent   Dec  482
1784  ANDREWS, James   AwW                                 Surry  Jny    1
1786  ANDREWS, James   "Hannibal" "L'Hector"               Pts    Mch  133
1796  ANDREWS, James                                       Middx  Nov  538
1797  ANDREWS, James Pettit, Esq.                          Middx  Aug  538
1799  ANDREWS, James                                       Essex  Jly  471
1767  ANDREWS, James de neufville                          SHant  Apr  120
1782  ANDREWS, Jane                                        Devon  Aug  390
1789  ANDREWS, otherwise ENDREWS, Jane                     Middx  Jny   23
1795  ANDREWS, otherwise ENDREWS, Jane   AwW of
        Gds unadm. W rgd Jny 1789                          Middx  May   --
1760  ANDREWS, Jeremiah                                    Middx  Apr  134
1781  ANDREWS, Jeremiah                                    Middx  Sep  417
1764  ANDREWS, otherwise ANDREW, Johannah
        otherwise Jone                                     Surry  Mch   78
1750  ANDREWS, John   AwW                                  Pts    Mch   66
1750  ANDREWS, John   AwW                        Pts -     SHant  Oct  313
1750  ANDREWS, John                                        Berks  Dec  376
1751  ANDREWS, John                                        Herts  Sep  250
1754  ANDREWS, Rev. John                                   Kent   Jny    1
1754  ANDREWS, John                                        Middx  Jny    1
1754  ANDREWS, John                                        Lond   Aug  217
1756  ANDREWS, John                                        Middx  Mch   58
1758  ANDREWS, John   AwW                                  Oxon   Aug  236
1759  ANDREWS, John                                        Devon  Oct  316
1760  ANDREWS, John                                        Middx  Mch   --
1760  ANDREWS, John                                        Middx  Aug  312
1762  ANDREWS, John                                        Pts    Feb   37
1762  ANDREWS, John                                        Devon  Nov  444
1762  ANDREWS, John                                        Pts    Dec  491
1763  ANDREWS, John                                        Kent   Nov  493
1764  ANDREWS, John
1766  ANDREWS, John                                        Wilts  May  166
1767  ANDREWS, John                                        Surry  Mch   82
1768  ANDREWS, John                                        Glos   Aug  305
1769  ANDREWS, John                                        Middx  Apr  110
1774  ANDREWS, John, Esq. (By Sentence rgd Jne 465)Middx  Jne  213
1776  ANDREWS, John   AwW unadm. W rgd 1763,493 Kent      Jly   --
1776  ANDREWS, John                                        Devon  Nov  447
1778  ANDREWS, John                                        Middx  Oct  385
1779  ANDREWS, John                                        Lond   Dec  482
```

1780	ANDREWS, John	AwW unadm. W rgd 1763,493			
	Last Grant Jly 1776		Kent	May	--
1782	ANDREWS, John	"Pallas" & "Guadaloupe"	Pts	Jne	261
1783	ANDREWS, John	E.I.S. "Chapman"	Pts	Apr	159
1783	ANDREWS, John	"Pallas"	Pts	Aug	397
1783	ANDREWS, John		Surry	Nov	549
1783	ANDREWS, John	Ser."Penelope" & "Port			
	Morant"		Devon	Dec	597
1784	ANDREWS, John		Middx	May	243
1786	ANDREWS, John	W rgd Jne 1782	Pts	May	--
1787	ANDREWS, John		Kent	Sep	395
1788	ANDREWS, John	"Hero"	Pts	Jly	381
1793	ANDREWS, John, Esq.		Durhm	Feb	61
1795	ANDREWS, John		Berks	Mch	136
1796	ANDREWS, John		Berks	Apr	159
1798	ANDREWS, John	Ser. "Majestic"	Pts	May	306
1783	ANDREWS, Jonathan		Pts	Aug	397
1764	ANDREWS, otherwise ANDREW, Jone other-				
	wise Johannah		Surry	Mch	78
1753	ANDREWS, Joseph		Dorst	Apr	100
1753	ANDREWS, Joseph		Middx	May	126
1758	ANDREWS, Joseph		Middx	May	139
1762	ANDREWS, Joseph		Pts	Sep	365
1764	ANDREWS, Joseph MC		Pts	Jly	272
1766	ANDREWS, Joseph		Middx	Jly	256
1767	ANDREWS, Joseph		Middx	May	162
1772	ANDREWS, Joseph	AwW unadm. W rgd 1766,256	Middx	Feb	--
1788	ANDREWS, Joseph	"Polyphemus","Sphynx"			
	& "Wasp"		Pts	Jny	1
1788	ANDREWS, Joseph		Essex	Jly	335
1799	ANDREWS, Joseph	AwW	Camb	May	332
1779	ANDREWS, Joshua		Pts	Jny	1
1771	ANDREWS, Judith		Lond	Jny	1
1758	ANDREWS, Laetitia		SHant	Oct	282
1761	ANDREWS, Lancelot		Pts	Aug	275
1782	ANDREWS, Margaret ASHCROFT, formerly		Norf	Jly	333
1750	ANDREWS, Martha		Essex	Mch	66
1770	ANDREWS, Martha		Middx	Feb	39
1777	ANDREWS, Martha		Bath	Dec	495
1799	ANDREWS, Martha Early		Middx	Nov	755
1799	ANDREWS, Martin		Lond	Feb	89
1751	ANDREWS, Mary		Berks	Apr	101
1751	ANDREWS, Mary		Lond	Sep	250
1759	ANDREWS, Mary		Middx	Jny	1
1760	ANDREWS, Mary		Middx	Jne	225
1762	ANDREWS, Mary	AwW	Surry	Aug	330
1764	ANDREWS, Mary		Middx	May	162
1770	ANDREWS, Mary		Middx	Feb	39
1777	ANDREWS, Mary	AwW	Sfolk	Jny	2
1778	ANDREWS, Mary		Lond	Dec	474
1780	ANDREWS, Mary		Middx	Mch	119
1787	ANDREWS, Mary	3 Cods proved in follow'g			
	month		Devon	Sep	395

1787	**ANDREWS**, Mary 3Cods **W** rgd Sep last	Devon	Oct	436
1789	ANDREWS, Mary	Middx	Jne	296
1795	ANDREWS, Mary	Bucks	Apr	232
1796	ANDREWS, otherwise ANDREWES, Mary	Som	Sep	440
1797	ANDREWS, Mary	SHant	Oct	624
1783	ANDREWS, Mathew	Pts	May	210
1763	ANDREWS, Michael	Salop	May	211
1783	ANDREWS, Michael	Pts	Sep	441
1750	ANDREWS, Mordecai	Middx	Feb	35
1800	ANDREWS, Rev. Mordecai	Essex	Feb	80
1786	ANDREWS, Moses "Superb" & "Sultan"	Pts	Mch	133
1786	ANDREWS, Moses W rgd this month "Hannibal" "Superb"	Pts	Mch	--
1750	ANDREWS, Nathaniel	Middx	Jne	185
1756	ANDREWS, Nathaniel	Lond	Jne	157
1766	ANDREWS, Nathaniel	Lond	Jny	1
1789	ANDREWS, Nicholas	Glos	Apr	186
1789	ANDREWS, Nicholas AwW	Pts	Nov	520
1782	ANDREWS, otherwise ANDERSON, Oliver	Pts	Nov	527
1774	ANDREWS, Patrick	Glos	Jly	253
1756	ANDREWS, Peter Pts -	Corn	Dec	317
1761	ANDREWS, Peter	Pts	Apr	115
1778	ANDREWS, Peter	Pts	Aug	309
1768	ANDREWS, Philip	Middx	Jny	1
1755	**ANDREWS**, Prudence	Surry	Dec	303
1774	ANDREWS, Rachel	Essex	Jny	1
1791	ANDREWS, Rev. Randal	Lancs	Nov	493
1756	ANDREWS, Richard	Kent	Jne	157
1761	ANDREWS, Richard	Pts	May	157
1761	ANDREWS, Richard	Devon	Jne	199
1762	ANDREWS, Richard	Berks	Jny	1
1764	ANDREWS, Richard	Wilts	Jne	210
1765	ANDREWS, Richard	Middx	Dec	438
1766	ANDREWS, Richard	Middx	May	166
1771	**ANDREWS**, Richard	Middx	Oct	395
1773	ANDREWS, Richard AwW	Middx	Apr	144
1778	ANDREWS, Richard	Lond	Feb	45
1778	ANDREWS, Richard	Lond	Jne	230
1780	ANDREWS, Richard	Surry	May	233
1785	ANDREWS, Richard, Esq. AwW	SHant	Mch	110
1786	ANDREWS, Richard AwW	Middx	Sep	461
1787	ANDREWS, Richard AwW of Gds unadm. W rgd Mch 1735	SHant	Apr	--
1787	ANDREWS, Richard	Leics	May	194
1787	ANDREWS, Richard	Lond	May	194
1791	ANDREWS, Richard	Kent	Apr	164
1794	ANDREWS, otherwise ANDREW, Richard AwW	Yorks	Nov	535
1797	ANDREWS, Richard "Marlbro'"&"Formidable" Pts		Feb	65
1800	ANDREWS, Richard Ser. "Triumph"	Pts	Jly	501
1754	ANDREWS, Robert	Pts	Dec	317
1755	ANDREWS, Robert AwW	Kent	Nov	275
1763	ANDREWS, Robert, Esq.	Middx	Sep	415
1763	ANDREWS, Robert	SHant	Dec	537

1765	ANDREWS, Robert		Pts	Dec	438
1771	ANDREWS, Robert		Surry	Dec	467
1773	ANDREWS, Robert		Middx	Jly	276
1788	ANDREWS, Roger		Middx	Sep	424
1795	ANDREWS, Salter		SHant	Nov	620
1750	ANDREWS, Samuel		SHant	Aug	250
1787	ANDREWS, Samuel		Middx	Jny	1
1754	ANDREWS, Sarah		Middx	Nov	291
1756	ANDREWS, Sarah		Middx	Sep	236
1762	ANDREWS, otherwise DAVIS, otherwise DAVIES, Sarah, formerly AwW		Herts	Aug	336
1784	ANDREWS, Sarah		SHant	Mch	117
1794	ANDREWS, Sarah		Kent	Feb	59
1795	ANDREWS, Solomon		Kent	Feb	61
1762	ANDREWS, Stephen		Surry	Oct	409
1768	ANDREWS, Susannah		SHant	Oct	367
1776	ANDREWS, Susannah		Herts	Apr	160
1777	ANDREWS, Susannah		Middx	Sep	374
1798	ANDREWS, Susannah AwW of Gds unadm. W rgd 1776, 160		Herts	Jne	--
1757	ANDREWS, Thomas		SHant	Mch	72
1759	ANDREWS, Rev. Thomas		Glos	Jny	1
1762	ANDREWS, Thomas		Wilts	Sep	365
1763	ANDREWS, Thomas		Surry	Feb	41
1766	ANDREWS, Thomas AwW		Pts	Feb	44
1766	ANDREWS, Thomas		Surry	Nov	395
1767	ANDREWS, Thomas		Middx	Jly	250
1775	ANDREWS, Thomas		Kent	May	168
1778	ANDREWS, Thomas		Middx	Jly	271
1779	ANDREWS, Thomas		Middx	Jny	1
1783	ANDREWS, Thomas		Kent	May	210
1785	ANDREWS, Thomas		Middx	Mch	110
1789	ANDREWS, Thomas		Middx	Dec	571
1793	ANDREWS, Thomas		Chich	Oct	487
1798	ANDREWS, Thomas E.I.S."Henry Addington"		Pts	May	306
1798	ANDREWS, Thomas		Essex	Sep	581
1800	ANDREWS, Thomas		Leics	May	338
1782	ANDREWS, Thomas Glover		Middx	May	210
1756	ANDREWS, William		Middx	Nov	286
1768	ANDREWS, William		Herfd	Feb	41
1770	ANDREWS, William	Pts -	Surry	Mch	84
1770	ANDREWS, William		Oxon	Jne	218
1770	ANDREWS, William		Pts	Aug	283
1781	ANDREWS, William		Hants	Jny	1
1783	ANDREWS, William "Hope" "Edgar"		Pts	Jny	1
1783	ANDREWS, William "Agamemnon"		Pts	Sep	441
1784	ANDREWS, William		Som	Feb	60
1784	ANDREWS, William "Sceptre" & "Thames"		Pts	Jne	302
1784	ANDREWS, William		Leics	Oct	535
1786	ANDREWS, William		Surry	Jny	1
1788	ANDREWS, William		Herts	Feb	53
1788	ANDREWS, William, Esq.		Kent	Sep	423
1789	ANDREWS, William		Lond	May	232

```
1792   ANDREWS, William                                      Kent    Feb   53
1794   ANDREWS, William                                      Dorst   Jne  295
1796   ANDREWS, otherwise ANDREW, William                    Carmn   Oct  485
1798   ANDREWS, William  "Egmont" & "Tor"                    Pts     Jny    2
1798   ANDREWS, William                                      Leics   Dec  755
1799   ANDREWS, William                                      Essex   Aug  560
1773   ANDREWS, William Eaton                                Middx   Apr  144
1767   ANDREWS, William John                                 Lond    Jne  204
1760   ANDRIES, Jan                                          Pts     Apr  134
1782   ANDRIESSEN, Elisabeth                                 Pts     Oct  478
1776   ANDRIESZ, Jean DEUTZ, Esq.  Ltd AwW                   Pts     Aug  354
1770   ANDRIEU, Susanne                                      Middx   Mch   84
1756   ANDRIOLI, Bartholomeus                                Pts     Nov  286
1761   ANDROS, Charles, Esq.  AwW                            Guery   Sep  307
1764   ANDROS, John  AwW                                     Guery   Aug  295
1784   ANDROS, Mary  AwW                                     Guery   Apr  185
1774   ANDRUS, Cuthbert                                      Kent    Apr  125
1788   ANDRUS, John                                          Kent    Dec  572
1780   ANDRUS, Susanna                                       Kent    Nov  503
1787   ANDRUS, Thomas Fox                                    Kent    Sep  395
1768   ANDUS, William                                        Middx   Mch   93
1775   ANELEY, MC, otherwise MC ANELY, otherwise
       MC ANNALLY, Philip  (poor)                            Pts     Aug  318
1787   ANELLY, Philip MC  AwW  "Alcide","Sultan",
       "San Carl.","Burford","Worcester"                     Pts     Feb   83
1775   ANELY, MC, otherwise MC ANNALLY, other-
       wise MC ANELEY, Philip  (poor)                        Pts     Aug  318
1773   ANESLEY, otherwise ANSLEY, Richard                    Surry   May  190
1780   ANGAS, Joseph                                         Surry   May  234
1785   ANGEL, Edward                                         Surry   Jly  351
1788   ANGEL, Edward Shephard                                Lond    Apr  170
1788   ANGEL, Flower                                         Middx   May  224
1793   ANGEL, George                                         Surry   Apr  179
1777   ANGEL, James                                          Pts     Dec  495
1757   ANGEL, John                                           Pts     Jly  211
1769   ANGEL, Joseph                                         Essex   Oct  331
1751   ANGEL, Saint John                                     Pts     Nov  320
1763   ANGEL, Thomas                                         Pts     Feb   41
1763   ANGEL, Thomas  W rgd this month                       Pts     Feb   42
1781   ANGEL, William Ser.                                   Hants   Aug  374
1758   ANGELE, Henere, otherwise ANGELL, Henry
                                            Pts - Middx      Nov  319
1786   ANGELIE, Thomas                                       Middx   Nov  552
1766   ANGELIS, Angelo DE                                    Middx   Feb   45
1789   ANGELKOT, Geertruiyd  (Ltd Pr)                        Pts     Apr  184
1783   ANGELKOT, Herman  (Ltd Pr)                            Pts     Nov  548
1791   ANGELKOT, Jan  (Ltd Pr)                               Pts     Mch  108
1788   ANGELKOT, Judith  (Ltd Pr)                            Pts     Apr  171
1794   ANGELKOT, Margaretha Catharina, other-
       wise Catarina  (Ltd Pr)                               Pts     Jly  344
1780   ANGELL, Anna                                          Middx   Nov  503
1786   ANGELL, Benedict, Esq. formerly BROWNE                Wilts   May  259
1789   ANGELL, Benedict, Esq, formerly BROWNE
       (Dble Pr) W rgd 1786, 259                             Wilts   Sep   --
```

Year	Name	Place	Month	Page
1762	ANGELL, Elizabeth	Lond	Dec	491
1780	ANGELL, Ellyot Always Hill	Middx	Jly	345
1792	ANGELL, George	Surry	Aug	413
1790	ANGELL, Grace	Dorst	Oct	450
1758	ANGELL, Henry otherwise ANGELE, Henere Pts –	Middx	Nov	319
1780	ANGELL, James AwW	Pts	Feb	53
1751	ANGELL, John, Esq.	Surry	Mch	68
1764	ANGELL, John	Middx	Apr	128
1780	ANGELL, John	Dorst	Dec	550
1782	ANGELL, John	Middx	Dec	569
1785	ANGELL, John, Esq. AwW (by int dec)	Surry	Dec	583
1786	ANGELL, John, Esq. AwW unadm. W rgd Dec last	Surry	May	––
1783	ANGELL, Joseph	Surry	Jly	333
1776	ANGELL, Luke	Middx	Dec	484
1776	ANGELL, Luke	Middx	Dec	485
1781	ANGELL, Mary	Wilts	Oct	459
1793	ANGELL, Rachel	Wilts	Oct	487
1789	ANGELL, Richard AwW	Herts	Apr	185
1775	ANGELL, Sarah	Middx	Nov	399
1755	ANGELL, Thomas	Surry	Mch	65
1778	ANGELL, Thomas Ser.	Devon	Nov	428
1781	ANGELL, William AwW	Wilts	Oct	459
1783	ANGELLO, otherwise ANGELO, Anthony	Pts	Apr	159
1783	ANGELO, otherwise ANGELLO, Anthony	Pts	Apr	159
1756	ANGELO, Francis AwW	Pts	Oct	266
1793	ANGELY, John	Middx	Jly	––
1781	ANGES, otherwise ANGUS, James	Pts	May	221
1795	ANGEWORTH, William, Esq.	Salop	Aug	492
1783	ANGIER, Bezaleel	Essex	Jne	278
1764	ANGIER, Charles	Middx	Dec	452
1775	ANGIER, Elizabeth	Middx	Dec	454
1775	ANGIER, John	Notts	Mch	81
1752	ANGIER, Samuel	Middx	Mch	56
1781	ANGIRE, Elizabeth	Surry	Feb	54
1760	ANGIS, Robert AwW	Pts	Aug	312
1775	ANGLE, Jane DE L'	Glos	Feb	47
1753	ANGLE, Merrick DE L'	Kent	Jne	169
1763	ANGLE, Theophilus DE L'	Kent	Sep	425
1750	ANGLES, Amos AwW	Kent	Aug	250
1782	ANGLES, Amos	Surry	Jne	261
1750	ANGLES, Jane	Kent	Aug	250
1780	ANGLICUM, Hendrick, otherwise INGLEKEN, Henry	Pts	Nov	502
1755	ANGOVE, Reynold	Pts	Jly	180
1781	ANGRAVE, Mary	Notts	Jly	326
1759	ANGUILAR, Pereira Moses Lopes DE	Lond	Aug	274
1778	ANGUISH, George	Pts	Sep	345
1765	ANGUISH, Hannah	Kent	Dec	438
1782	ANGUISH, Joseph	Pts	Dec	569
1765	ANGUISH, Thomas, otherwise ALLIN, Sir Thomas AwW	Sfolk	Nov	397

```
1786  ANGUISH, Thomas                              Middx Jny    1
1780  ANGUS, Alexander                             Pts   Jne  300
1773  ANGUS, Andrew                                Middx Aug  318
1783  ANGUS, Andrew  Ser                           NBrit Nov  548
1757  ANGUS, Charles                               Pts   Aug  238
1759  ANGUS, David  AwW                            Pts   Jny    1
1763  ANGUS, David  AwW                            Pts   Apr  163
1764  ANGUS, Elizabeth                             Surry Mch   79
1777  ANGUS, George  AwW  Anor Grant Oct 1775
         (by int dec)                             Pts   Mch   --
1779  ANGUS, George                                Pts   May  186
1781  ANGUS, otherwise ANGES, James                Pts   May  221
1757  ANGUS, Jane                                  Middx Sep  265
1790  ANGUS, Joseph                                Lond  Jny    2
1790  ANGUS, Margaret                              Lond  Apr  168
1754  ANGUS, Walter                                Pts   Mch   66
1755  ANGUS, William                               Pts   Jly  180
1790  ANGWIN, John, Esq.  No ship                  Pts   May  221
1791  ANGWIN, Richard  Spec AwW                    Corn  Dec  553
1792  ANKCORN, Stephen                             Kent  May  256
1780  ANKCORN, William                             Kent  May  233
1754  ANKEVEEN, High Noble Born Maria Elizabeth
         DE WALE VAN  (Ltd Pr)                     Pts   Jne  184
1785  ANKIN, Gloss, otherwise HANKIN, Klass
         E.I.S. "Norfolk", "Superb"                Pts   May   --
1781  ANLAY, Alexander MC, Esq.  AwW               Dubln Aug  397
1799  ANLEY, Ferdinand                             Middx Aug  561
1766  ANLEZARK, John  AwW                          Pts   Nov  396
1766  ANNABLE, John                                Middx Oct  360
1775  ANNABLE, William                             Middx Oct  365
1791  ANNAL, Margaret                              Middx Aug  369
1799  ANNALL, otherwise ARNOLD, John  Ser          Pts   Oct  694
         "Invincible"
1758  ANNALLY, Christopher MC                      Pts   Dec  375
1775  ANNALLY, MC, otherwise MC ANELY, other-
         wise MC ANELEY, Philip  (poor)            Pts   Aug  318
1785  ANNALLY, MC, otherwise Samuel MC ANNELLY     Middx Aug   --
1750  ANNAND, James  AwW unadm rgd Aug 1746        Middx Feb   --
1762  ANNANDALE, Most Noble Charlotta, Marchio-
         ness Dowager of-in NBrit  Ltd AwW         Middx Dec  492
1792  ANNANDALE, Most Noble Charlotta, Marchio-
         ness Dowager of-in NBrit  Ltd AwW & Cod
         of Gds unadm. W rgd 1762,497                    Jly   --
1789  ANNANIAS, Edward                             Kent  Feb   70
1777  ANNARE, otherwise ANNIER, Thomas             Pts   Jny    1
1785  ANNE, Mary                                   SHant Feb   61
1800  ANNELER, Christian John                      Berks Jly  501
1779  ANNELLY, John MC                             Pts   Aug   --
1785  ANNELLY, MC, otherwise Samuel MC ANNALLY     Middx Aug   --
1799  ANNELY, Joseph                               Middx Apr  239
1750  ANNELY, Richard                              Pts   Oct  313
1786  ANNESLEY, Arthur                             Middx Jny    1
1793  ANNESLEY, Rev. Dr. Arthur Henry, D.D.        Som   Feb   62
```

98

Year	Name	Place	Month	Page
1750	ANNESLEY, Francis, Esq. (Ltd Pr)	Middx	Apr	101
1760	ANNESLEY, James, Esq.	Kent	Jne	225
1761	ANNESLEY, John	Pts	May	157
1763	ANNESLEY, John	Pts	Aug	366
1776	ANNESLEY, otherwise ANSLEY, John	Glos	Nov	447
1797	ANNESLEY, otherwise ANNSLEY, Mary	Berks	Mch	124
1792	ANNESLEY, Rachel	Middx	Aug	415
1763	ANNESLEY, otherwise FOWLER, Dame Sarah	Middx	Dec	550
1793	ANNESLEY, William, Esq.	Middx	Oct	489
1776	ANNETT, Ann	Middx	Mch	108
1800	ANNETT, John	Middx	Mch	171
1782	ANNETTS, Elizabeth	Surry	Aug	390
1777	ANNIER, otherwise ANNARE, Thomas	Pts	Jny	1
1773	ANNIES, John	Middx	Mch	89
1774	ANNING, Henry	Devon	Feb	36
1765	ANNING, James	Devon	Nov	398
1774	ANNING, William	Middx	Jne	213
1786	ANNING, William	Devon	Mch	134
1799	ANNINGSON, Luck, Esq.	Middx	Oct	693?
1772	ANNIS, Benjamin	Nhant	Nov	390
1752	ANNIS, Hannah	Wark	Jne	145
1761	ANNIS, Henry	Middx	Sep	307
1775	ANNIS, James	Middx	Jne	218
1793	ANNIS, John	Surry	Jly	349
1799	ANNIS, John	Leics	Apr	241
1780	ANNIS, Sarah	Middx	Sep	425
1765	ANNIS, William	Lincs	Nov	397
1766	ANNIS, William AwW unadm. W rgd Nov 1765	Lincs	Jly	--
1792	ANNISON, Elizabeth	Oxon	May	253
1756	ANNISON, William	Essex	Jne	156
1795	ANNISON, William	Lond	Mch	137
1755	ANNISSON, Samuel	Middx	Sep	232
1781	ANNON, MC, otherwise MACKEENEN, otherwise MC KUNAN, otherwise MC KANNON, Duncan	Pts	Sep	444
1789	ANNOTT, otherwise ARNAT, otherwise AWNOTT, James "Monmouth" & "Defence"	Pts	May	232
1797	ANNS, Ann	Middx	Mch	124
1756	ANNS, Elizabeth	Lond	Jne	156
1752	ANNS, John	Surry	Mch	56
1797	ANNSLEY, otherwise ANNESLEY, Mary	Berks	Mch	124
1788	ANNULLY, Henry MC	Oxon	Sep	--
1776	ANQUETIL, Diana	Middx	Nov	447
1785	ANQUETIL, otherwise POMME, otherwise DAVAL, Mary AwW of Gds unadm. W rgd 1739, 87	Jersy	Jly	--
1787	ANQUETIL, otherwise POMME, otherwise DAVAL, Mary AwW of Gds unadm. W rgd 1739, 87	Jersy	Apr	--
1775	ANQUETIL, Susanna AwW	Middx	Nov	401
1764	ANS, Elizabeth J'	Surry	Mch	99
1773	ANS, Francis J' AwW Former Grant Aug last	Middx	Oct	--
1764	ANS, Michael J' AwW of Gds unadm. W rgd Apr 1760	Surry	Apr	--

1759	ANS, Thomas J'	Yorks	Jne 205
1796	ANSCHEUTZ, Valentine	Middx	Aug 393
1782	ANSCOMB, John	Surry	Jly 332
1758	ANSCOMBE, Patience	Sussx	Jny 1
1768	ANSELIN, Easther	Lond	Jly 265
1761	ANSELIN, Edward	Essex	Mch 81
1791	ANSELINE, Joseph No ship	Pts	Sep 414
1771	ANSELL, Ann	Middx	Aug 328
1800	ANSELL, Ann	Middx	Mch 171
1776	ANSELL, Anthony	Middx	Jny 1
1783	ANSELL, Benjamin	Middx	Apr 158
1783	ANSELL, Benjamin	Camb	May 210
1793	ANSELL, Catherina	Middx	Jny 1
1793	ANSELL, Edward	Oxon	Jny 1
1789	ANSELL, Eleanor (by int dec)	Surry	Mch 131
1778	ANSELL, Elizabeth	Middx	Oct 385
1779	ANSELL, Elizabeth	Bucks	Dec 482
1782	ANSELL, Elizabeth	Lond	May 210
1785	ANSELL, Elizabeth PATTEN, formerly	Middx	Feb 94
1797	ANSELL, George	Surry	Jne 394
1799	ANSELL, George	Kent	Aug 560
1773	ANSELL, Hannah	Berks	Feb 41
1788	ANSELL, James	Lond	Jly 335
1757	ANSELL, John	Middx	Jny 1
1757	ANSELL, John	Surry	Apr 108
1759	ANSELL, John AwW	Herts	Jly 223
1761	ANSELL, John	Surry	Feb 43
1761	ANSELL, John	Bucks	Jne 199
1768	ANSELL, John	Surry	Aug 305
1773	ANSELL, John	Surry	Apr 144
1773	ANSELL, John	Middx	Jly 277
1787	ANSELL, John	Middx	Jny 1
1760	ANSELL, Joseph	Pts	Jly 270
1799	ANSELL, Joseph Ser. "Brillt." &		
	"Resistance"	Pts	Dec 820
1795	ANSELL, Judith	Herts	Jne 360
1756	ANSELL, Margaret	Middx	Apr 93
1757	ANSELL, Margaret	Oxon	May 144
1800	ANSELL, Margaret	Kent	Mch 172
1775	ANSELL, Mary	Middx	May 168
1786	ANSELL, Mary	Middx	Jly 360
1753	ANSELL, Rebeccah	Surry	Mch 69
1774	ANSELL, Richard	Herts	May 165
1782	ANSELL, Richard	Middx	Jny 1
1771	ANSELL, Robert	Herts	Dec 466
1782	ANSELL, Robert	Middx	Nov 526
1799	ANSELL, Robert Ser. "Callo'n.","Druid"		
	& "Amaz'n."	Devon	Apr 240
1780	ANSELL, Samuel	Middx	Jly 345
1789	ANSELL, Samuel AwW	Surry	Nov 528
1761	ANSELL, Sarah ARNOLD, formerly Ltd AwW	Surry	Sep 307
1766	ANSELL, Thomas	Middx	Oct 360
1785	ANSELL, Thomas Ser. "Inflexible" AwW	Pts	Feb 61

1790	ANSELL, Thomas		Middx	Jny 1
1795	ANSELL, Thomas		Sfolk	Jly 426
1766	ANSELL, William		Herts	Nov 395
1766	ANSELL, William AwW		Surry	Dec 439
1770	ANSELL, William		Herts	Mch 85
1794	ANSELL, William		Herts	Dec 593
1777	ANSELME, Rebecca		Middx	Jny 1
1781	ANSILL, James AwW		Middx	Aug 374
1775	ANSLEY, Elizabeth		Brstl	Dec 454
1776	ANSLEY, otherwise ANNESLEY, John		Glos	Nov 447
1795	ANSLEY, John, Esq.		Lond	Jne 359
1753	ANSLEY, Mary		Middx	Dec 307
1750	ANSLEY, Richard AwW	Pts -	Lond	Jne 185
1752	ANSLEY, Richard		Middx	Nov 267
1764	ANSLOW, James		Kent	Apr 129
1764	ANSNEY, otherwise HANSLEY, David		Middx	Jne 210
1782	ANSON, Anna		Staff	Jne 261
1775	ANSON, Brian J'		Kent	Aug 313
1784	ANSON, Edward		Essex	May 243
1770	ANSON, Francis I'		Lond	Apr 149
1762	ANSON, Lord George, Rt Hon Baron of Soberton in Cty of SHant AwW		Middx	Jne 230
1764	ANSON, George AwW		Brstl	Apr 128
1782	ANSON, Rt Hon George, late Lord, Baron of Soberton in Cty of SHant AwW unadm W rgd 1762, 230		Oct	--
1790	ANSON, George, Esq.		Staff	Feb 55
1767	ANSON, Hannah		Bucks	Nov 399
1799	ANSON, Isabella		Middx	Jny 3
1787	ANSON, Joana, otherwise Joanna		Staff	Apr 155
1799	ANSON, John, otherwise JACOBSON, John, otherwise JACOBZ, Jorgen M.S."Dalaford" W rgd last month		Pts	Oct 693
1800	ANSON, John J', Esq.		Middx	Mch 210
1763	ANSON, Oliver, otherwise HANSON, Halver	Pts	Oct	457
1773	ANSON, Thomas, Esq.		Staff	Apr 144
1792	ANSON, William		Middx	Jny 2
1792	ANSON, William Anor Pr. W rgd last month	Middx	Feb	--
1800	ANSON, William J'		Notts	Dec 871
1795	ANSTEAD, John		Middx	Aug 492
1792	ANSTED, William		Bucks	Jne ---
1785	ANSTEE, Hannah		Bucks	Jne 288
1758	ANSTER, John		Pts	Feb 28
1751	ANSTEY, Christopher		Camb	Apr 101
1780	ANSTEY, John AwW		Kent	Jny 1
1798	ANSTEY, John		Devon	Sep 580
1754	ANSTEY, Mary		Middx	Jly 187
1783	ANSTEY, Richard		Som	Jly 332
1775	ANSTEY, Thomas		Som	Sep 332
1792	ANSTEY, Thomas		Surry	Mch 127
1797	ANSTEY, Thomas "Africa" &"Ambuscade"		Pts	Aug 538
1794	ANSTEY, William		Poole	Nov 535
1800	ANSTID, Jane		Lond	Jny 1

```
1782  ANSTID, John                                      Pts    Nov 527
1790  ANSTID, Thomas                                    Lond   May 221
1779  ANSTIE, John                                      Wilts  Jly 283
1796  ANSTIS, Ann                                       Devon  Nov 538
1764  ANSTIS, Rev. George                               Devon  Jly 248
1799  ANSTIS, Rev. George  AwW of Gds unadm
        W rgd 1764, 248                                 Devon  Oct
1754  ANSTIS, John, Garter King of Arms                 Surry  Dec 317
1768  ANSTIS, John, Garter King of Arms, Doctor
        of Laws  AwW of Gds unadm. W rgd 1754,317Surry  Nov    --
1776  ANSTIS, John                                      Corn   Mch 108
1794  ANSTIS, John, Esq. Garter Principal King
        at Arms  AwW of Gds unadm. W rgd 1744,60 Surry  Apr    --
1765  ANSTRUTHER, Charles, Esq.                         Pts    Jny   1
1754  ANSTRUTHER, Sir John, Bart  AwW                   NBrit  Aug 217
1792  ANSTRUTHER, John                                  Middx  Dec 593
1799  ANSTRUTHER, Sir John, Bart  (Ltd Pr)             Middx  Jly 472
1761  ANSTRUTHER, Hon Lt Gen Philip, Esq.              NBrit  May 157
1773  ANSTRUTHER, Robert, late Maj Gen of H M
        Forces  AwW                                     NBrit  Aug 318
1784  ANSTY, John  No ship  AwW                         Pts    Nov 583
1751  ANSTY, Mary  W rgd 1738, 53                       Dorst  Jly   --
1781  ANSWORTH, Harland                                 Middx  Dec 569
1758  ANSWORTH, James                                   Lond   Oct 282
1781  ANSWORTH, James                                   Kent   May 221
1769  ANSWORTH, Mary                                    Lond   Mch  73
1772  ANSWORTH, Susanna, otherwise Susannah             SHant  Jne 202
1757  ANTELL, James                                     Surry  May 144
1769  ANTHER, John                                      Surry  Jly 233
1774  ANTHERINISSEN, Jan                                Pts    Dec 418
1767  ANTHOINE, Joanna Maria Josepha                    Pts    Oct 360
1781  ANTHOINE, Hon Lady Maria Alexandrina
        Josepha  (Ltd Pr)                               Pts    Jly 326
1778  ANTHONIESZ, Weeveringh, otherwise ANTZ,
        Maarten Weveringh (Ltd Pr)                      Pts    Feb  46
1772  ANTHONY, Ann                                      Surry  Feb  34
1762  ANTHONY, Anne                                     Middx  Mch  89
1750  ANTHONY, Berry                                    Pts    Jne 185
1778  ANTHONY, Daniel                                   Bucks  Apr 141
1788  ANTHONY, David                                    Middx  Jly 335
1778  ANTHONY, Emanuel                                  Pts    Oct 385
1789  ANTHONY, Francis  "Crown"                         Pts    Apr 184
1762  ANTHONY, George  AwW                              Devon  Dec 491
1799  ANTHONY, George, Esq.                             Devon  Mch 162
1781  ANTHONY, Hannah                                   Middx  Jne 280
1761  ANTHONY, James                                    Pts    Mch  81
1798  ANTHONY, James                                    Dorst  Feb  75
1782  ANTHONY, Joan                                     Corn   May 210
1764  ANTHONY, John  AwW                                Pts    Apr 128
1778  ANTHONY, John  AwW                                Pts    Mch  93
1781  ANTHONY, John  AwW  W rgd Mch 1778                Pts    Nov   --
1782  ANTHONY, John                                     Middx  Oct 478
1784  ANTHONY, John                                     Corn   Apr 186
```

1790	ANTHONY, John	Lond	Jne 275
1800	ANTHONY, John	Bucks	Oct 696
1757	ANTHONY, Joseph	Devon	Jly 211
1771	ANTHONY, Judith	Middx	Mch 91
1795	ANTHONY, Martha	Lond	Feb 60
1776	ANTHONY, Mary	Middx	Nov 447
1787	ANTHONY, Nathaniel	Corn	Aug 353
1763	ANTHONY, Nicholas	Pts	Mch 105
1767	ANTHONY, Thomas Ser	Devon	Sep 330
1791	ANTHONY, Thomas	Yorks	Dec 552
1796	ANTHONY, Thomas	Devon	Dec 590
1799	ANTHONY, Thomas	Middx	Jne 413
1761	ANTHONY, William	Pts	Dec 416
1763	ANTHONY, William	Bucks	Feb 41
1765	ANTHONY, William	Middx	Sep 319
1788	ANTHONY, Rev. William	Berks	Jly 335
1796	ANTHONYO, Joze, otherwise ANTONIO, Josia		
	E.I.M.S."Woodford" AwW	Pts	May 232
1784	ANTHONYSZ, Jan Rygerbos (Ltd Pr)	Pts	Jly 363
1770	ANTON, James	Pts	Jly 251
1760	ANTON, Margaret	Lond	Feb 46
1761	ANTONEY, otherwise ANTONIO, Thomas AwW	Pts	Aug 275
1761	ANTONI, otherwise ANTONIE, Peter	Pts	Aug 275
1753	ANTONIE, Anne	Middx	Apr 100
1751	ANTONIE, Nicholas	Pts	Jne 164
1761	ANTONIE, otherwise ANTONI, Peter	Pts	Aug 275
1772	ANTONIE, Richard, Esq.	Beds	Feb 33
1772	ANTONIE, Richard, Esq. (Dble Pr) W rgd		
	last month	Beds	Mch ——
1776	ANTONIO, Francis	Pts	Nov 447
1776	ANTONIO, Joachin	Pts	Apr 159
1796	ANTONIO, Josia, otherwise ANTHONYO, Jose		
	E.I.M.S."Woodford" AwW	Pts	May 232
1796	ANTONIO, Julian M.S."Dover"	Pts	Nov 538
1761	ANTONIO, otherwise ANTONEY, Thomas AwW	Pts	Aug 275
1783	ANTOPE, otherwise HUNTROADS, otherwise		
	HUNTRODS, John Lovelace	Pts	Jly ——
1761	ANTRAM, George	SHant	Aug 275
1761	ANTRAM, Susanna	Middx	Aug 275
1779	ANTRAM, William	SHant	Jny 2
1752	ANTRIM, Anne Hester	Essex	Jly 176
1787	ANTROBUS, Edmund, Esq.	Middx	Oct 436
1798	ANTROBUS, Edward AwW	Kent	Jny 3
1773	ANTROBUS, Elizabeth	Camb	Oct 379
1782	ANTROBUS, George	Middx	Feb 59
1766	ANTROBUS, Rev. Henry	Worcs	Dec 439
1785	ANTROBUS, James "Eagle" AwW	Pts	Jly 350
1794	ANTROBUS, John AwW	Middx	Jly 343
1750	ANTROBUS, Mary	Bucks	Jny 1
1750	ANTROBUS, Mary	Chest	Apr 102
1754	ANTROBUS, Mary AwW unadm W rgd Jny 1750	Bucks	Jny ——
1767	ANTROBUS, Robert	Herts	Apr 120
1767	ANTROBUS, Robert	Herts	Apr 121

1757	ANTROBUS, Sanuel AwW		Pts	Aug	238
1762	ANTRON, John		Pts	Jny	2
1776	ANTRUM, Richard		Surry	Oct	410
1766	ANTRUM, William AwW		Surry	May	166
1764	ANTWHISTLE, John		Pts	Jny	1
1778	ANTZ, Maarten Weveringh, otherwise				
	ANTHONIESZ, Weeveringh (Ltd Pr)		Pts	Feb	46
1783	ANVERS, Daniel RICH D' Esq.		Berks	Jny	--
1794	ANVERS, Meriel D' AwW		Nhant	Dec	--
1799	ANVERS, Meriel D' AwW (by int dec)		Oxon	Jny	29
1751	ANVISS, John		Pts	May	130
1767	ANWYLL, Lewis		Denbh	Nov	399
1797	ANWYL, Thomas Lloyd		Salop	Sep	583
1775	APARTE, John		SHant	Feb	38
1799	APEDAILE, Rev. George		Worcs	Apr	238
1750	APEDELL, Thomas		Lond	Nov	345
1757	APLEFORD, Mary		Lond	Oct	293
1795	APLETREE, Mary		Oxon	Mch	136
1760	APLEY, William		Essex	Apr	134
1773	APLIN, Benjamin		Oxon	Sep	350
1759	APLIN, George		Pts	Dec	381
1800	APLIN, Rebecca		Kent	Mch	172
1793	APORT, otherwise ALPORT, John		Middx	Dec	578
1785	APOSTOOL, Gonda (Ltd Pr)		Pts	Oct	489
1799	APPEL, Willem DEN Esq. (Ltd Pr)		Pts	May	348
1750	APPELBE, William		Middx	Jny	1
1752	APPELBEE, James		Surry	Jly	176
1800	APPELBY, Mary AwW		Middx	Jny	4
1752	APPELBY, Susanna		Lond	Jny	1
1762	APPELS, Hermanus (Ltd Pr)		Pts	Nov	444
1783	APPERLEY, Anne		Denbh	Oct	494
1799	APPERLEY, Rev. Anthony		Wark	Dec	820
1758	APPERLEY, John, Esq.		Pts	Jny	1
1779	APPERLEY, John		Herfd	Dec	482
1785	APPERLEY, John E.I.S."Pigot"		Pts	Oct	489
1776	APPLEBEE, Alice		Surry	Sep	380
1792	APPLEBEE, Elizabeth		Oxon	Feb	53
1783	APPLEBEE, Rev. George		Lond	Aug	397
1795	APPLEBEE, Isaac		Middx	Feb	60
1800	APPLEBEE, Isaac AwW of Gds unadm W rgd				
	Feb 1795 (Esq)		Middx	Dec	
1754	APPLEBEE, Jane		Corn	Oct	264
1756	APPLEBEE, Jane		Corn	Jly	186
1750	APPLEBEE, John (by dec)		Lond	Feb	35
1762	APPLEBEE, Mary		Surry	Feb	37
1772	APPLEBEE, William		Oxon	Mch	81
1776	APPLEBEE, William		Surry	May	209
1762	APPLEBURY, Rebecca		Surry	Sep	365
1766	APPLEBURY, Rebecca AwW of Gds unadm				
	W rgd Sep 1762		Surry	Apr	--
1753	APPLEBURY, Thomas		Surry	Jne	159
1779	APPLEBY, Ann		Lond	Jne	230
1800	APPLEBY, Ann		Lond	Mch	172
1796	APPLEBY, Anthony AwW		Lond	Jny	2

1766	APPLEBY,	Elizabeth				Herts	May	167
1774	APPLEBY,	Elizabeth				Middx	Jly	253
1763	APPLEBY,	George				Middx	Dec	537
1768	APPLEBY,	George				Lond	Dec	437
1773	APPLEBY,	George	AwW	unadm	W rgd 1768,437	Lond	Jny	--
1787	APPLEBY,	Jane				Middx	Dec	527
1759	APPLEBY,	John	AwW			Pts	Jly	223
1800	APPLEBY,	John				Chest	Dec	833
1787	APPLEBY,	Mary				Middx		528
1783	APPLEBY,	Mathew				Pts	Oct	493
1773	APPLEBY,	Susanna				Lond	Feb	42
1765	APPLEFORD,	Elizabeth				Middx	Aug	282
1751	APPLEFORD,	Thomas				SHant	Oct	273
1775	APPLEFORD,	Thomas				Middx	Feb	37
1756	APPLEGARD,	John				Bath	Mch	58
1763	APPLEGARD,	John	AwW of Gds unadm. W rgd					
		1756, 58				Bath	Feb	--
1750	APPLEGARTH,	Alice				Middx	Mch	66
1750	APPLEGARTH,	Ann	AwW unadm	W rgd Feb				
		1748/9				Middx	Apr	--
1777	APPLEGARTH,	Henry				Middx	Mch	93
1765	APPLEGARTH,	Mary				Lond	May	166
1775	APPLEGARTH,	Robert	AwW			SHant	Feb	37
1779	APPLEGARTH,	William				Berks	Mch	86
1759	APPLEGATE,	Thomas				Dorst	May	155
1754	APPLEGATH,	John				Glos	Feb	31
1756	APPLEGATH,	Pelly				Surry	Jly	187
1785	APPLEGATH,	William	No ship		Pts -	Middx	Jly	349
1774	APPLETON,	Ann				Lond	Nov	384
1782	APPLETON,	Charles				Pts	Feb	59
1761	APPLETON,	Christian				Middx	Mch	81
1784	APPLETON,	Daniel				Essex	Sep	489
1795	APPLETON,	Elizabeth				Salop	Mch	136
1788	APPLETON,	George				Middx	Oct	468
1753	APPLETON,	James	AwW			Middx	May	126
1754	APPLETON,	James	AwW unadm W rgd May 1753			Middx	Jne	--
1754	APPLETON,	James	Ser			SHant	Jly	187
1783	APPLETON,	John				Middx	Dec	597
1784	APPLETON,	John				Salop	Jne	302
1786	APPLETON,	John				Brstl	Oct	499
1787	APPLETON,	John	(Dble Pr) W rgd Oct last			Brstl	Feb	--
1788	APPLETON,	John	98th Regt.			Pts	Mch	114
1764	APPLETON,	Joshua				Pts	Sep	335
1753	APPLETON,	Margaret				Middx	Oct	262
1789	APPLETON,	Mary				Yorks	Apr	184
1750	APPLETON,	Richard				Lond	Sep	285
1789	APPLETON,	Robert, Esq.				Yorks	Jly	343
1800	APPLETON,	Teavil, Esq.				Yorks	May	336
1760	APPLETON,	Thomas	AwW			Middx	Dec	449
1783	APPLETON,	Thomas				Brstl	Aug	397
1756	APPLETON,	William				Pts	Jny	1
1764	APPLETON,	William				Berks	Feb	37
1788	APPLETON,	William				Middx	Jny	1

1765	APPLEWHAITE, Henry	Sfolk	May	167
1775	APPLEWHAITE, Henry	Sfolk	Dec	453
1769	APPLEYARD, Alice	Camb	Dec	403
1799	APPLEYARD, James	Rutld	Aug	560
1796	APPLEYARD, Mary	Rutld	Aug	394
1800	APPLEYARD, Mary	Hull	May	335
1789	APPLEYARD, Mordecai	Hull	Jne	297
1795	APPLEYARD, Robert	Middx	Mch	138
1754	APPLEYARD, Thomas	Middx	Jny	1
1777	APPLIN, Betty	Dorst	Mch	93
1769	APPLIN, Edmund	Middx	Mch	74
1760	APPLIN, William	Pts	Jne	227
1771	APPLING, William	Devon	Dec	466
1766	APPS, Abraham	Surry	Jne	209
1751	APPS, Edward	Lond	Sep	250
1777	APPS, Elizabeth	Chich	May	194
1785	APPS, otherwise ABBS, John "Sultan"	Pts	Jne	288
1767	APPS, Owen	Chich	Jne	204
1776	APPS, Philip	Middx	Apr	159
1799	APPS, William	Kent	Sep	639
1772	APPSLEY, Edward	SHant	May	154
1763	APPY, John, Esq. (Ltd Pr)	Pts	May	210
1784	APREECE, Dorothy	Middx	Jne	303
1783	APSDEN, Jenet, otherwise Jennet	Middx	Apr	158
1766	APSEY, John	Camb	Jne	209
1795	APSEY, John	Kent	Mch	137
1798	APSEY, Sarah	Kent	May	306
1796	APSEY, William M.Ss. "Nymph","Talbot" & "Burt" Pts –	Middx	Oct	485
1791	APSLEY, Elizabeth	Kent	Aug	369
1751	APSLEY, George	Kent	Jly	197
1761	APSLEY, John	Kent	Apr	116
1766	APSLEY, John	Pts	Mch	88
1770	APSLEY, John, Esq.	Sussx	Feb	39
1781	APSLEY, John	Surry	Jny	2
1798	APSLEY, Leonard	Herts	Aug	522
1774	APSLEY, Thomas	Kent	Mch	77
1762	APSLEY, William	Surry	Oct	409
1774	APSLEY, William	Pts	Sep	328
1783	APTED, Mary GARNHAM, formerly	Kent	Jny	––
1750	APTHORP, Elizabeth	Worcs	May	134
1758	APTHORP, Frances	Camb	Oct	282
1773	APTHORP, John	Pts	Feb	42
1783	APTHORP, John (Dble Pr) W rgd 1773,42	Pts	Nov	––
1790	APTHORP, Rev. Dr. Stephen, D.D.	Bucks	Dec	535
1800	APTHORP, William Rice AwW No ship	Pts	Feb	80
1758	ARABIN, John, Esq.	Pts	Apr	99
1759	ARABIN, John, Esq. (Dble Pr) W rgd Apr last	Pts	Jny	––
1780	ARABIN, Jane Mary	Middx	Feb	53
1772	ARAM, Humphry	Devon	Feb	35
1788	ARAM, Peter	Surry	Apr	171
1774	ARAMAN, John	Surry	Jly	252

1781	ARANDA, Elizabeth D'	Surry	May	221
1798	ARANDA, Mary D'	Surry	Nov	704
1783	ARANJO, Bento DE'	Pts	Aug	408
1784	ARASENFSKIN, otherwise YOTSOFKEE, otherwise YATOSKIE, Ephrim "Portland" "Gibralter"	Pts	Jne	362
1757	ARBONNIER,D', otherwise DE ST SAPHORN, otherwise DE PESMES, Esther, formerly	Pts	Mch	101
1794	ARBOUIN, Frances	Kent	Jne	294
1763	ARBOUIN, Francis	Lond	Sep	416
1788	ABROUIN, Gideon	Bath	Jly	335
1765	ARBOUIN, Martha	Lond	Dec	439
1792	ARBOUIN, Matthew	Lond	Oct	495
1789	ARBOUIN, Peter AwW	Middx	Nov	529
1791	ARBOUIN, Peter AwW of Gds unadm W rgd Nov 1789	Middx	Aug	--
1788	ARBUCKEL, John M.Ss. "Daphne","Recovery" & "Reasonable"	Kent	Apr	170
1773	ARBUCKLE, Charles Anor grant last month	Middx	Feb	42
1779	ARBUTHNOT, George, Esq.	Middx	Sep	364
1762	ARBUTHNOT, James AwW	Pts	Aug	330
1763	ARBUTHNOT, James AwW	Pts	Nov	493
1797	ARBUTHNOT, John, Esq. Royal Artillery	Pts	Mch	124
1799	ARBUTHNOT, John AwW	Irel	Oct	693
1794	ARBUTHNOT, Marriot, Esq. Admiral of the Blue in H.M.Navy	Surry	Mch	119
1788	ARBUTHNOT, Richard AwW	Dorst	Apr	171
1762	ARBUTHNOT, Robert AwW	Pts	May	182
1773	ARBUTHNOT, Thomas	Middx	Aug	318
1800	ARBUTHNOT, Alexander, Esq. Lt Col 67th Regt	NBrit	Jny	2
1754	ARBUTHNOTT, Mary AwW	NBrit	May	123
1752	ARBUTHNOTT, Robert	Kent	Mch	56
1796	ARBUTHNOTT, Robert, Esq. 31st Regt	Pts	Dec	590
1784	ARBUTHNOTT, Romeo	Middx	Jny	1
1759	ARCH, John	Middx	Nov	346
1790	ARCH, John	Middx	Feb	54
1800	ARCH, William	Lond	Oct	696
1800	ARCH, William W rgd last month	Lond	Nov	--
1777	ARCHAMBO, John	Middx	May	195
1767	ARCHAMBO, Peter	Middx	Aug	294
1768	ARCHAMBO, Peter AwW	Middx	Jny	1
1768	ARCHAMBO, Peter (Dble Pr) W rgd Aug last	Middx	Feb	--
1783	ARCHBALD, John	Pts	Mch	107
1762	ARCHBOD, otherwise ARCHBOLD, Ralph AwW	Pts	May	182
1793	ARCHBOLD, Elizabeth	Bwick	Aug	397
1766	ARCHBOLD, John	Pts	Sep	327
1770	ARCHBOLD, John	Nhant	Sep	319
1762	ARCHBOLD, otherwise ARCHBOD, Ralph AwW	Pts	May	182
1783	ARCHBOLD, Stephen, Esq.	Pts	Sep	441
1800	ARCHBOLD, Thomas	Nhant	Mch	173
1779	ARCHBOULD, Ann	Middx	Feb	36
1790	ARCHBOULD, Ralph	Camb	Jne	276

1753	ARCHBOULD, Thomas		Pts	Oct	262
1763	ARCHBOULD, William Yeamans, Esq.		Brstl	Apr	163
1766	ARCHDAKON, Michael (poor) AwW		Pts	Apr	125
1762	ARCHDEACON, Elizabeth		SHant	Feb	38
1755	ARCHDEACON, John		Pts	Aug	209
1793	ARCHDEACON, John, Esq. (Ltd Pr)		Pts	Jne	296
1795	ARCHDEACON, John		Hunts	Oct	578
1783	ARCHDEACON, otherwise ARCHDICKON, Patrick				
	AwW		Pts	May	210
1751	ARCHDEACON, Peter		Pts	Feb	34
1790	ARCHDEACON, Thomas		Middx	Dec	535
1796	ARCHDEACON, William		Middx	Feb	52
1783	ARCHDICKON, otherwise ARCHDEACON, Patrick				
	AwW		Pts	May	210
1753	ARCHER, Ann		Middx	Jny	1
1755	ARCHER, Ann		SHant	Dec	303
1762	ARCHER, Ann		Middx	Aug	330
1770	ARCHER, Ann AwW		Lond	Apr	128
1771	ARCHER, Ann		Norf	Apr	140
1780	ARCHER, Ann Ltd A. granted in Apr 1780		Lond	Aug	383
1759	ARCHER, Anna AwW of Gds unadm. W rgd				
	1729,156 Last grant May 1747		Lond	Jny	--
1750	ARCHER, Anne		Kent	Aug	250
1767	ARCHER, Rev. Benjamin		Dorst	Mch	22
1796	ARCHER, Benjamin, Esq.		Dubln	May	232
1779	ARCHER, Charles		Middx	Feb	36
1800	ARCHER, Charles		Berks	Apr	251
1771	ARCHER, Christopher		Essex	Apr	142
1750	ARCHER, David		Glos	Sep	285
1782	ARCHER, David		Essex	Jny	1
1770	ARCHER, Dorothy		Lond	Oct	348
1797	ARCHER, Dorothy Ayre AwW		Corn	Jne	394
1750	ARCHER, Edward		Lond	May	134
1789	ARCHER, Dr. Edward Dr. of Physick		Middx	Apr	184
1793	ARCHER, Edward		Middx	May	238
1789	ARCHER, Eleanor		Middx	Jne	296
1776	ARCHER, Elisha		Middx	Nov	447
1758	ARCHER, Elizabeth		Essex	Jly	207
1762	ARCHER, Elizabeth		Bucks	Oct	408
1789	ARCHER, Rt Hon Lady Elizabeth		Middx	Jny	1
1750	ARCHER, Emely		Kent	SepVoid	
1774	ARCHER, George		Herts	May	165
1794	ARCHER, George		Middx	Oct	484
1794	ARCHER, Hannah		Sfolk	Dec	594
1750	ARCHER, Henry		Middx	Jny	1
1759	ARCHER, Henry		Essex	Dec	381
1768	ARCHER, Henry, Esq.		SHant	Mch	93
1797	ARCHER, Heron Ser "Polyphemus"		Pts	Nov	673
1757	ARCHER, Hugh		Pts	Jny	1
1773	ARCHER, Jacob		Middx	Mch	89
1770	ARCHER, James AwW		Herts	Feb	40
1798	ARCHER, James		Herts	Feb	74
1774	ARCHER, Jane otherwise Jean		Middx	Jne	213

1764	ARCHER, Job	Pts	Feb	36
1752	ARCHER, John	Middx	Jny	176
1762	ARCHER, John	Pts	May	182
1765	ARCHER, John	Middx	May	167
1765	ARCHER, John	Herts	Oct	359
1768	ARCHER, John	Surry	Feb	265
1769	ARCHER, John	Middx	Mch	73
1770	ARCHER, John	Surry	Jly	251
1771	ARCHER, John (poor) Pts –	Kent	Jne	240
1771	ARCHER, John	Middx	Jly	283
1782	ARCHER, John	Essex	Feb	59
1782	ARCHER, John	Essex	May	211
1785	ARCHER, John	Middx	Jly	350
1785	ARCHER, John	Surry	Nov	536
1788	ARCHER, John Ser "Ambuscade", "Cumberland" & "Eagle"	Pts	Nov	519
1789	ARCHER, John	Essex	May	232
1789	ARCHER, John	Essex	Sep	447
1790	ARCHER, John	Wark	Mch	114
1791	ARCHER, John	Herts	May	208
1792	ARCHER, John	Lond	Jny	2
1793	ARCHER, John AwW of Gds unadm. W rgd Nov 1785	Surry	Aug	--
1794	ARCHER, John (Dble Pr) W rgd Jny 1792	Lond	Apr	--
1796	ARCHER, John	Bucks	Sep	439
1799	ARCHER, John, Esq. Lt Gen in H.M.Army	SHant	Oct	694
1800	ARCHER, John, Esq.	Glos	Nov	762
1756	ARCHER, Joseph AwW	Middx	Apr	93
1757	ARCHER, Joseph	Pts	Jly	212
1772	ARCHER, Joseph	Middx	Jly	243
1779	ARCHER, Joseph Ser	Middx	Mch	87
1792	ARCHER, Keziah	Herts	Aug	413
1799	ARCHER, Lawrence	Wark	Aug	560
1757	ARCHER, Mary	Kent	Apr	108
1761	ARCHER, Mary	Middx	Feb	44
1762	ARCHER, Mary	Brstl	May	182
1766	ARCHER, Mary	Essex	May	166
1779	ARCHER, Mary	Essex	Jne	230
1783	ARCHER, Mary	Surry	Apr	158
1786	ARCHER, Mary	Lond	Mch	132
1763	ARCHER, Michael	Herts	Aug	367
1758	ARCHER, Myles	Essex	Feb	28
1761	ARCHER, Oliver AwW	Pts	Jne	199
1769	ARCHER, Oliver AwW of Gds unadm. W rgd 1761, 199	Pts	Jne	--
1799	ARCHER, Peter	Middx	Jne	413
1766	ARCHER, Rebeckah	Surry	Feb	44
1761	ARCHER, Richard	Lond	Mch	80
1775	ARCHER, Richard	Wark	Nov	399
1782	ARCHER, Richard AwW	Pts	Mch	108
1787	ARCHER, Richard	Oxon	May	195
1800	ARCHER, Richard	Wark	Jny	1
1767	ARCHER, Robert	Glos	Oct	360

1788	ARCHER, Robert		Middx	Jly	335
1793	ARCHER, Robert		Middx	Sep	451
1757	ARCHER, Sarah		Essex	Jny	1
1763	ARCHER, Sarah		Essex	May	210
1765	ARCHER, Sarah		Wark	May	167
1782	ARCHER, Sarah		Middx	Apr	163
1798	ARCHER, Sarah		Middx	Feb	74
1761	ARCHER, Susanna		Lincs	Mch	80
1789	ARCHER, Swete Nicholas, Esq.		Corn	Jny	1
1757	ARCHER, Thomas		Essex	Jly	211
1759	ARCHER, Thomas, Esq.		Essex	Aug	255
1761	ARCHER, Thomas		Pts	Oct	335
1762	ARCHER, Thomas AwW		Wark	Oct	409
1767	ARCHER, Rev. Thomas		Lond	Jly	250
1768	ARCHER, Rt Hon Lord Thomas, Baron of				
	Umberslade in Co. of Wark		Essex	Oct	367
1772	ARCHER, Thomas		Middx	Jne	202
1776	ARCHER, Thomas		Essex	Sep	380
1776	ARCHER, Thomas AwW		Sfolk	Oct	410
1783	ARCHER, Thomas "Canada"		Pts	Jne	278
1786	ARCHER, Thomas		Middx	Jly	361
1788	ARCHER, Thomas		Herts	Oct	468
1791	ARCHER, Thomas		Essex	Jly	314
1794	ARCHER, Thomas		Middx	Dec	594
1798	ARCHER, Thomas		Bucks	Sep	581
1763	ARCHER, Valentine		Kent	Mch	105
1769	ARCHER, Walter		Essex	Feb	31
1753	ARCHER, William		Wark	Feb	37
1754	ARCHER, William AwW		Lond	Jly	187
1756	ARCHER, William		Pts	Nov	287
1757	ARCHER, William AwW		Pts	Nov	319
1757	ARCHER, William		Pts	Dec	348
1759	ARCHER, William		Sfolk	May	155
1763	ARCHER, otherwise ERCHER, William		Pts	Mch	104
1766	ARCHER, William		Herts	Oct	360
1772	ARCHER, otherwise SMITH, William		Pts	Oct	382
1780	ARCHER, William, Esq.		Chest	Aug	383
1782	ARCHER, William		Lond	Jly	334
1782	ARCHER, William		Surry	Sep	438
1786	ARCHER, William		Lond	Jny	2
1786	ARCHER, William		Nhant	Jne	318
1795	ARCHER, William		Middx	Aug	492
1795	ARCHER, William (Dble Pr) W rgd 1786,2		Lond	Sep	--
1795	ARCHER, William (Dble Pr) W rgd 1786,2				
	Anor Grant last month		Lond	Oct	--
1797	ARCHER, William		Kent	Jly	468
1786	ARCHETT, William		Berks	Apr	201
1774	ARCHEUEQUE, John L' AwW		Middx	Jly	273
1798	ARCHIBALD, Anthony		Surry	Feb	74
1763	ARCHIBALD, James		Pts	Jly	320
1800	ARCHIBALD, James		Middx	Aug	573
1761	ARCHIBALD, John		Pts	Sep	307
1773	ARCHIBALD, Margaret LILLIE, formerly		NBrit	Oct	398

```
1779  ARCHIBALD, William                              Rad    Dec 482
1787  ARCUS, otherwise HARCUS, otherwise HAWKES,
      James  AwW  "Plymouth" & "Hero"                 Pts    Feb  51
1795  ARCY, Margaret D'                               Middx  Jne  --
1765  ARD, Charles                                    Pts    May 168
1765  ARDEN, Ann                                      Strat  Sep 319
1755  ARDEN, Daniel  AwW                              Dorst  Aug 209
1799  ARDEN, Elizabeth                                Salop  Aug 560
1751  ARDEN, George                                   Pts    Sep 250
1799  ARDEN, George                                   Worcs  Jny   2
1800  ARDEN, George  Ser  "Queen Charlotte"           Pts    Dec 833
1772  ARDEN, James  (Ltd Pr)  (by int dec)            Worcs  Feb  34
1778  ARDEN, James  Ser                               Kent   Dec 475
1787  ARDEN, John, Esq.                               Yorks  Jny   1
1761  ARDEN, otherwise ATHERON, Joseph                Yorks  Apr 116
1789  ARDEN, Mary                                     Kent   Feb  70
1794  ARDEN, Richard                                  Glos   Nov 535
1768  ARDEN, Rev. William  AwW                        Nhant  Nov 400
1762  ARDERN, otherwise ARDERNE, Nathan               Lancr  Aug 331
1762  ARDERN, otherwise ARDERNE, Nathan
      W rgd Aug last                                  Lancr  Nov  --
1800  ARDERNE, Elizabeth                              Lancr  Feb  80
1762  ARDERNE, otherwise ARDERN, Nathan               Lancr  Aug 331
1762  ARDERNE, otherwise ARDERN, Nathan
      W rgd Aug last                                  Lancr  Nov  --
1773  ARDERNE, Ralph                                  Surry  Dec 456
1775  ARDESOIF, Diana                                 Middx  Dec 453
1756  ARDESOIF, Francis                               Middx  Sep 236
1799  ARDESOIF, Isaac, Esq.                           Middx  Nov 756
1789  ARDESOIF, John, Esq.                            Middx  Apr 184
1787  ARDESOIF, Stephen Demar                         Middx  Aug 354
1770  ARDESOIF, Susannah Desmare                      Middx  May 170
1774  ARDESOIF, Thomas                                Middx  Nov 385
1786  ARDIN, Martha                                   Middx  Dec 597
1795  ARDING, Caleb                                   Surry  Mch 137
1772  ARDING, Caroline                                Brstl  Feb  34
1769  ARDING, George                                  Middx  Nov 363
1775  ARDING, John                                    Berks  Feb  37
1760  ARDING, Mary                                    Brstl  Jly 270
1770  ARDING, Richard  AwW                            Oxon   Mch  84
1771  ARDING, Richard                                 Brstl  Feb  42
1765  ARDINOIS, Catharine Francoise (Ltd Pr)          Pts    Mch  84
1763  ARDINOIS, Jacobus  (Ltd Pr)                     Pts    Mch 105
1766  ARDINOIS, formerly DUTILH, Judith (Ltd Pr)Pts   Dec 439
1766  ARDIOUN, Mary                                   Middx  Jny   1
1770  ARDLE, Patrick MC                               Brstl  Dec 441
1774  ARDLEY, Benjamin                                Middx  May 165
1795  ARDLEY, Elizabeth                               Middx  Feb  61
1751  ARDLEY, Isaac                                   Essex  Nov 298
1784  ARDLEY, John                                    Surry  Jny   1
1785  ARDLEY, John                                    SHant  Jly 351
1791  ARDLEY, John, Esq. (Dble Pr) W rgd 1785
         351                                          SHant  Sep  --
```

111

1795	ARDLEY, Joseph.	Essex	Nov	621
1772	ARDLEY, Samuel, Esq. (Ltd Pr)	Pts	Oct	349
1789	ARDLEY, Susanna	SHant	Apr	186
1787	ARDLY, Daniel Charles	Surry	Dec	528
1798	ARDMOIS, Sara	Pts	Oct	632
1771	ARDOUIN, Ann	Kent	Jly	282
1794	ARDOUIN, Charlotte	Kent	Aug	402
1772	ARDOUIN, Daniel	Oxon	Feb	35
1756	ARDOUIN, Michael	Middx	Jly	186
1781	ARDRON, Lydia	Kent	Sep	417
1760	ARDRON, William	Herts	Feb	45
1757	ARENTZ DE WIT, Jan (Ltd Pr)	Pts	Jly	237
1752	ARESKIN, Major	Pts - Kent	May	115
1752	ARESKIN, Major (by int dec)	Kent	Dec	292
1763	ARESKINE of Tinwald, Rt Hon Lord Charles, Lord Justice Clerk in that pt of GtBrit called Scotland		Jne	263
1758	ARESKINE, John	Middx	Oct	282
1763	ARESKINE, John AwW of Gds unadm. W rgd 1758, 282	Middx	Mch	--
1763	ARESKINE, Rose	Middx	Mch	103
1771	AREY, John	Pts	Nov	428
1751	ARGENT, Abel AwW	Chich	Aug	228
1761	ARGENT, otherwise DRAKE, otherwise DRACCO, Ann, formerly	Pts	Jly	245
1793	ARGENT, Clement	Herts	Nov	538
1751	ARGENT, George	Sfolk	Oct	273
1761	ARGENT, George	Middx	Apr	115
1768	ARGENT, John	Essex	May	184
1776	ARGENT, Mary	Middx	Feb	48
1781	ARGENT, Samuel	Essex	Dec	568
1796	ARGENTEAU, Count Florimond Claude de Mercy (Ltd Pr)	Middx	Sep	439
1797	ARGENTEAU, Count Florimond Claude de Mercy, Minister Plenipotentiary of HM the Emperor for the affairs of present War & formerly His Ambassador in France Spec AwW of Rest of Gds. Ltd Pr passed in Sep last	Middx	Jny	2
1781	ARGHES, John	Camb	Apr	179
1790	ARGILL, Thomas	Surry	Feb	55
1792	ARGILL, Thomas	Berks	Jly	457
1774	ARGLES, John	Bucks	May	165
1782	ARGLES, John	Sussx	Oct	478
1789	ARGLES, Mary	Kent	Dec	572
1755	ARGLES, Thomas	Kent	Nov	275
1769	ARGLES, Thomas	Sussx	Oct	331
1791	ARGLES, Thomas AwW of Gds unadm. W rgd 1736, 74	Kent	Jly	--
1761	ARGYLL, The Most Noble Lord Archibald, late Duke of	Middx	May	157
1770	ARGYLL, The Most Noble John, Duke of	Middx	Nov	387
1767	ARGYLL and GREENWICH, Lady Jane, Dowager Duchess of	Middx	Apr	120

```
1767   ARIGAN, otherwise ARRIGON, Patrick    Ser    Pts     Sep 330
1775   ARIS, Benjamin                               Middx   May 168
1763   ARIS, Edward                                 Nhant   Nov 493
1797   ARIS, Edward                                 Surry   Jne 393
1773   ARIS, Eldridge                               Brstl   Aug 318
1790   ARIS, John                                   Berks   Feb  55
1766   ARIS, Nicholas                               Middx   Nov 395
1763   ARIS, Prudence                               Wark    Jny   1
1761   ARIS, Thomas                                 Wark    Oct 336
1765   ARIS, Thomas   AwW of Gds unadm. W rgd
         Oct 1761                                   Wark    Aug  --
1781   ARIS, Thomas                                 Oxon    Sep 417
1786   ARIS, William                                Nhant   Nov 551
1772   ARKEL, Rt Noble Rudolph Frederick Baron
         VAN, otherwise Rudolph Ferdinand VAN
         ARKEL  (Ltd Pr)                            Pts     Jne 237
1784   ARKENBOUT, Leeuderd  (Ltd Pr)                Pts     Nov 583
1794   ARKILL, John                                 Corn    Feb  59
1795   ARKILL, John  "Impregnable"  W rgd Feb1794   Pts     Jne  --
1791   ARKINSTALL, Sarah                            Herts   Mch 108
1763   ARKINSTALL, Thomas                           Middx   May 211
1784   ARKLEY, Ann                                  Berks   Dec 627
1768   ARKLEY, Hon Jeremiah             Pts  -      Surry   Dec 437
1770   ARKLEY, Ralph  AwW                           Yorks   Aug 283
1762   ARKUSS, William                              Pts     Jly 282
1792   ARKWRIGHT, Sir Richard, Knt.  AwW of Gds
         unadm.  W rgd 1759, 255         Pts  -     Derby   Sep 458
1752   ARLIDGE, Jacob                               Wark    Jne 145
1794   ARMAGH, Most Rev Rt Hon Father in God,
         Richard by Divine Providence Lord Arch-
         bishop of, Primate and Metropolitan of
         all Ireland and Baron ROKEBY of Armagh
         in the Kingdom of Ireland  (Ltd Pr)        Brstl   Nov 534
1800   ARMAGH, Lord William, Most Rev Father in
         God by Divine Providence Lord Archbishop
         of Armagh                                  Irel    Jne 430
1783   ARMAN, Mark                                  Pts     Oct 493
1774   ARMAN, formerly BLOSS, Mary                  Middx   May 165
1777   ARMAN, Thomas                                Herts   Feb  49
1792   ARMANO, Rachel MACKENZIE, formerly           Surry   Oct 523
1755   ARMBROST, Hendrik                            Pts     Nov 274
1752   ARMENAULT, Daniel                            Pts     Dec 292
1799   ARMESTEAD, Mary                              Nhant   Feb  89
1762   ARMETAGE, Robert                             Surry   Jne 230
1762   ARMETAGE, Robert  AwW of Gds unadm.  W
         rgd Jne last                               Surry   Dec  --
1795   ARMETT, Charles                              Chest   Sep 533
1756   ARMETT, William                              Staff   Sep 461
1789   ARMIGER, Frances                             Middx   Jne 297
1778   ARMIGER, Jeremiah                            Essex   Nov 427
1777   ARMIGER, John                                Beds    Dec 495
1795   ARMIGER, Margarett                           Essex   Oct 579
1770   ARMIGER, Robert  Lt Gen of HM Forces         --      Apr 128
```

1768	ARMINER, Joseph	SHant	Aug 305
1799	ARMINER, Joseph	SHant	Nov 757
1782	ARMINER, Sarah	SHant	Nov 526
1761	ARMINER, Thomas	Pts – SHant	Nov 378
1776	ARMINER, Thomas	SHant	May 209
1800	ARMINGER, Christopher Ser "Prince of Wales"	Nwich	Nov 760
1800	ARMINGER, John	Nwich	May 336
1793	ARMINGER, William	Middx	Oct 488
1780	ARMIRANT, Christopher	Bath	Jly 345
1769	ARMISTEAD, Elizabeth	Nhant	Jny 1
1754	ARMISTEAD, Richard	Yorks	Jny 2
1781	ARMISTEAD, Robert	Middx	Nov 510
1792	ARMITAGE, otherwise ARMYTAGE, Ann	Surry	May 253
1799	ARMITAGE, Elizabeth	Middx	Jny 3
1781	ARMITAGE, George	Kent	Jly 326
1777	ARMITAGE, Jane	Middx	Feb 50
1750	ARMITAGE, otherwise HERMITAGE, John	Pts	Feb 36
1769	ARMITAGE, John	Surry	Dec 402
1784	ARMITAGE, John, Esq.	Surry	Mch 118
1787	ARMITAGE, John	Middx	Jny 2
1787	ARMITAGE, John	Middx	Dec 528
1796	ARMITAGE, John	Beds	Jly 342
1798	ARMITAGE, Dr. John (Dr of Physic)	Derby	Nov 692
1766	ARMITAGE, Joseph	Middx	Jly 255
1791	ARMITAGE, Joseph	Middx	Jny 1
1791	ARMITAGE, Joseph, Esq.	Yorks	Apr 164
1781	ARMITAGE, Joshua	Middx	Jny 2
1791	ARMITAGE, Mary	Middx	Aug 368
1787	ARMITAGE, Robert	Middx	Nov 480
1793	ARMITAGE, Robert	Middx	Apr 180
1786	ARMITAGE, Sarah	Middx	Mch 134
1797	ARMITAGE, Sarah	Beds	May 290
1751	ARMITAGE, Thomas	Middx	Nov 298
1755	ARMITAGE, Thomas	Middx	Dec 303
1796	ARMITAGE, Thomas	Surry	Jly 342
1777	ARMITSTEAD, Bartholemew	Surry	Mch 94
1753	ARMITSTEAD, John	Lond	Dec 307
1794	ARMITSTEAD, John	Glos	Nov 534
1754	ARMITSTEAD, Richard (Dble Pr) W rgd Jny last	Yorks	Mch 66
1775	ARMITSTEAD, Richard	Middx	Jly 259
1767	ARMITSTEAD, William	Middx	Mch 82
1752	ARMITSTEED, Elizabeth	Middx	Oct 241
1764	ARMOND, William	Pts	Dec 452
1774	ARMORER, Ann	Middx	May 165
1757	ARMORER, David	Lond	Jly 211
1779	ARMORER, otherwise FIDLING, Grace	Middx	Aug 333
1769	ARMORER, Robert	Lond	Apr 111
1780	ARMORER, William	Pts	Jny 1
1756	ARMOUR, Andrew	Pts	Sep 236
1759	ARMOUR, Hector AwW	Pts	Jly 223
1753	ARMOUR, James	Lond	Jny 1

```
1764  ARMOUR, John                                    Pts    Aug 295
1765  ARMOUR, Thomas  AwW                             Pts    Jny   1
1751  ARMOUR, William                                 Lond   Jly 197
1793  ARMOURER, Thomas  Ltd AwW                       Pts    Aug 397
1763  ARMROID, Charles                                Surry  Feb  41
1773  ARMROID, William                                Lond   Nov 414
1797  ARMROID, William                                Middx  Feb  66
1795  ARMROYD, Catherine                              Middx  Mch 137
1800  ARMS, Assable otherwise Asfable                 Herfd  Nov 760
1766  ARMS, Mary                                      Middx  Jne 210
1789  ARMSON, John                                    Lincs  Apr 185
1783  ARMSTEAD, Ann                                   Lond   Mch 106
1779  ARMSTEAD, John                                  Lond   Jny   1
1781  ARMSTEAD, John                                  Pts    Jne 281
1786  ARMSTEAD, Thomas                                Nhant  Aug 418
1799  ARMSTON, Ann                                    Middx  Dec 820
1795  ARMSTON, John                                   Leics  Dec 666
1793  ARMSTRONG, Abel  AwW                            Kent   Jly 350
1795  ARMSTRONG, Abel  AwW of Gds unadm.
      W rgd Jly 1793                                  Kent   Jne  --
1758  ARMSTRONG, Abraham                              Middx  Jne 175
1756  ARMSTRONG, Adam                                 Pts    May 128
1764  ARMSTRONG, Andrew                               Pts    Aug 295
1796  ARMSTRONG, Rev. Andrew                          Nland  Jly 342
1763  ARMSTRONG, Ann                                  Lond   Feb  41
1800  ARMSTRONG, Ann                                  Lond   Jne 429
1790  ARMSTRONG, Anna Maria                           Kent   Jne 275
1764  ARMSTRONG, Barbary  AwW                         Middx  Apr 128
1762  ARMSTRONG, Bazil                                Pts    Sep 365
1768  ARMSTRONG, Benjamin                             Berks  May 184
1794  ARMSTRONG, Bigoe, Esq.  Gen of HM Forces Middx  Jly 344
1800  ARMSTRONG, Charles  "St Albans","Jupiter"
      & "Daphne"                                      Pts    Jne 429
1775  ARMSTRONG, Christopher                          Middx  Mch  81
1762  ARMSTRONG, Daniel                               Middx  Feb  37
1797  ARMSTRONG, Deborah                              Lincs  May 291
1797  ARMSTRONG, Edmund, Esq.  AwW                    Middx  Nov 672
1781  ARMSTRONG, Elizabeth                            Middx  May 222
1797  ARMSTRONG, Elizabeth Rebecca                    Lond   Feb  66
1764  ARMSTRONG, Ellinor                              Yorks  Jly 248
1767  ARMSTRONG, Francis                              Middx  Oct 360
1784  ARMSTRONG, Francis  "Worcester"   Pts - SHant   Aug 425
1752  ARMSTRONG, George, Esq.  AwW                    Middx  Sep 227
1758  ARMSTRONG, George                               Pts    Feb  28
1783  ARMSTRONG, George              Pts - Essex      Nov 548
1793  ARMSTRONG, George  W rgd 1783, 548
      "Superbe" & "Nymphe"                            Essex  Dec  --
1795  ARMSTRONG, George  Ser  "Boyne"                 Middx  Aug 492
1800  ARMSTRONG, George                               Kent   Aug 574
1796  ARMSTRONG, Henrietta                            Nwich  Jly 343
1752  ARMSTRONG, James              Pts - Surry       Oct 241
1771  ARMSTRONG, James                                Surry  Jne 240
1780  ARMSTRONG, James                                Pts    Dec 550
```

1783	ARMSTRONG, James Ser			Devon	Jne	279
1799	ARMSTRONG, James Ser "Carnatic"			Pts	Jny	2
1768	ARMSTRONG, Jane			Cumb	Jne	224
1751	ARMSTRONG, John			Essex	Jly	197
1752	ARMSTRONG, John			Pts	Apr	82
1756	ARMSTRONG, John			Pts	Dec	317
1758	ARMSTRONG, John AwW			Pts	Aug	236
1760	ARMSTRONG, John			Middx	Nov	413
1761	ARMSTRONG, John AwW			Pts	Apr	115
1779	ARMSTRONG, John			Middx	Sep	364
1786	ARMSTRONG, John			Middx	Feb	62
1786	ARMSTRONG, John			Surry	Sep	461
1789	ARMSTRONG, John, Esq.			Cumb	Jne	296
1792	ARMSTRONG, John			Middx	Aug	413
1798	ARMSTRONG, John, Esq.			Irel	Apr	230
1798	ARMSTRONG, John			Middx	Dec	754
1800	ARMSTRONG, John			Surry	Apr	250
1791	ARMSTRONG, Joseph			Lond	Apr	164
1800	ARMSTRONG, Joseph			Surry	May	337
1764	ARMSTRONG, Mary			Middx	Feb	36
1784	ARMSTRONG, Mary			Middx	May	243
1784	ARMSTRONG, Mary			Middx	Aug	425
1786	ARMSTRONG, Mary			Kent	Jly	360
1790	ARMSTRONG, Mary			Middx	Feb	54
1757	ARMSTRONG, Michael, Esq.			Middx	Sep	266
1762	ARMSTRONG, Michael, Esq. AwW of Gds unadm.			Middx	Jly	--
	W rgd 1757, 266					
1766	ARMSTRONG, Patrick AwW			Pts	May	166
1783	ARMSTRONG, Patrick Ser			SHant	Jly	331
1778	ARMSTRONG, Peter			Middx	Dec	474
1755	ARMSTRONG, Philip			Middx	Sep	232
1789	ARMSTRONG, Priscilla			Middx	Apr	184
1783	ARMSTRONG, Robert "Isis"			Pts	Jly	333
1784	ARMSTRONG, Robert (Dble Pr) W rgd Jly1783			Pts	Jly	--
1800	ARMSTRONG, Ruth			SHant	Sep	642
1769	ARMSTRONG, Sarah			Berks	Apr	110
1779	ARMSTRONG, Sarah			Middx	Nov	441
1752	ARMSTRONG, Thomas			Pts	Jny	1
1758	ARMSTRONG, Thomas			Wilts	Sep	257
1764	ARMSTRONG, Thomas			Dorst	Mch	78
1764	ARMSTRONG, Thomas			Lond	Oct	376
1766	ARMSTRONG, Thomas			Essex	Nov	396
1786	ARMSTRONG, Thomas AwW			Dubln	Aug	417
1786	ARMSTRONG, Thomas "Swallow"			Pts	Sep	461
1791	ARMSTRONG, Thomas, Esq.			SHant	Jne	264
1794	ARMSTRONG, Thomas			Durhm	Mch	120
1756	ARMSTRONG, William			Berks	Feb	26
1766	ARMSTRONG, William			Pts	Apr	125
1766	ARMSTRONG, William			Middx	Jly	256
1769	ARMSTRONG, William			Middx	Feb	32
1770	ARMSTRONG, William			Surry	Aug	283
1779	ARMSTRONG, William			Middx	Dec	482
1783	ARMSTRONG, William			Kent	Jne	277

1784	ARMSTRONG, William "Sultan"		Pts	Apr 186
1784	ARMSTRONG, William		Middx	Oct --
1793	ARMSTRONG, William		Bath	Jny 1
1796	ARMSTRONG, William Ser "Agamemnon" & "Dido"		Pts	Aug 394
1796	ARMSTRONG, William Wingfield		Kent	Jny 2
1792	ARMYTAGE, otherwise ARMITAGE, Ann		Surry	May 253
1767	ARMYTAGE, Elizabeth		Nhant	Mch 83
1764	ARMYTAGE, John, Esq.		Yorks	Jly 248
1784	ARMWRIGHT, John	Pts -	Exter	Jly 363
1753	ARNALD, Michael		Middx	Dec 307
1755	ARNALD, otherwise ARNOLD, John		Middx	Jne 153
1777	ARNALD, Rev. John		Nhant	Apr 143
1754	ARNALD, William AwW unadm. W rgd 1729,239		Beds	Nov --
1763	ARNALL, George		Pts	Jly 320
1778	ARNALL, Hannah		Middx	Apr 141
1781	ARNALL, Hannah		Nwich	Oct 459
1775	ARNALL, Henry		Middx	Dec 454
1776	ARNALL, Henry (Dble Pr) W rgd Dec 1775		Middx	May --
1771	ARNALL, John		Lincs	May 191
1786	ARNALL, John		Kent	Nov 552
1778	ARNALL, William		Pts	Jly 271
1793	ARNAM, Frances		Nwich	Dec 578
1788	ARNAM, Rev. John		Norf	Feb 52
1789	ARNAT, otherwise ANNOTT, otherwise AWNOTT, James "Monmouth"&"Defence"		Pts	May 232
1799	ARNATT, Jonathan		Oxon	Mch 163
1754	ARNATT, Mary AwW		Sussx	Nov 292
1765	ARNAUD, Antoine D' Ltd W		Pts	Mch 84
1772	ARNAUD, Elias		SHant	Oct 347
1784	ARNAUD, Hannah		SHant	Jly 363
1767	ARNAUD, Mary		Middx	May 161
1765	ARNAUD, Mary Magdalen		Lond	Aug 282
1753	ARNAUD, Peter		Middx	May 126
1753	ARNAUD, Peter (Dble Pr) W rgd May last		Middx	Jly --
1785	ARNAUD, Peter		SHant	Dec 584
1779	ARNAUD, Sarah		SHant	Mch 85
1758	ARNAULD, otherwise ARNODIN, Susanna		Middx	Mch 61
1798	ARNDELL, Anthony		Middx	Sep 581
1784	ARNDELL, otherwise ARUDELL, otherwise ARUNDELL, Hannah		Durhm	May 244
1797	ARNDELL, Mary Ann		Middx	Sep 583
1797	ARNDELL, Mary Ann W rgd last month		Middx	Oct 625
1792	ARNDELL, Thomas		Middx	Apr 189
1778	ARNE, Dr. Thomas Augustine (Dr in Music)		Middx	Mch 94
1778	ARNE, Dr. Thomas Augustine (Dr in Music) (Dble Pr) W rgd this month		Middx	Mch --
1784	ARNEL, otherwise ARNOLD, Robert AwW "Stirling Castle"		Pts	Jny 1
1763	ARNELL, otherwise ARNOLD, George		Pts	Mch 105
1767	ARNELL, otherwise ARNOLD, John		Pts	Jny 1
1762	ARNELL, William		Pts	Mch 89
1763	ARNES, otherwise ERNEST, John Mathias		Middx	Jny 14

```
1777  ARNETT, Ann                                    Middx Jne 250
1764  ARNETT, otherwise ARNOTT, Decimus              Lond  Aug 295
1781  ARNETT, George                                 Pts   Sep 418
1774  ARNETT, Godfrey                                Middx Apr 125
1764  ARNETT, Henry                                  Kent  Jne 209
1771  ARNETT, William                                Middx Mch  91
1760  ARNEY, Edmund                                  SHant Jny   1
1755  ARNEY, Jane                                    Nhant May 121
1775  ARNEY, John                                    Middx Oct 365
1775  ARNEY, John  (Dble Pr)  W rgd this month       Middx Oct  --
1775  ARNEY, John  (Tble Pr)  W rgd Oct last
         Last Grant                                  Middx Nov  --
1780  ARNEY, John                                    Pts   Dec 550
1794  ARNO, Charles                                  Devon Dec 594
1758  ARNODIN, otherwise ARNAULD, Susanna            Middx Mch  61
1779  ARNOL, otherwise ARNOLD, John                  Middx May 186
1758  ARNOLD, Ann                                    Lond  Dec 355
1760  ARNOLD, Ann                                    SHant Jne 225
1760  ARNOLD, Ann                                    Glos  Sep 346
1775  ARNOLD, Ann  AwW                               Middx Jly 259
1776  ARNOLD, Ann                                    Middx Sep 380
1784  ARNOLD, Ann                                    Surry Mch 118
1788  ARNOLD, Ann                                    Middx Jly 335
1790  ARNOLD, Ann  AwW                               NBrit Aug 363
1795  ARNOLD, Ann                                    Middx Jne 295
1795  ARNOLD, Ann                                    Wark  Jly 428
1799  ARNOLD, Ann Awdry                              Wilts Oct 694
1761  ARNOLD, Benjamin                               Middx Mch  81
1760  ARNOLD, Charles                                Pts   Oct 378
1764  ARNOLD, Charles                                Pts   Oct 376
1774  ARNOLD, Charles                                Lond  Nov 384
1784  ARNOLD, Charles                                Kent  Jly 363
1758  ARNOLD, Christopher                            Middx Aug 236
1755  ARNOLD, Constable Hassell  AwW                 Pts   Aug 209
1759  ARNOLD, Daniel                                 Middx Jly 223
1784  ARNOLD, Edward                                 Rutld Jny   2
1789  ARNOLD, Edward                                 Middx Dec 571
1751  ARNOLD, Elizabeth  AwW                         Devon May 130
1756  ARNOLD, Elizabeth                              Surry Feb  26
1762  ARNOLD, Elizabeth                              Middx Oct 408
1765  ARNOLD, Elizabeth                              Middx Mch  83
1766  ARNOLD, Elizabeth  AwW unadm. W rgd Mch
         last                                        Middx Jny  --
1767  ARNOLD, Elizabeth                              Middx Nov 399
1771  ARNOLD, Elizabeth                              Middx Mch  91
1777  ARNOLD, Elizabeth                              Surry Jny   1
1778  ARNOLD, Elizabeth                              SHant May 182
1789  ARNOLD, Elizabeth                              Essex Nov 528
1794  ARNOLD, Elizabeth                              Kent  Sep 443
1750  ARNOLD, Fleet                                  Pts   Jly 220
1751  ARNOLD, George, Esq. One of Aldermen of
         City of Lond                                Surry Jly 197
1763  ARNOLD, otherwise ARNELL, George               Pts   Mch 105
```

```
1764   ARNOLD, George                                          Pts    Aug  296
1766   ARNOLD, George                                          Nhant  Mch   88
1771   ARNOLD, George                                          Som    Jne  240
1772   ARNOLD, George   (Dble Pr) W rgd Jne 1771 Som           Jly    --
1777   ARNOLD, George                                          Middx  Jly  296
1785   ARNOLD, George, Esq.                                    Kent   Aug  400
1791   ARNOLD, George                                          Essex  Oct  449
1773   ARNOLD, Henry                                           Middx  Sep  350
1778   ARNOLD, Rev. Dr. Henry, D.D.                            Wells  Nov  427
1779   ARNOLD, Rev. Dr. Henry, D.D.   AwW unadm.
         W rgd Nov 1778                                        Som    Sep   --
1797   ARNOLD, Henry                                           Wilts  Apr  220
1797   ARNOLD, Henry                                           Kent   May  290
1782   ARNOLD, Isaac                                           Kent   Mch  108
1775   ARNOLD, Isabel                                          Middx  Oct  365
1799   ARNOLD, Isack   "Thundr."                               Pts    Oct  693
1753   ARNOLD, James                                           Middx  Aug  222
1760   ARNOLD, James                                           Lond   Nov  413
1770   ARNOLD, James                                           Surry  Apr  128
1776   ARNOLD, James                                           Lond   Jne  253
1783   ARNOLD, James                                           Pts    Sep  441
1788   ARNOLD, James                                           Surry  Feb   52
1788   ARNOLD, James                                           Som    Aug  381
1767   ARNOLD, Jane                                            Middx  Apr  120
1786   ARNOLD, Jane                                            Middx  Jne  318
1750   ARNOLD, John                                            Pts    May  135
1753   ARNOLD, John                                            Middx  May  126
1754   ARNOLD, John   AwW                                      Lond   May  123
1755   ARNOLD, otherwise ARNALD, John                          Middx  Jne  153
1756   ARNOLD, John                                            Middx  Jly  186
1759   ARNOLD, John                                            Coven  Feb   44
1759   ARNOLD, John                                   Pts -   Middx  Apr  115
1761   ARNOLD, John                                            Middx  Nov  378
1762   ARNOLD, John                                            Middx  Jny    1
1762   ARNOLD, John                                            Middx  Oct  408
1767   ARNOLD, otherwise ARNELL, John                          Pts    Jny    1
1769   ARNOLD, John                                            Surry  Jny    2
1771   ARNOLD, John                                            Sfolk  May  191
1773   ARNOLD, John                                            Surry  Mch   90
1774   ARNOLD, John                                            Bath   Mch   77
1776   ARNOLD, John                                            Wark   Feb   47
1779   ARNOLD, John                                            Surry  Jny    1
1779   ARNOLD, John                                            Sfolk  Apr  138
1779   ARNOLD, otherwise ARNOL, John                           Middx  May  186
1781   ARNOLD, John                                            Pts    Dec  568
1789   ARNOLD, John                                            Middx  Apr  186
1789   ARNOLD, John                                            Surry  May  232
1793   ARNOLD, John                                            Middx  Sep  451
1794   ARNOLD, John                                            Middx  Jne  295
1795   ARNOLD, John                                            Surry  Sep  533
1799   ARNOLD, John   EIMS "Boddam"                            Pts    Mch  161
1799   ARNOLD, otherwise ANNALL, John   Ser
         "Invincible"                                          Pts    Oct  694
```

1800	ARNOLD, John	Brstl	Jny	3
1796	ARNOLD, Jonathan William	Berks	May	231
1761	ARNOLD, Joseph	Middx	Mch	80
1787	ARNOLD, Joseph	Lond	Feb	51
1792	ARNOLD, Joseph AwW	Surry	Sep	458
1797	ARNOLD, Joseph "Salisbury"	Pts	Feb	67
1781	ARNOLD, Latham, Esq.	Lond	Mch	107
1781	ARNOLD, Lumley	Nhant	May	221
1789	ARNOLD, Lumley, Esq. Spec AwW of Gds unadm. W rgd 1781, 221	Nhant	Jny	--
1771	ARNOLD, Margaret	Lond	Jne	240
1774	ARNOLD, Margaret	Wells	May	165
1782	ARNOLD, Margaret AwW of Gds unadm. W rgd 1774, 165	Wells	Dec	--
1772	ARNOLD, Martha AwW	Surry	Oct	348
1777	ARNOLD, Martha (Ltd Pr)	Middx	Nov	445
1786	ARNOLD, Martha AwW	Lond	Mch	134
1795	ARNOLD, Martha AwW of Gds unadm. W rgd 1786, 134	Lond	Jne	--
1755	ARNOLD, Mary AwW	Middx	Jly	180
1765	ARNOLD, Mary	Middx	Sep	319
1766	ARNOLD, Mary	Herfd	Nov	395
1767	ARNOLD, Mary	Wark	Feb	33
1770	ARNOLD, Mary	Middx	May	169
1775	ARNOLD, Mary AwW	Pts	Feb	38
1789	ARNOLD, Mary AwW	Winch	Jne	297
1757	ARNOLD, Mathew	Middx	Jny	1
1761	ARNOLD, Mathew	Sfolk	Aug	275
1760	ARNOLD, Matthew	SHant	Jne	225
1771	ARNOLD, Matthew AwW	Middx	Feb	42
1788	ARNOLD, Matthew Ltd AwW of Gds unadm. W rgd 1771, 42	Middx	Dec	--
1785	ARNOLD, Nathaniel	Kent	Feb	61
1754	ARNOLD, Richard	Middx	Mch	66
1768	ARNOLD, Richard AwW	Middx	Jny	1
1782	ARNOLD, Richard	Nhant	Jny	1
1789	ARNOLD, Richard	Surry	Sep	447
1792	ARNOLD, Richard	Nhant	Dec	593
1795	ARNOLD, Richard	Surry	Dec	666
1765	ARNOLD, Robert	Middx	Jne	205
1773	ARNOLD, Robert	Middx	Nov	413
1784	ARNOLD, otherwise ARNEL, Robert AwW "Stirling Castle"	Pts	Jny	1
1788	ARNOLD, Robert	Mon	Dec	572
1753	ARNOLD, Samuel	Wilts	Oct	262
1759	ARNOLD, Samuel	Pts	Nov	346
1795	ARNOLD, Samuel Ser "Minerva"	Pts	Jne	360
1761	ARNOLD, Sarah ANSELL, formerly Ltd AwW	Surry	Sep	307
1765	ARNOLD, Sarah	Middx	May	166
1767	ARNOLD, Susanna	Surry	May	161
1753	ARNOLD, Thomas AwW of Gds unadm ltd W rgd 1746, 107	Surry	May	--
1755	ARNOLD, Thomas	Surry	Aug	209

1761	ARNOLD, Thomas			Middx	Jne	199
1767	ARNOLD, Thomas			Middx	Nov	399
1770	ARNOLD, Thomas			Surry	May	170
1776	ARNOLD, Thomas			Surry	Apr	159
1789	ARNOLD, Thomas			Middx	Feb	71
1794	ARNOLD, Thomas			Middx	Apr	180
1797	ARNOLD, Thomas "Ranger"			Pts	Jny	2
1753	ARNOLD, William			Surry	Apr	100
1753	ARNOLD, William			Middx	Dec	307
1755	ARNOLD, William			Herts	Nov	274
1758	ARNOLD, William			Pts	Aug	236
1759	ARNOLD, William			Herts	Jny	1
1760	ARNOLD, William			SHant	Apr	134
1763	ARNOLD, William			Pts	Mch	103
1766	ARNOLD, William			Middx	Dec	439
1769	ARNOLD, William			SHant	Nov	363
1777	ARNOLD, William			Middx	May	195
1779	ARNOLD, William Ser			Middx	Apr	139
1779	ARNOLD, William			Lond	Nov	440
1783	ARNOLD, otherwise ARNOLL, William	Ser		Lond	Sep	441
1783	ARNOLD, otherwise ARNOLL, William	Anor				
	grant last month			Lond	Oct	493
1784	ARNOLD, William			Kent	Aug	425
1790	ARNOLD, William (Spec Pr)			Middx	Oct	451
1792	ARNOLD, William			Surry	Dec	593
1792	ARNOLD, Rev. William Filbridge			Leics	Jny	2
1763	ARNOLL, John			Pts	Aug	367
1793	ARNOLL, John			Surry	Apr	179
1766	ARNOLL, Robert AwW			Pts	Jne	209
1765	ARNOLL, William			Middx	Jly	244
1783	ARNOLL, otherwise ARNOLD, William	Ser		Lond	Sep	441
1783	ARNOLL, otherwise ARNOLD, William	Anor				
	grant last month			Lond	Oct	493
1783	ARNOLS, William			Brstl	Mch	107
1778	ARNOP, Edward			Sussx	Apr	142
1792	ARNOP, Mary			Sussx	Nov	542
1797	ARNOP, William			Surry	Feb	65
1756	ARNOT, Elizabeth			Middx	Aug	215
1761	ARNOT, John			Pts	Aug	275
1765	ARNOT, Mary			Oxon	Jny	1
1756	ARNOT, Michael			Surry	Jny	1
1767	ARNOT, Thomas Ltd Aw Testy Sched annxd			Pts	Sep	332
1771	ARNOT, Thomas			Pts	Aug	328
1772	ARNOT, Thomas (Dble Pr) W rgd Aug last			Pts	Jny	--
1756	ARNOTT, Alexander Ser AwW			Pts	Jly	186
1765	ARNOTT, Ann			Middx	Mch	84
1792	ARNOTT, Catharine			Lond	May	253
1757	ARNOTT, David AwW			Pts	Mch	72
1757	ARNOTT, David			Middx	Aug	238
1764	ARNOTT, otherwise ARNETT, Decimus			Lond	Aug	295
1764	ARNOTT, Edward			Middx	Jny	1
1763	ARNOTT, Jacob AwW			Pts	May	210
1750	ARNOTT, John			Middx	Mch	66

1750	ARNOTT, John	Middx	Mch	66
1750	ARNOTT, Sir John	Yorks	Jne	185
1754	ARNOTT, John AwW unadm. W rgd 1738, 279	Surry	Dec	317
1762	ARNOTT, John	Middx	Nov	444
1774	ARNOTT, Sir John, Bart.	Pts	Mch	76
1777	ARNOTT, John	Middx	Dec	495
1773	ARNOTT, Mary	Notts	Jne	233
1783	ARNOTT, Mary	Worcs	Apr	158
1795	ARNOTT, Mary	Middx	Jne	360
1800	ARNOTT, Matthew Robert, Esq.	Yorks	May	335
1769	ARNOTT, Richard	Herts	Jny	1
1760	ARNOTT, Robert	Yorks	Aug	312
1781	ARNOTT, Robert Ser	Pts	Dec	569
1762	ARNOTT, Thomas	Pts	Apr	136
1787	ARNOTT, Thomas	Essex	Apr	155
1797	ARNOTT, Thomas, Esq.	NBrit	Sep	583
1782	ARNOTT, Sir William	NBrit	Sep	438
1798	ARNOTT, William Ser "Arethusa" & "San Damo."	Devon	Mch	151
1766	ARNOUD, Margaret	Middx	Dec	440
1778	ARNOULD, John	Berks	Oct	385
1796	ARNOULD, Joseph	Berks	Nov	538
1796	ARNOUX, John	Surry	Nov	538
1775	ARNSBY, Edward	Nhant	Jne	217
1795	ARNSBY, William	Nhant	Sep	532
1797	ARNTZENIUS, Hendrick Otto No ship	Pts	May	291
1764	ARNTZENIUS, Otto (Ltd Pr)	Pts	Jny	1
1762	ARNULL, Samuel	Sfolk	Mch	89
1800	ARNULL, Samuel	Camb	Feb	81
1779	ARNULL, William	Middx	Apr	138
1769	ARONIO, Lord John Jerome Delevigne	Pts	Jny	1
1793	ARONS, David Lion (Ltd Pr)	Pts	Nov	537
1781	ARONSON, otherwise AARONSON, Aaron	Pts	Nov	510
1760	AROW, otherwise ARROW, Ann AwW	Middx	Feb	45
1762	AROWSMITH, Sarah	Middx	May	182
1787	AROY, Sarah (Ltd Pr)	Pts	Nov	479
1767	ARP, Mattheus VAN	Pts	Sep	358
1768	ARPEN, Ann	Herts	Sep	336
1752	ARPIN, Thomas	Herts	Apr	82
1786	ARPIN, William	Beds	Jne	318
1791	ARPIN, William	Middx	Apr	164
1800	ARPTHORP, otherwise ARPTHORPE, John	Herts	Mch	171
1800	ARPTHORPE, otherwise ARPTHORP, John	Herts	Mch	171
1770	ARQUET, Hon Hendrick D' (Ltd Pr)	Pts	Feb	51
1759	ARRAN, Rt Hon Charles, Earl of	Middx	Jny	2
1757	ARRAN, Rt Hon Elizabeth, Countess of	Middx	Feb	37
1783	ARRELLANO, otherwise LAMA, Emanuel Ser	SHant	Jne	279
1791	ARREST, Hon Abraham D'	Pts	Nov	509
1791	ARRHENIUS, Hans Christiern, Esq.	Middx	May	208
1767	ARRIGON, otherwise ARIGAN, Patrick Ser	Pts	Sep	330
1781	ARRIGONI, Charles Ferdinando	Lond	Jny	1
1800	ARRIPÉ, Isaac Augustus D' 15th Regt Foot	Dubln	Dec	853
1781	ARRIVE, Peter AwW	Jersy	Sep	418

1750	ARROSMITH, Jane	Surry	Jny	1
1760	ARROW, otherwise AROW, Ann AwW	Middx	Feb	45
1777	ARROW, Ann	Surry	May	194
1798	ARROW, Elizabeth	Surry	Mch	150
1754	ARROW, James	Middx	Mch	66
1791	ARROW, James, Esq.	Middx	Sep	414
1775	ARROW, John Ser	Pts	Apr	126
1789	ARROW, Rev. John	Sfolk	Aug	417
1784	ARROW, otherwise HARROW, otherwise HORNSBY, Joseph Ser "Ramillies", "Princess Amelia" & "Monarca"	Pts	Aug	453
1756	ARROWSMITH, Benjamin	Berks	Jly	186
1779	ARROWSMITH, Charles	Dorst	Oct	401
1764	ARROWSMITH, Christiana	Lond	May	162
1760	ARROWSMITH, Rev. Edward	Lond	Feb	45
1793	ARROWSMITH, Elisabeth	Surry	Jny	3
1762	ARROWSMITH, Elizabeth	Bucks	Feb	37
1771	ARROWSMITH, Elizabeth	Lond	Nov	428
1791	ARROWSMITH, Elizabeth	Middx	May	208
1799	ARROWSMITH, Elizabeth	Middx	Jny	3
1786	ARROWSMITH, Frances	Middx	May	257
1786	ARROWSMITH, George "Magnanime"&"Active"	Middx	Aug	418
1791	ARROWSMITH, George	Herts	Nov	492
1780	ARROWSMITH, Hannah	Middx	May	233
1794	ARROWSMITH, Henry AwW	Beds	Apr	181
1796	ARROWSMITH, James Ser "Ganges"	Lancs	Dec	590
1754	ARROWSMITH, Jane	Lond	Oct	264
1771	ARROWSMITH, John	Middx	Dec	466
1786	ARROWSMITH, John	Salop		62
1752	ARROWSMITH, Joseph	Nhant	Jne	145
1793	ARROWSMITH, Joseph	Berks	Jly	349
1781	ARROWSMITH, Leybourne Ser	Pts	Oct	459
1781	ARROWSMITH, Noble Ser	Pts	May	221
1774	ARROWSMITH, Robert	Essex	Oct	357
1776	ARROWSMITH, Robert	Lond	Dec	484
1794	ARROWSMITH, Robert	Middx	Jne	294
1765	ARROWSMITH, Sarah	Lond	Feb	40
1790	ARROWSMITH, Sarah	Lond	Oct	450
1759	ARROWSMITH, Stephen	Lond	Oct	317
1774	ARROWSMITH, Susanna AwW W rgd 1756,58	Oxon	Sep	--
1756	ARROWSMITH, Susannah	Oxon	Mch	58
1753	ARROWSMITH, Thomas	Middx	Oct	262
1753	ARROWSMITH, Thomas AwW	Middx	Dec	307
1775	ARROWSMITH, Thomas	Glos	Sep	333
1765	ARROWSMITH, William	Middx	Oct	359
1781	ARROWSMITH, Yerrow	Worcs	Jne	281
1788	ARSCOTT, John, Esq.	Devon	Mch	112
1799	ARSCOTT, Margery	Cumb	Aug	561
1796	ARSCOTT, Thomazin	Corn	Apr	159
1753	ARSKIN, otherwise ERESKINE, otherwise ERSKIN, Philip	Pts	Nov	289
1750	ARSKIN, otherwise ASKINS, William	Pts	Oct	313
1761	ARSLET, Margaret	Middx	Jne	199

1798	ARTELL, James Ser "Suffolk"	Surry	Aug	523
1762	ARTER, William	Pts	Dec	491
1782	ARTERES, otherwise ARTERS, Richard	Pts	Apr	163
1785	ARTERES, otherwise ARTERS, Richard			
	AwW of Gds unadm. W rgd Apr 1782	Pts	Aug	--
1769	ARTERS, Hon Elizabeth	Middx	Jny	2
1782	ARTERS, otherwise ARTERES, Richard	Pts	Apr	163
1785	ARTERS, otherwise ARTERES, Richard			
	AwW of Gds unadm. W rgd Apr 1782	Pts	Aug	--
1765	ARTHER, Hannah	Herts	Dec	438
1757	ARTHER, Nathaniel	Brstl	Apr	108
1757	ARTHER, otherwise AUTHER, Samuel,Ser.AwW	Pts	Nov	319
1757	ARTHER, otherwise BAGNAL, Winifride Mary			
	commonly called Lady Winifride Mary	Middx	Jny	3
1750	ARTHINGTON, Cyril, Esq.	Oxon	Jne	186
1751	ARTHINGTON, Jane	Middx	Jly	197
1779	ARTHINGTON, John	Yorks	Apr	139
1784	ARTHINGTON, Robert	Yorks	Apr	185
1771	ARTHINGTON, Timothy	Surry	Jly	283
1781	ARTHUR, Addis, Esq.	Devon	Jny	2
1760	ARTHUR, Alexander	Pts	Jly	270
1773	ARTHUR, Alexander	Middx	Jly	301
1789	ARTHUR, Anna	Exter	Sep	464
1796	ARTHUR, Archibald MC "Adventure"	Pts	Apr	--
1764	ARTHUR, Catherine AwW	Corn	Feb	36
1783	ARTHUR, Charles	Glos	Dec	596
1800	ARTHUR, Charles, Esq. AwW No ship	Pts	Jne	429
1761	ARTHUR, Christina AwW	Middx	Jly	239
1785	ARTHUR, David, Esq.	Glos	Jly	350
1778	ARTHUR, Deborah	Brstl	May	182
1750	ARTHUR, Elinor	Kent	Oct	313
1757	ARTHUR, Elizabeth	Devon	Apr	108
1796	ARTHUR, Elizabeth	Surry	Jny	2
1783	ARTHUR, George	Pts	May	210
1767	ARTHUR, otherwise AFTHUR, Hannah	Corn	May	161
1794	ARTHUR, Hannah	Middx	Dec	594
1760	ARTHUR, John	Devon	Oct	378
1764	ARTHUR, John	Corn	Jny	1
1764	ARTHUR, John	Middx	Mch	79
1766	ARTHUR, John Ser AwW	Pts	Sep	327
1771	ARTHUR, John	Middx	Dec	467
1772	ARTHUR, John	Bath	Aug	282
1772	ARTHUR, John MC	Middx	Dec	449
1774	ARTHUR, John AwW	Yorks	Aug	289
1783	ARTHUR, John	Pts	Mch	106
1783	ARTHUR, John Ser "Sampson"&"Warspite"	SHant	Apr	158
1788	ARTHUR, John, Esq. (Spec Pr)	Devon	Apr	170
1794	ARTHUR, John	Surry	Jny	2
1797	ARTHUR, John	Middx	Aug	538
1750	ARTHUR, Mainwaring	Yorks	May	134
1755	ARTHUR, Margaret	Surry	Mch	65
1794	ARTHUR, Mary	Bucks	Jly	343
1794	ARTHUR, Mary	Surry	Nov	535

1751	ARTHUR, Robert	Pts	Dec	326
1761	ARTHUR, Robert	Middx	Oct	335
1781	ARTHUR, Robert MC	Middx	Apr	204
1781	ARTHUR, Rogers	Pts	Feb	54
1793	ARTHUR, Samuel	Corn	Jny	1
1799	ARTHUR, Sarah	Berks	Dec	819
1750	ARTHUR, Thomas AwW	Pts	Jly	220
1766	ARTHUR, otherwise ARTHURS, Thomas AwW (by in dec)	Pts	Jly	255
1800	ARTHUR, Thomas	Pts	Feb	80
1774	ARTHUR, Williams	Corn	Nov	384
1781	ARTHUR, William	Pts	Jny	1
1782	ARTHUR, William	Pts	Jny	2
1782	ARTHUR, William	Surry	Apr	161
1798	ARTHUR, William	Middx	May	522
1753	ARTHURE, Benedict, Esq.	Irel	Apr	109
1799	ARTHURS, Francis	Middx	Apr	239
1800	ARTHURS, Sarah	Staff	Jly	499
1766	ARTHURS, otherwise ARTHUR, Thomas AwW (by int dec)	Pts	Jly	255
1760	ARTHURSON, otherwise ATHURSON, otherwise ATTERSON, Benjamin AwW	Pts	Jny	1
1786	ARTIERES, Joseph	Middx	Jny	1
1781	ARTILLACT, Judith Bourigand D' (Ltd Pr)	Pts	Oct	473
1756	ARTIS, Collingwood	Middx	Sep	236
1788	ARTIS, Michael	Middx	Aug	381
1795	ARTLEY, Elizabeth	Surry	Feb	62
1785	ARTUS, Claude	Middx	Aug	400
1798	ARTY, Daniel MC "Tisiphone"	Pts	Jly	499
1800	ARTZ, Mary (Spec Gen Pr)	Surry	Dec	833
1784	ARUDELL, otherwise ARNDELL, otherwise ARUNDELL, Hannah	Durhm	May	244
1778	ARUNDALL, John	Middx	Nov	427
1778	ARUNDALL, otherwise ARUNDELL, John W rgd last month	Middx	Dec	—
1757	ARUNDEL, Rt Hon Anne, Lady Dowager	Wilts	Nov	319
1757	ARUNDEL OF WARDOUR, Rt Hon Lord Henry	Wilts	Jny	2
1763	ARUNDEL, Thomas	Pts	Apr	164
1778	ARUNDEL, Willoughby	Middx	May	182
1757	ARUNDELL, Alexander	Exter	Dec	348
1778	ARUNDELL, Rt Hon Ann	Bath	Oct	386
1763	ARUNDELL, Charles	Pts	Jny	1
1754	ARUNDELL, Elizabeth	Bucks	Aug	217
1767	ARUNDELL, Elizabeth	Corn	Aug	294
1769	ARUNDELL, Rt Hon Lady Frances, commonly called Lady Frances	Yorks	Dec	402
1754	ARUNDELL, Francis	Som	Sep	243
1785	ARUNDELL, Fream	Glos	Jne	288
1789	ARUNDELL, Fream AwW of Gds unadm. W rgd 1785, 288	Glos	Jne	—
1784	ARUNDELL, otherwise ARNDELL, otherwise ARUDELL, Hannah	Durhm	May	244
1776	ARUNDELL, Harriott	Nhant	Dec	504

1774	ARUNDELL, Rt Hon Henry William, Lord			
	Viscount GALLWAY of Kingdom of Irel	Notts	Mch	76
1778	ARUNDELL, John, Esq.	Dorst	Nov	429
1778	ARUNDELL, otherwise ARUNDALL, John			
	W rgd last month	Middx	Dec	--
1784	ARUNDELL, John, Esq.	Som	Apr	186
1798	ARUNDELL, John Lane	Berks	Aug	522
1778	ARUNDELL, Joseph	Berks	May	182
1766	ARUNDELL, Mary	Bucks	Jne	209
1769	ARUNDELL OF WARDOUR, Rt Hon Mary, Lady			
	Dowager	Middx	Mch	74
1772	ARUNDELL, Mary	Bucks	Jny	1
1799	ARUNDELL, Mary	Wilts	Oct	694
1758	ARUNDELL, Hon Richard Esq.	Yorks	Feb	28
1766	ARUNDELL, Richard	Berks	Mch	88
1767	ARUNDELL, Robert, Esq.	Corn	Aug	295
1786	ARUNDELL, Samuel	Glos	May	258
1789	ARUNDELL, Samuel, Esq. AwW	Glos	Apr	186
1781	ARUNDELL, Sarah	Middx	Sep	417
1781	ARUNDELL, Sarah (Dble Pr) W rgd last			
	month	Middx	Oct	--
1752	ARUNDELL, Hon Thomas, Esq.	Middx	Apr	82
1754	ARUNDELL, Thomas, Esq.	Corn	Sep	243
1768	ARUNDELL, Hon Thomas	NSarm	Jly	265
1784	ARUNDELL, Thomas, Esq.	Bath	Apr	186
1774	ARUNDELL, William Ser AwW	Pts	Nov	384
1775	ARUNDELL, William (by int dec)	Pts	Jly	259
1791	ARUNDELL, William	Surry	Sep	415
1779	ARVIN, William	Surry	Apr	139
1762	ARXHOUCK, Johannes VAN	Pts	Apr	178
1751	ARY, Robert	Middx	Nov	298
1795	ARYILL, Charles	Essex	Aug	492
1789	ASAPH, Lord Johnathan SHIPLEY, Rt Rev			
	Father in God, Bishop of ST.		Sep	447
1769	ASAPH, Lord Richard NEWCOME, Rt Rev			
	Father in God, Lord Bishop of ST.	Middx	Jne	226
1769	ASAPH, Lord Richard NEWCOME, Rt Rev			
	Father in God, Lord Bishop of ST.			
	(Dble Pr) W rgd last month	Middx	Jly	--
1790	ASAPH, Lord Samuel, Rt Rev Father in God			
	by Div Perm, Lord Bishop of ST.	Middx	Mch	159
1783	ASBRIDGE, Jeremiah	Middx	May	210
1776	ASBRIDGE, Joseph AwW	Cumb	Aug	342
1785	ASBRIDGE, Margaret NEATE, formerly	Middx	Feb	91
1777	ASBURY, John	Lond	Jne	251
1788	ASBURY, Sarah AwW	Salop	Jne	282
1765	ASBY, George	Pts	Dec	438
1780	ASCHARMAN, otherwise ASHEMAN, John Henry	Middx	Nov	502
1773	ASCHAT, Rt Hon Jan Agges Scholten, Lord of	Pts	Jne	269
1773	ASCHOFF, Margareta VOSDING, formerly			
	(Ltd Pr)	Pts	Oct	410
1759	ASCOON, otherwise ASKING, otherwise			
	ASKEN, John	Pts - SHant	Mch	80

1771	ASCOUGH, otherwise ASOUGH, Attkins	Herts	Jly	282
1793	ASCOUGH, Catherine	Middx	Apr	179
1799	ASCOUGH, George Merrick, Esq.	Lond	Jne	414
1787	ASCOUGH, Thomas	Yorks	Dec	528
1775	ASCROFT, Martha	Essex	Oct	365
1750	ASCROFT, Philip	Pts	Feb	35
1766	ASDON, Aerron AwW	Pts	Jly	255
1783	ASELBY, Thomas	Brstl	Jly	331
1780	ASFORD, Benjamin AwW of Gds twice unadm.			
	W rgd Mch 1776, Last Grant Sep 1777	SHant	Nov	--
1765	ASGILL, Arthur, Esq.	Essex	Jne	205
1788	ASGILL, Sir Charles, Bart.	Middx	Sep	423
1790	ASGILL, Harriot Maria	Middx	May	221
1773	ASGILL, John	Lancr	Apr	144
1772	ASGILL, Margaret	Essex	Feb	33
1790	ASH, Ann AwW	Wark	Mch	115
1771	ASH, Christopher	Yorks	Jly	283
1785	ASH, Dove	Middx	Dec	583
1792	ASH, Faithfull	Som	May	253
1784	ASH, Francis Ser	Kent	Jny	1
1792	ASH, Gregory	Brstl	Feb	--
1768	ASH, Humphrey	Som	Jny	1
1763	ASH, James	Pts	Jly	319
1755	ASH, John	Oxon	Nov	274
1761	ASH, John Ser	Pts	Sep	307
1795	ASH, John	Middx	Jne	360
1783	ASH, Jonathan	Derby	Jly	333
1762	ASH, Joseph	Middx	Jne	230
1764	ASH, Joseph W rgd Jne 1762	Pts	Jny	--
1762	ASH, Malachi	Devon	Dec	491
1785	ASH, Margaret	Kent	Oct	489
1776	ASH, Martha	Middx	Jne	253
1763	ASH, Mary	Middx	Feb	41
1794	ASH, Mary	Middx	Apr	181
1796	ASH, Mary AwW of Gds unadm. W rgd Apr			
	1794	Middx	Oct	--
1758	ASH, Matthew	Pts	May	139
1783	ASH, Paul	Kent	May	211
1771	ASH, Richard	Pts	Mch	91
1785	ASH, Richard	Brstl	Mch	110
1753	ASH, Robert	Herts	Dec	307
1771	ASH, Samuel	Pts	Mch	91
1780	ASH, Samuel, Esq.	Herts	Apr	168
1760	ASH, Silas	Pts	Mch	85
1780	ASH, Thomas	Middx	May	233
1759	ASH, William	Lond	Jne	192
1762	ASH, William	Bucks	Aug	330
1783	ASH, William	Pts	Aug	397
1784	ASH, William	Middx	Apr	185
1769	ASHALD, John	Middx	May	149
1779	ASHAR, John AwW	Surry	Jne	230
1789	ASHBEE, Elizabeth	Kent	Jly	344
1788	ASHBEY, Francis	Yorks	Apr	170

1790	ASHBEY, Samuel	Yorks	Jly	317
1756	ASHBEY, Thomas	Pts	Apr	93
1765	ASHBRIDGE, John	Pts	Jny	2
1781	ASHBRIDGE, Robert	Essex	Jny	2
1759	ASHBROOK, Rt Hon Lady Elizabeth, Viscountess Dowager	Middx	Feb	44
1753	ASHBROOK, Rt Hon Henry, Lord Viscount in Kingdom of Irel		Jne	158
1758	ASHBROOK, Joseph AwW	Pts	Sep	257
1780	ASHBROOK, Rt Hon William, Lord Viscount of Kingdom of Irel	Berks	Oct	458
1779	ASHBURN, Ann	Surry	Nov	441
1774	ASHBURN, Frances	Surry	Dec	418
1786	ASHBURN, Thomas No ship	Pts	Oct	501
1765	ASHBURNER, Dorothy	Lond	Sep	319
1766	ASHBURNER, Elizabeth	Middx	Feb	45
1770	ASHBURNER, Elizabeth	Middx	Mch	86
1754	ASHBURNER, Hannah	Lond	Oct	264
1772	ASHBURNER, John AwW	Pts	Jly	244
1750	ASHBURNER, Thomas	Lond	Mch	66
1775	ASHBURNER, Thomas	Pts	Oct	365
1797	ASHBURNHAM, Rt Rev Father in God, Sir William, Lord Bishop of Chichester	Chich	Oct	624
1783	ASHBURTON, Lord John, Baron of Ashburton in Cty of Devon, formerly DUNNING, John, Esq.	Devon	Sep	442
1789	ASHBY, Alicia	Wark	Jny	2
1766	ASHBY, Ann	Middx	Jly	255
1771	ASHBY, Ann AwW unadm. W rgd 1766, 255	Middx	Oct	--
1784	ASHBY, Ann	Sussx	Jny	1
1785	ASHBY, Anne	Herts	Nov	536
1791	ASHBY, Anne	Herts	Jne	264
1773	ASHBY, Benjamin	Middx	Mch	90
1757	ASHBY, Charles	Herts	May	144
1773	ASHBY, Charles	Essex	Oct	379
1775	ASHBY, Edmund	Nhant	Feb	37
1786	ASHBY, Edmund	Salop	Jny	1
1759	ASHBY, Edward	Herts	Sep	287
1765	ASHBY, Elizabeth	Bath	Feb	40
1796	ASHBY, Elizabeth AwW	Middx	Aug	393
1787	ASHBY, Elizabeth Judith	Nhant	Mch	102
1774	ASHBY, Frances	Kent	Dec	418
1798	ASHBY, Francis, Esq.	Derby	Nov	692
1782	ASHBY, Henry	Nhant	Sep	438
1782	ASHBY, otherwise ECHBACK, Jacob	Lond	Apr	173
1764	ASHBY, Jemina	Leics	Jly	248
1763	ASHBY, John	Middx	Feb	42
1765	ASHBY, John	Essex	Nov	398
1779	ASHBY, John, Esq.	Salop	Mch	85
1793	ASHBY, John	Middx	Mch	124
1795	ASHBY, John	Herts	Oct	579
1795	ASHBY, Joseph	Glos	Jne	361
1753	ASHBY, Judith	Middx	Jny	1

1798	ASHBY, Lydia	Oxon	Feb	74
1754	ASHBY, Mary	Kent	Dec	317
1765	ASHBY, Mary	Herts	Sep	319
1789	ASHBY, Mary	Sussx	May	232
1761	ASHBY, Michael	Pts	Jne	199
1794	ASHBY, Patience	Bucks	Mch	119
1769	ASHBY, Richard	Leics	Apr	110
1792	ASHBY, Richard	Middx	Jne	314
1767	ASHBY, Robert	Middx	Dec	435
1769	ASHBY, Robert, Esq.	Middx	Aug	271
1782	ASHBY, Robert	Surry	Jne	261
1784	ASHBY, Robert	Oxon	Mch	117
1767	ASHBY, Samuel	Middx	Apr	121
1777	ASHBY, Sarah	Middx	Mch	93
1791	ASHBY, Sarah	Middx	Sep	414
1750	ASHBY, Shukbrugh, Esq.	Leics	May	136
1792	ASHBY, Shukbrugh, Esq.	Leics	May	252
1750	ASHBY, Stephen, Esq. AwW unadm. W rgd 1744, 27	Worcs	Nov	--
1752	ASHBY, Stephen	Middx	Nov	267
1767	ASHBY, Stephen, Esq. AwW twice unadm. W rgd 1744, 27, Last Grant Nov 1750	Worcs	Oct	--
1797	ASHBY, Stephen, Esq. AwW of Gds thrice unadm. W rgd 1744,27,Last Grant Oct 1767	Worcs	May	--
1760	ASHBY, Susanna	Beds	**Dec**	**449**
1771	ASHBY, Thomas AwW	Middx	Aug	328
1771	ASHBY, Thomas, Esq.	Middx	Sep	364
1771	ASHBY, Thomas	Beds	Nov	428
1776	ASHBY, Thomas	Middx	Aug	343
1779	ASHBY, Thomas	Bucks	May	185
1780	ASHBY, Thomas	Wark	Jne	299
1797	ASHBY, Thomas	Herts	Jly	468
1762	ASHBY, William	Middx	Jne	230
1780	ASHBY, William	Surry	Mch	118
1788	ASHBY, William	Nhant	Sep	424
1800	ASHBY, William	Surry	Jne	431
1773	ASHCROFT, Easter	Beds	Sep	350
1757	ASHCROFT, Elizabeth	Surry	Apr	108
1782	ASHCROFT, Margaret, formerly ANDREWS, Margaret	Norf	Jly	333
1761	ASHCROFT, Nicholas AwW	Pts	Jne	199
1768	ASHCROFT, Rev. Thomas	Camb	Mch	93
1787	ASHCROFT, otherwise STEEL, Thomas	Surry	Dec	527
1772	ASHDOWN, David	Kent	Oct	347
1800	ASHDOWN, Henry	Surry	May	335
1794	ASHDOWN, Mary	Middx	Jny	2
1751	ASHDOWN, Susanna	Kent	Nov	298
1793	ASHDOWN, Thomas	Kent	Apr	180
1764	ASHDOWN, William	Kent	Sep	335
1765	ASHDOWNE, John	Lond	Mch	84
1793	ASHDOWNE, John	Kent	Jny	1
1773	ASHDOWNE, Sarah	Kent	Oct	379
1754	ASHDOWNE, William	Kent	Jly	187

```
1794   ASHE, Ann                                           Middx Jny    1
1776   ASHE, Bridget    AwW                                 Middx Nov 447
1782   ASHE, Bridget    AwW of Gds unadm.
       W rgd 1776, 447                                      Middx Jne   --
1770   ASHE, Dulcibella                                     Middx Jne  218
1756   ASHE, Edward, Esq.   Ltd AwW unadm.
       W rgd 1748, 169                                      Wilts Mch   --
1750   ASHE, Elizabeth                                      Middx Jny    1
1763   ASHE, Frances                                        Nhant Feb   41
1771   ASHE, Isaac, Esq.                                    Middx Jny    1
1754   ASHE, John  AwW unadm.  W rgd 1721,194               Middx Apr   97
1781   ASHE, John                                           Middx Jny    2
1799   ASHE, John                                           Middx Oct  693
1770   ASHE, Metcalfe                                       Kent  Sep  319
1769   ASHE, Pierce A'COURT, Esq.   (sent)                  Wilts Feb   32
1774   ASHE, Rev. Robert                                    Wilts Feb   36
1780   ASHE, Rev. Robert                                    Shant Jly  345
1769   ASHE, William                          Pts - Devon Nov  364
1781   ASHE, William A'COURT, Esq. General of
       H.M.Forces                                           Wilts Aug  374
1780   ASHEMAN, otherwise ASCHARMAN, John Henry Middx Nov 502
1764   ASHENDEN, James                                      Lond  Dec  452
1768   ASHENHURST, Hannah                                   Middx Aug  305
1800   ASHER, formerly LEVY, otherwise HART,
       Esther, otherwise Hester, formerly
       (Spec Pr)                                            Middx May  372
1790   ASHETON, Rev. Edmund    AwW                          Glos  Oct  450
1767   ASHFEILD, Thomas                                     Worcs Jne  204
1797   ASHFIELD, James                                      Norf  Apr  220
1795   ASHFORD, Amos                                        Som   Jly  428
1784   ASHFORD, Edward                                      Kent  Oct  535
1777   ASHFORD, John                                        Kent  Jny    1
1783   ASHFORD, Joseph                                      Pts   Feb   56
1787   ASHFORD, Mary                                        Exter Feb   51
1795   ASHFORD, Mary                                        SHant Apr  233
1786   ASHFORD, Richard                                     Devon Nov  552
1757   ASHFORD, Samuel                                      Pts   Feb   37
1794   ASHFORD, Thomas    AwW                               Wark  Jly  468
1800   ASHFORD, Thomas                                      Lond  Oct  696
1780   ASHFORD, William    Ser                              Devon Sep  426
1768   ASHFORDBY, Ann                                       Middx Jny    1
1774   ASHFORDBY, Frances                                   Herts Apr  125
1778   ASHFORDBY, John, Esq.                                Wilts Nov  427
1754   ASHFORTH, Joseph                                     Middx Jne  157
1788   ASHHURST, Diana                                      Oxon  Jny    1
1796   ASHHURST, Diana                                      Oxon  Oct  485
1773   ASHHURST, Elizabeth                                  Middx May  190
1784   ASHHURST, Frances                                    Pts   Dec  627
1782   ASHHURST, Harriot                                    Middx Jly  333
1784   ASHHURST, Harry                                      Middx Jny    1
1792   ASHHURST, John                                       Middx Jne  313
1753   ASHHURST, Sarah                                      Middx Jne  158
1782   ASHHURST, Sarah                                      Middx Dec  569
```

```
1753   ASHHURST, Samuel, Esq.                        Middx Nov 284
1765   ASHHURST, Thomas                              Essex May 168
1777   ASHHURST, Thomas (Dble Pr) W rgd 1765,168 Essex Apr  --
1773   ASHHURST, William Prichard, Esq.             Herts Jne 233
1791   ASHHURST, William Prichard  AwW of Gds
         unadm. W rgd 1773, 233                      Herts Jne  --
1798   ASHILL, Thomas  AwW                           Nwich Jly 456
1751   ASHILLE, Philip                               Pts   Jne 164
1785   ASHINGTON, Edward "Rattlesnake", "Bristol"
         "Superb" & "Sultan"                         Pts   Oct 489
1796   ASHINGTON, Elizabeth                          Middx Mch 106
1793   ASHINGTON, Thomas                             Middx Jly 349
1788   ASHLE, otherwise ASHLEE, Elizabeth            Bucks Jny   1
1782   ASHLEE, Edward                                Middx Jne 262
1788   ASHLEE, otherwise ASHLE, Elizabeth            Bucks Jny   1
1763   ASHLETT, otherwise ASLETT, Edward             Pts   Aug 367
1773   ASHLETT, James                                Middx Jny   1
1771   ASHLETT, Richard                              Essex May 191
1776   ASHLETT, Sarah                                Essex Mch 108
1783   ASHLEY, Amos, otherwise Emos                  Pts   Aug 398
1754   ASHLEY, Ann                                   Lond  Nov 291
1775   ASHLEY, Charles                               Middx Oct 365
1788   ASHLEY, Daniel                                Middx May 224
1764   ASHLEY, Edward                                Pts   Apr 129
1754   ASHLEY, Elizabeth                             Middx Nov 291
1783   ASHLEY, Elizabeth                             Middx Aug 397
1794   ASHLEY, Elizabeth                             Surry Mch 120
1783   ASHLEY, Emos, otherwise Amos                  Pts   Aug 398
1790   ASHLEY, George                                Wilts Mch 114
1800   ASHLEY, George                                Middx Mch 171
1776   ASHLEY, Hannah                                Middx Feb  48
1757   ASHLEY, Isaac, Esq.                           Nhant Apr 108
1762   ASHLEY, James  AwW                            Pts   Jne 230
1771   ASHLEY, James                                 Middx Nov 428
1776   ASHLEY, James                                 Lond  Jly 295
1785   ASHLEY, James                                 Middx Mch 110
1795   ASHLEY, James                                 Middx Jne 361
1784   ASHLEY, Jane                                  Nhant Jne 303
1751   ASHLEY, John, Esq.             Pts -         Kent  Oct 273
1759   ASHLEY, John                                  Berks Dec 381
1760   ASHLEY, John  AwW of Gds unadm. First
         Grant Dec last                              Berks May  --
1761   ASHLEY, John, Esq.                            Nhant Sep 307
1770   ASHLEY, John                                  Lond  Apr 128
1779   ASHLEY, John                                  Middx Oct 401
1785   ASHLEY, otherwise ASHLY, John  Ser
         "Europe", "Antelope" & "Janus"              Pts   Nov 536
1799   ASHLEY, John, Esq,                            Berks Jny   3
1798   ASHLEY, Joseph                                Nhant Aug 523
1769   ASHLEY, Joyce  AwW                            Lond  May 150
1756   ASHLEY, Mary                                  Middx Mch  58
1758   ASHLEY, Mary                                  Nhant Dec 354
1772   ASHLEY, Mary                                  Middx Oct 346
```

1763	ASHLEY, Peter		Middx May	210
1788	ASHLEY, Phebe		Lond Oct	468
1795	ASHLEY, Philip		Lincs Jny	1
1789	ASHLEY, Rachel		Middx Jly	343
1750	ASHLEY, Richard		Middx Jly	220
1766	ASHLEY, Richard		Middx Jne	209
1767	ASHLEY, Richard		Middx Jny	1
1780	ASHLEY, Richard		Lond Apr	168
1784	ASHLEY, Richard		Middx Feb	59
1761	ASHLEY, Robert		Kent Oct	335
1775	ASHLEY, Solomon, Esq.		Middx Feb	38
1775	ASHLEY, Stephen		Essex May	168
1783	ASHLEY, Susanna		Hunts May	210
1780	ASHLEY, Susannah		Middx Jly	345
1764	ASHLEY, Thomas		Surry Feb	36
1771	ASHLEY, Thomas		Middx Aug	328
1751	ASHLEY, Walter		Middx Mch	70
1756	ASHLEY, William		Lond Oct	266
1760	ASHLEY, William		Middx Dec	449
1771	ASHLEY, William	Pts -	Devon Aug	328
1779	ASHLEY, William		Pts Sep	364
1782	ASHLEY, William		Surry Jly	334
1792	ASHLEY, William		Surry Feb	53
1791	ASHLEYE, Arabella		Middx Aug	370
1784	ASHLIN, John Ser "Pondicherry"		Middx Jne	302
1765	ASHLIN, Sarah		Kent Mch	83
1767	ASHLIN, William		Middx Nov	399
1762	ASHLING, Dorothy		Lincs Sep	365
1750	ASHLING, Richard		Lincs May	135
1785	ASHLY, otherwise ASHLEY, John Ser "Europa","Antelope" & "Janus"		Pts Nov	536
1784	ASHLY, Mary		Kent Apr	186
1786	ASHLY, otherwise FIELDER, Michael "Princess Amelia","Berwick"&"Latona"		Pts Oct	--
1778	ASHLYNG, Mary		Lond Dec	474
1758	ASHMALL, Robert, Esq.		Middx Nov	319
1767	ASHMAN, Ann		Lond Apr	121
1761	ASHMAN, Christopher		Jne	199
1751	ASHMAN, James		Pts Feb	34
1772	ASHMAN, James		Middx Oct	346
1765	ASHMAN, John		Middx May	167
1758	ASHMAN, William AwW unadm. W rgd 1737,48		Middx May	--
1771	ASHMEAD, Thomas		Glos Oct	**395**
1775	ASHMEADE, John		Brstl Jly	259
1789	ASHMOOR, Charles		Middx Dec	572
1784	ASHMORE, Ann		Middx Oct	534
1775	ASHMORE, Henry		Worcs Nov	400
1759	ASHMORE, James		Middx Dec	381
1765	ASHMORE, John Ser	Pts -	Lond Sep	319
1766	ASHMORE, John		Pts Jne	210
1778	ASHMORE, John		Middx Jny	1
1766	ASHMORE, Peter		Middx Sep	327
1787	ASHMORE, Thomas		Middx Aug	353

1765	ASHMORE, William			Surry	Apr	127
1798	ASHPINSHAW, John			Middx	Oct	631
1800	ASHREN, Richard			Lincs	Jly	499
1770	ASHTON, Ann			Middx	Aug	283
1766	ASHTON, Christopher			Hunts	Dec	440
1780	ASHTON, Dorothy			Middx	Feb	53
1799	ASHTON, Dorothy AwW of Gds unadm. W rgd 1780, 53			Middx	Mch	--
1764	ASHTON, Edmund			Lond	Jly	248
1775	ASHTON, Edmund			Middx	Jne	217
1779	ASHTON, Elizabeth			NBrit	Dec	483
1799	ASHTON, Elizabeth AwW			Middx	Apr	239
1750	ASHTON, Frances 6th Pr	W rgd	1727, 283	Lond	May	134
1754	ASHTON, Frances 7th Pr	W rgd	1727, 283	Lond	Jny	1
1769	ASHTON, Frances 8th Pr	W rgd	1727, 283	Lond	Aug	272
1770	ASHTON, Frances 9th Pr	W rgd	1727, 283	Lond	Aug	283
1773	ASHTON, Frances 10th Pr	W rgd	1727, 283	Lond	Nov	413
1780	ASHTON, Frances 11th Pr	W rgd	1727, 283	Lond	Nov	--
1782	ASHTON, Frances 12th Pr	W rgd	1727, 283	Lond	Sep	438
1785	ASHTON, Frances 13th Pr	W rgd	1727, 283	Lond	Oct	489
1792	ASHTON, Frances 14th Pr	W rgd	1727, 283	Lond	Sep	459
1793	ASHTON, Frances 15th Pr	W rgd	1727, 283	Lond	Nov	537
1788	ASHTON, George			Kent	Jne	281
1793	ASHTON, George			Middx	Jne	296
1776	ASHTON, Henry, Esq. AwW unadm. W rgd 1731, 221			Middx	Jly	--
1777	ASHTON, Isaac			Yorks	Dec	495
1762	ASHTON, James			SHant	Nov	444
1763	ASHTON, James			Surry	May	210
1763	ASHTON, James			Nhant	Sep	416
1790	ASHTON, Rev. James			Oxon	Apr	169
1780	ASHTON, Jane			Middx	Apr	169
1798	ASHTON, Jane			Sussx	Dec	455
1765	ASHTON, John			Middx	Mch	83
1768	ASHTON, John, Esq.			Surry	Apr	138
1779	ASHTON, John			Chest	Sep	364
1784	ASHTON, John			Middx	Apr	186
1798	ASHTON, John			Middx	Feb	74
1799	ASHTON, John			Herts	Jne	413
1758	ASHTON, Joseph			Middx	Jly	207
1789	ASHTON, otherwise AISHTON, Joseph			Som	May	232
1751	ASHTON, Mary			Lond	Jny	1
1750	ASHTON, Rebecca			Lond	Nov	345
1768	ASHTON, Richard			Middx	Apr	138
1799	ASHTON, Richard			Essex	Nov	756
1800	ASHTON, Richard			Middx	Jny	2
1782	ASHTON, Sarah			Middx	Jly	334
1764	ASHTON, Rev. Stephen			Lincs	Feb	36
1766	ASHTON, Stephen			Kent	Oct	360
1751	ASHTON, Thomas			Middx	Jne	164
1775	ASHTON, Rev. Dr. Thomas, D.D.			Lond	Mch	81
1773	ASHTON, Weston			Middx	Mch	89
1786	ASHTON, Wilkinson No ship			Pts	Jly	360

1764	ASHTON, William	Middx	Apr	128
1775	ASHTON, William	Middx	Sep	332
1799	ASHTON, William	Middx	Aug	561
1786	ASHURST, Elizabeth	Middx	Mch	135
1753	ASHURST, Judith	Derby	Apr	100
1755	ASHURST, Sarah	Lond	Apr	92
1786	ASHWEEK, Melleora AwW	Devon	May	257
1773	ASHWELL, Agnes	Beds	Mch	90
1793	ASHWELL, Benjamin	Bucks	Jny	2
1762	ASHWELL, Edward	Herts	Nov	444
1795	ASHWELL, Edward, Esq.	Beds	Apr	232
1755	ASHWELL, Hannah	Glos	Dec	303
1753	ASHWELL, James	Beds	Jly	192
1792	ASHWELL, James, Esq.	Essex	Aug	413
1763	ASHWELL, John	Middx	Mch	103
1768	ASHWELL, John	Middx	Sep	336
1774	ASHWELL, Martha	Herts	Oct	357
1777	ASHWELL, Thomas	Herts	Jny	2
1786	ASHWELL, William	Essex	Dec	597
1758	ASHWIN, Richard	Glos	Dec	354
1772	ASHWIN, Richard	Worcs	Jne	203
1791	ASHWIN, Richard AwW of Gds unadm. W rgd 1758, 354	Glos	Nov	—
1766	ASHWIN, Sarah	Glos	Dec	439
1764	ASHWOOD, Benjamin	Salop	Jne	209
1779	ASHWOOD, Charles	Lond	Jny	1
1783	ASHWOOD, Dorothy	Salop	Jne	277
1790	ASHWOOD, Mary	Surry	May	221
1772	ASHWOOD, Thomas Porter	Salop	Jly	243
1753	ASHWOOD, William AwW of Gds unadm. W rgd 1740, 59	Salop	Mch	—
1783	ASHWORTH, otherwise ASTWORTH, otherwise STRANDING, Abraham Ser AwW	Pts	Jny	—
1766	ASHWORTH, Ann	Kent	Jly	255
1776	ASHWORTH, Rev. Dr. Caleb, D.D.	Nhant	Jny	1
1790	ASHWORTH, Carolina	Glos	Feb	55
1762	ASHWORTH, Edward	Lond	Feb	37
1783	ASHWORTH, Henry	Shant	Jly	331
1759	ASHWORTH, James	Pts	Oct	316
1781	ASHWORTH, James Ser	Surry	Jny	1
1786	ASHWORTH, John	Nhant	Mch	135
1788	ASHWORTH, John E.I.S."Rose"	Pts	Jly	335
1768	ASHWORTH, Sarah	Lond	Jly	266
1790	ASHWORTH, Thomas	Pts – Mon	Jny	1
1779	ASKE, Thomas Ser	Middx	Dec	483
1775	ASKELL, Michael AwW unadm. W rgd 1697,195	Wark	Nov	—
1775	ASKELL, Susanna AwW unadm. W rgd 1700, 94	Wark	Nov	—
1759	ASKEN, otherwise ASCOON, otherwise ASKING, John	Pts – SHant	Mch	80
1775	ASKEW, Dr. Adam Dr of Physick	Newcl	Jne	216
1791	ASKEW, Rev. Adam	Essex	Mch	108
1774	ASKEW, Dr. Anthony Dr of Physick	Middx	Mch	76
1771	ASKEW, Elizabeth	Middx	Jly	282

1783	ASKEW, Ferdinando, Esq.		Wilts	May	211
1784	ASKEW, Ferdinando, Esq. AwW unadm. W rgd May 1783		Wilts	Apr	--
1800	ASKEW, George		Middx	Oct	696
1796	ASKEW, Henry, Esq.		Durhm	Apr	158
1789	ASKEW, Leonard		Lond	Sep	447
1795	ASKEW, Mary		Kent	Nov	620
1760	ASKEW, Millicent		Surry	Dec	449
1753	ASKEW, John		Pts	Jly	193
1753	ASKEW, John AwW (by int dec)		Pts	Aug	222
1773	ASKEW, John		Essex	Oct	379
1784	ASKEW, John "Warwick" & "St.Albans"		Pts	Jny	1
1770	ASKEW, Richard		Essex	Mch	84
1755	ASKEW, otherwise ASKEY, Robert	.	Som	Feb	31
1756	ASKEW, Robert		Middx	Jne	156
1769	ASKEW, Robert		Middx	Feb	32
1771	ASKEW, Sarah		Essex	Dec	466
1781	ASKEW, Thomas		Lond	Oct	459
1782	**ASKEY**, Ann		Berks	Aug	390
1792	ASKEY, Henry		Middx	Mch	124
1755	ASKEY, otherwise ASKEW, Robert		Som	Feb	31
1793	ASKEY, Robert		Som	Nov	537
1784	AS**K**HAM, Ann		Camb	Mch	118
1781	ASKHAM, Dingley, Esq.		Camb	May	221
1783	ASKHAM, Frances		Camb	Apr	158
1792	ASKHAM, Thomas		Yorks	Mch	126
1773	ASKIN, John		Pts	Jny	2
1780	ASKIN, John		Pts	Apr	169
1759	ASKING, otherwise ASKEN, otherwise ASCOON, John	Pts -	SHant	Mch	80
1763	ASKINGS, otherwise ERESKINE, John AwW		Pts	May	212
1750	ASKINS, otherwise ARSKIN, William		Pts	Oct	313
1759	ASKQUETH, Obedience AwW		Middx	Jny	1
1783	ASKREN, Mary		Middx	Nov	548
1766	ASKY, Rev. Francis, D.D.		Beds	Nov	395
1797	ASLAM, otherwise ASYLAM, John 8th & 15th Regt.		Pts	Jne	394
1787	ASLAT, Richard		Middx	Aug	353
1786	ASLETT, Ann		SHant	Jny	2
1763	ASLETT, otherwise ASHLETT, Edward		Pts	Aug	367
1786	**ASLETT**, James		Middx	Jne	318
1792	**ASLETT**, John		SHant	Apr	189
1800	ASLETT, Sarah		Sussx	Dec	833
1783	ASLEY, Elizabeth AwW unadm. W rgd Aug last		Middx	Oct	--
1756	ASLIN, Robert		Pts	Jny	1
1782	ASLOTT, Susanna		Lond	Aug	390
1784	ASLOTT, Thomas		Kent	Oct	534
1753	ASLOTT, William		Pts	Jly	192
1771	ASOUGH, otherwise ASCOUGH, Attkins		Herts	Jly	282
1771	ASP, Daniel		Middx	Jly	282
1768	ASP, Samuel		Pts	Mch	93
1760	**ASPEGREEN**, John, otherwise ASPEGREN, Johan Laurents		Pts	May	180

1760	ASPEGREN, Johan Laurents, otherwise ASPEGREEN, John		Pts	May	180
1789	ASPELL, otherwise HOSPILL, John Anor grant Feb last		Pts	Jny	--
1780	ASPENALL, otherwise ASPENELL, William Ser		Pts	Nov	502
1781	ASPENALL, otherwise ASPENELL, William W rgd Nov last		Pts	Aug	--
1780	ASPENELL, otherwise ASPENALL, William Ser		Pts	Nov	502
1781	ASPENELL, otherwise ASPENALL, William W rgd Nov last		Pts	Aug	--
1773	ASPEREN and LANGERAK, Hon Philip Jacob Grave VAN DEN BOETZELAER, Baron, otherwise ASPEREN, Philip Jacob, Earl of BOETZELAER, Baron of		Pts	Jne	271
1763	ASPEY, otherwise ESPY, David		Pts	Nov	493
1754	ASPILLIN, William		Middx	Feb	31
1769	ASPIN, Ann		Sfolk	Aug	271
1764	ASPIN, Christopher		Pts	Jly	248
1764	ASPIN, Dorothy		Sfolk	Apr	128
1791	ASPIN, Rev. Harvey		Sfolk	Jne	263
1753	ASPIN, Israel		Kent	May	126
1782	ASPINAL, Francis		Lond	Oct	478
1800	ASPINAL, Thomas AwW Ser "Trident"		Pts	Mch	172
1785	ASPINALL, Alexander		Lond	Feb	61
1754	ASPINALL, Ann		Middx	Jny	2
1779	ASPINALL, Ann		SHant	Jly	283
1792	ASPINALL, Humphrey		Middx	Mch	124
1764	ASPINALL, James		Middx	Nov	413
1756	ASPINALL, John		Middx	Feb	26
1759	ASPINALL, John		Middx	Mch	80
1784	ASPINALL, John		Middx	Apr	186
1785	ASPINALL, John, Esq.		Lancs	Sep	452
1785	ASPINALL, John 100 Regt		Pts	Oct	489
1772	ASPINALL, Mary		Middx	Feb	35
1770	ASPINALL, Sarah		Herts	Mch	85
1771	ASPINALL, Stanhope AwW	Pts –	Middx	May	191
1789	ASPINWALL, Catherine		Middx	Jne	297
1758	ASPINWALL, John		Lond	Mch	61
1766	ASPITALL, William		Pts	Aug	290
1754	ASPLEY, Anne		Lond	Oct	264
1758	ASPLEY, Frances		Lond	Apr	99
1799	ASPLIN, Francis		Essex	Jne	413
1758	ASPLIN, Rev. William		Glos	Jne	175
1773	ASPLOM, otherwise ABSOLON, Richard		Berks	Oct	379
1760	ASPRAY, Thomas		Bucks	Jly	270
1800	ASPRAY, Thomas AwW No ship		Pts	Jly	501
1798	ASPRY, John AwW		Lond	Jly	456
1792	ASQUITH, Amos		Surry	Apr	189
1789	ASQUITH, Christopher		Middx	Jly	343
1790	ASQUITH, David		Surry	May	221
1764	ASQUITH, Sarah		Lond	Mch	78

1777	ASSBRIDGE, Betty	Middx	Jly	296
1762	ASSCHENBERG, Abraham (Ltd Pr)	Pts	Jly	282
1773	ASSCHENBERGH, formerly LAM, Maesken	Pts	Jly	276
1766	ASSELIN, Susanna	Middx	Apr	125
1773	ASSELIN, Susanna (Dble Pr) W rgd 1766,125	Middx	Jly	--
1751	ASSELT, Gerrit VAN	Middx	Oct	295
1794	ASSENBORGH, Adriaan VAN	Pts	Nov	--
1756	ASSENBORGH, Louis (Ltd Pr)	Pts	Jny	1
1771	ASSENDELFT, Adriana Christina VAN, formerly VAN HOEY (Ltd Pr)	Pts	Feb	87
1784	ASSENDELFT, Rt Hon Barthout Adriaan VAN (Ltd Pr)	Pts	Oct	579
1751	ASSENDELFT, Rt Hon Daniel Pompeus VAN (Ltd Pr)	Pts	Jly	225
1786	ASSENDELFT, Elizabeth VAN, otherwise CAROLINA, Elizabeth, otherwise VAN DER STRATEN, Elizabeth, formerly (Ltd Pr)	Pts	Oct	--
1760	ASSENDELFT, Gerard VAN	Pts	May	221
1788	ASSENDELFT, Gerard VAN (Ltd Pr)	Pts	Jly	375
1782	ASSENDELFT, Isaac VAN	Essex	Mch	156
1752	ASSENDELFT, Jacob VAN (Ltd Pr)	Pts	Apr	110
1766	ASSENDELFT, Jacob Adriaan VAN, Esq.	Pts	May	204
1756	ASSENDELFT, The Worshipful Jean Deutz VAN, Lord of Assendelft and Van Assumburg, Lord of Heemskerk and Meesterknaap Van Brederode AwW	Pts	Apr	94
1776	ASSENDELFT, Johan VAN AwW	Pts	May	249
1763	ASSENDELFT NENOORT, Lord of Hey, Otto Jan Willem DU FAGET D' (Ltd Pr)	Pts	Apr	163
1756	ASSER, Edmund	Middx	Jly	186
1760	ASSER, Isaac	Kent	Jly	270
1798	ASSEY, John	Sfolk	Apr	231
1781	ASSHETON, Elizabeth	Glos	Nov	510
1773	ASSHETON, Harriet AwW	Lancs	Feb	42
1800	ASSHETON, Dr. Richard, D.D.	Lancs	Nov	760
1774	ASSHETON SMITH, Thomas, Esq.	Chest	May	166
1788	ASSHETON, Thomas	Lond	Dec	572
1788	ASSIRE, Benjamin	Middx	Apr	171
1753	ASSIZE, David	Middx	Feb	37
1779	ASTBURY, Thomas	Pts	Mch	86
1789	ASTBURY, Rev. Thomas	Worcs	Dec	571
1769	ASTELEY, Rev. William	Derby	May	149
1758	ASTELL, Ann	Surry	Jly	207
1793	ASTELL, Ann	Leics	Jne	296
1762	ASTELL, Edward	Nhant	Jny	1
1771	ASTELL, John	Leics	Oct	395
1777	ASTELL, Richard	Hunts	Feb	49
1789	ASTEN, Johannes Josephus VAN (Ltd Pr)	Pts	Jly	407
1773	ASTEN, Maria Theresia Catharina VAN formerly DE MENLENAER (Ltd Pr)	Pts	Jny	37
1761	ASTERLEY, David	Surry	Jne	199
1772	ASTERLEY, John	Salop	Jne	203
1771	ASTERLEY, Mary	Middx	Mch	91

1770	ASTEROTH, John	Middx	Nov	387
1761	ASTEY, Ambrose, Esq.	Herts	Nov	378
1750	ASTEY, Thomas	Middx	Dec	376
1785	ASTEY, Thomas No ship	Pts	Sep	451
1775	ASTHAY, otherwise ASTHY, Samuel AwW	Guery	Oct	365
1775	ASTHY, otherwise ASTHAY, Samuel AwW	Guery	Oct	365
1779	ASTIE, Mary	Middx	Dec	483
1795	ASTIE, Peter	Middx	Jny	1
1796	ASTIE, Richard	Lond	Dec	591
1771	ASTILL, Benjamin	Middx	Jny	1
1757	ASTILL, Charles	Surry	Apr	108
1763	ASTILL, William	Oxon	Jly	320
1768	ASTIN, Mary	Berks	Mch	94
1763	ASTLE, John	Herts	Sep	416
1762	ASTLE, Joseph	Beds	Dec	491
1785	ASTLE, Robert	Leics	Aug	400
1757	ASTLE, Sarah	Beds	Apr	109
1777	ASTLES, George	Middx	Sep	374
1761	ASTLEY, Abraham	Middx	May	158
1757	ASTLEY, Ann	Herts	Nov	319
1752	ASTLEY, Anne AwW of Gds unadm. W rgd 1733, 304	Lincs	Mch	--
1753	ASTLEY, Anne AwW of Gds twice unadm. W rgd 1733,304, Last grant Mch 1752	Lincs	Apr	--
1795	ASTLEY, Anne	Bath	Jne	361
1788	ASTLEY, Rev. Bernard	Norf	Dec	572
1766	ASTLEY, Rev. Edward	Glos	May	166
1768	ASTLEY, Elizabeth	Salop	Jly	266
1760	ASTLEY, Sir Jacob	Norf	Jny	1
1790	ASTLEY, James	Middx	Apr	168
1789	ASTLEY, Jane	Staff	Jly	343
1772	ASTLEY, Sir John, Bart.	Wilts	Feb	34
1783	ASTLEY, John	Worcs	Mch	106
1788	ASTLEY, John, Esq.	Chest	Feb	53
1795	ASTLEY, John	Middx	Apr	233
1773	ASTLEY, Lydia	Lond	Dec	456
1756	ASTLEY, Mary	Oxon	Nov	287
1779	ASTLEY, Richard, Esq.	Middx	Feb	36
1781	ASTLEY, Richard	Surry	Jny	1
1764	ASTLEY, Dame Sarah	Bath	Sep	335
1756	ASTLEY, Thomas	Middx	Oct	236
1759	ASTLEY, Thomas	Middx	Apr	115
1753	ASTLING, Samuel Boren	Middx	Mch	69
1752	ASTON, Abraham	Pts	May	116
1753	ASTON, Ann	Wark	Jly	193
1762	ASTON, Ann	Middx	Aug	330
1751	ASTON, Anne	Middx	Aug	228
1769	ASTON, Hon Catherine AwW	Chest	Feb	31
1762	ASTON, Edward	Staff	Apr	136
1780	ASTON, Edward	Som	Nov	502
1793	ASTON, Edward	Middx	Jny	1
1756	ASTON, Elizabeth	Bath	Apr	93
1781	ASTON, Elizabeth	Som	Jne	282

1786	ASTON, Elizabeth	Lichd	Jny	1
1800	ASTON, Elizabeth	Middx	Jny	2
1785	ASTON, Henry, Esq.	Chest	Sep	451
1799	ASTON, Henry Hervey, Esq.	Pts	Nov	755
1751	ASTON, Rt Hon Lord James, Baron of Forfar in NBrit	Staff	Dec	325
1753	ASTON, John AwW of Gds unadm. W rgd 1738, 168	Middx	Mch	--
1755	ASTON, John AwW twice unadm. W rgd 1738, 168 Last grant Mch 1753	Middx	Mch	--
1752	ASTON, Dame Katherine	Chest	May	115
1789	ASTON, Mary	Bucks	Sep	447
1774	ASTON, Matthew	Sfolk	Mch	76
1789	ASTON, Matthew AwW of Gds unadm. W rgd 1774, 76	Sfolk	Apr	--
1794	ASTON, Matthew	Brstl	Feb	59
1778	ASTON, Sir Richard (One of Justices of H.M.Court of King's Bench)	Middx	Mch	93
1796	ASTON, Richmond, Esq.	Staff	May	231
1754	ASTON, Thomas	Staff	Nov	291
1756	ASTON, Thomas	Wark	Oct	236
1780	ASTON, Thomas	Wark	Feb	53
1769	ASTON, William, Esq.	Middx	Feb	32
1800	ASTON, William AwW	Herfd	Jne	430
1778	ASTREY, Mary	Oxon	Jny	1
1768	ASTREY, Robert	Oxon	Jly	266
1760	ASTRY, Ann	Middx	Jne	225
1754	ASTRY, Francis	Oxon	Jne	157
1757	ASTRY, Susanna	Middx	Feb	37
1789	ASTWOOD, Mary	Middx	Feb	70
1783	ASTWORTH, otherwise STRANDING, otherwise ASHWORTH, Abraham Ser AwW	Pts	Jny	--
1753	ASTY, Elizabeth	Herts	Jne	159
1763	ASTY, Elizabeth	Herts	Dec	537
1784	ASTY, Hannah	Lond	Feb	59
1775	ASTY, John	Sussx	Nov	399
1774	ASWELL, Thomas AwW	Kent	Jny	1
1797	ASYLAM, otherwise ASLAM, John 8th & 15th Regt	Pts	Jne	394
1789	ATCHELER, James	Middx	Aug	417
1756	ATCHERLEY, Elizabeth	Salop	Mch	58
1796	ATCHERLEY, Elizabeth AwW of Gds unadm. W regd 1756, 58	Salop	Apr	--
1777	ATCHERLEY, John	Glos	Aug	339
1750	ATCHERLEY, Richard	Salop	Oct	313
1796	ATCHERLEY, Richard AwW of Gds unadm. W rgd 1750, 313	Salop	Apr	--
1762	ATCHISON, Andrew	Middx	May	182
1760	ATCHISON, David	Nhant	Mch	85
1785	ATCHISON, David	Nhant	Feb	61
1773	ATCHISON, Elizabeth	Middx	Nov	413
1759	ATCHISON, James	Dorst	Jne	191
1800	ATCHISON, James	Dorst	Apr	251

1751	ATCHISON, John		Lond	Oct	273
1771	ATCHISON, John		Bucks	May	191
1773	ATCHISON, John	Pts —	Middx	Aug	318
1766	ATCHISON, Mary		Middx	Jne	209
1761	ATCHISON, William AwW Ser		Pts	Nov	378
1799	ATCHLEY, William		Middx	Apr	240
1767	ATFIELD, Edmund		Surry	Oct	360
1791	ATFIELD, John		Surry	Dec	552
1793	ATFIELD, John		Surry	Jny	1
1794	ATHAWES, Dawson		Kent	Dec	594
1767	ATHAWES, Edward, Esq. AwW		Lond	Nov	399
1796	ATHAWES, Edward, Esq.		Lond	May	233
1787	ATHAWES, Joseph		Kent	Feb	51
1794	ATHAWES, Mary		Surry	Aug	402
1758	ATHAWES, Samuel		Kent	Jny	1
1764	ATHAWES, Thomas		Lond	Aug	295
1772	ATHAY, Samuel		Som	Jny	1
1759	ATHER, Ann		Surry	Dec	381
1784	ATHERDEN, Edward		Kent	Mch	117
1793	ATHERFOLD, Ann		Kent	Mch	125
1763	ATHERFOLD, Edward		Kent	Oct	457
1762	ATHERFOLD, John		Kent	May	182
1776	ATHERFOLD, Thomas		Surry	Feb	47
1800	ATHERFOLD, Thomas		Kent	Jny	3
1766	ATHERFOLD, William		Middx	Mch	88
1784	ATHERIDGE, Hester Katharine		Middx	May	244
1775	ATHERIDGE, Richard		Surry	Nov	401
1768	ATHERIDGE, William		Middx	Mch	93
1769	ATHERLEY, Arthur AwW of Gds unadm. W rgd 1742, 112		SHant	Aug	——
1795	ATHERLEY, Arthur AwW of Gds twice unadm. W rgd 1742, 142 Last grant Aug 1769		SHant	May	——
1767	ATHERLEY, Richard		NSarm	Nov	399
1761	ATHERON, otherwise ARDEN, Joseph		Yorks	Apr	116
1794	ATHERTON, Atherton Legh, Esq.		Lancs	May	240
1784	ATHERTON, Betty		Devon	Feb	59
1751	ATHERTON, George AwW		Pts	Jne	164
1751	ATHERTON, James		Middx	Jly	197
1763	ATHERTON, John		Pts	Aug	366
1782	ATHERTON, John		Middx	Sep	437
1786	ATHERTON, John, Esq.		Lancr	Aug	418
1792	ATHERTON, John		Som	Aug	415
1757	ATHERTON, Joseph		Essex	Nov	319
1752	ATHERTON, Mary		Berks	Jny	1
1783	ATHERTON, Mary		Middx	Jny	1
1777	ATHERTON, Rev. Philip		Devon	Apr	143
1800	ATHERTON, Peter, Esq.		Lancr	Jny	2
1756	ATHERTON, Sarah		Herts	Jne	156
1798	ATHERTON, Sarah		Brstl	Dec	756
1758	ATHERTON, Thomas		Middx	Mch	61
1781	ATHERTON, Thomas		Pts	Mch	107
1753	ATHIAS, otherwise ATTIAS, Daniel AwW		Pts	Jly	192
1769	ATHIAS, DA COSTA, otherwise DA COSTA, Soloman		Lond	Nov	372

```
1794  ATHILL, Charles                                  Middx Apr 180
1752  ATHOL, Joseph  AwW                               Sussx Jny   1
1750  ATHOLL, Most Noble Jane, Duchess of
         formerly LANNOY   AwW unadm. W rgd
         Jne 1748                                      Middx Aug  --
1779  ATHOLL, Most Noble John, late Duke of            NBrit Mch  87
1772  ATHORPE, Henry Esq.                              Yorks May 154
1758  ATHOW, Rebecca                                   Herts Apr  99
1760  ATHURSON, otherwise ARTHURSON, otherwise
         ATTERSON, Benjamin  AwW                       Pts   Jny   1
1775  ATKENS, otherwise ATKINS, Thomas                 Pts   Jne 217
1799  ATKENSON, otherwise ATKINSON, Thomas
         GV "Cracker"                                  Kent  Sep 640
1777  ATKIN, Ann                                       Exter Mch  93
1757  ATKIN, Dorothy                                   Herts Apr 108
1767  ATKIN, John  AwW of Gds unadm.W rgd 1733,
         252                                           Exter Oct  --
1798  ATKIN, John                                      Middx Jne 376
1788  ATKIN, Mary                                      Exter Feb  52
1758  ATKIN, Sarah (poor)                              Lond  Nov 318
1784  ATKIN, Rev Thomas Vernon                         Kent  Feb  59
1761  ATKIN, William                                   Devon Jny   1
1779  ATKIN, William                                   Lond  May 185
1761  ATKINES, Jane                                    Middx Mch  81
1778  ATKINES, Jane (Dble Pr) W rgd 1761, 81           Middx May  --
1750  ATKINGSON, otherwise ATKINSON, John  AwW         Pts   May 134
1782  ATKINS, Abraham                                  Cntby Feb  59
1792  ATKINS, Abraham, Esq.                            Surry Mch 125
1784  ATKINS, Alice                                    Middx Oct 534
1779  ATKINS, Andrew                                   Som   May 185
1752  ATKINS, Ann                                      Middx Feb  27
1758  ATKINS, Ann                                      Middx Jne 175
1778  ATKINS, Ann                                      Surry Mch  93
1767  ATKINS, Arnold                                   Essex Jny   1
1759  ATKINS, Benjamin                                 Middx Dec 381
1776  ATKINS, Bless                                    Essex Jny   1
1797  ATKINS, Catherine  AwW                           Surry May 290
1775  ATKINS, Charles                                  Middx Aug 298
1783  ATKINS, Charles                                  Pts   Jly 333
1795  ATKINS, David  Ser  "St Albans"                  Pts   Apr 232
1754  ATKINS, Edward                                   Surry Jny   1
1793  ATKINS, Edward, Esq.                             Middx Mch 123
1796  ATKINS, Edward                                   Oxon  Apr 160
1799  ATKINS, Edwin Martin, Esq.                       Berks Sep 639
1760  ATKINS, Elias  AwW                               Pts   Jly 270
1763  ATKINS, otherwise ADKINS, formerly
         SHELDON, Elizabeth Ltd AwW                    Surry Aug 366
1769  ATKINS, otherwise ATTKINS, Elizabeth             Leics Feb  32
1773  ATKINS, Elizabeth                                SHant Jne 233
1785  ATKINS, Elizabeth                                Bucks May 228
1786  ATKINS, Elizabeth                                Lond  Nov 551
1798  ATKINS, Ezekiel                                  Surry Sep 581
1776  ATKINS, Frances                                  Middx Dec 485
```

1796	ATKINS, Rev. Francis	Sussx	May	232
1787	ATKINS, Frank	Kent	Mch	101
1755	ATKINS, George, Esq.	SHant	Jny	1
1759	ATKINS, George	Brstl	Jne	191
1765	ATKINS, George AwW of Gds unadm.1745,264	Nhant	Aug	---
1769	ATKINS, Hannah	Sussx	Jly	233
1780	ATKINS, Hannah	Glos	Aug	383
1780	ATKINS, Henry	Lond	Dec	550
1782	ATKINS, Henry	Devon	Jly	333
1799	ATKINS, Henry	Surry	Nov	757
1786	ATKINS, Hugh AwW	Lond	Nov	551
1788	ATKINS, Isabella	Bath	Dec	572
1761	ATKINS, James	Kent	Nov	378
1763	ATKINS, James AwW	Pts	Jly	320
1768	ATKINS, James	SHant	May	184
1786	ATKINS, James	Bath	Jny	2
1788	ATKINS, James (by int dec) Anor W proved Jny 1786	Bath	Nov	518
1794	ATKINS, James	Middx	Jly	344
1799	ATKINS, James	Wilts	Dec	820
1784	ATKINS, Jane	SHant	May	243
1783	ATKINS, otherwise ADKINS, Jeremiah	Essex	Apr	158
1763	ATKINS, Job	Wark	Feb	41
1750	ATKINS, John AwW	Pts	Jly	220
1753	ATKINS, John	Surry	Feb	37
1754	ATKINS, John	Middx	Jne	157
1757	ATKINS, John	Lond	Aug	238
1757	ATKINS, John	Lond	Sep	265
1757	ATKINS, John	Essex	Dec	348
1758	ATKINS, John (by dec)	Lond	Apr	99
1765	ATKINS, otherwise MONTGOMERY, John	Pts	Jny	1
1765	ATKINS, John Ser AwW	Pts	Jly	244
1770	ATKINS, John	SHant	Jne	218
1773	ATKINS, John	Surry	Aug	318
1784	ATKINS, John AwW E.I.S."Northumberland" Pts -	Surry	Jly	373
1784	ATKINS, John Ser "Magnificent"	Pts	Sep	488
1786	ATKINS, John	Surry	Dec	597
1787	ATKINS, John	Rutld	Aug	353
1793	ATKINS, John S."Trusty" AwW	Pts	Dec	578
1797	ATKINS, John	Leics	Sep	584
1798	ATKINS, John	Lond	Apr	230
1799	ATKINS, John	Middx	Feb	89
1777	ATKINS, John Pace	Lond	Nov	445
1759	ATKINS, Jonathan	Pts	May	155
1763	ATKINS, Jonathan	Wark	Mch	104
1751	ATKINS, Joseph	Surry	Jny	1
1765	ATKINS, Joseph AwW	Wark	Sep	319
1780	ATKINS, Joseph	Beds	Oct	458
1783	ATKINS, Joseph Ser	Som	Nov	549
1791	ATKINS, Joseph No ship	Pts	Nov	492
1793	ATKINS, Joseph	Middx	Sep	451
1797	ATKINS, Joseph AwW of Gds unadm. W rgd Sep 1793	Middx	Dec	---

1767	ATKINS, Margaret		Middx	Jny	1
1778	ATKINS, Mary		Wark	Oct	385
1752	ATKINS, Michael, Esq.		SHant	Feb	27
1763	ATKINS, Michael, Esq.		Brstl	Apr	163
1767	ATKINS, Michael		SHant	Mch	82
1791	ATKINS, Rebecca		Middx	Jly	314
1792	ATKINS, Rebekah		Middx	Dec	593
1756	ATKINS, Sir Richard, Bart.		Surry	Jne	156
1790	ATKINS, Richard		Middx	Jne	275
1750	ATKINS, Robert		Middx	Aug	250
1756	ATKINS, Robert		Pts	Sep	236
1767	ATKINS, Robert		Pts	Jny	1
1768	ATKINS, Robert		Leics	Sep	336
1774	ATKINS, Robert Ser		Pts	Dec	418
1777	ATKINS, Robert		Bath	Jne	250
1782	ATKINS, Robert		Leics	Dec	569
1784	ATKINS, otherwise AITKEN, otherwise AITKAN, Robert AwW Ser "Barfleur"		Pts	Jny	2
1771	ATKINS, Sarah		Middx	Apr	140
1752	ATKINS, Samuel		Middx	Apr	82
1765	ATKINS, Samuel, Esq.		SHant	Oct	360
1770	ATKINS, Samuel (Dble Pr) W rgd 1765,360		SHant	Jly	--
1782	ATKINS, Samuel, Esq. (Tble Pr) W rgd 1765, 360		SHant	Feb	--
1799	ATKINS, Samuel		SHant	May	331
1757	ATKINS, Samuell		Lond	Apr	109
1797	ATKINS, Susanna		Devon	Oct	625
1756	ATKINS, Thomas		Lond	May	128
1768	ATKINS, Thomas AwW		Middx	Jne	224
1772	ATKINS, Thomas AwW unadm. W rgd 1768,224		Middx	Nov	--
1775	ATKINS, otherwise ATKENS, Thomas		Pts	Jne	217
1779	ATKINS, Thomas		Surry	Oct	401
1793	ATKINS, otherwise ATTKINS, Thomas		Pts	Sep	451
1795	ATKINS, Thomas		Middx	Apr	233
1754	ATKINS, William		Middx	May	123
1755	ATKINS, William		Nhant	Jly	180
1758	ATKINS, William		Surry	Aug	236
1778	ATKINS, William		Middx	Feb	46
1781	ATKINS, William Ser		Pts	Jly	326
1781	ATKINS, William AwW		Pts	Aug	375
1790	ATKINS, William		SHant	Dec	535
1799	ATKINS, William		Essex	Dec	820
1763	ATKINSON, Abraham		Middx	Oct	457
1762	ATKINSON, Ann AwW		Surry	Nov	444
1789	ATKINSON, Ann		Yorks	Sep	447
1796	ATKINSON, Ann		Yorks	Jny	1
1797	ATKINSON, Ann		Yorks	May	290
1770	ATKINSON, Anna Maria		Middx	Mch	84
1775	ATKINSON, Anthony		Kent	Nov	399
1777	ATKINSON, Caleb		Middx	Jny	1
1786	ATKINSON, Catherine		Durhm	Jne	318
1778	ATKINSON, Charles		Newcl	Apr	142
1770	ATKINSON, Christopher		Pts	Nov	387

1770	ATKINSON, David, Esq.	Lincs	May	170
1797	ATKINSON, Dorothy AwW	Lond	Jly	468
1757	ATKINSON, Edward	Surry	Jly	212
1759	ATKINSON, Edward	Surry	Jny	1
1762	ATKINSON, Edward AwW	Pts	Oct	409
1767	ATKINSON, Edward	SHant	Jny	1
1776	ATKINSON, Edward	Middx	Aug	343
1786	ATKINSON, Edward AwW "Anson"	Pts	Jne	318
1789	ATKINSON, Edward	Essex	Aug	417
1786	ATKINSON, Eleanor	Middx	Oct	500
1760	ATKINSON, Elizabeth AwW	Surry	May	180
1762	ATKINSON, Elizabeth	Middx	Feb	37
1785	ATKINSON, Elizabeth	Durhm	May	228
1786	ATKINSON, Elizabeth	Middx	Jne	318
1790	ATKINSON, Elizabeth	Kent	Apr	168
1794	ATKINSON, Elizabeth	Surry	Jly	344
1797	ATKINSON, Elizabeth	Middx	Jne	394
1795	ATKINSON, Esther	Middx	Mch	136
1797	ATKINSON, Esther AwW of Gds unadm.			
	W rgd Mch 1795	Middx	Apr	--
1783	ATKINSON, Francis AwW	Pts	Dec	596
1800	ATKINSON, Francis Ltd AwW	Middx	Dec	833
1762	ATKINSON, George AwW	Pts	Sep	365
1770	ATKINSON, George	Pts	Mch	84
1771	ATKINSON, George	Surry	Apr	140
1777	ATKINSON, George	Middx	May	194
1783	ATKINSON, George	Berks	Jne	279
1792	ATKINSON, George	Surry	Oct	495
1793	ATKINSON, George, Esq.	Pts	Nov	537
1797	ATKINSON, George AwW of Gds unadm.			
	W rgd Oct 1792	Surry	Mch	--
1763	ATKINSON, Gilbert	Middx	Nov	493
1778	ATKINSON, Grace	Herts	Aug	308
1797	ATKINSON, Hannah	Exter	Feb	66
1784	ATKINSON, Harry	Yorks	Jne	302
1759	ATKINSON, Isaac AwW	Surry	Aug	255
1756	ATKINSON, Isabella AwW	Middx	Apr	93
1757	ATKINSON, James AwW	Pts	Jne	179
1786	ATKINSON, James	Newcl	Nov	551
1796	ATKINSON, James	Herts	Feb	53
1797	ATKINSON, James	Middx	Mch	124
1799	ATKINSON, James	Middx	Jly	471
1786	ATKINSON, James Paul	Middx	Aug	417
1755	ATKINSON, Jane	Lond	Jny	2
1767	ATKINSON, Jane	Mgomy	Mch	83
1777	ATKINSON, Jane otherwise Jean	Lond	Mch	93
1779	ATKINSON, Jane otherwise Jean W rgd Mch			
	1777	Lond	Feb	--
1787	ATKINSON, Jane	Middx	Sep	395
1777	ATKINSON, Jean otherwise Jane	Lond	Mch	93
1779	ATKINSON, Jean otherwise Jane W rgd Mch			
	1777	Lond	Feb	--
1777	ATKINSON, Jeremiah	Lond	Aug	340

1778	ATKINSON,	Jeremiah		Kent	Aug	308
1750	ATKINSON,	otherwise ATKINGSON, John AwW		Pts	May	134
1751	ATKINSON,	John		Pts	Apr	101
1752	ATKINSON,	John		Pts	Apr	82
1753	ATKINSON,	John		Lond	Jne	159
1754	ATKINSON,	John		Middx	Dec	317
1757	ATKINSON,	John		Pts	Apr	109
1757	ATKINSON,	John		Middx	Aug	238
1758	ATKINSON,	John Ser		Pts	Dec	355
1759	ATKINSON,	John		Lond	Jny	1
1760	ATKINSON,	John			Jne	225
1763	ATKINSON,	John	Pts –	Middx	Jny	1
1764	ATKINSON,	John		Middx	Feb	36
1764	ATKINSON,	otherwise ACHISON, John		Pts	Aug	295
1765	ATKINSON,	John AwW		Lond		205
1767	ATKINSON,	John		Lond	Mch	82
1769	ATKINSON,	John		Devon	Sep	299
1770	ATKINSON,	John		SHant	Apr	128
1770	ATKINSON,	John		Middx	Jne	218
1777	ATKINSON,	John		Surry	Jne	250
1782	ATKINSON,	John		Pts	Sep	437
1782	ATKINSON,	John AwW		Pts	Oct	478
1783	ATKINSON,	John		Lond	Jne	279
1783	ATKINSON,	John		Pts	Oct	494
1784	ATKINSON,	John		Middx	Jny	3
1784	ATKINSON,	John No ship		Lancs	Mch	118
1784	ATKINSON,	John		Middx	Jne	303
1784	ATKINSON,	John "Champion","L'Aimable" &				
		"LeCaton"		Pts	Sep	488
1784	ATKINSON,	Rev. John		Chich	Nov	584
1785	ATKINSON,	John		Middx	Oct	489
1786	ATKINSON,	John		Kent	May	257
1786	ATKINSON,	John "Gibraltar"		Pts	May	257
1789	ATKINSON,	John		Surry	Oct	481
1793	ATKINSON,	John		Surry	Mch	124
1794	ATKINSON,	John		Surry	Jne	294
1796	ATKINSON,	John		Herts	May	232
1800	ATKINSON,	John		Yorks	Jne	429
1800	ATKINSON,	John		Cumb	Sep	641
1791	ATKINSON,	John Anson AwW		Pts	Jne	263
1756	ATKINSON,	Jonathan	Pts –	SHant	Mch	58
1765	ATKINSON,	Jonathan		Lond	Jly	244
1782	ATKINSON,	Jonathan		Pts	Aug	390
1784	ATKINSON,	Jonathan AwW		Pts	Jly	363
1755	ATKINSON,	Joseph AwW		Middx	Jly	180
1760	ATKINSON,	Joseph		Middx	Oct	378
1780	ATKINSON,	Joseph		Surry	May	234
1782	ATKINSON,	Joseph		Lond	Jne	262
1790	ATKINSON,	Joseph		Essex	Jny	1
1790	ATKINSON,	Joseph		Durhm	Dec	535
1782	ATKINSON,	Josiah, Esq.		Middx	Jne	262
1796	ATKINSON,	Mark		Herts	Aug	394
1750	ATKINSON,	Mary		Surry	Feb	35

1750	ATKINSON, Mary AwW unadm. W rgd 1736,1	Lond	Dec	--
1764	ATKINSON, Mary	Middx	Jne	209
1767	ATKINSON, Mary	Middx	Jne	204
1772	ATKINSON, Mary	Surry	Jny	1
1785	ATKINSON, Mary	Yorks	Jny	1
1798	ATKINSON, Mary	Middx	Dec	754
1762	ATKINSON, Mathew AwW	Pts	Nov	444
1800	ATKINSON, Mathew	SHant	Jly	499
1800	ATKINSON, Myles	Lond	Aug	573
1788	ATKINSON, Nathaniel	Middx	Nov	519
1762	ATKINSON, Nicholas	Pts	Dec	491
1787	ATKINSON, Nicholas	Essex	Jly	308
1762	ATKINSON, otherwise ACHISON, Poorteen	Pts	May	182
1759	ATKINSON, Rachel	Lond	Oct	316
1768	ATKINSON, Rebecca	Nhant	May	184
1777	ATKINSON, Reuban	Surry	Feb	50
1755	ATKINSON, Richard	Middx	Oct	252
1769	ATKINSON, Richard	Surry	Mch	73
1772	ATKINSON, Richard	Lond	Jne	202
1776	ATKINSON, Richard	Lond	Feb	47
1776	ATKINSON, Richard	Middx	Jne	253
1786	ATKINSON, Richard, Esq. late one of Alder- men of City of Lond	Lond	Sep	460
1786	ATKINSON, Richard, Esq. late one of Alder- men of City of Lond (Dble Pr) W rgd this month	Lond	Sep	--
1787	ATKINSON, Richard, Esq. late of of Alder- men of City of Lond (Tble Pr) W rgd Sep 1786	Lond	Jly	--
1787	ATKINSON, Richard, Esq. late of of Alder- men of City of Lond (4th Pr) W rgd Sep 1786	Lond	Sep	--
1790	ATKINSON, Richard	Lancr	Jny	2
1757	ATKINSON, Robert	Herts	Jny	2
1761	ATKINSON, Rev. Robert	SHant	Dec	416
1779	ATKINSON, Robert	Surry	Jne	230
1788	ATKINSON, Robert, Esq.	Nhant	Jly	335
1797	ATKINSON, Robert	Devon	May	291
1762	ATKINSON, Samuel	Essex	May	183
1767	ATKINSON, Samuel	Herts	Feb	33
1773	ATKINSON, Samuel, Esq.	Surry	Nov	413
1774	ATKINSON, Samuel (Dble Pr) W rgd Nov last	Surry	Jny	--
1792	ATKINSON, Samuel, Esq.	Herts	Apr	189
1785	ATKINSON, Sarah	Kent	Aug	400
1790	ATKINSON, Sarah	Middx	Oct	450
1794	ATKINSON, Sarah AwW	Essex	Feb	59
1769	ATKINSON, otherwise ATKISSON, Solomon	Kent	Sep	299
1783	ATKINSON, Susanna	Lond	Mch	106
1783	ATKINSON, Susannah	Middx	Oct	493
1783	ATKINSON, Theodore, Esq. AwW	Pts	Oct	493
1752	ATKINSON, Thomas	Middx	Mch	56
1756	ATKINSON, Thomas	Middx	Oct	266
1756	ATKINSON, Thomas	Pts	Oct	266

1761	ATKINSON, Thomas AwW	Pts	Feb	44
1764	ATKINSON, Thomas	Pts	Apr	128
1769	ATKINSON, Thomas	Lond	Apr	111
1774	ATKINSON, Thomas	Pts	Jly	252
1775	ATKINSON, Thomas	Surry	Dec	454
1777	ATKINSON, Thomas AwW	Pts	Mch	93
1778	ATKINSON, Thomas	Middx	Dec	474
1785	ATKINSON, Thomas	Kent	Mch	110
1791	ATKINSON, Thomas	Mon	Dec	552
1793	ATKINSON, Thomas (Dble Pr) W rgd 1775,454	Surry	Aug	--
1795	ATKINSON, Thomas, Esq.	SHant	Jne	360
1796	ATKINSON, Thomas, Esq.	Lond	Mch	106
1796	ATKINSON, Thomas, Esq. (Dble Pr) W rgd Jne 1795	SHant	Oct	--
1798	ATKINSON, Thomas	Yorks	Oct	631
1798	ATKINSON, Thomas "Star"	Pts	Nov	691
1799	ATKINSON, otherwise ATKENSON, Thomas G.V."Cracker"	Kent	Sep	640
1750	ATKINSON, William	Middx	Oct	313
1751	ATKINSON, William	Lond	May	130
1752	ATKINSON, William	Lond	Jne	145
1757	ATKINSON, William	Herts	Jny	1
1758	ATKINSON, William AwW unadm. W rgd 1735, 91	Middx	Sep	--
1762	ATKINSON, William	Brstl	Sep	365
1763	ATKINSON, William	Pts	Apr	163
1765	ATKINSON, Rev. William	Wilts	Aug	282
1766	ATKINSON, William Ltd AwW of Gds unadm. W rgd 1750, 313	Middx	May	--
1766	ATKINSON, William	Middx	Jly	255
1768	ATKINSON, William	Lond	Feb	41
1770	ATKINSON, William	Middx	May	169
1777	ATKINSON, William	Lond	Oct	406
1784	ATKINSON, William	Middx	Mch	118
1784	ATKINSON, William	Surry	Nov	583
1784	ATKINSON, William	Middx	Nov	584
1794	ATKINSON, otherwise ATTKINSON, William	Middx	Jny	2
1795	ATKINSON, William AwW	Pts	Jly	428
1797	ATKINSON, William	Devon	Feb	66
1797	ATKINSON, William	Essex	May	290
1800	ATKINSON, William No ship	Pts	Oct	697
1780	ATKINSON, William Brudenell	Essex	May	234
1762	ATKINSON, Rev. Worsopp	Herts	Jly	282
1790	ATKIS, Richard	Lancr	Jne	276
1795	ATKIS, Sarah	Chest	Oct	578
1769	ATKISSON, otherwise ATKINSON, Solomon	Kent	Sep	299
1782	ATKYNS, Ann	Lond	Oct	478
1782	ATKYNS, Ann W rgd Oct last	Lond	Dec	--
1791	ATKYNS, Christopher	Surry	Jny	1
1767	ATKYNS, Dorothy	Lond	Jne	204
1751	ATKYNS, Edward, Esq.	Norf	Mch	68
1765	ATKYNS, Edward	Lond	Mch	83
1765	ATKYNS, Edward (Dble Pr) W rgd last month	Lond	Apr	--

1750	ATKYNS, John		Surry	Feb	35
1752	ATKYNS, Robert		Kent	Oct	241
1771	ATKYNS, Thomas		Surry	Oct	395
1793	ATLEE, Anthony		Middx	Mch	125
1782	ATLEE, James		Berks	Sep	437
1756	ATLEE, John AwW		Pts	Aug	215
1762	ATLEE, John		Middx	May	183
1764	ATLEE, John		Lond	Aug	294
1774	ATLEE, John AwW unadm. W rgd 1764,294		Lond	Jly	——
1780	ATLEE, John		Pts	Jly	345
1785	ATLEE, John		Middx	Dec	584
1774	ATLEE, Joseph, Esq.		Surry	Jly	252
1788	ATLEE, Joseph AwW of Gds unadm. W rgd 1774,253		Surry	May	——
1765	ATLEE, Mary		Bucks	Aug	283
1774	ATLEE, otherwise ATTLEE, Peter		Wark	Oct	357
1800	ATLEE, Priscilla		Newcl	Nov	760
1752	ATLEE, Thomas		Pts	Jly	176
1763	ATLEE, William		Surry	Oct	458
1792	ATRICK, William		Middx	Oct	495
1785	ATRISTAIN, Pedro DE		Middx	Jly	
1766	ATTAWAY, Isaac		Herts	Jny	1
1753	ATTELSEY, Jane		Norf	Apr	100
1754	ATTELSEY, Peter AwW unadm. W rgd 1730,146		Norf	Apr	97
1797	ATTENBORROW, Rachel		Camb	May	290
1786	ATTENBORROW, Thomas AwW		Sussx	Jny	2
1775	ATTENHOVEN, Christina Elizabeth VAN (Ltd Pr)		Pts	Jne	254
1797	ATTENHOVEN, Elizabeth Maria VAN (Ltd Pr)		Pts	Mch	211
1776	ATTENHOVEN, Pieter VAN (Ltd Pr)		Pts	Mch	
1784	ATTERBURY, Abraham		Lond	Jly	364
1779	ATTERBURY, Austin		Pts	Nov	441
1788	ATTERBURY, Elizabeth		Lond	Nov	519
1776	ATTERBURY, Henry		Lond	Nov	447
1795	ATTERBURY, Henry		Bucks	May	292
1796	ATTERBURY, Luffman		Middx	Dec	590
1783	ATTERBURY, Mary		Lond	May	210
1781	ATTERBURY, Robert		Wark	Jny	2
1758	ATTERBURY, Thomas		Pts	May	139
1752	ATTERBURY, William (Dble Pr) W rgd Aug 1749		Middx	Jne	——
1795	ATTERBURY, William		Nhant	Mch	136
1774	ATTERSOLL, Hannah		Sussx	Jny	1
1798	ATTERSOLL, John		Herts	Mch	151
1779	ATTERSOLL, Joseph		Berks	Oct	401
1750	ATTERSOLL, Samuel		Pts	Jne	185
1770	ATTERSOLL, Susanna		Sussx	May	169
1760	ATTERSON, otherwise ARTHURSON, otherwise ATHURSON, Benjamin AwW		Pts	Jny	1
1750	ATTEWELL, John		Kent	Sep	285
1753	ATTEWELL, John		Middx	Feb	37
1766	ATTFEILD, James		Middx	Feb	45
1798	ATTFIELD, Edward		Middx	Aug	523

```
1777   ATTFIELD, Elizabeth                              Middx  Apr  144
1772   ATTFIELD, Sarah                                  Surry  Dec  429
1784   ATTFIELD, William                                Surry  Jny    1
1799   ATTIAS, Abram otherwise Abraham Raffael          Pts    Nov  757
1753   ATTIAS, otherwise ATHIAS, Daniel  AwW            Pts    Jly  192
1781   ATTICK, John  Ser                                Pts    Jly  326
1769   ATTKINS, otherwise ATKINS, Elizabeth             Leics  Feb   32
1794   ATTKINS, John                                    Staff  Mch  119
1752   ATTKINS, Thomas                                  Bucks  Jny    1
1793   ATTKINS, otherwise ATKINS, Thomas                Pts    Sep  451
1794   ATTKINSON, otherwise ATKINSON, William           Middx  Jny    2
1786   ATTLAY, Stephen, Esq.                            Herts  Apr  201
1796   ATTLE, William  Ser  "Raisonable"                Wark   Dec  590
1762   ATTLEBOROUGH, John                               Lond   Jne  230
1770   ATTLEBOROUGH, John  AwW unadm. W rgd
          1762, 230                                     Lond   May   --
1769   ATTLEBOROUGH, Mary  AwW                          Surry  Jne  193
1774   ATTLEE, otherwise ATLEE, Peter                   Wark   Oct  357
1800   ATTLEY, George                                   Middx  Sep  642
1769   ATTLEY, Jane                                     Surry  Sep  299
1770   ATTMAR, Esther                                   Kent   Apr  128
1766   ATTON, otherwise HATTON, Thomas                  Middx  Feb   44
1786   ATTREE, Jesse                                    Surry  May  258
1765   ATTRICK, Daniel                                  Wark   Mch   83
1772   ATTRIDGE, Ann SHROWSBRIDGE, formerly             Middx  Oct  384
1758   ATTRIDGE, Joseph                                 Middx  Jne  175
1797   ATTWATER, Benjamin                               Kent   Nov  673
1785   ATTWEEK, Richard, Esq.                           Middx  Sep  452
1780   ATTWELL, William                                 Devon  Jne  299
1766   ATTWICK, Elizabeth  AwW                          SHant  Jny    1
1766   ATTWICK, Elizabeth  AwW of Gds unadm.
          W rgd last month                              SHant  Feb   --
1764   ATTWICK, otherwise WEEKS, James                  Pts    Jly  248
1763   ATTWICK, Jeremiah                                Pts    May  210
1754   ATTWICK, Mary                                    SHant  May  123
1773   ATTWICKE, Margery                                Surry  May  190
1750   ATTWOOD, Christopher                             Worcs  Feb   35
1754   ATTWOOD, Clement                                 Pts    Mch   66
1782   ATTWOOD, Collin                                  Pts    Feb   59
1778   ATTWOOD, Edward                                  Middx  Mch   94
1766   ATTWOOD, Elizabeth                               Brstl  Oct  360
1790   ATTWOOD, Elizabeth                               Middx  May  221
1796   ATTWOOD, Elizabeth CHAPMAN, formerly             Middx  Dec  590
1800   ATTWOOD, otherwise ATWOOD, Elizabeth             Middx  Jny    2
1787   ATTWOOD, George  AwW                             Pts    Aug  353
1750   ATTWOOD, Hannah                                  Middx  Oct  313
1787   ATTWOOD, otherwise ATWOOD, Hosea                 Middx  Aug  353
1751   ATTWOOD, James                                   Middx  Jne  164
1757   ATTWOOD, James                                   Pts    Feb   37
1779   ATTWOOD, John                                    Pts    Aug  333
1779   ATTWOOD, John                                    Middx  Sep  364
1793   ATTWOOD, John  AwW of Gds unadm. W rgd
          1779, 364                                     Middx  May   --
```

1797	ATTWOOD, John	Hunts	Mch	124
1783	ATTWOOD, otherwise ATWOOD, Joseph	Pts	Aug	397
1797	ATTWOOD, Lucretia	SHant	Feb	66
1755	ATTWOOD, Mary	Glos	Aug	209
1768	ATTWOOD, Mary	Middx	Sep	336
1795	ATTWOOD, Mary	Middx	Sep	531
1793	ATTWOOD, Ralph	Kent	Nov	537
1755	ATTWOOD, Richard Ltd AwW	Glos	Aug	209
1752	ATTWOOD, Thomas	Middx	Feb	27
1779	ATTWOOD, Thomas Ser	Kent	Feb	36
1798	ATTWOOD, Thomas	Middx	Jne	376
1759	ATTWOOD, William	Pts	Sep	287
1780	ATTWOOD, William	Middx	May	234
1786	ATTWOOD, William	Surry	Jne	318
1798	ATTWOOD, William	Middx	Jny	1
1798	ATTWOOD, William	Glos	Apr	230
1773	ATTWOOLL, Richard	Surry	Mch	90
1799	ATTY, Sarah	Middx	Feb	89
1794	ATWELL, Jane	Middx	May	240
1752	ATWELL, John	Pts	Jny	1
1752	ATWELL, John	Pts	Aug	204
1768	ATWELL, Joseph, D.D.	Glos	Sep	336
1788	ATWELL, Michael	Berks	May	224
1751	ATWELL, Thomas	Sarum	Jly	197
1771	ATWICK, Henry	Middx	Aug	328
1787	ATWOOD, Abraham AwW	Wilts	Jny	2
1772	ATWOOD, Ann	Lincs	Feb	33
1793	ATWOOD, Ann	Surry	Mch	124
1779	ATWOOD, Berthya	Middx	Dec	483
1765	ATWOOD, Elizabeth	Middx	Jny	1
1765	ATWOOD, Elizabeth	Surry	Jne	206
1800	ATWOOD, otherwise ATTWOOD, Elizabeth	Middx	Jny	2
1754	ATWOOD, Rev. George, Archdeacon of Taunton	Som	Jly	187
1758	ATWOOD, George	Lond	Oct	282
1777	ATWOOD, Rev. George, B.D. Archdeacon of Taunton, AwW of Gds unadm. W rgd 1754, 187	Som	Apr	--
1787	ATWOOD, otherwise ATTWOOD, Hosea	Middx	Aug	353
1761	ATWOOD, John, Esq.	Surry	Sep	307
1762	ATWOOD, , John	Middx	Jny	1
1767	ATWOOD, John	Bath	Jny	1
1777	ATWOOD, John	Bath	Jny	2
1781	ATWOOD, John	Cntby	Mch	109
1783	ATWOOD, otherwise ATTWOOD, Joseph	Pts	Aug	397
1753	ATWOOD, Katharine	Lincs	Aug	222
1757	ATWOOD, Mary	Middx	Mch	72
1785	ATWOOD, Mary	Middx	May	228
1781	ATWOOD, Richard	Middx	Dec	568
1775	ATWOOD, Richard John	Middx	May	168
1752	ATWOOD, Thomas AwW of Gds unadm. W rgd 1719, 98	Middx	Jne	--
1766	ATWOOD, Thomas	Worcs	Jny	1
1771	ATWOOD, Thomas	Bath	Mch	91

```
1765   ATWOOD, William                                      Brstl  Oct  360
1793   ATWOOD, William                                      Wilts  Aug  397
1800   ATYEO,  William                                      Som    May  335
1767   ATZENHEIM, Hon Friedrichphilip VON                   Pts    Feb   78
1754   AUBAN, Rt Hon Lady Marianne Sophia Theo-
         dora DE BOUCOUR, otherwise PAPE de ST. Pts         Jly  193
1773   AUBAN, Rt Hon Lady Marianna Sophia Theo-
         dora DE BOUCOUR, otherwise PAPE ST.
         AwW of Gds unadm.  W rgd 1754, 193                 Pts    Feb   --
1769   AUBANEL, Jean otherwise John                         Middx  Jne  193
1779   AUBANET, Jean otherwise John  AwW unadm.
         W rgd 1769, 193                                    Middx  Feb   --
1775   AUBER, Henrietta                                     Lond   Jne  219
1783   AUBER, James                              Pts - Lond Nov  548
1800   AUBER, Jane                                          Glos   Nov  764
1767   AUBER, Jaques                                        Lond   Mch   83
1798   AUBER, Rev. John                                     Glos   Jly  457
1766   AUBER, Peter                                         Middx  Oct  361
1787   AUBER, Peter, Esq.                                   Herts  Aug  353
1750   AUBER, Robert                                        Middx  Nov  345
1780   AUBER, Susanna                                       Herts  Dec  550
1798   AUBERT, Alexander                                    Middx  Dec  755
1780   AUBERT, Anthony                                      Lond   Mch  118
1774   AUBERT, Claude                                       Lond   Dec  419
1796   AUBERT, Jaques Louis                                 Pts    Oct  485
1796   AUBERT, Jane, otherwise Jeanne                       Pts    Apr  158
1783   AUBERT, John  AwW                                    Lond   Dec  597
1764   AUBERT, John Augustin                                Dorst  Aug  295
1772   AUBERT, Margaret, otherwise Marquerite
         LALONET, formerly                                  Pts    Mch   98
1784   AUBERT, Peter                                        Pts    Sep  488
1773   AUBERT, William                                      Pts    Nov  413
1772   AUBERTIN, John                                       Middx  Mch   81
1787   AUBERY, Ann   AwW                                    Bath   Feb   51
1758   AUBERY, Rev. Edmund                                  Som    Jny    1
1773   AUBERY, Elizabeth                                    Middx  Oct  379
1783   AUBERY, Isabella                                     Middx  Mch  106
1758   AUBERY, John                                         Middx  Feb   28
1767   AUBERY, Rachel                                       Middx  Dec  435
1750   AUBIGNY, Most Noble Charles, Duke of
         RICHMOND LENOX and                                        Sep  306
1752   AUBIGNY, Most Noble Charles, Duke of
         RICHMOND LENOX and  (Dble Pr) W rgd
         Sep 1750                                           -      Jny   --
1752   AUBIGNY, Most Noble Sarah, Duchess Dowager
         of RICHMOND LENOX and                             -      Jny   21
1752   AUBIN, Catherine DE ST. otherwise DERICQ
         DE ST. AUBIN, Catherine                            Middx  Jny    7
1779   AUBIN, Elizabeth AwW                                 Jersy  Feb   36
1756   AUBIN DERICQ, Henrietta ST.                          Middx  May  128
1760   AUBIN DERICQ, Henrietta ST. (Dble Pr)
         W rgd 1756, 128                                    Middx  Dec   --
1751   AUBIN, Judith  AwW                                   Jersy  Jne  164
```

```
1761   AUBIN, Mary  AwW                              Jersy  Jny    1
1783   AUBIN, D', otherwise DIVEEN, otherwise
          DOBBYN, Michael    AwW                     Pts    Aug   --
1751   AUBIN, Peter John                             Lond   Apr  101
1751   AUBIN, Peter John  AwW of Gds unadm.
          W rgd Apr last                             Lond   Aug   --
1783   AUBIN, Philip, otherwise Philip James         Middx  Sep  442
1774   AUBIN, Sophia D'                              Glos   Jly  261
1782   AUBINS, Christopher                           Mgomy  Aug  390
1791   AUBONE, Jane                                  Newcl  Aug  369
1792   AUBREY, Anne                                  Herfd  Jly  362
1778   AUBREY, Arabella COLE, formerly               SHant  Jny   10
1800   AUBREY, Arrabella                             Middx  Jny    3
1800   AUBREY, Eleanor Gough                         Glam   Oct  696
1757   AUBREY, Elizabeth                             Herfd  Jne  179
1758   AUBREY, Herbert, Esq.                         Herfd  Dec  355
1796   AUBREY, Rev. James Gough                      Glam   Dec  590
1758   AUBREY, John                                  Middx  Nov  318
1770   AUBREY, John                                  SHant  Jne  218
1759   AUBREY, Laetitia (Dble Pr) W rgd 1746, 107    Middx  Feb   --
1793   AUBREY, Margaret                              Glam   Apr  179
1765   AUBREY, Peter  (Ltd Pr)                       Pts    Nov  397
1762   AUBREY, Dame Prudence  Ltd AwW                Lond   Sep  363
1787   AUBREY, Sir Thomas, Bart.                     Glam   Feb   51
1783   AUBREY, Ursula, otherwise Urslua              Lond   Feb   56
1794   AUBREY, William  "Minerva"                    Pts    Aug  402
1764   AUBUREY, Mary                                 Essex  Mch   78
1761   AUBUREY, Robert                               Essex  Apr  116
1770   AUBUREY, Robert                               Surry  Dec  421
1791   AUBUREY, otherwise AUBURY, Sarah              Surry  Nov  493
1791   AUBURY, otherwise AUBUREY, Sarah              Surry  Nov  493
1772   AUBYN, Sir John ST., Bart.                    Corn   Oct  384
1797   AUBYN, Sir John ST., Bart.  AwW of Gds
          unadm., W rgd 1772, 384                    Corn   Mch   --
1770   AUBYN, Martha ST.                             Middx  Mch
1797   AUBYN, Rachel, formerly LE GALLAIS   AwW      Jersy  Jne  393
1796   AUCHENCLOSS, Robert  No ship  AwW             Pts    Mch  107
1786   AUCHINLECK, John, Esq.  "Achilles"            Pts    Dec  597
1757   AUCHINLECK, Robert                            Pts    May  144
1786   AUCHMUTY, Arthur Forbes                       Pts    Mch  133
1753   AUCHMUTY, Rev. James  (Ltd Pr)               Middx  May  126
1790   AUCHMUTY, James Smith  Ltd AwW                Pts    Dec  535
1751   AUCHMUTY, John  AwW                           Pts    Sep  250
1788   AUCHMUTY, Robert, Esq.                        Middx  Dec  573
1790   AUCHMUTY, Robert  AwW of Gds unadm.
          W rgd 1788, 573                            Middx  Jly   --
1795   AUCHMUTY, Robert Ardesoil  17th Regt          Pts    Mch   --
1793   AUCHTERLONEY, David E.I.S."Busbridge"         Pts    Sep  451
1771   AUCKELE, Friderick          Pts - Middx       Jly  282
1795   AUCKLAND, John                                Middx  May  292
1796   AUCKLAND, Mary                                Middx  Aug  393
1781   AUDAIN, Abraham, Esq. Ltd Pr wW               Pts    Jne  280
1776   AUDAIN, Ann                                   Middx  Jly  296
```

1791	AUDAS, Thomas	Middx	Dec	552
1777	AUDEMAR, Judith	Middx	Sep	374
1785	AUDEMAR, Mary	Middx	Dec	583
1793	AUDIBERT, Jacob	Middx	Mch	125
1763	AUDIBERT, John Peter, Esq.	Pts	Feb	41
1780	AUDINET, Jenne	Middx	Feb	53
1760	AUDINET, Paul AwW	Middx	May	180
1768	AUDLEE, James	Middx	Feb	41
1792	AUDLEY, Elizabeth	Wark	Jny	1
1792	AUDLEY, Elizabeth (Dble Pr) W rgd Jny 3			
	1792	Wark	Jne	––
1777	AUDLEY, George	Chest	Apr	143
1769	AUDLEY, Rt Hon James, Earl of CASTLEHAVEN	Wilts	Aug	272
1779	AUDLEY, John	Camb	Mch	85
1782	AUDLEY, Rev. Dr. John, D.D.	Wark	May	210
1796	AUDLEY, Rev. Dr. John, D.D. AwW of Gds			
	unadm. W rgd 1782, 210	Wark	Mch	––
1799	AUDLEY, Rev. Dr. John, D.D. AwW of Gds			
	twice unadm. W rgd 1782,210 Last grant			
	Mch 1796	Wark	Mch	––
1777	AUDLEY, Baron Lord in the Kingdom of Gt			
	Brit. and Rt Hon John Talbot TUCKET,			
	Earl of CASTLEHAVEN in the Kingdom of			
	Ireland	Wilts	May	244
1780	AUDLEY, Lucy	Norf	Dec	550
1788	AUDLEY, Robert	Middx	May	224
1796	AUDLEY, Thomas "Nonsuch"	Middx	May	231
1767	AUDOUIN, William	Middx	Feb	33
1759	AUDRE, Elizabeth ST.	SHant	Apr	146
1775	AUDROUIN, Solomon	Herts	Nov	399
1774	AUDRY, Edward	SHant	Nov	384
1756	AUDSLEY, James	Middx	Aug	215
1783	AUDSLEY, Laetitia	Middx	Apr	158
1799	AUDSLEY, Matthew Carverley	Kent	Sep	640
1781	AUFRERE, Rev. Anthony	Nwich	Jne	281
1758	AUFRERE, Rev. Isaac Anthony	Middx	Apr	100
1751	AUFRERE, Mary, formerly SMITH	Norf	Apr	101
1757	AUGER, Lawrence, otherwise OGARD, Lawrance	Kent	Dec	367
1786	AUGHTON, otherwise HOUGHTON, otherwise			
	HAUGHTON, otherwise OUGHTON, Daniel			
	"Antigua","Star","Pegasus","Barbados"			
	& "Berwick" AwW	Lancr	Jne	––
1792	AUGIER, Burrage, Esq.	Essex	Dec	593
1757	AUGIER, David Hilary Seigneuron	Lond	Nov	319
1763	AUGIER, Elizabeth	Middx	Sep	416
1759	AUGIER, otherwise CHAVAT, Geertd.	Pts	Jny	10
1761	AUGIER, Samuel	Middx	Feb	43
1773	AUGIER, Susan	Lond	Feb	42
1752	AUGIZEAU, Mary	Devon	Feb	27
1766	AUGIZEAUX, Mary	Middx	Mch	89
1792	AUGOT, Catherina (Spec Pr)	Pts	Jny	1
1760	AUGUST, Elizabeth	Kent	Jne	225
1791	AUGUST, Elizabeth, otherwise Elisabeth	Bucks	Aug	368

1754	AUGUST, Samuel AwW		Middx	Jne	157
1756	AUGUST, Samuel AwW W rgd Jne 1754		Middx	Aug	--
1781	AUGUST, William		Pts	Oct	459
1751	AUGUSTINE, Thomas		Pts	Apr	102
1763	AUGUSTUS, John		Pts	Jny	1
1766	AUKWARD, otherwise ORFORD, John AwW		Pts	Jny	1
1764	AULAY, Archibald MAC		Pts	Feb	60
1771	AULAY, MC, otherwise MC KAULEY, Aullay				
		Pts -	Kent	Mch	115
1784	AULAY, MC, Aulay, otherwise MC AULY,Auly				
	Ser "Gibraltar"		Pts	Dec	653
1800	AULAY, James MC		Brstl	Jly	539
1769	AULAY, Peter MC		Pts	Dec	425
1784	AULAY, Philip MC "Panther" "Terror Bomb "				
	"San Carlos"		Pts	Jne	335
1778	AULD, Allan (Ltd Pr)		Pts	Dec	475
1779	AULD, Allan (Ltd Dble Pr) W rgd Dec last		Pts	Feb	--
1759	AULD, George AwW		Pts	Feb	44
1775	AULD, Samuel		Bucks	Feb	37
1775	AULD, Samuel (Dble Pr) W rgd Feb last		Bucks	Apr	--
1783	AULIFFE, Timothy MC		Pts	Dec	--
1794	AULIUS, Angelica Henrietta D' (Ltd Pr)		Pts	Jny	16
1764	AULT, Rev. George		Beds	Mch	79
1773	AULT, Mary		Middx	May	190
1773	AULT, Nathaniel		Middx	Apr	144
1787	AULT, Rosamond		Herts	Jne	251
1762	AULTON, John		Salop	Dec	491
1784	AULY, MC, Auly, otherwise MC AULAY, Aulay				
	Ser "Gibraltar"		Pts	Dec	653
1763	AULY, Hector MC		Pts	Oct	478
1787	AUMONIER, Peter		Middx	Mch	101
1754	AUMONNIER, Peter		Middx	Jny	1
1778	AUMONNIER, otherwise AUMOUNIER, Susannah				
	Margaret		Middx	Nov	429
1778	AUMOUNIER, otherwise AUMONNIER, Susannah				
	Margaret		Middx	Nov	429
1770	AURBACK, Augustus		Middx	Mch	85
1780	AURBACK, Honour		Middx	Mch	117
1771	AURBACK, Winifred		Essex	Mch	92
1778	AURIOL, Elisha		Lond	Feb	45
1799	AURIOL, Elizabeth		Middx	May	331
1753	AURIOL, Peter		Pts	Jly	192
1754	AURIOL, Peter AwW		Middx	Nov	291
1761	AUSSET, Paul		Pts	Jly	239
1781	AUSSY, Charles D', Esq.		Hants	Nov	520
1785	AUSSY, Charles D', Esq. (Dble Pr) W rgd				
	1781, 510		SHant	Nov	--
1778	AUST, Daniel		Wilts	Mch	94
1772	AUSTELL, Stephen		Middx	Feb	33
1791	AUSTELL, William		Essex	Nov	492
1753	AUSTEN, Ann		Middx	Aug	222
1758	AUSTEN, Ann		Kent	Aug	236
1772	AUSTEN, Ann		Middx	May	154

154

1758	AUSTEN,	Charles	Kent	May	139
1764	AUSTEN,	Earl	Kent	Apr	128
1760	AUSTEN,	Edward	Kent	Nov	412
1761	AUSTEN,	Edward	Kent	Feb	43
1755	AUSTEN,	Elizabeth	Denbh	Apr	92
1788	AUSTEN,	Elizabeth	Kent	Feb	52
1791	AUSTEN,	Francis	Kent	Jly	313
1772	AUSTEN,	George	Middx	Mch	81
1781	AUSTEN,	Hannah	Kent	Nov	510
1787	AUSTEN,	Henry	Poole	May	195
1796	AUSTEN,	Henry Ser "Raisonable"	Pts	May	232
1770	AUSTEN,	James	Sussx	Feb	40
1785	AUSTEN,	James	Kent	Dec	583
1791	AUSTEN,	James "Nymph"	Pts	Nov	493
1799	AUSTEN,	James AwW of Gds unadm. W rgd 1785, 583	Kent	Jly	--
1751	AUSTEN,	Jane	Middx	Nov	298
1763	AUSTEN,	Jane AwW of Gds unadm. W rgd 1751, 298	Middx	Feb	--
1769	AUSTEN,	Joan	Surry	Feb	32
1764	AUSTEN,	John	Pts	Sep	335
1765	AUSTEN,	John	Kent	May	168
1771	AUSTEN,	John	Middx	Apr	142
1785	AUSTEN,	John	Devon	Aug	400
1763	AUSTEN,	Joseph	Pts	Aug	366
1765	AUSTEN,	Martha	Surry	Jne	205
1766	AUSTEN,	Mary	Middx	Feb	45
1780	AUSTEN,	Mary	Kent	Jne	300
1788	AUSTEN,	Mary	Middx	Jny	1
1791	AUSTEN,	Mary	Kent	Apr	164
1785	AUSTEN,	Nathaniel	Kent	May	229
1778	AUSTEN,	Nicholas Pts -	Devon	Dec	474
1790	AUSTEN,	Philip	Kent	Jny	1
1790	AUSTEN,	Richard Spec AwW	Middx	Mch	114
1759	AUSTEN,	Sir Robert AwW of Gds unadm. W rgd 1743,328	Kent	Mch	--
1759	AUSTEN,	Robert, Esq.	Surry	Sep	287
1763	AUSTEN,	Robert, Esq. AwW of Gds unadm. W rgd 1728, 256	Kent	Feb	--
1772	AUSTEN,	Sir Robert	Kent	Feb	34
1797	AUSTEN,	Robert, Esq.	Middx	Dec	721
1773	AUSTEN,	Sarah	Sussx	Jne	233
1797	AUSTEN,	Sarah	Kent	Feb	66
1800	AUSTEN,	Sarah	Middx	Jly	499
1758	AUSTEN,	Sheffield ST. Ltd AwW	Irel	Nov	319
1751	AUSTEN,	Stephen	Lond	Jny	1
1768	AUSTEN,	Susanna	Kent	Oct	367
1773	AUSTEN,	Dame Susanna	Kent	Jny	1
1774	AUSTEN,	Dame Susanna (by int dec) Cod. W rgd Jny 1773	Kent	May	166
1753	AUSTEN,	Thomas AwW of Gds twice unadm. W rgd 1743,64 Last grant Nov 1747	Kent	Jly	--
1772	AUSTEN,	Thomas	Kent	Apr	119

1790	AUSTEN,	**Rev. Thomas**	Kent	Oct	450
1794	AUSTEN,	Thomas	Kent	Feb	59
1799	AUSTEN,	otherwise AUSTIN, Thomas	Irel	Jly	472
1794	AUSTEN,	Valentine	Kent	Mch	119
1784	AUSTEN,	William	Kent	Jly	364
1793	AUSTEN,	William	Kent	Jly	350
1796	AUSTEN,	William AwW	Kent	**Nov**	538
1763	AUSTERS,	William	Pts	Oct	457
1785	AUSTIN,	Alice	Middx	Mch	110
1789	AUSTIN,	Ann	Derby	Jly	343
1794	AUSTIN,	Ann	Lond	Mch	120
1794	AUSTIN,	Ann	Surry	Jly	344
1794	AUSTIN,	Ann	Middx	Dec	593
1766	AUSTIN,	Benjamin AwW	Middx	Jne	209
1788	AUSTIN,	Charles No ship	Pts	May	224
1785	AUSTIN,	Edward	Bucks	Oct	489
1755	AUSTIN,	Eleanor	Nhant	Dec	303
1793	AUSTIN,	Eleanor	Middx	Jny	2
1771	AUSTIN,	Elizabeth	Middx	Mch	91
1772	AUSTIN,	Elizabeth	Middx	Jny	1
1778	AUSTIN,	Elizabeth	Middx	Sep	345
1781	AUSTIN,	Elizabeth	Middx	Dec	568
1782	AUSTIN,	Elizabeth W rgd Dec last	Middx	Feb	--
1783	AUSTIN,	Elizabeth	Middx	Oct	493
1786	AUSTIN,	Elizabeth	Middx	Apr	201
1795	AUSTIN,	Elizabeth	Hunts	May	292
1798	AUSTIN,	Elizabeth	Middx	Sep	581
1771	AUSTIN,	Emanuel	Lond	Dec	466
1774	AUSTIN,	George, Esq.	Salop	Jly	252
1758	AUSTIN,	Grace	Middx	Jne	175
1793	AUSTIN,	Hannah	Wark	May	238
1799	AUSTIN,	Hannah	SHant	Jny	2
1781	AUSTIN,	Henrietta	Middx	Dec	568
1750	AUSTIN,	Henry	Middx	Oct	313
1787	AUSTIN,	Hugh, Esq. AwW	Pts	Dec	527
1790	AUSTIN,	James	Middx	Mch	115
1757	AUSTIN,	Joanna	Lond	Dec	348
1751	AUSTIN,	John AwW	Lond	Sep	250
1752	AUSTIN,	John	Nhant	Apr	82
1752	AUSTIN,	John	Pts	May	115
1752	AUSTIN,	John	Middx	Oct	241
1764	AUSTIN,	John	Pts	Feb	36
1765	AUSTIN,	Rev. John	Nhant	Apr	128
1767	AUSTIN,	John	Lond	Jne	204
1769	AUSTIN,	John	Middx	Feb	32
1772	AUSTIN,	John	Middx	Jly	244
1774	AUSTIN,	John AwW unadm. W rgd 1767, 204	Lond	Sep	--
1775	AUSTIN,	John	Oxon	Aug	298
1776	AUSTIN,	John	Lond	Nov	447
1778	AUSTIN,	John Ser	Devon	Feb	47
1783	AUSTIN,	John	Middx	Jny	1
1784	AUSTIN,	John	Herts	Nov	584
1798	AUSTIN,	John	Middx	Aug	523

1799	AUSTIN,	John "Namur" AwW	Pts	Nov	756
1756	AUSTIN,	Joseph	Herts	Dec	317
1773	AUSTIN,	Joseph	Lond	Jne	233
1779	AUSTIN,	Joseph	Middx	Oct	401
1780	AUSTIN,	Joseph Ser	Pts	Apr	169
1789	AUSTIN,	Joseph	Worcs	Mch	131
1797	AUSTIN,	Joseph	Mon	Dec	721
1760	AUSTIN,	Katherine	Bucks	Nov	412
1751	AUSTIN,	Mary	Rutld	Jne	164
1754	AUSTIN,	Mary	Beds	Mch	66
1755	AUSTIN,	Mary	Bucks	Jly	180
1756	AUSTIN,	Mary AwW	Lond	Jny	1
1767	AUSTIN,	Mary	Middx	Sep	331
1770	AUSTIN,	Mary	Middx	Apr	128
1771	AUSTIN,	Mary	Middx	Feb	42
1771	AUSTIN,	Mary	Lond	May	191
1775	AUSTIN,	Mathias	Middx	Jne	219
1784	AUSTIN,	Morgan	Middx	Dec	627
1774	AUSTIN,	Peter	SHant	Mch	76
1800	AUSTIN,	Philip, otherwise Phillip	Middx	Apr	250
1759	AUSTIN,	formerly ROTHERY, Rachel (Ltd Pr)	Middx	Sep	287
1761	AUSTIN,	Sir Ralph	Surry	Sep	307
1784	AUSTIN,	Ralph	Lond	Sep	489
1762	AUSTIN,	Richard AwW Pts —	Middx	May	182
1793	AUSTIN,	Richard	Lond	Feb	61
1754	AUSTIN,	Robert (Dble Pr) W rgd 1744,1	Middx	Oct	264
1763	AUSTIN,	Robert	Pts	Apr	163
1766	AUSTIN,	Robert	Middx	Feb	45
1754	AUSTIN,	Samuel AwW	Pts	Jny	1
1761	AUSTIN,	Samuel	Middx	Feb	44
1770	AUSTIN,	Samuel AwW unadm. W rgd 1761,44	Middx	Nov	—
1797	AUSTIN,	Sarah	Derby	Sep	583
1754	AUSTIN,	Southerton	Middx	Nov	292
1784	AUSTIN,	Tabitha	Essex	Aug	425
1751	AUSTIN,	Thomas	Surry	Nov	298
1753	AUSTIN,	Thomas	Derby	Jne	158
1755	AUSTIN,	Thomas (Dble Pr) W rgd Jne 1753	Derby	Apr	—
1763	AUSTIN,	Thomas	Pts	Aug	366
1764	AUSTIN,	Thomas	Middx	Jly	248
1768	AUSTIN,	Thomas	Glos	Jny	1
1777	AUSTIN,	Thomas	Surry	Mch	93
1779	AUSTIN,	Thomas	Kent	Feb	36
1786	AUSTIN,	Thomas	Lond	Jly	360
1796	AUSTIN,	Thomas "Victory" Ltd AwW	Pts	Feb	52
1799	AUSTIN,	otherwise AUSTEN, Thomas	Irel	Jly	472
1800	AUSTIN,	Thomas	Middx	Feb	80
1800	AUSTIN,	Thomas	Middx	Oct	696
1757	AUSTIN,	William	Nhant	Jny	2
1759	AUSTIN,	William	Middx	Jny	1
1759	AUSTIN,	William AwW	Pts	Nov	347
1767	AUSTIN,	William	Middx	Sep	330
1773	AUSTIN,	William	Middx	Mch	89
1774	AUSTIN,	William	Lond	Oct	357

1778	AUSTIN, William	Surry	Nov	429
1779	AUSTIN, William	Surry	May	185
1783	AUSTIN, William, Esq.	Oxon	Jly	333
1784	AUSTIN, William	Middx	Apr	186
1784	AUSTIN, William	Surry	Jly	363
1784	AUSTIN, William	Middx	Nov	584
1789	AUSTIN, William No ship	Pts	Aug	417
1793	AUSTIN, Dr. William, Dr. of Physic	Middx	Jny	2
1800	AUSTIN, William (by int dec)	Lond	Dec	833
1777	AUSTIS, Thomas	Devon	Aug	339
1783	AUSTON, John	Pts	Apr	159
1776	AUSTREY, Ann	Middx	Jne	253
1776	AUSTREY, Thomas AwW	Middx	Jne	253
1757	AUSTWICK, Amor	Surry	Dec	348
1752	AUSTWICK, Joseph	Middx	Apr	82
1763	AUSTWICK, Joseph	Middx	May	210
1778	AUSTWICK, Joseph AwW unadm. W rgd 1763,210	Middx	Jny	—
1754	AUSTWICK, William	Lond	Nov	292
1782	AUTERAC, Mary	Middx	Dec	569
1757	AUTHER, otherwise ARTHER, Samuel AwW	Pts	Nov	319
1752	AUTRAM, William	Pts	Feb	27
1777	AUVACHE, John	Middx	Aug	339
1785	AUVACHE, Mary	Lond	Oct	489
1800	AUVERGNE, James D', Esq. A Maj-Gen in H.M.Forces	SHant	Jny	—
1753	AUVERQUERQUE, Rt Hon William Maurice D' late Count de Nassau	Pts	Jly	202
1777	AUVERS, Michael D'	Nhant	Feb	62
1750	AUVRAY, Claudius	Pts	May	136
1782	AUVRAY, Mary	Middx	Jne	262
1789	AUVRAY, Mary (Dble Pr) W rgd 1782, 262	Middx	Feb	—
1767	AUVRAY, Michiel	Pts	Apr	121
1779	AVANT, Ann	Devon	Dec	483
1797	AVARD, Sarah	Sussx	Dec	721
1796	AVARD, Thomas	Sussx	Jne	291
1769	AVARNE, Job Jeffries, otherwise AVERNE, Jefferys AwW	Staff	Aug	271
1795	AVARNE, Jonah Jefferies	Wark	May	294
1784	AVARNE, Rev. Thomas	Staff	Mch	118
1787	AVEARY, otherwise AVEREY, Elizabeth	Surry	Sep	395
1778	AVELINE, Anne	Middx	Mch	93
1772	AVELINE, Daniel	Middx	Sep	316
1756	AVELINE, Elizabeth	Middx	Nov	286
1795	AVELINE, Samuel	Herfd	Jne	359
1756	AVENAL, Alice	Lond	Dec	317
1773	AVENANT, Charles D'	SHant	Aug	327
1798	AVENANT, Thomas D', Esq.	Salop	Aug	532
1799	AVENELL, George	Surry	Jne	414
1785	AVENELL, Henry	Wilts	Oct	489
1787	AVENELL, Henry	Wilts	Jne	251
1767	AVENELL, John	Sussx	May	161
1793	AVENELL, John	Middx	Jny	1
1758	AVENT, James	Pts	Oct	282

1783	AVENT, John	Corn	Jly	331
1760	AVENT, otherwise HEAVENS, Philip AwW	Pts	Mch	85
1775	AVENT, Tristram AwW	Devon	Apr	126
1769	AVERA, otherwise AVORY, Mary	Pts	Dec	402
1792	AVERALL, otherwise AVERELL, Rachel	Middx	May	254
1774	AVERAY, John	Brstl	Apr	125
1762	AVERDALL, otherwise EVERDELL, Richard	Pts	Sep	375
1792	AVERELL, otherwise AVERALL, Rachel	Middx	May	254
1787	AVEREY, otherwise AVEARY, Elizabeth	Surry	Sep	395
1768	AVEREY, William	Lond	Feb	41
1758	AVERHOULT, D', otherwise Rt Hon Lady Anna Jacoba HOEUFFT (Ltd Pr)	Pts	Feb	28
1788	AVERHOULT, Anna Magdalena D'	Pts	Feb	
1786	AVERHOULT, Isabella Agneta D', otherwise Isabella Agnes D'	Pts	Jne	
1788	AVERHOULT, Isabella Agneta D', otherwise Isabella Agnes D' (Dble Pr) W rgd Jne 1786	Pts	Feb	
1790	AVERIS, John	Middx	Feb	56
1775	AVERNAS, Hon Antonio Lopes Suasso D', Baron (Ltd Prs)	Pts	Dec	479
1769	AVERNE, otherwise AVARNE, Job Jeffries, otherwise Jefferys AwW	Staff	Aug	271
1792	AVERY, Alpheus	Surry	Nov	542
1751	AVERY, Ann	Surry	Dec	325
1752	AVERY, Ann	Berks	Feb	27
1762	AVERY, Ann	Surry	May	182
1772	AVERY, Anne	Cntby	Oct	348
1796	AVERY, Anne BICKERSTETH, formerly	Wmord	Sep	446
1764	AVERY, Dr. Benjamin, Dr of Laws	Surry	Aug	295
1764	AVERY, Benjamin	Middx	Sep	336
1784	AVERY, Benjamin "Formidable"&"Glorieux"	Pts	Oct	534
1763	AVERY, David AwW	Middx	Mch	104
1763	AVERY, David AwW W rgd Mch last	Middx	Nov	—
1763	AVERY, Diana	Chich	Aug	366
1763	AVERY, Edward AwW	Pts	Jly	319
1779	AVERY, otherwise EVORY, Edward	Middx	Mch	100
1798	AVERY, Edward	Kent	Feb	75
1788	AVERY, Elizabeth	Dorst	Apr	170
1797	AVERY, Elizabeth	Surry	Jny	1
1798	AVERY, Elizabeth	Middx	Oct	631
1787	AVERY, Esther	Middx	Jne	257
1753	AVERY, Francis (sent)	Middx	Feb	37
1787	AVERY, George	Middx	Mch	102
1755	AVERY, Henry	Berks	Nov	274
1797	AVERY, Henry Thomas	Middx	May	291
1786	AVERY, Isabel	Middx	Feb	60
1771	AVERY, James	Wilts	Jly	283
1793	AVERY, James	Middx	Jny	1
1799	AVERY, James	Devon	Oct	694
1757	AVERY, John	SHant	Sep	265
1770	AVERY, John	Lond	Nov	387
1775	AVERY, John	Middx	Dec	452

```
1778  AVERY, John                                          Kent   Aug 308
1780  AVERY, John  AwW unadm. W rgd 1775, 452              Middx  Sep  --
1800  AVERY, John                                          Surry  Dec 833
1753  AVERY, Joseph                              Pts -     Surry  Dec 307
1756  AVERY, Joseph  AwW unadm. W rgd 1747,300             Middx  Feb  --
1777  AVERY, Martha                                        Surry  Dec 495
1798  AVERY, Martha Christian                              Bucks  Oct 631
1750  AVERY, Mary                                          Lond   Aug 250
1753  AVERY, Mary                                          Middx  Feb  37
1754  AVERY, Mary  AwW                                     Middx  Dec 317
1771  AVERY, Mary                                          Lond   Apr 142
1775  AVERY, Mary                                          Surry  May 168
1778  AVERY, Mary                                          Middx  Jne 230
1798  AVERY, Mary                                          Middx  Oct 631
1771  AVERY, Richard                                       Berks  Jny   1
1759  AVERY, Robert                              Pts -     Middx  May 155
1751  AVERY, Samuel                                        Lond   Jny   1
1760  AVERY, Samuel                                        Middx  Nov 412
1762  AVERY, Samuel                                        Yorks  Mch  89
1783  AVERY, Sarah                                         Nhant  Nov 548
1795  AVERY, Sarah                                         Surry  Aug 492
1756  AVERY, Stephen                                       Middx  Feb  26
1762  AVERY, Thomas                                        Surry  Jny   1
1768  AVERY, Thomas  Ser  AwW                              Pts    Apr 138
1766  AVERY, William                                       Middx  Jne 209
1772  AVERY, William                                       Middx  Apr 119
1797  AVES, James                                          Sfolk  Mch 125
1772  AVESAET, Catharina VOSCH VAN  (Ltd Pr)     Pts       Oct 387
1782  AVESAET, Hon Lady Maria Anna VOSCH VAN
        (Ltd Pr)                                           Pts    May 256
1776  AVESAET, Ysbram VOSCH VAN, Esq. (Ltd Pr) Pts         Mch  10
1760  AVESON, Richard                                      Middx  Jly 270
1752  AVESS, otherwise AVIS, otherwise JAVIS,
        Thomas  AwW                            Pts -     Devon  Nov 267
1761  AVILA, Aron                                          Middx  Dec 415
1790  AVINS, John                                          Worcs  Jly 317
1782  AVINS, Sarah                                         Middx  Oct 478
1752  AVIS, Elizabeth                                      Berks  Mch  56
1775  AVIS, Hannah                                         Surry  Jly 259
1777  AVIS, John                               Pts -     Kent   Feb  50
1790  AVIS, Richard                                        Devon  Feb  56
1775  AVIS, Robert                                         Surry  Aug 298
1778  AVIS, Robert  AwW unadm. W rgd Aug 1775    Surry  May  --
1752  AVIS, otherwise JAVIS, otherwise AVESS,
        Thomas  AwW                            Pts -     Devon  Nov 267
1771  AVISON, Charles  AwW or Testy Sched        Newcl  Feb  42
1783  AVISON, Edward                                       Newcl  Dec 596
1782  AVISON, Esther, otherwise Hester                     Bucks  Nov 526
1782  AVISON, Thomas  AwW                                  Bucks  Dec 569
1769  AVORY, otherwise AVERA, Mary                         Pts    Dec 402
1764  AVOY, John MC                                        Pts    Jne 233
1800  AVRON, Pierre Sebastian                              Middx  May 337
1800  AVRON, Pierre Sebastian                              Middx  May  --
```

```
1797   AWARD, Henry                                      Surry  Dec 721
1785   AWART, otherwise EWART, otherwise ILEVERT,
       otherwise HEVERT, John  "Major" &
       "Monmouth"  Anor Grant Jly last                   Pts    Apr
1768   AWBERY, Edward                                     Berks  Mch  94
1774   AWBERY, otherwise ABUEARY, otherwise
       AUBERY, Elizabeth                                  Berks  Jly 252
1775   AWBERY, Rev. John                                  Berks  Oct 365
1765   AWBREY, Francis                                    Middx  Sep 319
1784   AWBREY, John William, Esq.                         Bath   Mch 118
1763   AWBREY, Mary                                       Berks  Jne 263
1762   AWBREY, Samuel                                     Berks  May 182
1758   AWBREY, William                                    Lond   Jly 207
1784   AWBREY, William  "Princessa","Ranger" &
       "Gibraltar"                                        Pts    Jne 302
1797   AWCOCK, Thomas                                     Kent   Jny   1
1773   AWDLEY, Thomas                                     Norf   Jly 276
1750   AWDRY, Ann  AwW                                    Wilts  Jne 185
1800   AWDRY, Jane                                        Wilts  Jne 431
1754   AWDRY, Jeremiah, Esq.                              Wilts  Nov 291
1797   AWDRY, John, Esq.                                  Wilts  May 291
1769   AWDRY, Martha                                      Wilts  Aug 271
1800   AWDRY, Mary  AwW                                   Wilts  Jne 431
1789   AWNOTT, otherwise ARNAT, otherwise ANNOTT,
       James "Monmouth"&"Defence"                         Pts    May 232
1783   AWOOD, Thomas  AwW                                 Lond   Oct 493
1762   AWSE, James                                        Devon  Feb  37
1769   AWSE, James  AwW of Gds unadm. W rgd
       1762, 37                                           Devon  Aug  --
1776   AWSE, James  AwW of Gds twice unadm.
       W rgd 1762,37  Last grant Aug 1769                 Devon  Oct  --
1764   AWSE, Robert, Esq.                                 Devon  Oct 376
1787   AWSITER, John                                      Middx  Mch 101
1753   AWSON, Thomas                                      Coven  Jly 192
1750   AWSON, Tonns, otherwise LARSON, Tola              Pts    Mch  84
1775   AXEL, Abraham                                      Pts    Jly 259
1797   AXELL, John                                        Middx  Jne 393
1756   AXFORD, Benjamin                                   Lond   Jne 156
1776   AXFORD, Benjamin  AwW                              SHant  Mch 107
1777   AXFORD, Rev. Benjamin  AwW of Gds unadm.
       First grant Mch 1776                               SHant  Sep  --
1770   AXFORD, Dorothy                                    Lond   Dec 420
1776   AXFORD, Eleanor                                    Wilts  Jly 295
1779   AXFORD, Eleanor  AwW unadm. W rgd Jly,1776 Wilts  Jne  --
1750   AXFORD, Jonathan                                   Som    Nov 344
1791   AXFORD, Jonathan                                   Surry  Mch 108
1794   AXFORD, Jonathan  AwW of Gds unadm.  W
       rgd Mch 1791                                       Surry  Mch  --
1778   AXFORD, Sarah                                      SHant  Jny   1
1767   AXFORD, Susannah  Ltd AwW                          Middx  Jly 250
1771   AXFORD, Thomas                                     Middx  Dec 466
1799   AXFORD, Thomas                                     Surry  Jly 472
1760   AXFORD, William                                    Pts    Mch  85
```

1780	AXFORD, William	Lond	Sep	425
1792	AXFORD, William "Iris" & "Southampton"	Kent	Jne	313
1770	AXTELL, Elizabeth	Lond	Jny	1
1769	AXTELL, Francis	Middx	Mch	73
1775	AXTELL, Henry	Middx	Feb	38
1758	AXTELL, John	Herts	Dec	354
1763	AXTELL, John	Surry	Jne	263
1777	AXTELL, John	Middx	Jne	250
1774	AXTELL, Joseph	Middx	Jny	1
1795	AXTELL, William	Surry	Sep	531
1764	AXTON, Rev. Thomas	Kent	Mch	78
1759	AXX, Joseph	Pts	Nov	347
1775	AYANSSON, Swann	Middx	Jny	1
1754	AYARS, Ann	Middx	Jly	187
1784	AYARS, otherwise AYERS, John Ser "Bellona","Fortune"&"Monmouth"	Middx	Mch	117
1752	AYARS, Richard	Middx	May	115
1798	AYCRIGG, Benjamin	Worcs	Feb	74
1800	AYDON, Ann	Middx	Jly	499
1779	AYEARST, Thomas	Kent	Oct	401
1760	AYER, Richard AwW	Lond	May	180
1795	AYER, Thomas AwW	Essex	Jne	361
1759	AYERS, Edward	Pts	Jny	1
1784	AYERS, otherwise EYRE, otherwise AYRES, Elizabeth	Middx	May	244
1758	AYERS, John	Wilts	Apr	100
1760	AYERS, otherwise EARS, John	SHant	Jne	225
1784	AYERS, otherwise AYARS, John Ser "Bellona","Fortune"&"Monmouth"	Middx	Mch	117
1787	AYERS, otherwise AYRES, John	Essex	Nov	479
1772	AYERS, Joseph	Wilts	Jly	243
1761	AYERS, Margaret	Middx	Jly	239
1784	AYERS, otherwise AYRES, Mary AwW	Wilts	Sep	489
1754	AYERS, Matthew	Surry	Aug	217
1776	AYERS, Phillis	Middx	Jne	253
1781	AYERS, Thomas	Beds	Nov	510
1750	AYERS, William	Middx	Apr	101
1755	AYERS, William	Lond	Oct	252
1760	AYERST, Catherine AwW	Roch	May	180
1766	AYERST, Catharine AwW of Gds unadm. W rgd May 1760	Roch	Mch	--
1777	AYERST, Jane	Kent	Oct	406
1765	AYERST, Dr. William, D.D.	Cntby	May	167
1763	AYESCOUGH, Mary	SHant	Mch	105
1756	AYLEN, otherwise ALLEN, Richard	Pts	May	141
1789	AYLES, Barnabas	SHant	Mch	131
1789	AYLES, James	Sussx	Oct	481
1780	AYLES, John	Dorst	Sep	425
1783	AYLES, otherwise EALES, John Ser W rgd Sep 1780	Dorst	Apr	--
1800	AYLES, William	Middx	Sep	641
1784	AYLESBURY, Eleanor	Wark	Jne	302
1761	AYLESBURY, Sarah	Wark	May	157

1753	AYLESBURY, Wilson, Esq.	Wark	Jne	158
1757	AYLESFORD, Rt Hon Heneage, Earl of	Surry	Jly	211
1777	AYLESFORD, Rt Hon Heneage, Earl of	Middx	May	195
1772	AYLETT, George AwW	Essex	Jne	202
1782	AYLETT, George, Esq.	Berks	Oct	478
1783	AYLETT, Meliora AwW	Essex	Aug	397
1783	AYLETT, Sarah AwW	Essex	Aug	397
1793	AYLETT, Sarah AwW	Middx	Mch	124
1800	AYLETT, Thomas	Lond	Oct	696
1796	AYLETT, William	Middx	Feb	53
1756	AYLEWORTH, Jonathan	Middx	Jly	186
1780	AYLIFF, Heneritta, otherwise Henrietta	Surry	Mch	117
1770	AYLIFF, Mary	Middx	Mch	84
1780	AYLIFF, William AwW	Surry	Mch	117
1778	AYLIFFE, Elizabeth	Middx	Jne	230
1756	AYLIFFE, George	Middx	Dec	317
1758	AYLIFFE, George (Dble Pr) W rgd Dec 1756	Middx	Jne	—
1770	AYLIFFE, Henry	Surry	Jny	1
1761	AYLIFFE, Joseph	Lond	Apr	115
1781	AYLIFFE, Robert	Pts	Dec	568
1800	AYLIN, Henry	Middx	May	336
1797	AYLING, Elizabeth	SHant	Aug	538
1761	AYLING, John	Sussx	Feb	44
1751	AYLING, Mary	Surry	Dec	325
1770	AYLING, Mary	Surry	Oct	348
1771	AYLING, otherwise AYLWIN, Peter	Sussx	Jly	283
1771	AYLING, Richard	Sussx	Apr	142
1785	AYLING, Richard, Esq.	Sussx	Jly	349
1785	AYLING, Richard, Esq. (Dble Pr) W rgd Jly last	Sussx	Oct	—
1797	AYLING, Richard	Surry	May	291
1800	AYLING, Thomas	SHant	Sep	639
1751	AYLING, William AwW	Pts	Oct	273
1772	AYLING, William	Sussx	Apr	119
1779	AYLISSE, Samuel	Pts	Jly	283
1750	AYLLETT, William AwW	Kent	May	135
1766	AYLLETT, William	Essex	Jne	209
1788	AYLMER, Betty	Haver	Jne	281
1795	AYLMER, George	Lond	May	292
1754	AYLMER, Rt Hon Henry, late Lord	Kent	Jly	187
1766	AYLMER, Rt Hon Henry, Lord	SHant	Dec	439
1800	AYLMER, John	Middx	Apr	250
1776	AYLMER, Sir Mathew, Bart.	Dubln	May	209
1780	AYLMER, Richard, Esq.	Dubln	Feb	54
1769	AYLMER, Rev. Robert	Surry	Sep	299
1761	AYLMER, Whitgift, Esq. AwW	Pts	Dec	415
1781	AYLOFFE, Sir Joseph, Bart.	Surry	May	221
1797	AYLOFFE, Dame Margaret	Surry	Mch	125
1755	AYLOFFE, Dr. William, Dr of Laws AwW unadm. W rgd 1728, 102	Camb	Mch	—
1765	AYLOFFE, Dr. William, Dr of Laws AwW of Gds twice unadm. W rgd 1728,102 Last grant Mch 1755	Camb		

1796	AYLOTT, Samuel		Herts Apr 158
1796	AYLOTT, otherwise ELLIOT, Samuel W rgd		
	last month		Herts May 158
1786	AYLWARD, Elizabeth		Kent Oct 499
1763	AYLWARD, John	Pts -	SHant Dec 537
1762	AYLWARD, Mary		Essex May 182
1750	AYLWARD, Peter		Pts Aug 250
1797	AYLWARD, Peter		SHant Jne 394
1781	AYLWARD, Robert		Hunts Nov 510
1760	AYLWARD, William		Pts Feb 45
1799	AYLWIN, John		Surry Sep 639
1771	AYLWIN, otherwise AYLING, Peter		Sussx Jly 283
1767	AYLWIN, Richard		Sussx Oct 360
1792	AYLWIN, Richard		SHant Mch 124
1799	AYLWORTH, Samuel, Esq.		Wark Mch 161
1786	AYLY, Elizabeth		Middx Mch 133
1781	AYMER, David		Middx Nov 510
1798	AYMES, Mary		Middx Oct 631
1772	AYNGE, John		Lond Mch 81
1781	AYNGE, Richard		Middx Feb 54
1769	AYNGE, William		Pts Apr 110
1793	AYNSCOMB, Anthony		Surry Sep 451
1800	AYNSCOMB, Benjamin		Surry May 336
1787	AYNSCOMB, Catherine		Surry Nov 479
1798	AYNSCOMB, Edward		Surry May 306
1755	AYNSCOMB, Mary		Kent Jne 153
1793	AYNSCOMB, Mary		Kent Oct 488
1800	AYNSCOMB, Mary		Surry Mch 171
1784	AYNSCOMB, William AwW		Surry Mch 118
1799	AYNSCOMBE, Charlotte Anne		Surry Apr 239
1800	AYNSWORTH, Frances		Middx Mch 172
1754	AYNSWORTH, George		Pts Feb 31
1789	AYNSWORTH, John		Staff Mch 131
1761	AYNSWORTH, Lawrence		Berks Aug 275
1774	AYNSWORTH, Rowland, Esq.		Middx Jny 1
1791	AYNSWORTH, Rowland, Esq.		Middx Dec 553
1788	AYNSWORTH, Samuel		Herts Oct 468
1776	AYNSWORTH, Sarah		Middx Jny 1
1750	AYNSWORTH, Susanna		Bath Nov 344
1795	AYNSWORTH, Thomas		Wark Jny 2
1761	AYRAY, William (Dble Pr) W proved Nov		
	1760		Middx Jne --
1765	AYRE, Charity		Surry Dec 438
1765	AYRE, Hester		Lond Jny 1
1781	AYRE, John		Surry Jny 1
1795	AYRE, John, Esq.		Leics Sep 531
1794	AYRE, Martha AwW		Norf Jne 294
1790	AYRE, Ralph		Middx Apr 169
1769	AYRE, Sarah		Kent Jny 1
1784	AYRE, Thomas		Essex Mch 117
1800	AYRE, Thomasine, otherwise Thomsin		Devon Apr 250
1755	AYRE, William		Pts Oct 252
1759	AYRE, William AwW (by int dec)		Pts Apr 115

```
1775  AYRE, William                                            Leics Nov 401
1779  AYRE, William                                            Som   Oct 401
1779  AYRES, Benjamin                                          Som   Aug 333
1757  AYRES, Charles                                           Lond  Jne 179
1769  AYRES, David  AwW                                        Pts   May 150
1762  AYRES, Elizabeth                                         Herts May 182
1784  AYRES, otherwise AYERS, otherwise EYRE,
        Elizabeth                                              Middx May 244
1789  AYRES, Francis                                           Chest Nov 528
1763  AYRES, Gabriel, Esq.                                     Sussx Nov 493
1769  AYRES, George                                            Lond  May 150
1780  AYRES, George                                            Middx Sep 425
1791  AYRES, George                                            Kent  Jny   1
1768  AYRES, James                            Pts - Middx Aug 305
1777  AYRES, otherwise AIRES, James                            Pts   Nov 445
1758  AYRES, John                                              Surry Jny   1
1758  AYRES, John                             Pts - Devon Aug 236
1766  AYRES, John                                              Middx Jne 209
1766  AYRES, John, Esq.                                        Middx Dec 439
1769  AYRES, John  AwW unadm. W rgd 1758                       Surry Jly  --
1771  AYRES, John                                              Middx Feb  42
1774  AYRES, John  AwW unadm. W rgd Feb 1771                   Middx Jne  --
1783  AYRES, John  AwW of Gds unadm. W rgd 1771,
        42 Last grant Jne 1774                                 Middx Oct  --
1787  AYRES, otherwise AYERS, John                             Essex Nov 479
1763  AYRES, John Saully                                       Surry Mch 103
1772  AYRES, Joseph                                            Berks Dec 430
1788  AYRES, Joseph                                            Middx Dec 572
1799  AYRES, Joseph                                            Oxon  Apr 240
1762  AYRES, Margaret                                          Middx Jne 230
1800  AYRES, Margaret                                          Essex Jly 500
1760  AYRES, Mary                                              Lond  Jny   1
1776  AYRES, Mary                                              Surry Mch 108
1784  AYRES, otherwise AYERS, Mary  AwW                        Wilts Sep 489
1767  AYRES, Peter                                             Middx Dec 435
1785  AYRES, Phineas  "Active"                                 Pts   Sep 451
1794  AYRES, Rachel                                            Kent  Nov 534
1755  AYRES, Richard  AwW                                      SHant Oct 252
1780  AYRES, Robert                                            Pts   Oct 458
1781  AYRES, Samuel                                            Pts   Sep 418
1790  AYRES, Susanna                                           Beds  Feb  55
1780  AYRES, Susannah                                          Middx Nov 503
1753  AYRES, Thomas  AwW of Gds unadm.  W rgd
        1714, 1                                                Middx Mch  --
1771  AYRES, Thomas  AwW                                       Kent  Jly 282
1776  AYRES, Thomas                                            Surry Mch 107
1776  AYRES, Thomas  AwW                                       Surry Mch 108
1796  AYRES, Thomas                                            Kent  Jne 291
1799  AYRES, Walter  Ser  "Salisbury"                          Pts   Mch 163
1763  AYRES, William                                           SHant May 211
1783  AYRES, William                                           Lond  Dec 596
1795  AYREY, Jannet                                            Middx Aug 492
1782  AYREY, William, Esq.                                     Middx Jny   1
```

1784	AYRLEY, otherwise EARLY, James			
	"Richmond" & "Gibraltar"		Pts	Jly 381
1754	AYSCOGHE, Edward, Esq. AwW unadm.			
	W rgd 1741, 329		Lincs	Dec 317
1776	AYSCOUGH, Anne		Middx	Apr 159
1792	AYSCOUGH, Catherine VENN, formerly		Hunts	May 303
1799	AYSCOUGH, Elizabeth		Lincs	Aug 560
1763	AYSCOUGH, Dr. Francis, D.D.		Brstl	Sep 415
1757	AYSCOUGH, Gabriel		Pts	Jny 1
1759	AYSCOUGH, James		Lond	Nov 346
1789	AYSCOUGH, James, Esq.	Pts -	SHant	Nov 520
1768	AYSCOUGH, John, Esq. AwW		Pts	Feb 41
1787	AYSCOUGH, John AwW		SHant	May 195
1767	AYSCOUGH, Martha		Lond	Jny 1
1765	AYSCOUGH, Mary		Essex	Feb 40
1760	AYSCOUGH, Richard		Pts	Nov 412
1768	AYSCOUGH, Richard AwW unadm. W rgd 1760,			
	412		Pts	Jny --
1775	AYSCOUGH, Thomas		Lond	Jly 259
1791	AYSCOUGH, Rev. William		Berks	May 208
1800	AYSCOUGH, William		Lond	Jne 429
1754	AYSHCOMBE, John		Wark	Feb 66
1775	AYSHFORD, Daniel		Berks	Jne 217
1750	AYSHFORD, Frances		Berks	Mch 66
1798	AYTON, Ann		Middx	Jny 1
1769	AYTON, James		Middx	Sep 299
1777	AYTON, John		Coven	May 194
1787	AYTON, John, Esq.		Middx	Dec 528
1796	AYTON, Obadiah		Coven	May 232
1753	AYTON, William		Middx	Mch 69
1798	AYTON, William		Lond	Oct 631
1800	AYTON, William		Chest	Jly 499
1752	AYTONE, Charles AwW		Pts	Jny 1
1773	AZEBI, otherwise AZUBI, David (Ltd Pr)		Pts	Aug 318
1785	AZEBI, Sabitay Vintura		Pts	Nov 536
1785	AZEL, otherwise AZELE, John Ser "Sampson"		Pts	Jny 1
1785	AZELE, otherwise AZEL, John Ser "Sampson"		Pts	Jny 1
1784	AZEYEDO, Moses Cohen D'		Lond	Oct 547
1773	AZUBI, otherwise AZEBI, David (Ltd Pr)		Pts	Aug 318

Year	Name	Notes	Place	Month	Page
1781	BAACK, John Albert				
	alias John Abrot		Middlesex	Aug	375
1795	Mary		Middlesex	Jun	365
1762	BAAD, Adam	Pts	Middlesex	Sep	370
1793	BAALDE, Jan	Ltd Prob	Pts	Dec	582
1778	Magdalena Hendrietta,				
	alias Henrietta		Pts	Feb	47
1761	BAAR, Edward, alias BEER		Middlesex	Oct	340
1773	BAARE, Elizabeth van de		Pts	Jan	37
1775	BAARNAART, Anna Johanna				
	formerly VERHAMME	Ltd Prob	Pts	Oct	367
1771	BAART, Abraham,				
	alias BAERT		Pts	Sep	365
1773	BAART, Johannes		Pts	May	193
1786	BAARTMANS, Abraham, Esq	Ltd Prob	Pts	Mar	144
1783	Nicolaas	Ltd Prob	Pts	May	218
1766	Pieter	Ltd Prob	Pts	Aug	293
1767	BAAS, Joachim Gerhard		London	Apr	123
1778	Joachim Gerhard	A with W unad			
		W regd 123 Legard	London	Jan	-
1785	Joachim Gerhard	A with W unad			
		W regd 123 Legard			
		By Int Decree			
		Another Grant, Jan 1778	London	Feb	-
1789	Mary		Middlesex	Aug	419
1798	Mary		Norfolk	May	307
1752	BABAULT, Isaac	A with W	Guernsey	May	117
1771	BABB, Edward		Hertford	May	193
1789	Elizabeth		Middlesex	Jan	9
1754	John		Pts	Feb	32
1756	John		Surrey	Aug	216
1795	John		Surrey	Jan	6
1772	Joseph		Essex	Aug	283
1786	Joseph		Middlesex	Oct	503
1793	Joseph		Cornwall	May	245
1756	Martha		Devon	Jan	2
1796	Michael		Middlesex	Dec	595
1776	Moses	Ser	Pts	Jun	255
1762	Robert		Pts	Jul	286
1761	Thomas	Ser	Pts	Aug	277
1761	William		Hertford	May	159
1791	William		Cornwall	Jul	318
1794	William		Middlesex	May	241
1796	William		Lincoln	Feb	54
1751	BABBAGE, John				
	alias BABBIDGE		Pts	Aug	229
1751	BABBIDGE, John				
	alias BABBAGE		Pts	Aug	229
1759	Mary		Surrey	Aug	258
1783	BABBINGTON, Ann		Middlesex	May	218
1783	Ann	W regd last month	Middlesex	Jun	

Year	Name	Notes	Place	Month	No.
1750	BABBS, Benjamin				
	alias BEBB alias BOBBS		Pts	Apr	106
1768	Elizabeth		Essex	Jul	267
1771	Elizabeth	A with W unad			
		W regd Jul 1768	Essex	Nov	
1779	Elizabeth	A with W twice unad			
		W regd 267 Secker			
		Last grant Nov.1771	Essex	Oct	
1784	Sarah		Hertford	Sep	492
1794	Susannah		Essex	Aug	405
1771	BABELL, Peter		Middlesex	Oct	396
1769	BABER, Catherine		Bath	Feb	33
1756	John		Bristol	Sep	238
1788	John	A with W	Middlesex		576
1792	John	A with W of goods unad			
		W regd 376 Calvert	Middlesex	Oct	
1780	Katherine		Essex	May	238
1750	Sophia		Somerset	Apr	106
1783	Thomas Draper, Esq	A with W	Cambridge	May	216
1766	BABHAM, Elizabeth		Buckinghamshire	Jan	4
1786	Thomas		Buckinghamshire	Sep	464
1756	BABINGTON, Catharine		Middlesex	Feb	30
1788	Elizabeth		Middlesex	Feb	56
1798	Ferdinando		Warwick	Jun	383
1752	John		N'hamptonshire	Jan	2
1790	John		Surrey	Feb	60
1791	Lydia		Leicestershire	Sep	420
1797	Rev. Matthew		Leicestershire	Mar	127
1776	Thomas		Leicester	Jul	300
1778	Thomas		Middlesex	Sep	347
1774	BACARI, Baptista	poor	Surrey	Jul	255
1799	BACCANEAU, Lydia				
	alias BACONNEAU		Winchester	May	338
1784	BACHHURST, Richard		London	Jan	5
1797	BACCHUS, Edward		London	Nov	675
1767	Henry		Pts	Jul	254
1770	John		N'hamptonshire	Dec	421
1781	John		Pts	Apr	181
1781	John	A with W	Middlesex	Jul	328
1777	Richard		Hertfordshire	Nov	446
1779	Richard		Buckinghamshire	Mar	88
1788	William		Surrey	Jun	288
1779	BACCUS, John		London	Oct	404
1782	BACH, John Christian		Middlesex	Feb	64
1774	Mary, formerly SOAMES		Middlesex	May	169
1798	Robert		Middlesex	Aug	526
1760	William		Hereford	May	181
1772	BACHARACH, Livy		London	Dec	433
1756	BACHE, Elizabeth		Stafford	Jun	160
1783	Frances		Middlesex	Oct	499
1794	Humphry, Esq		Middlesex	Oct	485
1757	John	W regd 35 Seymour	Shropshire	Dec	
1761	John		Stafford	Apr	121

	BACHE (contd)				
1786	John		Hertford	Jul	364
1767	Mary		Warwick	Oct	361
1787	Rebekah		Shropshire	Dec	532
1752	Sarah		Shropshire	May	117
1783	Thomas		Shropshire	Jun	280
1796	William	A with W	Southampton	Jan	5
1797	BACHELARD, David		Kent	Jun	398
1752	BACHELER, Giles		Bristol	Mar	57
1764	Lepine John	A with W	Middlesex	Feb	38
1763	BACHELLE, LE, Charlotte		Pts	Feb	72
1784	BACHHURST, Richard		London	Jan	5
1798	BACHIENE, Philip Jan, Esq	Ltd Prob	Pts	Mar	154
1799	BACHILLOR, Thomas				
	alias BATCHILLOR		Middlesex	Mar	163
1778	BACHMAIR, John James		Middlesex	Mar	99
1750	BACHMAN, Jacob		Pts	Jun	188
1774	Jan Fredick	Ltd Prob	Pts	Nov	385
1780	BACHOP, Tobias		Middlesex	Apr	170
1777	BACK, The Right Hon Adriaan				
	alias Adrianus Cornelis de	Ltd Prob	Pts	Jan	8
1770	Edward	Pts	Devon	Jun	220
1770	Edward	Pts Dble Prob			
		W regd Jun last	Devon	Aug	
1757	BACK, DE, Geertruyd	Ltd Prob	Pts	Sep	267
1775	Henrietta Anna				
	formerly VAN SCHINNE		Pts	Feb	40
1764	Isabella Maria				
	formerly NOLTHENIUS		Pts	Sep	338
1770	Jan		Pts	Nov	387
1766	John	Ltd Prob	Pts	Aug	294
1783	BACK, Mary		Kent	Jun	280
1760	Thomain alias Thomazin		London	Apr	137
1759	Thomas		Kent	Jan	4
1771	Thomas		Kent	Feb	48
1784	Thomas	A with W of goods unad			
		W regd 4 Arran	Kent	Mar	
1760	Thomazin alias Thomain		London	Apr	137
1766	BACKER, Catharina				
	formerly DE LA COURT	Ltd Prob	Pts	Mar	98
1759	Catharina Cornelia				
	formerly MUNTER				
	alias BICKER		Pts	Jul	242
1775	Cornelis				
	alias The Worshipful BACKER, Cornelis				
	Lord of BACKERSHAGEN		Pts	Jun	222
1780	Henrick	Ltd Prob	Pts	May	241
1768	Jan de, Lord of				
	Noordwykerhaut and Zick	Ltd Prob	Pts	Feb	42
1778	Jan, Doctor of Laws	Ltd Prob	Pts	Mar	97
1761	The Hon Jan Hendrik	Ltd Prob	Pts	May	158
1782	Jannetje	Ltd Prob	Pts	Oct	482
1770	John alias BECKER				
	alias BAKER		Middlesex	Nov	390

Year	Name	Note	Place	Month	No.
	BACKER (contd)				
1773	John		Hertford	May	194
1771	Maria	Ltd Prob	Pts	May	192
1783	Sarah		Hertford	Jul	335
1762	Wilhelmina				
	alias VAN MIDLUM	Ltd Prob	Pts	Apr	164
1778	BACKERS, Americus		Middlesex	Jan	4
1775	BACKERSHAGEN, Lord of				
	alias BACKER, Cornelius				
	alias BACKER, The Worshipful				
	Cornelius		Pts	Jun	222
1781	BACKHOUSE, Ann		Buckinghamshire	May	229
1761	Cecilia		London	Jan	6
1771	Charles alias BACKHUSE		Essex	May	195
1798	Eleanor		Southampton	Jun	383
1788	Elizabeth		Cumberland	Jul	338
1764	George		Pts	Jul	251
1775	The Rev George		Bedford	Aug	300
1754	Hannah		Middlesex	Dec	317
1768	John		Surrey	Dec	439
1754	James		Middlesex	Mar	69
1790	The Rev James		Cambridge	Oct	452
1798	James		Durham	May	313
1770	Joseph		York	Jul	253
1771	Mary		Middlesex	May	194
1792	Mary		Bedford	Oct	500
1772	Rebeckah		Middlesex	Jul	247
1783	Richard		Pts	May	219
1787	Richard		Buckinghamshire	Feb	52
1765	Robert		Warwickshire	Jan	4
1791	Robert		Hertford	Jan	2
1789	Susanah alias Susannah		Essex	Feb	71
1761	Thomas, Esq		Pts	Jan	5
1765	Thomas		Pts	Jun	208
1782	Thomas		Pts	Dec	574
1796	Rev Thomas		Northampton	Apr	163
1800	Thomas, Esq		Buckinghamshire	Jul	509
1784	William		London	Nov	587
1788	William, Doctor of Divinity		Kent	Oct	471
1788	William, Doctor of Divinity	Dble Prob			
		W regd Oct last	Kent	Nov	
1792	William		Surrey	Apr	198
1799	William	A with W of goods unad			
		Will regd Apr 1792	Surrey	May	
1779	William Henry		Essex	Aug	337
1779	William Henry	Dble Prob			
		Will regd last month	Essex	Sep	
1772	BACKHOLTZ, John		Middlesex	Jun	207
1772	John	Will regd June last	Middlesex	Aug	
1784	BACKHURST, Elizabeth		Kent	Aug	427
1780	BACKHUS, Edward		Oxford	Jan	3

Year	Name	Note	County	Month	Page
1771	BACKHUSE, Charles				
	alias BACKHOUSE		Essex	May	195
1787	BACKLER, Benjamin		London	Jun	252
1781	BACKLIN, John		Pts	Aug	378
1761	BACKON, Thomas				
	alias BACON	A with W	Pts	Jan	6
1793	BACKSHALL, Josiah		Sussex	Feb	70
1799	Mary		Surrey	Aug	572
1750	BACKSHELL, John, Dr of Laws		Chichester	Dec	379
1794	Thomas		Sussex	Jan	10
1784	BACKSTER, Thomas				
	alias BAXTER		Surrey	Mar	120
1766	BACKUS, Johanna		Pts	Aug	293
1799	BACKWAY, Amelia				
	formerly SEABORNE		Middlesex	Dec	827
1771	BACKWELL, Catherine	A with W	N'hampton	Mar	92
1779	Catherine	A with W				
		Will regd 92 Trevor	N'hampton	Jul	
1788	Charlotte		Middlesex	Nov	521
1761	Esther		London	Apr	121
1775	Jane		Middlesex	Nov	402
1785	Jane		Middlesex	May	230
1797	Lucy		Middlesex	Nov	673
1772	Martha	A with W	Monmouth	Oct	350
1779	Richard, Esq	A with W	N'hampton	Jul	290
1764	Sarah		Middlesex	Jul	252
1797	Sarah		Buckingham	Sep	585
1784	Tyringham		Buckinghamshire	Aug	218
1770	William, Esq		Middlesex	Jan	4
1770	William, Esq	Dble Prob				
		Will regd this month	Middlesex	Jan	
1770	BACON, Alice		Middlesex	Jul	253
1762	Ann		Middlesex	Jun	231
1793	Ann		Surrey	Oct	490
1797	Ann formerly WARBOYS	A with W	Middlesex	May	
1787	Anthony	Dble Prob				
		Will Regd Feb 1786	Glamorgan	Mar	
1793	Barbara		Suffolk	Oct	493
1776	Basil		Surrey	Feb	49
1771	Castell, Esq		Norfolk	Mar	93
1771	Catherine		Suffolk	Mar	95
1798	Catherine		Oxford	Apr	233
1755	Sir Edmund, Baronet		Norfolk	Jun	155
1784	Edward		London	Sep	494
1786	Edward, Esq		Middlesex	Mar	142
1793	Edward, Esq	Another Prob				
		Will regd 142 Norfolk	Norfolk	Nov	
1770	Elizabeth		Peterborough	Sep	321
1793	Elizabeth		Middlesex	May	245
1796	Elizabeth		Middlesex	Feb	61
1796	Elizabeth	Will regd Feb last	Middlesex	Apr	
1799	Elizabeth		Middlesex	Jul	481

	BACON (contd)				
1754	Fairchild		Middlesex	Jan	5
1766	Frances		Norwich	Nov	398
1759	George		Pts	Oct	319
1771	George		Middlesex	Jun	244
1783	George		Surrey	Apr	163
1779	Hannah		Middlesex	Dec	488
1757	Henry		Suffolk	Jun	182
1776	Henry		Suffolk	Mar	109
1759	James		Essex	Apr	117
1789	James		Wells	Feb	74
1752	John, Esq		Durham	Jul	178
1759	John		Middlesex	Nov	351
1764	John		Middlesex	Mar	81
1767	John		Berkshire	Dec	438
1772	John		London	Sep	317
1788	John		Suffolk	Jan	5
1799	John, Esq		Middlesex	Aug	565
1780	John Errington		Pts	Jun	304
1788	Joseph		Wells	Apr	173
1792	Joseph		Lincoln	Nov	545
1770	Lawrence		Middlesex	Apr	131
1775	Lydia	A with W	Oxford	Apr	132
1791	Mary		Middlesex	Jan	3
1757	Mathew, Esq		London	Mar	73
1800	Matthew		Southampton	Apr	253
1768	Montagu, Doctor of Physick		Suffolk	Feb	42
1788	Montagu, Doctor of Physick	A with W of goods unad Will regd 42 Secker	Suffolk	Dec	
1762	Nathaniel		Devon	Dec	494
1797	Nicholas, The Rev	By Sent	Suffolk	Dec	724
1761	Nollard		Surrey	Aug	276
1756	Philippa		Essex	Dec	320
1781	Rebecca		Suffolk	Dec	572
1763	Richard		Pts	Sep	418
1786	Samuel		Middlesex	Oct	505
1788	Sarah		Suffolk	Sep	429
1753	Stephan		Wiltshire	Jul	197
1756	Thomas	A with W	Pts	Oct	267
1761	Thomas alias BACKON	A with W	Pts	Jan	6
1787	Thomas		Middlesex		254
1800	The Rev Phannel, Dr of Div	Dble Prob W regd 216 Comwallis Dble Prob Feb 1786	Oxford	Sep	
1768	Tollemach		Suffolk	May	185
1783	William		Middlesex	Jun	280
1787	William		Surrey	Jul	311
1793	William		Norfolk	Oct	495
1796	William		Norfolk	Mar	107
1796	William		Middlesex	Nov	541
1799	BACONNEAU, Lydia alias BACCANEAU		Winchester	May	338
1778	Nicolas		Winchester	Dec	478

1769	BACOT, John		Middlesex	Oct	333
1790	William		Middlesex	Oct	452
1762	BACRAFT, John		Middlesex	Oct	412
1791	BADAM, Catharine		Middlesex	Mar	109
1774	John		London	May	169
1753	William		Monmouth	Dec	308
1789	William		Monmouth	Jul	349
1797	BADCOCK, Abraham	A with W	London	Apr	226
1796	Benjamin		Berkshire	May	238
1785	Francis		Oxford	Feb	63
1768	George		Middlesex	Apr	139
1767	Hannah		Gloucester	Apr	122
1774	Hannah		Middlesex	Dec	421
1777	Isaac	A with W	Middlesex	Sep	376
1763	James		Gloucester	Aug	371
1793	James		Southampton	Sep	453
1751	John	Pts A with W	Cornwall	May	130
1756	John		Middlesex	Mar	58
1786	John Neale, Esq		Devon	Feb	69
1783	Joseph Lanning		Bristol	Jan	2
1800	Mary		Oxford	Apr	255
1767	Robert	A with W annexed	Berkshire	Feb	34
1755	Richard		Middlesex	Nov	277
1763	Richard		Middlesex	Mar	110
1783	Richard Neale, Esq		London	Sep	445
1798	Richard Neale, Esq	A with W of goods unad Will regd 445 Cornwallis	London	Dec	
1765	Samuel		Pts	May	168
1796	Samuel	Ser "Majestic"	Pts	Jul	345
1779	Sarah		Berkshire	Apr	144
1759	William		Canterbury	Jan	6
1774	William		Surrey	Mar	78
1796	William		Surrey	Feb	61
1784	BADDELEY, James		Middlesex	Jan	6
1787	James	Dble Prob Will regd Jan.1784	Middlesex	Dec	
1794	Robert		Middlesex	Dec	597
1783	BADDELY, James, Esq		Southampton	Jul	334
1786	Lucy		Southampton	Jun	319
1769	Susanna		Southampton	Dec	406
1776	BADDILEY, Benjamin		Worcester	Feb	55
1781	Elizabeth		Worcester	Jul	329
1782	Elizabeth	Dble Prob Will regd July last	Worcester	May	
1788	Joseph		Berkshire	Apr	178
1799	BADDILY, Ann		Somersetshire	Jan	9
1794	The Rev William		Somersetshire	May	301
1771	BADDISON, Susanna		Middlesex	Feb	49
1770	Thomas, Esq		Middlesex	Jul	253
1800	BADELEY, Mary		Suffolk	Nov	767
1780	Samuel		Suffolk	Dec	553
1782	BADEN, James	A with W	London	Dec	570
1797	Mary		Wiltshire	Nov	678

1791	BADGE, John		Devon	Jun	265
1751	BADGER, Charles		Gloucester	Nov	300
1800	Charles		Kent	May	343
1768	Daniel		Durham	Mar	98
1777	Edward		Berkshire	May	198
1792	Edward		Oxford	Mar	132
1774	Elizabeth		Kent	Sep	330
1775	Elizabeth		Oxford	Dec	459
1781	Elizabeth		Berkshire	Aug	375
1794	Henry		Middlesex	Mar	124
1752	James		Nottingham	Aug	206
1771	James		Essex	Apr	144
1778	Joan		Gloucester	Feb	51
1754	John		Pts	Aug	220
1766	John		Pts	Jun	213
1757	Joseph		London	Jun	181
1762	Joseph		Warwick	Sep	370
1762	Joseph	A with W	Worcester	Nov	448
1783	Joseph		Staffordshire	Jul	338
1797	Joseph		Worcester	Jul	471
1789	Mary		Surrey	Apr	187
1770	Nathaniel		Worcester	May	176
1785	Nathaniel	A with W of Goods unad Will regd 176 Jenner	Worcester	Dec	
1775	Overbury		Gloucester	Oct	367
1799	Phoebe		Worcester	Aug	567
1750	Richard		Pts	Jan	3
1767	Sarah		Worcester	Aug	297
1768	Sarah		Nottingham	Dec	438
1771	Thomas	A with W	Kent	Jun	244
1779	Thomas		Middlesex	May	188
1752	Wildsmith		Worcester	Nov	268
1758	William		Surrey	May	143
1761	BADHAM, Betty		Berkshire	Dec	421
1763	Charles, alias BAHAM		Bath	Jan	6
1756	John		Worcester	Jan	2
1763	John	A with W	Surrey	Jan	7
1771	John		London	Feb	48
1786	Margaret		Bath	Jul	366
1758	Mary		London	Dec	357
1754	William		Bath	Nov	294
1756	William	A with W	Worcester	Apr	96
1757	William		London	Mar	74
1756	BADHESHALL, James	Ser	Middlesex	Oct	268
1786	BADLAND, William		Hereford	Dec	599
1778	BADLEY, Anthony		Stafford	Nov	433
1783	Anthony	A with W of goods unad Will regd Nov 1778	Staffordshire	Jun	
1783	Elizabeth	A with W	Staffordshire	Jun	284
1783	Ellen		Staffordshire	Jun	284
1783	Henry		Worcester	Jun	284
1790	John		Lincoln	Sep	413
1768	Sarah		Worcester	Jan	5

Year	Name	Notes	Place	Month	Page
1790	BADMAN, Henry		Middlesex	Mar	119
1769	BADNALL, John		Middlesex	May	153
1763	William		Surrey	Nov	496
1784	BADNEDGE, Elizabeth		London	Sep	494
1779	BADRICK, Elizabeth		Buckinghamshire	Jun	232
1792	BADSEY, Sarah		Hereford	Oct	500
1791	BADYER, Joseph		Worcestershire	Apr	166
1788	BAELDE, Hendrick	Ltd Prob	Pts	Jul	338
1771	Michiel	Ltd Prob	Pts	Apr	146
1764	Pieter, The Hon	Ltd Prob	Pts	Jan	4
1773	Rudolph	Ltd Prob	Pts	Apr	146
1779	BAER, Peter		Pts	Jul	289
1762	BAERD, James				
	alias BEARD		Gloucester	Nov	450
1762	BAERE, LA, Peter				
	alias LA BARE				
	alias LA BARRE	A with W	Pts	Jun	
1787	BAERLE, VAN, Henrietta				
	Catharina Elisabeth	Ltd Prob	Pts	Apr	191
1790	Margareta Maria	Ltd Prob	Pts	Mar	162
1782	Sara Maria	Ltd Prob	Pts	Nov	564
1785	BAERLMAN, Hermanus	Ltd Prob	Pts	Dec	586
1771	BAERT, Abraham				
	alias BAART		Pts	Sep	365
1784	Catharina Adriana		Pts	Aug	430
1782	Cornelia, formerly				
	HARTMAN	Ltd Prob	Pts	Aug	394
1777	Passchier, The				
	Hon Dr,				
	Doctor of Physic		Pts	May	198
1776	Peter		Pts	Jun	254
1769	BAES, Brechtelandt				
	The Hon Lady	Ltd Prob	Pts	Jan	2
1788	BAETS, Margaret				
	alias BATES		Surrey	May	226
1800	BAGALEY, Thomas	No Ship	Pts	Jan	6
1777	BAGGALLEY, William		Middlesex	Aug	342
1757	BAGE, Ann		Middlesex	Oct	294
1780	BAGEHOT, Thomas		Somerset	Nov	504
1784	BAGER, Zachariah		Brecon	Feb	60
1783	BAGG, James		Pts	Jul	334
1776	Stephen		Bristol	Jun	256
1784	William	"Defence"			
		A with W	Pts	Aug	372
1768	BAGGALEY, John	A with W	Surrey	Jun	230
1778	Robert		Surrey	Dec	476
1793	BAGGALLEY, James		Middlesex	Feb	69
1777	William		Middlesex	Aug	342
1800	BAGGARLEY, Jonathan		Surrey	Dec	834
1791	BAGGE, Charles				
	Doctor in Divinity		Norfolk	Nov	494
1799	Charles Elsden		Norfolk	Jun	416
1762	William, Esq		Norfolk	Nov	448

1793	BAGGELEY, Rebecca				
	alias BAGGLEY		Surrey	Apr	181
1765	BAGGELY, Hellen		York	Feb	44
1771	BAGGERLY, John		Middlesex	Apr	146
1761	Thomas		Northampton	Feb	45
1783	BAGGETT, Phillip		Pts	Oct	497
1789	BAGGLEY, Priscilla		Wiltshire	Jan	12
1793	Rebecca, alias BAGGELEY		Surrey	Apr	181
1761	BAGGOT, John		Middlesex	Aug	278
1767	John		Middlesex	Oct	363
1769	John		Middlesex	Jan	3
1773	Phillips, Esq		Essex	Jun	238
1792	Phillips, alias BAGOTT		Essex	May	259
1778	Susanna		Middlesex	Sep	346
1791	BAGGRIDGE, Richard		Middlesex	Sep	418
1788	BAGGS, Eleanor		Oxford	Nov	520
1789	Isaac		Pts	Jan	13
1777	John		Middlesex	Aug	341
1792	Martha		Worcester	Jan	7
1773	Richard		Berkshire	Apr	147
1751	Robert		Pts	Mar	75
1779	BAGHOT, Kinard, Rev.		Gloucester	Feb	41
1770	BAGILHOLL, Mary		Devon	Apr	130
1763	BAGLEHOLE, Henry		Surrey	Jun	265
1774	Henry	A with W			
		Will regd 265 Caesar	Surrey	Jun	
1790	BAGLEY, Abigail		London	Aug	367
1791	Alice		Surrey	Oct	449
1763	Hannah		Middlesex	Oct	460
1764	John		Kent	Aug	296
1770	John	A with W	Kent	Nov	388
1780	John		Middlesex	Sep	426
1783	John		Buckinghamshire	Sep	445
1765	Joseph		Surrey	Aug	285
1778	Mary		Middlesex	Dec	477
1800	Orlando	Ser "Edgar" "Argonaut" "Excellent"	Devon	Mar	176
1774	Richard		London	Apr	129
1785	Richard		Surrey	Aug	404
1775	Sarah		Surrey	May	174
1780	Sarah	A with W	Buckinghamshire	Mar	120
1761	Thomas		Buckinghamshire	Dec	419
1768	Thomas		Oxford	Dec	441
1778	Thomas		Middlesex	Jan	3
1781	Thomas	Ser. A with W	Pts	Sep	421
1755	BAGNAL, George, Esq		Middlesex	Apr	94
1754	William	Ltd A with W unad			
		Will regd 90 Dorset	Worcestershire	Jul	
1757	Winifride Mary				
	called Lady ARTHER		Middlesex	Jan	3
1796	BAGNALL, Ann		Kent	Aug	397
1758	Anna Maria		Middlesex	Dec	357
1763	Barbara		Rutland	Jan	7

BAGNALL (contd)

Year	Name	Note	County	Month	No.
1789	Capell		Hereford	Feb	75
1770	Dorothy		Suffolk	Feb	41
1758	Elizabeth		Berkshire	May	143
1758	Gibbons	Will regd 146 Boycott	Berkshire	May	
1790	Hannah, alias BAGNEL		Warwickshire	Nov	494
1769	James		Middlesex	Jul	233
1788	James		Berkshire	Jun	283
1766	John	A with W	London	May	169
1769	John		Chester	Jul	234
1775	John		London	May	171
1782	John		Middlesex	Dec	573
1776	Robert		Pts	Jan	3
1769	Samuel	A with W	Chester	Jul	234
1785	Sarah		Middlesex	Jun	289
1795	Sarah		Middlesex	Jan	3
1771	Thomas		Pts	Apr	146
1772	Thomas		Stafford	Jul	247
1750	William		Rutland	May	139
1755	William		Surrey	Jan	3
1790	BAGNEL, Hannah alias BAGNALL		Warwickshire	Nov	494
1781	BAGNELL, John	Ser	Pts	Sep	421
1781	Thomas		Pts	Mar	120
1762	BAGNIOT, Abram		Pts	Dec	495
1752	BAGNOL, Anne		Middlesex	Sep	227
1754	John		Pts	Jul	189
1756	Mary Anne	A with W	Pts	Nov	289
1756	BAGNOLD, George		Essex	Jun	159
1792	Jeffery		Staffordshire	May	263
1781	Susanna		Bristol	Aug	377
1776	BAGOT, Egerton, Esq		Warwickshire	Feb	52
1776	The Hon Ignatius, Rev	A with W	Pts	Dec	486
1761	John		Cambridge	Aug	277
1776	John		Pts	Dec	486
1798	Richard, Esq	"Queen Charlotte" "Concord" "Trent"	Pts	Nov	696
1768	Sir Walter Wagstaffe	Further Grant May 1768	Staffordshire	Feb	49
1798	The Rt Hon Lord William		Middlesex	Nov	696
1792	BAGOTT, Phillips alias BAGGOTT		Essex	May	259
1788	BAGSHAW, Ann		Leicestershire	Mar	118
1792	Ann		Middlesex	Nov	543
1770	Elizabeth		Kent	Apr	131
1772	Jane		Middlesex	Jul	245
1779	John		Surrey	Jan	3
1792	John, Esq		Derby	Apr	199
1792	John	Special A with W	Cambridge	Nov	546
1797	Joseph	No Ship	Pts	Nov	676
1758	Mary	A with W	Derby	Mar	65
1780	Nathaniel		Middlesex	Oct	461

BAGSHAW (contd)

Year	Name	Note	Place	Month	Page
1792	Prudence		Derby	Feb	60
1750	Richard, Esq		Derby	Jun	189
1766	Robert, Esq		Middlesex	Aug	294
1780	Sarah		Middlesex	May	240
1800	Sarah		Worcestershire	Mar	176
1755	Thomas		Surrey	Sep	234
1769	Thomas		Surrey	Aug	274
1772	Thomas		Surrey	Aug	285
1787	The Rev Thomas		Kent	Nov	487
1794	Thomas		London	Dec	595
1755	William		Northampton	Aug	211
1757	William	A with W	Derby	Aug	242
1785	William, Esq		Derby	Dec	587
1763	BAGSHAWE, Samuel		Derby	Jan	4
1758	BAGSHOTT, William	A with W	Monmouth	Oct	283
1762	BAGSTER, Elizabeth		Kent	May	184
1760	George, alias BAXTER		Pts	May	182
1795	George		Dorset	Dec	667
1765	Mill, Esq		Hertfordshire	May	172
1768	Sarah		Hertfordshire	Dec	370
1779	Thomas	A with W	Pts	Apr	140
1785	Thomas, Esq	A with W	Leicestershire	May	235
1800	BAGUE, George		Middlesex	Dec	837
1773	Nehemiah		Warwick	Apr	145
1774	BAGULEY, Michael		Middlesex	Nov	387
1765	BAGWELL, Andrew		London	Feb	45
1758	Elizabeth		Middlesex	Jan	3
1763	John		London	Mar	109
1767	Margaret	A with W annexed	Berkshire	Nov	401
1783	Margaret	A with W twice unad Last Grant Oct.1777 Will regd 401 Legard	Berkshire	Apr	
1783	Martha		Berkshire	Apr	160
1770	Mary		Surrey	Oct	348
1785	Peter		Surrey	Dec	586
1762	Susanna		London	Jun	234
1777	Thomas	A with W of Goods unad Will regd 401 Legard	Berkshire	Oct	
1760	BAGWORTH, Henry		Pts	Mar	91
1763	BAHAM, Charles alias BADHAM		Bath	Jan	6
1779	BAIER, James alias LEBURG Jens Johanson		Pts	Nov	444
1763	BAIG, James alias BEEG		Pts	May	216
1751	BAIGNOUX, Lawrence James alias BAYGNEW, James		London	Feb	36
1776	Margaret		London	Feb	55
1762	BAIJEN,VAN, The Hon Alexander	Ltd Prob	Pts	Jul	
1771	BAIJER, John Otto	A with W	Middlesex	May	193

	BAIJER (contd)				
1791	John Otto, Esq		Devon	Jun	
1778	Rachel Otto		Wiltshire	Jul	295
1763	BAIKIE, Charles				
	alias BAYKEE		Pts	Aug	371
1783	Mungo	Pts	Southampton	Aug	401
1781	BAIL, Edward	A with W	Pts	Aug	378
1787	BAILARD, John		Somerset	Mar	107
1766	BAILE, Hugh				
	alias BAILEY				
	alias BAILY				
	alias BALIE	By Sent	Pts	Dec	443
1762	Richard				
	alias BEALLE		Pts	May	185
1800	William		Essex	Jun	439
1778	BAILES, Ann				
	formerly WELLBELOVED		Middlesex	Jul	275
1757	Anthony	A with W	Durham	Apr	112
1785	Mary		Middlesex	Apr	173
1770	Thomas		Pts	Jun	222
1766	William		Middlesex	Oct	361
1773	BAILEY, Abigail		Derby	Jun	239
1784	Abigail	A with W of goods unad			
		Will regd 239 Stevens	Derby	Mar	
1766	Alexander				
	alias BAYLEY	By Int Decree	Pts	Jan	4
1771	Ambrose		Middlesex	Dec	472
1756	Amos	Ser	Surrey	Jan	2
1757	Ann		Middlesex	Jan	4
1788	Ann		Middlesex	Jan	7
1792	Ann, alias BALEY		Middlesex	Jan	6
1797	Anna		Middlesex	Jun	395
1782	Anthony		London	Mar	112
1786	Anthony	A with W unad			
		Will regd Mar.1782	London	Oct	
1759	Arthur		Pts	Oct	319
1764	Arthur	Ltd A with			
		W of goods unad			
		Will regd 251 Barns	Middlesex	Nov	
1770	Barney		Middlesex	May	174
1780	Benjamin		Middlesex	Jul	346
1787	Benjamin		Kent	Jan	7
1797	Benjamin	A with W	Middlesex	May	298
1763	Charles		Pts	Sep	416
1788	Charles, alias BAILY		Southampton	Feb	55
1799	Edmund		Middlesex	Jan	10
1750	Edward		Essex	May	138
1751	Edward		Middlesex	Mar	71
1756	Edward	A with W	Hertfordshire	Feb	28
1770	Edward	A with W annexed			
		Will regd 71 Busby	Middlesex	Mar	
1777	Edward, alias BAYLEY		Essex	Oct	408

BAILEY (contd)

Year	Name	Note	Place	Month	Page
1778	Edward		Southampton	Sep	347
1788	Edward		Northampton	Apr	171
1792	Edward		Surrey	Sep	461
1752	Elizabeth		Kent	Oct	241
1760	Elizabeth		Berkshire	Sep	348
1767	Elizabeth, alias BAYLEY		Middlesex	Oct	362
1780	Elizabeth, alias BAYLEY		Kent	Dec	554
1783	Elizabeth		Huntingdon	May	215
1784	Elizabeth, alias BAILY alias HILL		Middlesex	Feb	61
1799	Elizabeth		Buckinghamshire	Nov	761
1781	Frances		Buckinghamshire	Oct	461
1752	Francis		Middlesex	Dec	292
1768	Ffrancis		Middlesex	Sep	340
1786	Francis		Middlesex	Jun	321
1783	George		Surrey	Feb	58
1768	Henry		Buckinghamshire	Jul	266
1774	Henry		Kent	Apr	127
1766	Hugh, Esq		Litchfield	Sep	328
1766	Hugh, alias BAILY, alias BALIE, alias BAILE	By Sent (regd Dec 431)	Pts	Dec	443
1750	Humphry	Poor	London	Sep	288
1775	James		Pts	Jul	260
1776	James		Middlesex	Jun	256
1779	James		London	Jan	2
1781	James		Middlesex	Oct	466
1783	James	"Resistance"	Surrey	Feb	59
1790	James		Berkshire	Apr	170
1764	Jane		Surrey	Nov	418
1759	Jasper		Pts	Dec	385
1782	Jasper		Gloucester	Nov	531
1756	John		Pts	Feb	27
1759	John, alias HUSSEY	Pts	Dorset	Dec	402
1760	John		Southampton	May	184
1762	John		Gloucester	May	187
1776	John		Berkshire	Oct	413
1777	John		Huntingdonshire	Jun	254
1780	John, alias BALEY		Cambridge	Nov	505
1782	John		Middlesex	Jan	3
1782	John		Pts	Jul	336
1783	John, alias BAYLEY, alias BAILIFF	"Defiance", "Ramilies", "Providence" & "Monarch"	Pts	Jul	324
1786	John		Gloucester	Feb	66
1787	John		Essex	Jul	308
1789	John	"Isis"	Pts	Mar	135
1790	John		Surrey	Feb	62
1793	John		Somerset	Mar	126
1794	John		London	Nov	538
1795	John		Dorset	Oct	582
1797	John		Leicestershire	Feb	70

BAILEY (contd)

Year	Name	Note	Place	Month	No.
1797	John		Middlesex	Mar	127
1797	John	"Monmouth"	Pts	Jun	395
1759	Joseph		London	Jan	5
1773	Joseph		Middlesex	May	193
1782	Joseph		London	Dec	574
1793	Katherine		Huntingdon	Mar	129
1793	Katherine	Dbl Prob Will regd March last	Huntingdon	Jun	129
1767	Margaret		Middlesex	Jul	251
1767	Margaret, alias Marigret		Middlesex	Sep	334
1761	Mary		Gloucester	May	160
1774	Mary		London	Jun	218
1781	Mary		Middlesex	Aug	376
1789	Mary		Oxford	Jun	301
1791	Mary		Middlesex	Oct	454
1797	Mary		Middlesex	Mar	135
1753	Minton, alias BAYLEY, alias, BAYLY		Middlesex	Apr	102
1790	Oades		Devon	Dec	540
1800	Patrick	"Maidstone"	Pts	Aug	576
1765	Phillip	A with W	Middlesex	Aug	285
1766	Philip	A with W	Berkshire	Oct	363
1797	Rebecca		Middlesex	Mar	131
1763	Richard, alias BAYLY		Middlesex	Oct	458
1767	Richard		Hertford	May	164
1771	Richard		Southampton	Mar	94
1772	Richard	A with W	Pts	Jul	247
1774	Richard		Middlesex	Feb	38
1781	Richard		Middlesex	Aug	376
1781	Richard, alias BAILLIE		Pts	Dec	569
1786	Richard	no Ship	Pts	Nov	553
1800	Richard		Southampton	Feb	90
1760	Robert, alias BAYLY		Pts	Nov	416
1795	Robert		Somerset	Nov	623
1800	Robert		Berkshire	Aug	575
1757	Samuel		Middlesex	Aug	239
1775	Samuel		Middlesex	Dec	458
1799	Samuel		Middlesex	May	335
1751	Sarah, alias BAYLEY		Middlesex	Feb	38
1762	Sarah		Lincoln	Jul	283
1783	Sarah		Kent	Sep	442
1784	Sarah		Middlesex	Jan	7
1782	Stephen		Middlesex	May	215
1784	Susannah, alias BAILY		London	May	248
1762	Thomas		Southampton	Apr	139
1764	Thomas		London	Dec	454
1765	Thomas		Middlesex	Mar	87
1773	Thomas		London	Mar	95
1778	Thomas		Pts	Dec	478
1782	Thomas		Surrey	May	214
1786	Thomas		Kent	Jun	321
1784	Thomas		Suffolk	Mar	122

	BAILEY (contd)				
1786	Thomas	A with W "Eagle"	Pts	Aug	420
1792	Thomas		Surrey	Jan	6
1796	Thomas		Essex	Feb	59
1800	Thomas		Essex	May	346
1777	Walter		Cambridge	Oct	409
1750	William	Pts	London	Feb	37
1762	William		Pts	Jan	3
1763	William		Middlesex	Mar	107
1764	William		Middlesex	Nov	413
1766	William		Middlesex	Dec	441
1773	William		Gloucester	May	190
1773	William		Surrey	Aug	321
1776	William		Middlesex	Apr	163
1780	William, alias Wiley	Ser	Pts	Nov	504
1781	William		Pts	Sep	422
1783	William		Pts	Oct	496
1784	William	"Exeter" & "Pondicherry"	Pts	Feb	63
1787	William		Middlesex	Oct	436
1789	William	A with W of goods unad Will regd 352 Strahan	Middlesex	Jul	
1792	William		Bath	Aug	416
1797	William		Gloucester	Dec	728
1798	William, alias BAILLEY	E.I.S. "Fort William"	Pts	Jan	6
1787	William Phillips	Will regd last month	Southampton	Jan	
1777	BAILIE, Hannah alias BAILLIE, alias BAYLIFF		Westminster	Jul	297
1763	James		Pts	May	216
1797	William		Middlesex	Jun	398
1770	BAILIES, Mary alias MESSEDER		Middlesex	May	1
1781	BAILLEY, Catherine alias BAILY	A with W	Hampshire	Jun	286
1789	Elizabeth		Surrey	Jul	348
1798	William, alias BAILEY	E.I.S."Fort William"	Pts	Jan	6
1800	William, Esq		Pts	Feb	81
1764	BAILLIE, Alexander		Pts	Sep	337
1781	Alexander		Middlesex	Mar	110
1799	Alexander, Esq		N Britain	Aug	570
1751	Ann		Middlesex	Dec	327
1800	Ann, formerly BROUGHTON		N Britain	Jun	441
1758	Anne		Southampton	Nov	320
1797	David	Ltd A with W	Pts	Oct	631
1793	Frederick		Middlesex	Oct	489
1759	Grisel, Dame alias MURRAY		N Britain	Aug	
1777	Hannah, alias BAYLIFF alias BAILIE		Westmoreland	Jul	297
1776	Hugh, Dr. Doctor of Laws		Middlesex	Aug	348
1793	James, Esq		Middlesex	Oct	494
1795	James, Esq		N Britain	Dec	671

	BAILLIE (contd)				
1797	James Smith, Esq	99th Regt	N Britain	Feb	72
1751	John		Pts	Nov	299
1765	John		Pts	Jun	209
1795	John		N Britain	Dec	671
1757	Robert, Esq	A with W	Middlesex	Nov	321
1799	Robert, Esq		N Britain	Jul	477
1781	Richard, alias BAILEY	Ser	Pts	Dec	569
1787	Thomas		Pts	Jul	311
1751	William, alias BAYLEY		Pts	Nov	301
1764	William, Esq	Ltd A with testamentary schedule annexed	Pts	Nov	414
1797	William Hall		Middlesex	Mar	128
1783	BAILLIEU, Joannes Franciscus alias Jean Francois		Pts	Jul	334
1773	BAILLEUL, Peter		Middlesex	Feb	47
1752	BAILLIF, Ester		Middlesex	Nov	268
1783	John, alias BAYLEY, alias BAILEY	"Defiance", "Ramilies", "Providence" & "Monarch"	Pts	Jul	324
1787	BAILISS, Richard alias BAYLISS		Gloucester	Dec	529
1780	BAILLY, Ann		London	Nov	505
1770	BAILLY,LE, Jane alias BAILLY, now DENTON		Jersey	Sep	
1788	BAILLY, Hugues	A with W	Pts	Jan	4
1787	Mary, alias Marie alias BERNARD	A with W	Pts	May	196
1758	BAILLY,LE, Mathieu, alias MATTHEW	A with W	Middlesex	Apr	102
1773	Nicholas		Devon	Aug	336
1777	Sarah, now COUMBE		Devon	Sep	380
1755	BAILMAN, Ann		Surrey	May	123
1758	BAILS, John	Pts	Kent	Aug	237
1788	BAILWARD, Ann		Wiltshire	Sep	428
1761	BAILY, Abraham	Ser	Devon	Jan	3
1781	BAILY,LE, Ann	Will regd last Nov	Middlesex	Mar	
1785	BAILY, Benjamin		Middlesex	May	233
1786	Benjamin	A with Will unad Will regd May 1785	Middlesex	Apr	
1750	Caleb, Esq		Wiltshire	Sep	287
1781	Catherin, alias BAILLEY, Catherine	A with W	Hampshire	Jun	286
1788	Charles, alias BAILEY		Southampton	Feb	55
1775	Dinah		Wiltshire	Mar	86
1784	Elizabeth, alias BAILEY, alias HILL		Middlesex	Feb	61
1791	Elizabeth		Berkshire	Mar	113
1767	Giles		Bristol	Feb	38
1783	Henry		Wiltshire	Oct	497
1766	Hugh, alias BAILEY, alias BALIE, alias BAILE	By Sent (regd Dec 431)	Pts	Dec	443

BAILY (contd)

Year	Name	Notes	County	Month	No.
1762	James		Middlesex	Jun	235
1771	James		Southampton	Jun	242
1798	James		Middlesex	Jul	459
1770	John		Wiltshire	Jul	251
1774	John		Somerset	Aug	290
1776	John		Middlesex	Jul	298
1781	John	A with W unad Will regd 252 Fenner	Somerset	May	
1783	John		Wiltshire	May	212
1785	John, Esq		Devon	Jan	9
1785	John		Wiltshire	Oct	496
1790	John		Berkshire	Oct	451
1791	John		Wiltshire	Dec	560
1798	John		Gloucester	May	310
1799	John		Wiltshire	Mar	164
1767	Joseph	A with W	Wiltshire	Jun	206
1777	Leonard		Middlesex	Jul	299
1760	Major		Wiltshire	May	185
1785	Major		Wiltshire	Jul	355
1776	Mary	A with W	Southampton	Apr	163
1781	Mary		Somerset	Jul	332
1784	Mary	Ltd Prob	Pts	Nov	589
1751	Richard		Berkshire	May	131
1753	Richard		Berkshire	Dec	309
1756	Richard		London	Jul	188
1763	Richard		Pts	Feb	47
1786	Richard, Esq		Middlesex	Dec	598
1798	Richard	Lieut. Chatham Division of Marines	Berkshire	May	309
1751	Robert		Pts	Nov	300
1752	Robert		Wiltshire	Apr	82
1791	Robert		Wiltshire	Dec	557
1761	Sarah		Middlesex	Dec	420
1781	Sarah		Essex	May	229
1763	Susanna		London	Dec	543
1784	Susannah, alias BAILEY		London	May	248
1797	Thomas		Middlesex	Mar	132
1764	William	A with W	Pts	Jan	5
1779	William		Middlesex	Feb	43
1782	William	A with W	Pts	Dec	574
1791	William, Rev.		Somerset	Aug	376
1786	William Phillips		Southampton	Dec	603
1772	BAILYE, Eleanor, alias Eliner		Coventry	Jan	3
1800	Richard		Lichfield	May	339
1797	Samuel		Coventry	Dec	723
1786	William		Lichfield	May	263
1753	BAIMBRIDGE, John		Southampton	May	127
1765	BAIN, David	A with W	Pts	Nov	402
1783	George	Ser. A with W "Terrible"	Pts	Oct	497

184

	BAIN (contd)				
1763	James		Middlesex	Mar	105
1775	James		Middlesex	May	174
1781	James, alias BEAIN		Pts	Aug	375
1795	Janet, alias MURDOCK	A with W	Edinburgh	Sep	
1795	John	"Melampus" Ser	Pts	Sep	534
1752	Mary		Middlesex	Jul	179
1794	Michael	no Ship	Pts	Jun	296
1782	William, alias BAYNE	A with W "Canada"	Pts	Mar	109
1793	William		Middlesex	Oct	495
1754	BAINARD, Mary,				
	alias BAYNARD		Dorset	Sep	244
1792	BAINBRIDGE, Ann		Middlesex	Mar	131
1788	Cuthbert	Ltd A with W annexed	Durham	Aug	382
1750	Eleazer		London	Jan	3
1780	Elizabeth		Surrey	May	234
1790	Elizabeth		London	Nov	494
1793	Elizabeth		Middlesex	Dec	580
1769	Forster		Middlesex	Sep	302
1768	Ffrances		Essex	Mar	94
1759	Hugh		Surrey	Jan	5
1789	Isabella	A with W	Middlesex	Nov	532
1779	James		London	Mar	90
1785	Jane		Surrey	Jun	294
1797	Jane		Durham	Jun	398
1763	John		Middlesex	Sep	417
1763	John		Surrey	Apr	167
1775	John		Middlesex	May	170
1777	Joseph		Middlesex	Apr	145
1782	Nathaniel Holdoman	A with W	Middlesex	Jan	6
1779	Samuel		Middlesex	Feb	43
1781	Thomas		Durham	Sep	419
1785	Thomas	"Thetis"	Pts	May	232
1787	Thomas	A with W of goods unad Will regd May 1785 "Thetis"	Pts	Nov	
1754	BAINBRIGG, Elizabeth		Middlesex	Jun	159
1750	John		Middlesex	Oct	315
1758	BAINBRIGGE, The Rev. John		Leicester	Oct	284
1800	Philip		Pts	Feb	81
1769	Philip Harley		Leicester	Sep	302
1780	William, Esq		Leicester	May	240
1761	BAINE, Eleanor		Surrey	Mar	83
1784	Mary		Gloucester	Jun	308
1775	Paul, Esq		Warwick	Aug	299
1761	William		Pts	Nov	380
1759	BAINES, Frances				
	alias WYLLIS Francas		Cambridge	Nov	351
1794	Frances		Cambridge	Apr	183
1768	John		London	Oct	369
1776	John		Suffolk	Feb	53
1785	John	Ser "Marlborough"	Pts	Jun	293

	BAINES (contd)				
1767	Mary		Essex	Nov	404
1765	Richard		Middlesex	Apr	129
1768	Richard	Dbl Prob	Middlesex	Oct	
		Will regd April 1765			
1796	Richard		Rutland	Oct	487
1799	Richard		York	Feb	90
1775	Robert		Essex	May	170
1772	Thomas		Suffolk	Mar	82
1776	Thomas, alias BEANS		Devon	Jan	6
1784	William		Kent	Jul	367
1795	William		Rutland	Jun	367
1764	BAINS, William		Pts	Jul	252
1775	William, alias BYNES		Pts	Aug	299
1781	BAINSFAIR, Hugh	Pts	Middlesex	Jun	285
1780	BAINTON, Benjamin		Winchester	Aug	386
1775	Charles	By Int Decree			
		A with W	London	Aug	299
1752	Elizabeth		Huntingdon	Oct	241
1757	Elizabeth	A with W of goods unad.			
		Will regd 241 Bettesworth	Huntingdon	Jun	
1770	Elizabeth		London	Aug	288
1761	James		London	Dec	421
1777	BAIRD, Archibald	Ltd Prob	Pts	Jul	300
1788	Archibald	By Int Decree			
		Special Prob			
		A W or Test.Schedule			
		regd 300 Collier	Pts	Mar	116
1759	David	A with W	Pts	Nov	351
1763	David, alias BEARD	A with W	Pts	Sep	419
1772	George	A with W	Pts	Oct	350
1752	James	A with W	Pts	Feb	30
1760	James, alias BEARD		Pts	Mar	89
1765	James, alias BEARD		Pts	Aug	285
1768	James		Middlesex	Jun	226
1784	James	"Alcide"	Pts	May	248
1764	John, alias BEIARD,				
	alias BEARD	A with W	Pts	Dec	457
1800	John	"Tryal", "Kite" &"Cynthia"	Pts	Aug	580
1784	Joseph		Buckinghamshire	Dec	630
1783	Josiah, alias Josia	Ser.	Pts	Apr	162
1783	Nicholas		Pts	Feb	60
1761	Patrick , Esq		Pts	Aug	279
1761	Patrick	A with W	Pts	Oct	340
1751	Robert		Pts	Feb	34
1761	Thomas		Pts	Apr	121
1750	William		Pts	Jan	3
1757	William	Pts	Middlesex	Jun	180
1795	BAIRNER, George		Middlesex	Jan	6
1763	BAISE, Jonathan,				
	alias BAISS	A with W	Pts	Sep	418
1774	BAISEY, William		Essex	Jun	216
1774	BAISLEY, Edmund		Essex	May	170

1787	BAISMARE, Mary alias BAISMORE		Middlesex	Mar	106
1787	BAISMORE, Mary alias BAISMARE		Middlesex	Mar	106
1763	BAISS, Jonathan, alias BAISE	A with W	Pts	Sep	418
1772	BAISSOY, Jean, alias John	A with W. Ser.	Pts	Jan	4
1785	BAISY, Count Roose de Jean Alexander Joseph Baron of Bouchout		Pts	Feb	
1785	BAISY de, Jean Alexander Joseph Count Roose alias de BAISY Pierre Jean Alexander Count Roose Baron of Bouchout &c	W regd last month	Pts	Mar	
1787	BAITSON, William		Lancashire	Jul	310
1783	BAITT, David, alias BEATT	A with W Ser	N Britain	Nov	551
1752	BAIZE, Marten		Pts	Aug	207
1768	BAJIER, Isabella Otto alias BAYER		Middlesex	Jul	268
1761	BAKEN, Jude		Devon	Apr	120
1795	BAKER, Aaron		London	Apr	235
1773	Abigall, alias Abigail		London	Dec	456
1752	Abraham		Leicester	Feb	28
1769	Adriana		London	Jan	3
1785	Alvery, alias Elvery		Surrey	Jul	351
1764	Andrew, Esq		Worcester	Mar	83
1750	Ann		Kent	Jun	186
1750	Ann		London	Jul	223
1759	Ann	A with W	Essex	May	160
1762	Ann		Wiltshire	Aug	332
1763	Ann	A with W	Surrey	Feb	45
1767	Ann		Bristol	Jun	209
1770	Ann		London	May	171
1771	Ann		Surrey	Jul	285
1777	Ann		Middlesex	Mar	95
1784	Ann		Surrey	Sep	494
1786	Ann		Middlesex	Aug	422
1787	Ann		Ireland	Oct	439
1793	Ann		Surrey	Jan	9
1795	Ann		Somerset	Mar	142
1796	Ann		Hertford	Mar	110
1799	Ann		Middlesex	Jan	9
1752	Anne		Middlesex	Mar	58
1771	Anthony		Southampton	Jul	285
1785	Anthony		Kent	Jul	353
1787	Anthony, Rev		Middlesex	Feb	52
1753	Arthur		Somerset	May	130
1774	Arthur		Middlesex	Mar	80
1790	Augustus, alias Augustes	"Jupiter"	Pts	Aug	367

BAKER (contd)

Year	Name	Notes	County	Month	No.
1796	Barnard		Middlesex	Jan	6
1754	Benjamin		Essex	Sep	244
1758	Benjamin		Devon	Oct	287
1771	Benjamin		Middlesex	May	193
1771	Benjamin		Bristol	Oct	397
1772	Bernard		Middlesex	Aug	282
1776	Bernard	Dbl Prob Will regd Aug. 1772	Middlesex	Feb	
1784	Bernard	Treble Prob Will regd 282 Taverner	Middlesex	May	
1795	Betty, formerly GILLARD		Somerset	May	296
1776	Bramston		Essex	May	211
1763	Catherine		Northampton	Feb	43
1750	Charles		Essex	Nov	345
1753	Charles		Pts	Jan	5
1773	Charles	Sp A with W unad Will regd 345 Greenly	Essex	Aug	
1761	Charles		Pts	Apr	119
1786	Charles		London	Jan	4
1792	Charles		London	Apr	197
1791	Charles Augustus Frederick	Ser "Arrogant"	Pts	Sep	418
1758	Charles Bowles		London	Jun	178
1782	Charles Swaine		Pts	Dec	570
1784	Charles Vaughan, Rev		Sussex	Aug	431
1781	Cordelia, alias Cordelie		Middlesex	Apr	180
1764	DE HELD, Cornelia, formerly BROUWER		Pts	May	164
1753	Daniel		Bristol	Feb	37
1790	Daniel		Surrey	Jul	319
1792	David		Essex	Dec	594
1764	Deborah		Kent	May	165
1789	Deborah	A with W of goods unad Will regd 165 Simpson	Kent	Jun	
1780	Dorothy		Middlesex	Jan	4
1800	Dorothy		Surrey	Aug	580
1754	Edward		Lincoln	Jan	5
1757	Edward	Pts	Essex	May	148
1762	Edward		Gloucester	Oct	412
1763	Edward		Pts	Jan	8
1772	Edward, Esq		Wiltshire	Oct	350
1776	Edward		Middlesex	Jan	2
1779	Edward		London	Feb	38
1796	Edward		Salisbury	Nov	541
1797	Edward		Kent	Nov	674
1798	Edward	A with W	Somerset	Dec	757
1767	Edward		London	Jan	4
1755	Elisha		Wiltshire	Apr	94
1761	Elishaba		Middlesex	Dec	416
1755	Elizabeth		London	Feb	34

BAKER (contd)

1755	Elizabeth		Lincoln	Dec	304
1757	Elizabeth		Suffolk	Feb	38
1759	Elizabeth, alias ROSE	A with W of Goods unad Will regd 123 Henchman	Surrey	Dec	
1760	Elizabeth		Surrey	Oct	381
1761	Elizabeth		Surrey	Jun	200
1762	Elizabeth, alias BAKOR		Middlesex	Nov	448
1763	Elizabeth		Kent	Feb	47
1764	Elizabeth		London	Oct	379
1765	Elizabeth		Surrey	Nov	400
1765	Elizabeth		Kent	Dec	439
1766	Elizabeth		Middlesex	Mar	90
1766	Elizabeth		Berkshire	Jun	215
1767	Elizabeth		Surrey	Aug	297
1769	Elizabeth		London	Feb	34
1769	Elizabeth		Middlesex	May	151
1771	Elizabeth		Kent	Jun	243
1773	Elizabeth		Cambridge	Mar	92
1778	Elizabeth		Somerset	Jul	275
1779	Elizabeth		Kent	Oct	404
1780	Elizabeth		Berkshire	May	240
1780	Elizabeth		Middlesex	Aug	386
1782	Elizabeth		Essex	Jan	3
1785	Elizabeth		Devon	Jul	351
1787	Elizabeth		Kent	Sep	397
1788	Elizabeth		Devon	Jul	337
1788	Elizabeth		London	Dec	
1789	Elizabeth		Kent	Jan	3
1789	Elizabeth		Middlesex	Feb	76
1790	Elizabeth		Northamptonshire	Mar	120
1790	Elizabeth		Middlesex	Oct	452
1790	Elizabeth		Kent	Dec	540
1791	Elizabeth		Oxford	May	209
1791	Elizabeth		Norfolk	Dec	559
1791	Elizabeth		Kent	Dec	560
1792	Elizabeth		Hertford	Sep	460
1793	Elizabeth		Somerset	Sep	453
1793	Elizabeth		Norfolk	Oct	495
1795	Elizabeth		Middlesex	Dec	674
1796	Elizabeth		Middlesex	Jul	347
1797	Elizabeth		London	Jan	5
1797	Elizabeth	Will regd last month	London	Feb	5
1797	Elizabeth		London	Mar	132
1797	Elizabeth		Dorset	Oct	625
1798	Elizabeth		Middlesex	Sep	583
1769	Emm		Middlesex	Mar	74
1772	Euselius		Somerset	Apr	121
1754	Felix		London	Jul	188
1763	Fortune		Devon	Aug	367
1757	Frances		London	Jun	180
1762	Frances		Southampton	Sep	369

	BAKER (contd)				
1779	Frances		Middlesex	May	186
1799	Frances		Kent	Oct	698
1778	Ffrancis		Middlesex	Jun	232
1786	Francis		London	Mar	135
1796	Francis		Middlesex	Apr	164
1753	Gabriel		Berkshire	Mar	70
1753	George		Middlesex	Feb	38
1758	George		Surrey	Mar	64
1759	George		Sussex	Aug	255
1763	George		Devon	Jul	322
1771	George, Esq		London	Jan	7
1772	The Revd George		Exeter	Mar	85
1775	George, alias JAMESON		Kent	Jun	223
1786	George		Dorset	Feb	70
1788	George		Kent	Jul	336
1789	George		Kent	Feb	75
1793	George		Suffolk	May	246
1800	George	Ltd Prob	Pts	Feb	88
1790	George Stamp		Middlesex	Nov	493
1754	Giles		Southampton	Jun	158
1757	Giles		Kent	May	148
1771	Grace		Middlesex	Oct	398
1800	Grace		Bristol	Feb	83
1779	Groves		Suffolk	Sep	366
1762	Hannah		Middlesex	Oct	411
1787	Hannah		Middlesex	Jul	309
1793	Hannah		Middlesex	Jan	9
1793	Hannah	Another grant last mth	Middlesex	Feb	9
1775	Hayward		Kent	Oct	368
1757	Henry		Worcester	Apr	112
1760	Henry		Surrey	Mar	89
1761	Henry		Surrey	Jun	204
1762	Henry		Pts	Jul	287
1762	Henry		Warwick	Nov	446
1773	Henry		Cambridge	Apr	147
1774	Henry, Esq		Middlesex	Dec	420
1775	Henry, Esq		Middlesex	Feb	39
1778	Henry	A with W; Ser	Devon	May	187
1780	Henry	A with W	Surrey	Mar	120
1785	Henry	A with W "Milford" "Meredith" "Culloden" "Resolution" & "Triumph"	Pts	Aug	405
1787	Henry	No Ship	Dublin	Jun	253
1796	Henry		Middlesex	Jan	4
1762	Hercules	A with W of goods unad Will regd 274 Anstis	Kent	Dec	
1791	Hercules, Esq	Will regd 274 Anstis Last grant Dec.1762	Kent	Aug	
1776	Hester		London	Jun	256
1790	Hester		London	Mar	119

BAKER (contd)

1750	Horatia		Middlesex	Sep	286
1753	Hugh	Pts	Middlesex	Oct	263
1798	Hugh		Essex	Feb	79
1772	Isabella		Surrey	Oct	350
1792	Isabella		Sussex	Jul	365
1786	Issabell		Middlesex	Jan	6
1793	Jacob	Merchant Ship "Hope"	London	Jul	354
1750	James		Pts	Jul	222
1757	James		Pts	May	144
1757	James		Pts	Sep	267
1759	James		Warwick	Jun	192
1762	James		Middlesex	Apr	137
1762	James		Pts	Jun	235
1764	James		Middlesex	Nov	416
1765	James		Surrey	Apr	128
1765	James		Surrey	Dec	443
1766	James		Surrey	Jan	4
1766	James, poor	Ltd A with W	Pts	Feb	45
1766	James, Esq		Pts	Aug	294
1766	James		Middlesex	Dec	442
1767	The Revd James, Doctor of Physick		Buckinghamshire	Dec	436
1771	James		Warwick	Feb	45
1773	James		Derby	Nov	417
1781	James	Ser	Pts	Mar	119
1784	James		Middlesex	Jul	367
1788	James		Middlesex	Jul	339
1792	James		Sussex	Jun	314
1793	James		Middlesex	Aug	398
1795	James		Middlesex	Mar	144
1796	James		Gloucester	Jul	345
1797	James	"Intrepid"; Ser	Pts	Feb	70
1798	James		Berkshire	Feb	84
1798	James		Oxford	May	314
1753	Jane		Middlesex	Feb	39
1766	Jane		Sussex	Apr	128
1774	Jane		Middlesex	Nov	385
1782	Jane		Essex	Aug	393
1799	Jane		Middlesex	Oct	699
1800	Jane		Kent	May	340
1800	Jane		Salisbury	Sep	648
1765	Jefford		Pts	Oct	364
1798	Jeremy, Esq		Gloucester	Jul	457
1758	Joanna		Worcester	Jun	179
1750	John		Pts	Mar	67
1750	John		London	Apr	104
1750	John		Kent	Jul	224
1750	John		Middlesex	Dec	376
1751	John		Surrey	Apr	102
1752	John		Surrey	Jul	180
1753	John		Herts	Aug	222

BAKER (contd)

Year	Name	Note	Note2	County	Month	Page
1753	John			Suffolk	Dec	310
1754	John			Somerset	Jun	160
1757	John			Kent	Nov	323
1758	John			Pts	Mar	65
1758	John			Middlesex	Apr	102
1759	John			Middlesex	May	157
1759	John, Esq			Buckinghamshire	Nov	350
1760	John, Esq	Dbl Prob Will regd Nov. last		Buckinghamshire	Jan	
1760	John			Warwick	Oct	382
1762	John			Middlesex	Jan	3
1762	John			Oxford	Apr	140
1762	John			Pts	Jul	286
1763	John			Pts	May	216
1763	John			Southampton	Jul	323
1763	Revd John			London	Sep	420
1763	John			Gloucester	Sep	421
1764	John	A with W		Southampton	Feb	38
1764	John			Northampton	Aug	296
1764	John			Herts	Aug	298
1765	John	A with W		London	Nov	400
1767	John			Somerset	Feb	36
1768	John			Salisbury	Jun	221
1768	John			Middlesex	Sep	336
1770	John			Worcester	Apr	131
1770	John			Northampton	Sep	322
1770	John, alias BECKER, alias BACKER			Middlesex	Nov	390
1771	John			Middlesex	Mar	96
1771	John			Essex	Jul	283
1771	John			Somerset	Nov	428
1774	John			Kent	Apr	131
1775	John, Esq			Middlesex	Feb	42
1775	John			Essex	Apr	127
1775	John			London	Oct	368
1777	John			Devon	Feb	55
1777	John	A with W		London	May	196
1777	John			Southampton	Dec	496
1778	John			London	Jun	230
1779	John			Surrey	Apr	140
1780	John			Middlesex	Feb	57
1780	John			Southampton	Mar	119
1780	John			Pts	May	235
1781	John	Pts		Kent	Aug	376
1781	John	Dbl Prob Will regd Feb. 1780		Middlesex	Oct	
1781	John			Hereford	Nov	512
1781	John			Bath	Nov	514
1781	John			Essex	Dec	573
1782	John			Pts	Jan	3
1782	John	Pts		Devon	Mar	111
1782	John			London	Jun	264

BAKER (contd)

Year	Name	Note	Place	Month	No.
1783	John	A with W of Goods unad Will regd June last	London	Feb	
1783	John		Middlesex	Jun	284
1784	John		Newcastle u Tyne	Jun	304
1784	John	E I S "Busbridge"	Pts	Aug	428
1786	John, Esq		Kent	Sep	465
1786	John		Essex	Oct	505
1787	John, Esq		Worcester	Jan	6
1787	John	No regiment	Pts	Jul	309
1789	John, Esq		Salisbury	Feb	71
1789	John	A with W	Hertfordshire	Feb	76
1789	John		London	Oct	484
1790	John		Middlesex	Mar	119
1790	The Revd John		Berkshire	Jun	276
1790	John		Hertfordshire	Jul	317
1791	John		Hertfordshire	Jan	3
1791	John		Southampton	Feb	58
1792	John		Middlesex	Aug	416
1792	John		Norfolk	Aug	419
1792	John		Surrey	Nov	543
1793	John		Middlesex	Apr	181
1793	John		Essex	May	244
1793	John		Kent	Jul	351
1795	The Revd Dr John Doctor in Divinity		Derby	Jun	365
1795	John	Ser "Boyne"	Pts	Sep	537
1796	John, Esq	A with W of Goods unad Will regd 131 Bargrave	Kent	Sep	
1796	John, Esq		Surrey	Sep	445
1796	John		Stafford	Nov	541
1797	John	"Latona"	Pts	Mar	135
1797	John	A with W	Northampton	Jul	474
1797	John		Middlesex	Oct	628
1798	John, Esq		York	Jan	7
1798	John		Essex	Apr	234
1798	John		Surrey	May	314
1798	John	"Diomide"	London	Jun	378
1798	John		Sussex	Jun	379
1798	John		Surrey	Jun	382
1798	John		London	Jul	463
1798	John		Surrey	Dec	756
1799	John		Kent	Feb	96
1799	John	A with W	Middlesex	May	335
1799	John	Ser: "Cerberus"	Pts	Aug	572
1800	John		Hertford	Jan	5
1800	John		Surrey	Jan	5
1800	John		Worcester	Jan	5
1800	John		Cornwall	Jun	439
1800	John		Middlesex	Nov	757
1800	John		Surrey	Nov	768
1768	John Andrewes, Esq		Middlesex	Oct	369
1793	John Brickenden		Kent	Jul	352

BAKER (contd)

1791	John Carpenter		Middlesex	Jan	6
1788	John Valentine		Middlesex	Feb	56
1762	Jonas		Pts	Sep	369
1769	Jonathan		Pts	Aug	273
1780	Jonathan		Northampton	Mar	124
1751	Joseph		Pts	Nov	301
1753	Joseph		Middlesex	Aug	222
1759	Joseph		Middlesex	Aug	256
1764	Joseph		Surrey	Jan	3
1771	The Revd Joseph		Middlesex	Sep	366
1778	Joseph		Middlesex	Sep	346
1781	Joseph		Middlesex	Jul	330
1784	Joseph		Lancashire	Aug	427
1782	Joseph		Pts	Nov	532
1786	Joseph	"Active" "Burford" & "Worcester" "Coventry"		Jan	6
1791	Joseph, Esq		Chichester	Nov	498
1795	Joseph		Suffolk	Jul	432
1761	Joshua		Middlesex	Feb	47
1761	Joshua	Ser	Devon	Oct	340
1776	Joshua		Pts	Jun	259
1787	Joshua		London	Mar	107
1800	Joshua	A with W	Middlesex	Apr	254
1763	Josiah		Southampton	Mar	109
1798	Josiah		Middlesex	May	308
1753	Judith		Middlesex	Jan	5
1755	Loe	Pts	Kent	Aug	211
1785	Margaret		Surrey	Sep	453
1798	Maria		Berkshire	Nov	694
1753	Martha		Pts	Jan	5
1754	Martha		Middlesex	Feb	33
1765	Martha		Warwick	Jan	3
1771	Martha		Middlesex	Jan	5
1775	Martha		Middlesex	Apr	129
1793	Martha		Norwich	Aug	397
1781	Marthanna		Sussex	Jan	3
1753	Mary		Kent	Oct	263
1755	Mary		London	Feb	33
1755	Mary		Middlesex	May	123
1756	Mary		Middlesex	Jan	2
1756	Mary		Middlesex	Feb	27
1757	Mary		Berkshire	Jun	180
1759	Mary		Devon	Dec	384
1762	Mary		Kent	Apr	141
1763	Mary		Middlesex	Jun	265
1766	Mary		Kent	Jun	212
1769	Mary		Middlesex	Aug	273
1770	Mary		Surrey	Jun	222
1772	Mary, alias BARKER		Middlesex	Jul	247
1772	Mary		London	Sep	317

BAKER (contd)

Year	Name	Note	Place	Month	No.
1774	Mary		Kent	Dec	421
1776	Mary	A with W	Middlesex	Oct	411
1777	Mary		Middlesex	Feb	54
1777	Mary		Exeter	Aug	341
1780	Mary		Middlesex	Jan	3
1782	Mary		Buckinghamshire	Jan	5
1785	Mary		Middlesex	Jul	353
1786	Mary	A with W	Salisbury	Feb	64
1787	Mary		Surrey	May	198
1787	Mary		Middlesex	Oct	441
1787	Mary	Another grant last month	Middlesex	Nov	
1788	Mary	A with W of Goods unad Will regd 341 Collier	Exeter	Sep	
1789	Mary		Southampton	Jun	300
1791	Mary		Middlesex	Mar	117
1792	Mary		Bristol	Feb	61
1792	Mary		Norwich	Feb	62
1796	Mary		Kent	Aug	399
1798	Mary		Kent	Jan	10
1800	Mary		Middlesex	Apr	254
1788	Merchant		Norwich	Jun	292
1750	Michael, Esq		Sussex	Sep	287
1754	Michael		Surrey	Aug	220
1771	Michael, Esq		Sussex	Apr	145
1787	Millecent		Cambridge	May	199
1771	Molin, alias Moline		Hereford	Jul	284
1751	Nathaniel		Pts	Jul	198
1754	Nicholas		Kent	Dec	317
1766	Nicholas	A with W	Pts	Jan	3
1795	Nicholas		Essex	Jul	433
1798	The Revd Nicholas		Somerset	Dec	756
1761	Oliver		Middlesex	Mar	81
1770	Patience		Berkshire	Jun	219
1800	Paul	A with W	Ireland	Jun	432
1791	Penelope		Devon	Dec	561
1755	Peter		Dorset	Mar	68
1755	Peter		Middlesex	Dec	304
1769	Petronela		Middlesex	Nov	366
1787	Phanny		Middlesex	Aug	358
1759	Philip		Pts	Jul	224
1760	Philip, Esq		Middlesex	Jun	228
1797	The Revd Philip		Southampton	Jan	5
1768	Phillip		Middlesex	Apr	141
1795	Phillip, alias BEAKER	"Leopard"	Lancaster	Oct	583
1795	Prudence		Lincoln	Oct	583
1760	Rachell	A with W	Surrey	Oct	379
1754	Rebecca		Surrey	Nov	294
1798	Rebecca		Southampton	Apr	234
1751	Richard		Middlesex	Apr	105
1758	Richard		Middlesex	Oct	286
1762	Richard		Kent	Feb	40
1764	Richard	Dbl Prob Will regd 141 Strahan	London	Sep	

Year	Name	Notes	Place	Month	No.
	BAKER (contd)				
1764	Richard	Dbl Prob Will regd 141 Strahan Another Grant this mth	London	Sep	
1765	Richard	Will regd 286 Hutton	Middlesex	Mar	
1765	Richard		Southampton	Aug	285
1767	Richard, Esq		London	Nov	401
1769	Richard		Southampton	Aug	272
1770	Richard		Sussex	Jan	3
1771	Richard	By Int. Decr.	Pts	Nov	430
1772	Richard		Salop	Sep	318
1774	Richard, Esq		Norfolk	Sep	329
1775	Richard		Middlesex	Oct	366
1779	Richard	Pts	Kent	Jul	289
1780	Richard		London	Mar	122
1784	Richard		Southampton	Oct	538
1789	Richard	A with W of Goods twice unad. Will regd 98 Derby. Last grant May 1744	London	Dec	
1795	Richard		Kent	Jul	433
1795	Richard		Kent	Aug	494
1798	Richard		Surrey	May	308
1753	Robert		Somerset	Jun	164
1759	Robert		Pts	Feb	44
1760	Robert		Surrey	May	185
1764	Robert		Pts	May	162
1775	Robert		Surrey	Apr	131
1775	Robert		Bristol	Dec	456
1785	Robert		Suffolk	Mar	112
1789	Robert, Esq		Middlesex	Mar	135
1791	Robert		Sussex	Feb	55
1796	Robert		Berkshire	May	238
1765	Rowland		London	Nov	401
1752	Samuel, Esq		London	Nov	269
1754	Samuel		Middlesex	Mar	67
1761	Samuel		Southampton	Nov	383
1762	Samuel	Dbl Prob Will regd Nov. last	Southampton	Jan	
1762	Samuel		Pts	Oct	412
1769	Samuel		Suffolk	Sep	302
1788	Samuel		Kent	Dec	579
1789	Samuel		Middlesex	Apr	190
1795	Samuel		Worcester	Mar	138
1796	Samuel		Sussex	Apr	161
1797	Samuel	Roy. Regt. Artillery	Pts	Mar	129
1799	Samuel		Middlesex	Dec	826
1793	Samuel Undershell		Essex	Aug	399
1798	Samuel Undershell	A with W of Goods unad Will regd Aug. 1793	Essex	Oct	
1752	Sarah		Middlesex	Aug	205
1759	Sarah		Bedford	Mar	84

BAKER (contd)

Year	Name	Note	County	Month	No.
1764	Sarah		Oxford	Oct	377
1765	Sarah		Middlesex	Feb	45
1765	Sarah		Essex	Sep	321
1766	Sarah		Kent	Jul	259
1768	Sarah		Surrey	Mar	98
1776	Sarah, alias BEAKER		Gloucester	Dec	490
1778	Sarah		Surrey	Jul	276
1779	Sarah		Kent	Mar	87
1789	Sarah		Essex	Jun	304
1790	Sarah		Surrey	Nov	495
1791	Sarah		Staffordshire	Jan	2
1793	Sarah	A with W	Middlesex	Dec	582
1796	Sarah		Kent	Dec	592
1756	Solomon		Middlesex	Feb	27
1751	Stephen		Kent	Jul	197
1767	Stephen	Pts	Surrey	Jun	208
1793	Stephen		Southampton	May	242
1788	Susanna	A with W	Kent	Dec	580
1793	Susanna		Somerset	Nov	538
1793	Susanna		Middlesex	Nov	539
1795	Susanna		Salisbury	Dec	673
1799	Susanna	A with W	Middlesex	Dec	822
1788	Susannah, alias Susanah		Surrey	Apr	175
1790	Susannah		Salisbury	Mar	118
1794	Susannah		Middlesex	Aug	403
1760	Sybil		Hereford	Mar	87
1752	Theophilus		London	Oct	242
1753	Thomas		Somerset	Dec	310
1754	Thomas		Berkshire	Oct	266
1756	The Revd Thomas		Gloucester	May	131
1756	Thomas	Serv. A with W	Devon	Mar	59
1760	Thomas		Pts	Jan	3
1760	Thomas		Kent	Mar	88
1761	Thomas		Kent	Jun	201
1763	Thomas		Essex	Jan	7
1763	Thomas		Kent	Apr	164
1763	Thomas		London	May	212
1765	Thomas		Berkshire	Nov	402
1767	Thomas		Canterbury	Jan	3
1768	Thomas		Suffolk	Jan	3
1768	Thomas		Middlesex	Dec	439
1769	Thomas		Surrey	Oct	333
1770	Thomas		Norwich	Mar	89
1771	Thomas		Middlesex	May	195
1772	Thomas	A with W of Goods unad. Will regd 266 Pinfold	Berkshire	Apr	
1774	Thomas		London	Mar	79
1775	Thomas		Kent	Jun	222
1777	Thomas		Middlesex	Apr	144
1777	Thomas		Middlesex	May	198

BAKER (contd)

1777	Thomas		Pts	Aug	340
1777	Thomas		Middlesex	Sep	377
1778	Thomas	Ser	Surrey	Jun	234
1779	The Revd Thomas		Middlesex	Jun	231
1779	Thomas		Gloucester	Jun	236
1779	Thomas	Pts	Kent	Aug	336
1779	Thomas		London	Dec	485
1780	Thomas, Esq		Pts	Nov	505
1781	Thomas, Esq		Salisbury	May	227
1782	Thomas		Middlesex	Mar	110
1782	Thomas		Sussex	Jul	337
1783	Thomas		Surrey	Dec	601
1784	Thomas	Ser "Shrewsbury"	Exeter	May	245
1788	Thomas		Herefordshire	Jul	336
1788	Thomas		Middlesex	Oct	471
1788	Thomas		Middlesex	Nov	523
1789	The Revd Thomas		Southampton	Apr	190
1789	Thomas		Suffolk	Aug	419
1789	Thomas		Kent	Dec	574
1790	Thomas		Bristol	Mar	116
1791	Thomas		Kent	Dec	554
1792	Thomas		Kent	Aug	419
1793	Thomas		London	Feb	62
1793	Thomas, Esq		London	Feb	68
1793	Thomas		Kent	Apr	182
1794	Thomas, Esq		Surrey	Feb	60
1796	The Revd Thomas		Sussex	Feb	58
1798	Thomas	Pts. "Minotaur"	Devon	Aug	525
1798	Thomas	"La Nymphe"&"Excellt."	Pts	Dec	760
1799	Thomas		Sussex	Apr	247
1799	Thomas		Somerset	Apr	250
1800	Thomas		Middlesex	Sep	644
1800	Thomas		Gloucester	Dec	835
1770	Walter		Middlesex	Apr	129
1750	William	Pts	Surrey	Jun	186
1752	William	Pts	Devon	Jun	148
1753	William		Berkshire	Feb	40
1755	William		Middlesex	Mar	65
1757	William		Sussex	Apr	110
1759	William		Middlesex	Jan	5
1760	William		Devon	Jan	2
1761	William	Ser	Southampton	May	160
1764	William, Esq		Cambridge	Aug	299
1764	William		Pts	Aug	299
1763	William		London	Feb	45
1763	William	A with W of Goods unad. Will regd 186 Greenly. Pts	Surrey	Feb	
1763	William	Pts		Mar	106
1763	William	Pts		Aug	371
1766	William	Pts		Feb	46

	BAKER (contd)				
1766	William		Surrey	Dec	441
1768	William	A with W	Bristol	Dec	441
1769	William, Esq		Pts	Apr	112
1770	Sir William Knight one of the Aldermen of the City of London		London	Feb	41
1770	William		Surrey	Mar	87
1774	William, Esq		Middlesex	Feb	40
1774	William		Kent	Jul	253
1774	William		Middlesex	Aug	291
1774	William		Essex	Nov	386
1775	William		Devon	Oct	366
1776	William		Middlesex	Aug	345
1778	William, Esq	A with W unad. Will regd Feb.1774	Middlesex	Mar	
1778	William		Middlesex	Oct	388
1779	William		Somerset	Feb	43
1779	William		Somerset	May	186
1779	William		Middlesex	Oct	405
1779	William	Pts	Southampton	Nov	444
1780	William		Middlesex	Feb	55
1780	William	A with W	Warwickshire	May	240
1781	William		Pts	Dec	570
1783	William		Surrey	Apr	163
1784	William		Middlesex	Apr	188
1784	William	A with W "Milford," "DuGuay", "Trouin"	Pts	May	246
1786	William		Kent	Mar	141
1786	William		Kent	Apr	204
1787	William		London	Mar	106
1788	William	A with W of Goods unad. Will regd 5 Arran	Middlesex	Jan	
1789	William		Hertfordshire	Nov	531
1790	William		Kent	Jul	319
1791	William		Berkshire	Apr	166
1791	William		Surrey	Apr	168
1791	William		Southampton	Jun	265
1791	William		Kent	Nov	499
1793	William		Kent	Dec	579
1794	William		Lincoln	Sep	446
1796	William	"Raisonable"	Pts	Feb	53
1796	William		Lincoln	Jul	346
1798	William		Middlesex	Oct	632
1798	William		Southampton	Nov	697
1799	William		Surrey	Jul	474
1799	William	A with W	Somerset	Sep	645
1800	William		Bristol	Jun	437
1795	William Augustus		London	Apr	237
1781	BAKERS, Adrianas		Pts	Jul	327
1759	BAKES, Mary		London	Aug	257

Year	Name	Notes	Place	Month	Page
1798	BAKEVELL, Lucy				
	alias BAKEWELL		Derby	Jul	458
1770	BAKEWELL, Elizabeth		Kent	Sep	322
1781	Elizabeth		Leicester & Derby	Jul	327
1794	Henry		Staffordshire	Mar	124
1766	Joanna		Nottingham	Aug	295
1755	John	A with W	London	Jun	154
1800	John		Chester	Sep	647
1798	Lucy, alias BAKEWELL		Derby	Jul	458
1772	Richard		Middlesex	Mar	85
1753	Robert		Derby	Mar	72
1794	Robert, Esq		Leicester	Jan	5
1795	Robert		Leicester	Oct	583
1770	Samuel		Middlesex	Oct	351
1798	BAKKER, Pieter		Pts	Nov	698
1792	Symon		Pts	Jul	364
1762	BAKOR, Elizabeth				
	alias BAKER		Middlesex	Nov	448
1760	BALAAM, Charles		Pts	Dec	453
1788	John		Middlesex	Oct	471
1794	William		Northampton	May	241
1768	BALACK, Thomas		Middlesex	May	187
1772	BALAGUIER, John Anthony	Dbl Prob.			
		Will regd 212 Simpson	Middlesex	Jan	
1764	BALAQUIER, John Anthony		Middlesex	Jun	212
1770	BALBERNEY, William				
	alias BALBERNIE		Middlesex	Jun	222
1770	BALBERNIE, William				
	alias BALBERNEY		Middlesex	Jun	222
1788	BALBI, Francis Marie Anthony. His Excellency Count of Siroela, Marquis of Arrard, alias Son of Constantine, Count of Siroela		Pts	Jan	7
1797	The Most Illus. Giacomo alias Giacomo Antonio		Pts	Sep	590
1786	BALCAM, Michael		Jersey	Dec	602
1769	BALCH, Edward		Essex	Dec	406
1769	Joanna		Essex	Apr	115
1756	Katherine		Middlesex	Dec	319
1774	Meary, alias Mary		Kent	Jun	218
1779	Meary, alias Mary	A with W of Goods unad. Will regd 218 Bargrave	Kent	May	
1773	Robert		Chester	Aug	319
1779	Robert, Esq		Bath	Jun	234
1780	BALCHEN, Henry		Middlesex	Apr	171
1750	James	A with W	London	Mar	69
1750	John	A with W unad Will regd in May 1748			
		Pts	Southampton	Jul	

	BALCHEN (contd)				
1761	John		Pts	Sep	308
1763	John	By Int Decr	Pts	Jul	320
1783	John		Surrey	May	217
1785	John		Middlesex	Jan	6
1786	Mary		Surrey	Nov	555
1788	Sarah		Surrey	May	226
1755	Dame Susannah		Middlesex	Jul	177
1758	Dame Susannah	Dbl Prob			
		Will regd 177 Bettesworth	Middlesex	Jun	
1765	William		Middlesex	Sep	322
1783	BALCHIN, Ann		Middlesex	Jan	2
1788	Ann		Surrey	Dec	576
1769	Henry, alias BALLCHIN		Surrey	May	152
1775	Peter		Middlesex	Mar	82
1793	BALCOMB, Thomas		Sussex	Jun	302
1790	BALCOMBE, William		Kent	May	226
1777	BALD, Charles	A with W Pts	N Britain	Nov	448
1794	Elizabeth		London	May	245
1786	William		London	Feb	65
1751	BALDCHIN, Joan		Surrey	Jun	165
1751	BALDE, The Right Hon.				
	Lord Jan		Pts	Dec	327
1763	Jan	Ltd Prob	Pts	Nov	496
1765	The Right Noble Lady				
	Sophia, alias DE BAS				
	formerly MARCELIS		Pts	Mar	85
1795	BALDEN, John	"Alligator"	Pts	May	300
1762	BALDERSTON, Barth		Norwich	Feb	43
1784	Charles		Middlesex	Jan	4
1799	David	"Crown"	Kent	Apr	248
1797	George	"Speedwell"			
		Lieut. Navy	Kent	Jul	474
1771	Mary		London	Feb	48
1773	Robert		Surrey	Aug	321
1765	Timothy		Norwich	Jan	2
1780	William		Middlesex	May	239
1751	BALDING, John		London	Nov	298
1752	John	Dbl Prob			
		Will regd Nov. last	London	Jan	
1783	Thomas, alias				
	BALDWIN	A with W	Surrey	Sep	443
1782	BALDIS, Francess,				
	alias BAULDAY, Francis		Pts	Mar	109
1770	BALDO, The Right Noble				
	and Awful Lord Ysbrant				
	Kieft	Ltd Prob	Pts	Jun	
1798	BALDOCK, Arabella		Kent	Mar	153
1799	David		Middlesex	Dec	823
1780	Edward		Kent	Nov	505
1790	Edward		Kent	Feb	61
1787	George		Hertford	Jan	6

BALDOCK (contd)

1783	Isabella		London	Mar	110
1768	James		Middlesex	Mar	97
1786	John		London	Jun	320
1765	Joseph		Middlesex	Apr	131
1783	Mary		Kent	May	217
1765	Michael	A with W	Pts	Dec	442
1768	Robert		Kent	Jun	227
1777	Robert		Pts	Dec	496
1758	Thomas	Pts	Middlesex	Jan	3
1767	Thomas		Hertford	Sep	332
1793	William		Hertford	Aug	401
1799	William		Hertford	Mar	166
1775	BALDRICK, Robert Halsey		Middlesex	Aug	303
1795	BALDRY, Benjamin				
	alias BOLDRY	"Irresistible" Ser.	Pts	Mar	147
1788	Judith Julie		Pts	May	231
1769	BALDWIN, Adee		Buckinghamshire	Jan	3
1763	Amy		Middlesex	Jul	324
1753	Ann		Oxford	May	127
1767	Ann, alias BOLDWEN		Middlesex	Mar	88
1783	Ann		Middlesex	Jun	283
1785	Ann Susanna		Suffolk	Oct	491
1785	Anne		Middlesex	Jun	295
1765	Bridges, Sir		Ireland	Nov	402
1756	Catherine		Kent	Dec	318
1786	Charles		Middlesex	Mar	142
1750	Christopher		Middlesex	Nov	345
1800	Daniel		London	Jul	506
1750	Drusilla		Middlesex	Apr	106
1755	Edward		Berkshire	Dec	304
1764	Edward		Coventry	Sep	338
1758	Elizabeth		Kent	Dec	356
1781	Elizabeth		Middlesex	Mar	115
1783	Elizabeth		Middlesex	Nov	552
1785	Elizabeth		Kent	May	232
1798	Elizabeth		Buckinghamshire	Nov	695
1753	Freeman	A with W	Middlesex	Jun	163
1799	George	A with W	Leicester	Jan	3
1756	Henry	A with W	Gloucester	Nov	290
1777	Henry		Surrey	Sep	375
1783	Henry		Kent	Jul	337
1764	James		Wiltshire	May	164
1768	James	A with W	Buckinghamshire	Jun	2
1768	James		Middlesex	May	184
1774	James		Buckinghamshire	Jan	3
1793	James		Middlesex	Jun	302
1766	Jane		Middlesex	Nov	399
1789	Jane		Berkshire	Feb	78
1769	Joan		Middlesex	Apr	114
1750	John	A with W	Pts	Oct	314
1753	John		Middlesex	May	128

BALDWIN (contd)

Year	Name	Notes	County	Month	No.
1754	John		Surrey	Dec	319
1760	John		Surrey	Apr	134
1761	John	Pts	Surrey	Oct	339
1762	John	A with W of Goods unad. Will regd 319 Pinfold	Surrey	Apr	
1766	John, alias BURNINGHAM		Southampton	Jul	260
1770	John		Norfolk	Jun	221
1771	John, Esq	Ltd A (with copy of W annexed)	Pts	Aug	332
1785	John		Buckinghamshire	Nov	538
1793	John		Kent	Sep	453
1757	Joseph		Bristol	Feb	41
1800	Joseph	Ltd Prob	London	Apr	257
1760	Joshua		Hertfordshire	Sep	348
1761	Margaret		Surrey	Sep	308
1762	Mary		Middlesex	Feb	38
1773	Mary		Kent	Dec	459
1784	Mary		Bath	May	246
1764	Ralph		London	Sep	336
1775	Richard		Surrey	Jul	261
1777	Richard		Warwick	Jan	6
1762	Robert		Berkshire	Jul	283
1784	Robert	A with W	Kent	Jun	309
1791	Robert		London	Oct	450
1760	Samuel		Middlesex	Apr	134
1773	Sarah		Middlesex	Jul	279
1783	Sarah		Surrey	Nov	554
1797	Shadrach		Kent	Jul	471
1770	Stephen		Buckinghamshire	Jan	6
1782	Susanna		Middlesex	May	213
1765	Susannah		Middlesex	Sep	322
1751	Thomas		Middlesex	Oct	277
1768	Thomas		London	Apr	138
1778	Thomas		Buckinghamshire	Nov	432
1783	Thomas	Ser	Pts	Jul	335
1783	Thomas, alias BALDING	A with W	Surrey	Sep	443
1786	Thomas		Surrey	Feb	67
1791	Thomas	E. I. S. "Ceres" A with W	Pts	Oct	451
1795	Thomas		Surrey	May	294
1785	Tryphena		Middlesex	Apr	173
1755	William		Dorset	Mar	66
1765	William		Surrey	May	169
1777	William	A with W of Goods unad. Will regd 186 Seymer	Southampton	Mar	
1781	William		Surrey	Jul	328
1786	William	Pts	Coventry	Feb	67
1795	William		Berkshire	Jun	368
1769	BALDWYN, Ann		Berkshire	Jun	197
1781	Ann		Salop	Jun	286

	BALDWYN (contd)					
1789	Barbara		Bath	Jan	11
1751	Charles		Stafford	Jun	166
1790	Edith		Buckinghamshire	Dec	537
1772	Edward		Salop	Jun	207
1769	Frances, Dame		Bath	Jun	197
1774	George	A with W	Salop	Mar	78
1795	George		Kent	Apr	241
1779	John	Ser	Middlesex	May	189
1756	Joyce		Surrey	Apr	94
1791	John, Esq		Monmouthshire	Mar	110
1758	Mary		Salop	Nov	322
1795	Mary		Surrey	Mar	139
1779	Samuel, Esq		Lancaster	Nov	442
1769	Susannah		Buckinghamshire	Mar	77
1754	Thomas		Middlesex	Nov	293
1758	William		Bedford	Jun	178
1774	BALDY, John		Pts	Mar	82
1774	Robert		Middlesex	Jan	3
1797	Robert	Ser	Sussex	Mar	132
1795	William	A with W	Devon	Oct	582
1761	BALE, Ann		Essex	Nov	380
1794	Charles		Middlesex	Sep	448
1791	Elizabeth		Middlesex	Feb	57
1781	Gabriel		Essex	Nov	511
1792	Hellen, alias Helen	Ltd Prob	Winchester	Apr	194
1794	James		Devon	Aug	403
1752	John	A with W	Pts	Apr	84
1789	Mary		Surrey	Apr	187
1796	Rachael, alias Rachell		Bath	Jul	347
1783	Robert, alias BEALE	Ser	Pts	Oct	500
1770	Sackville, Esq		Essex	Oct	350
1799	Simon		Norfolk	Aug	571
1769	Thomas	A with W	Middlesex	Feb	33
1798	BALEINE, James, alias BALLEINE		Jersey	Feb	84
1792	BALEMANN, Peter Henry, Esq		Middlesex	Apr	198
1781	BALENGALL, Thomas		Pts	Aug	378
1760	BALES, Robert		Surrey	Dec	451
1789	BALEY, Abraham, Esq		Sussex	Apr	187
1792	Ann, alias BAILEY		Middlesex	Jan	6
1763	John		Pts	Mar	106
1766	John		Essex	Aug	292
1777	John		Essex	Jun	252
1780	John, alias BAILEY		Cambridge	Nov	505
1791	Mary		Essex	Mar	117
1751	Nicholas		Southampton	Nov	299
1760	Stephen		Pts	Jul	273
1758	BALFE, Richard	A with W	Pts	Nov	320
1750	BALFOUR, Alexander	A with W	Pts	Jun	189
1750	Charles, Esq		Middlesex	Mar	67
1760	Christopher	A with W	London	Feb	48

	BALFOUR (contd)				
1761	David		Pts	Oct	340
1794	George		Southampton	Jul	348
1754	James, Esq		Middlesex	Jan	4
1756	John		Pts	Dec	319
1759	John		Pts	Apr	120
1768	John, alias CRAWFURD, Esq		N Britain	Jun	
1782	John		Pts	Aug	395
1760	Margaret		Middlesex	Jun	227
1783	Robert		Middlesex	Sep	443
1799	Thomas, Esq		Bath	Oct	697
1793	William, Esq		Middlesex	Jun	301
1752	BALFOURE, William		Pts	Jul	180
1769	BALGAY, Elizabeth		Northampton	Jan	4
1757	Elmes		Middlesex	Apr	110
1763	Frances		Middlesex	Mar	111
1774	Frances	Dbl Prob W Regd III Caesar	Middlesex	Feb	
1785	BALGOWAN, George	A with W	Middlesex	Oct	495
1788	BALGUERIE, David		Pts	Aug	385
1796	Johanna		Pts	Dec	
1753	The Rev John		Middlesex	Jul	196
1795	BALGUY, The Rev Thomas		Winchester	Feb	63
1758	BALICOURT, Simon		London	Jun	179
1766	BALIE, Hugh, alias BAILEY, alias BAILY, alias BAILE	By Sent (regd Dec 431)	Pts	Dec	443
1766	BALISS, Joseph		London	Jul	258
1757	BALK, Richard		Pts	Sep	266
1787	BALL, Adam		London	Jul	311
1751	Alice		London	Oct	276
1752	Ann		Middlesex	May	117
1777	Ann		Lincoln	Feb	53
1796	Ann		Southampton	Jan	5
1798	Ann		Middlesex	Mar	158
1763	Anthony		Devon	May	219
1776	Anthony	A with W unad. Will regd 219 Caesar	Devon	Jun	256
1789	Barbara		Middlesex	Jan	7
1763	Benjamin		Hertford	May	214
1788	Catherine Weller	A with W	Chester	Apr	173
1757	Christopher		Pts	May	145
1766	Cicelia		Bristol	Aug	296
1797	David		Middlesex	Jan	32
1765	Diana		Middlesex	Feb	45
1794	Edmund		Oxford	Feb	61
1765	Edward		Cornwall	Jul	247
1777	Edward		Essex	Jun	253
1784	Edward		Kent	Oct	540
1794	Edward		Middlesex	May	241
1800	Edward	A with W of goods unad. Will regd 540 Rockingham	Kent	Feb	

	BALL (contd)				
1752	Elizabeth		London	Jul	178
1753	Elizabeth		Wiltshire	Jun	163
1756	Elizabeth		Surrey	Mar	61
1758	Elizabeth		Warwick	Apr	102
1765	Elizabeth		Essex	Dec	440
1767	Elizabeth	A with W	Middlesex	Feb	35
1768	Elizabeth		Kent	May	185
1772	Elizabeth		Northampton	May	156
1770	Elizabeth		Warwick	Jan	5
1771	Elizabeth		Chester	May	196
1775	Elizabeth	A with W of Goods unad.			
		Will regd 196 Trevor	Chester	Dec	
1780	Elizabeth		Stafford	Sep	427
1793	Elizabeth		Middlesex	Feb	70
1795	Elizabeth		London	Feb	65
1800	Elizabeth		London	Jan	5
1754	Ffrances	Will regd 71 Seymer	Middlesex	Feb	32
1763	Frances		Essex	Apr	167
1776	Francis		Middlesex	Mar	110
1764	George		Middlesex	Mar	81
1767	George, alias BIALL	A with W	Pts	Aug	295
1779	George	A with W unad.			
		Will regd 287 Browne	Somerset	Mar	
1781	George		Pts	Jul	330
1790	George		Chester	Jul	318
1776	Gertrude	A with W	Lincoln	Nov	448
1767	Hannah		Wiltshire	Jun	207
1770	Hannah		Gloucester	Jan	3
1781	Hannah		Essex	Sep	422
1792	Hannah		Buckinghamshire	Sep	459
1800	Hannah		Buckinghamshire	Feb	85
1763	Heman	A with W	Somerset	Jan	7
1756	Henry		Hertford	Jan	2
1765	Henry		Herts	Mar	86
1789	Henry		Devon	Feb	72
1796	Henry		Hertford	Nov	539
1757	Hugh		Pts	Sep	268
1785	Isabel		Essex	Mar	111
1767	Jacob	A with W annexed of goods unad.			
		Will regd 141 Strahan	Southampton	Jan	
1760	James		Pts	Feb	47
1760	James		Middlesex	Jul	274
1776	James		Cornwall	May	211
1787	James	2nd Regiment	Dublin	Jun	253
1790	James		Middlesex	Jul	321
1771	Jane		Devon	May	194
1750	John		Pts	Feb	39
1758	John		Hertford	Apr	100
1760	John		Pts	Dec	451
1762	John		London	May	187

BALL (contd)

Year	Name	Notes	Place	Month	Page
1763	John		Bristol	Aug	368
1764	John		Buckinghamshire	Sep	338
1770	John		London	Dec	424
1773	John		Middlesex	Feb	45
1774	John		Chester	Aug	290
1774	John, Esq	Ltd A with W annexed of goods unad. Will regd 3 Price	Durham	Aug	
1779	John, Dr of Physick		London	Oct	406
1768	John		Northampton	Feb	44
1776	John		Cardigan	Jun	254
1780	John		Pts	Jun	301
1780	John		London	Sep	428
1783	John		Devon	Aug	400
1785	John		Middlesex	Feb	64
1785	John		Buckinghamshire	May	231
1787	John		Devon	Jul	311
1797	John	Dbl Prob Will regd 311 Major	Devon	Dec	
1799	John		Pts	Mar	166
1762	John Paul		Middlesex	Dec	496
1760	Joseph, Esq		Essex	Mar	91
1778	Joseph		Pts	Jul	273
1781	Joseph	Ser	Kent	Sep	421
1784	Joseph		Middlesex	Jan	6
1791	Joseph		Somerset	Jan	3
1755	Joyce, formerly JONES		Salop	Oct	254
1800	Judith		Norfolk	Apr	253
1783	Lydia		Suffolk	Jul	337
1783	Margaret		Chichester	Aug	399
1783	Maria Henrietta		Rutland	Jun	283
1759	Martha		Hertfordshire	Jan	6
1751	Mary		Bristol	Jul	200
1767	Mary		Buckinghamshire	Jun	208
1788	Mary		Devon	Jan	6
1794	Mary	A with W	Kent	Mar	123
1795	Mary		Northampton	Nov	624
1772	Matthew	A with W	Pts	Jan	2
1800	Matthew		Middlesex	Aug	583
1760	Michael		Middlesex	Aug	315
1751	Nathaniel		London	Feb	38
1758	Nathaniel		Buckinghamshire	Feb	32
1766	The Rev Nathaniel		Surrey	Oct	362
1791	Nathaniel	A with W	Buckinghamshire	Dec	556
1774	Olive, formerly RAYNSFORD	A with W	Middlesex	May	170
1781	Patrick	A with W	Pts	Mar	114
1790	Peter		Wiltshire	Nov	496
1795	Peter		Middlesex	Nov	623
1758	Philip		Pts	May	139
1776	Philip		Pts	Jan	4

	BALL (contd)				
1780	Rachell, formerly				
	EDWARDS		Middlesex	Mar	123
1769	Rebecca, alias				
	Reebacker		Middlesex	Dec	404
1800	Rebecca		Middlesex	Mar	175
1763	Richard		Leicester	Mar	107
1763	Richard		Surrey	Oct	459
1763	Richard		Middlesex	Nov	498
1774	Richard		Southampton	Sep	329
1784	Richard		Middlesex	Jul	372
1786	Richard	A with W unad			
		Will regd Jul 1784	Middlesex	Apr	
1786	Richard	A with W twice unad.			
		Will regd Jul 1784			
		Last Grant April last	Middlesex	May	
1787	Richard		Surrey	Jun	253
1789	Richard, Rev		Southampton	Nov	530
1796	Richard		Surrey	Dec	541
1759	Robert		Pts	Jan	3
1759	Robert		Pts	Feb	46
1762	Robert	A with W	Pts	Dec	495
1795	Robert		Middlesex	Mar	145
1756	Samuel		Suffolk	Feb	27
1782	Samuel	Pts	Middlesex	Oct	479
1788	Samuel		Surrey	Jul	340
1795	Samuel		Middlesex	Feb	66
1752	Sarah		Middlesex	Aug	205
1764	Sarah		London	Sep	339
1770	Sarah		Buckinghamshire	Nov	389
1795	Sarah		Surrey	Jul	432
1794	Sarah Sprigg		Middlesex	Jan	9
1763	Stephen	A with W	Middlesex	Jan	5
1766	Susannah		Surrey	Oct	363
1771	Susannah		Warwick	Jul	284
1776	Susannah		Middlesex	Feb	50
1753	Thomas	A with W	Pts	Jan	1
1753	Thomas		Middlesex	Mar	70
1753	Thomas		Stafford	Mar	70
1758	Thomas		Middlesex	Jun	177
1759	Thomas		Middlesex	Sep	288
1763	Dr Thomas, Doctor in				
	Divinity		London	Jul	322
1769	Thomas		London	Apr	114
1770	Rev Thomas		Sussex	Dec	422
1773	Thomas		Middlesex	Mar	92
1776	Thomas	Ltd Prob			
		Will regd 422 Jenner	Sussex	Dec	
1785	Rev Thomas	A with W of Goods unad.			
		Will regd 422 Jenner	Sussex	Nov	
1786	Thomas		Bath	Oct	506
1788	Thomas		Kent	Jun	291

	BALL (contd)				
1788	Thomas	A with W of Goods unad Will regd 506 Norfolk	Bath	Oct	
1789	Rev Thomas, Doctor in Divinity		Suffolk	Jul	345
1791	Thomas		Middlesex	Jan	7
1793	Thomas		Middlesex	Sep	453
1795	Thomas		Middlesex	Feb	63
1795	Thomas		Stafford	Jul	434
1796	Rev Thomas		Middlesex	May	240
1796	Thomas		Middlesex	Aug	401
1796	Timothy	A with W	Warwick	Jan	4
1755	William, Esq		Hereford	Sep	233
1758	William	A with W	Pts	May	141
1763	William		Pts	May	217
1764	William	Pts	Devon	Dec	457
1766	William		Oxford	Aug	293
1770	William	Pts	Middlesex	Jan	6
1778	William	A with W	Somerset	Oct	387
1782	William, alias BALLE		Pts	Mar	109
1784	William	Ser	Devon	Jul	366
1792	William, Esq		Dublin	Dec	596
1794	William		Buckinghamshire	Dec	599
1795	William		London	Dec	671
1800	William		Coventry	Dec	840
1764	Woolworth		Pts	Aug	299
1798	BALLACHEY, Joanna		Oxford	Jan	9
1793	Panayoty		Oxford	Aug	399
1791	BALLAM, Elizabeth		Middlesex	Aug	374
1787	Joseph		Dorset	Dec	533
1784	BALLAMY, Abraham, alias BELLAMY	A with W	Surrey	Jul	369
1775	Samuel		Middlesex	Oct	369
1788	Samuel	A with W of Goods unad Will regd 369 Alexander	Middlesex	Nov	
1799	BALLANCE, Francis		London	Sep	643
1796	George Augustus		Devon	Dec	591
1786	Mary		Middlesex	Oct	503
1754	BALLANDS, Augustine		Kent	Feb	33
1762	BALLANGER, Anne		Middlesex	Jul	283
1772	BALLANTINE, Alexander		Middlesex	Oct	352
1757	Andrew, alias BALLATINE		Pts	Aug	239
1795	Eleaner		Kent	Feb	66
1761	John, alias BALLANTYNG	A with W	Pts	Dec	422
1784	John	A with W "Ceres"	Pts	Mar	122
1782	James		N Britain	Jul	337
1786	Mary		Surrey	Jun	323
1792	Ninian		London	Feb	58
1781	Richard		Surrey	Jul	331
1762	Thomas	Pts	Kent	Apr	138

1782	BALLANTYNE, Alexander		Salisbury	Dec	572
1763	John, Esq		North Britain	Oct	460
1789	Sarah, alias BALLENTYNE		Surrey	Mar	133
1761	BALLANTYNG, John,				
	alias BALLANTINE	A with W Ser	Pts	Dec	422
1775	BALLARD, Caroline	A with W	Kent	Aug	303
1771	Charles Taylor		Southampton	Mar	95
1799	Cookes Ann	A with W	Middlesex	Aug	568
1787	Daniel		Gloucester	Nov	486
1771	The Rev Edward,				
	Doctor in Divinity		Berkshire	Aug	330
1796	Edward		London	Feb	60
1766	Elizabeth		London	May	171
1778	Elizabeth		Salop	Apr	145
1798	Elizabeth		London	Oct	633
1751	George, Esq		Surrey	Feb	35
1755	George		Oxford	Sep	232
1794	George		Middlesex	Apr	184
1767	Grace		Oxford	May	162
1757	Hannah	A with W	London	Oct	294
1764	Hannah	A with W	Worcester	Jul	254
1755	Henry	Pts	Surrey	Jul	182
1757	James		Bristol	Aug	241
1794	James	A with W	Middlesex	May	247
1762	John		Middlesex	Nov	447
1763	Rev John		Wiltshire	Mar	107
1773	John		Warwick	Mar	95
1778	John	Ser	Southampton	Apr	143
1778	John	By Int Decr	Wiltshire	Apr	143
1788	John, The Rev		Winchester	Jan	5
1795	John		Middlesex	Jul	431
1797	John		London	Mar	132
1767	Jonathan		Pts	Apr	122
1799	Joseph, Esq		Middlesex	Jan	14
1785	Josiah		Middlesex	Nov	540
1759	Margaret		Middlesex	Jan	5
1774	Martin		Essex	Apr	130
1772	Mary		Gloucester	Dec	431
1782	Mary		Essex	Oct	482
1789	Mary		Winchester	Jun	304
1797	Mary		Gloucester	Jun	395
1757	Michael		Pool	Feb	40
1764	Philip		Hereford	Jul	254
1766	Philip		Southampton	Jan	3
1770	The Rev Reeve,				
	Doctor in Divinity		Middlesex	Jul	252
1756	Richard		London	Apr	96
1780	Richard		Warwick	May	241
1769	Robert		Pts	Oct	333
1782	Robert, Esq		Southampton	Apr	164
1795	Robert		Southampton	Jan	8
1786	Samuel		Surrey	Aug	420

Year	Name	Notes	Place	Month	No.
	BALLARD (contd)				
1755	Thomas		Gloucester	Jan	3
1764	Thomas		London	May	162
1771	Thomas	A with W	Essex	May	196
1772	Thomas		Gloucester	Sep	320
1790	Thomas		Kent	Apr	172
1762	Warden	Pts	Surrey	Aug	331
1756	William		Southampton	Sep	238
1758	William	Pts		May	139
1758	William		London	May	142
1760	William		Warwick	Dec	451
1762	William	A with W of Goods unad. Will regd May 1758	London	Aug	
1763	William		London	Jun	268
1770	William		London	Apr	129
1797	William		Essex	Sep	584
1751	BALLASH, Stephen, alias BELLACHE	By Int Decree	Pts	Feb	34
1757	BALLATINE, Andrew alias BALLANTINE		Pts	Aug	239
1769	BALLCHIN, Henry alias BALCHIN		Surrey	May	152
1759	BALLDARSON, Thomas		Pts	Oct	317
1784	BALLE, DE LA, Francis		Middlesex	May	254
1759	BALLE, Isaac		Middlesex	May	156
1758	BALLE, DE LA, Lewis		Surrey	Nov	328
1798	Thomas		Exeter	Apr	240
1782	William, alias BALL		Pts	Mar	109
1798	BALLEINE, James alias BALEINE		Jersey	Feb	84
1751	BALLENDEN, James		Middlesex	Sep	252
1793	James		Middlesex	Jan	3
1794	The Rt Hon Sarah Cuming, Lady		Middlesex	Dec	605
1788	BALLENDINE, Alexander		Middlesex	Nov	525
1764	BALLENGER, John		Herts	Jun	213
1774	BALLENTIN, Archbald alias BALLENTINE, Archibald		Pts	Aug	292
1774	BALLENTINE, Archibald alias BALLENTIN, Archbald		Pts	Aug	292
1750	George, alias BELLINGTON	A with W By Int Decree	Pts	Jan	2
1780	John		Pts	Apr	170
1789	BALLENTYNE, Sarah, alias BALLANTYNE		Surrey	Mar	133
1791	BALLER, Rev Joseph		Devon	Jan	6
1750	William		Hertford	Jul	222
1750	BALLETT, John, Esq	Pts	Southampton	Aug	253
1755	John, Esq	.	Middlesex	Feb	33
1796	Mary		Middlesex	Sep	446

Year	Name	Notes	Place	Month	No.
1784	BALLEUR, Martha		Pts	Feb	64
1784	Martha	Will regd Feb. last	Pts	Apr	
1780	BALLEY, Abigail		Essex	Feb	58
1772	Jeremiah		Essex	Sep	319
1781	Jeremiah		Kent	Jan	7
1759	BALLIFF, Jane		Essex	Feb	47
1786	BALUN, Abraham		London	Feb	65
1790	BALLIN, Alexander		London	Jul	320
1789	Esther		London	Jul	346
1785	Samuel		London	Dec	586
1788	Simon		London	Dec	575
1792	Zeporah		London	Nov	547
1789	BALLINER, Joseph		London	Aug	418
1772	BALLINGALL, George		Pts	Nov	392
1763	James		Pts	Mar	105
1766	John		Pts	May	168
1793	William		London	Dec	578
1799	BALLINGER, Charles		Gloucester	Apr	245
1798	James		Chester	Jun	379
1774	John		Hertford	Aug	293
1798	Martha		Gloucester	Sep	585
1775	BALLINGHAM, James		Middlesex	Nov	406
1778	BALLINTINE, James	Ser	Surrey	Oct	386
1798	BALLMAN, Henry		Dorset	May	307
1778	BALLMER, Thomas		Pts	Jun	232
1795	BALLMO, Mary, alias BALLOW		Buckinghamshire	Sep	537
1760	BALLOW, James		Middlesex	Jun	229
1762	Joseph, alias BELLOOU		Pts	Jul	284
1795	Mary, alias BALLMO		Buckinghamshire	Sep	537
1765	BALLOWE, Dorothy		Middlesex	May	172
1782	Henry, Esq		Middlesex	Jul	340
1754	Mary		Surrey	Nov	292
1794	BALLS, Benjamin	"Russell"	Pts	Jul	354
1800	Elizabeth		Suffolk	Jan	7
1755	John, Esq		Norwich	Jul	181 & 332
1768	Mark		Cambridge	Nov	400
1783	BALLY, Edward		Bath	Sep	445
1777	BALLYMAN, Robert		Devon	Aug	341
1789	BALMAIN, James		London	Oct	485
1767	Thomas		Pts	Sep	334
1775	William		Pts	Mar	81
1784	William		Pts	Sep	493
1782	BALMANNO, David		Pts	Jul	340
1795	BALME, Anne		Derby	Mar	143
1763	Sarah		Middlesex	Sep	417
1768	Sarah	A with W unad. Will regd Sep.1763	Middlesex	Jul	
1767	BALNE, James		Pts	Jan	2
1790	BALNAVES, James, alias BALNEAVES	E I S 'Hertford" A with W	Pts	Apr	173

Year	Name	Notes	Place	Month	No.
	BALNAVES (contd)				
1759	Patrick		Middlesex	Dec	384
1790	BALNEAVES, James,	EIS "Hertford"			
	alias BALNAVES	A with W	Pts	Apr	173
1785	BALNEAVIS, John, Esq		Middlesex	Jun	294
1761	BALNEVIS, Patrick		Kent	Jan	4
1798	BALLON, DE, Louis				
	Francois Guyard		Pts	Jun	394
1758	BALS, Charles	A with W	Pts	Oct	283
1786	BALSA, Barbara Rose		Pts	Sep	479
1764	BALSANT, Thomas,				
	alias BALSON		Pts	Apr	130
1780	BALSHAW, Margaret,				
	alias Margret		Middlesex	Oct	460
1787	BALSHAW, Thomas		Middlesex	Mar	105
1764	BALSON, Thomas,				
	alias BALSANT		Pts	Apr	130
1760	BALSTER, John	A with W	Dorset	Mar	89
1785	BALSTON, Mary	A with W	Dorset	May	232
1751	BALTIMORE, Lord of				
	the Kingdom of Ireland				
	The Right Hon Charles		Kent	Apr	106
1772	The Right Hon Frederick				
	Lord	Ltd Prob	Pts	Jan	5
1772	The Right Hon Frederick				
	Lord		Pts	Mar	83
1772	The Right Hon Frederick	Dbl Prob			
	Lord	Will regd in Mar. last	Pts	Jul	
1774	BALTIN, DE, Francois				
	Maximiliaen		Pts	Apr	127
1764	BALVAIRD, Peter		Pts	Jul	249
1780	BALY, Martin		Middlesex	Nov	507
1778	Thomas		Middlesex	May	183
1767	BALZLOW, Sarah		Middlesex	Jul	250
1751	BAMBER, Dorothy		Wiltshire	Oct	274
1763	Elizabeth		Middlesex	Nov	498
1753	Dr John, Dr of Physic		Essex	Nov	285
1753	Mary		Winchester	Feb	38
1781	William	Ser	Hampshire	Jun	286
1756	BAMBREY, Richard	Ser	Surrey	Aug	217
1792	BAMBRICK, Henry	"Crown"	Pts	Jun	316
1783	William		Middlesex	Oct	500
1785	BAMBRIDGE, Elizabeth		London	Sep	454
1790	Elizabeth		Kent	Apr	170
1779	John	Ser	London	Aug	334
1783	John	Ser	Pts	Sep	443
1769	Thomas		Middlesex	Jan	2
1784	Thomas	A with W of Goods unad.			
		Will regd 2 Bogg	Middlesex	Apr	
1759	BAMBROUGH, John	A with W	Middlesex	Jan	5
1791	William		Northumberland	Jun	264
1773	BAMBURY, Elizabeth		London	Oct	382

Year	Name	Note	Place	Month	No.
	BAMBURY (contd)				
1798	Elizabeth		London	May	311
1774	John		Warwick	May	172
1779	BAMFIELD, Anne		Middlesex	Jan	4
1773	James		Middlesex	Sep	353
1753	John		Middlesex	Aug	222
1779	BAMFORD, Ann		Lancaster	Jun	231
1757	Cornelius		Middlesex	May	145
1781	Dorothy		Kent	May	227
1790	John		London	Dec	537
1796	Martha		Middlesex	Jun	291
1790	Matthew Paul	A with W	Somerset	May	222
1800	Richard		Kent	Jun	436
1800	Robert	Ser."Thunderer"	Pts	Jul	508
1762	Sarah		Middlesex	Mar	90
1773	Thomas		Pts	Sep	352
1777	William	A with W	London	Nov	449
1793	William		London	Jul	351
1776	BAMFORTH, Margaret		York	Apr	163
1751	BAMFYLDE, John Esq		Somerset	Mar	74
1797	BAMINGS, Ernest Bernard		London	Nov	674
1751	BAMPFIELD, Frances		Middlesex	Jul	200
1754	John		Middlesex	Jan	3
1784	John, alias BAMPFILD	"Atlas"	Pts	Aug	429
1799	John		Devon	Mar	165
1791	Thomas		Middlesex	Dec	557
1758	William		Pts	Nov	319
1784	BAMPFILD, John, alias BAMPFIELD	"Atlas"	Pts	Aug	429
1791	BAMPFYLDE, Coplestone Warre Esq		Somerset	Nov	494
1776	Sir Richard Warwick, Bt		Devon	Aug	349
1794	BAMPSTEAD, Anne		Essex	Nov	537
1752	BAMPTON, Andrew		Middlesex	Apr	86
1759	Ann		Gloucester	Jun	193
1796	Elizabeth		Middlesex	Jan	3
1796	Elizabeth	Will regd last month	Middlesex	Feb	
1765	Henry		Middlesex	Apr	131
1770	Henry		Gloucester	Nov	388
1751	John		Salisbury	Jun	166
1767	Richard	Pts	Southampton	Oct	361
1773	Samuel		London	Dec	457
1798	Samuel Esq		Buckinghamshire	Mar	154
1777	Susanna		Gloucester	Jul	301
1777	Susanna	Dbl Prob Will regd last Month	Gloucester	Aug	
1763	Thomas		Middlesex	Jul	322
1772	Thomas		Surrey	Sep	317
1789	Thomas	E I S "Essex"	Middlesex	Aug	417
1797	William Esq		Middlesex	May	295
1799	William		London	Feb	97
1770	BANASTER, Charles		Middlesex	Aug	286

	BANASTER (contd)				
1773	Jane, alias				
	COLLINSON	Ltd Prob	Southampton	Apr	
1751	BANASTRE, Elizabeth, Dame		Middlesex	Jan	3
1768	Elizabeth		Middlesex	Oct	369
1777	BANBURY, Edmund		Warwick	May	198
1778	Elizabeth		Worcester	Feb	50
1763	George, alias BENBURY		Pts	Jun	269
1773	James		Bath	Jul	281
1787	John		Middlesex	Jul	311
1793	John		Middlesex	Jul	350
1771	The Right Hon Martha				
	Countess Dowager of		Oxford	Nov	429
1797	Mary		Northampton	Oct	625
1775	Rebecca		Middlesex	Mar	85
1755	Richard Esq		Surrey	May	124
1770	Richard	A with W	London	May	171
1770	Richard	A with W unad.			
		Will regd this month	London	May	
1772	Richard	A with W unad.			
		Will regd May 1770			
		Last Grant May 1770	London	Oct	
1774	Samuel		Devon	Dec	419
1792	The Rev Thomas Radcliffe	A with W	Devon	Jul	363
1793	The Rt Hon Thomas Woods				
	Earl of				
	Viscount Wallingford and				
	Baron Knollis		Oxford	May	241
1763	William		Gloucester	Jun	264
1776	The Rt Hon William, Earl				
	of BANBURY Viscount				
	Wallingford & Baron Greys				
	in the County of Oxford			Sep	380
1789	William		Worcester	May	236
1790	BANC, DE, Susan Louise,				
	alias DEBANE		Middlesex	Oct	
1793	BANCE, Ann		Berkshire	Jun	302
1768	Francis		Southampton	Nov	402
1755	John Esq		Berkshire	Mar	67
1768	John		Buckinghamshire	Nov	400
1769	John	A with W of Goods unad.			
		Will regd 67 Paul	Berkshire	May	
1774	BANCHEM, VAN, Anna				
	Elisabeth	Ltd Prob	Pts	Feb	71
1788	BANCKS, Christopher		Worcester	May	228
1767	James		Worcester	Jan	2
1753	Seth		Dorset	Jan	5
1775	BANCRAFT, Thomas		Bristol	Feb	40
1796	BANCROFT, Benjamin		Chester	Aug	399
1770	George		Middlesex	Sep	322
1762	John		Middlesex	Mar	94
1769	John		Middlesex	May	153

BANCROFT (contd)

Year	Name	Notes	Place	Month	No.
1785	John	"Monmouth", "Elizabeth"	Pts	Sep	457
1796	Joseph		Lancaster	Oct	491
1777	Mary		Exeter	Sep	376
1790	Mary Barbon		Middlesex	Sep	410
1797	Peter		Chester	Sep	586
1799	Richard		Chester	Aug	566
1751	Thomas		Derby	Jun	165
1787	BANCUTT, Alice		Hertford	Apr	157
1787	Jane		Northampton	Oct	438
1759	Thomas		Hertfordshire	Feb	44
1787	Thomas	A with W of Goods unad. Will regd 44 Arran	Hertford	Jun	
1787	BAND, Bridget		Exeter	Apr	159
1772	Catherine	A with W	Middlesex	Mar	81
1763	Francis	A with W	Pts	Jun	267
1773	James Osmond		Somerset	Sep	353
1799	John	A with W	Ireland	Mar	163
1768	B ANDINEL, Ffrancis		Pts	May	187
1755	Judith	Will regd Mar.1753	Jersey	Oct	
1781	Philip Esq	Pts. A with W	Jersey	Oct	464
1784	Philip		Jersey	Jun	305
1791	Philip	Dbl Prob Will regd 305 Rockingham	Jersey	Jun	
1774	Rachel, formerly LE FEBVRE	A with W	Guernsey	Nov	400
1800	BANDINELL, Mary		Leicester	May	339
1790	BANDT, DEN, Anna Maria	Ltd Prob	Pts	Oct	
1775	Margaretha, formerly UYLENBERG		Pts	Apr	135
1764	BANDY, Susannah		Middlesex	Dec	456
1794	Thomas		Middlesex	Apr	184
1750	BANE, Hugh		Pts	Nov	346
1788	Michael		Middlesex	Apr	177
1792	BANES, Daniel, alias BEWES		Middlesex	Oct	498
1793	John		Essex	Oct	490
1765	Sarah, alias BANS		Middlesex	Dec	440
1760	Sobieski Elizabeth, formerly MORICE		Buckinghamshire	Mar	111
1783	BANFATHER, Joseph		Norwich	Nov	553
1773	BANFF, The Rt Hon Alexander late Lord		North Britain	Mar	94
1784	Lady Mary, commonly called KEMP		Middlesex	Feb	86
1755	BANFEILD, Richard		Dorset	Jan	3
1773	George		Hertford	Oct	380
1763	BANFORD, Bernard, alias BANGER		Pts	May	216
1762	John		Middlesex	May	187
1759	Philip		Pts	Nov	349
1799	BANGAFIELD, George		London	Jun	417

1795	BANGAY, Samuel		Middlesex	Feb	68
1763	BANGER, Bernard				
	alias BANFORD		Pts	May	216
1760	John		Pts	Mar	87
1794	John Light		Dorset	Oct	489
1762	Thomas		Dorset	Apr	137
1782	Timothy		Hertford	Apr	162
1765	William		Dorset	Oct	362
1758	BANGHAM, Edward	A with W annexed of Goods unad. Will regd 201 Farrant	Hereford	May	
1760	Edward Esq	A with W	Middlesex	Aug	314
1790	BANGLEY, Jane		Bristol	Jun	277
1774	BANGOR, The Rt Rev Father in God John by Divine Permission Lord Bishop of		Worcester	Dec	419
1800	John, The Right Rev Father in God John by Divine Permission Lord Bishop of		Middlesex	Apr	290
1783	BANGS, Charles		Hertford	Oct	496
1799	Charles		Hertford	Oct	700
1799	BANGY, DE, Mary	A with W	Guernsey	Apr	260
1796	BANHAM, John		Middlesex	May	235
1751	William, alias BENHAM	A with W	Pts	Nov	300
1758	BANIS, Watson		Middlesex	Feb	31
1792	BANISTER, Ann		Salop	Feb	57
1789	Anthony		Oxford	Oct	485
1767	Edward		Sussex	May	164
1775	Elizabeth		Monmouth	Nov	403
1784	Elizabeth		Kent	Dec	630
1789	Elizabeth		Middlesex	May	238
1788	Hariot, alias BANNISTER		Middlesex	Jul	338
1768	Isaac		Bristol	Jun	227
1753	James	A with W	London	Oct	263
1772	James		Bristol	Nov	392
1785	James		Berkshire	Apr	172
1774	John		Middlesex	Mar	80
1782	John		Salop	Apr	164
1783	John		Surrey	Mar	114
1789	Rev John		Huntingdon	Oct	485
1792	John		Berkshire	Mar	128
1793	John	Spec.A with W of Goods unad. Will regd 80 Bargrave	Middlesex	Sep	
1799	John		London	Feb	92
1799	John		Surrey	Aug	564
1770	Joseph		Middlesex	Jan	2
1783	Joseph		Oxford	Aug	399
1783	Joseph, alias BANNISTER		Middlesex	Dec	600

	BANKES (contd)				
1758	Richard Esq	A with W unad. Will regd 318 Greenly	London	Mar	
1796	Richard		Middlesex	Nov	539
1763	Thomas		London	Dec	542
1762	William		Surrey	Mar	89
1766	William		Pts	Apr	125
1787	BANKIN, Ann		Kent	Feb	53
1754	Mary		Kent	Nov	292
1777	Nicholas		Sussex	Apr	148
1777	BANKS, Adam		Essex	Jun	256
1763	Alexander	A with W	Pts	Aug	371
1775	Alexander		Middlesex	Feb	40
1789	Alice		Middlesex	Jan	5
1775	Ann		Middlesex	Feb	39
1792	Ann		Middlesex	Apr	198
1795	Ann		London	Sep	535
1797	Ann		Oxford	May	298
1763	Barbara		Middlesex	Jul	321
1756	Benjamin		Warwick	Jul	190
1777	Benjamin		Pts	Feb	52
1795	Ben jamin		Salisbury	Mar	145
1764	Christian		Middlesex	Aug	299
1755	Collingwood Esq		Lincoln	Jul	181
1779	Edward		Middlesex	Dec	488
1780	Eleanor		Nottingham	Jan	4
1771	Elizabeth		Middlesex	Jan	7
1771	Elizabeth		Essex	Mar	95
1776	Elizabeth		Northampton	Jun	254
1788	Elizabeth		Kent	May	228
1788	Elizabeth		London	Dec	580
1792	Elizabeth		Middlesex	Mar	132
1799	Frances		Bristol	Mar	166
1751	George		Pts	Jun	165
1766	George		Wiltshire	Feb	47
1773	George		Middlesex	Jun	234
1791	George		Middlesex	Aug	376
1798	George	"Charon" & "Bellona"	Pts	Jan	3
1798	George		Essex	May	314
1764	Goldstone		Kent	Mar	80
1796	Hugh	Ser."Bellona"	Pts	Aug	402
1754	James		Essex	Feb	32
1760	James		Pts	Feb	47
1763	James	A with W	Pts	Jan	6
1775	James	A with W. Pts	Middlesex	Dec	458
1757	Jan e		London	Mar	73
1767	Jane		Middlesex	Apr	123
1797	Jane		Lincoln	Apr	226
1756	John		Middlesex	Dec	319
1761	John	Ser	Pts	Feb	46
1761	John		Pts	Aug	276
1763	John	A with W	Pts	Aug	368

BANKS (contd)

Year	Name	Notes	Place	Month	No.
1767	John		Lincoln	Jun	207
1774	John		Middlesex	Mar	84
1780	John		London	Jan	3
1781	John		Essex	Dec	571
1784	John		Pts	Jan	4
1788	John		Middlesex	Aug	385
1791	John		London	Oct	453
1792	John		Surrey	Jun	314
1797	John		Southampton	May	298
1799	Rev John		Suffolk	Jul	475
1800	John	"Ariadne"	Pts	Feb	85
1761	Joseph	A with W.Ser	Pts	Aug	278
1777	Joseph		Wiltshire	May	199
1788	Joseph Esq		Surrey	Oct	470
1755	Joshua		Middlesex	Mar	68
1757	Letice Mary	A with W	Lincoln	Dec	348
1799	Martha		Essex	Apr	249
1781	Mary		Essex	Mar	114
1781	Mary	Dbl Prob. Will regd this month	Essex	Mar	
1785	Mary		Middlesex	Jan	3
1789	Mary	A with W	Middlesex	Dec	576
1791	Mary		Surrey	Sep	419
1750	Oliver		Middlesex	Nov	348
1785	Peter		Southampton	May	232
1752	Rachael		Northampton	Apr	84
1784	Rhoda		Essex	Jan	8
1750	Richard		Surrey	Jun	187
1759	Richard	A with W	Pts	Nov	348
1786	Richard		Middlesex	May	262
1800	Richard	"Brilliant"	London	Feb	90
1763	Robert		Pts	Aug	371
1777	Robert		Middlesex	Jun	253
1790	Robert, alias BRANKSTON		Middlesex	Aug	368
1788	Samuel		Cambridgeshire	Jul	340
1793	Sarah		Middlesex	Jun	297
1794	Sarah Savidge		Middlesex	Jan	7
1751	Susanna		Dorset	Mar	71
1765	Susanna		Surrey	Jan	3
1798	Susanna		Wiltshire	Jul	462
1759	Thomas		Pts	Mar	82
1763	Thomas	Pts	London	Aug	370
1773	Thomas		Northampton	May	191
1784	Thomas	A with W "Proteus"	Pts	Mar	121
1785	Thomas	"Stirling Castle"	Pts	Sep	453
1793	Thomas		Surrey	May	127
1800	Thomas	Ser "Ganges"	Pts	Aug	575
1800	Thomas	"Pomona"	Pts	Aug	580
1752	William Esq		Pts	Dec	292
1755	William		Middlesex	Aug	210
1758	William		Pts	Oct	284
1758	William		Pts	Dec	355

	BANKS (Contd)				
1761	William Esq		Lincoln	Oct	337
1770	William Esq		Pts	Feb	42
1771	William	Dbl Prob			
		Will regd in Feb.1770	Pts	Mar	
1775	William Esq		York	Dec	457
1776	William		Middlesex	Jul	303
1778	William		Cambridge	Jun	231
1778	William		Middlesex	Jul	273
1785	William	Ser: "S. Russel"	Pts	Jun	352
1787	William		London	Jul	309
1788	William		Wiltshire	Feb	57
1789	William		London	Mar	133
1789	William		Middlesex	Jun	302
1799	William		Surrey	Jun	416
1800	William		Lancaster	Jul	507
1785	BANNAM, Matthew		Middlesex	Dec	589
1765	BANNATYNE, John		Pts	Feb	44
1781	BANNELL, John	A with W	Pts	Sep	423
1798	BANNER, Ann		Warwick	Jan	6
1784	Henry		Middlesex	Oct	536
1787	James		Middlesex	Apr	158
1788	John		London	Aug	383
1793	John		Middlesex	Apr	187
1799	John		Kent	Oct	700
1750	Dr Richard,				
	Doctor in Divinity		Oxford	May	140
1775	Richard	A with W unad			
		Will regd 28 Anstis	Warwick	May	
1750	Samuel	Pts	Surrey	Aug	251
1797	William John		Warwick	Dec	725
1756	BANNERMAN, Alexander	A with W.	Pts	Sep	239
1797	James	A with W	Middlesex	Mar	131
1785	John Esq		Middlesex	Feb	64
1793	Thomas	Ship	Pts	Feb	70
1798	BANNERMANN, Adam	A with W	Pts	May	311
1770	BANNES, Anthony		Middlesex	Aug	287
1758	BANNESTAR, John,				
	alias BANNISTER		Buckinghamshire	Jun	176
1775	BANNICK, John		Devon	Oct	366
1776	John	Will regd Oct. last	Devon	Feb	
1783	BANNING, Ann		Surrey	Jan	3
1772	Annamoriah		Wiltshire	Jun	206
1793	Dinah, formerly				
	BENWELL	A with W	Wiltshire	Jan	5
1766	Thomas		Wiltshire	Jun	212
1776	Thomas		Middlesex	Dec	488
1757	BANNION, Nathan		Middlesex	Jul	213
1750	BANNISTAR, Ann		Middlesex	Feb	36
1775	BANNISTER, Amy		Berkshire	Aug	303
1778	Elizabeth		Surrey	Sep	347
1769	Giles		Pts	Jan	4

	BANNISTER (contd)				
1792	Hannah		Middlesex	Oct	499
1788	Hariot, alias				
	BANISTER		Middlesex	Jul	338
1778	Jacob		Middlesex	Jan	3
1760	James	By Int Dec	Pts	Feb	47
1766	James		Berkshire	Mar	92
1757	John	Pts	Kent	Nov	322
1758	John, alias				
	BANNESTAR		Buckinghamshire	Jun	176
1762	John		Kent	Apr	140
1762	John		Buckinghamshire	Oct	409
1766	John		Middlesex	Jun	214
1777	John		London	Sep	378
1783	Joseph, alias				
	BANISTER		Middlesex	Dec	600
1779	Lawrance		Pts	May	187
1775	Richard, alias				
	BANISTER		Surrey	May	171
1777	Sarah		Surrey	Sep	375
1790	Susannah		Buckinghamshire	Jul	321
1762	Thomas		Middlesex	Jul	286
1764	Thomas, alias				
	BANISTER		Pts	Jul	251
1772	Thomas		Middlesex	Feb	42
1753	BANNTON, George		Somerset	Mar	72
1800	BANQUES, Thomas		Middlesex	Jun	442
1798	BANQUET, Pierre		Pts	Mar	157
1765	BANS, Sarah,				
	alias BANES		Middlesex	Dec	440
1791	BANSA, Remigius,				
	alias Remy		Pts	Oct	449
1786	BANSLEBEN, Ann		Middlesex	Dec	601
1764	BANSON, Barlee		Hertfordshire	Nov	418
1750	Jane		Middlesex	Nov	345
1776	The Rev John		Kent	Jun	256
1783	BANT, Francis		Pts	Oct	496
1786	Frans Jan Baptiste		Pts	Jul	363
1764	BANTHAM, Thomas	A with W	Pts	Jun	210
1756	BANTING, Elizabeth		Berkshire	Nov	289
1755	BANTOCK, Hugh		Essex	Oct	254
1780	BANTON, Samuel	Ser	Southampton	Jan	2
1761	BANYARD, Charles		Middlesex	Feb	47
1762	Charles	A with W of Goods unad. Will regd Feb.1761	Middlesex	Apr	
1792	John		Berkshire	Jun	315
1794	John		Middlesex	Feb	62
1781	Mary		Norfolk	Jan	4
1758	Thomas		Middlesex	Mar	62
1764	BANYER, Jane		London	Jan	2
1756	Jennet		London	Mar	60
1798	Laurence Esq		Kent	Jun	380

BANYER (contd)

Year	Name	Notes	Place	Month	No.
1759	Mary		Cambridge	May	159
1772	Sarah	A with W unad Will regd May 1771	Middlesex	Sep	
1751	BAP, John Esq		Middlesex	May	131
1781	BAPLIS, Walter		Middlesex	Apr	183
1799	BAPTIE, John	Pts, "Santa Margarita"	Southampton	Sep	645
1797	BAPTIST, John, alias BAPTISTO	A with W "Le Caton" Ser.	Devon	Oct	625
1774	Joseph, alias BAPTISTO		Middlesex	Mar	78
1780	BAPTISTA, John		Pts	Nov	503
1774	Mark		Pts	Nov	386
1786	BAPTISTE, Anthony	"Spider" & "Vansittart"	Pts	Nov	554
1761	John		Pts	Jun	200
1784	BAPTISTO, Ann		Devon	Dec	628
1750	John		Pts	May	137
1797	John, alias BAPTIST	A with W "Le Caton" Ser.	Devon	Oct	625
1774	Joseph, alias BAPTIST		Middlesex	Mar	78
1767	BARACHIN, Marguerite		Middlesex	Jan	2
1754	BARATIER, Francis	A with W	Pts	July	188
1754	BARATT, Henry	A with W	Oxford	Feb	31
1770	John, alias BARRATT		Middlesex	Jan	5
1770	John, alias BARRATT	A with W unad Will regd Jan. last	Middlesex	Apr	
1771	BARATTY, John	A with W	Pts	Dec	468
1797	Margaret		Essex	Feb	67
1765	BARBAR, Abraham Esq		Chester	Sept	321
1764	Adam		Middlesex	Jun	212
1782	Edward, alias BARBER	Pts		May	215
1773	James		Somerset	Apr	147
1789	James, Esq.		Southampton	Mar	132
1799	James, alias BARBER		Southampton	June	416
1792	Thomas, Esq.		Devon	Aug	420
1776	BARBARA, Elizabeth		London	Aug	345
1755	BARBAROUX, Elizabeth		Middlesex	Jan	2
1770	Joseph		London	Nov	390
1799	William		Nottingham	Aug	571
1750	BARBAT, John		Middlesex	Dec	376
1755	BARBAULD, Revd. Ezechiel		Middlesex	Aug	211
1764	Mary Charlotte		Middlesex	May	164
1763	Susanna Mary		Middlesex	June	267
1779	The Revd. Theophilus Lewis		Pts	Mar	89
1751	BARBAULT, Abraham		Pts	Sep	252
1780	BARBAY, Catherine		Middlesex	Jun	301
	Catherine	Dbl Prob Will regd this month	Middlesex	Jun	
1771	Ferdinand		Middlesex	Mar	95
1799	BARBE, ST., Alexander, Esq.		Dorset	Nov	806
1764	Andrew, alias BARBEE		Pts	Apr	130
1790	Anna Maria Elisabeth	Ltd Prob	Pts	Aug	368

	BARBE (contd)				
1788	Marguerite, alias Margueritte, alias Margueritte Elisabeth, The Rt Hon Lady		Pts	Nov	522
1779	ST., William		Southampton	Nov	474
1764	BARBEE, Andrew, alias BARBE		Pts	Apr	130
1754	BARBER, Abraham	A with W unad Will regd 231 Brook	Buckinghamshire	Dec	
1777	Abraham		Hertfordshire	Aug	342
1760	Ann		Middlesex	May	183
1769	Ann, heretofore LEE	Ltd Prob	Devon	June	197
1773	Ann		Middlesex	Dec	459
1776	Ann		Middlesex	May	211
1782	Ann		Devon	Aug	393
1785	Ann		Kent	Apr	170
1783	Benjamin		Middlesex	Aug	401
1757	Bennit		Middlesex	Oct	294
1798	Catherine		Hertfordshire	Feb	82
1794	Charles		Middlesex	Aug	402
1800	Charles Esq		Pts	Apr	253
1759	Dorothy		Middlesex	Oct	318
1759	Edward, Esq.	A with W	Oxford	May	158
1762	Edward, Esq.		Middlesex	Aug	333
1770	Edward		Warwickshire	Feb	42
1782	Edward, alias BARBAR		Pts	May	215
1752	Elizabeth		Kent	Apr	83
1754	Elizabeth		Middlesex	Jul	188
1766	Elizabeth		London	Oct	364
1779	Elizabeth	A with W	Yorkshire	Nov	444
1780	Elizabeth		Middlesex	Feb	60
1780	Elizabeth		Litchfield	Nov	503
1785	Elizabeth	A with W of Goods unad Will regd 444 Warberton	Yorkshire	Mar	
1788	Elizabeth		Nottinghamshire	Jan	5
1772	Francis		Middlesex	Sept	317
1782	Francis		Derbyshire	Jul	336
1751	George		Pts	Feb	34
1765	George		Yorkshire	Apr	129
1783	George, Esq.		Middlesex	May	212
1800	George	Ser: "Duke" & "Prince of Wales"	Southampton	Aug	576
1795	Henry		Essex	Feb	63
1785	Isaac		Middlesex	Mar	114
1750	James		Southampton	Jan	3
1767	James		Middlesex	Jan	3
1779	James		Southampton	May	190
1783	James	Ser	Southampton	May	214
1791	James		Hertfordshire	Jan	4
1799	James		Cambridge	May	339
1799	James, alias BARBAR		Southampton	Jun	416

BARBER (contd)

Year	Name	Notes	County	Month	No.
1799	James	A with W of Goods unad Will regd. Jan 1791	Hertfordshire	Dec	
1771	Jane		Essex	Jan	3
1752	John		London	Feb	30
1757	John		Middlesex	Jun	180
1760	John		Middlesex	Jun	229
1766	John		Pts	Oct	361
1767	John		Worcestershire	May	167
1767	John		Middlesex	Sep	334
1771	John	Pts	Southampton	Jun	242
1773	John, Esq.		Oxford	Sep	351
1774	John		Middlesex	Jan	2
1775	John		Exeter	Jun	221
1781	John		Middlesex	Jun	283
1782	John		Pts	July	340
1785	John		London	Dec	589
1788	John		Kent	May	226
1789	John		Middlesex	Apr	188
1797	John, alias BARBOR	Ser	Cornwall	Feb	68
1797	John		Wiltshire	Aug	542
1800	John		Berkshire	Aug	579
1797	John Butler	Ser: "Leda"	Pts	Mar	130
1754	Jonathan		London	Dec	319
1763	Joseph		Lon don	Feb	47
1767	Joseph	A with W unad Will regd February 1763	London	May	
1776	Joseph		Middlesex	Apr	163
1777	Joseph		Middlesex	Aug	341
1790	Joseph		London	Jan	5
1791	Joseph		London	Jun	268
1765	Judith	A with W	Middlesex	Dec	443
1799	Margaret		Middlesex	Feb	96
1753	Margret		Middlesex	May	128
1778	Martha		Suffolk	Feb	50
1754	Mary	A with W unad Will regd 86 Anstis	Buckinghamshire	Dec	
1758	Mary		Wiltshire	Jun	179
1767	Mary		Bedford	May	163
1773	Mary		Middlesex	Apr	145
1785	Mary		Middlesex	Aug	402
1797	Mary		Suffolk	Dec	727
1750	Mercy	A with W	London	Aug	251
1772	Nathaniel		Middlesex	Aug	284
1764	Nicholas, alias Nicolas		Middlesex	Dec	457
1764	Nicolas, alias Nicholas		Middlesex	Dec	457
1754	Peter		Cornwall	Jun	159
1782	Peter		Pts	Dec	574
1785	Rebecca		Middlesex	Jul	354
1753	Richard		Devon	Apl	102

BARBER (contd)

Year	Name	Notes	Place	Month	No.
1759	Richard		Devon	Oct	317
1790	Richard, Esq.		Derbyshire	Jan	3
1750	Robert		London	Aug	252
1752	Robert, Esq.	A with W unad Will regd. 100 Brown	Wiltshire	Apr	
1773	Robert		Middlesex	Feb	47
1778	Robert		London	May	182
1778	Robert, Esq.	Special A with W unad Will regd. 277 Cheslyn	Staffordshire	May	
1782	Robert		Middlesex	Apr	162
1783	Robert	"Mercury"&"Princessa"	Pts	July	339
1784	Robert		Hertfordshire	Aug	431
1768	Sampson, Esq.		Bath	Nov	402
1783	Samuel	Ser	Pts	Oct	500
1751	Sarah		Middlesex	Apr	104
1771	Sarah		London	Mar	92
1772	Sarah		Middlesex	Dec	431
1789	Sarah		Coventry	Sep	448
1791	Sarah		Surrey	Sep	417
1786	Solomon		Hertfordshire	Mar	140
1784	Stephen		Staffordshire	Dec	630
1763	Thomas		Middlesex	Jan	2
1763	Thomas	A with W of Goods unad Will regd. January last	Middlesex	Apr	
1765	Thomas	A with W	Kent	Aug	285
1769	Thomas		Surrey	Aug	274
1775	Thomas		Bedford	Mar	83
1788	Thomas		Middlesex	Dec	574
1795	Thomas		Kent	Feb	62
1800	Thomas		Newcastle /Tyne	Jul	506
1754	William		Hertfordshire	Nov	293
1762	William		Monmouthshire	Jan	5
1762	William		Middlesex	Feb	40
1768	William		Surrey	Jan	4
1768	William		Essex	Jun	227
1769	William		Middlesex	Apr	113
1777	William		Exeter	Jan	7
1781	William		Pts	Mar	118
1781	William	A with W	Pts	Apr	180
1781	William		Middlesex	Oct	464
1782	William	A with W	Southampton	Mar	111
1783	William		Hertfordshire	Sep	446
1786	William		Middlesex	May	261
1794	William		London	Mar	124
1795	William		Middlesex	Aug	495
1799	William		Middlesex	Dec	827
1767	BARBET, James Leonard alias Jacque Eleour		Middlesex	Mar	88

	BARBET (contd)				
1783	Stephen		Guernsey	Apr	162
1753	BARBIER, Daniel		Middlesex	Mar	71
1794	Jan, alias John Denis		Middlesex	May	247
1757	Jane		Middlesex	Dec	350
1771	John Pere, alias John Peter		Oxford	Nov	432
1760	Paul		Middlesex	Dec	451
1790	BARBIN, Catharina, alias Catarina Elisabeth	Ltd A with W	Pts	Jun	279
1797	Jeanne Marie	Ltd Prob	Pts	Jan	32
1764	Paul	Ltd Prob	Pts	Oct	379
1790	Paul, alias Paulus	Ltd Prob	Pts	May	222
1752	BARBO, Isabella		Kent	Oct	242
1765	BARBOR, Barbara		London	Feb	42
1777	Elizabeth		Essex	May	201
1750	Gabriel		Essex	Nov	347
1768	Gabriel		London	Feb	48
1788	George, Esq.		Devon	Apr	174
1757	John		Surrey	Apr	110
1797	John, alias BARBER	Ser	Cornwall	Feb	68
1782	Michael		London	Jun	267
1761	Robert, Esq.		Stafford	Aug	277
1782	Robert, Esq.	Special A with W unad Will regd. 277 Cheslyn Last Grant May 1778	Stafford	Mar	
1782	Robert, Esq.	Pts	Middlesex	Dec	573
1775	Sarah		Surrey	Apr	128
1768	William, Dr.	Doctor of Physick	Devon	Mar	94
1785	William, Dr.	Doctor of Physick A with W of Goods unad Will regd. 94 Secker	Devon	Mar	
1791	BARBOSS, James, alias BARWIS	"Crown" &"Prss. Royal"		May	216
1766	BARBOT, John		Middlesex	Apr	129
1752	Mary		Middlesex	Apr	86
1766	Susanna		London	Oct	364
1780	BARBOTTIN, Cornelia		Surrey	Feb	59
1762	BARBOUD, Peter		Pts	Nov	445
1766	BARBU, Catherine		Middlesex	Nov	396
1775	Joseph		Middlesex	Sep	335
1765	Magdalen		Middlesex	Nov	398
1774	BARBUR, Andrew		Middlesex	Jan	5
1766	Herbert		Middlesex	Jan	4
1772	Martha, formerly YARROW		Middlesex	Mar	82
1793	BARBUT, Ann	Special Prob	Surrey	Sep	452
1782	James, Esq.		Huntingdonshire	May	213
1794	Stephen		Middlesex	Jul	354
1795	Stephen	Double Prob Will regd. July 1794	Middlesex	Jun	
1774	BARBUTT, Horatio Pearse	A with W	Middlesex	Sep	328
1770	BARCHARD, Joseph	A with W	Surrey	Sep	322
1769	Morris		Rutland	Jan	2

1764	BARCHMAN WUYTIERS Lady Johanna Charlotta Cornelia	Ltd Prob	Pts	Oct	377
1752	Maria Richardina, alias KARSSEBOOM	A with W	Pts	Mar	58
1762	BARCHMAN WUYTIERS Maria Richardina, alias KARSSEBOOM	Will regd. 58 Bettesworth	Pts	May	
1756	BARCKEMEYER, Albertus		Pts	Jan	2
1770	Elisabett,formerly JANNETTE	Ltd Prob	Pts	Jun	222
1760	BARCKLAND, Hans		Pts	Jul	274
1750	BARCKLAY, John, alias BARCKLEY	A with W	Pts	Feb	37
1750	BARCKLEY, John alias BARCKLAY	A with W	Pts	Feb	37
1784	BARTLEY, Alexander, alias BARCLAY	Ser "Thorne,""Isis,""Renown," "Hero"	Pts	Jul	367
1798	BARCLAY, Andrew	Ser "Prince of Wales"	Pts	Jul	461
1750	David		London	Apr	102
1769	David		Middlesex	Apr	113
1770	David		London	Mar	89
1770	David	Ser A with W	Pts	Aug	286
1783	David		Middlesex	Aug	400
1795	David	"Irresistible" Ser	Pts	May	294
1793	Elizabeth Isabella		Middlesex	Apr	184
1755	George		Middlesex	Oct	253
1756	George		Middlesex	Jun	160
1764	George	A with W of Goods unad Will regd 253 Paul	Middlesex	Aug	
1786	Hugh	"Tarton"&"Royal Admiral"	Pts	Jul	361
1754	Isaac, alias BARTLEY		Pts	Oct	267
1750	James		Pts	Apr	106
1765	James, Esq.	Ltd Prob	Pts	Apr	130
1766	James		London	Jun	210
1778	James, The Revd.		Middlesex	Aug	311
1793	James, Sir, Baronet		Pts	Sep	455
1758	John		Pts	Aug	237
1778	John		Pts	Mar	96
1788	John		Middlesex	Feb	56
1798	Joseph, Esq.	Int. Decree	Middlesex	Feb	76
1796	Margaret		Lancashire	Nov	541
1798	Margret, alias Margaret alias BARLAY, formerly CRAIG		Edinburgh	Sep	583
1757	Patience, alias FORBES	Ltd Prob	N.Britain	Jul	220
1780	Priscilla		Warwickshire	Apr	172
1783	Robert		N.Britain	Aug	398
1789	Robert, Esq.		Pts	Dec	572
1760	Samuel	A with W	Pts	Nov	414

	BARCLAY (contd)				
1760	Sarah, alias BARKLAY		London	Jun	229
1780	Susannah		Bath	Apr	170
1785	Thomas		Wiltshire	Jan	5
1784	Ursula		Berkshire	Aug	431
1759	BARCLEY, James	A with W	Pts	Jan	6
1756	William		Pts	Jun	160
1777	BARCOMBE, Ann		Middlesex	Mar	96
1754	BARCROFT, Gilbert		Bristol	Feb	33
1751	James		Exeter	May	134
1800	John		Yorkshire	Oct	698
1783	Phebe		Surrey	Jul	339
1758	William		Essex	Mar	61
1782	BARCUSS, Aaron, alias BURKUS, Aron	Pts	Devon	Feb	60
1757	BARD, Thomas, alias BIRD		Pts	Oct	293
1784	BARDAN, James	No Ship	Pts	Jun	309
1784	BARDEN, Edward, alias BARDING	Ser "Magnamine"	Pts	Jul	369
1797	BARDIN, Charles	A with W	Middlesex	Jun	395
1798	Dorothy		Middlesex	Feb	78
1755	John, alias Jean		Ireland	Sep	233
1769	John		Middlesex	Mar	78
1781	John		Middlesex	Aug	377
1791	John		Middlesex	Apr	167
1777	BARDINE, Isaac		Middlesex	Jun	252
1773	John, alias BORDON, alias BORDEN	A with W	Pts	Jun	235
1784	BARDING, Edward alias BARDEN	Ser "Magnamine"	Pts	Jul	369
1775	BARDOLPH, John		Middlesex	May	173
1752	Nathaniel		London	Nov	270
1784	BARDON, Elizabeth		Middlesex	Dec	630
1767	Richard		Middlesex	Dec	438
1788	BARDSLEY, Elizabeth		Middlesex	Jan	5
1753	Samuel		London	Dec	311
1754	Samuel, alias BAZLEY	Will regd. December last	London	Jan	
1777	Samuel		London	Jul	302
1794	BARDWELL, John		Essex	Sep	446
1786	Sarah		Essex	Feb	66
1785	BARE, Mary, alias BEAR	By Int Dec Another Grant in July 1784	London	Jul	354
1762	BARE, LA, Peter, alias LA BAERE, alias LA BARRE	A with W	Pts	Jun	
1773	BARED, John		London	Apr	145
1796	William		Hertfordshire	Feb	54
1788	BAREFOOT, Margaret		Southampton	May	226
1781	Mary		Winchester	Dec	577
1771	Robert		Southampton	Nov	428

	BAREFOOT (contd)				
1760	William		Kent	Nov	413
1799	William		Essex	Jul	475
1786	BAREMAN, Benjamin, alias BEERMAN	"Cockatrice"	Pts	Jan	7
1766	BARENS, Albert, alias BARENTS, alias BARNES		Pts	Sep	329
1766	BARENTS, Albert, alias BARENS, alias BARNES		Pts	Sep	329
1793	BARENTZ, Hans		Pts	Jul	352
1777	BARERK, William, alias BARRACK	A with W	Pts	Jan	6
1763	BARES, John, alias BARNES		Pts	Sep	420
1786	BARET, Hesta		Norwich	Aug	422
1774	Robert, Esq.		Norwich	Feb	37
1753	BAREY, Pieter, alias Peter, alias BERRY	By Int Dec	Pts	May	130
1800	BARFOOT, Alice		Stafford	Oct	699
1766	Benjamin	Poor Pts	Surrey	Mar	90
1796	Henry		Lincolnshire	Aug	399
1771	Lydia		Poole	Feb	48
1798	James	"Helen" & "Greyhound"	Pts	Oct	635
1774	John		Middlesex	Jul	254
1793	John	Special A with W of Goods unad.Will regd. 254 Bargrave	Middlesex	Mar	
1796	Mary		Devon	Jul	344
1751	Richard		Surrey	Dec	326
1797	Richard		Middlesex	Jan	3
1766	Robert		Dorset	May	169
1779	Robert		Leicestershire	Feb	39
1799	Thomas		Leicestershire	Aug	562
1766	William		Poole	Nov	397
1792	BARFORD, Anne		Somerset	Oct	497
1789	Edward		Warwickshire	Jun	298
1789	Frances		Salisbury	Mar	132
1772	John		Salisbury	Oct	351
1788	John		Somerset	Oct	473
1782	Jonathan Martha		Salisbury	Jul	336
1782	Mary		Middlesex	Oct	481
1796	Mary		Lichfield	Sep	442
1762	Richard		Wiltshire	Oct	413
1769	Richard, Revd.	Doctor in Divinity A with W	Northampton	Dec	407
1784	Richard		Salisbury	Apr	190
1774	Thomas		Bedfordshire	Mar	80
1781	Thomas	A with W unad Will regd. 9 Bargrave	Bedfordshire	Dec	
1780	William, The Revd.		Wiltshire	Jun	304
1793	William, The Revd. Dr.	Doctor in Divinity	Hertfordshire	Jan	10
1797	BARGE, William	Pts WIS"Meliora"	Middlesex	Jun	397

Year	Name	Notes	County	Month	Page
1770	BARGEAU, James		Kent	Jan	6
1785	BARGENDAL, Roloff	"3 Brothers"	Pts	Jan	8
1762	BARGES, Daniel	A with W	Staffordshire	Oct	411
1772	BARGIGNAC,(formerly)Benine, now DUREGE		Pts	Aug	283
1763	BARGOT, Andrew, alias Andries BORGHAR		Pts	Jul	324
1765	BARGRAVE, Charles		Kent	Mar	88
1772	Christian		Middlesex	Dec	431
1800	Isaac		Kent	Jun	436
1764	Mary		London	May	163
1774	Robert, Esq.	Late one of the Procurators General of the Arches Court of Canterbury	Surrey	May	166
1780	Robert		Kent	Apr	171
1772	Sarah		Kent	Feb	39
1775	BARGROVE, Edward		Kent	Mar	85
1794	Thomas		Kent	Oct	490
1782	William		Kent	Aug	391
1757	BARHAM, Charles	Pts	Southampton	Jan	6
1787	Edmund		Kent	Nov	485
1756	Elizabeth		Middlesex	Jul	188
1759	Elizabeth	Double Prob Will Regd. 188 Glasier	Middlesex	Oct	
1762	Elizabeth	A with W	Middlesex	May	185
1790	Elizabeth	A with W	Middlesex	May	223
1768	Harris		Canterbury	Feb	46
1763	John	A with W	Pts	Mar	110
1785	John	"Termagant"	Pts	June	293
1794	John		Surrey	Jul	349
1794	John		Kent	Dec	596
1799	John		Essex	Aug	567
1789	Joseph Foster, Esq.		Salop	Aug	420
1750	Mary	A with W	Sussex	May	138
1768	Mary		Surrey	Sep	339
1790	Moses		Essex	Apr	173
1792	Natthaniel, alias Nathaniel		Sussex	Feb	54
1793	Refrain		Southampton	Aug	399
1785	Richard, Esq.		Canterbury	Jan	6
1795	Richard Harris, Esq.		Canterbury	Sep	537
1773	BARIL, Ann Louisa		London	Mar	94
1796	Bercher, Esq.		Southampton	Feb	54
1798	James, Esq.		London	Jan	7
1761	Lewis		London	Apr	120
1770	Susannah		London	Dec	421
1770	BARINER, Peter	A with W	Pts	June	220
1766	BARING, Elizabeth		Devon	May	167
1799	Sarah		Surrey	Feb	96
1780	BARINGER, John, alias BARRENGER		Buckinghamshire	Feb	60
1786	Mary, alias BARRINGER		Southampton	May	262
1789	BARINGTON, John Harris		Montgomeryshire	Jul	347

BARINGTON, (contd)

Year	Name	Notes	County	Month	Page
1765	Paul		Middlesex	Aug	283
1765	Paul	Double Prob	Middlesex	Dec	
		Will regd. August last			
1794	BARJEAN, Abraham	A with W of Goods	Middlesex	Nov	
		Unad Will Regd			
		109 Edmonds			
1781	BARK, Barbara, alias BARKE		Kent	Sept	420
1781	Edward	Ser	Pts	May	228
1779	John		Middlesex	Feb	40
1792	Mary		Derbyshire	Mar	127
1792	William, alias BARKE		Warwickshire	Mar	129
1762	BARKA, John	A with W	Pts	Dec	492
1781	BARKAS, Frances		Middlesex	Nov	514
1781	BARKE, Barbara,alias BARK		Kent	Sep	420
1790	Elizabeth		Middlesex	Oct	451
1772	George		Middlesex	Apr	122
1761	John	A with W	Kent	May	158
1781	John	A with W unad	Kent	Nov	
		Will regd. 158 Cheslyn			
1781	Thomas	A with W	Nottinghamshire	Aug	377
1792	William, alias BARK		Warwickshire	Mar	129
1782	BARKELL, Richard,		Pts	Feb	65
	alias BUCKNELL				
1795	BARKELY, Isabella, alias BARKLEY		Middlesex	Oct	583
1794	BARKER, Abram	"Leviathan"	Pts	Jul	352
1771	Dame Alice, alias		Suffolk	Nov	429
	BROKE, Alice				
1770	Ann		Leicester	Aug	284
1772	Ann		Oxford	Jun	204
1781	Ann		Worcestershire	Oct	461
1789	Ann		Winchester	Jan	6
1800	Ann		Surrey	May	339
1794	Anna	A with W	Middlesex	Feb	63
1800	Anne		Middlesex	May	345
1781	Annetje		Pts	Jan	9
1763	Anthony		Pts	Feb	46
1778	Averina		Middlesex	Oct	387
1764	Benjamin		Middlesex	Jul	251
1773	Betty		Middlesex	Jul	280
1764	Bogge	A with W	Pts	Jun	213
1777	Catherina		Middlesex	Feb	52
1793	Catherina	A with W of Goods	Middlesex	Aug	
		unad Will regd. 52 Collier			
1800	Catherine		Middlesex	Jun	434
1750	Charles	Pts	Middlesex	Jul	223
1751	Charles		Middlesex	Sep	252
1772	Charles		Kent	Jan	3
1798	Charlotte		Middlesex	Jan	3
1796	Christopher		Yorkshire	Feb	53
1783	Cordelia	A with W	Middlesex	Feb	60
1779	Cornelia Jacoba		Pts	Mar	91

BARKER, (contd)

1767	Cornelius JANSZ, The Hon	Ltd Prob	Pts	Mar	
1786	Cornelius		Middlesex	May	262
1800	Daniel		Oxford	Apr	258
1783	Dorothy		Bath	Dec	602
1791	Dorothy	A with W of Goods unad	Bath	May	
		Will regd 602 Cornwallis			
1750	Edmund		London	Dec	377
1800	Edmund	Mt.S. "Bellona" Pts	Surrey	May	345
1759	Edward, Esq.		Middlesex	June	194
1778	Edward	A with W	Southampton	Oct	388
1780	Edward		Norfolk	Jul	346
1783	Edward		Kent	Dec	601
1756	Elizabeth		Surrey	Feb	28
1759	Elizabeth	A with W	Middlesex	Dec	385
1763	Elizabeth		Hertfordshire	Sep	416
1768	Elizabeth		Hertfordshire	Dec	440
1774	Elizabeth		Middlesex	Nov	386
1778	Elizabeth		Hertfordshire	Apr	143
1782	Elizabeth		Surrey	Jul	335
1784	Elizabeth		Denbigh	Dec	629
1781	Elizabeth Adriana	Ltd Prob	Pts	Feb	58
1794	Esther		Chester	Dec	596
1798	Esther		Gloucestershire	Dec	761
1769	Frances		Kent	Feb	34
1798	Francis		Middlesex	Aug	524
1799	Francis	Ser. "Venge"	Middlesex	Aug	564
1751	Freelove		Kent	Jun	166
1750	George		Middlesex	May	137
1761	George		Middlesex	Apr	119
1762	George, alias BERKER	Pts	Middlesex	Jun	234
1779	George		Hertfordshire	Feb	43
1784	George	Ser. "Experiment"	Pts	Dec	629
1796	George		Kent	Dec	596
1757	Grace		Middlesex	May	148
1791	Harriot		Middlesex	May	210
1758	Henry	Ser.	Middlesex	Jun	175
1761	Henry		Northampton	Nov	380
1775	Henry, Esq.		Berkshire	Jun	225
1793	Henry, Esq.	A with W of Goods unad	Berkshire	Aug	
		Will regd 225 Alexander			
1751	Hugh	Ltd A with W of Goods unad	Pts	Jan	
		Will regd 216 Wake			
1766	James		Middlesex	Jun	210
1768	James, Rev.	A with W of Goods unad	Sussex		
		Will regd. 195 Derby			
1780	James	Ser	Middlesex	Dec	553
1791	James		Kent	Dec	561
1793	James		Exeter	Nov	539
1755	Jeremiah	A with W	Pts	Nov	276

BARKER, (Contd)

Year	Name	Note	Place	Month	No.
1751	John		Middlesex	Feb	36
1751	John		Middlesex	May	134
1753	John		Middlesex	May	128
1754	John		Middlesex	Sep	244
1754	John		Pts	Oct	267
1757	John, Sir		Suffolk	Jul	213
1758	John, Esq.		Flintshire	May	140
1759	John	A with W	Pts	Apl	118
1762	John		Surrey	Jun	235
1762	John		Pts	Dec	496
1763	John		Pts	Sep	419
1768	John		Middlesex	Sep	337
1771	John		Yorkshire	Apr	146
1773	John		Northamptonshire	May	195
1775	John		Bedfordshire	Dec	456
1776	John		Surrey	Feb	54
1781	John		Bristol	Jan	8
1782	John		London	Oct	480
1781	John, Esq.		Litchfield	Sep	420
1783	John	Ser	Pts	Jan	4
1783	John		Westmoreland	May	215
1785	John		Surrey	Oct	497
1786	John	Pts	Gibralter	Jun	320
1787	John, Esq.		Middlesex	Nov	483
1792	John, Esq.		Devon	Apr	196
1794	John		Nottingham	Nov	539
1795	John, Esq		Derbyshire	Dec	669
1797	John		Derbyshire	May	292
1799	John		Surrey	Dec	824
1766	John Fytch, Sir.		Suffolk	Feb	48
1781	Jonathan	Ser.	Durham	May	229
1788	Jordan, alias Jordon		Middlesex	Jul	340
1750	Joseph		Gloucester	Jul	223
1750	Joseph		Suffolk	Oct	316
1755	Joseph		Somerset	Nov	277
1768	Joseph		Middlesex	Feb	43
1768	Joseph		Surrey	Jun	229
1786	Joseph		Surrey	Dec	602
1784	Joseph		Middlesex	Aug	428
1782	Lewis		Pts	May	215
1785	Lucretia		Essex	Apr	172
1761	Margaret		Middlesex	Jan	5
1798	Margaret		Kent	Sep	583
1798	Maria	Ltd Prob	Pts	Sep	583
1753	Martha		Bedford	Jan	4
1753	Martha		Surrey	Apl	102
1767	Martha		Middlesex	Jun	209
1796	Martha		Yorkshire	Jul	346
1754	Mary		Middlesex	Apr	99
1759	Mary		London	Sep	288
1760	Mary	Double Prob	London	Mar	

Will regst. September last

BARKER (Contd)

1760	Mary		Kent	Mar	86
1772	Mary, alias BAKER		Middlesex	Jul	247
1775	Mary		London	Feb	39
1780	Mary		Middlesex	Dec	551
1781	Mary		Middlesex	June	287
1786	Mary		Oxford	Jun	321
1789	Mary	A with W	Yorkshire	Jun	301
1792	Mary		Cambridge	May	257
1792	Mary		Kent	Oct	500
1797	Mary		Middlesex	Sep	586
1798	Mary		Southampton	Sep	581
1800	Mary	Double Prob Will regd Oct 1792	Kent	Nov	
1753	Matthias		Kent	Mar	69
1800	Michael		Middlesex	Dec	835
1770	Moses		Surrey	Jan	2
1762	Pentecost		Devon	Oct	412
1784	Pentecost	Ltd A with W of Goods Unad Will regd 412 St Eloy	Devon	Aug	
1783	Peter		Middlesex	Aug	401
1751	Rachel		Northampton	Jan	4
1799	Ralph		Wiltshire	Feb	97
1750	Richard		Pts	May	136
1750	Richard	Pts	Southampton	Jul	222
1759	Richard	Pts	Middlesex	Oct	318
1764	Richard		Somerset	Aug	298
1766	Richard		Essex	Mar	91
1770	Richard		Chichester	Oct	352
1772	Richard		London	Jun	204
1776	Richard, Esq	Double Prob. Will regd Oct 1770	Chichester	Jun	
1766	Robert		London	Nov	400
1779	Robert		Norwich	Mar	90
1784	Robert		Essex	Mar	122
1784	Robert		Middlesex	Oct	536
1789	Robert, Sir, Baronet		Middlesex	Oct	483
1795	Robert		Middlesex	Dec	669
1797	Robert, The Rev		Derby	Jun	395
1799	Robert		Middlesex	Aug	567
1768	Ruth	A with W	Middlesex	Jul	269
1752	Sacheverel	A with W	Suffolk	May	116
1759	Samuel, Esq		Rutland	Nov	347
1772	Samuel	A with W	Surrey	Feb	40
1781	Samuel		Middlesex	Jul	329
1793	Samuel		Essex	Apr	187
1762	Sarah		Berkshire	Apr	142
1773	Sarah	A with W annexed	Berkshire	Apr	144
1777	Sarah		Middlesex	Feb	51
1785	Sarah		Kent	May	230

BARKER (Contd)

Year	Name	Note	County	Month	Page
1800	Sarah		Surrey	Sep	646
1798	Scory		Southampton	Mar	156
1750	Thomas, Esq		Berkshire	Jan	4
1750	Thomas		London	May	139
1750	Thomas		Northampton	Jul	223
1752	Thomas	A with W of Goods Unad. Will regd Jul 1750	Northampton	Feb	
1754	Thomas		Bedford	Jan	4
1755	Thomas		Derby	Feb	32
1755	Thomas		Kent	Jul	182
1755	Thomas		Suffolk	Nov	277
1762	Thomas		Derby	Jun	232
1762	Thomas		Gloucester	Jun	235
1765	Thomas	A with W	Middlesex	Aug	285
1770	Thomas		Surrey	Aug	287
1773	Thomas		Hertford	May	195
1779	Thomas	A with W Unad Will regd 195 Stevens	Hertford	Jun	
1773	Thomas, Esq		Dorset	Oct	382
1777	Thomas		Huntingdon	Feb	52
1779	Thomas, Esq		Pts	Oct	406
1784	Thomas		Middlesex	May	249
1785	Thomas		Hertford	Mar	118
1785	Thomas, The Rev Doctor in Divinity		Oxford	Oct	490
1787	Thomas		Middlesex	Apr	157
1791	Thomas		Dorset	Oct	452
1792	Thomas		Lancaster	Sep	460
1793	Thomas		Kent	Jul	351
1793	Thomas	Double Prob Will regd 249 Rockingham	Middlesex	Nov	
1794	Thomas		Middlesex	Apr	184
1795	Thomas		Cambridge	Apr	235
1795	Thomas		Surrey	Dec	673
1796	Thomas		Huntingdon	Jan	7
1796	Thomas	"Joana"	Pts	Mar	110
1796	Thomas		Kent	Dec	595
1798	Thomas		Hertford	Feb	83
1750	William		Hertford	May	137
1751	William		Oxford	Apr	102
1754	William		Surrey	May	125
1758	William, Esq		Berkshire	Sep	259
1759	William		Pts	Oct	319
1767	William		Essex	Apr	122
1777	William		Middlesex	Jul	302
1782	William		Pts	Sep	439
1783	William	A with W "Barfleur"	Pts	Dec	602
1787	William		Essex	Jan	5

	BARKER (Contd)				
1789	William		Middlesex	Nov	532
1791	William, alias HOULTON	"Minerva"Pts	Essex	Aug	385
1795	William		Middlesex	Feb	64
1796	William	Ser'Excellent"	Pts	Nov	542
1797	William		Middlesex	Sep	587
1798	William		Kent	Jun	382
1791	The Revd. William Bell		Suffolk	Mar	112
1765	BARKERS, Magtils formerly VANDER BECK		Pts	Mar	86
1764	BARKHAM, George	A with W	London	Oct	379
1776	Thomas		London	Aug	346
1770	William, Esq	Ltd Prob	Pts	Jun	222
1780	BARKINGTON, Ann		Middlesex	Jul	346
1780	Ann, alias BARTINGTON	Will regd this Month	Middlesex	Jul	
1757	BARKLAY, John		Middlesex	Mar	72
1779	John, alias BARKLY	Ser	Pts	Jul	286
1760	Sarah, alias BARCLAY		London	Jun	229
1776	BARKLEY, Charles	A with W Pts	Middlesex	Mar	110
1795	Elizabeth		Middlesex	Oct	580
1795	Isabella, alias BARKELY		Middlesex	Oct	583
1752	John		Middlesex	Mar	59
1753	Samuel	A with W	London	Jun	162
1758	Thomas		Pts	Mar	65
1779	BARKLY, John alias BARKLAY	Ser	Pts	Jul	286
1750	BARKOFFER, DE, Dame Henrietta Amelie Agnes, alias DE DREVON		Pts	Apr	110
1754	BARKS, Joshua		Pts	Mar	68
1771	BARKSDALE, Lucy		Middlesex	Apr	143
1754	BARKWELL, Barnaby, Esq		Middlesex	Oct	265
1770	BARKWITH, John		Middlesex	Jul	253
1788	BARLAND, George		Middlesex	Sep	427
1769	Helaner		Middlesex	Apr	111
1798	BARLAY, Margret, alias Margaret alias BARCLAY, formerly CRAIG		Edinburgh	Sep	583
1785	BARLEE, Charles Barlee		London	Jan	7
1792	Charles Barlee	A with W of Goods Unad Will regd 7 Ducarel	London	Mar	
1757	Palgrave, Esq		Essex	May	149
1765	William Spring	A with W	Essex	Jun	208
1785	BARLEUS, Machelina, alias Macgelina, alias Machtalina	Ltd Prob	Pts	May	231
1750	BARLEY, Ann		Hertford	Mar	69
1773	James		Devon	Jun	239

BARLEY (Contd)

Year	Name	Notes	County	Month	No
1772	Richard, alias BARLY		Middlesex	Feb	41
1767	Robert	By Decree	Surrey	May	164
1753	Ruth		Hertfordshire	Oct	263
1757	William		Berkshire	Feb	68
1788	BARLING, Aaron		Wiltshire	Jun	286
1767	George		London	Oct	362
1795	John Smith, Esq		Kent	Mar	140
1762	Thomas		Pts	Dec	492
1770	Thomas		Kent	Jan	5
1750	William		London	Jan	3
1760	William	Pts	Southampton	Aug	314
1778	BARLOW, Alethea		Surrey	Jun	230
1797	Alice		Worcester	Jul	
1775	Andrew		London	Nov	405
1777	Ann		York	May	200
1800	Ann Sophia Ann		Middlesex	Nov	765
1795	Anne		Pembroke	Dec	668
1787	Arabella		Devon	Feb	54
1759	Bartholomew		Lincoln	May	156
1759	Benjamin		Southampton	Nov	348
1783	Benjamin		Lincoln	Mar	113
1797	Benjamin		Surrey	Feb	73
1763	Edward		Buckinghamshire	Mar	105
1788	Edward		Middlesex	Aug	382
1755	Elisha		Suffolk	Aug	209
1750	Elizabeth		Kent	Oct	315
1762	Elizabeth		Surrey	May	186
1762	Elizabeth		Surrey	Jul	284
1769	Elizabeth	A with W of Goods Unad Will regd 284 St Eley	Surrey	Feb	
1774	Elizabeth		Middlesex	Feb	40
1777	Elizabeth		Middlesex	Nov	447
1789	Elizabeth		Pembroke	Feb	74
1795	Elizabeth		Middlesex	Feb	67
1771	Francis, Esq		York	Dec	472
1799	Francis		Middlesex	Jan	10
1781	Francis Ligo		Buckinghamshire	Aug	378
1755	George		Middlesex	Jun	153
1767	George		Middlesex	Jul	251
1775	George, Sir, Bart	A with W	Pts	Dec	456
1785	George	Pts	Gibralter	Mar	113
1787	George, Esq	A with W	York	Mar	105
1791	George	A with W Another Grant Mar 1787	York	Feb	
1795	George		London	Apr	235
1782	Henry		Essex	Nov	528
1763	Hugh		Pembroke	Dec	539
1764	Hugh	Codicil – Will regd in Dec last	Pembroke	Sep	338

1792	Jane	A with W	Buckinghamshire	Aug	415
1752	John	By Int Dec	Middlesex	Jun	148
1756	John		Middlesex	Nov	287
1757	John	A with W Unad Will regd Nov 1756	Middlesex	Feb	
1759	John		Middlesex	Jul	224
1770	John		Middlesex	Dec	422
1777	John	A with W	Pts	Dec	499
1781	John, alias WRIGHT		Pts	Dec	577
1783	John	A with W Pts	Dublin	Sep	443
1788	John, Esq		Bristol	Jun	286
1794	John		Surrey	Jan	5
1780	Joseph		London	Jun	302
1792	Joseph		Surrey	Nov	543
1795	Joseph		Middlesex	Mar	142
1768	Margaret		Essex	Dec	438
1772	Mary		Wiltshire	May	158
1779	Mary		Southampton	Oct	405
1785	Mary		Middlesex	Sep	457
1776	Matthew		Wiltshire	Jul	296
1766	Michael		London	Oct	363
1787	Nathaniel, Esq		Pts	Jan	7
1798	Nathaniel		Essex	Jun	377
1763	Rachel		Middlesex	Feb	48
1768	Rebecca		Middlesex	Dec	438
1751	Richard		Middlesex	Feb	38
1759	Richard		Middlesex	Oct	317
1787	Richard		Warwickshire	Feb	52
1796	Richard		Essex	Jul	348
1765	Robert		Middlesex	May	171
1791	Robert		Lincoln	Nov	500
1795	Robert		Winchester	Jul	429
1774	Sophia, spinster	By Sent (regd Jun 465) A with W	York	Jul	255
1763	Thomas, Esq		Middlesex	Jul	323
1766	Thomas		Middlesex	Dec	441
1779	Thomas		Berkshire	Dec	484
1782	Thomas, Esq		Middlesex	Jul	335
1798	Thomas		Middlesex	Mar	156
1750	William		Pts	May	138
1753	William		Devon	Dec	309
1756	William		Middlesex	May	129
1767	William		Middlesex	Dec	436
1779	William		London	Jan	5
1779	William		Southampton	Mar	89
1779	William		Middlesex	Aug	335
1781	William		Middlesex	Feb	57
1783	William	Ser	Pts	Sep	443
1790	William		Middlesex	Dec	538
1790	William, Esq		Lancaster	Dec	541

	BARLOW (Contd)				
1798	William, Esq		Bath	Jul	459
1800	William George		London	Sep	642
1772	BARLY, Richard,		Middlesex	Feb	41
	alias BARLEY				
1768	BARMCOTT, Mary,	By Sent	Middlesex	Nov	436
	alias WISEMAN				
1786	BARMONT, DE, Andrew		Jersey	Dec	
	Grenier				
1798	BARMORE, William		Middlesex	Jan	7
1759	BARNAART, Engeltje	Ltd Prob	Pts	Mar	83
	alias VAN HOOVEN				
1781	Jacobus	Ltd Prob	Pts	Jan	8
1781	Philip Willem	Ltd Prob	Pts	Aug	375
1780	The Hon Willem	Ltd Prob	Pts	Mar	121
1751	BARNABE, Maria Isabella		Pts	Dec	328
	Clara, alias GORIS				
1755	BARNABY, Henry		Middlesex	May	121
1763	BARNACLE, George		Warwick	May	214
1791	BARNARD, Alice	Ltd Prob	Surrey	Nov	498
1762	Ann		Surrey	Jan	2
1778	Ann		Middlesex	Nov	429
1787	Ann		Northampton	Jun	252
1799	Ann		Essex	Apr	245
1799	Ann Bathsheba			Aug	568
1792	Anna, alias Ann		Surrey	Nov	544
	alias BERNARD				
1763	Anthony		Middlesex	Nov	495
1783	Boldero Leuyus, Esq		York	Jun	281
	alias BOLDERO, Leuyus				
1761	Catherine		Hertford	Nov	380
1775	Catherine, alias Cathrine		Middlesex	Jun	224
1785	Charles		York	Dec	585
1798	Ciselly		Kent	Oct	639
1795	Collier		Cambridge	Feb	66
1798	Daniel, Esq		Surrey	Jun	380
1760	Edward		London	Aug	315
1770	Edward		Middlesex	Sep	319
1775	Edward		Southampton	Dec	458
1781	The Revd Edward,		Buckinghamshire	Dec	573
	Doctor in Divinity				
1784	The Revd Dr Edward	Will regd Dec 1781	Buckinghamshire	Dec	
	Doctor in Divinity				
1791	Edward		Berkshire	Jun	267
1774	Eleanor, alias Elener		Southampton	Sep	324
1800	Eleanor		Southampton	Sep	648
1800	Eleanor	A with W Unad	Southampton	Nov	
		Will regd Sep last			
1752	Elizabeth		Pts	Jul	179
1762	Elizabeth		Middlesex	Jul	286
1775	Elizabeth, alias HARDY	Ltd Prob	Essex	May	187

BARNARD (Contd)

1778	Elizabeth, alias FFIGGINS Ltd Prob		Surrey	Apr	146
1782	Elizabeth		Essex	Jun	263
1789	Edward		Kent	Oct	482
1770	Frances		Sussex	Oct	351
1756	Francis, Dr in Divinity		Cambridge	Oct	267
1760	George		Bedford	Jul	273
1764	George		Hertfordshire	Dec	454
1767	George		London	Jan	2
1775	George		Middlesex	Jul	262
1755	Hannah		Middlesex	Sep	233
1761	Henry		Hertford	Jul	241
1766	Henry		Essex	Jun	215
1776	Henry		Suffolk	Jul	296
1791	Henry		London	May	215
1752	James		Middlesex	Jun	148
1752	James	Double Prob Will regd this month	Middlesex	Jun	
1775	James		Hertford	Jan	1
1778	James		Somerset	Jul	275
1786	James	By Int Decree	Hertford	Mar	139
1763	Jane, alias BERNARD		Middlesex	May	215
1751	John		Middlesex	Aug	229
1755	John		Essex	Apr	93
1756	John		Pts	May	130
1762	John		Middlesex	May	186
1762	John		Surrey	Aug	334
1763	John, Esq		Southampton	Sep	418
1764	John		Surrey	Sep	337
1765	John		Kent	Jun	209
1766	John		Berkshire	Jun	213
1769	John		Essex	Feb	34
1773	John		Middlesex	Jun	238
1773	John, Esq	A with W	Middlesex	Jul	279
1774	John		Berkshire	Jun	216
1774	John		Middlesex	Dec	423
1775	John	A with W Unad Will regd 93 Paul	Essex	Sep	
1778	John		Middlesex	Feb	49
1784	John, Esq		Middlesex	Nov	588
1787	John		Hertford	Sep	397
1791	John, Esq		Surrey	Oct	453
1793	John		Middlesex	May	240
1797	John		Suffolk	Jul	473
1798	John		Middlesex	May	311
1800	John		Bath	Jul	508
1767	John Barners		Middlesex	Nov	402
1783	John Beardwell, Esq		Pts	Nov	550
1785	Jonathan	A with W	Kent	Oct	490
1761	Joseph		Berkshire	Apr	116
1781	Joseph		Surrey	Nov	513

BARNARD (Contd)

Year	Name	Notes	County	Month	Page
1784	Joseph		Pts	Apr	187
1769	Lucina		Kent	Apr	112
1791	Margaret		Surrey	Dec	555
1755	Mary		Middlesex	Jul	182
1775	Mary		Middlesex	Oct	369
1794	Mary		Yorks	Feb	63
1797	Mary		Middlesex	Aug	542
1799	Mary		York	May	333
1799	Mary		Hertford	Aug	566
1763	Matthew		London	May	215
1760	Nathaniell		London	Feb	49
1779	Noah		Middlesex	May	190
1779	Noah	Double Prob Will regd this month	Middlesex	May	
1760	Rachel		Essex	Sep	347
1769	Rebeca, alias Rebecca	A with W	Devon	May	153
1764	Richard, Esq		Sussex	Dec	453
1770	Richard		Essex	Mar	89
1771	Richard		Middlesex	Jun	244
1772	Richard		London	Jun	207
1779	Richard		Essex	Jul	288
1783	Richard	A with W Unad Will regd 244 Trevor	Middlesex	May	
1781	Robert		Essex	May	227
1788	Robert		Surrey	Dec	579
1797	Robert		Middlesex	Apr	221
1791	Sacheverell		London	Sep	418
1774	Samuel		Essex	May	169
1800	Samuel		Kent	Mar	178
1756	Sarah		Surrey	Apr	94
1751	Susanna		Surrey	Jun	166
1775	Susanna	A with W Unad Will regd 166 Busby	Surrey	Mar	
1757	Thomas		London	Feb	40
1757	Thomas		Pts	Mar	73
1757	Thomas		Middlesex	Nov	322
1769	Thomas		Surrey	Jun	195
1770	Thomas		Middlesex	Jun	221
1775	Thomas	A with W	Gloucester	Jul	260
1777	Thomas		London	Jul	299
1780	Thomas		Buckinghamshire	Apr	170
1781	Thomas, Esq		Middlesex	Dec	571
1781	The Revd Thomas		Suffolk	Dec	575
1783	Thomas		London	May	213
1785	The Revd Thomas		Buckinghamshire	Jan	3
1786	Thomas		Essex	Apr	205
1794	Thomas		Rutland	Apr	182
1795	The Revd Thomas		Cambridge	Feb	66
1799	The Revd Thomas		Norfolk	Dec	824
1800	Thomas		Hertford	May	340

	BARNARD (Contd)				
1788	Thomas Allen		Middlesex	Sep	427
1758	William		Middlesex	Jul	208
1760	William		Middlesex	Jun	230
1768	William Lord, Rt Revd Father in God. Doctor of Divinity by Divine permission Late Lord Bishop of Derry in the Kingdom of Ireland		Ireland	Feb	42
1777	William		Southampton	Jul	302
1782	William		Pts	Dec	574
1786	William		Middlesex	Jun	324
1787	William		Middlesex	Sep	399
1790	William	A with W	London	Sep	433
1795	William		Kent	Mar	145
1798	William	Ser. "Melpomene"	Pts	Dec	757
1786	BARNARDISTON, Arthur	A with W	Middlesex	Apr	202
1762	Clarke		Middlesex	Feb	41
1755	Grace		London	Jan	3
1757	Dame Kath^e		Middlesex	Dec	350
1779	The Revd John, Doctor in Divinity		Cambridge	Oct	405
1777	Joseph	A with W	Hertfordshire	Jun	252
1795	Margate, alias Margret, alias Margaret		Middlesex	Jul	432
1760	Mary		Gloucester	Aug	315
1788	Mary		Middlesex	Jun	291
1771	Nathaniel		Middlesex	Jan	6
1776	Nathaniel, Esq		London	Jul	303
1752	Thomas	Serjeant at Law	Middlesex	Nov	268
1771	BARNARDON, Gaston		Ireland	Aug	331
1786	BARNBY, Elizabeth		Norfolk	Oct	506
1773	BARNDEN, William		Sussex	Feb	43
1758	BARNE, Elizabeth	A with W	Middlesex	Jan	4
1780	George		Hertford	Mar	122
1757	Henry		Middlesex	Apr	110
1752	John		Essex	Aug	205
1765	Miles		Middlesex	Apr	130
1781	Miles, Esq		Suffolk	Mar	112
1784	BARNEBY, Bartholomew Richard, Esq		Hereford	Feb	62
1785	Betty		Worcester	Jun	291
1764	BARNER, Juriaann, alias Juriaan		Pts	Apr	132
1764	Juriaan, alias Juriaann		Pts	Apr	132
1756	Thomas		Pts	Nov	287
1750	BARNERD, Ernest, Esq		Middlesex	Jun	187
1791	BARNES, Abraham		Middlesex	Dec	561
1759	Adam		Suffolk	Sep	288

BARNES (Contd)

Year	Name	Notes	Place	Month	Page
1766	Albert, alias BARENTS alias BARENS		Pts	Sep	329
1762	Andrew, alias BAUTS		Pts	Oct	411
1752	Ann		Worcester	Jul	179
1759	Ann	A with W	Wiltshire	Aug	258
1763	Ann		London	Nov	497
1765	Ann		Middlesex	Feb	45
1770	Ann	A with W Unad Will regd 45 Rushworth	Middlesex	Feb	
1770	Ann		Middlesex	May	195
1777	Ann		Warwick	Nov	448
1782	Ann		Middlesex	Apr	164
1795	Ann		Middlesex	Apr	238
1789	Anne		Derby	May	238
1750	Anthony		Middlesex	Nov	349
1769	Aubrey, Esq	A with W	Monmouth	Jan	4
1790	Aubry, Esq		Monmouth	Jun	277
1790	Barbara		Oxford	Jun	278
1758	Baynham		Monmouth	Oct	284
1768	Benjamin		Middlesex	Jun	228
1784	Benjamin	E.I.S."Deptford"	Pts	Mar	120
1770	Cassandra		Surrey	Feb	44
1759	Catherine		Northampton	Jul	225
1759	Charles		Pts	Oct	319
1764	Charles		Middlesex	Oct	379
1767	Charles		Norfolk	Feb	34
1787	Charles		Surrey	Nov	486
1767	Cornelius	A with W annexed of Goods Unad Will regd in Jun last	Southampton		
1792	Cornelius		Middlesex	Jul	363
1782	Daniel		Middlesex	Jul	339
1752	Edward		Surrey	Dec	292
1764	Edward		Middlesex	Feb	37
1764	Edward		Pts	Apr	130
1773	Edward		Middlesex	May	193
1781	Edward, alias BARNS		Pts	Dec	577
1781	Edward, alias BARNS		Pts	Dec	577
1782	Edward		Pts	Feb	59
1796	Edward, Esq		Middlesex	Dec	597
1767	Eleanor		Norwich	Nov	404
1779	Eleanor		Rutland	Feb	39
1781	Elianor, alias Eleanor		Monmouth	Dec	569
1752	Elizabeth		Middlesex	Jun	146
1754	Elizabeth		Suffolk	Jun	159
1764	Elizabeth		Middlesex	Mar	81
1764	Elizabeth		Kent	Oct	377
1766	Elizabeth		Derby	Apr	128
1768	Elizabeth		Sussex	Feb	45
1768	Elizabeth	A with W	Middlesex	Sep	337

BARNES (Contd)

Year	Name	Note	Place	Month	Page
1769	Elizabeth	A with W	Gloucester	Feb	33
1775	Elizabeth		Middlesex	Feb	39
1781	Elizabeth		Middlesex	Jan	9
1784	Elizabeth		Bath	Oct	537
1785	Elizabeth		Middlesex	Feb	67
1786	Elizabeth, alias BARNS		Middlesex	Mar	136
1789	Elizabeth		Middlesex	Jan	11
1797	Elizabeth		Wiltshire	May	297
1797	Elizabeth		Gloucester	Aug	540
1798	Elizabeth		Surrey	Mar	152
1799	Elizabeth		Bath	Mar	166
1763	Elizabeth Berry		London	Nov	494
1763	Frances		Oxford	Nov	494
1767	Frances		London	Apr	124
1778	Ffrances		Wiltshire	Mar	96
1798	Frances	A with W	Monmouth	Jun	383
1767	Francis		Middlesex	Sep	333
1800	Francis		Wiltshire	Dec	837
1778	Gabriel		Gloucester	Mar	95
1751	George		Worcester	Feb	35
1757	George	A with W	Surrey	Feb	41
1761	George	Ser	Pts	Aug	278
1762	George		Pts	Jun	235
1788	George		Middlesex	Dec	577
1789	George	A with W of Goods Unad Will regd Dec last	Middlesex	Sep	
1795	George	A with W	Kent	Feb	63
1751	Grace		Surrey	Sep	252
1771	Hannah		Worcester	Aug	329
1779	Hannah		Hertford	Dec	484
1753	Henry	A with W of Goods Unad Will regd 189 Boycott	Monmouth	Feb	
1761	Henry		Worcester	Jan	2
1766	Henry, alias BARNS	Ser	Pts	Jan	2
1767	Henry		Middlesex	Mar	84
1772	Henry	A with W	Southampton	Jun	208
1773	Henry, Esq		London	Jun	239
1775	Henry		London	Dec	460
1788	Henry		Surrey	Nov	524
1792	Henry	A with W	London	May	257
1800	Henry		Middlesex	Nov	765
1758	Hester	A with W Unad Will regd 161 Richmond	Middlesex	Dec	
1786	Humphrey	A with W	Somerset	Jul	366
1764	Isaac	A with W	Middlesex	Jul	252
1777	Isaac		Middlesex	Dec	497
1779	Isabella		Middlesex	Feb	38
1751	Jacob		Pts	Oct	275

BARNES (Contd)

1795	Jacob		Essex	Aug	495
1779	James, alias BARNS		Pts	Jun	236
1779	James		Stafford	Dec	485
1780	James	Double Prob Will regd Dec last	Stafford	Feb	
1780	James	Ser	Pts	Jun	303
1781	James		Huntingdon	Jun	283
1753	Jane	A with W	Dorset	Sep	245
1782	Jane		Surrey	Nov	527
1792	Jane Des		Canterbury	Oct	506
1796	Jane		Monmouth	Apr	160
1797	Joan		Middlesex	Mar	126
1751	Job		Somerset	Jun	166
1750	John		Middlesex	Feb	36
1751	John		Huntingdon	Apr	104
1752	John		Monmouth	May	118
1754	John		Middlesex	Dec	319
1757	John		Middlesex	Apr	110
1759	John		Pts	Apr	118
1759	John	A with W	Berkshire	May	159
1759	John		Monmouth	May	161
1759	John		Pts	Jul	223
1760	John		Suffolk	Dec	452
1761	John	Ser	Kent	Jul	241
1761	John		Gloucester	Sep	308
1763	John	Pts	Surrey	Feb	48
1763	John, alias BARES		Pts	Sep	420
1764	John	A with W of Goods Unad Will regd Jul 1761	Kent	Oct	
1765	John		Huntingdon	Nov	402
1765	John		Southampton	Dec	440
1765	John		London	Dec	442
1766	John		Middlesex	Jul	258
1768	John		Essex	May	187
1769	John		London	Apr	111
1770	John		Cambridge	Feb	42
1771	John		Middlesex	Apr	143
1778	John		Surrey	Nov	430
1774	John, alias BARNS		Middlesex	Sep	329
1780	John		Surrey	Jun	301
1781	John		Middlesex	Mar	112
1782	John		Middlesex	Jan	3
1782	John		London	Apr	163
1782	John	By Int Decree	London	Aug	392
1783	John	Ser	Lancaster	Mar	112
1783	John		Northampton	May	213
1783	John		Middlesex	Nov	552
1784	John, alias ROBERTS	Ser "Shrewsbury" "Prince William"	Middlesex	Jan	3

	BARNES (Contd)				
1785	John		Surrey	Jan	4
1786	John		Middlesex	Dec	601
1791	John		London	Feb	55
1795	John		Middlesex	Sep	535
1796	John	A with W Pts "Egmont"	Devon	Jul	344
1796	John		Southampton	Sep	445
1797	John		Sussex	Jun	399
1797	John	No ship	Pts	Oct	627
		A with W			
1799	John		Dorset	May	335
1799	John		Surrey	Jun	417
1752	Jonathan		Pts	Oct	241
1769	Jonathan		London	Mar	79
1754	Joseph		Warwick	Apr	99
1756	Joseph	A with W	Middlesex	Nov	288
1758	Joseph	A with W	Pts	Oct	286
1764	Joseph		Pts	Dec	457
1775	Joseph		Worcester	May	172
1781	Joseph	A with W Unad	London	Feb	
		Will regd 197 Potter			
1783	Joseph	A with W of Goods	London	Jun	
		twice Unad			
		Will regd 197 Potter 1781			
1787	Joseph		Surrey	Feb	52
1791	Joseph		Surrey	Mar	113
1800	Joseph	A with W	Hereford	Sep	642
1772	The Revd Joshua		Southampton	Feb	42
1769	Josias	A with W	Cornwall	Feb	33
		Pts			
1794	Lucy		Northampton	Oct	486
1791	Margret, alias	A with W	Middlesex	Dec	559
	BARNS, Margaret				
1766	Martha		Chichester	Feb	48
1774	Martha		Middlesex	Mar	80
1800	Martha		Stafford	May	342
1759	Martin		Kent	Oct	317
1760	Mary		Berkshire	Apr	138
1777	Mary		Warwick	Nov	448
1778	Mary	A with W	Bristol	May	183
1779	Mary		Gloucester	Jul	289
1780	Mary		Essex	Oct	462
1791	Mary	A with W	Devon	Jan	7
1796	Mary		Essex	May	109
1776	Michael		Surrey	Feb	54
1770	The Revd Nathaniel,		Worcester	Dec	425
	alias Nathanael				
1751	Penelope		Kent	Feb	34
1779	Peter		Wiltshire	Jan	4
1768	Philip		Wiltshire	Jan	3
1752	Richard	A with W	Pts	May	117

BARNES (Contd)

1764	Richard		Kent	Oct	377
1785	Richard		Essex	May	235
1786	Richard		Essex	Dec	602
1756	Robert		Pts	Sep	238
1759	Robert		London	Jan	7
1762	Robert		Pts	Sep	365
1790	Robert, Esq		Southampton	Jul	317
1768	Samuel		Southampton	Feb	48
1772	Samuel	Ser	Pts	Jul	248
1778	Samuel		Surrey	May	185
1783	The Revd Samuel		Wiltshire	May	214
1784	Samuel		Middlesex	Jan	8
1784	Samuel		Middlesex	Nov	589
1791	Samuel	A with W	Middlesex	Oct	450
1794	Samuel		Surrey	Jul	352
1800	Samuel		Middlesex	Feb	86
1753	Sarah		Kent	Feb	39
1763	Sarah		Middlesex	Dec	540
1767	Sarah		Middlesex	Apr	124
1768	Sarah		Middlesex	Jul	267
1772	Sarah		London	Sep	318
1783	Sarah		Surrey	Jun	285
1786	Sarah	Double Prob Will Regd June 1783	Surrey	Apr	
1789	Sarah		Middlesex	Sep	449
1778	Sarah Bewley		Suffolk	Dec	478
1779	Sarah Bewley	Will Regd Dec last	Suffolk	Jan	
1760	Stephen		Sussex	Aug	316
1777	Stephen Light		Middlesex	Dec	498
1750	Thomas		Pts	Apr	106
1760	Thomas		Pts	Aug	314
1760	Thomas		Somerset	Dec	451
1762	Thomas, Esq		Middlesex	May	183
1763	Thomas	A with W	Pts	Jan	2
1763	Thomas		Kent	Feb	43
1765	Thomas		Middlesex	Sep	320
1767	Thomas		Bath	Oct	362
1768	Thomas		London	Mar	97
1769	Thomas		Pts	Nov	366
1771	Thomas		Middlesex	Jul	286
1775	Thomas		Pts	Jun	224
1777	Thomas		Middlesex	Jun	255
1777	Thomas		Pts	Jul	300
1780	Thomas		London	Jul	347
1785	Thomas	"Eagle" Pts	Kent	Nov	538
1786	Thomas	"Lark""Vigilant" "Bl ond" A with W	Pts	Feb	67
1788	Thomas		Berkshire	May	230
1791	Thomas		Gloucester	Oct	451
1797	Thomas		Oxford	Jun	399
1766	Timothy		Gloucester	May	167

	BARNES (Contd)				
1776	Walter		Dorset	Jun	258
1756	William		Huntingdon	Jun	158
1760	William		Devon	Jan	4
1760	William		Kent	Jun	228
1761	William		Middlesex	Apr	121
1764	William		Middlesex	Mar	80
1765	William		Kent	Sep	322
1767	William	Will regd 158 Glazier	Huntingdon	Jul	
1769	William		Middlesex	Jun	195
1770	William		Middlesex	Jan	6
1773	William		Middlesex	Nov	415
1774	The Revd William		Hereford	Apr	126
1775	William		Huntingdon	Jul	261
1778	William	A with W Unad Will regd 322 Rushworth	Kent	Dec	
1779	William		Worcester	May	189
1779	William, Esq		Bristol	Jun	235
1779	William		Surrey	Dec	486
1783	William		Middlesex	Aug	402
1786	William	"Monarca"	Pts	Feb	68
1788	William		Gloucester	Dec	580
1789	William		Buckinghamshire	Apr	189
1790	William	Pts	Cumberland	Sep	413
1790	William		Middlesex	Oct	455
1793	William		Middlesex	Aug	398
1798	William		Hertford	Jul	464
1798	William		Middlesex	Sep	584
1800	William		Middlesex	Dec	836
1766	The Revd William George		Middlesex	Mar	89
1774	BARNESLEY, Elizabeth, alias GWYNNE		Hereford	Jan	14
1794	Elizabeth, alias GWYNNE	A with W of Goods Unad. Will regd 14 Bargrave	Hereford	Sep	
1777	Frances, alias MEYRICKE	Ltd Prob Will regd Nov last	London	Feb	
1773	Henry		London	Dec	457
1777	Henry	A with W of Goods Unad. Will regd Dec 1773	London	Feb	
1779	Mary		Middlesex	Apr	140
1777	Rebecca		Surrey	Apr	148
1794	Samuel		Middlesex	Aug	403
1794	Samuel John		Surrey	Sep	445
1773	William		Salop	Feb	46
1765	William Weeks		Middlesex	Jan	3
1780	BARNET, Edward		Rutland	May	241
1794	George, alias BARNETT		Berkshire	May	245
1759	John		Middlesex	Aug	256
1763	John	Pts	Middlesex	Sep	419
1761	Peter, alias BERNOT or BERNDT		Pts	May	161

	BARNET (Contd)				
1776	Richard	A with W Unad Will regd 233 St Eloy	Kent	Jun	
1800	Thomas	A with W	Oxford	May	344
1769	BARNETT, Ann	A with W	Middlesex	Jun	195
1783	Ann, alias POWELL	Ltd Prob	Middlesex	Jan	3
1784	Ann		Middlesex	Apr	187
1766	Anna		Middlesex	Nov	399
1765	Arthur		Northumberland	Mar	88
1800	Caleb		Middlesex	Jun	442
1788	Charles		Buckinghamshire	Apr	178
1760	Christopher		Pts	Dec	453
1792	Curtis, Esq	A with W Unad Will regd 171 Potter		Jan	
1776	Ebenezer	A with W	Gloucester	Jun	256
1752	Edward		Middlesex	Apr	82
1785	Edward		Middlesex	Feb	68
1794	George, alias BARNET		Berkshire	May	245
1775	Hannah		Leicester	May	172
1799	Hannah, alias CLARK		Middlesex	May	346
1799	Harry		Middlesex	Aug	562
1784	Henry		Worcester	Jul	367
1787	Henry		Warwick	Nov	486
1776	James		Middlesex	Jul	302
1783	James		Pts	Feb	59
1789	James	No ship Pts	Southampton	Jun	302
1762	Jane		Berkshire	Nov	446
1750	Jarvis	A with W	Middlesex	Aug	251
1750	John		Pts	Dec	376
1757	John		York	Apr	113
1760	John		Middlesex	Jan	5
1760	John		London	Mar	90
1773	John		London	Apr	145
1780	John		Pts	Feb	59
1781	John		Surrey	Feb	55
1782	John	A with W	Pts	Mar	109
1785	John	A with W Pts	Worcester	May	233
1794	John		Middlesex	May	246
1795	John		Kent	May	297
1796	John	Ser'Raisonable"& "Assistance"	Middlesex	Jun	293
1798	John		Salop	Mar	154
1770	Margreat, alias Margaret		Surrey	Jun	223
1760	Mary		Middlesex	Apr	138
1779	Mary, alias BARRNETT		Middlesex	Feb	38
1786	Michael		Devon	Jan	8
1788	Molly, alias ALDRIDGE		Buckinghamshire	May	225
1763	Nicholas		Warwick	Dec	539

BARNETT (Contd)

1762	Richard		Kent	Jun	233
1786	Richard		Surrey	Oct	503
1792	Richard	A with W	Middlesex	Jan	6
1778	Robert		Middlesex	Nov	431
1781	Robert		Westmoreland	Sep	419
1793	Robert		London	Apr	184
1763	Samuel, Esq	Pts	London	Feb	47
1774	Sarah		Buckinghamshire	Mar	78
1793	Sarah		Surrey	Jan	4
1782	Solomon	A with W	Middlesex	Apr	163
1769	Thomas		Middlesex	Dec	406
1780	Thomas, alias	Ser	Pts	Jun	302
	BEARNETT				
1795	Thomas		Middlesex	Jan	6
1800	Thomas	A with W	Middlesex	Aug	580
1753	William		Surrey	Oct	262
1758	William		Surrey	Jan	2
1776	William		Middlesex	Feb	51
1797	William		Kent	Jan	3
1797	William		Worcester	May	297
1798	William		Stafford	Oct	636
1800	William		Worcester	Jul	508
1775	BARNEVELD, VAN,		Pts	Jul	293
	Anthony, alias Anthoney	Ltd Prob			
1800	BARNEVELT, VAN, Clara		Pts	Feb	161
	Catharina				
1769	BARNEVELT, Elizabeth		Middlesex	May	150
1786	Robert		London	Feb	63
1782	BARNEWALL, The Hon.	Ltd A with W	Dublin	Mar	111
	Elizabeth, commonly				
	called Lady TRIMLESTOUN				
1782	The Hon. Elizabeth,	Ltd A with W	Dublin	Oct	
	commonly called Lady	Will regd Mar last			
	TRIMLESTOUN				
1780	George, Esq	A with W	Pts	May	239
1786	Mary		Middlesex	Feb	68
1787	John Curson, Esq		Oxford	Aug	362
1798	Nicholas, Esq		Devon	Nov	693
1756	Patrick, Esq	Poor	Middlesex	Jun	160
1788	Robert	No ship	Pts	Mar	115
1786	Silvester		Middlesex	Nov	555
1772	BARNEY, Catherine		Middlesex	Apr	122
1770	Joseph		Middlesex	Mar	88
1755	Mary		Middlesex	Dec	304
1796	Sarah, alias FREEMAN		Middlesex	Oct	498
1767	Stephen		Southampton	Nov	400
1789	Timothy		Salop	Jun	304
1791	BARNFATHER, Frances		Northampton	Dec	556
1793	John, Esq		Middlesex	Sep	456
1782	Thomas		Hertford	Dec	573

1784	BARNFEATHER, Elizabeth		Kent	Apr	188
1759	BARNFIELD, Francis		Middlesex	Sep	289
1763	Francis		Middlesex	May	215
1764	John		Gloucester	Aug	297
1751	Thomas	Pts	Kent	Jun	166
1774	BARNGART, Hester, alias VAN LENNEP	Ltd Prob	Pts	Mar	
1766	BARNHAM, Charles		Berkshire	Oct	362
1767	James		Norwich	Mar	84
1770	James		Middlesex	Aug	285
1770	Joseph		Middlesex	Nov	389
1761	BARNHARD, Francis		Middlesex	Apr	120
1756	BARNICOAT, George	Serv	Middlesex	May	129
1779	John	A with W Unad Will regd 215 Tyndall	London	Apr	
1764	BARNICOTT, William alias BENNICUTT	A with W Pts	Middlesex	Jul	252
1767	BARNIER, Edward		Middlesex	Oct	363
1799	BARNITT, James		Chester	Apr	242
1769	BARNJAM, Sarah		London	Dec	405
1783	BARNJUM, John		Middlesex	Aug	402
1784	BARNOP, John, alias BEARNUP	Ser Pts	Exeter	Jul	368
1770	BARNOUIN, The Revd James Francis		Bristol	Oct	352
1797	The Revd Isaac John		Southampton	Apr	223
1793	Margaret Frederica Elizabeth		Middlesex	Jan	5
1765	Susannah		Pts	Oct	365
1760	BARNS, Andrew, alias BARNSON, alias BENSON		Pts	Sep	348
1783	Clark		Essex	Nov	554
1766	Cornelius	A with W annexed	Southampton	Jun	214
1781	Edward, alias BARNES		Pts	Dec	577
1758	Elizabeth		London	Apr	103
1786	Elizabeth, alias BARNES		Middlesex	Mar	136
1766	Henry, alias BARNES	Ser	Pts	Jan	2
1792	Henry		Warwick	Nov	547
1754	James		Berkshire	Jan	5
1779	James, alias BARNES		Pts	Jun	236
1784	Joel		London	May	247
1758	John	Pts	Lincoln	Apr	104
1760	John		Pts	Oct	379
1763	John	Pts	Southampton	Dec	539
1764	John		Warwick	Aug	296
1774	John, alias BARNES	Serv	Middlesex	Sep	329
1785	John		London	Apr	175
1799	John		Cumberland	May	337
1782	Joseph, alias FURNEAUX		Devon	Mar	110

Year	Name		Place	Month	No.
	BARNS (Contd)				
1791	Margret, alias	A with W	Middlesex	Dec	559
	BARNES, Margaret				
1777	Mary		Somerset	Nov	450
1794	Mary		Northampton	May	243
1785	Moses	Ser Pts	Worcestor	Feb	66
1750	Richard	Poor Pts	Somerset	Oct	318
1777	Richard	A with W	Middlesex	Aug	342
1786	Richard		Warwick	Jan	7
1782	Samuel		London	Dec	572
1771	Susan		Suffolk	Nov	431
1754	Thomas		Pts	Oct	266
1780	Thomas		Surrey	Jun	302
1784	Thomas	"Powerful"	Pts	Apr	188
1798	Thomas		Hertford	Oct	635
1798	William		Essex	Feb	81
1800	William		Kent	Apr	258
1789	BARNSBY, Jennet		London	Sep	449
1762	William		Pts	Feb	41
1792	BARNSLEY, Benjamin		Middlesex	Dec	597
1793	Dashwood William		Middlesex	Apr	187
1770	Elizabeth		Middlesex	Jan	3
1770	Elizabeth		Bristol	Feb	44
1767	John		Gloucester	Jul	251
1776	John, Esq		Surrey	Dec	488
1779	John, Esq		Gloucester	Apr	141
1757	Joshua		Surrey	May	149
1800	Mary		Warwick	May	342
1774	Thomas, Esq		Pts	Sep	328
1756	William		Middlesex	Dec	319
1765	William		Worcester	Feb	45
1760	BARNSON, Andrew,		Pts	Sep	348
	alias BARNS, alias				
	BENSON				
1786	BARNSTABLE, George	"Druid"	Pts	Jul	363
1783	John	A with W	Bristol	Apr	163
1799	BARNSTON, Elizabeth		Chester	Dec	827
1755	Letitia, alias MYTTON	Ltd Prob	Bath	Dec	306
1784	Robert		Chester	Dec	629
1783	The Revd Roger		Chester	Mar	109
1762	Thomas	A with W	Pts	Dec	495
1771	Trafford, Esq	A with W	Chester	Jul	286
1784	William Gregg, Esq		Essex	Aug	426
1785	BARNWELL, Anne Wilson,		Norfolk	Jul	352
	alias WARNER				
1750	Elizabeth	A with W	Essex	Nov	347
1755	Elizabeth		Hertford	Apr	93
1750	John	A with W Unad	Essex	Nov	
		Will regd in May 1749			
1761	John		Hertford	May	158
1760	Mary		Middlesex	Feb	49

BARNWELL (Contd)

1760	Mary		Kent	Nov	414
1787	Mary		Norfolk	Jul	310
1772	Peter	A with W	Surrey	Jan	4
1762	Richard	A with W of Goods Unad Will regd 24 Isham Last Grant July 1745	London	Mar	
1794	BARON, Ann		Berkshire	Apr	185
1786	Anthony, Esq		Glamorgan	Feb	70
1765	Barbara		Middlesex	Mar	85
1762	Bernard		Middlesex	Feb	42
1770	Bernard, Esq		Middlesex	Jun	219
1773	Catherine		Middlesex	Apr	146
1755	Charles		Hertford	May	121
1767	Charlotte		Middlesex	Dec	439
1767	Christopher, Esq		Middlesex	Dec	435
1786	Edmund		Cambridge	Jun	324
1765	Elizabeth		Devon	Jun	209
1796	Elizabeth, alias Elisseth		Cornwall	Apr	162
1789	The Revd Francis, Doctor in Divinity		Leicester	Jan	12
1785	Gennaro		Norfolk	Jul	355
1775	Gerrard		Cambridge	Aug	302
1786	James, Esq		Somerset	Dec	600
1794	James		Southampton	Jun	296
1799	Jasper, Esq		Cornwall	Jun	416
1755	John		Hereford	Feb	34
1759	John		Cambridge	Jul	226
1760	John	Ltd Prob	Pts	Nov	413
1763	The Revd John		Northampton	Mar	107
1765	John		Middlesex	Apr	128
1766	John	By Int. Dec	Northampton	Jul	258
1770	John		London	Jun	220
1794	John	London Packet	Pts	Jan	6
1771	The Revd Jonathan		Cornwall	Feb	48
1800	Judith		Surrey	Oct	702
1763	Letitia		Middlesex	Dec	540
1760	Mariane, alias MENIEL		Pts	Oct	398
1793	Marie Magdalena	Ltd A with W	Pts	Nov	540
1760	Mary		Pts	Feb	49
1780	Mary		Derby	Apr	169
1767	Nicholas, Esq		Suffolk	May	163
1786	Oliver, Esq		Surrey	Jun	320
1793	Oliver William		Middlesex	Jun	297
1766	Pierce, alias BARRON	A with W Ser	Pts	Jun	213
1768	The Revd Richard		Kent	Mar	95
1773	Sir Richard		Essex	Apr	146
1786	Robert	By Int Decree	Devon	Jul	365
1791	Robert		Devon	Feb	58
1794	Sarah		Surrey	Jul	352

Year	Name	Notes	Place	Month	No.
	BARON (Contd)				
1766	Thomas		Gloucester	Dec	440
1781	Thomas	Ser	Pts	Aug	376
1789	Thomas	Another Grant Aug 1781 Will regd 376 Webster "Laurel"		Sep	
1751	William	Pts	Devon	Sep	252
1755	William		Huntingdon	Jul	183
1776	BARONNEAU, Benjamin		Essex	Jun	254
1795	Mary Frances		Kent	Jan	8
1765	BARONS, Ann		Hertfordshire	Nov	398
1783	Benjamin, Esq		Kent	Apr	161
1794	George		Devon	Dec	599
1781	Samuel		Middlesex	Aug	376
1785	BARQUET, Mary	A with W	Guernsey	Feb	62
1762	BARR, Alexander		Southampton	Jun	235
1782	Archibald		Pts	Apr	166
1798	Eleanor		Middlesex	May	309
1760	Elizabeth		Essex	Mar	86
1766	Elizabeth		Middlesex	Oct	365
1789	James		Middlesex	Apr	187
1781	John	A with W Ser	Pts	Feb	57
1790	John		Berkshire	Jan	3
1795	John		Middlesex	Apr	238
1787	Joseph		Middlesex	May	197
1793	Pleasant		Middlesex	Dec	580
1779	Richard		Northampton	Feb	39
1774	Tamar		Middlesex	Nov	386
1763	BARRACK, Hendrick, alias BERG, alias BARRETT		Pts	Mar	107
1781	James	A with W Ser	Pts	Dec	570
1777	William, alias BARERK	A with W	Pts	Jan	6
1789	BARRACLOUGH, Stephen	A with W Ser "Adamant", "Assurance" "Rhinoceros", "Mentor"	Pts	Dec	573
1773	William		York	Feb	47
1762	BARRADALE, Jacob, Esq	A with W	Pts	Apr	139
1796	Thomas		Middlesex	Apr	166
1757	BARRADALL, Frances		Middlesex	Feb	38
1757	Katherine		Middlesex	May	147
1787	BARRADELL, Mary		Middlesex	Jun	255
1766	William		Middlesex	Feb	47
1796	BARRAN, John		Warwick	Jan	3
1791	BARRAND, John		Lincoln	Dec	556
1790	BARRANS, Giles		Middlesex	Jan	4
1773	BARRAR, Henry		Berkshire	Mar	96
1776	BARRAS, Ann		Middlesex	Apr	163
1788	Elizabeth		London	Mar	116

	BARRAS (Contd)				
1762	John		Middlesex	Nov	445
1797	Joseph	Ltd A with W of Goods	Middlesex	Jun	
		Unad			
		Will regd 34 Brooke			
1762	Joshua		Pts	Nov	446
1797	Rebeccah		Middlesex	Apr	222
1796	Samuel		Essex	Mar	110
1760	BARRASS, John		Middlesex	Jan	5
1786	John		London	Jan	3
1774	Thomas	A with W	Pts	Jul	255
1789	BARRAT, Isabella, alias		London	May	234
	BARRETT				
1787	John, alias BARRET	A with W	Pts	Jul	312
		"Stormont"			
1750	Peter		Pts	Aug	251
1777	BARRATCLOUGH, Joseph		Pts	Jul	299
1754	BARRATIER, Anne, alias		Pts	Sep	245
	CHARLES				
1776	BARRATT, Ann		Essex	Mar	111
1789	Ann		Middlesex	Oct	482
1793	Ann		Essex	Feb	66
1759	Christopher		Essex	Mar	84
1783	Edward		Pts	Jun	280
1785	Elizabeth, alias ADAMS,	Ltd Prob	Buckinghamshire	Apr	173
	alias BROOKES				
1779	Francis		Pts	Dec	488
1750	James		Middlesex	Dec	379
1778	James	A with W	Ireland	Jun	231
		Pts			
1799	James		Middlesex	Dec	827
1751	John		Wiltshire	Jul	198
1756	John		Gloucester	May	129
1759	John		Wiltshire	Mar	81
1764	John		Southampton	Apr	131
1770	John, alias BARATT		Middlesex	Jan	5
1771	John	Poor	Middlesex	Apr	146
1774	John		Middlesex	Dec	422
1775	John	Double Prob	Middlesex	Jan	
		Will regd last month			
1775	John		Kent	Nov	403
1776	John	A with W Unad	Kent	Nov	
		Will regd Nov 1775			
1780	John		London	Feb	54
1796	John		Surrey	Mar	110
1783	Joseph, alias BARRETT	Ser	Pts	Jul	335
1775	Joseph		Warwick	Jan	1
1799	Joseph		Surrey	May	340
1772	Mary		Bedford	Aug	284
1755	Philip	A with W unad	London	Dec	
		Will regd 1 Plymouth			

	BARRATT (Contd)				
1756	Phineas		Middlesex	Mar	60
1769	Richard	Ser	Pts	Sep	304
1788	Robert		Gloucester	Aug	384
1776	Samuel, alias BARRETT	A with W	Gloucester	May	213
1783	Samuel, alias BARRETT	Ser	Pts	May	218
1762	Thomas, Esq		Middlesex	Nov	449
1798	Thomas		Warwick	Dec	759
1800	Thomas Pendrill		Warwick	Aug	582
1760	William	A with W	Pts	Sep	346
1776	BARRATTY, Jane		Kent	Sep	381
1778	BARRAUD, Ffrances		Middlesex	Jan	4
1762	BARRE, LA, Peter, alias	A with W	Pts	Jun	
	LA BAERE, alias				
	LA BARE				
1762	BARREL, George		Pts	Dec	495
1775	BARRELL, Ann, alias		Middlesex	Nov	437
	PILGRIM				
1757	Benjamin		Pts	Jul	212
1765	The Revd Edmund		Kent	Mar	88
1774	The Revd Edmund	A with W Unad	Kent	Jun	
		Will regd 88 Rushworth			
1786	Frances		Middlesex	Jan	8
1772	Francis, Esq		Middlesex	Mar	81
1754	Henry		Kent	Sep	245
1790	Henry		Middlesex	May	225
1783	Jane		Southampton	May	212
1773	John		Middlesex	Feb	48
1795	John		London	Mar	143
1767	Savage		Pts	Dec	438
1772	Savage, Esq		Middlesex	Jul	248
1780	BARRENGER, John, alias		Buckinghamshire	Feb	60
	BARINGER				
1784	BARRENS, Lawrence	"Childers" & "Vaughan"	Pts	Feb	65
1761	BARRER, Henry		Worcester	May	159
1777	BARRES, DES, Francis		London	Jun	261
1750	BARRESFORD, Michael,	A with W	Pts	Nov	349
	alias BORISFORT				
1785	BARRET, Amyas, alias	"Monarch"	Pts	Jun	291
	BARRETT, Amias Deane				
1790	Edward		Essex	Mar	116
1766	Elizabeth		Berkshire	Jan	5
1787	John, alias BARRAT	A with W	Pts	Jul	312
		"Stormont"			
1779	Joseph, Esq	Ltd Prob of a Codicil	Pts	Jan	
		Will regd Nov last			
1786	Stephen, alias BARRETT		Kent	Aug	421
1752	BARRETA, Fillece, alias		Pts	Jun	148
	BERRETTS, Felice				
1794	BARRETT, Alice		Middlesex	Feb	60

BARRETT (Contd)

Year	Name	Ship/Note	Place	Month	Page
1785	Amias Deane, alias BARRET, Amyas	"Monarch"	Pts	Jun	291
1800	Andrew	A with W	Surrey	Jul	505
1755	Ann		Sussex	Jun	155
1763	Ann		Kent	Sep	417
1771	Ann		Berkshire	Jun	240
1796	Ann		Stafford	May	239
1791	Anthony		Wiltshire	Aug	374
1785	Ashley		Essex	Oct	494
1763	Barbara		Middlesex	Mar	106
1799	Bryan	"Duke of Gloucester" "Resolution" & "Lyne"	Pts	Nov	760
1766	Charles		Hertford	Jan	5
1782	Christopher		Surrey	Sep	442
1789	Cornelius		Northampton	Dec	575
1762	Cottrell		Middlesex	May	185
1760	Damaris		Middlesex	Mar	89
1786	Edward		Middlesex	Sep	464
1797	Edward	"Experiment"	Pts	Jan	4
1799	Edward		Pts	Aug	572
1760	Elizabeth		Surrey	Jan	4
1771	Elizabeth		Middlesex	Jan	4
1792	Elizabeth	A with W	Salop	Apr	198
1794	Elizabeth		Berkshire	Nov	569
1779	Elizabeth Mary	Ltd Prob	Pts	Jan	3
1754	Ffrancis		Surrey	Feb	32
1763	Francis, alias BARRITT		Pts	May	213
1751	George		London	Feb	34
1762	George		Bristol	Jun	235
1783	George		Pts	Apr	161
1782	Griffith		Middlesex	Oct	479
1785	Hannah		Cornwall	Nov	538
1763	Hendrick, alias BERG, alias BARRACK		Pts	Mar	107
1762	Henry		Middlesex	Apr	141
1783	Henry John		Pts	Apr	160
1779	Hester		Kent	Dec	485
1792	Isaac		Middlesex	May	258
1789	Isabella, alias BARRAT		London	May	234
1760	James		Pts	Apr	136
1761	James		Pts	Feb	45
1765	James		Pts	Mar	87
1784	James	"Medway"& "Bruno"	Pts	Jan	5
1792	James		Middlesex	May	262
1796	James	"Adventure." Ser	Pts	Mar	107
1798	James		London	Apr	231
1752	John	A with W of Goods Unad Will regd 1 Strahan	Middlesex	Dec	
1753	John	A with W of Goods Unad Will regd 248 Potter	Pts	Feb	

BARRETT (Contd)

Year	Name	Notes	Place	Month	No.
1756	John	A with W Pts	Middlesex	Jan	1
1758	John		Gloucester	Apr	104
1759	John	A with W of Goods Unad Will regd 1 Strahan	Middlesex	Dec	
1760	John	By Int Dec A with W of Goods Unad Will regd 1 Strahan	Middlesex	Jul	
1763	John		Stafford	Oct	462
1764	John	A with W	Pts	Sep	338
1767	John		Berkshire	Mar	85
1767	John		Hereford	May	163
1770	John, alias BARROW		Pts	Apr	131
1770	John		London	May	173
1771	John		Middlesex	Sep	366
1773	John		Dorset	Aug	322
1780	John		Essex	Mar	120
1782	John		Devon	Jul	338
1785	John	EIS "Southampton"	Pts	Jun	295
1788	John		Buckinghamshire	Jun	291
1789	John	"Vestal"	Pts	Apr	190
1796	John		Middlesex	Apr	165
1796	John	A with W	Middlesex	Jun	292
1796	John		Berkshire	Aug	402
1797	John, Esq		Stafford	Jan	4
1798	John	Ser (1st) A with W	Pts	Apr	240
1798	John		Somerset	Sep	585
1799	John		Warwick	Feb	90
1799	John	Ser: "Ganges"	Pts	Oct	696
1798	John Hickman		Middlesex	Sep	582
1777	Joseph		Pts	Nov	446
1778	Joseph, Esq	Double Prob Will regd Nov 1777	Pts	Dec	
1783	Joseph, alias BARRATT	Ser	Pts	Jul	335
1785	Joseph	"Superb"	Pts	Jul	354
1790	Joseph Bryant, Esq		Berkshire	Apr	171
1785	Katherine		Kent	Jun	290
1782	Mark		Surrey	Jan	4
1757	Mary		London	Jul	214
1766	Mary		London	Nov	397
1768	Mary		Middlesex	May	187
1771	Mary		Middlesex	Nov	429
1783	Mary		Surrey	Apr	164
1795	Mary		Surrey	Jun	363
1785	Matthew		Middlesex	Nov	537
1800	Matthew		Surrey	Feb	90
1762	Michael	A with W	Pts	Dec	493
1764	Michael		Pts	Sep	339
1796	Nathan		Stafford	Oct	486

BARRETT (Contd)

1789	Nathaniel, Esq		Suffolk	Jun	304
1793	Nathaniel, Esq		Stafford	Jun	299
1766	Nicholas		London	Sep	328
1764	Onslow		Pts	Mar	81
1791	Rebecca		Middlesex	Jun	268
1750	Richard		London	Mar	69
1755	Richard		Surrey	Mar	67
1764	Richard		Kent	Apr	130
1798	Richard		Middlesex	Dec	758
1799	Richard		Lincoln	Dec	823
1756	Robert		Middlesex	Jun	160
1765	Robert	A with W	Pts	Apr	129
1760	Sampson		Surrey	Apr	136
1752	Samuel		Somerset	Sep	227
1776	Samuel, alias BARRATT	A with W	Gloucester	May	213
1783	Samuel, alias BARRATT	Ser	Pts	May	218
1779	Sarah		Wiltshire	Mar	92
1791	Sarah	A with W	London	Mar	115
1796	Sarah		Suffolk	Nov	540
1758	The Revd Serenus		Sussex	Feb	29
1771	Serenus		London	Apr	147
1780	Simon		Pts	Nov	507
1786	Stephen, alias BARRET		Kent	Aug	421
1752	Susanna		Salop	Feb	29
1755	Thomas		London	Mar	68
1757	Thomas	A with W	Pts	Aug	240
1770	Thomas		Southampton	Nov	388
1775	Thomas		Pts	Apr	128
1775	Thomas		Middlesex	May	168
1776	Thomas		Pts	Jun	254
1781	Thomas		Kent	Jun	284
1788	Thomas, alias HARRISON,"Princess Royal" alias HARRIESON		Pts	Aug	387
1756	William		Pts	Apr	95
1758	William		Pts	Apr	101
1760	William		Pts	Mar	86
1765	William		Devon	Oct	363
1766	William	Ser	Southampton	Sep	327
1767	William	A with W Unad Will regd 101 Hutton	Pts	Aug	
1769	William		Middlesex	Feb	33
1777	William		Pts	Jun	251
1778	William		Pts	Dec	478
1783	William		Oxford	Oct	497
1784	William	"Monarca" & "Coventry"	Pts	Jun	309
1784	William		Worcester	Dec	630
1790	William		Somerset	Feb	58
1791	William	MS"Venus"	Pts	Feb	53
1799	William		London	Apr	242
1784	BARRIBALL, John	Ser."Sceptre"	Devon	Apr	190

BARRIBALL (Contd)

Year	Name		Place	Month	No.
1784	John	Pts "Sceptre" Will regd April last	Devon	Aug	
1760	Thomas		Pts	Jun	230
1782	BARRICK, John		Middlesex	Feb	59
1784	William	"Cornwall"	Pts	Jan	5
1785	BARRICKSTRUM, Peter, alias BINGSTROM		Pts	Mar	112
1775	BARRIE, Robert		Pts	Aug	300
1773	BARRIFF, Thomas		Middlesex	Apr	148
1771	William		Middlesex	Jan	3
1783	BARRILL, William, alias BURRILL	Ser	Southampton	Jan	5
1774	BARRINGER, John		Sussex	Oct	358
1755	Joseph		Cambridge	Apr	94
1778	Joseph		Buckinghamshire	May	185
1786	Mary, alias BARINGER		Southampton	May	262
1772	Sarah	A with W	Middlesex	May	155
1767	Thomas		Buckinghamshire	Mar	88
1754	BARRINGTON, Ann		Bath	Aug	219
1797	Ann		Essex	May	293
1797	Benedic		Somerset	Oct	628
1800	Daines, The Hon		London	Mar	175
1792	Sir Fitz Williams, Baronet		Essex	Oct	496
1772	Francis, alias VARINGTON		Pts	May	160
1797	Jane, Dame		Middlesex	Apr	225
1776	John, Baronet		Southampton	May	212
1788	John		Essex	May	227
1790	John, Esq	Another Grant May 1788 By Inty Decree	Essex	Aug	367
1764	Mary, Viscountess		Berkshire	Nov	414
1800	Samuel, Esq	Adm. of the White in His Majesty's Navy	Middlesex	Sep	642
1779	Sarah		Hertford	Mar	88
1850	Dame Susanna		Herts	Oct	313
1756	Thomas, Esq		London	Mar	61
1786	Thomas	"Blanche"	Pts	Jan	
1793	The Right Hon. William Wildman Lord Barrington Viscount of the Kingdom of Ireland		Middlesex	Feb	65
1782	BARRIS, George	A with W	London	Dec	571
1795	BARRISFIELD, George	"Bellona". Ser	Kent	Oct	581
1770	BARRISTRUM, Andrew, alias BIENSTRUM, Hans	A with W	Pts	Jul	254
1798	BARRIT, Peter		Middlesex	Jun	379
1760	Robert		Pts	Jun	229

	BARRIT (Contd)				
1784	William		London	Dec	628
1768	BARRITT, Charles		London	Mar	94
1763	Francis, alias BARRETT		Pts	May	213
1757	Niclaes		Pts	Jan	6
1772	Robert		Middlesex	Dec	431
1781	Thomas		Middlesex	Jan	5
1784	William Tonson	A with W	London	Oct	537
1779	BARRNETT, Mary, alias BARNETT		Middlesex	Feb	38
1770	BARRON, Ann		Middlesex	May	173
1795	Ann		Warwick	Mar	148
1798	Ann		Surrey	Jul	463
1788	Anna		Middlesex	Apr	173
1799	Charles		Middlesex	Jan	9
1785	Edith		Surrey	May	232
1773	Edward	A with W	Middlesex	Jan	3
1751	Elizabeth		Middlesex	Jul	199
1763	Frances	A with W	Middlesex	Aug	368
1778	George		Middlesex	Jan	4
1791	Hugh, Esq		Middlesex	Sep	418
1761	James	A with W	Middlesex	Jun	201
1786	James		Cambridge	Dec	598
1772	John		Haverford West	Jan	5
1787	John		Kent	Jan	3
1797	John		Cambridge	Apr	225
1787	Joseph		Middlesex	Jan	3
1766	Pierce, alias BARON	A with W Ser	Pts	Jun	213
1774	Robert		Middlesex	Aug	291
1794	Robert		London	Nov	536
1789	Susannah		Middlesex	Apr	189
1763	Thomas		Pts	Dec	538
1786	Thomas		Middlesex	Jun	320
1797	BARROSS, Thomas, alias BURROUGHS	100th Regt A with W	Pts	May	299
1775	BARROT, Edward		Pts	May	172
1771	BARROUGHBY, Anne		Middlesex	Oct	396
1762	BARROUGHBY, John		Middlesex	Jan	3
1782	BARROW, Ann		Berkshire	Jul	335
1789	Ann		Middlesex	Apr	190
1762	Anthony		Southampton	Oct	412
1765	Charles		Berkshire	Apr	132
1788	Charles		Berkshire	Jan	6
1789	Sir Charles, Baronet		Gloucester	Sep	448
1752	Edward		London	May	116
1796	Edward	EIMS"Taunton Castle"	Pts		540
1754	Elizabeth		London	Sep	244
1761	Elizabeth		Middlesex	Apr	121
1762	Elizabeth		Middlesex	Dec	494

BARROW (Contd)

Year	Name	Note	Place	Month	No.
1763	Elizabeth		Gloucester	Jan	7
1792	Elizabeth		Salop	Oct	497
1794	Elizabeth		Middlesex	Nov	541
1795	Elizabeth		Middlesex	Mar	140
1750	Grace		Middlesex	Apr	105
1773	Grace		Somerset	Jul	280
1798	Jacob		London	Sep	586
1750	James	Double Prob Will regd in June last	Middlesex	Feb	
1762	James		Surrey	Nov	447
1772	James		Middlesex	Apr	123
1794	James		Westmoreland	Oct	490
1752	Jane		Middlesex	Feb	28
1753	John		London	Apr	102
1754	John		Kent	May	124
1757	John	By Int Dec A with W	Middlesex	Jan	2
1766	John		Middlesex	Jun	211
1769	John		Middlesex	Apr	113
1770	John, alias BARRETT		Pts	Apr	131
1773	John		Middlesex	Jul	280
1773	John		Surrey	Sep	353
1780	John		Essex	Jan	1
1789	John		Middlesex	Feb	79
1791	John	A with W	Gloucester	Sep	417
1798	Joney		Gloucester	Jan	8
1776	Joseph		Middlesex	Oct	414
1750	Letitia		Essex	Dec	378
1754	Margaret		Middlesex	May	125
1765	Martha		Middlesex	Dec	442
1772	Martha		Middlesex	May	158
1754	Mary		London	Jun	157
1765	Mary		London	Nov	402
1783	Mary		Middlesex	Jul	338
1787	Mary		Lancashire	Sep	397
1762	Maurice		London	May	184
1778	Maurice		Sussex	Dec	477
1777	Ralph		Middlesex	Sep	374
1782	Rebecca		London	Aug	392
1754	Rebekah		Chichester	May	124
1777	Richard		Gloucester	Dec	497
1800	The Revd Richard		Lancashire	Sep	645
1783	Robert		Middlesex	Jul	336
1754	Thomas		London	Jul	190
1773	Thomas		Berkshire	May	195
1776	Thomas		Middlesex	Nov	450
1780	Thomas	A with W Unad Will regd 195 Stevens	Berkshire	Feb	
1780	Thomas, Esq		Middlesex	Nov	505
1781	Thomas		Surrey	Jul	329

BARROW (Contd)

1788	Thomas		Middlesex	Nov	526
1789	Thomas		Middlesex	Aug	419
1792	Thomas		Salop	Apr	191
1792	Thomas		Berkshire	May	260
1753	William		London	Jul	196
1755	William	A with W Unad Will regd July 1753	London	Jan	
1768	William		Lincoln	Aug	307
1770	William	Ser	Pts	Jun	223
1771	William		Bristol	Nov	429
1772	William		Kent	Jun	207
1778	William	A with W	London	Mar	94
1794	BARROWBY, Francis, alias BARROWLEY	"Wm & Henry"	Surrey	Aug	403
1758	Dr William	Doctor in Physic	Southampton	Nov	321
1794	BARROWLEY, Francis, alias BARROWBY	"Wm & Henry"	Surrey	Aug	403
1783	BARROWMAN, John	Ser	Pts	Aug	399
1763	BARROWS, John		Pts	May	215
1775	Thomas		Middlesex	Jun	224
1760	BARRS, Mary		Middlesex	Feb	46
1787	BARRY, Ann		Essex	Nov	483
1797	Ann Dorothy Smith		Middlesex	Dec	728
1750	Anne, alias HOTCHKIS	Ltd A with W annexed	Middlesex	Jan	14
1751	Anthony		Pts	Mar	72
1771	The Hon Arthur		Chester	Jan	4
1750	Barratt, alias BERRY		Pts	Sep	286
1799	Betty	A with W	Suffolk	Jan	13
1789	Boothby		Middlesex	Aug	419
1775	Catharine		Gloucester	Apr	127
1794	Catherine Smith		Middlesex	Jan	5
1786	Charles		London	Oct	505
1796	Daniel	"Powerful" & "Europa"	Pts	Apr	160
1764	David	A with W	Middlesex	Jan	6
1796	David	Ser: "St George"	Pts	Jul	345
1756	Dorothy Smith	A with W	Chester	Feb	52
1758	Edward	Pts	Southampton	Oct	283
1760	Edward		Devon	Jul	275
1777	Sir Edward, Baronet		Bath	Jan	3
1764	Elizabeth		Kingston U Hull	Dec	454
1770	Elizabeth		Wiltshire	May	171
1774	Elizabeth		London	Jan	2
1778	Elizabeth		Middlesex	Nov	434
1792	Elizabeth		Surrey	Mar	130
1798	Elizabeth		Middlesex	May	310
1760	Francis		Devon	Mar	86
1799	Francis		Berkshire	Aug	561
1763	Garrett		Pts	Aug	369
1777	Gerard	Ltd A with W	Pts	Aug	342
1758	James, alias BERRY	A with W	Pts	Aug	237
1761	James	Ser: A with W	Oxford	Dec	421
1762	James		Hertfordshire	May	183

BARRY (Contd)

1762	James, Esq		Kingston U Hull	Jul	284
1783	James	"Torbay" & "Centurion"	Pts	Nov	550
1763	John		London	Jul	322
1763	John		Pts	Sep	420
1763	John		Devon	Oct	461
1765	John		Pts	Sep	320
1772	John		Pts	Jun	209
1780	John	A with W	Middlesex	Jan	3
1782	John	Pts	Southampton	May	214
1783	John	"Warwick" A with W	Pts	Nov	551
1786	John	Pts "Vigilant" "Pigmy" &"Sampson"	Middlesex	Jun	324
1797	John		Middlesex	Apr	223
1797	John		Southampton	Dec	724
1798	John	Ser: "Triumph"	Pts	Nov	694
1799	John	Double Prob Will regd April 1797	Middlesex	Feb	
1765	Jonas		Pts	Jan	5
1762	Joseph		Devon	Jun	233
1791	Joseph		Surrey	Apr	168
1757	Margaret		Middlesex	Jul	214
1771	Mary		Essex	May	194
1781	Mary		London	Mar	111
1782	Nathaniel		Pts	Feb	61
1795	Sir Nathaniel, Bart.		Middlesex	Mar	141
1763	Patrick		Devon	Mar	108
1784	Patrick, alias BERRY	"Martin"	Pts	Oct	537
1783	Peter		Pts	Jul	335
1754	Rachell		Middlesex	Sep	245
1770	The Rev Richard		Gloucester	May	173
1788	Richard, Hon		Chester	Apr	177
1797	Richard, alias BARY		Leicester	Jul	468
1759	Robert		Middlesex	Apr	117
1759	Robert, alias BERRY		Pts	Jun	193
1774	Robert		Northampton	Dec	424
1775	Robert	Double Prob Will regd December last	Northampton	Mar	
1793	Robert		York	Oct	491
1777	Spranger		Middlesex	Feb	50
1800	Susanna		Middlesex	Jan	7
1750	Thomas		Pts	Apr	105
1752	Thomas		Pts	Jun	147
1770	Thomas, Esq		Surrey	Oct	350
1783	Thomas		Surrey	Jun	280
1760	Walter		Middlesex	Mar	87
1758	William		Pts	Jun	179
1761	William		Pts	Jun	200
1762	William, alias BERRY		Pts	Apr	140
1763	William		Pts	Feb	42

	BARRY (Contd)				
1763	William	A with W of Goods Unad Will regd February last	Pts	July	
1764	William		Kingston U Hull	Sep	339
1781	The Revd William	Doctor in Divinity	Bristol	Apr	180
1789	The Revd William	A with W of Goods Unad Will regd 180 Webster	Bristol	Dec	
1800	William	Merchant Ship "Calcutta" A with W	Pts	Apr	255
1783	Willoughby, Dr	Doctor of Physick	Essex	Nov	553
1791	Willoughby	A with W of Goods Unad Will regd 553 Cornwallis	Essex	Feb	
1768	Winefred		Bath	Jul	269
1781	BARRYMORE, The Rt Hon Emily, Countess of,		Middlesex	Apr	181
1753	The Rt Hon James, Earl of		Ireland	Jul	194
1791	Margaret, Countess Dowager of	A with W	Ireland	Mar	109
1794	Margaret, Countess Dowager of	A with W Will regd March 1791	Ireland		
1785	BARSBY, Elizabeth		Middlesex	Mar	112
1756	John		London	Dec	320
1777	John	A with W of Goods Unad Will regd 320 Glasier	London	Jun	
1776	Margaret		Middlesex	Jan	4
1768	Mary		Berkshire	Jul	268
1784	Samuel		Middlesex	Mar	122
1767	Thomas		London	Nov	402
1777	Thomas	A with W of Goods Unad Will regd 402 Legard	London	Jun	
1765	BARSEET, Jacob, alias BRASSETT		Pts	Dec	440
1782	BARSHAM, Elizabeth		London	Feb	61
1775	The Rev Philip	A with W	Hertford	Feb	42
1777	Thomas		London	May	200
1766	BARSILAY, Hanna		Pts	Apr	127
1750	Lea	A with W	Pts	Jan	2
1773	BARSON, Thomas		Surrey	Apr	148
1753	BARSOTTI, Michael, Esq		Pts	Dec	309
1783	BARSTABLE, Solomon	"Sandwich"	Pts	Jul	337
1783	BARSTON, Jane		Surrey	Nov	553
1784	BARSTOW, Eleanor		York	May	247
1794	Michael		Pts	Sep	448
1787	Thomas		York	Jun	257
1765	BARSUCK, William, alias BASSETT		Pts	Feb	41
1779	BART, John		London	Dec	485
1795	BARTAUD, Angelique, alias Anglique		Middlesex	Nov	622

1789	BARTELL, Edward George		Mid	Oct	484
1776	BARTELS, Anna		Pts	Mar	112
1784	Josephus Albertus		Pts	Sep	492
1770	Petronella Elisabeth, alias VAN UCHELEN	Ltd Prob	Pts	Jul	
1795	BARTEMU, Charles		Surrey	May	303
1785	BARTENSHLAG, John Rodolph		London	Jul	353
1798	BARTENSTEIN, DE, Baroness, alias Barbara Maria OSSY alias Barbara Maria OSY		Pts	Jan	18
1772	BARTER, Ann		Southampton	Aug	284
1774	Edward	By Sent (regd Nov 465)	Middlesex	Nov	385
1779	Edward	A with W Unad Will regd November 1774	Middlesex	Mar	
1781	Frances		Exeter	Apr	180
1800	Henry	A with W	Kent	Jun	442
1759	James		Pts	Feb	47
1782	James		Gloucester	Jun	267
1783	John		Wiltshire	Mar	112
1797	John		Gloucester	Jul	478
1799	John		Wiltshire	Nov	760
1752	Joseph		Pts	Jun	146
1766	Richard		Southampton	Jun	214
1777	Stephen		Pts	Mar	96
1763	Thomas		Wiltshire	Jun	265
1792	Thomas		Wiltshire	Apr	193
1755	William		Middlesex	Mar	66
1779	William		Devon	Dec	487
1783	William	Special A with W Unad Will regd 66 Paul	Middlesex	Apr	
1759	BARTEY, Philip, alias BARTLEY, alias BARTLET		Pts	Feb	47
1787	BARTH, Christopher alias BATH	Merchant Ship "Harrison"	Pts	Aug	356
1753	BARTHE, Peter		Middlesex	Oct	263
1773	BARTHELEMIN, James		Pts	Dec	458
1771	BARTHELEMY, Elisabeth, alias Elizabeth Louise		Pts	Sep	364
1766	BARTHETT, Elizabeth		Surrey	Apr	126
1764	BARTHEUIL, Elizabeth, alias BARTHOIL		Middlesex	Nov	413
1790	BARTHOLAM, Margaret		Salop	Aug	363
1781	BARTHOLD, Grace, alias BERTHOLD, alias BERTHOL		Middlesex	Aug	377
1755	BARTHOLMEW, Joanah, alias BARTHOMU Joana		Surrey	Feb	32

1790	BARTHOLMEW, John, alias BARTHOLOMEW		Middlesex	Mar	116
1772	Philipp, Esq	A with W Unad Will regd 29 Auber Last Grant January 1731		Nov	
1756	BARTHOLOMEW, Ann		Surrey	Apr	96
1774	Ann		Middlesex	Mar	79
1775	Ann		Kent	Dec	459
1795	Edward		Berkshire	Nov	621
1795	Edward	A with W	Berkshire	Nov	621
1770	Elizabeth		Middlesex	Feb	45
1784	Elizabeth		Middlesex	Jul	372
1795	Elizabeth		Surrey	Jan	6
1766	Francis		Surrey	Dec	441
1786	Henry		Surrey	Jun	320
1765	Dr Humphrey	Dr of Physic	Kent	Feb	44
1758	James	A with W	Pts	Oct	286
1799	James		Kent	Jan	7
1764	John		Warwick	Jul	252
1764	John		London	Apr	132
1772	John		Middlesex	Oct	351
1774	John		Surrey	Jul	257
1784	John		Middlesex	Jun	311
1790	John, alias BARTHOLMEW		Middlesex	Mar	116
1792	John		Kent	May	259
1795	John		Buckinghamshire	May	296
1757	Leonard, Esq		Kent	Jun	180
1757	Leonard, Esq	Double Prob Will regd this month	Kent	Jun	
1775	Martha		Derby	Jul	261
1775	Mary		Kent	Aug	301
1780	Mary		Surrey	Dec	553
1783	Mary		Surrey	Oct	496
1786	Mary		Surrey	Feb	64
1781	Peter	A with W	Middlesex	Jun	282
1798	Richard, Esq		Oxford	Apr	236
1766	Robert		Middlesex	Feb	46
1768	Sarah		Middlesex	Feb	44
1792	Sarah		Southampton	Feb	55
1792	Sarah	Double Prob Will regd Feb 55	Southampton	May	
1753	Thomas		Sussex	Jan	2
1754	Thomas		London	Feb	31
1763	Thomas		Southampton	Jan	6
1766	Thomas		Middlesex	Jun	213
1767	Thomas		Middlesex	Jan	4
1778	Thomas		Pts	Jul	274
1787	William		Berkshire	Feb	54
1784	BARTHOLOMY, Jeremiah	EIS"Winterton"	Pts	Aug	426

Year	Name	Notes	Place	Month	No.
1770	BARTHOLOTTI, Lady Anna Francoise Vanden Heuvel at Beichlingen Said, alias SADELYN		Pts	Aug	
1755	BARTHOMU, Joana, alias BARTHOLMEW, Joanah		Surrey	Feb	32
1755	BARTHONNEAU, Mary, alias DESMONTIS alias BERTHONNEUX, Marie	Further Grant May	Hertford	Apr	99
1787	BARTHROP, Christopher		Middlesex	Feb	55
1753	Jonathan Esq	A with W of Goods Unad Will regd 19 Vere	Middlesex	Mar	
1780	Mary	Ltd Prob	Pts	Oct	462
1772	BARTIE, Bustian	A with W	Pts	Jan	4
1759	William		Middlesex	Aug	258
1759	William	A with W of Goods Unad Will regd August last	Middlesex	Nov	
1780	BARTINGTON, Ann alias BARKINGTON	Will regd this month July 1780 346	Middlesex	Jul	
1797	BARTLAM, Ann		Warwick	Nov	677
1790	Mary	A with W	Chester	Aug	365
1764	BARTLAT, Andrew alias BARTLETT		Pts	Aug	298
1799	BARTLE, John	Ser:"Charon"	Pts	May	339
1798	Richard		Wiltshire	Jul	463
1791	BARTLEMAN, Susanna		London	Mar	113
1782	William		Middlesex	Aug	395
1795	BARTLEMORE, Elizabeth		Oxford	Nov	621
1761	BARTLET, Benjamin		Sussex	Sep	308
1776	alias BARTLETT, Benjamin		Pts	Nov	450
1787	Benjamin, Esq		Hertford	Mar	103
1789	Elizabeth		Sussex	Dec	574
1788	James		Nth. Britain	Apr	178
1772	John		Surrey	Aug	283
1789	Newton		Hertfordshire	Jan	4
1759	Philip, alias BARTEY, alias BARTLEY		Pts	Feb	47
1758	Richard	Poor	Middlesex	Jul	208
1779	Richard	Ser	Pts	Jan	4
1751	Thomas		Middlesex	Oct	276
1783	BARTLETT, Abell		Dorset	Jul	334
1764	Andrew, alias BARTLAT		Pts	Aug	298
1760	Ann		Leicester	May	185
1762	Ann		Bristol	Sep	365
1767	Ann		Bristol	Jan	4
1770	Ann		Surrey	Feb	42
1773	Ann		Surrey	Jan	2
1773	Ann		Middlesex	Apr	147
1774	Ann		Devon	Mar	82

BARTLETT (Contd)

Year	Name	Note	County	Month	No.
1800	Ann		Devon	Mar	174
1794	Anne		Gloucester	Apr	184
1776	Benjamin, alias BARTLET		Pts	Nov	450
1765	Daniel		Southampton	Nov	399
1786	Edmund		Middlesex	Feb	70
1756	Edward		Gloucester	Feb	28
1771	Edward		Northampton	Apr	145
1782	Edward		Pts	Feb	60
1789	Edward		Somerset	Jun	303
1795	Edward		Buckingham	Mar	146
1790	Eleanor		Buckinghamshire	Oct	451
1771	Elizabeth		Hertford	Feb	48
1775	Elizabeth		Surrey	Jul	260
1781	Elizabeth		Hampshire	Oct	461
1784	Elizabeth		Gloucester	Jun	307
1792	Elizabeth		Surrey	Sep	460
1786	Ellis	Pts	Devon	Jul	365
1794	Esther		Oxford	Oct	488
1800	Fanny		Dorset	Apr	256
1777	Felix		Worcester	Aug	340
1793	Frances		Middlesex	May	242
1753	George		Devon	Mar	71
1768	Gideon		Middlesex	Aug	308
1763	Hannah		Surrey	Dec	538
1784	Henry		Buckinghamshire	Apr	187
1796	Henry	A with W	Surrey	Jan	4
1774	Hester		Middlesex	Mar	81
1760	James		Middlesex	May	185
1768	James, Esq		Salisbury	Aug	306
1775	James, Esq	A with W Unad Will regd 306 Secker	Salisbury	Nov	
1783	James		Middlesex	Nov	549
1784	James, Esq	A with W of Goods Unad Will regd 306 Secker	Salisbury	Jul	
1786	James	A with W Unad Will regd November 1783	Middlesex	Nov	
1788	James Perry, Revd	The Reverend	Devon	May	232
1787	Jane		Dorset	May	200
1787	Jane		Exeter	Nov	488
1795	Jane	A with W of Goods Unad Will regd 488 Major	Exeter	Dec	
1750	John		Pts	Jun	187
1753	John		Pts	Jul	197
1759	John		Cornwall	Dec	383
1763	John		Warwick	Jan	2
1773	John		Middlesex	Apr	146
1793	John		Berkshire	Sep	455
1796	John		Dorset	Jan	5

BARTLETT (Contd)

Year	Name	Note	Place	Month	Page
1779	John Morgan	Ser	Pts	Apr	144
1763	Jonathan		Southampton	Dec	539
1788	Jonathan		Middlesex	Dec	575
1759	Joseph		Pts	Dec	385
1761	Joseph		Middlesex	Mar	81
1780	Joseph		London	Mar	119
1779	Joshua		Gloucester	Mar	88
1755	Katharine		London	Feb	34
1760	Martha		Surrey	Apr	134
1753	Mary	Will regd 250 Spurway	Jersey	Jul	
1764	Mary		Middlesex	Jan	2
1769	Mary		Middlesex	May	153
1784	Mary		Oxford	Aug	431
1790	Molly		Bristol	Sep	412
1791	Paul		Devon	Feb	58
1771	Peter	Poor	Pts	Jun	243
1771	Peter	Will regd in June last	Pts	Jul	
1767	Phebe		Middlesex	Oct	361
1775	Philip		Middlesex	Aug	301
1799	Rebecca		Surrey	May	334
1754	Richard		Pts	Aug	220
1763	Richard, alias BEARTLETT		Southampton	Mar	106
1764	Richard		Pts	Sep	337
1781	Michael		Pts	Dec	570
1799	Richard	Ser"Favorite"	Dorset	Jan	10
1774	Ridly		Middlesex	May	169
1753	Robert		Southampton	Sep	244
1756	Robert		Middlesex	Jun	160
1759	Robert		Kent	Nov	349
1768	Robert, alias Robart		Surrey	Mar	96
1779	Robert		Buckinghamshire	Sep	367
1769	Roger		Dorset	Feb	34
1783	Rose		London	Sep	443
1795	Samuel	"Powerful"Ltd Prob Ser	Devon	Jan	6
1785	Simon		Oxford	Mar	114
1772	Susanna		Essex	Feb	42
1779	Theophilus		Dorset	Mar	88
1753	Thomas		Surrey	Apr	101
1755	Thomas		Middlesex	Sep	232
1758	Thomas		Pts	Mar	62
1759	Thomas		Middlesex	Feb	45
1760	Thomas		Surrey	Dec	452
1761	Thomas		Middlesex	Dec	417
1764	Thomas	A with W	Pts	Jun	210
1769	Thomas		Oxford	Apr	114
1772	Thomas		Mid	Dec	432
1778	Thomas		Surrey	Nov	432
1789	Thomas	A with W of Goods Unad Will regd 432 Taverner	Mid	Feb	

BARTLETT (Contd)

1791	Thomas		Devon	Apr	165
1798	Thomas		Berkshire	Feb	77
1799	Thomas		Oxford	Nov	761
1772	Unity		Salisbury	Nov	390
1782	Unity	A with W Unad Will regd 390 Taverner	Salisbury	Mar	
1764	Walter		Pts	Feb	38
1764	William, alias BARTLIET, alias BARTLEY		Pts	Jul	253
1769	William		Wiltshire	Feb	35
1770	William		Pts	Jul	254
1771	William		Gloucester	Sep	366
1780	William	Ser	Pts	Apr	169
1780	William		Pts	Dec	552
1783	William	"Experiment"	Pts	Sep	446
1786	William		Devon	Jul	366
1796	William		Surrey	Nov	541
1800	William	"Bedford" & "Assistance"	Pts	Mar	180
1800	William	Will regd 366 Norfolk	Devon	Jul	
1784	BARTLEY, Alexander alias BARCLAY	"Thome", "Isis", "Renown", "Hero" Ser	Pts	Jul	367
1789	George		Middlesex	Feb	74
1754	Isaac, alias BARCLAY		Pts	Oct	267
1759	Philip, alias BARTEY, alias BARTLET		Pts	Feb	47
1760	William		Surrey	Mar	89
1764	William, alias BARTLIET, alias BARTLETT		Pts	Jul	253
1764	BARTLIET, William, alias BARTLETT, alias BARTLEY		Pts	Jul	253
1753	BARTLY, Rebecca		Somerset	May	129
1776	BARTMAKER, John		Mid	Apr	165
1775	BARTOLOTTI VANDEN HEUVEL, The Rt Hon Geertruyd Cornelia, alias VAN ROUWENNOORT, alias VAN ROUWENOORT	Ltd prob	Pts	Sep	363
1760	BARTON, Abraham		Pts	Apr	135
1799	Ann		York	Apr	242
1792	Anna		Middlesex	Jan	3
1791	Anne		Worcestershire	May	216
1762	Revd Baptist Noel		Rutland	Jul	285
1752	Benjamin		Middlesex	May	116
1772	Catharine, alias Catherine		Southampton	Mar	84
1769	Charles		Middlesex	Jun	199
1770	Charles		Middlesex	Feb	46
1751	Christopher		Middlesex	Nov	299
1765	Cornelius		Middlesex	Mar	87

BARTON (Contd)

Year	Name	Note	Place	Month	Page
1751	Edward		Derby	Aug	229
1773	Edward		Kent	May	195
1762	Elizabeth		Middlesex	Oct	412
1769	Elizabeth		Middlesex	Feb	36
1785	Elizabeth		Wiltshire	Jan	6
1791	Elizabeth		Surrey	Dec	561
1788	Elizabeth Mary	A with W	Canterbury	May	228
1800	Elizabeth Mary	A with W of Goods Unad Will regd 228 Calvert	Canterbury	Dec	
1757	Ewart		London	Feb	40
1777	Francis		Essex	Oct	407
1760	George		Pts	Mar	90
1762	George	Pts	Middlesex	Dec	494
1788	George		Southampton	Aug	385
1750	Henry		Surrey	Aug	251
1765	Isobel		Middlesex	Feb	44
1751	James		London	Feb	35
1761	James, Esq	Pts	Lancaster	Mar	81
1763	James, Esq	Double prob Pts Will regd March 1761	Lancaster	May	
1774	James		Surrey	Dec	421
1800	Joseph		Surrey	Feb	81
1800	Jane		York	Mar	173
1751	John		Surrey	Mar	71
1751	John		Pts	Apr	104
1756	John		London	Nov	287
1758	John		Pts	Feb	29
1761	John		Middlesex	Jan	4
1761	John		Warwick	May	161
1763	John	A with W of Goods Unad Will regd January 1761	Pts	Aug	
1764	John		London	Jan	4
1766	John		Kent	Apr	128
1766	John		London	Jun	215
1777	John	A with Will	Cambridge	Apr	146
1779	John		Kent	Apr	141
1779	John	A with Will Unad Will regd 215 Tyndall	London	Apr	
1780	John		Pts	Apr	173
1784	John	"Conqueror"	Pts	Mar	123
1785	John		Wiltshire	Jan	6
1789	John		Hertfordshire	Jul	347
1790	John	A with Will	Pts	Jun	278
1793	John		Surrey	Mar	126
1799	John		Essex	Jan	11
1799	John		Kent	Jun	418
1800	John, Esq	Major of Artillery EIC	Pts	Jul	509
1800	John		Kent	Dec	842
1775	Joseph		Pts	Jul	260

BARTON (Contd)

1794	Joseph		Lincoln	Apr	183
1791	Judith		Worcestershire	Oct	452
1800	Judith		Lincoln	Oct	705
1774	Katharine		Berkshire	Jul	255
1762	Lewis		Middlesex	May	185
1783	Margaret		Canterbury	Oct	495
1789	Margaret	A with W of Goods Unad Will regd 495 Cornwallis	Canterbury	Feb	
1800	Margaret	A with W of Goods Twice Unad, Will regd 495 Cornwallis	Canterbury	Dec	
1800	Martha		Hertford	Nov	765
1753	Mary		Kent	Apr	102
1754	Mary		Middlesex	Oct	265
1757	Mary		London	Sep	267
1763	Mary		Middlesex	Sep	418
1768	Mary		Wiltshire	Jan	5
1778	Mary		Middlesex	Jan	4
1778	Mary		Somerset	Nov	431
1783	Mary	Int Decree	Middlesex	Jul	334
1796	Matthew, Esq	Adm of the White in His Majesty's Fleet	Middlesex	Jan	3
1779	Nathaniel		Pts	Mar	90
1768	Newton		Bath	Nov	401
1763	Perin		London	Aug	370
1763	Perin	Double Prob Will regd last month	London	Sep	
1765	Dr Philip	Dr of Laws	Oxford	Aug	284
1786	Rev Philip		Middlesex	May	266
1787	Rev Philip	Double Prob Will regd May 1786	Middlesex	May	
1795	Philip	"Europd"Ser	Pts	Jan	7
1796	Rev Philip		Exeter	Jul	347
1750	Richard		London	Mar	67
1778	Richard		Buckinghamshire	Mar	98
1779	Richard		Pts	Jan	4
1787	Richard		Cambridge	Nov	486
1792	Richard		Middlesex	Nov	545
1796	Richard		Southampton	Nov	540
1798	Robert, Esq		Southampton	Apr	238
1754	Roger	A with W Unad Will regd 196 Spurway	Flint	Mar	68
1756	Sarah		Surrey	Dec	319
1793	Silvanus		Berkshire	Jan	4
1753	Serena		London	Jul	195
1764	Solomon		London	Jun	210
1772	Stephen	A with W Unad Will regd 99 Wake	Southampton	Mar	
1778	Stephen		Dorset	Oct	387

BARTON (Contd)

1798	Stephen		Middlesex	Nov	693
1781	Susanna		Buckinghamshire	Jun	283
1793	Susanna		Middlesex	Nov	540
1757	Thomas		Middlesex	Jun	181
1761	The Revd Thomas		Sussex	Jan	4
1778	Thomas		Middlesex	May	182
1781	Thomas, Esq		Pts	Mar	119
1781	Thomas		Salop	Jul	328
1783	Thomas		Surrey	Oct	496
1787	Thomas		Kent	Mar	106
1791	Thomas, Esq		London	Nov	499
1796	Thomas		Kent	Nov	540
1799	Thomas		Lancaster	Oct	699
1760	Walter		Middlesex	Feb	47
1751	William		Surrey	Nov	301
1757	William		Somerset	Feb	39
1759	William		Wiltshire	Jan	5
1769	William		Kent	Oct	332
1771	William		Kent	Apr	142
1775	William		Middlesex	Jun	220
1777	William		Middlesex	Jul	298
1779	William		Surrey	May	186
1785	William		Surrey	May	231
1796	William	"Intrepid"	Pts	Feb	53
1756	BARTRAM, Ann		Worcester	Mar	58
1789	Catharine		Kent	Oct	482
1774	Elizabeth, alias MILLER	A with W	Bedford	Mar	78
1771	George Henry		Middlesex	Apr	147
1774	John		Dorset	Feb	37
1794	John	Double Prob Will regd July last	Surrey	Oct	349
1784	Margaret		Kent	Mar	123
1788	Richard		Kent	Jul	337
1800	Robert		Kent	Jun	442
1769	Thomas		Kent	Sep	302
1772	Thomas		Kent	Dec	431
1782	William		Middlesex	Oct	482
1799	BARTRUM, Elizabeth		Surrey	Jan	7
1774	John		Somerset	May	166
1797	Mary		Middlesex	Jan	32
1771	Philip	A with W	London	Nov	431
1785	Wright		Middlesex	Oct	490
1797	BARTS, George Frederick		Middlesex	Dec	725
1750	BARTTELOT, Catharine		Sussex	Jun	186
1767	Elizabeth		Sussex	Sep	333
1779	Isabel		Sussex	Sep	365
1764	Walter, Esq		Sussex	Jul	254
1792	BARTUM, James	"Phoenix"	Pts	Apr	193
1795	BARTWELL, Charles		Essex	Jan	28

1767	BARUCH CARAVAGLIO, Abraham of Jacob, alias ZITA BARUCH CARAVAGLIO, Abraham		Pts	Jan	5
1762	Moses	Ltd Prob	Pts	Aug	331
1769	Saul de Abraham, alias CARVALLO, Saul	A with W	Pts	Oct	332
1751	BARUCH, DE, Senior David, alias SENIOR, David		London	May	138
1775	BARUGH, John	A with W	Middlesex	Nov	401
1785	John	A with W of Goods Unad Will regd 401 Alexander	Middlesex	Mar	
1793	Magdalen		Essex	Dec	580
1752	BARUH LOUSADA, Jacob		London	Nov	271
1766	BARUH, Naftali		Middlesex	Feb	46
1793	BARVELL, Catherine		Norfolk	Apr	184
1757	BARWELL, Amy		Middlesex	Sep	267
1757	Amy	Double Prob Will regd September last	Middlesex	Dec	
1797	Arrabella Catherine		Northampton	Feb	71
1763	Charles		Leicester	Dec	541
1780	Daniel, Esq, alias Daniel Octavius	By Int Decree Another Grant August 1779	Pts	Dec	550
1799	Edward, Esq		Middlesex	Jan	9
1788	Eleanor		Middlesex	Oct	470
1756	Elizabeth		Middlesex	Aug	216
1790	Godfrey		Middlesex	May	222
1763	Henry		Northampton	Jun	266
1785	Henry, Esq		Pts/Middlesex	Nov	537
1793	Joseph	A with W	Wiltshire	May	243
1800	Margaret		Middlesex	Feb	85
1793	Nathaniel, Esq		Middlesex	Apr	188
1774	Osborn, Esq		Middlesex	Aug	289
1775	Richard, Esq		Surrey	Mar	82
1800	Richard, Esq		Sussex	May	345
1753	Robert		Middlesex	Aug	224
1772	Roger, Esq	Ltd A with W	Middlesex	Jul	244
1792	Roger , Esq	Another Grant July 1772	Middlesex	May	262
1756	William	A with W	London	Nov	289
1769	William, Esq		Surrey	Dec	403
1799	William, Esq		Middlesex	Nov	762
1781	BARWICK, Benjamin		Middlesex	Nov	512
1776	Edward, Esq		London	May	213
1766	Elizabeth		Bath	Jul	258
1772	Elizabeth	Double Prob Will regd 258 Tyndall	Bath	Apr	
1772	Elizabeth, alias WILLOUGHBY		Middlesex	Jun	207
1795	Elizabeth		Middlesex	Oct	574
1761	Francis		Middlesex	Feb	46
1761	James		Middlesex	Oct	341

BARWICK (Contd)

1754	John		Chichester	Jul	190
1760	John		Surrey	Feb	46
1791	John		Middlesex	Sep	419
1789	Mark Anthony		Middlesex	Jun	298
1767	Mary	A with W	Middlesex	Apr	122
1769	Mary		London	Feb	35
1780	Mary		London	Dec	552
1788	Mary		Kent	Jun	290
1780	Newe, Esq		Buckinghamshire	Mar	120
1750	Richard		Pts	Dec	380
1781	Sarah		Middlesex	Nov	514
1773	Thomas		London	Oct	381
1784	Thomas		Surrey	Sep	494
1792	Thomas, alias BERWICK		London	Apr	200
1776	William		Cambridge	Aug	349
1782	BARWIS, Dr Cuthbert	Dr in Divinity	Middlesex	Sep	440
1791	James, alias BARBOSS	"Crown"&"Princess Royal"		May	216
1796	BARWISE, Richard	A with W	Middlesex	Oct	490
1763	Thomas		Middlesex	May	213
1775	BARY, DE, Isabella, alias MARCET		Pts	Apr	149
1797	BARY, Richard, alias BARRY		Leicester	Jul	468
1777	BARY, DE, Sarah		Middlesex	May	206
1770	BARZEY, Thomas		Pembroke	Nov	388
1766	Thomas Bouveron, Esq		Pts	May	170
1787	BARZILAY, Jacob Jesuzum	·A with W	Pts	Oct	438
1754	Ribca		Pts	Dec	318
1759	BAS, David le		Middlesex	Dec	406
1791	George le		Middlesex	Feb	82
1765	Sophia de, The Right Noble Lady, alias BALDE, formerly MARCELIS		Pts	Mar	85
1773	BASAID, Sarah		Middlesex	Apr	144
1783	BASCHARD, Mary Ann		Bath	Dec	602
1750	BASCOM, Lawrence	A with W	Surrey	Feb	36
1797	BASCOMB, Joseph	A with W	Kent	Aug	542
1754	BASCOMBE, Mary		Middlesex	Jul	188
1781	BASDEN, Rebeckar		Kent	Apr	183
1758	Thomas		Berkshire	Feb	29
1771	Thomas		Kent	Dec	471
1778	Thomas		Middlesex	Oct	390
1785	Thomas	A with W unad Will regd 390 Hay	Middlesex	Jun	
1788	Thomas	A with W unad Will regd 390 Hay last grant Jun 1785	Middlesex	Jan	
1788	Thomas	A with W unad Will regd 390 Hay last grant Jan 1788	Middlesex	Mar	

1765	BASE, Ann		Canterbury	Mar	88
1782	John		Parts	Nov	530
1750	BASELEE, William,				
	alias BAZELEE,				
	alias BEEZLEY	Pts	Kent	Feb	40
1787	BASELEY, Henry, Revd		Leicester	Mar	106
1766	Job		Warwick	Jun	213
1774	Job		Warwick	Aug	291
1784	Thomas		Warwick	Jun	307
1795	Thomas		Norwich	Aug	494
1770	BASELL, George,				
	alias BASSILL		Hertford	Aug	284
1773	BASFORD, Peter		Middlesex	Feb	45
1773	Robert		Essex	Sep	352
1777	BASHAM, John		Dorset	Jun	253
1780	John	A with W unad			
		Will regd June 1777	Dorset	Oct	
1798	William	"Emerald"	Pts	Mar	153
1795	BASHFIELD, John,				
	alias BLASHFIELD		Radnor	Jul	431
1762	BASHLA, Peter Francis Le,				
	alias BOCHLO	A with W	Pts	May	
1751	BASHLEY, William		Middlesex	Oct	274
1779	BASIL, Edmund, Esq		Buckinghamshire	Dec	487
1775	Frances		Middlesex	Dec	455
1755	William, Esq		Buckinghamshire	Oct	252
1790	BASILL, Martha		Middlesex	Jul	321
1799	Sarah		Middlesex	Aug	572
1767	William		Middlesex	Mar	87
1784	BASING, John		Berkshire	May	245
1784	John	A with W	Berkshire	May	245
1791	William		Surrey	Mar	110
1753	BASINGTON, Sarah,				
	alias BASSINGTON	A with W	Middlesex	Jun	163
1770	BASIRE, Isaac	By Int Decree	Middlesex	Jun	219
1763	BASKCOMBE, John		Pts	May	217
1754	Thomas	A with W	London	Feb	32
1795	BASKERFIELD, Catherine		Bedford	Jan	4
1799	Thomas		Middlesex	Nov	758
1786	BASKERVILE, John	E. I. S. "Mansfield"	Pts	May	260
1799	John		London	Aug	570
1756	Joseph		London	Apr	95
1779	Rachel		Wiltshire	Nov	441
1756	Thomas		Surrey	Aug	217
1771	BASKERVILLE, Ann		Salop	Apr	144
1777	George		London	Dec	499
1782	George		London	Mar	111
1761	John		Wiltshire	Apr	118
1775	John		Warwick	Mar	83
1800	John		Wiltshire	May	344
1752	Pusey	A with W	Pts	Aug	206

	BASKERVILLE (Contd)				
1767	Rachel		London	Sep	333
1750	Robert		Salop	Apr	105
1784	Sarah		London	Feb	62
1788	Sarah		Warwick	Mar	119
1796	Sarah		London	Mar	108
1766	Simon		Salisbury	Sep	328
1795	Simon		Middlesex	Mar	144
1759	Thomas, Esq		Surrey	Nov	347
1760	Thomas		London	Oct	380
1779	Thomas		Wiltshire	Sep	367
1781	Thomas		Salisbury	Jun	283
1777	William		Southampton	Jan	5
1786	BASKES, Catharina	Ltd Prob	Pts	Jun	323
1786	BASKET, Mark,				
	alias BASKETT		Berkshire	Jan	8
1764	BASKETT, Lucy	A with W	Lincoln	Jun	211
1786	Mark,				
	alias BASKET		Berkshire	Jan	8
1767	Robert, Esq		Surrey	Jul	253
1756	Roger, Esq		Devon	Dec	324
1792	Ruth		Dorset	May	257
1793	Revd Samuel		Dorset	Mar	126
1783	Thomas	A with W	Dorset	Mar	112
1799	William	A with W			
		E.I.S. "Lord Hawkesbury"	Pts	Oct	699
1776	BASLEY, Richard		Berkshire	Jan	5
1780	Richard	Dble Prob			
		Will regd Jan 1776	Berkshire	Feb	
1752	BASNAGE DE BEAUVAL,				
	Marie, alias AMSINCQ	Ltd Prob	Pts	Jan	2
1784	BASNET, James	"Enterprize",			
		"Leander" &			
		"Princess Amelia"	Pts	Sep	492
1754	BASNETT, Elizabeth		Middlesex	Jul	189
1785	Elizabeth		Berkshire	Jan	7
1774	John		Salop	Sep	329
1756	Mary	A with W	Middlesex	Feb	30
1774	Nathaniel		Berkshire	Apr	130
1756	Peter		Salop	Jul	190
1763	Peter		Salop	Jan	8
1792	Peter		Salop	Jul	363
1764	Rebeckah	A with W	Surrey	Apr	130
1765	Richard		Salop	Feb	41
1774	Richard		Middlesex	Dec	423
1800	Revd Richard		Salop	Aug	575
1765	Thomas		Middlesex	Apr	132
1754	William		Middlesex	Jun	158
1779	William Birch, Esq			Jun	232
1798	BASNIP, George	Ser "Suffolk"			
		A with W	Pts	Sep	586

1751	BASON, Francis	A with W	Pts	Nov	300
1754	William		Buckinghamshire	May	125
1752	BASQUOIRT, Joseph,				
	alias BOSQUOIRT	A with W	Pts	Jan	3
1751	BASS, Ann		Oxford	Mar	71
1764	Ann		Middlesex	Jan	6
1765	Antonia,				
	alias BOIS, Anthony		Pts	Sep	321
1758	Daniel		Pts	Nov	321
1789	Frances		Essex	Jun	298
1771	George		Essex	Jun	241
1797	Hannah		Middlesex	Dec	728
1772	Joel		London	Feb	37
1753	John		Middlesex	Feb	38
1764	John	A with W	Leicester	Dec	455
1766	Revd John		Warwick	May	169
1771	John	Pts	Ireland	Apr	146
1786	John		London	Nov	554
1793	John		Essex	Aug	401
1794	John		Middlesex	Dec	598
1797	John	A with W of good unad			
		Will regd Aug 1793	Essex	Mar	
1782	Mary		Bristol	Dec	573
1792	Mary		Essex	Dec	594
1797	Samuel		Southampton	May	294
1782	Stephen		Middlesex	Feb	64
1768	Thomas	Ser	Middlesex	Oct	369
1784	Thomas		Kent	Feb	65
1788	Thomas	"Irresistible"	Pts	Sep	426
1783	William	Ser	Pts	Jun	285
1767	Wright		Middlesex	Feb	36
1786	BASSACK, Philadelphia,				
	alias BASSETT		Kent	Jul	364
1782	BASSAM, Rebecca	A with W	Middlesex	Oct	483
1790	William		Hertford	Nov	495
1772	BASSANO, Mark		Pts	Jun	204
1753	BASSE, Jane		Middlesex	Jun	163
1779	BASSECOUR, Anna de la	Ltd Prob	Pts	Feb	39
1773	Carel de la, The Worshipful,				
	alias Charles	Ltd Prob	Pts	Jul	277
1767	Jacob Willem de la, The				
	Noble Worshipful	Ltd Prob	Pts	Sep	333
1767	Nicolaas de la		Pts	Jun	216
1779	BASSILL, Thomas,	Another Will proved			
	alias BASSEL	in December last	Glamorgan	May	
1778	BASSELL, Thomas		Glamorgan	Dec	476
1793	BASSET, Anne		Glamorgan	May	125
1793	Elizabeth		Middlesex	Mar	125
1770	Francis, Esq		Cornwall	Mar	87
1782	Henry, Esq	A with W	Middlesex	May	212

	BASSET (Contd)				
1794	Thomas,				
	alias BASSETT	"Robust"	Pts	Jun	297
1791	BASSETT, Alexander, Esq		Surrey	Jan	3
1765	Ann		Surrey	May	88
1791	Ann,				
	alias EVANS	A with W	Glamorgan	Jul	316
1763	Anne		Devon	Mar	108
1798	Anne		Suffolk	Jan	5
1762	Christopher		Glamorgan	Jun	237
1764	Christopher, Esq		Glamorgan	Nov	418
1750	Daniel	Servt	Middlesex	Jan	4
1760	Daniel		Bristol	Sep	348
1764	David		Pts	Jul	249
1770	David		Kent	May	172
1800	Dorothy		Suffolk	Feb	90
1759	Edward		Kent	Jun	194
1751	Eiizabeth		Warwick	Mar	72
1776	Elizabeth		Kent	Aug	348
1788	Elizabeth		Essex	May	226
1792	Elizabeth	Another Probate Will regd May 1788 226 Calvert	Essex	Aug	
1762	Frances		Southampton	Sep	366
1754	George	A with W unad Will regd 61 Potter	Sussex	Aug	219
1797	George, Revd		Lincoln	Jan	4
1797	George		Kent	Dec	728
1798	James		Oxford	Jan	5
1796	Jane		Somerset	May	234
1750	John		Kent	Jun	190
1750	John		Kent	Jul	221
1758	John		Pts	Jan	5
1758	John, Esq		Devon	Feb	29
1765	John		Pts	Jul	248
1769	John		Kent	May	153
1781	John	Ser	Pts	Jul	333
1797	Judith		Suffolk	Dec	727
1760	Mary		London	May	185
1795	Mary	A with W	Warwick	Oct	582
1786	Philadelphia, alias BASSACK		Kent	Jul	364
1785	Rebekah		Northampton	Feb	66
1758	Richard		Pts	Oct	284
1765	Richard		Surrey	Jan	4
1791	Richard		Middlesex	May	211
1795	Revd Richard		Surrey	Feb	63
1762	Robert		Pts	Jan	2
1781	Stephen		Kent	Jun	287
1796	Stephen	A with W	Surrey	Apr	164
1750	Thomas		London	Feb	39

	BASSETT (Contd)				
1769	Thomas		Middlesex	Dec	407
1770	Thomas		Suffolk	Apr	131
1779	Thomas	Dble Prob			
		Will regd 131 Jenner	Suffolk	Jul	
1794	Thomas,				
	see BASSET			Jun	297
1795	Thomas		Warwick	Nov	625
1764	William		Surrey	Jun	213
1765	William,				
	alias BARSUCK		Pts	Feb	41
1766	William		Leicester	Nov	398
1769	William, Esq		Glamorgan	Dec	403
1770	William		Pts	Feb	43
1778	William		Surrey	Jan	3
1791	William		Wells	Dec	559
1796	William, Esq		Glamorgan	Nov	540
1797	William	Ser "Queen"	Pts	Oct	627
1776	BASSEVELD, Jan Franson,				
	alias BASSEVELD, Jan,				
	alias Jan Versevelt,				
	alias Jan Barssevelt	A with W	Pts	Dec	524
1784	BASSIL, Edward		Hertford	Jul	369
1769	George		Hertford	Nov	367
1792	BASSILL, Edward		Hertford	Nov	547
1770	George,				
	alias BASELL		Hertford	Aug	284
1799	BASSIL, George		Hertford	Apr	249
1772	BASSILL, John		Hertford	Dec	432
1779	Thomas,	Another Will proved in			
	alias BASSEL	December last	Glamorgan	May	
1792	William		Hertford	Feb	55
1779	BASSINGTON, John		Middlesex	Jul	287
1798	John		Middlesex	Sep	584
1753	Sarah,				
	alias BASINGTON	A with W	Middlesex	Jun	163
1789	BASSON, John		Oxford	Aug	420
1785	William	Poor	London	Jun	292
1755	BASSOON, Elizabeth,				
	alias BASSOUN		Middlesex	Feb	32
1755	Elizabeth,	Dble Prob			
	alias BASSOUN	Will regd in February last	Middlesex	Mar	
1755	BASSOUN, Elizabeth,				
	alias BASSOON		Middlesex	Feb	32
1755	Elizabeth,	Dble Prob			
	alias BASSOON	Will regd in February last	Middlesex	Mar	
1780	BASSTON, William		Devon	May	236
1781	BASSTONE, Grace		Exeter	Apr	179
1787	BASTABLE, John		Bristol	Sep	396
1775	BASTAIN, Samuel		Pts	Jun	220
1773	BASTARD, Baldwin Pollexfen,				
	Esq	A with W	Devon	Aug	319

BASTARD (Contd)

Year	Name	Note	Place	Month	No
1772	Benjamin		Dorset	May	158
1774	Bridget, The Right Honourable Lady		Devon	Apr	130
1773	Edmund, Esq		Devon	Jul	278
1785	Henary, alias Henry	Ser "Carysfort"	Pts	Jul	352
1758	John		Pts	May	143
1770	John		Dorset	May	176
1776	John		Dorset	Jan	4
1778	John		Middlesex	Sep	346
1757	Joseph		Kent	Jun	181
1794	Joseph		Southampton	Aug	404
1784	Margaret		Exeter	Dec	629
1759	Philip	A with W	Exeter	Dec	383
1772	Thomas		Dorset	Feb	37
1772	Thomas		Dorset	Nov	390
1793	Thomas		Dorset	Apr	183
1798	Thomas		Surrey	Mar	157
1767	William		Dorset	Mar	83
1771	William		Exeter	Aug	330
1782	William, Esq		Devon	Dec	573
1781	BASTER, George		Berkshire	Jan	8
1775	Job	Ltd Prob	Pts	Sep	334
1761	John		Wiltshire	Jul	240
1787	Joseph		Wiltshire	Jul	311
1790	Joseph		Berkshire	Aug	365
1765	BASTERT, Nicolaas	Ltd Prob	Pts	May	172
1770	BASTIAANSE, Cornelis Abraham	Ltd Prob	Pts	Jun	222
1770	Cornelis Abraham, alias BASTIAANSEN	Ltd Prob Will regd in this month	Pts	Jun	
1770	BASTIAANSEN, Cornelis Abraham, alias BASTIAANSE	Ltd Prob Will regd in this month	Pts	Jun	
1755	BASTIAN, Joanna		Surrey	Apr	94
1768	Martha		Oxford	Jun	225
1778	BASTICK, William		Essex	Jan	4
1797	BASTIDE, Abraham, Esq	Ltd Prob	Pts	Jul	477
1800	George, Esq		Southampton	Dec	840
1770	John Henry, Esq		Southampton	Sep	322
1754	Mary, de la		Surrey	Jun	158
1752	BASTIN, Amy		Berkshire	May	117
1795	George		Surrey	Mar	143
1775	John	A with W	Middlesex	Nov	401
1771	William		Oxford	Apr	144
1774	William		Middlesex	Jan	3
1783	BASTOCK, Thomas		Warwick	May	214
1784	BASTON, George	"Gibraltar"	Pts	Aug	426
1781	John		Pts	Feb	57
1795	Richard		London	Jan	3
1800	Turner		Bedford	May	345

1766	BASTONE, Elizabeth		Kent	Jul	256
1766	Robert		Kent	May	168
1755	BASTOW, George		London	Sep	234
1785	George	"Gibraltar"	Pts	May	229
1764	BAT, Jacob La		Middlesex	Sep	356
1763	BATAILHEY, Mary Ann,				
	alias GODIN		Pts	Dec	541
1797	BATAILLE, Anne		Middlesex	Apr	251
1751	Anne Louisa		Middlesex	Dec	326
1765	Elizabeth		Middlesex	Oct	364
1789	Revd Isaac		Norfolk	Jul	345
1759	James		Middlesex	Mar	84
1759	Jane		Middlesex	Nov	350
1791	Revd Martin William Andrew		Devon	Mar	114
1776	Peter		Middlesex	Jul	303
1750	BATAILLARD, Huldrich		London	Jul	224
1788	BATAT, John, Esq		Middlesex	Feb	59
1757	BATCH, Jane		Middlesex	Mar	74
1770	Jane	A with W unad			
		Will regd 74 Herring	Middlesex	Sep	
1763	BATCHELAR, James		Sussex	Mar	108
1797	John		Surrey	Jun	396
1782	BATCHELDER, Martha		London	Jan	5
1782	Martha,				
	alias BATCHELOR	Will regd January last	London	Aug	
1797	BATCHELER, James		Worcester	Feb	67
1783	John,				
	alias BATCHELOR		Middlesex	Sep	443
1785	Joseph		Middlesex	Dec	587
1764	Mary		Middlesex	Oct	378
1800	Sarah		Bristol	Jan	5
1759	BATCHELLER, Paul		Sussex	Sep	289
1795	Susanna, alias Susannah		Canterbury	Jan	7
1797	BATCHELLOR, Mary		Kent	Feb	71
1792	Robert		Middlesex	Jun	319
1797	Robert	Ser "Undaunted"	Kent	Sep	589
1770	BATCHELOR, Ann		Middlesex	Jul	253
1774	Anna Maria		Middlesex	Jun	217
1751	Archibald		Middlesex	Dec	326
1767	Benjamin		Middlesex	Jan	3
1765	Charles		Southampton	Dec	441
1787	Edmund		Southampton	May	198
1757	Elizabeth		Wiltshire	Jun	183
1762	Elizabeth		Stafford	Nov	446
1786	Elizabeth		Middlesex	Jan	7
1762	George		Pts	Oct	409
1775	James		Middlesex	Jan	3
1754	John		Sussex	Jan	2
1758	John		Pts	Aug	237
1779	John		Pts	Nov	443
1780	John, alias BATCHLOR,				
	alias BATCHER		Pts	May	241

	BATCHELOR (Contd)				
1781	John		Kent	Aug	377
1783	John,				
	alias BATCHELER		Middlesex	Sep	443
1797	John		Sussex	Nov	676
1782	Martha,				
	alias BATCHELDER	Will regd January last	London	Aug	
1751	Mary		Sussex	Jun	165
1759	Mary		Worcester	Nov	347
1798	Mary		Sussex	Oct	636
1791	Philip		Kent	Dec	556
1766	Thomas		Buckinghamshire	Nov	399
1777	Thomas		Buckinghamshire	Aug	341
1798	Thomas	A with W	Southampton	Jul	463
1790	Walter		Sussex	Aug	363
1753	William	A with W	Sussex	Feb	38
1783	William		Sussex	Apr	163
1792	William		Southampton	Sep	461
1780	BATCHER, John,				
	alias BATCHLOR,				
	alias BATCHELOR		Pts	May	241
1799	BATCHILLOR, Thomas,				
	alias BACHILLOR		Middlesex	Mar	163
1780	BATCHLOR, John,				
	alias BATCHELOR,				
	alias BATCHER		Pts	May	241
1764	BATE, Chambers Revd		Northampton	May	163
1766	Dorothy		Middlesex	Mar	91
1754	Elias		Pts	Aug	218
1785	Elizabeth		Salop	Sep	456
1798	Elizabeth		Warwick	Jun	379
1751	George, Esq	A with W	Essex	Jun	167
1762	Henry		Worcester	Nov	450
1778	Henry		Worcester	Jul	273
1798	Henry, alias BATES	"Laurel" "La Renomme"	Pts	Nov	698
1761	James	Ser	Pts	Apr	119
1762	James		Southampton	May	183
1768	James, Esq		Essex	Mar	95
1775	Revd James		Kent	Sep	334
1760	John		Middlesex	Dec	453
1761	Revd John		Middlesex	Nov	383
1771	Revd Julius		Sussex	May	195
1776	Katherine		Middlesex	Jul	296
1776	Margaret		Worcester	Apr	162
1782	Mary		Sussex	Jun	267
1792	Mary		Stafford	Mar	133
1775	Revd Richard		Northampton	Sep	336
1783	Robert	Ser	Pts	Jul	339
1758	Samuel		Worcester	Mar	62
1758	Samuel		Worcester	Nov	321
1756	Sarah		Worcester	Aug	216
1770	Thomas		Northampton	Dec	422

	BATE (Contd)				
1797	Thomas, alias BATES		Essex	Jan	3
1768	BATELY, John, Esq		Southampton	Feb	46
1786	John	Will regd 46 Secker	Southampton	Jan	
1773	William, Esq		Chichester	Oct	383
1790	William	A with W of goods unad			
		Will regd 383 Stevens	Chichester	Mar	
1788	BATEMAN, Ann		Derby	May	225
1755	Ann Yrnbetta		Middlesex	Dec	303
1769	Anne, The Right Honourable				
	Lady Vicountess Dowager of				
	the Kingdom of Ireland		Middlesex	Feb	35
1779	Anne	A with W	Derby	Oct	406
1790	Anthony		Norfolk	Jan	5
1760	Archibald		Pts	Aug	316
1779	Betty		Leicester	Nov	441
1781	Christopher		London	Mar	119
1785	Christopher	A with W of goods unad			
		Will regd 119 Webster	London	Dec	
1756	Daniel		Middlesex	Mar	59
1790	Daniel	A with W	Northumberland	Aug	366
1750	Deborah		Middlesex	Aug	251
1773	Dorcas		Lincoln	May	195
1762	Dorothea		Middlesex	Oct	411
1766	Dorothea	A with W	London	Sep	329
1751	Dr Edmund	Doctor in Divinity	Leicester	Jun	166
1781	Edward	A with W	Pts	Mar	121
1799	Elenor, alias Eleanor		Middlesex	Apr	286
1758	Elias		London	Oct	284
1763	Elizabeth		London	May	213
1765	Elizabeth		Middlesex	Apr	131
1775	Elizabeth		Derby	Feb	41
1776	Elizabeth	A with W unad			
		Will regd February 1775	Derby	Jun	
1776	Elizabeth	A with W twice unad			
		Will regd February 1775	Derby	Aug	
1781	Elizabeth		Berkshire	Jan	9
1781	Elizabeth		York	Mar	120
1776	Frances		Derby	May	212
1766	George		Middlesex	Aug	294
1791	George		Middlesex	Jul	317
1779	Henry		Middlesex	May	189
1798	Henry		Bristol	Apr	231
1795	Hester		Middlesex	Mar	143
1778	Hugh, Esq		Derby	Jan	6
1763	Isaac		London	Oct	458
1758	James, Esq	A with W annex'd	Lincoln	Apr	101
1793	Johanna	A with W	Middlesex	Jul	351
1750	John		Middlesex	Sep	285
1757	John	A with W	Pts	Aug	239
1760	John		Northampton	Aug	313
1760	John		Middlesex	Nov	414

BATEMAN (Contd)

Year	Name		Place	Month	No.
1762	John		Pts	Aug	333
1763	John		Surrey	Jan	5
1764	John		Middlesex	Feb	38
1766	John		Oxford	Jul	259
1768	John, Esq		Middlesex	Feb	46
1775	John		Middlesex	Dec	460
1776	John		Middlesex	Jul	303
1785	John, Esq	A with W	Northampton	Mar	119
1790	John		Middlesex	Feb	64
1793	John		Essex	Jul	353
1791	Jonathan		Middlesex	Aug	374
1800	Joseph		London	Dec	839
1758	Katherine		Middlesex	Apr	103
1762	Martha	A with W	London	Oct	410
1750	Mary		Middlesex	Jun	187
1761	Mary	A with W	Middlesex	Feb	44
1774	Mary		Kent	Oct	359
1789	Mary		Middlesex	May	236
1761	Matthew, Esq		Middlesex	Oct	337
1751	Maule		Pts	Aug	230
	alias BATMAN				
1763	Miles		Pts	Feb	45
1762	Moses		London	Aug	334
1783	Moses		Northampton	Jul	336
1798	Nathan, Esq		Middlesex	May	312
1761	Nathaniel, Esq		Surrey	Apr	122
1781	Nathaniel		Buckinghamshire	Jun	284
1798	Nathaniel, Esq		Gloucester	Jan	3
1761	Nicholas		Oxford	Nov	381
1757	Price		Pts	Sep	268
1764	Rebecca		London	Oct	378
1763	Richard, Esq		Derby	Jun	265
1773	Richard, Esq		Berkshire	Mar	94
1775	Richard	Poor	Middlesex	Mar	85
1782	Richard	A with W Will regd 265 Caesar	Derby	Sep	
1776	Robert, The Reverend	Dr of Phy sick	Cornwall	Aug	347
1751	Rowland		Pts/Kent	Mar	71
1760	Sarah	A with W of Goods Unad Will regd 57 Isham	London	Jun	
1779	Sarah		Middlesex	Apr	140
1797	Sarah		Middlesex	May	299
1754	Stephen	A with W Will regd 260 Lort	London	Oct	
1776	Susanna		Surrey	Nov	448
1756	Temperance		Pembroke	Aug	217
1752	Thomas		Kent	Feb	30
1761	Richard Thomas, The Reverend	Pts	London	Feb	47
1763	Thomas		Kent	Feb	46
1766	Thomas	A with W unad Will regd Feb 1763	Kent	Apr	

	BATEMAN (Contd)				
1781	Thomas		London	May	229
1784	Thomas	Ser."Minerva" "Gibraltar"	Pts	Aug	427
1791	Thomas		Haverford	Apr	167
1793	Thomas		Middlesex	May	239
1756	William		Derby	Sep	239
1763	William		London	Jul	322
1783	William, Hon		Middlesex	Jun	284
1787	William		London	Oct	438
1794	William		York	Jun	296
1794	Wright, Esq		Essex	Aug	403
1800	BATES, Alice		Middlesex	Apr	253
1757	Ann		Buckinghamshire	Aug	241
1782	Anne		Suffolk	Nov	531
1764	Benjamin		Pts	Mar	81
1781	Benjamin	Ser	Pts	Sep	422
1795	Daniel		Middlesex	Jun	368
1796	David	Ser "Fortitude"	Pts	Mar	109
1764	Edward	A with W	Pts	Aug	298
1768	Edward		Middlesex	Sep	339
1786	Edward		Middlesex	Feb	68
1776	Elizabeth		London	Jan	4
1798	Elizabeth		Newcastle/Tyne	Mar	153
1784	George		Suffolk	Feb	62
1762	Gilbert	A with W	Pts	Jun	234
1759	Henry	Ltd A with W or Testa- mentary sched annex'd	Buckinghamshire	May	160
1798	Henry alias BATE	"Laurel" "La Renomme"	Pts	Nov	698
1758	Isaac	A with W	Middlesex	Jul	208
1774	Isable		Newcastle/Tyne	Aug	293
1774	James		Surrey	Jun	218
1792	James		Surrey	Apr	191
1799	Joah, Esq		Middlesex	Jul	474
1751	John		Middlesex	Oct	277
1753	John	A with W	London	Feb	37
1753	John		Pts	May	128
1756	John	A with W	Pts/Southampton	Jan	3
1762	John alias BEAT		Pts	Oct	412
1767	John		Kent	Oct	363
1779	John		Buckinghamshire	Nov	441
1782	John		Pts	Oct	482
1785	John, Esq	Late one of the Aldermen of the City of London	London	May	235
1792	John	"Sirius"	Pts	Jul	365
1795	John, Esq		Berkshire	Aug	495
1799	John, Esq		Buckinghamshire	Feb	95
1800	John		Middlesex	May	345
1753	Joseph		London	Dec	307
1759	Joseph		Essex	Apr	119
1767	Joseph	A with W unad Will regd 367 Searle	London	Oct	

	BATES (Contd)				
1772	Joseph	A with W unad Will regd 307 Searle Last Grant Oct 1767	London	Aug	
1776	Joseph		Pts	Nov	449
1776	Margaret		Middlesex	Mar	111
1788	Margaret alias BAETS		Surrey	May	226
1771	Margery		Middlesex	Sep	366
1763	Martha		Essex	Apr	166
1788	Martha		Buckinghamshire	Jul	338
1751	Mary		Middlesex	May	132
1757	Mary		Middlesex	Jun	180
1763	Mary		Middlesex	Sep	419
1771	Mary		Southampton	Apr	145
1773	Mary		Middlesex	Oct	382
1776	Mary		Somerset	Jul	297
1782	Mary		Middlesex	Feb	61
1789	Mary		Middlesex	Jan	6
1790	Mary		Middlesex	Aug	366
1795	Mary		Middlesex	Aug	494
1798	Mary		Middlesex	Jul	458
1790	Mathew		Kent	Oct	454
1778	Michael		Middlesex	Jun	231
1798	Michael		London	Dec	759
1759	Phillippa Maria		Middlesex	Mar	84
1762	Rachel	A with W	London	Jul	287
1783	Ralph, Esq		Newcastle/Tyne	Sep	446
1750	Richard		London	Nov	348
1760	Richard	A with W	Pts	Aug	314
1788	Richard		Middlesex	Feb	56
1754	Robert		Buckinghamshire	Sep	244
1761	Robert		Warwick	May	158
1798	Sally		Middlesex	Nov	693
1764	Samuel, The Reverend		Wiltshire	Oct	377
1774	Samuel		Middlesex	Jun	215
1794	Sarah		Middlesex	Jan	5
1779	Susannah		Middlesex	Mar	91
1759	Tayler		London	Mar	80
1773	Tayler		Middlesex	Oct	383
1752	Thomas		Middlesex	Sep	227
1759	Thomas		Southampton	Jul	225
1760	Thomas		Pts	Feb	47
1782	Thomas		Middlesex	Jun	265
1790	Thomas		Middlesex	Apr	170
1795	Thomas, The Reverend Dr.Dr in Divinity		Northampton	Feb	66
1797	Thomas alias BATE		Essex	Jan	3
1765	William		Buckinghamshire	Mar	85
1765	William	A with W		Apr	128
1767	William		Middlesex	Jan	3

1768	BATHER, Robert		Salop	Oct	370
1796	Thomas		Salop	Jul	343
1782	BATHGATE, Mary		Middlesex	Nov	528
1788	BATHO, Lucy		Lincolnshire	Apr	174
1775	BATHURST, Allen, Lord		Gloucester	Oct	370
	The Right Honourable Earl				
1785	Barbara		Middlesex	Feb	67
1767	Benjamin, The Honourable		Gloucester	Feb	37
1768	Benjamin, Esq		Northampton	Feb	49
1796	Catherine		Northampton	Oct	490
1767	Charles		Kent	Feb	38
1786	Charles		London	Aug	419
1772	Edward, Esq		Middlesex	Nov	391
1757	Elizabeth		Surrey	Aug	240
1771	Elizabeth, The Right		Middlesex	Nov	430
	Honourable Lady				
1781	Elizabeth	A with W unadm Will regd Oct 1778	Surrey	Jul	
1788	Elizabeth		Herefordshire	May	229
1762	Finnetta		Somerset	Jul	285
1757	George	A with W	Pts	Jan	5
1794	Henry, Lord, The Right				
	Honourable Earl		Middlesex	Sep	446
1766	John		London	Jun	211
1777	John, Hon		Gloucester	Oct	410
1777	Margaret		Middlesex	Aug	343
1779	Margaret		Middlesex	Jul	288
1776	Mary		Kent	Apr	165
1793	Poole, Esq		Gloucester	Feb	67
1752	Ralph, Dr	Ltd A with W of Goods Unad Will regd 125 Ash	Oxford	Feb	
1757	Ralph, Dr Dr of Physic	A with W of Goods unad Will regd 125 Ash. Last Grant Feb. 1752	Oxford	Jun	
1756	Richard	A with W	Lincoln	Aug	216
1765	Robert		Gloucester	Oct	363
1791	Robert, Esq		Southampton	May	209
1777	Selina, Lady		Middlesex	Dec	497
1791	Susannah		Bath	May	214
1778	Thomas	A with W	Middlesex	Jan	6
1792	Thomas, Esq		Gloucester	Feb	56
1771	Walter		London	May	196
1792	BATHWAY, Sarah		Middlesex	Jan	6
1771	BATIE, De La. The Right Honourable Frances de Donop Baroness formerly TURRETTINI		Pts	Oct	402
1759	BATIGUE, Martha		Middlesex	Jun	192
1794	BATLEY, Benjamin, Esq		Surrey	Apr	184
1758	Grace		Hertford	Feb	32
1770	Henry		Middlesex	Sep	319
1782	John, Esq		Middlesex	Sep	441

BATLEY (Contd)

1787	John		Southampton	Feb	52
1798	John		Bedfordshire	Apr	235
1786	Robert		Suffolk	Apr	202
1780	William		Pts	Jun	301
	alias BOTLEY				
1751	BATMAN, Maule		Pts	Aug	230
	alias BATEMAN				
1771	BATON, William		Middlesex	Nov	430
1789	BATTRICK, Robert		Salop	Jun	298
	alias BATTRICH				
	alias BATRICH				
1800	BATSFORD, Edward		Middlesex	Nov	765
1798	Prosper		Southampton	Feb	77
1770	William		Middlesex	Apr	129
1775	BATSON, David	Ser	Devon	May	169
	alias BEATSON				
1763	Emanuel		Middlesex	Aug	371
1780	Henry	Poor	Pts	Aug	386
1780	Henry	Will regd last month	Pts	Sep	427
1774	Lucy		Middlesex	Apr	128
1752	James, Esq		Middlesex	Jan	3
1785	James, Esq		Berkshire	Jul	352
1787	Jane		York	Mar	105
1781	John, Esq		Rutland	May	225
1770	Thomas, Esq		London	Dec	423
	alias DAVIS, Edmund				
1781	William Scott		Pts	Jan	7
1791	BATSTONE, Clement		Surrey	Feb	53
	alias CEELY				
1792	BATT, Alice		Gloucester	Oct	498
1797	Ann		Dorset	Jun	398
1762	Benjamin		Pts	Oct	410
1765	Benjamin		Pts	Apr	130
1785	Catherine		Cumberland	Jun	289
1756	Christopher		Middlesex	Feb	30
1753	Cornelius		Somerset	Jul	194
1754	Daniel		Kent	Jan	3
1774	Deborah		London	Feb	39
1777	Deborah	A with W of Goods unad Will regd Feb 1774	London	May	
1750	Edward		Kent	Nov	346
1800	Edward		Oxford	Jan	4
1771	Elizabeth		Somerset	May	192
1783	Elizabeth		Middlesex	Sep	442
1784	Elizabeth	A with W	Wiltshire	Mar	122
1755	Frances	A with W unad Will regd 71 Seymour	Middlesex	Jan	
1787	Frances	A with W	Middlesex	Jul	312
1785	Francis		Berkshire	Oct	491
1784	Harry	"Monarca"	Pts/Southampton	May	245

	BATT (Contd)				
1799	Henry		Kent	Nov	759
1776	James		Kent	Jan	5
1776	James		Middlesex	Oct	414
1784	John, Esq		Cornwall	Oct	537
1762	John Thomas, Dr	Dr of Physic	Middlesex	Sep	367
1787	John Thomas	Dr of Physic. A with W of Goods unad Will regd 367 St Eloy		Dec	
1779	Margaret La alias LABOR		Middlesex	Mar	114
1758	Mark, Esq		Cornwall	Jul	209
1750	Mary		Middlesex	May	137
1764	Mary		Wiltshire	Sep	338
1772	Mary		Berkshire	Sep	319
1789	Mary		Middlesex	Jun	299
1799	Mary		Kent	Aug	566
1793	Nathaniel		Wiltshire	Jul	354
1761	Peter	Ser	Middlesex	Nov	378
1800	Robert		Middlesex	Jan	10
1750	Samuel		London	Jan	3
1777	Samuel	A with W of Goods unad Will regd 3 Greenly	London	May	
1789	Sarah		Surrey	Jul	346
1770	-RAWDEN, Thomas		Middlesex	Mar	119
1781	Thomas		Gloucester	Dec	577
1785	Thomas	"Eagle" Pts	Middlesex	Apr	173
1786	Thomas	By Int Decree A with W proved Apr 1785 "Eagle"	Middlesex	Feb	67
1763	William		Pts	May	217
1772	William, Esq		Wiltshire	Sep	317
1790	William		Surrey	Mar	118
1793	William, Esq	A with W	Wiltshire	Feb	65
1750	BATTAIL, James alias BATTAILLE		Canterbury	Jun	189
1754	BATTALL, James alias BATTAILE	A with W unad Will regd 190 Greenly	Kent	Feb	32
1785	BATTAILLE, Abraham		Middlesex	Jan	7
1750	David		Middlesex	Jan	3
1750	James alias BATTAIL		Canterbury	Jun	189
1789	BATTAILLE, Magdallin		Middlesex	Dec	576
1783	BATTAMS, Mary		Middlesex	May	217
1799	BATTARS, Elizabeth		Southampton	Feb	95
1789	Isaac	"Ajax","Royal Sovereign"	Southampton	Nov	532
1799	BATTCOCK, Thomas		Middlesex	Oct	701
1778	BATTELEY, Mary alias COX	Ltd Prob	Surrey	Feb	55
1797	BATTELL, Rebecca		Devon	Aug	541
1796	William	"Petterel"	Pts	Oct	486

1756	BATTELY, Ann		Middlesex	Jan	4
1752	Anne		Middlesex	Jul	179
1767	Dorothy		Bristol	May	166
1752	Elizabeth		Middlesex	Jun	148
1772	Elizabeth		Salop	Nov	392
1762	Oliver, Revd		Gloucester	Dec	494
1780	BATTEN, Ann		Berkshire	Jun	303
	alias Anne				
1792	Ann		Middlesex	May	260
1788	Edward		Middlesex	Apr	172
1770	Eleazar		Buckinghamshire	May	172
	alias Eleazer				
1757/	Elizabeth		Kent	Nov	320
1761	Elizabeth		Dorset	Apr	119
1792	Elizabeth		Kent	May	258
1768	George		Pts	Feb	42
1790	Henry		Somerset	Jun	277
1751	James		Pts/Devon	Oct	274
1760	John		Kent	Mar	87
1760	John		Berkshire	Mar	89
1764	John		Essex	Apr	131
1774	John		Berkshire	Dec	422
1783	John		Wiltshire	Apr	162
1788	John		Middlesex	Nov	526
1789	John		London	Jan	4
1791	John	Double Prob Will regd 87 Lynch	Kent	Jun	
1792	John		Kent	Mar	128
1792	John		Cornwall	May	262
1790	Lydia	A with W	London	Mar	116
1795	Mary		Middlesex	Nov	621
1766	Rebecca		Somerset	Oct	362
1755	Richard		Middlesex	Jul	183
1757	Richard		Surrey	Feb	38
1773	Robert		Somerset	Jul	278
1787	Robert		Berkshire	Nov	484
1780	Samuel		Middlesex	Oct	460
1750	Stephen	By Int Decree	Pts	Mar	68
1756	Walter, Esq	Sentence	Essex	Feb	28
1788	William		London	Apr	172
1798	William		Kent	Aug	525
1800	William		Bristol	Jul	505
1782	BATTENHAUS, John Frederick		Middlesex	Dec	570
1761	BATTENS, James		Somerset	Dec	418
1800	BATTERBEE, Zacharias		Middlesex	Dec	839
1752	BATTERILL, Ely		Northampton	Apr	86
1768	BATTERLY, Thomas		Middlesex	Aug	302
1799	BATTERS, John	Ser?"Terrible"	Pts	Feb	97
1758	Samuel		Pts	Mar	62
1759	BATTERSBY, Elizabeth		London	Mar	82

	BATTERSBY (Contd)			
1760	Elizabeth	Somerset	Nov	413
1752	John	Bristol	Jun	149
1776	John	Middlesex	Jan	5
1800	Robert	Middlesex	Jan	8
1782	Thomas	Middlesex	Mar	110
1777	William	Middlesex	Jun	254
1767	BATTERSHILL, John	Middlesex	Apr	123
1783	BATTERSON, Elizabeth	Surrey	Jan	4
1756	John	Pts	Nov	290
	alias BATTESON			
1769	Thomas	Middlesex	Apr	115
1760	William	Buckinghamshire	May	181
1756	BATTESON, John	Pts	Nov	290
	alias BATTERSON			
1750	BATTESTER, John	Pts	Jul	222
1799	BATTESSON, Joseph	Warwick	Sep	640
1780	BATTEUX, Stephen	Middlesex	Jul	346
1785	BATTEY, John	London	May	234
1772	Mary	Middlesex	Jul	248
1780	BATTIE, David Ser	Southampton	Jan	2
	alias BEATTIE			
1765	John	York	Nov	435
	alias WRIGHTSON			
1780	Ralph	Middlesex	Feb	56
1754	Thomas	Pts	Jun	157
1776	William	York	Mar	112
1776	William, Dr Dr of Physick	Middlesex	Jun	257
1776	William, Dr Dr of Physick Double Prob Will regd June last	Middlesex	Oct	
1771	BATTIER, John Jacob	London	Feb	46
1777	Nicholas	Pts	May	198
1777	BATTIN, James Magewick	Southampton	Nov	452
1781	James Magewick, Esq A with W unad Will regd Nov 1777	Hampshire	Feb	
1794	James Magewick, Esq A with W of Goods twice unad Will regd 452 Collier Last Grant Feb 1781	Southampton	Jun	
1763	John	Middlesex	Sep	421
1750	Margaret	London	Dec	376
1781	Mary	Hampshire	Feb	56
1791	Mary A with W of Goods unad Will regd 56 Webster	Southampton	Nov	
1800	Mary	Middlesex	Dec	840
	alias McCONCHY			
1786	Richard	Berkshire	Oct	502
1766	Samuel	Pts/London	Sep	327
1768	William	Middlesex	Apr	140
1770	BATTINE, William, Esq	Sussex	Apr	132
1777	BATTING, Ann	Buckinghamshire	Jun	254

1798	BATTING, Elizabeth		Buckinghamshire	Jul	464
1800	Elizabeth		Buckinghamshire	Jun	442
1774	James		Buckinghamshire	Apr	130
1780	James		Buckinghamshire	May	234
1767	James		Buckinghamshire	Dec	437
1767	Joan	A with W	Devon	May	163
1793	John		Buckinghamshire	Apr	188
1768	Thomas		Buckinghamshire	Feb	42
1787	Thomas		Buckinghamshire	Oct	439
1777	BATTISCOMB, John		Surrey	Apr	144
1789	BATTISCOMBE, Ann		Surrey	Oct	484
1794	Christopher		Somerset	Jun	298
1758	Giles		Dorset	Sep	257
1793	John		Middlesex	Oct	489
1757	Nathaniel		Dorset	Mar	75
1782	Richard		Dorset	Jul	336
1763	BATTISHILL, Jane	A with W	Exeter	Nov	498
1776	BATTISON, William		Middlesex	Aug	345
1777	William		Surrey	Jul	299
1758	BATTISSON, John		Northampton	Oct	287
1788	Loetitia		Bedford	Nov	520
1774	BATTLE, Elizabeth		Middlesex	Oct	360
1800	Henry		Essex	May	340
1774	James		Surrey	Jan	3
1790	James		Middlesex	Jul	320
1785	Mary		Middlesex	Dec	585
1778	Thomas		Pts	Apr	145
1787	BATTON, John	"Queen" & "La Fortune"	Pts	May	198
1789	BATTRICK, Robert		Salop	Jun	298
	alias BATTRICH				
	alias BATRICH				
1760	BATTS, Aaron	A with W	Pts	Feb	49
1785	Mary		Surrey	Nov	540
1780	Peter		Surrey	Mar	121
1779	BATTSON, William		Pts	May	188
1755	BATTURS, Samuel		Surrey	Jul	182
1773	BATTY, Abraham		Middlesex	Aug	318
1752	Alice		Middlesex	Nov	270
1765	Allison		Middlesex	Jan	5
1793	Ann		York	Feb	63
1800	Ann		Suffolk	Nov	769
1758	Edward		Essex	Nov	322
1780	Edward		Middlesex	Feb	56
1800	Elizabeth		Westmorland	Sep	643
1781	Hannah		Middlesex	Sep	418
1762	Henry		Pts	Nov	450
1773	Henry		Pts	Feb	47
1788	Henry		Middlesex	May	229
1769	James		Kent	Apr	114
1750	John		London	Mar	67
1750	John		Pts	Apr	105

	BATTY (Contd				
1756	John		Middlesex	Nov	290
1776	John		London	Feb	54
1788	John		Kent	Nov	520
1790	John	A with W	Worcestershire	Apr	170
1773	Mary	A with W	London	Jul	281
1762	Thomas	A with W	Pts	Nov	447
1781	Thomas, Esq		Lancashire	Mar	116
1784	Thomas	"Burford"	Pts	Jun	311
1785	Thomas		Middlesex	Nov	541
1795	Thomas		Devon	Sep	536
1796	Thomas		Middlesex	Jan	5
1759	William		Middlesex	Jun	194
1794	William		Kent	Jun	298
1796	William		Middlesex	Apr	165
1773	BATTYE, Elizabeth		Surrey	Dec	458
1799	BATTYN, Ann		Bristol	Apr	246
1799	William Dottin, Esq		Bristol	Jan	14
1752	BATUT, John		Middlesex	Nov	269
1757	Mary		Middlesex	Sep	268
1764	BATWELL, Elizabeth alias JERVIS	Ltd A with W	Middlesex	Mar	80
1765	BATYAS, William		Kent	Jul	247
1765	BATYE, John		Surrey	Jun	206
1755	BAUCELS, Louisa DE alias DE LAUGES DE BEAUVEZER		Pts	Dec	305
1782	BAUCHEM, Sir Nicholas Van	Ltd Probate	Pts	Mar	156
1773	BAUDAN, Antoine alias Anthony		Middlesex	Nov	418
1773	Antoine alias Anthony	Double Prob Will regd Last Month	Middlesex	Dec	
1776	Elizabeth Pautard		Pts	Jun	282
1752	BAUDESSOU, Mary	A with W	Middlesex	Jul	180
1752	Mary	A with Will of Goods unad Will regd July last	Middlesex	Sep	
1753	BAUDINEL, Judith	A with W	Jersey	Mar	73
1766	BAUDOUIN, Elizabeth alias BAUDOVIN		Surrey	May	168
1770	Margaret		Middlesex	Mar	89
1766	BAUDOVIN, Elizabeth alias BAUDOUIN		Surrey	May	168
1752	BAUDWIN, Elizabeth		London	Oct	242
1782	BAUER, Christian alias BOWERS		Pts	Apr	163
1762	BAUFRE, Jean Claude	A with W	Middlesex	Dec	494
1750	BAUGE, Henrietta Ann alias COHNAN	A with W By Int Decree	Middlesex	Dec	377
1799	BAUGH, Ann		Surrey	Sep	642
1759	Benjamin		Middlesex	Jul	224

BAUGH (Contd)

Year	Name	Note	County	Month	Page
1765	Benjamin		Salop	May	171
1799	Edmund	Ltd A with W	Worcestershire	Apr	243
1795	Edward, The Reverend		Salop	Jul	431
1764	Elizabeth		Middlesex	Nov	415
1793	Elizabeth		Somerset	Jan	3
1800	Elizabeth		Salop	Jan	4
1787	Isaac, Esq. Late one of the Aldermen of Bristol		Bristol	Jan	7
1757	Lancelot		Middlesex	Oct	293
1775	Lancelot		Southampton	Jun	220
1792	Lancelot, Esq		Middlesex	May	256
1792	Lancelot, Esq	Double Prob. Will regd this month	Middlesex	May	
1800	Mary		Salop	Sep	643
1771	Merien		Middlesex	Nov	429
1774	Theodosia		Middlesex	Sep	330
1762	Samuel		Bristol	Sep	368
1793	Thomas		Salop	May	245
1757	Thomas Folliot, Esq		Salop	May	148
1755	BAUGHAM, Edward	A with W twice unad Will regd 201 Farrant Last Grant Jan. 1747	Hereford	Dec	
1780	Edward		Surrey	May	241
1798	Edward	A with W of Goods unad Will regd 314 Lynch	Middlesex	May	
1795	Thomas		Middlesex	Mar	148
1779	BAUGHAN, George		Bath	Apr	143
1784	Samuel		Kent	Feb	60
1757	William		Middlesex	Feb	40
1792	BAUGHURST, John	Ltd Probate	Southampton	Apr	197
1772	Robert alias BOUGHST		Wiltshire	Oct	351
1767	BAULCOMB, Elizabeth		Essex	Dec	436
1782	BAULDAY, Francis alias BALDIS, Frances		Pts	Mar	109
1788	BAULDRY, Judith Julie		Pts	May	231
1788	Magdalona alias Madeline	A with W	Pts	Sep	426
1782	BAUMASTER, Gurgen		Pts	Aug	395
1782	BAUMGARTEN, John Ernst		Middlesex	Apr	166
1798	Samuel Christian Frederick		Middlesex	Aug	524
1796	BAUNTON, John		Somerset	Dec	591
1784	Mary		Middlesex	Jul	367
1768	BAURIN,		Middlesex	Dec	439
1790	Elizabeth		Middlesex	Sep	412
1761	Ester alias BOURIN	Will regd in June last	Middlesex	Jul	
1782	BAURINE, Ann		Middlesex	Jan	2

Year	Name	Notes	County	Month	Page
1752	BAUSLEBEN, Erhard		Middlesex	Jan	3
1762	BAUTS, Andris		Pts	Oct	411
	alias BARNES, Andrew				
1771	BAUYER, Sarah		Middlesex	May	192
1762	BAVAND, Jane		Middlesex	Apr	139
1777	John		Middlesex	Jun	254
1759	BAVEL, Cornelia VAN		Pts	Jan	37
	alias SNOECK				
	alias ROOS				
	alias SWEERTS				
1797	BAVELAAR, Cornelia	Ltd Probate	Pts	Jul	471
1769	Maria	Ltd Probate	Pts	Feb	35
1759	BAVEN, Martha		Middlesex	Jan	6
1762	BAVENT, Peter		Middlesex	Jun	235
1799	BAVERSTOCK, Isabella		Middlesex	May	335
1761	John		Essex	Apr	116
1768	John		Southampton	Jun	229
1798	William		Hertford	May	312
1771	BAVIN, Ann		Middlesex	Sep	366
1797	Elizabeth		Kent	May	296
1791	Thomas		Middlesex	Oct	453
1768	William		Essex	Oct	368
1751	BAVINK, Gerrit		Pts	Aug	228
1795	BAVOIS, DE, The Most	Ltd A with W	Pts	Sep	
	Illustr Lady Mary				
	Cormarque, Baroness				
1752	BAVWENS, Mary		Middlesex	May	116
	alias BAUWENS, Lady				
	Mary				
1750	BAWCOCK, Mary		Surrey	Oct	316
1777	BAWCOMB, Elizabeth		Surrey	Dec	495
1785	Richard		Surrey	Oct	497
1769	Thomas		Middlesex	Sep	301
1784	BAWDAN, Pearce	"St. Vincent"&"St.	Pts	Jun	311
	alias BOARDEN, Pierce	Eustatius"			
1777	BAWDEN, Ann		Devon	Nov	447
1785	Henry, Esq		Cornwall	Jun	294
1752	John		Pts	Jan	2
1798	John		Cornwall	Dec	759
1755	Jonathan	A with W	Pts	Jan	3
1788	Jonathan		Surrey		574
1788	Joshua, The Reverend		Devon	Jul	338
1769	Margaret		Surrey	Mar	79
1770	Margaret		Middlesex	Jun	222
1770	Margaret	Double Prob	Surrey	Aug	
		Will regd March 1769			
1767	Mary		Middlesex	Sep	332
1789	Mary Anne		Cornwall	Jul	345
1762	Richard		Devon	Mar	91
	alias BOWDEN				
1781	Richard, The Reverend		Devon	Sep	419

BAWDEN (Contd)

1795	Thomas	Ser.	Devon	Nov	622
1787	William		Bristol	Sep	396
1783	BAWDWEN, Thomas		Middlesex	Jan	4
1798	BAWN, William		Gloucestershire	Jul	461
1779	BAWNE, Mary		Essex	Nov	444
1782	BAWTREE, Elizabeth		Middlesex	Jun	264
1791	Grace		Essex	Jun	269
1782	Jane		Essex	Jul	340
1770	Thomas		Middlesex	Sep	322
1782	Sarah		Essex	Jan	2
1776	BAX, Ann	By Int Decree Ltd A with W and first codicil and copy of second codicil annexed of goods unad. Will and first codicil regd 88 Rushworth. Copy of second codicil regd in this month	Kent	Apr	162
1759	Anthony		Pts	Nov	348
1753	John	Pts	London	Jul	197
1796	Mary		Surrey	Jul	344
1755	Philip		Surrey	Sep	235
1790	Puryour		Kent	Jun	278
1782	Sarah		Kent	Jul	338
1759	Stephen		Kent	Jul	225
1770	Stephen		Kent	Apr	129
1792	William		Kent	Oct	496
1754	BAXCAMP, VAN, Joan	Ltd Probate	Pts	Oct	287
1754	BAXLEY, Alice		Middlesex	Apr	99
1794	BAXTER, Alexander, Esq		Southampton	Dec	599
1800	Alexander	"Sceptre"	Middlesex	May	343
1750	Anthony Thomas		Middlesex	May	138
1780	Barnaby		Middlesex	Oct	460
1770	Benjamin		Middlesex	May	177
1799	Charles		Oxford	Aug	569
1752	Daniel		Middlesex	Mar	57
1766	Dudley, Esq		Middlesex	Dec	443
1762	Edmund, Dr	Dr in Divinity	Chester	Dec	495
1755	Edward		Middlesex	Nov	276
1769	Edward		Middlesex	Feb	34
1780	Edward		Salop	Oct	459
1784	Edward	"Burford" "York"	Pts	Sep	492
1758	Elizabeth		Middlesex	Aug	237
1769	Elizabeth		Essex	Mar	77
1781	Elizabeth		Surrey	Jun	287
1791	Elizabeth		Montgomery	May	210
1756	Felix		London	Jan	4
1756	Francis	Ser	Surrey	May	129
1768	Francis		Surrey	Jun	221
1778	Francis, Esq	Ltd Probate	London	Nov	431
1795	Galpine		Hertford	Jul	433

	BAXTER (Contd)				
1760	George		Pts	May	182
	alias BAGSTER				
1777	George		Gloucester	Sep	377
1755	Grace		Middlesex	May	123
1761	James		Kent	Sep	309
1776	James		Middlesex	Mar	163
1786	James	No Ship	Pts	Jan	7
1788	James		Surrey	Nov	522
1797	James		Warwickshire	Oct	625
1767	Jane		London	Nov	404
1753	Joanna		Southampton	Oct	262
1752	John		Pts	Feb	30
1758	John		Pts	Jan	5
1758	John		Pts/Middlesex	May	143
1763	John		Sussex	Aug	368
1766	John		York	Jul	258
1766	John		Middlesex	Nov	399
1769	John		Kent	Apr	112
1770	John	A with W unad	Kent	Jul	
		Will regd April 1769			
1776	John		Surrey	Dec	490
1781	John		Pts	Oct	462
1782	John		Canterbury	May	216
1784	John	"Stork""Mentor""L'Aigle""Warwick" Pts		Jun	306
1784	John	"Raisonable"	Pts	Oct	541
1789	John, Esq		Montgomery	Dec	576
1798	John		Lincoln	Dec	757
1763	Margaret		Chester	Mar	108
1777	Margaret		London	Mar	95
1770	Mary		Middlesex	Jan	7
1775	Mary		Hertford	Apr	130
1783	Mary		Middlesex	Dec	597
1772	Michael		Warwick	Feb	37
1797	Michael, The Reverend		Staffordshire	May	293
1777	Patrick		London	Apr	144
1763	Penelope	A with W	Northampton	Jul	322
1764	Rebecca		Essex	Sep	339
1764	Richard		Surrey	Jun	211
1781	Robert	Ser	Middlesex	Apr	180
1783	Robert	Ser: A with W	Pts	Dec	599
		Barfleur			
1790	Robert, Esq		London	Jan	2
1766	Samuel		Pts	Sep	328
1798	Samuel		Kent	Mar	159
1771	Sarah		Bath	Apr	145
1772	Sarah		Middlesex	Mar	86
1777	Sarah		London	Aug	342
1781	Sarah		Lincolnshire	Sep	419
1754	Thomas		London	Mar	69
1755	Thomas	A with W	Middlesex	Oct	255

Year	Name	Note	Place	Month	No.
	BAXTER (Contd)				
1761	Thomas		Pts	Apr	121
1761	Thomas		Surrey	Dec	422
1764	Thomas		Pts	Oct	377
1766	Thomas		Derby	Jul	257
1774	Thomas	A with W	Middlesex	Jul	258
1782	Thomas	A with W	London	Mar	110
1784	Thomas		Surrey	Mar	120
	alias BACKSTER				
1753	William		Essex	Jul	195
1757	William		Middlesex	Jan	4
1761	William		Hertford	Oct	338
1765	William		Pts	Dec	442
1768	William, Esq		Kent	Oct	371
1769	William, Esq	A with W unad	Kent	Jul	
		Will regd Oct 1768			
1771	William	A with W unad	Essex	Jul	
		Will regd 195 Searle			
1779	William	Pts	Southampton	Jul	285
1782	William	A with W	Pts	Apr	164
1786	William		Middlesex	Jun	322
1786	William	A with W	Surrey	Aug	420
1797	William		Sussex	Mar	128
1776	BAXTOR, Richard		Kent	Apr	164
1760	BAY, John		Berkshire	Jun	230
1773	Thomas		Middlesex	May	195
1764	William		Middlesex	Jun	213
1781	BAYCOCK, William		Essex	Jul	330
1799	BAYDEN, Sarah		Kent	Jun	419
1792	Thomas		Kent	Oct	498
1779	BAYER, Edward Otto, Esq		Pts	Aug	334
1768	Isabella Otto		Middlesex	Jul	268
	alias BAJIER				
1762	Otto Rowland, Esq		Middlesex	Oct	411
1762	BAYES, Daniel		Leicester	Apr	138
1765	Elizabeth		Leicester	Feb	46
1765	James		Middlesex	Oct	361
1780	Mary		Middlesex	Feb	57
1780	Mary		Northampton	Apr	173
1764	Nathaniel		London	Dec	454
1779	Richard		Middlesex	Jan	2
1789	Samuel, Esq	A with W	Surrey	Oct	485
1761	Thomas		Kent	May	158
1791	Thomas		Warwick	Jul	315
1800	BAYFIELD, Mary		Norfolk	Mar	179
1790	BAYFORD, David, Dr	Dr of Physic	Middlesex	Sep	410
1761	Elizabeth		Essex	Sep	308
1751	Sarah		Surrey	Sep	253
1751	BAYGNEW, James		London	Feb	36
	alias BAIGNOUX,				
	Lawrence James				

1763	BAYKEE, Charles		Pts	Aug	371
	aliais BAIKIE				
1794	BAYLAY, Richard, Esq		Devon	Sep	447
1751	BAYLES, Henry	A with W of Goods unad	Surrey	Jul	
		Will regd 204 Isham			
1778	John		London	Feb	50
1771	John Husken		Kent	Dec	470
	alias Huskins				
1760	Lucy		Middlesex	Jun	227
1769	Martin		London	Jul	236
1750	Mary		Middlesex	Feb	38
1783	Mary Huskins	A with W	Kent	Jul	335
	alias BRANEN				
1767	Sarah		Middlesex	May	165
1770	Sarah		Middlesex	Mar	89
1787	Teresa		Middlesex	Apr	155
1775	Thomas		Essex	Sep	335
1775	Thomas		Surrey	Dec	455
1787	Thomas		Essex	Oct	439
1753	Thomas Trinder		Pts/London	May	130
1790	William Dennis		Pts	Jan	2
1778	BAYLESS, Joseph		Middlesex	Jun	232
1764	BAYLEY, Alexander		Pts	Mar	80
1766	Alexander	By Int Decree	Pts	Jan	4
	alias BAILEY				
1755	Ann		Essex	Oct	253
1763	Ann .		Middlesex	Jul	322
1781	Ann		Buckinghamshire	Feb	58
1793	Ann		Middlesex	Feb	69
1798	Ann		Surrey	Jun	380
1775	Anna		Suffolk	Jun	224
1755	Anthony		Middlesex	Aug	210
1765	Amy		Hertfordshire	Nov	400
1796	Arthur		Middlesex	Jul	345
1754	Benjamin		Kent	Oct	267
1779	Charles		Pts	Oct	405
1780	Christopher		Middlesex	Jan	4
1761	Daniel		Pts	Jun	200
1765	Daniel		Lancaster	Apr	130
1774	Daniel, Esq		Cambridge	May	171
1795	Daniel		London	Dec	671
1799	Daniel		Middlesex	Jun	419
1769	Deborah		Buckinghamshire	Nov	364
1755	Edward		Kent	Jun	155
1763	Edward		Pts/Middlesex	May	213
1777	Edward		Essex	Oct	408
	alias BAILEY				
1750	Elizabeth		Essex	Feb	38
1750	Elizabeth		Surrey	Jun	186
1767	Elizabeth		Middlesex	Oct	362
	alias BAILEY				

BAYLEY (Contd)

1769	Elizabeth		Nottingham	Apr	114
1769	Elizabeth		Middlesex	Apr	115
	alias BAYLY				
1780	Elizabeth		Kent	Dec	554
	alias BAILEY				
1783	Elizabeth		Middlesex	Nov	550
1786	Elizabeth		Surrey	Oct	501
1788	Elizabeth		London	Jul	339
1795	Elizabeth		London	Nov	623
1796	Elizabeth		Middlesex	Dec	594
1760	Esther		Huntingdon	Feb	49
1768	Frances		Rutland	Jun	230
1781	Frances		Derby	Oct	463
1785	Francis		Middlesex	Feb	67
1785	Francis		Essex	Sep	456
1764	George	A with W	London	Feb	37
1771	George		London	May	193
1766	Giles		London	Jan	2
1751	Henry	By Int Decree	Pts	Jul	199
1753	Henry		Hertfordshire	Apr	101
1762	Henry		Cornwall	May	183
1769	Henry		London	Dec	403
1773	Henry		Middlesex	Jan	4
1782	Henry		Pts/Essex	Jul	377
	alias RUSE				
1751	Isaac		Huntingdon	Dec	327
1786	Isaac		Leicester	Nov	557
1765	James, Esq		Chester	Jan	3
1765	James		Pts	Jun	208
1773	James		Warwickshire	Jun	236
1782	James	Double Prob Will regd 236 Stevens	Warwickshire	Dec	
1785	James		Worcestershire	Dec	588
1795	James		London	Feb	62
1782	Jane		Essex	Jun	265
1785	Jane		Middlesex	Sep	454
1800	Jane		Middlesex	Jun	441
1779	Jeremiah		Hertford	Feb	42
1755	John	By Decree	London	Mar	68
1756	John	By Int Decree	Middlesex	May	129
1757	John		Surrey	Jan	3
1770	John		Middlesex	May	175
1780	John	A with W	Salop	Apr	174
1780	John		London	May	238
1783	John	Ser. "Defiance," "Romilies," "Providence" and "Monarch"	Pts	Jul	324
	alias BAILEY				
	alias BAILIFF				
1784	John		Hertford	Jan	3
1784	John		Middlesex	Nov	586
1785	John		Chester	Oct	493

BAYLEY (Contd)

1787	John		York	Jun	251
1790	John		Huntingdon	Dec	536
1791	John		Middlesex	Mar	115
1793	John		Warwickshire	May	126
1794	John		Montgomery	Apr	186
1796	John		Surrey	Apr	165
1800	John		Surrey	Nov	765
1754	Joseph		Surrey	Mar	69
1769	Joseph		Essex	Jul	234
1774	Magdalen		Middlesex	Dec	420
1756	Martha		Surrey	Sep	238
1769	Martha		Kent	Apr	114
1778	Martha		Essex	Feb	47
1797	Martha		Surrey	Jun	395
1750	Mary		Kent	Oct	315
1759	Mary	A with W	Middlesex	Jan	7
1759	Mary	Will regd January last	Middlesex	Aug	
1762	Mary		Middlesex	Jul	285
1774	Mary		Middlesex	Oct	360
1786	Mary		London	Oct	504
1786	Mary		Essex	Oct	506
1788	Mary	A with W of Goods unad Will regd Oct 1786	London	Dec	
1762	Matthew		Northampton	Jun	232
1775	Matthew		Surrey	Dec	460
1753	Minton alias BAYLY alias BAILEY		Middlesex	Apr	102
1785	Phebe alias Phoebe		Stafford	Aug	402
1789	Rachel		London	Feb	74
1754	Richard		London	Jun	160
1758	Richard	Ser	Middlesex	May	142
1764	Richard		Essex	Mar	82
1764	Richard		Middlesex	Nov	415
1766	Richard		Warwickshire	Apr	126
1766	Richard		Berkshire	May	172
1771	Richard		Norfolk	Feb	49
1777	Richard		Middlesex	Mar	94
1780	Richard		Pts/Middlesex	Jan	5
1798	Richard		Kent	Aug	526
1754	Robert		Kent	Jan	2
1757	Robert		London	Dec	349
1780	Robert		Middlesex	Feb	58
1751	Roger		Middlesex	Sep	252
1752	Samuel		Wiltshire	Sep	227
1759	Samuel		Middlesex	Feb	47
1760	Samuel		Middlesex	Apr	135
1772	Samuel alias BELEY alias BELLEY		Pts	Oct	352

	BAYLEY (Contd)				
1799	Samuel	A with W	Surrey	Jul	478
1751	Sarah		Middlesex	Feb	38
	alias BAILEY				
1754	Sarah		Middlesex	Apr	100
1766	Sarah		Yorkshire	Apr	126
1771	Sarah		Middlesex	Feb	49
1771	Sarah	A with W	Surrey	Nov	430
1773	Sarah		Buckinghamshire	Nov	415
1793	Sarah		Hertfordshire	Jun	297
1769	Susanna		Essex	May	150
1760	Susannah		Middlesex	Nov	413
1755	Thomas		Middlesex	Aug	211
1761	Thomas		Middlesex	Jun	203
1762	Thomas		Buckinghamshire	Feb	42
1762	Thomas		Middlesex	Apr	139
1772	Thomas		Surrey	Nov	393
1773	Thomas		Cambridge	Dec	459
1775	Thomas		London	Mar	86
1777	Thomas		Essex	May	199
1778	Thomas		Surrey	Apr	143
1785	Thomas		Essex	Apr	171
1787	Thomas		Buckinghamshire	May	198
1791	Thomas		Middlesex	May	214
1799	Thomas		Pts	Oct	695
1764	Weston, Esq		Salop	Nov	417
1751	William		Pts	Nov	301
	alias BAILLIE				
1752	William		Nottingham	Jan	2
1775	William	A with W	Pts	May	174
1769	William		Essex	Apr	114
1777	William		Surrey	Apr	147
1786	Willaim		Middlesex	Apr	204
1787	William, Esq		Worcestershire	Jun	253
1793	William		Hertfordshire	Nov	540
1798	William		London	Apr	232
1798	William		Middlesex	Aug	527
1799	William		Surrey	Jul	478
1785	BAYLIE, Eleanor		Middlesex	Oct	496
1770	Martin, The Reverend		Suffolk	Nov	390
1771	William		Surrey	Oct	396
1765	BAYLIES, Jacob	By Sen. A with W	Worcester	Jan	3
1795	Martha		Stafford	Dec	671
1765	Mary		Middlesex	May	172
1760	William		Worcester	Apr	138
1787	William, Dr	Dr of physic	Pts	Sep	399
1770	BAYLIFF, Ann		Hertford	Oct	353
1751	Daniel	A with W	Hertford	Feb	37
1770	Elizabeth		Kent	Dec	421
1750	Featherston		Pts	Sep	285

	BAYLIFF (Contd)				
1777	Hannah		Westmorland	Jul	297
	alias BAILLIE				
	alias BAILIE				
1778	William		Middlesex	Aug	311
1758	BAYLIFFE, Charles	A with W unad	Wiltshire	Feb	
		Will regd 221 Druce			
1760	Mary		Wiltshire	Aug	314
1756	Susanna		Middlesex	Jan	2
1755	BAYLIS, Amelia		London	Aug	210
1786	Ann		Gloucestershire	Dec	601
1777	Benjamin		Gloucestershire	Jul	301
1796	Charles		Surrey	Jan	5
1767	Edward		Oxford	Jun	207
1775	Edward, Esq		Gloucestershire	Oct	369
1760	Eleanor		Worcestershire	Mar	88
1754	Elizabeth	A with W	Gloucestershire	Sep	245
1792	Elizabeth		Hereford	Feb	59
1798	Elizabeth	A with W	Gloucestershire	May	315
1799	Elizabeth	A with W of Goods unad	Hereford	Sep	
		Will regd Feb 1792			
1790	George		Gloucestershire & Berkshire	Feb	64
1799	George		Berkshire	Jan	11
1799	Henry		Worcestershire	Apr	243
1759	John		Worcestershire	Mar	83
1769	John		Worcestershire	May	151
1777	John		Worcestershire	Feb	55
1784	John		Gloucestershire	Nov	585
1788	John		Worcestershire	Jan	5
	alias BAYLISS				
1798	John		Gloucestershire	May	311
1799	John		Devon	Nov	759
1777	Joseph, The Reverend		Wiltshire	Mar	95
1778	Joseph		Middlesex	Jun	233
1786	Joseph		Hereford	May	263
1799	Joseph		Worcestershire	Feb	95
1782	Mary		Gloucestershire	Nov	529
1788	Mary		Worcestershire	Aug	386
1768	Randall		Middlesex	Jun	230
1766	Rebecca		Worcestershire	May	171
1799	Robert	A with W "L'Aigle"&"Mercury"	Pts	Jun	416
1780	Samuel		Gloucestershire	Jan	4
1763	Stephen		Middlesex	May	212
1754	Thomas		Gloucester	Apr	100
1798	Thomas		Warwickshire	May	311
1799	Thomas		Gloucestershire	Nov	763
1761	William		Worcestershire	May	162
1765	William		London	Dec	439
1781	William		Surrey	Apr	180

BAYLIS (Contd)

Year	Name		Place	Month	Page
1795	William		Hereford	Feb	67
1800	William		Worcestershire	May	342
1777	BAYLISS, Catherine		London	May	198
1779	Elizabeth		Hereford	Jun	232
1787	John		Surrey	Aug	358
1788	John		Worcestershire	Jan	5
	alias BAYLIS				
1787	Richard		Gloucestershire	Dec	529
	alias BAILISS				
1781	William		Worcestershire	Oct	466
1789	William		Middlesex	Oct	483
1756	BAYLLE, Paul	A with W	Pts/ Southampton	Feb	31
1753	BAYLY, Abel		Middlesex	Oct	263
1751	Abraham		Kent	Jun	165
1752	Ann		Bristol	Jun	147
1766	Ann		Surrey	Apr	126
1776	Ann		London	Oct	413
1764	Anne		Middlesex	Oct	379
1800	Anne		Gloucestershire	Jun	432
1782	Anselm Yates, Esq	A with W	Berkshire	Nov	530
1774	Anthony		Kent	Jul	257
1757	Bridget		Derby	Feb	38
1788	Caroline		Middlesex	Jun	290
1776	Charles		Kent	Apr	164
1768	Lady Dorothy	A with W	Ireland	Nov	400
1781	Edmund		Wiltshire	Mar	112
1786	Edward		Wiltshire	Dec	598
1792	Edward	A with W	Kent	Feb	58
1797	Edward, Esq		Gloucestershire	Jun	402
1800	Edward, Esq		Dorset	May	340
1756	Elizabeth		London	May	130
1763	Elizabeth		Middlesex	Feb	45
1769	Elizabeth		Middlesex	Apr	115
	alias BAYLEY				
1795	Elizabeth		Poole	Mar	139
1750	Frances		Oxford	Feb	38
1752	Francis		Lichfield	Feb	28
1796	Francis	A with W		Feb	58
1772	George, Dr	Dr of Physic	Chichester	Feb	36
1775	George	A with W	Dorset	Jul	262
1783	George		Surrey	Mar	112
1790	George		Dorset	Apr	163
1756	Hannah		Surrey	Mar	59
1762	Herbert		Middlesex	Nov	448
1753	James		Middlesex	Oct	262
1763	James		Middlesex	Jan	8
1764	James	A with W	Ireland	Jul	252
1773	James		Wiltshire	Feb	44
1774	Jane		Hertford	Mar	82

BAYLY (Contd)

Year	Name	Notes	Place	Month	Page
1775	Jennet		Middlesex	Nov	406
1758	John		Suffolk	Feb	32
1761	John		Surrey	Mar	84
1762	John		Bristol	Nov	446
1765	John		Wiltshire	Feb	42
1777	John		Wiltshire	Jul	303
1794	John		Kent	May	241
1790	John		Kent	Dec	537
1781	Joseph		Devon	Dec	576
1794	Joseph, The Reverend		Sussex	Apr	182
1758	Mary		Middlesex	May	140
1765	Mary		Oxford	Nov	400
1765	Mary		Middlesex	Dec	441
1769	Mary		Wiltshire	Dec	406
1778	Mary		Wiltshire	Oct	389
1787	Mary		Surrey	Aug	354
1777	Michael		Kent	Apr	147
1753	Minton alias BAYLEY alias BAILEY		Middlesex	Apr	102
1799	Nathaniel, Esq	No Ship	Pts	Jan	14
1783	Nicholas, Sir	Baronet	Anglesey	Jan	3
1766	Ralph		Oxford	Jul	260
1792	Ralph		Hertford	May	260
1763	Richard alias BAILEY		Middlesex	Oct	458
1768	Richard, Esq	A with W	Ireland	Nov	403
1795	Richard		Kent	May	296
1795	Richard, Esq	A with W	Gloucestershire	Jul	429
1760	Robert alias BAILEY		Pts	Nov	416
1778	Robert		Poole	Apr	142
1782	Robert		Pts	Oct	479
1778	Samuel		Middlesex	Feb	47
1761	Sarah		Wiltshire	Dec	418
1765	Sarah		Bristol	Nov	398
1768	Sarah		Somerset	Apr	140
1773	Sarah		Chichester	Dec	456
1777	Stephen		Monmouth	May	201
1754	Thomas	By Int Decree	Middlesex	Oct	265
1768	Thomas	A with W of Goods unad Will regd 317 Seymour	Surrey	Mar	
1785	Thomas		Norwich	Feb	66
1788	Thomas		Gloucestershire	Sep	427
1756	Vines		Middlesex	Oct	268
1768	William		Kent	May	188
1772	William		Wiltshire	Dec	434
1796	William		Leicester	Apr	166
1771	Zachary, Esq		Pts	Jun	241
1764	BAYNARD, Bisson		Middlesex	Dec	456

	BAYNARD (Contd)				
1797	Elizabeth		Kent	Nov	675
1764	Lydia		Kent	Apr	130
1792	John, Esq		Kent	Jul	364
1754	Mary		Dorset	Sep	244
	alias BAINARD				
1782	BAYNBRIDGE, Christopher		Middlesex	Dec	575
1762	Elizabeth		London	Oct	410
1775	Mary		London	Dec	457
1768	BAYNE, Alexander		Pts	Dec	369
1769	Daniel		Middlesex	Sep	301
1788	Daniel		London	Feb	57
1796	Donald	Pts	Devon	Nov	542
1784	Elenor		Middlesex	May	249
1767	Elizabeth		Middlesex	Mar	83
1797	George, Esq		Devon	May	294
1795	John, Esq	Ltd Probate	Middlesex	Nov	621
1771	Murdow		London	Jul	286
1799	Rachel		Middlesex	Oct	696
1768	Richard, Esq		York	Feb	47
1782	William	A with W "Canada"	Pts	Mar	109
	alias BAIN				
1797	William		Kent	May	293
1799	BAYNES, Ann		Southampton	May	338
1783	Anne		Sussex	May	214
1784	Anne	A with W	Gloucestershire	Jun	305
1789	Arthur, Esq		Southampton	Aug	418
1759	Edward		Pts	May	156
1756	Hellen		Middlesex	Nov	289
1758	Jane		Oxford	May	141
1766	John		Surrey	Feb	47
1770	John		Pts	Sep	321
1788	John		Middlesex	Jul	339
1793	John		London	May	244
1787	Joseph	A with W	Surrey	Jun	255
1771	Mary	A with W	Kent	Apr	143
1772	Mary	A with W unad	Kent	Feb	
		Will regd April 1771			
1780	Mary		Middlesex	Nov	506
1793	Mary		Gloucester	Apr	188
1783	Michael, The Reverend	A with W	Oxford	Jun	281
1774	Penelope		Middlesex	Mar	82
1779	Richard		Middlesex	Nov	441
1783	Robert, The Reverend		Suffolk	Oct	498
1789	Robert		Cumberland	Dec	575
1767	Samuel		Middlesex	Feb	37
1791	Susannah		Essex	Aug	371
1766	Thomas		Middlesex	Nov	399
1778	Thomas		Kent	Jul	272
1775	Walter, Esq		Bath	Nov	404
1765	William		Middlesex	Dec	441

	BAYNES (Contd)				
1769	William, The Reverend		Sussex	Apr	112
1778	William, The Reverend		Middlesex	Mar	95
1798	William, Esq		Middlesex	Dec	760
1786	BAYNHAM, Alice		Hereford	Apr	206
1795	Ann	A with W	Middlesex	Mar	143
1797	Emer		London	Apr	226
1778	Ffrancis		Surrey	Jul	276
1773	John		Middlesex	Apr	148
1779	John		Surrey	Feb	40
1788	Lucy	A with W	Worcestershire	Apr	178
1795	Martha		Surrey	Dec	671
1780	Mary		Middlesex	Apr	173
1755	Richard		Middlesex	Mar	65
1756	Richard Rowdon		Kent	Mar	61
1792	Samuel		Middlesex	Nov	543
1773	Sophia	A with W	Middlesex	Apr	144
1771	Thomas		Middlesex	Jan	6
1782	Thomas	A with W	Middlesex	Jul	339
1790	Thomas	A with W of Goods unad Will regd 6 Trevor	Middlesex	Jun	
1799	Thomas	A with W of Goods twice unad Will regd 6 Trevor Last Grant June 1790	Middlesex	Aug	
1754	BAYNTON, Lucy		Nottingham	Feb	33
1762	Mary		Warwick	Jun	237
1792	Richard		Middlesex	Sep	460
1797	Stephen		Middlesex	Sep	585
1753	William		Warwick	Feb	39
1775	William		Gloucester	May	171
1800	BAYNTUN ROLT, Sir Edward	Baronet	Wiltshire	Mar	174
1773	BAYNTUN, Stucley, Esq	By Sent (regd Feb 500)	Oxford	Mar	93
1785	William, Esq		Middlesex	Feb	64
1758	BAYS, Peter		Pts	Oct	283
1792	BAYSTER, John		York	Jun	318
1772	BAYTOP, James		Pts	Aug	284
1762	Thomas		Kent	Jun	237
1752	BAYZAN, John		Gloucester	Dec	293
1780	BAYZAND, Ann		Middlesex	Nov	505
1790	Charles		Gloucester	Apr	172
1760	Hannah		Middlesex	Feb	49
1759	John		Gloucester	Jan	4
1759	John	Codicil Will regd this month	Gloucester	Jan	4
1799	John		Middlesex	May	369
1769	Joseph		London	Jan	2
1786	Richard		Gloucester	Aug	419
1787	Robert		Middlesex	Sep	398
1785	William		London	Mar	113

Year	Name	Notes	Place	Month	No.
1750	BAZELEE, William alias BASELEE alias BEEZLEY	Pts	Kent	Feb	40
1759	BAZELY, Joseph		Pts	Jan	5
1769	BAZEN, Mary		London	Jan	4
1787	BAZIL, Susanna Louisa		London	Mar	107
1752	BAZIN, Anne Antoinette alias BOSE DE LA CALMETTE		P ts	Dec	292
1790	James Charles		Pts	Feb	62
1776	John Isaac		London	Jul	303
1764	Thomas		Middlesex	Dec	457
1794	BAZING, Thomas	A with W	Surrey	Jan	6
1799	Thomas	A with W of Goods unad Will regd Jan 1794	Surrey	Jul	
1781	BAZIRE, John		London	Aug	376
1774	Josiah		London	Oct	360
1800	Mary		Suffolk	Nor	766
1788	BAZLEY, James		Bristol	Jul	340
1781	John Griffiths alias BEASLEY	Ser	Pts	Jun	287
1754	Samuel alias BARDSLEY	Will regd Dec last	London	Jan	
1770	Thomas		Middlesex	Jul	254
1766	BAZWIN, Benjamin		Middlesex	Jul	260
1772	BEACH, Dorothy		Somerset	Apr	123
1767	Elias		London	Aug	297
1771	Elizabeth		London	Aug	329
1785	Elizabeth		Bath	Dec	585
1798	Elizabeth		Devon	Apr	233
1794	Henrietta Maria		Surrey	Apr	183
1760	Henry		London	Jan	3
1770	Martha alias BEECH		Middlesex	Jan	3
1776	Mary		Dorset	Sep	380
1795	Mary Hannar		Middlesex	Jan	8
1752	James		Devon	Jul	179
1756	James		Pts/Kent	Sep	237
1765	Joan		Somerset	Aug	285
1756	John		London	Nov	288
1775	John		Southampton	Feb	41
1796	John, Esq		Middlesex	Oct	486
1797	John	Double Prob Will regd Oct last	Middlesex	Mar	
1794	Joseph		Kent	Jan	3
1781	Richard, Esq		Devon	Sep	418
1783	Richard		Berkshire	May	218
1790	Richard		Berkshire	Aug	364
1799	Richard	65th Reg	Pts	Jan	7
1771	Robert		Middlesex	Mar	95
1787	Sophia		Somerset	Sep	397

	BEACH (Contd)				
1753	Thomas, Esq		Wiltshire	Mar	71
1788	Thomas, Esq		London	Jul	337
1795	Thomas		Wiltshire	Jun	364
1759	William		Kent	Mar	83
1788	William, Esq	Ltd Probate. No Ship	Pts	Mar	117
1790	William, Esq		Wiltshire	Jun	279
1798	BEACHAM, Eleanor		Somerset	Jun	379
1782	Elizabeth		Middlesex	Feb	61
1777	Francis	Will regd Jan last	Middlesex	Mar	
	alias BEAUCHAMP				
1759	James		Middlesex	Dec	385
1769	John		Surrey	Jan	2
1800	John		Surrey	Feb	82
1763	Joseph		Middlesex	Jun	265
	alias BETCHAM				
1798	Richard		Middlesex	Dec	761
1760	Samuel		Somerset	Mar	91
1767	Thomas		Middlesex	Mar	84
1767	BEACHCROFT, Elizabeth		Essex	Jun	209
1759	Matthew, Esq		Essex	Aug	256
1758	Joseph, Esq		Middlesex	Jan	2
1784	Joseph Matthews		London	Aug	428
1767	Nathaniel		Essex	Feb	35
1776	Robert, The Reverend		Essex	Jan	4
1781	Robert Porter		London	Jul	332
1774	Samuel		Middlesex	Mar	79
1796	Samuel, Esq		London	May	237
1757	BEACHFEILD, Susanna		Middlesex	Sep	268
1778	BEACRAFT, William		Kent	Aug	311
1752	BEADELL, James		Pts	Dec	292
1782	BEADER, John		London	Oct	482
1763	BEADLE, Ann		London	Feb	45
1796	Daniel		Essex	Apr	166
1796	Daniel	Double Prob	Middlesex	Apr	166
		Will regd this month			
1754	James		Middlesex	Apr	99
1762	James		Kent	Oct	410
1751	John		Kent	Dec	326
1766	John		Sussex	May	172
1761	Mary		Middlesex	Nov	282
1790	Mary		Surrey	Dec	541
1760	Stephen		Hertfordshire	Dec	452
1799	Stephen		Hertfordshire	Jan	11
1755	Susanna		Essex	Jul	182
1791	Thomas		Essex	Sep	417
1800	Thomas	"Thunderer"	Pts	Sep	648
1791	William		Hertford	Aug	373
1782	BEADLEN, George		Pts	Jul	334
1761	John	Ser	Southampton	Sep	308
	alias BEDLAND				

1799	BEADMAN, John		Surrey	Apr	245
1764	BEADMEAD, John		Pts	Feb	37
1777	BEADON, Christopher		Somerset	Nov	454
1782	Edward, The Reverend		Devon	Dec	571
1769	Elizabeth		Middlesex	Apr	115
1778	George	A with W	Somerset	Jan	3
1764	Richard, Esq		Somerset	Jun	212
1762	BEADS, James		Pts	Feb	40
1763	BEAFORD, Francis	A with W	Pts	Feb	44
	alias BEEFORD				
	alias BEFETT				
1758	BEAGHAN, Elizabeth		Middlesex	May	142
1758	John, Esq		Pts	Jul	211
1776	Katherine		Middlesex	Jun	257
1777	Penelope		Middlesex	Jul	299
1758	BEAGIN, John	Ser	Middlesex	Jul	208
1790	BEAGUE, John, Esq		Somerset	Jul	320
1781	BEAIN, James		Pts	Aug	375
	alias BAIN				
1786	BEAK, Ann		Kent	Jun	319
	alias BEEK				
1777	Mary		Middlesex	Aug	340
	alias BICK				
1795	BEAKE, Mary		Kent	Apr	240
1753	Mary Anne	A with W	Middlesex	Dec	309
1788	Robert		Kent	Apr	172
1795	BEAKER, Philip	"Leopard"	Lancaster	Oct	583
	alias BAKER, Phillip				
1776	Sarah		Gloucestershire	Dec	490
	alias BAKER				
1762	BEAKEY, James		Pts	Sep	369
1788	BEAKHURST, James		Wiltshire	Nov	522
1751	BEAKLEY, Margaret		Surrey	Apr	105
1759	BEAL, Avelin		Middlesex	Jul	224
1773	Edward	Ser	Devon	Apr	146
1750	James		Pts	Jun	189
1758	Jane		Middlesex	Nov	320
1756	John		Middlesex	Oct	267
1772	Mary		Middlesex	May	156
1786	Robert		Kent	Mar	144
1781	Thomas	Ser	Devon	Jul	328
	alias BEALL				
1755	William		Surrey	May	122
1760	William		Pts/Surrey	Feb	50
1760	William		Middlesex	Oct	378
1761	William	A with W unad	Middlesex	Jun	
		Will regd Oct 1760			
1782	William		Pts	Nov	530
1785	William		Middlesex	Jan	2
1756	BEALBY, John	A with W	Pts	Sep	239
	alias BEILBY	Ser			

Year	Name	Notes	County	Month	No.
1790	BEALBY, William		Middlesex	Sep	409
1758	BEALE, Abigail		Sussex	Aug	238
	alias COUSINS				
1757	Alexander, Esq		Surrey	Mar	73
1757	Ann	Ltd Probate	London	Apr	110
	alias YEATES				
1758	Ann		Middlesex	Mar	62
1768	Ann		Staffordshire	Feb	46
1768	Ann	Double Probate Will regd Feb 1768	Staffordshire	Sep	
1782	Ann		Middlesex	Mar	110
1782	Ann		Middlesex	Aug	393
1794	Ann		Kent	Mar	123
1800	Ann		Surrey	Aug	575
1777	Anne	A with W	Kent	May	201
1760	Anthony		Pts	May	184
1783	Batt		Kent	Mar	109
1776	Benjamin		Kent	Apr	163
1786	Benjamin		Worcester	Oct	501
1751	Dorothy		Worcester	Dec	329
1759	Edridge		Middlesex	Oct	317
1762	Elizabeth		Middlesex	Aug	331
1766	Elizabeth		Middlesex	Nov	398
1789	Elizabeth		Worcester	Dec	575
1762	Francis		Middlesex	Aug	331
1793	Hannah		Gloucestershire	Jan	6
1750	Henry		Wiltshire	Jul	223
1766	Henry		Sussex	Nov	396
1788	Henry	Special A with W of Goods unad. Will regd 396 Tyndall	Sussex	Dec	
1775	Increase		Middlesex	Sep	336
1760	James		Pts	Nov	415
1773	James		Sussex	May	195
1784	James		Surrey	Sep	490
1791	James	A with W of Goods unad Will regd 195 Stevens	Southampton	May	
1751	John		Pts	Oct	274
1756	John		Pts	Jun	158
1757	John		Pts	Jun	182
1759	John		Sussex	May	157
1766	John		Oxford	Oct	363
1774	John		Gloucester	Oct	358
1775	John		London	Jan	3
1777	John		Middlesex	Aug	342
1784	John	"Centurion"&"Monmouth"	Pts	Jul	365
1789	John		Wiltshire	May	238
1792	John		London	Oct	500
1799	John		Surrey	Jun	418
1800	John		Devon	Mar	174
1770	Joseph		Middlesex	May	172
1777	Joseph	A with W of Goods unad Will regd 172 Jenner	Middlesex	Apr	

BEALE (Contd)

Year	Name	Notes	Place	Month	No.
1795	Joseph	Ser."Trident"	Southampton	Jul	433
1789	Loyd		Surrey	May	236
1764	Martha	A with W	Lincoln	Aug	298
1766	Martha	A with W Will regd in August 1764	Lincoln	Jun	
1789	Mary		Gloucestershire	Oct	484
1800	Mary		Gloucestershire	Nov	764
1752	Michael		Cambridge	Jun	146
1761	Nathaniel		London	Jul	241
1755	Robert		Kent	May	123
1783	Robert alias BALE	Ser.	Pts	Oct	500
1758	Richard		Kent	Jan	2
1766	Richard		London	Apr	127
1768	Richard		Middlesex	Mar	95
1769	Richard	Double Probate Will regd March 1768	Middlesex	Jun	
1771	Richard		Surrey	Jun	241
1783	Richard		Middlesex	Apr	159
1787	Richard, Esq		Kent	Jan	6
1799	Richard		Sussex	Jul	476
1765	Sarah		Sussex	Dec	442
1788	Sarah		Sussex	Sep	425
1796	Sarah		Essex	Jan	6
1789	Seaman Cooke		Surrey	May	239
1756	Stephen		Sussex	Aug	215
1751	Thomas		Middlesex	Aug	229
1775	Thomas	A with W unad Will regd 76 Bogg	London	Mar	
1769	Thomas		London	Mar	76
1784	Thomas	By lnt Decree "Sceptre" Another Grant last month	Pts	Mar	122
1792	Thomas		Bath	Jan	6
1792	Thomas		Middlesex	Aug	417
1800	Thomas, Esq		Salop	Apr	255
1751	William		Warwick	Apr	105
1768	William		Essex	Nov	400
1772	William, The Reverend		Cambridge	Sep	317
1776	Thomas		Salop	Feb	51
1777	William		Middlesex	Mar	94
1794	William		Dorset	Jul	351
1796	William		Hertford	Sep	442
1755	BEALES, Benjamin		Cambridge	Mar	65
1778	John		Pts/Gloucester	Jul	273
1792	Patrick, Esq		Cambridge	Oct	500
1783	Robert		Surrey	Mar	113
1791	Thomas alias BEALY		Middlesex	Oct	450
1776	BEALL, Lionel		Pts	Apr	165

Year	Name	Notes	Place	Month	No.
1784	BEALL, Lionell	Double Probate Will regd 165 Bellas	Pts	Jun	
1781	Thomas alias BEAL	Ser.	Devon	Jul	328
1762	BEALLE, Richard alias BAILE		Pts	May	185
1776	BEALS, Daniel		Middlesex	Nov	448
1776	Daniel	Double Probate Will regd last month	Middlesex	Dec	
1791	BEALY, Thomas alias BEALEY		Middlesex	Oct	450
1780	BEAMAN, Elizabeth	A with W	Middlesex	May	240
1765	John		London	May	169
1778	Mary		Middlesex	Feb	48
1783	Richard		Middlesex	May	213
1761	BEAMISH, George		Surrey	Jul	241
1782	Richard		Pts	Apr	164
1772	William		Ireland	Jul	248
1785	BEAMMAND, Susannah		Middlesex	Jan	
1795	BEAMON, Thomas		Somerset	Feb	64
1751	BEAMOND, Michael, Esq		Middlesex	May	132
1769	Michael		Surrey	Sep	302
1757	BEAMONT, William		Pts	Jan	2
1781	BEAMS, Ambrose		Cornwall	Oct	463
1789	BEAN, Alexander		Middlesex	Nov	533
1791	Alexander, Esq		Middlesex	Jan	2
1778	Ann		Middlesex	Mar	94
1784	Charles	"Superb" A with W	Pts	Sep	489
1766	Daniel		Kent	Dec	440
1792	Daniel	E IS "Hindostan"	Pts	Apr	194
1785	David	"Eagle"	Pts/Middlesex	Mar	119
1785	Edith		London	Jan	2
1780	Frances		London	Jan	2
1772	Francis		London	Feb	36
1762	George	A with W	Pts	Jun	232
1772	George		Pts	Mar	86
1767	James		York	Aug	298
1767	James	Double Probate Will regd in August last	York	Dec	
1788	James		Middlesex	Mar	120
1797	James	Treble Probate Will regd 298 Legard	York	May	
1760	John		Pts/Southampton	Jan	2
1763	John		Pts	Jul	325
1767	John		Middlesex	Mar	85
1768	John		Surrey	Oct	368
1770	John	A with W	Pts	Oct	353
1780	John		Pts	Jan	2
1782	John		N. Britain	Jan	4
1784	John	"Sceptre"	Pts	Jun	306
1785	John		Sussex	Jan	8

BEAN (Contd)

1785	John		N. Britain	Aug	404
1789	John		Kent	Aug	418
1776	Joseph		Middlesex	Jun	256
1781	Margaret		Middlesex	May	230
1792	Margaret		Middlesex	Sep	461
1800	Mark Mc-	"Cerberus"&'Excellent"	Pts	Oct	736
1785	Mary		Hertford	Nov	537
1798	May		N. Britain	Oct	666
	alias MOUATT				
1781	Michael		Pts	Jun	283
1756	Morris	Ser.	Middlesex	Jul	189
1779	Peter		Middlesex	Jul	289
1786	Peter	"Inflexible","Eagle"	Pts	Feb	67
1777	Reginald, The Reverend		Somerset	Feb	52
1783	Robert		Pts	Apr	161
1792	Robert, The Reverend		Surrey	Dec	597
1797	Silvester Pryor, Esq		Somerset	Jun	395
1774	Vincent		Kent	May	170
1760	William		Pts/Middlesex	Nov	414
1797	William		Middlesex	Mar	129
1774	BEANE, Ann		Kent	Apr	130
1752	John		London	Jul	177
1765	Thomas		Kent	Mar	85
1763	BEANEY, John		Middlesex	Oct	459
	alias BENEY				
1791	Moses		Middlesex	Nov	495
1773	BEANHAM, Joseph		Oxford	Apr	167
	alias BEAUHAM				
1776	BEANS, Thomas		Devon	Jan	6
	alias BAINES				
1772	BEAR, Elizabeth		Surrey	Feb	39
1795	John A		Berkshire	Oct	578
1781	Jonathan		Kent	Aug	378
1797	Jonathan		Kent	Jan	32
1785	Mary	By Int Decree	London	Jul	354
	alias BARE	Another Grant July 1784			
1769	Richard		Berkshire	Aug	274
1795	Sarah		Kent	Mar	140
1765	Thomas _		Kent	Jan	4
1785	BEARBLOCK, Elizabeth	A with W	Kent	Mar	117
1784	Gilbert, Esq		Middlesex	Apr	191
1761	John		London	Oct	336
1762	John		Middlesex	Dec	492
1784	John, The Reverend		Kent	Jul	365
1785	John, The Reverend	A with W of Goods unad Will regd July last	Kent	Mar	
1793	BEARCROFT, Edward, Esq		Worcester	Apr	189
1796	Edward, Esq		Middlesex	Dec	596
1763	Elizabeth		Surrey	Nov	498
1755	Jane		Surrey	Aug	211

BEARCROFT (Contd)

Year	Name	Note	County	Month	Page
1770	Mary		Surrey	Aug	285
1777	Mary		Middlesex	Nov	446
1791	Samuel		Middlesex	Jul	316
1763	Sarah		Middlesex	Apr	167
1800	Sarah		Middlesex	Jan	9
1753	William		Surrey	Aug	223
1760	BEARD, Abigail		Oxford	Jan	4
1759	Andrew		Pts	Oct	317
1782	Andrew		Lancaster	Jan	3
1794	Ann		Surrey	Apr	182
1799	Ann		Surrey	Mar	170
1799	Ann	Will regd March last	Surrey	May	
1756	Anthony		Pts	Aug	217
1795	Arthur		Devon	Sep	535
1769	Barbara		Sussex	Apr	111
1762	Benjamin		Pts	Jun	233
1783	Daniel		Pts	Jun	281
1763	David	A with W	Pts	Sep	419
	alias BAIRD				
1772	David		Essex	Nov	393
1799	Dorothy		Stafford	May	340
1755	Elizabeth		Middlesex	Dec	305
1767	Elizabeth		Essex	Apr	124
1773	Elizabeth		Sussex	Aug	322
1779	Elizabeth		Middlesex	Sep	367
1786	Elizabeth		London	Jan	3
1768	Frances		London	Aug	307
1781	Frances		Middlesex	Sep	423
1783	Francis		Pts	Mar	110
1784	Francis		Pts	Jan	7
1760	George	A with W	Middlesex	Nov	416
1786	George, The Reverend		Sussex	Sep	462
1782	Hannah		Cornwall	Jul	339
1754	Henry		Kent	Apr	97
1796	Henry		Surrey	Jan	6
1763	Isaac		Kent	Jan	7
1779	Isaac		Middlesex	May	189
1798	Jacob		Middlesex	Sep	584
1760	James		Pts	Mar	89
	alias BAIRD				
1762	James		Gloucester	Nov	450
	alias BAERD				
1765	James		Pts	Aug	285
	alias BAIRD				
1768	James	Poor	Pts	Jul	269
1775	James		Pts	May	173
1791	Joan		Gloucestershire	Sep	419
1754	John		Middlesex	Jul	189
1757	John		Essex	Aug	241

	BEARD (Contd)				
1764	John	A with W	Pts	Dec	457
	alias BAIRD				
	alias BEIARD				
1767	John		Southampton	Dec	435
1789	John		Surrey	Nov	532
1791	John, Esq		Middlesex	Mar	114
1759	Joseph		Surrey	May	160
1790	Lydia, spinster	By Sent (regd Dec 1789 626)	Cornwall	Aug	368
1780	Mary		Sussex	Jul	347
1782	Mary		Devon	Sep	441
1797	Mary		Berkshire	Apr	227
1776	Nathaniel, Esq		London	Dec	485
1779	Richard		Bristol	Dec	485
1781	Robert	Ser	Hampshire	Aug	377
1787	Robert		Surrey	Jul	309
1757	Roger		Somerset	Apr	111
1765	Samuel		London	Jun	207
1789	Sarah		Berkshire	Nov	530
1756	Thomas		Pts	Jul	189
1756	Thomas		Berkshire	Dec	319
1758	Thomas		Gloucester	Feb	30
1786	Thomas		Essex	Jul	364
1760	William	A with W	Pts	Nov	413
1761	William		London	Sep	308
1761	William		London	Sep	311
1778	William		Berkshire	Oct	391
1788	William		Surrey	Dec	579
1791	William, Esq		Staffordshire	Nov	496
1771	BEARDMORE, Arthur, Esq		London	Jan	7
1779	Dorothy		Essex	Oct	405
1790	Isabella		London	Mar	115
1750	John		Middlesex	May	140
1758	John		Middlesex	Apr	101
1784	John	"Coventry"	Pts	Sep	491
1790	John		Middlesex	Mar	117
1786	Jonathan		London	Feb	66
1775	Joshua		London	Sep	336
1784	Joshua	Will regd 336 Alexander	London	Dec	
1778	Mary		Middlesex	Dec	478
1784	Mary		London	Dec	627
1787	Mary		Wiltshire	May	199
1753	William		Middlesex	May	130
1782	William	A with Will	Middlesex	Apr	164
1775	BEARDSELL, George		London	Jul	260
1792	BEARDSLEY, Ann		Middlesex	Dec	596
1775	Elizabeth		Warwick/Stafford	Dec	456
1760	George		Devon	May	185
1772	John		Warwick	Jul	247
1782	John	Ltd A with W unad	Warwick	Jun	
		Will regd 247 Taverner			

	BEARDSLEY (Contd)				
1761	Mary		Middlesex	May	160
1757	Peter		Middlesex	Nov	321
1761	Samuel		Stafford	Jan	5
1769	Samuel		Pts/Middlesex	Dec	408
1800	Samuel	Ser. "Suffolk"	Pts	Jan	5
	alias SMITH, George				
1789	Susanna		Middlesex	Feb	76
1794	Thomas		London	Jul	351
1779	BEARDSWORTH, Elizabeth		Kent	Jul	286
1767	Nicholas		Surrey	May	162
1777	BEARDWELL, James	A with W	Middlesex	Jun	256
1768	John		Suffolk	Mar	96
1755	BEARDWORTH, Richard		Pts	Jul	181
1776	BEARE, Lydia		Wiltshire	Nov	449
	alias BEER				
1788	Mary		Middlesex	Oct	472
1781	Thomas		Middlesex	Jan	5
1759	William	By Int. Decree	Oxford	Feb	45
1773	BEAREN, William	Ser	Devon	Oct	382
	alias BYRNE				
1781	BEARER, John		Pts	Nov	514
	alias BEARING				
1797	BEARFOOT, Ann		Berkshire	Jun	395
1781	BEARING, John		Pts	Nov	514
	alias BEARER				
1790	BEARLEY, Dorothy		Wiltshire	Mar	115
1783	Ezkiel		Pts	Jul	339
	alias BEASLAY				
	alias BEEZLEY				
1774	BEARMAN, Elizabeth		Middlesex	May	167
1752	George		Pts	May	117
1781	George		Middlesex	Oct	465
1782	George	A with W unad	Middlesex	May	
		Will regd October last			
1789	Simon		Middlesex	Jun	304
1767	William		Middlesex	Feb	36
1780	William	Ser	Pts	Apr	172
1796	William	A with W	Dorset	Aug	399
1780	BEARNETT, Thomas	Ser	Pts	Jun	302
	alias BARNETT				
1782	BEARNS, Peter	A with W	Pts	Feb	61
	alias BURN				
1784	BEARNUP, John	Ser."Exeter"	Pts	Jul	368
	alias BARNOP				
1769	BEARPACKER, Edward		Gloucester	Dec	405
1760	George		Gloucester	Oct	379
1780	Judith		Bristol	Nov	504
1785	BEART, Charles		Suffolk	Nov	542
1765	John		Pts/Devon	Jan	5
1754	Roger	A with W unad	Suffolk	Mar	
		Will regd 141 Anstis			

Year	Name	Notes	Place	Month	No.
1763	BEARTLETT, Richard alias BARTLETT		Southampton	Mar	106
1752	BEARSLEY, Allison		London	Sep	227
1790	Margaret		New Sarum	Apr	171
1762	Peter		Middlesex	Mar	90
1762	Peter	Double Prob Will regd March last	Middlesex	Jun	
1762	Peter	Two Codicils Will regd March last	Middlesex	Jun	234
1799	Richard William		Glamorgan	Jun	417
1778	William		Middlesex	Jun	232
1785	William	Double Probate Will regd 232 Hay	Middlesex	May	
1783	BEASLAY, Ezkiel alias BEARLEY alias BEEZLEY		Pts	Jul	339
1783	BEASLEAY, Job		Middlesex	Apr	162
1762	BEASLEY, Ann		London	May	186
1759	Edward		Bristol	Jun	193
1756	Gilbert		Surrey	Jan	3
1759	John		London	May	161
1769	John		London	May	152
1795	John		Middlesex	Sep	533
1781	John Griffiths alias BAZLEY	Ser	Pts	Jun	287
1794	Luke		Middlesex	Mar	127
1755	Thomas		Middlesex	Dec	305
1784	BEASOM, Francis alias BISSOM	Ser. A with W "Monmouth"	Pts	Sep	491
1762	BEASANT, John		London	Jul	284
1787	BEASTALL, John		London	Sep	396
1764	BEASTEW, Cassandra		Middlesex	Mar	83
1784	BEASLY, John alias BEEZLEY		Pts	Mar	120
1762	BEAT, John alias BATES		Pts	Oct	412
1759	BEATER, Andrew	Nuncupative Will	Pts/Devon	Nov	351
1769	BEATES, Mary		Kent	Jul	235
1783	BEATIE, Alexander alias BEATTIE	"Alfred"& "L'Hector"	Pts	Oct	496
1758	BEATH, John	Ser. A with W	Pts	Feb	32
1769	Mathew		Middlesex	Sep	303
1770	William		Pts	Aug	285
1791	BEATNIFFE, Jane		Lincoln	Mar	109
1793	Richard		York	Mar	130
1758	BEATON, David		Pts	Jan	5
1789	Elizabeth		Somerset	Jul	350
1800	Hector		Bath	Jan	4
1763	Honour		Dorset	Apr	164
1767	John		Bristol	May	165
1783	John	"America"	Pts	Nov	552

	BEATON (Contd)				
1795	John	"Leopard"	Pts	Jun	364
1797	John		Middlesex	Jan	4
1757	Jonathan	A with W of Goods unad Will regd 4 Tenison	Dorset	Nov	
1791	Mary alias DAVIS		London	Aug	374
1796	Robert		Middlesex	Dec	596
1785	Samuel		Somerset	Jun	293
1763	BEATSON, Alexander	A with W	Pts	Sep	419
1775	David alias BATSON	Ser	Devon	May	169
1758	James		Pts	Nov	321
1794	James		Hertfordshire	Nov	541
1800	John		London	Jun	435
1767	Peter		Middlesex	May	166
1783	BEATT, David, alias BAITT	A with W Ser.	N. Britain	Nov	551
1762	BEATTER, Richard		Middlesex	Mar	93
1783	BEATTIE, Alexander alias BEATIE	"Alfred"& "L'Hector"	Pts	Oct	496
1780	David alias BATTIE	Ser	Southampton	Jan	2
1778	Walter alias BEATTY		N. Britain	Apr	144
1794	Walter	"Union"	Pts	Sep	445
1789	BEATTY, Elizabeth		Middlesex	Dec	575
1754	Francis		Pts	Dec	317
1750	James		Hertford	Oct	314
1785	Robert	"Victor"	Pts	Jun	293
1778	Walter alias BEATTIE		N. Britain	Apr	144
1752	William		Hertfordshire	Nov	267
1778	William		Hertfordshire	Jun	233
1774	BEATY, Adam		Oxford	Aug	289
1796	Ann		Surrey	Aug	394
1797	Elizabeth		Middlesex	May	297
1784	John	"Princessa""Ranger""Gibralta"	Pts	Jun	309
1742	Joseph	A with W	Pts	Feb	42
1770	Richard		Cambridge	Sep	321
1786	Richard		Northampton	Jan	7
1797	Richard		Middlesex	May	296
1794	Thomas		Surrey	Jan	5
1791	Walter		Buckinghamshire	Jun	269
1776	William		Pts	Nov	449
1777	William	Double Prob Will regd Nov last	Pts	Aug	
1792	William	No ship	Pts	Nov	546
1773	BEAU, James		Middlesex	Aug	323
1757	Mary le alias CREW	Limited Probate	Middlesex	Mar	72
1786	BEAUCHAMP, Anthony		Surrey	Nov	556

BEAUCHAMP (Contd)

Year	Name	Note	County	Month	No
1751	Christopher		Surrey	Oct	275
1750	Edward		Middlesex	Nov	347
1778	Elizabeth	A with W	Northampton	Sep	346
1788	Elizabeth	A with W unad	Northampton	May	
		Will regd 346 Hay			
1783	Finetta		Kent	Jan	4
1774	Francis, Esq		Cornwall	Apr	126
1777	Francis		Middlesex	Jan	9
1777	Francis	Will regd Jan last	Middlesex	Mar	
	alias BEACHAM				
1771	BEACHAMP, George		Essex	May	192
	The Reverend				
1780	BEAUCHAMP, John, Esq		Cornwall	Feb	58
1798	PROCTOR, Loetitia, Dame		Middlesex	Mar	159
1799	Maria		Gloucestershire	Dec	823
1763	Martha		Kent	Aug	367
1785	Martin		Surrey	Apr	172
1756	Maurice		London	May	130
1750	Perleta		Kent	Sep	285
1754	Philip		Surrey	Feb	31
1789	Richard		Middlesex	Sep	449
1799	Richard		Surrey	Aug	572
1777	Rose		London	Dec	496
1774	Thomas		Middlesex	Nov	387
1798	Thomas		Middlesex	Sep	586
1753	BEAUCHAMPE, Mary		London	Feb	39
1770	BEAUCLERCK, The Right Honourable Lady Charlotte		Middlesex	Jul	253
1768	The Right Honourable George, commonly called Lord George BEAUCLERCK		Middlesex	May	187
1755	BEAUCLERK, The Right Honourable Lady Catherine		Southampton	Nov	276
1775	Charles, Esq		Middlesex	Sep	335
1761	The Right Honourable Henry, commonly called Lord Henry BEAUCLERK		Middlesex	Jan	5
1787	James, The Right Reverend Father in God by Divine Permission Lord Bishop of Hereford		Hereford	Oct	440
1792	Lady Margaret commonly called Lady George BEAUCLERK		Southampton	Nov	545
1788	Martha, commonly called Lady Henry BEAUCLERK		Middlesex	Mar	118
1766	The Right Honourable Mary commonly called Lady Sidney BEAUCLERK		Middlesex	Dec	440

1780	BEAUCLERK, Topham, Hon		Middlesex	Mar	124
1777	BEAUFAIN, De, Claire		Pts	Oct	409
	alias DE BERENGER				
	De Beaufain, Claire				
1767	Hector de	Limited Probate	Pts	Feb	36
	Beringer				
1755	BEAUFILS, Elizabeth		London	Feb	34
1794	Elizabeth		Middlesex	Mar	121
1754	BEAUFORD, James		Pts	Jul	190
1750	John	Dr in Physick	Middlesex	Oct	316
1771	Sarah		Middlesex	Sep	378
1786	BEAUFORT, DE, The	Limited Probate	Pts	May	
	Right Honourable				
	Lady Ann Agatha				
1756	The Most Noble	Lord	Gloucester	Dec	320
	Charles Noel Duke				
	of BEAUFORT				
1799	The Most Noble	Duchess	Middlesex	Apr	250
	Elizabeth Duchess				
	Dowager of BEAUFORT				
	Baroness of Botetourt				
1799	DE, Jacob Marinus,	The Hon.	Pts	Mar	179
		Limited Probate			
1768	DE, The Lady Johanna		Pts	Sep	340
	Levina				
1772	The Right Honourable	Limited Probate	Pts	Aug	298
	Maria Adriana DE LO,				
	formerly				
	Lady BEAUFORT				
1783	DE, Maria Elisabet	Limited Probate	Pts	May	
	alias Elizabeth				
1768	Peter Bernard, Esq		Pts	May	186
	The Right Honourable				
1752	William		Middlesex	Feb	29
1795	BEAUFOY, Henry, Esq		Middlesex	May	303
1776	John		Kent	Apr	164
1782	Mark		Surrey	Jun	266
1799	Sarah	A with W	Bristol	Jul	476
1773	BEAUHAM, Joseph		Oxford	Apr	167
	alias BEANHAM				
1766	BEAULAND, John		Surrey	Oct	362
1761	BEAULIEU, John		Middlesex	Oct	340
1779	BEAUMAN, John		Kent	Aug	336
1781	John	Double Probate	Kent	Sep	
		Will regd Aug 1779			
1792	BEAUME, LA, Melchior		Carlisle	Feb	94
1770	BEAUMGARTEN, John		Oxford	Dec	423
	Henry				
1756	BEAUMONT, Abraham		Middlesex	Nov	287
1782	Agnes	A with W	Hull	Dec	570
1757	Alice		Bedford	Apr	112
1763	Alice		Surrey	May	217

BEAUMONT (Contd)

1768	Alice		Bedford	Sep	338
1767	Amy		Middlesex	Feb	35
1754	Anne		Leicester	Feb	31
1776	Anselm		Middlesex	Feb	52
1779	Anselm	Double Probate Will regd Feb 1776		Mar	
1754	Arabella		Leicester	Feb	33
1766	Arabella	A with W unad Will regd 31 Lisle	Leicester	Aug	
1774	Benjamin		London	Feb	36
1793	Betty		Nottingham	Dec	579
1773	Braint John		Middlesex	Jul	278
1799	Catharine alias Catherine		Essex	May	339
1796	Catherine		Middlesex	Apr	166
1754	Charles		Kent	Jun	159
1756	Charles		Suffolk	Nov	289
1774	Charles, Esq		London	Dec	422
1791	Cornelis Johan	A with W	Pts	Dec	604
1792	Cornelis Johan van	A with W of Goods unad Will regd Dec last	Pts	Mar	
1753	Daniel		Middlesex	Jan	2
1754	Elizabeth		Kent	Apr	99
1763	Elizabeth		Surrey	Oct	461
1764	Elizabeth		Kent	Jun	211
1792	Elizabeth		Suffolk	Aug	421
1762	Esther van alias VAN BYUKERSHOEK		Pts	May	224
1792	Everhard Gysbert van		Pts	Feb	117
1763	Sir George		Essex	Feb	45
1787	George		Middlesex	Apr	157
1763	Hannah	A with W	Somerset	Mar	107
1757	James		Middlesex	Jun	182
1780	James		Middlesex	Nov	504
1756	John		Middlesex	Sep	238
1769	John		Bedford	Jan	2
1769	John, Esq		Derby	Feb	35
1779	John		London	Jun	231
1788	John		Pts	Sep	430
1794	John		Surrey	Jun	299
1795	John		Bedford	Jun	369
1797	John George		Middlesex	Jan	32
1756	Joseph	A with W	Suffolk	May	130
1773	Joseph		Lancaster	Apr	148
1757	Judith		Bedford	Jan	5
1764	Lewis de alias DE LA PORTE Chevalier DE BEAUMONT	Limited Probate	Pts	Mar	82

BEAUMONT (Contd)

1761	Mary		Middlesex	Apr	119
1796	Mary		Surrey	Oct	490
1750	Michael		Suffolk	Jan	3
1787	Percivall		Middlesex	Jun	254
1754	Richard	A with W unad Will regd 225 Henchman	London	Jan	3
1756	Richard alias BEMEN	Ser	Middlesex	Sep	239
1788	Robert		Middlesex	May	228
1784	Susanna		Suffolk	May	246
1750	Theophilus		Ireland	Mar	68
1764	Theophilus, Esq	Ltd A with W of Goods unad. Will regd 68 Greenly	Ireland	Mar	
1751	Thomas		Sussex	Dec	326
1754	Thomas		Surrey	Mar	69
1755	Thomas	Double Probate Will regd Mar 1754	Surrey	Mar	
1756	Thomas		London	Dec	318
1759	Thomas		London	Nov	348
1766	Thomas		Surrey	Sep	329
1771	Thomas		Nottingham	Jun	243
1777	Thomas	A with W of Goods unad Will regd 329 Tyndall	Surrey	Jan	
1794	Thomas	A with W of Goods unad Will regd 329 Tyndall, Last Grant January 1774	Surrey	Sep	
1795	Thomas		Surrey	Jul	433
1796	Thomas		Surrey	Aug	400
1797	Thomas		Essex	Dec	723
1800	Thomas Robert	M. S. "Penny"	Pts	Jun	442
1764	William, Esq		Surrey	Nov	415
1764	William		Somerset	Dec	454
1784	William		Middlesex	Feb	65
1785	William		Bedford	Dec	588
1788	William		Middlesex	Feb	55
1789	William		Bedford	Jan	4
1793	William		Hertfordshire	Jul	354
1794	William, Esq		Middlesex	Dec	596
1787	BEAUPRE BELL, William Greaves, Esq		Cambridge	Mar	108
1759	BEAUPUY, Jane		Middlesex	Dec	382
1772	BEAUVAIS, John		Middlesex	Oct	350
1754	Lewis		Middlesex	Jun	159
1796	Louis		Middlesex	May	233
1752	BEAUVAL, BASNAGE DE, Marie alias AMSINCQ	Limited Probate	Pts	Jan	2
1755	BEAUVEZER, DE, Louisa DE LAUGES alias DE BAUCELS, Louisa		Pts	Dec	305

1772	BEAUVOIR, Elizabeth		Essex	Feb	37
1763	James de		Guernsey	Jun	268
1771	James, Esq		Essex	Oct	398
1757	Osmond		Essex	Feb	39
1789	Osmond,The Reverend	Dr in Divinity	Middlesex	Jul	350
1780	Richard, Esq		Essex	Aug	386
1763	BEAVAN, Henry		Somerset	Apr	166
1783	John		Kent	Jan	1
1795	John		Middlesex	Aug	493
1795	Mary		Middlesex	Apr	235
1796	Mary		Kent	Jun	293
1776	Thomas		London	Feb	55
	alias BEVAN				
1788	Thomas		Devon	May	226
1778	William		Middlesex	Mar	95
1787	BEAVEAN, Joseph		Brecon	Apr	159
	alias BEVAN				
1775	BEAVEN, Heasther		Wiltshire	Jun	220
	alias Hester				
1788	Henry		Wiltshire	Jun	286
1766	John (2d)		Devon	Sep	329
	alias BEAVIN				
	alias BEVANS				
	alias BEVIN				
1787	John Awbray		Ireland	Nov	488
1794	Samuel		Wiltshire	May	242
1750	Thomas		Pts	Aug	252
	alias BEAVN				
1789	Thomas		London	Jan	9
1795	William		Wiltshire	Apr	241
1789	BEAVER, Benjamin		Berkshire	Mar	133
1797	Edward		Northampton	Feb	68
1773	Eleanor		Sussex	Jun	235
1787	Elizabeth		Berkshire	Jul	311
1794	Elizabeth		Northampton	Jul	349
1791	Francis		Middlesex	Mar	112
1799	Herculus		Middlesex	Sep	643
1799	James		London	Aug	564
1752	John		Middlesex	Feb	28
1763	John		Cambridge	Aug	367
1762	Joseph		Middlesex	Jun	233
1764	Mary		Middlesex	Oct	378
1772	Patience		Middlesex	Oct	351
1762	Peter, Esq		Ireland	Aug	333
1778	Peter, Esq		Surrey	Oct	388
1779	Rhoda		Surrey	Jan	2
1776	Samuel		Middlesex	Sep	380
1785	Thomas		Liverpool	May	229
1787	Thomas		Middlesex	Aug	358
1793	Thomas		Berkshire	Jul	350
1798	Thomas		Rutland	Jul	461

	BEAVER (Contd)				
1784	William		Middlesex	Oct	540
1750	BEAVERS, John		Middlesex	Aug	252
1766	BEAVIN, John (2d)		Devon	Sep	329
	alias BEVIN				
	alias BEAVEN				
	alias BEVANS				
1783	BEAVIS, Charles		Kent	Nov	550
1756	George		London	Jun	158
1758	Henry	A with W	Devon	Feb	31
1793	Jeremiah		Surrey	Jul	350
1765	Sabina		Stafford	Dec	443
1772	Sarah		Devon	Jul	248
1783	Sarah		Middlesex	Mar	113
1760	William		London	Aug	314
1799	BEAVITT, George		Pts	Mar	166
1800	Mary	A with W	London	Nov	767
1793	BEAVON, Elizabeth		Salop	Jan	7
1761	BEAW, Ann		Oxford	Jul	242
1773	BEAYS, Domingo	A with W	Southampton	Nov	417
1765	BEAZANT, Mary		Kent	Jan	2
1798	BEAZER, James	Ser. "Alarm"	Pts	May	314
1759	BEAZLEY, David Thomas		Middlesex	Jun	193
1782	Isaac John		Middlesex	Feb	61
1777	Jane		Surrey	Nov	448
1782	Joseph		Middlesex	Apr	163
1769	Richard	A with W	Middlesex	Feb	34
1795	Sarah		Middlesex	Mar	144
1787	Thomas		Wiltshire	Aug	354
1759	Walsingham, Esq		Middlesex	Dec	384
1796	BEAZLY, John	Ser "Intrepid"	Pts	Jun	294
1750	BEBB, Benjamin		Pts	Apr	106
	alias BABBS				
	alias BOBBS				
1798	George, Esq		York	May	313
1781	John, Esq		Hertford	Dec	573
1781	William		Montgomery	Jul	327
1763	BEBBER, VAN, Matthys		Pts	Jan	36
1762	BEBEE, Edward		Pts	Sep	370
1761	BEBINGTON, Mary		Middlesex	May	83
1769	Samuel		Middlesex	Jul	233
1751	BECCELER, Mary		Surrey	Feb	36
1799	BECHER, Craufield		Bristol	Jun	415
1764	George		Middlesex	Jan	3
1766	Elizabeth		Middlesex	Aug	292
1793	Hannah	Ltd Probate	Kent	Mar	31
	alias JENKINS				
1784	John, Esq	A with W	Pts/Staffordshire	Jan	3
1760	Michael		Bristol	Apr	138
1764	Michael, Esq		Pts/Bristol	Apr	131
1788	Richard, Esq	Ltd Probate	Pts	Nov	519

	BECHER (Contd)				
1754	Samuel		Southampton	Jul	188
1751	William, Esq		Bedford	Jul	198
1774	BECHEY, Ann		Berkshire	Nov	385
1761	BECHINOE, Benjamin		Middlesex	Mar	83
1775	Reuben		Middlesex	Sep	334
1777	Samuel		Essex	Nov	448
1773	BECIUS, Assuerus		Pts	Mar	96
1774	Hendrick		Pts	Jul	253
1800	BECK, Andrew	Ser."Seahorse"	Pts	Jan	8
1765	Ann		Middlesex	Apr	132
1788	Ann		Essex	Jan	5
1797	Ann		Middlesex	Sep	585
1778	Alice		Southampton	Jul	272
1764	Benson		Middlesex	Apr	131
1788	Catherine, spinster	By Sent (regd Nov 636)	Middlesex	Apr	175
1785	Charlotta		Essex	Jan	8
1772	Christopher		London	Sep	319
1782	Christopher alias BEEAK		Southampton	Jul	340
1787	Cornelius	Ltd Probate	Pts	Nov	488
1776	Daniel	Ltd Probate	Pts	Apr	163
1777	Daniel	A with W	Surrey	Jul	297
1755	Edward		Middlesex	Feb	31
1786	Edward	"Eagle"	Devon	May	260
1796	Eleanor		Kent	May	234
1780	Elizabeth		Bedford	Feb	59
1793	Elizabeth		Berkshire	Jul	353
1763	Francis		Middlesex	Apr	165
1777	George		Hertfordshire	Jun	255
1781	George		Middlesex	May	228
1783	George		Pts	Aug	401
1781	Gilbert		Buckinghamshire	Apr	182
1770	Hannah		Middlesex	Dec	424
1771	Hans Bernard	Ltd Probate	Pts	Jul	286
1767	James		Buckinghamshire	Jul	251
1788	James		Middlesex	May	230
1750	John	A with W	Middlesex	Mar	69
1762	John		Middlesex	Feb	40
1769	John		Hereford	Sep	303
1774	John	A with W unad Will regd 168 Potter	Surrey	May	
1780	John		London	Dec	554
1794	John		Hertford	Dec	597
1795	John	75 Regt E.I.S.	Pts/Middlesex	Feb	62
1799	John		Bristol	Sep	646
1763	Joseph		Pts	Feb	46
1765	Joseph		London	Oct	362
1772	Joseph		Bristol	Jul	244
1782	Joseph		Stafford	Feb	65
1793	Joseph		Gloucester	Apr	185
1764	Justys Denis	Sir	Essex	Jan	4

BECK (Contd)

Year	Name	Note	Place	Month	Page
1765	Magtils vander alias BARKERS		Pts	Mar	86
1781	Maria Elizabeth		Pts	Dec	574
1751	Mary		Oxford	Mar	74
1762	Mary		Middlesex	Jun	235
1794	Mary		Bath	Jan	6
1795	Mary		Buckinghamshire	Oct	580
1795	Mary	Will regd last month	Buckinghamshire	Nov	
1797	Mary		Sussex	Sep	587
1799	Mary		Bristol	Apr	247
1786	Middlemoore	A with W	London	May	
1751	Nathaniel		Hertford	Nov	300
1799	Percival	Ser. "Phoeton"	Pts	Nov	787
1779	Picter, The Right Honourable, Lord	Ltd Probate	Pts	Feb	40
1786	Robert		Buckinghamshire	Jun	322
1787	Roger		Surrey	Feb	53
1774	Sophia	A with W unad Will regd 272 Potter	Surrey	May	
1755	Thomas		Pts	Apr	93
1772	Thomas		Oxford	Sep	319
1774	Thomas		Berkshire	Jun	216
1779	Thomas		Middlesex	Dec	485
1791	Thomas	A with W	Hertfordshire	Aug	373
1794	Thomas		Salop	Dec	595
1766	William	Will Nuncupative	Surrey	Apr	126
1769	William		Middlesex	Nov	365
1772	William		Surrey	Sep	318
1780	William		Berkshire	Feb	56
1784	William	"Exeter"	Pts	Dec	627
1785	William		Kent	Apr	174
1789	William, Esq alias CHURCH, William		Hertfordshire	Dec	580
1795	William		Oxford	Apr	234
1758	BECKE, Thomas		Lincoln	Mar	62
1796	Thomas	Ltd A with W of Goods unad. Will regd 62 Hutton	Lincoln	Dec	
1766	BECKER, Catherina Elisabeth alias DE WAERT		Pts	Sep	358
1772	Johan Melchior		Middlesex	Feb	38
1770	John alias BACKER alias BAKER		Middlesex	Nov	390
1784	Michel		Kent	Jul	369
1751	BECKERLEG, Richard alias BECKERLEY		Cornwall	Oct	274
1751	BECKERLEY, Richard alias BECKERLEG		Cornwall	Oct	274

1776	BECKET, Anne	Special A with W	Middlesex	Dec	490
1785	Anne	Special A with W of Goods unad. Will regd 490 Bellas	Middlesex	Nov	
1750	John		Surrey	Aug	251
1771	John, Dr	Dr of Physick	Middlesex	Jan	6
1767	Margaret	A with W	Gloucestershire	Sep	335
1784	Richard	"Eagle"	Pts	Jul	366
1798	BECKETT, Ann Martha		Middlesex	May	307
1782	Anne		Kent	Feb	65
1761	Benjamin		Middlesex	Sep	308
1795	Elizabeth		Middlesex	Dec	670
1791	George	E.I. Mt.S. "Abergavenny"	Surrey/Pts	Aug	375
1794	George		Worcestershire	Aug	405
1800	George		Surrey	May	338
1767	Hannah		Middlesex	Dec	438
1790	Isaac		Staffordshire	Feb	58
1789	James		Kent	Feb	78
1794	James		Surrey	Mar	126
1767	John	Ser	London	May	166
1767	John		Middlesex	Sep	334
1788	John		Kent	Oct	471
1762	Joseph		Surrey	Jun	234
1787	Joseph		Middlesex	Apr	156
1786	Katharine		Surrey	Jul	366
1756	Rawley		Surrey	Aug	217
1759	Samuel		Middlesex	May	158
1753	Sarah		Surrey	Feb	38
1763	Sarah		Middlesex	Jun	264
1756	Thomas		Kent	Feb	30
1761	Thomas alias BEKITT	Ser	Pts	Sep	309
1791	Thomas		Middlesex	Aug	375
1800	Thomas		Surrey	Jul	506
1772	William		Surrey	Aug	283
1775	William		Buckinghamshire	Oct	368
1782	William	A with W	Pts	May	215
1800	William		Surrey	Feb	90
1792	BECKFORD, Ann		Surrey	Dec	596
1751	Bathshua		Middlesex	Feb	36
1786	Bathshua	A with W	Middlesex	Jul	364
1763	Dorothea		Surrey	Mar	109
1769	Elienor		Middlesex	Jun	196
1768	Francis , Esq		Middlesex	Dec	440
1792	John		Berkshire	Jan	6
1765	Julines, Esq	A with W	Pts	May	173
1798	Maria		Middlesex	Aug	527
1784	Mary		Wiltshire	Nov	587
1772	Matthew alias BEDFORD		Pts	Jul	247
1757	Peter, Esq	A with W of Goods unad Will regd 101 Derby	Pts	May	

	BECKFORD (Contd)				
1791	Ralph		Surrey	Mar	116
1756	Richard, Esq. late one of the Aldermen of the City of London		Pts	Mar	59
1758	Richard, Esq. late one of the Aldermen of the City of London	Double Probate Will regd in March 1756	Pts	Apr	
1796	Richard, Esq	A with W	Middlesex	Sep	446
1764	Simon		Pts	Aug	298
1789	Susanna		Middlesex	Sep	448
1757	Thomas, Esq		Surrey	Mar	72
1765	Thomas		Pts	Jul	245
1796	Thomas, Esq	Ltd A with W of Goods unad. Will regd 72 Herring	Surrey	Mar	
1753	William		Oxford	Feb	39
1770	William, The Right Honourable, late Lord Mayor of the City of London			Jul	256
1799	William, Esq		Middlesex	Feb	96
1751	BECKINGHAM, Anne		Middlesex	Apr	103
1766	Catherine		Kent	Sep	329
1767	Hanah		Middlesex	May	162
1752	Henry		Middlesex	Jan	2
1794	James		Middlesex	Nov	530
1757	Mary	A with W	Wiltshire	May	145
1756	Stephen, Esq		Kent	Oct	267
1796	BECKINGTON, Ann		Middlesex	Nov	540
1774	Mary		Middlesex	Jun	215
1779	BECKINSALE, Francis		Middlesex	Jun	236
1761	BECKITT, Thomas alias BECKETT	Ser	Pts	Sep	309
1751	BECKLEY, Emanuel	A with W of Goods unad Will regd 290 Seymour	London	May	
1770	John		Berkshire	Dec	422
1800	John		London	Nov	766
1760	Lucy		Middlesex	Jan	2
1797	Thomas William	Ser."Isis"& "Ganges"	Pts	Feb	73
1766	BECKMAN, Dedirick		London	Aug	293
1787	Margaret Magdalen		Middlesex	Dec	533
1778	Peter Adoph		Pts	Sep	348
1758	BECQUE, Mary de la		Kent	May	123
1792	BECKTON, Adam	A with W	Northampton	Apr	194
1790	Ann	A with W	Middlesex	Jun	277
1769	BECTON, Robert, The Reverend		Hereford	Feb	33
1789	BECUDA, John		London	Jun	300
1773	BECKWITH, Catharine		Durham	Jul	277
1765	Edward		Kent	Nov	401

BECKWITH (Contd)

Year	Name	Note	County	Month	No.
1776	Elizabeth		Middlesex	Jan	4
1781	George	Ser	Pts	Aug	377
1791	Hannah		Kent	Nov	498
1800	Henry		Essex	Oct	704
1779	Jacob		Suffolk	Jan	3
1763	James		Pts	Jul	324
1775	John		Essex	Jul	260
1779	John		Durham	May	190
1780	John		Middlesex	Mar	122
1767	Jonah		Essex	Dec	436
1789	Onslow, Esq		Kent	Nov	532
1800	Ray, Dr	Dr of Physick	York	Jan	9
1758	Sarah		Buckinghamshire	Mar	62
1787	Stephen		York	Apr	158
1784	Susanna		Middlesex	Jan	8
1785	William		Middlesex	Nov	540
1777	BECKWORTH, Eleanor		Middlesex	Feb	55
1775	Francis		Surrey	Sep	333
1772	Humphrey		Middlesex	Jan	4
1763	Richard		Middlesex	Mar	110
1769	BEDALL, John		Middlesex	Jun	196
1784	BEDARD, Charles	"Monmouth"	Pts	Mar	119
1760	Francis		Pts	Aug	313
1785	BEDAFF, VAN, Gommaerus The Reverend		Pts	Jan	
1780	BEDBURY, Joseph		Bristol	Apr	170
1781	William		Somerset	Dec	577
1775	BEDBOROUGH, Robert		Wiltshire	Mar	84
1786	BEDBROUGH, Arthur		Sussex	Oct	505
1794	BEDCOTT, Elizabeth		Middlesex	Nov	538
1798	Elizabeth	A with W of Goods unad Will regd Nov 1794	Middlesex	Sep	
1754	James		Middlesex	Jun	161
1760	William		Middlesex	May	183
1797	BEDDALL, James		Middlesex	Feb	67
1775	Richard		Buckinghamshire	May	169
1784	BEDDARD, Edward	"Repulse"	Lancaster	Mar	121
1767	BEDDEK, Richard		Devon	Mar	87
1757	BEDDOES, George	A with W of Goods unad Former Grant Nov. 1728 Will regd 315 Brook	Montgomery	Sep	
1754	BEDDER, Thomas		Berkshire	Oct	267
1758	Thomas	A with W unad Will regd 59 Spurway	Buckinghamshire	May	
1778	BEDDERIDGE, Ann alias TANNER		Middlesex	Jul	302
1759	BEDDINGFIELD, Jane		Berkshire	Apr	121
1782	BEDDINSON, Andrew alias BODDISTON		Pts	Jun	265
1788	BEDDOES, George		Salop	Feb	54

1782	BEDDOES, Susanna		Middlesex	Dec	574
	alias BEDDOSS				
	Suesanna				
1795	BEDDOME, Benjamin	Clerk	Gloucester	Sep	535
	The Reverend				
1757	John		Bristol	Nov	323
1794	Joseph		Bristol	Feb	61
1758	Rachel		Bristol	Oct	286
1782	BEDDOSS, Suesanna		Middlesex	Dec	574
	alias BEDDOES, Susanna				
1762	BEDDOW, Andrew		Middlesex	Jun	235
1790	Henry		Surrey	Jun	277
1789	Joshua		Surrey	Jul	349
1784	Nathan		Middlesex	Nov	585
1784	William	Ser."Renown"	Pts	Nov	589
	alias BEDDS				
1784	BEDDS, William	Ser."Renown"	Pts	Nov	589
	alias BEDDOW				
1760	BEDELL, Ann		Kent	Mar	87
1782	Charles		Middlesex	Feb	60
1768	Henry		London	Feb	49
1793	James		Kent	May	243
1758	John		Kent	Dec	356
1768	Martha		Middlesex	Apr	139
1783	Michael		Surrey	Jun	284
1795	Michael		Kent	Nov	621
1790	Susanna		Surrey	Sep	412
1790	William		London	Apr	174
1772	BEDELLS, Henry		Surrey	May	159
1758	William		Surrey	Sep	258
1772	William		London	Jul	245
1788	BEDFORD, Ann		Southampton	Jul	337
1791	Ann		Hertford	Jul	315
1799	Ann		Bath	May	338
1788	Charles, The		Cornwall	Mar	120
	Reverend				
1798	Charles		Southampton	Feb	82
1800	Cheesman Welstead		Southampton	Jan	4
	alias Westead				
1763	Elizabeth		Bedford	Nov	497
1776	Elizabeth		Middlesex	Apr	163
1782	Elizabeth		Somerset	Mar	112
1790	Elizabeth		Middlesex	Oct	453
1795	Elizabeth		Huntingdon	Oct	581
1797	Elizabeth		Bedford	Dec	727
1755	Francis		Cornwall	Dec	305
1794	Gertrude, Lady		Middlesex	Jul	348
	The Most Noble Duchess				
	Dowager of BEDFORD				
1771	Grosvenor, Esq		Surrey	Nov	430
1797	Henrietta		Southampton	Jun	398

BEDFORD (Contd)

1779	Hilkiah, Esq		Durham	Sep	365
1781	Hilkiah, Esq	Double Probate Will regd Sept 1779	Durham	Oct	
1797	Isaac		Essex	Apr	223
1761	James		Southampton	Feb	46
1770	James		London	Apr	132
1771	James		Hertford	Jun	241
1798	James, Esq		Southampton	Feb	81
1793	Jenny		Cornwall	Dec	581
1752	John		Pts	Jun	146
1763	John		Pts	Apr	165
1769	John		Middlesex	May	153
1771	The Most Noble John late Duke of		Middlesex	Feb	42
1776	John, Dr	Dr of Physick	Durham	Feb	49
1782	John		Middlesex	Feb	59
1784	John, The Reverend		Devon	Jun	306
1789	John	E.I.M.S. Talbot	Pts/Surrey	May	233
1792	John		Glamorgan	Dec	598
1796	John		Wiltshire	Apr	162
1796	John		Surrey	Jul	343
1775	Joseph, Esq		Middlesex	Feb	40
1766	Martha		Middlesex	Oct	364
1772	Mary		Middlesex	Feb	41
1777	Mary	A with W	Berkshire	Jan	8
1780	Mary		Bedford	Jan	4
1772	Matthew alias BECKFORD		Pts	Jul	247
1792	Penelope		Essex	Oct	500
1751	Richard		Southampton	Jul	198
1778	Richard		Pts	Jul	274
1794	Richard		Buckinghamshire	Dec	597
1762	Robert		Surrey	May	183
1782	Sarah alias PHILLIPS		Bedford	Feb	94
1791	Sarah		Warwickshire	Feb	58
1781	Stephen		Warwickshire	May	228
1762	Susanna		London	Jan	2
1760	Thomas		Kent	Feb	46
1773	Thomas		Derby	Mar	95
1783	Thomas		Northampton	Jun	285
1789	Thomas, The Reverend		Ireland	Sep	449
1754	William		Bedford	Jul	189
1771	William	A with W	Stafford	Aug	329
1779	William		Hertford	Jun	236
1783	William, The Reverend		Kent	Nov	552
1784	William		Southampton	Jan	4
1784	William		Surrey	Aug	430
1784	William	A with W of Goods unad Will regd 329 Trevor		Dec	
1793	William		Worcestershire	Jun	298

	BEDFORD (Contd)				
1798	William		Surrey	Mar	156
1787	BEDGEGOOD, Josiah		Gloucestershire	Feb	55
1751	BEDINGFELD, Ann	A with W	Middlesex	Jun	166
1797	Bacon, The Reverend alias BEDINGFIELD		Norfolk	Sep	584
1775	Catherine		Bath	May	173
1758	Edmund		Kent	Jul	208
1761	Edmund	A with W unad Will regd July 1758	Kent	Jan	
1757	Elizabeth		Suffolk	Nov	321
1750	Henrietta		Middlesex	Aug	251
1787	John, Esq		Norfolk	May	197
1761	Margaret		Sussex	Nov	380
1769	William		Middlesex	Jan	2
1761	BEDINGFIELD, Ann	A with W unad Will regd 166 Busby	Middlesex	Jul	
1797	Bacon, The Reverend alias BEDINGFELD		Norfolk	Sep	584
1760	Henry, Sir	A with W	Norfolk	Oct	378
1770	Mary		York	Mar	88
1794	Susan		Norwich	Sep	446
1800	William Derisley		Suffolk	Dec	834
1761	BEDLAND, John alias BEADLIN	Ser.	Southampton	Sep	308
1787	BEDLESTON, John	98th Regiment	Pts	Dec	
1763	BEDO, Hugh		Middlesex	Jul	324
1767	Mary		London	Aug	297
1785	BEDOORS, John	"Union"&"Solitaire"	Pts	Aug	405
1752	BEDOU, Stephen		Middlesex	Feb	29
1788	BEDSAR, William alias BEDSER		Surrey	Aug	386
1799	BEDSER, Ann		Middlesex	Oct	696
1778	William		Surrey	May	183
1788	William alias BEDSAR		Surrey	Aug	386
1755	BEDSON, Joseph		Middlesex	Mar	65
1782	BEDWARD, Jordan		Pts	Jul	334
1769	BEDWELL, Arthur		London	Apr	114
1763	Bernard		Berkshire	Aug	372
1760	Christian		Oxford	Aug	314
1783	Edward		Pts	Jul	338
1783	Edward	Ser	Pts	Jul	338
1769	Elizabeth		Southampton	Oct	332
1765	Francis		Middlesex	Jan	3
1776	Francis		Middlesex	Mar	110
1785	Hannah		Oxford	Dec	587
1769	John		Gloucestershire	Nov	366
1792	John		Gloucestershire	Feb	56
1793	John	Double Probate Will regd Feb 1792	Gloucestershire	Feb	

BEDWELL (Contd)

1798	John	Ltd A with W of Goods unad (thrice) Will regd 107 Brodrepp. Last Grant Jan 1741	Middlesex	Aug	
1799	John		Berkshire	Sep	641
1783	Martha		Gloucestershire	Nov	549
1776	Mary		Surrey	Jan	4
1773	Richard		Oxford	Jun	237
1770	Samuel		Middlesex	Mar	90
1756	Sarah		Surrey	Jan	1
1765	Stephen		Pts	Nov	399
1750	Thomas		Middlesex	Jul	221
1764	Thomas		Middlesex	Feb	39
1793	BEDWIN, Francis		Oxford	Jan	5
1782	George		Berkshire	Aug	394
1762	Thomas		Pts	Apr	142
1771	Thomas		Middlesex	Feb	45
1795	BEDWORT, Alice		Surrey	Apr	240
1785	BEE, Benjamin William		Devon	Jan	2
1753	Henry		Essex	Mar	69
1778	James	Ser	Middlesex	Oct	389
1780	Mary		Middlesex	Aug	386
1765	Thomas		Middlesex	Mar	88
1775	Thomas		Middlesex	Jul	262
1755	William		Middlesex	Sep	234
1760	William	A with W	Pts	Dec	450
1799	William		Kent	Jul	481
1782	BEEAK, Christopher alias BECK		Southampton	Jul	340
1759	BEEBE, Frances		Middlesex	Jan	5
1759	William	A with W	Middlesex	Jul	224
1787	BEEBEE, Edward	A with W	Middlesex	Feb	52
1799	John		Staffordshire	Oct	695
1786	Thomas, Esq		Hereford	Jul	365
1771	BEEBEY, Sarah		Kent	Oct	396
1775	BEEBY, Elizabeth		Middlesex	Nov	402
1754	John		Leicester	Oct	292
1778	Robert		Middlesex	Mar	94
1788	Thomas		Huntingdonshire	Mar	120
1762	BEECH, Ann	A with W	Hertfordshire	Sep	367
1779	Ann		Middlesex	Aug	336
1767	Anthony		Middlesex	Dec	439
1797	Charles		Kent	Jan	2
1790	Dorothy		Middlesex	Feb	63
1751	Edward		Pts	Oct	276
1753	Elias		London	Feb	39
1770	Elizabeth		Worcester	Mar	90
1795	Elizabeth		Bedford	Apr	240
1765	Henry	A with W	Pts	Mar	86
1769	Henry		London	Mar	75

	BEECH (Contd)				
1752	Jane		Salop	Mar	58
1784	John	A with W	London	Nov	587
1793	John		Middlesex	Jan	9
1755	Joseph		Southampton	Oct	255
1770	Martha		Middlesex	Jan	3
	alias BEACH				
1800	Mary		Middlesex	Dec	839
1758	Michael		Pts/Middlesex	Feb	29
1764	Parker		London	Nov	414
1795	Sarah		Middlesex	Jul	433
1755	Thomas		Hertford	Oct	253
1765	Thomas, Esq		Middlesex	Apr	129
1767	Thomas		Kent	Jun	208
1788	Thomas		Middlesex	Feb	56
1750	William		Salop	May	139
1763	William		Derby	May	214
1765	William	A with W of Goods unad Will regd 190 Romney	Middlesex	Jul	
1768	William		Middlesex	May	186
1772	William		Middlesex	Mar	82
1781	William		Lincolnshire	Nov	513
1797	BEECHAM, King		Middlesex	Nov	674
1783	William		Middlesex	Mar	114
1763	BEECHEN, John		Kent	May	212
1790	BEECHER, Mary		Sussex	Mar	117
1750	James		Kent	Apr	102
1796	BEECHEY, James		Middlesex	Jan	3
1783	BEECHIN, Samuel	A with W	Pts	Oct	499
1750	BEECK, Henry		Surrey	Jul	224
1750	Henry	Double Probate	Surrey	Aug	
	alias VERBEECK	Will regd in July last			
1793	Van, Jan Frederick		Pts	Oct	532
1776	Van, Thomas		Pts	Jan	42
1791	William		Surrey	Sep	417
	alias BEEK				
1774	BEECKMAN, Lady Adriana Constantia alias Adriana Constantia Sise	Ltd Probate	Pts	Sep	350
1791	BEECRAFT, Thomas		Lincoln	Oct	454
1780	BEECROFT, Christiana		Kent	Apr	173
1796	Joseph		Middlesex	Jan	5
1774	Thomas		Middlesex	Apr	129
1767	BEED, George		Pembroke	Nov	400
1760	John	A with W	Pts	Oct	382
1753	Walter		Kent	Mar	69
1773	William		Pts	Feb	47
1761	BEEDALL, John		Middlesex	Sep	309
1780	Samuel		Middlesex	Mar	122
1798	BEEDEN, Ann		Middlesex	Jun	378
1798	John		Middlesex	Jun	378

1769	BEEDHAM, Thomas		London	May	152
1786	BEEDING, John		Chichester	Oct	503
1776	BEEDLE, Ambrose		Somerset	Jun	257
1785	Elizabeth		Middlesex	Apr	173
1797	James	"Aurora"	Devon	Mar	127
1789	Thomas		Devon	Jul	347
1779	BEEDO, William		Kent	Jul	286
1789	BEEDOM, John		Hertford	Nov	530
1782	Mary		Hertford	Oct	482
1797	Richard		Hertford	May	296
1775	BEEELL, Mary alias LEWIS	Will regd July last	Middlesex	Dec	
1784	BEEF, Peter	"Invincible,""Vengeance" "Cumberland"	Pts	Jun	307
1763	BEEFORD, Francis alias BEAFORD alias BEFETT	A with W	Pts	Feb	44
1791	BEEFTINGH, Frans Van		Pts	Apr	
1797	Hendrick Van	Limited Probate	Pts	Dec	773
1793	Johanna Adriana Van	Limited Probate	Pts	Mar	175
1782	Petronella Van alias Van LOCKHORST	Limited Probate	Pts	Dec	615
1796	Pieter Van	A with W	Pts	Oct	
1771	Shalkeus, Esq alias Shalkens	Limited Probate	Pts	May	235
1763	BEEG, James alias BAIG		Pts	May	216
1786	BEEK, Ann alias BEAK		Kent	Jun	319
1773	Bernardus Van Der	Limited Probate	Pts	Jul	315
1763	Elizabeth alias BICK	A with W	London	Dec	542
1787	Hermina	Limited Probate	Pts	May	197
1784	William	"Preston"	Pts	Jul	367
1791	William alias BEECK		Surrey	Sep	417
1798	BEEKE, Christopher, The Reverend		Devon	Apr	237
1753	BEEKHOVEN, Elizabeth Van		Pts	Oct	282
1754	BEEKLEY, Thomas		Middlesex	Feb	32
1762	BEEKMAN, Swen		Pts	Sep	369
1784	BEEKS, Joan	"Burford"	Pts/Southampton	Jul	365
1755	BEELAERTS, Christina	Limited Probate	Pts	May	124
1790	Christina alias Christiana	Limited Probate	Pts	Mar	116
1790	Gerard, The Right Honourable	Hon. Limited Probate	Pts	Dec	541
1797	Pieter Matthys, The Honourable	Hon. Limited Probate	Pts	Apr	221
1786	Susanna Adriana	Limited Probate	Pts	Dec	601
1774	BEELDEMAKER, Francois, Esq alias Frans		Pts	Oct	359

Year	Name	Type	Place	Month	No.
	BEELDEMAKER (Contd)				
1785	Gerardina Barbara	Limited Probate	Pts	Apr	173
1784	Willan	Limited Probate	Pts	Dec	628
1765	BEELDSNIDER, Francois	Lord. Limited Probate	Pts	May	171
	The Right Noble Lord				
1800	BEELDSNYDER, Catharina		Pts	Jan	9
1798	Francois Gerard		Pts	Sep	581
1771	Gerard	Limited Probate	Pts	Jan	5
1799	Jacobus Schlosser		Pts	Jan	12
1754	Susanna	Limited Probate	Pts	Dec	319
	alias Van HERNERT				
1794	BEELE, Elizabeth		Worcestershire	Dec	594
1758	William, The Reverend		Devon	Feb	32
1789	BEELS, Marten Adriaan	Limited Probate	Pts	Jul	346
1784	Richard		Surrey	Oct	537
1780	Robert	A with W	Middlesex	May	240
1775	Theodorus, Dr	Dr of Laws. Ltd Probate	Pts	Sep	334
1773	BEEN, Diana		Middlesex	Jul	280
	alias GAWTON				
1787	Diana	A with W of Goods unad	Middlesex	Feb	
	alias GAWTON	Will regd 280 Stevens			
1773	Joseph		Middlesex	Aug	320
1761	Thomas		Middlesex	Dec	418
1770	William		Middlesex	Jul	253
1787	William	A with W of Goods unad	Middlesex	Feb	
		Will regd 253 Fenner			
1786	BEENAN, Edward		Kent	May	260
1787	BEER, Ann		Middlesex	Jun	253
1796	Ann		Middlesex	Jan	4
1784	Anne		Middlesex	Sep	493
1770	Cornelis de	Limited Probate	Pts	May	173
1754	Edward		Pts	Oct	265
1761	Edward		Middlesex	Oct	340
	alias BAAR				
1758	Enoch		Pts	Mar	64
1758	George		Pts/Southampton	Mar	65
1781	Gertruyda de, Lady	Limited Probate	Pts	Feb	
1777	DE MEULEBEQUE,		Pts	Jan	29
	Hubertine de,				
	alias Marie Hubertine				
	Francoise de Beer de				
	Meulebeque				
1760	Hugh		Devon	Oct	381
1779	James		Middlesex	Jul	288
1782	James		Kent	Oct	482
1780	John		Middlesex	Feb	58
1784	John		Devon	Apr	190
1791	John	"Bombay Castle"	Pts	Jan	7
1781	Laurens de	Limited Probate	Pts	Oct	471
1776	Lydia		Wiltshire	Nov	449
	alias BEARE				
1767	Richard	Ser	Kent	Jun	206

	BEER (Contd)				
1751	Thomas		Pts/Devon	Oct	276
1750	William		Pts/Devon	Mar	67
1782	William		Middlesex	Jan	7
1791	BEERLING, Henry		Middlesex	Jan	6
1786	BEERMAN, Benjamin	"Cockatrice"	Pts	Jan	7
	alias BAREMAN				
1760	Samuel		London	Nov	415
1797	William	"Boyne" "Veteran"&"Alarm"	Pts	Aug	541
1770	BEERS, St. John		Ireland	Apr	131
1754	BEESLEY, Benjamin		Worcestershire	Apr	98
1798	Eleanor		Middlesex	Jul	460
1791	Elizabeth	A with W	Oxford	May	214
1793	Henry		Worcestershire	May	241
1783	BEESLEY, John		Middlesex	Nov	551
1800	Joseph		Worcester	Nov	770
1776	Thomas		Oxford	Mar	111
1797	Thomas		Worcestershire	Apr	226
1782	John		Surrey	Jun	268
1793	BEESLY, John	A with W	Berkshire	Dec	579
1800	Mary		Surrey	Oct	702
1772	Michael		Berkshire	Jul	246
1777	BEESON, John		London	Jan	5
1780	Margaret		Middlesex	Feb	54
1770	Sarah		Middlesex	Dec	421
1799	Thomas		Leicestershire	Dec	821
1767	William		Middlesex	Apr	123
1797	BEEST, Hendrik	Limited Probate	Pts	Sep	621
	Justus van				
1768	Maria van	Limited Probate	Pts	Sep	364
1776	Maria Hillegonda van	Limited Probate	Pts	Feb	107
1755	BEESTON, Anne		Berkshire	Feb	32
1766	Catherine		Berkshire	Mar	89
1776	Elizabeth		Oxford	Dec	488
1751	Francis		Stafford	Dec	326
1768	George		Middlesex	Dec	441
1774	Hannah		Middlesex	Oct	360
1795	Paul		Kent	Mar	147
1760	Richard		Kent	May	184
1782	BEET, Thomas		Leicestershire	Mar	110
1782	Thomas		Leicestershire	Jul	339
1784	Thomas		York	May	249
1784	William		Essex	May	248
1777	BEETE, James		Bath	Jul	303
1787	Jeene		Middlesex	Feb	56
	alias Jane				
1785	John	Special Probate	Pts	Dec	588
1786	Joseph		Berkshire	Sep	464
1797	BEETENSON, Mary		Salop	Jul	469
1754	William		Middlesex	Apr	99
1761	BEETHAM, Robert		Surrey	Jul	241

	BEETHAM (Contd)				
1784	Thomas		Middlesex	May	246
1784	William		Middlesex	May	246
1781	BEETHELL, Ann		Dorset	Jun	282
1782	George, Esq		Southampton	Apr	165
1778	Jane		Dorset	Sep	347
1773	Mary		Dorset	Sep	351
1770	BEETON, Jabez		Middlesex	Oct	352
1795	John	"Sceptre"	Pts	Apr	236
1784	Malcolm	"Isis"	Pts	Jul	367
	alias Malkim				
1788	May		Middlesex	Apr	172
1782	Sarah		Middlesex	Feb	65
1768	BEETS, Martin	A with W	Pts	Dec	370
1789	BEETT, George		Surrey	Dec	572
	alias BETT				
1757	William		London	Mar	73
1795	BEETTELL, Thomas, Esq	E.I. "Canton"	Middlesex	Sep	534
1787	BEETTLESTONE, John		Kent	Jul	312
1758	BEETY, Godfrey		Middlesex	Dec	357
1788	BEEVER, John		York	Sep	425
1756	BEEVINS, Thomas		Pts/Devon	Feb	27
1751	BEEVOR, Henry		Middlesex	Mar	74
1773	Henry		London	Sep	351
1750	Thomas		York	Sep	286
1783	BEEZLEY, Ezkiel		Pts	Jul	339
	alias BEASLAY				
	alias BEARLEY				
1784	John		Pts	Mar	120
	alias BEASLY				
1755	Jonathan		Middlesex	Sep	234
1785	Sarah		Middlesex	Jul	356
1750	William	Pts	Kent	Feb	40
	alias BASELEE				
	alias BAZELEE				
1763	BEFETT, Francis	A with W	Pts	Feb	44
	alias BEEFORD				
	alias BEAFORD				
1777	BEFFORD, Elizabeth		Salisbury	Jun	256
1787	Thomas		Salisbury	May	200
1759	BEGART, Garett		Pts	Jun	193
1788	BEGBIE, Robert	E.I.S."Contractor"	Pts	Mar	119
1761	BEGER, William		Middlesex	Jun	204
1799	BEGG, Alexander		Middlesex	Feb	97
	alias BEGGS				
1763	Charles		Pts	Feb	47
1783	Mark		Ireland	Sep	444
1785	BEGGE, Le, Petrus		Pts	Nov	
	Josephus				
1799	BEGGS, Alexander		Middlesex	Feb	97
	alias BEGG				

Year	Name	Type	Place	Month	Page
1783	BEGLEY, Terry alias BEGLY	Ser.	Devon	Aug	399
1783	BEGLY, Terry alias BEGLEY	Ser	Devon	Aug	399
1757	BEGON, Elizabeth alias GALLATIN	Limited Probate	Pts	Aug	247
1762	John Andrew, Esq	A with W	Middlesex	Jan	4
1777	BEGOZ, Isaac Ralph		London	Oct	408
1769	BEGRAM, Cornelia alias VANDER HEYDEN	Limited Probate	Pts	May	152
1779	Jan	Limited Probate	Pts	Jul	284
1753	BEGUIN, John Joseph		Middlesex	Sep	245
1787	BEHARRELL, Alice		Montgomery	Nov	483
1773	BEHO, Cathrine alias Catherine		Middlesex	May	191
1761	George		Berkshire	Aug	278
1794	BEHRENDS, Philipp Friedrich alias Philip Frederik		Pts	May	215
1764	BEIARD, John alias BAIRD alias BEARD	A with W	Pts	Dec	457
1770	BEICHLINGEN Lady Anna Francoise Vanden Heuvel at BEICHLINGEN said Bartholotti formerly Sadelyn		Pts	Aug	
1782	BEIEKEN, Hans Hinrek alias BEINKEN	A with W	Pts	May	212
1772	BEIGHTON, Mary		Surrey	Aug	285
1766	Rebecca		Cambridge	Jan	3
1766	Samuel		Surrey	Mar	92
1771	Thomas, The Reverend		Surrey	Oct	398
1789	BEIJEM, Johan Franco alias BEIJEN	A with W	Pts	Dec	574
1789	BEIJEN, Johan Franco alias BEIJEM	A with W	Pts	Dec	574
1784	BEIL, Elizabeth	Limited Probate	Middlesex	Nov	586
1761	BEILBY, Ann		Kent	Jan	6
1774	Ann		Middlesex	Dec	422
1769	Benjamin, Esq		York	Dec	404
1761	Dinah		London	Jan	3
1776	Elizabeth		York	Mar	165
1763	Henry alias BILBEE	A with W	Pts	Jan	5
1756	John alias BEALBY	Ser. A with W	Pts	Sep	239
1761	Richard	Ser.	Pts	Mar	81
1757	Robert alias BILBY		London	Feb	38

1782	BEINKEN, Hans Hinrick alias BEIEKEN	A with W	Pts	May	212
1789	BEITH, John		Surrey	Apr	188
1782	BEKE, Vander, Cornelis, Esq. The Right Honourable	Limited Probate	Pts	Nov	564
1772	The Right Honourable Lady Gysberta Elizabeth Vander	Limited Probate	Pts	Jun	30
1754	Vander, Johanna Elizabeth alias VANOVERBEKE		Pts	Mar	93
1772	BEKKER, Lamina alias CORRICK alias CORRECH	Limited Probate	Pts	Jan	6
1774	BEL, Van, Agatha alias PILLETIER		Pts	Jun	247
1788	Van, Gabriel Jansz		Pts	Dec	
1764	BELAIN, James alias BLY		Middlesex	Dec	454
1776	Jean Louis alias BELIN		Pts	Aug	344
1774	BELASYSE, Bridget		Durham	Apr	128
1750	Penelope, The Right Honourable Lady		Middlesex	Apr	106
1768	Rowland The Honourable	A with W	Middlesex	May	188
1769	William, , Esq		Middlesex	Mar	74
1757	BELBAN, William alias BELBIN		Pts	May	147
1785	BELBIN, James		Middlesex	Apr	171
1786	Joshua		Middlesex	Apr	203
1757	William alias BELBAN		Pts	May	147
1792	BELCEY, Richard		Kent	Apr	190
1780	BELCH, Elizabeth		London	Feb	56
1791	George		Devon	Mar	111
1767	Henry		Buckinghamshire	Oct	362
1798	Henry	A with W of Goods unad Will regd 362 Legard	Buckinghamshire	Dec	
1783	James	A with W	Pts	Oct	495
1787	John		Hertford	Jul	309
1791	Mary		Middlesex	Jan	2
1765	Sarah		Hertford	Feb	44
1792	William		Surrey	Aug	422
1781	William		London	Oct	463
1777	BELCHAM, John		London	Oct	409
1753	William		Essex	Jun	164
1782	BELCHER, Anne Maria		Oxford	Aug	391
1775	Benjamin		Gloucester	Jul	262
1776	Charles		Cornwall	Mar	112

BELCHER (Contd)

Year	Name		Place	Month	No.
1781	Daniel		Hampshire	Jan	7
1800	Daniel		Kent	Aug	575
1789	Elizabeth		Kent	Jan	7
1789	Elizabeth		Gloucestershire	Feb	72
1792	Elizabeth	A with W	London	Oct	497
1757	James		Pts	Dec	349
1750	John		London	Jun	187
1765	John		Essex	Mar	85
1765	John		Middlesex	Nov	401
1771	John	A with W	Middlesex	Nov	432
1782	John		Pts	Mar	109
1798	John		Berkshire	Apr	234
1767	Paul	A with W	Pts	Nov	402
1766	Rebecca		Surrey	Mar	89
1780	Richard		London	Aug	386
1786	Richard		Berkshire	May	264
1799	Richard		Oxford	Jan	13
1799	Richard		Berkshire	Nov	758
1760	Samuel		Kent	Jul	274
1782	Samuel	A with W unad Will regd 274 Lynch	Kent	Aug	
1796	Samuel, Esq	A with W of Goods unad Will regd 274 Lynch Another Grant Aug 1782	Kent	Jun	
1753	Thomas		Berkshire	Jan	3
1784	Thomas		Middlesex	Mar	120
1788	Thomas Smith		Oxford	May	226
1798	William		Berkshire	Oct	633
1800	BELCHERE, Henry		Middlesex	Jun	439
1756	BELCHIER, Elizabeth		Bristol	Jun	158
1753	Hannah		Surrey	Nov	286
1785	John		London	Feb	68
1788	Mary		Surrey	Aug	383
1775	Nathaniel	A with W	Pts/Kent	Sep	335
1750	Thomas		Monmouth	Oct	317
1773	William	A with W	Surrey	Sep	350
1785	William		Northampton	Sep	455
1786	William	A with W unad Will regd 350 Stevens	Surrey	Sep	
1796	William	A with W of Goods unad Will regd 455 Ducarel	Northampton	Dec	
1799	William		Northampton	Jan	11
1777	BELDAM, Elizabeth	A with W	Hertfordshire	Jan	3
1788	Hester		Cambridge	Oct	470
1770	John		Cambridge	Dec	424
1764	James		Hertfordshire	Oct	377
1777	Mary	A with W	Hertfordshire	Dec	497
1778	Mary		Hertfordshire	May	185
1762	Samuel		Hertfordshire	Jul	284
1769	Samuel		Essex	Nov	365
1765	Valentine	A with W	Hertfordshire	Jun	207

Year	Name	Note	Place	Month	No.
	BELDAM (Contd)				
1762	William		Middlesex	Nov	446
1766	William	A with W	Cambridge	Dec	441
1787	William, Esq		Middlesex	Apr	158
1752	BELDEN, Nicholas		Pts	May	117
	alias BILDEN				
1755	BELDER, Ephraim		Middlesex	Jul	183
1782	BELDOM, John		Surrey	Dec	572
1787	Thomas		London	Apr	155
1750	William		Middlesex	Aug	251
1781	BELDON, Sarah		Hertford	Jun	285
1790	Thomas		London	Apr	173
1761	BELEY, Johanna		Middlesex	Mar	83
1767	Mary		Kent	Dec	437
1781	Noah	Ser.	Pts	Mar	115
1795	BELFEILD, Henry		Hertfordshire	Nov	623
1765	BELFIELD, Edward	A with W	Southampton	Feb	44
1797	Elizabeth		Hertfordshire	Mar	129
1789	Henry, The Reverend		Hertfordshire	Feb	79
1795	Henry	Ser."Victory"	Pts	May	300
1751	John		London	Nov	299
1763	John		London	Feb	45
1762	David		Pts/Middlesex	Dec	493
1772	Martha		Kent	Dec	430
1780	William, Esq		Kent	Aug	384
	General of His				
	Majesties Forces				
1779	BELFOUR, Ann		Middlesex	Sep	367
1759	Bartholomew		Pts	Apr	119
1771	John		Middlesex	Feb	46
1793	John		Middlesex	Nov	539
1773	Michael		Middlesex	Aug	318
1764	BELFRIDGE, John		Kent	Dec	455
	alias BELVRIDGE				
1775	BELGROVE, William		Hertfordshire	Jan	2
1797	BELGRAVE, Ann		Leicester	Jun	397
1777	Con, The Reverend		Rutland	Nov	451
1757	Cornelius, The		Rutland	Jun	182
	Reverend				
1795	George		Rutland	May	296
1795	George	Will regd this month	Rutland	May	
1753	William		Rutland	Jul	196
1781	William		Leicester	Jul	332
1796	BELHAVEN, William	Lord	Middlesex	Sep	
	HAMILTON, commonly				
	called Lord Belhaven				
1762	BELIN, Allard		London	Jun	234
1776	George	Ltd A with W	Middlesex	Mar	110
1796	George	Ltd A with W of Goods unad. Will regd 110 Bellas	Middlesex	Oct	

	BELIN (Contd)				
1776	Jean Louis		Pts	Aug	344
	alias BELAIN				
1796	Mary		Middlesex	Apr	167
1793	Mary Magdalen		Pts	Feb	67
	alias Marie Magdelaine				
	alias Magdeleine				
1761	BELING, Peter Gottfriedt		London	Jun	200
1762	BELITHA, John		Pts	Jun	233
	alias BELITHO				
1781	Mary		Surrey	Jan	6
1776	Samuel		Pts	Feb	54
	alias BOLITHA				
1762	Thomas		Surrey	Jun	236
1759	Warren, Esq		Cornwall	Apr	119
1759	William, Esq		Middlesex	Apr	119
1784	BELITHER, James		Middlesex	Jun	305
	alias BOLITHAR				
1762	BELITHO, John		Pts	Jun	233
	alias BELITHA				
1792	BELJEAN, Samuel		Middlesex	May	260
1780	BELK, William		Middlesex	Aug	384
1766	BELL, Abraham	A with W	Surrey	Jan	3
1760	Alexander		Surrey	Jun	230
1763	Alexander	A with W	Surrey	Jun	267
1773	Alexander		London	Jan	2
1771	Alice		Middlesex	Jun	244
	alias Alles				
1779	Amey		Middlesex	Nov	443
1779	Amey	By Int Decree	Middlesex	Nov	445
		Another Will proved this month			
1792	Amy		Wiltshire	Jun	316
1761	Andry	A with W	Pts	Dec	419
	alias Andrew				
	alias Henry				
1756	Ann		Surrey	Aug	217
1758	Ann		Berkshire	Jul	210
1773	Ann		Berkshire	Jun	235
1777	Ann	A with W	Kent	May	201
1797	Ann		Newcastle/Tyne	Apr	221
1761	Anna Maria		London	Oct	337
1793	Vander, Anna Maria		Pts	Jun	345
1797	Augustine	E.I.S."Prince Wm. Henry"	Pts	Mar	134
1752	Benjamin		London	Nov	270
1782	Benjamin		Pts	Jul	340
1793	Benjamin	Poor	Kent	Aug	398
1795	Benjamin		Surrey	Jun	369
1797	Bridget		Devon	Apr	225
1790	Charity		Bedford	Mar	119
1755	Charles		Middlesex	Jun	154

BELL (Contd)

1764	Charles		Devon	Dec	454
1792	Charles		N.Britain	Mar	131
1754	Christopher		London	Sep	244
1762	Christopher		Middlesex	Aug	331
1788	Christopher		Norfolk	Jun	290
1793	Christopher		Middlesex	Jul	352
1781	Coulson, Esq		Norfolk	Mar	118
1800	Coulson, Esq		Norfolk	May	347
1758	Daniel		Middlesex	Mar	63
1762	Daniel		Middlesex	Jan	4
1762	Daniel		Middlesex	Apr	136
1778	Daniel		Pts/Devon	Aug	309
1752	David	A with W	Pts	Aug	206
1757	David	A with W of Goods unad	Middlesex	May	
		Will regd 209 Brodrepp			
1758	David		Pts	Jan	5
1773	David, Esq		Chichester	Apr	147
1799	Dorothy		Lincoln	Apr	248
1782	Edmund		Middlesex	Oct	479
1751	Edward		Pts/Surrey	Oct	274
1752	Edward		Pts	Jun	147
1760	Edward		Middlesex	Feb	48
1767	Edward		Pts	May	162
1796	Eleanor		Staffordshire	Sep	446
1782	Elijah		Pts	Jan	2
1751	Elizabeth	.	Buckinghamshire	May	132
1758	Elizabeth		Surrey	Apr	101
1766	Elizabeth		Middlesex	Jan	3
1769	Elizabeth	A with W	Durham	Dec	406
	alias COCKRAM				
1770	Elizabeth		Middlesex	Nov	389
1780	Elizabeth		Hertfordshire	Apr	174
1784	Elizabeth		Middlesex	Oct	539
1786	Elizabeth		Staffordshire	Sep	479
1789	Elizabeth		Surrey	Mar	137
1789	Elizabeth		Cornwall	Apr	191
1789	Elizabeth		Surrey	Aug	418
1799	Elizabeth		Buckinghamshire	Nov	759
1781	Ellen	A with W	Lincoln	Jun	287
1762	Esther		Kent	Mar	91
1789	Esther		Middlesex	Nov	532
1773	Fleming Pinkstan		Pts	Aug	319
1761	Francis	Ser. A with W	Pts	Dec	418
1773	Francis		Northampton	May	193
1785	Francis	Ser. "Hector"	Pts	Aug	403
1750	Frances		Norfolk	Jul	222
1761	Frances		London	May	160
1763	Frances		London	Jun	268
1768	Frances	A with W unad	London	Apr	
		Will regd June 1763			

BELL (Contd)

Year	Name	Notes	Place	Month	No.
1768	Frances	A with W unad Will regd 268 Caesar Last Grant April last	London	Dec	439
1772	Frances		Hertford	May	159
1781	Frances		Surrey	Dec	573
1799	Frances		Middlesex	Jan	13
1750	George	Pts	Middlesex	Oct	315
1759	George		Pts	Mar	81
1762	George		Surrey	Dec	493
1763	George		Middlesex	Jun	269
1764	George	A with W	Pts	Nov	413
1767	George	Ltd A with W	Pts	Mar	87
1771	George, The Reverend		Bath	Sep	366
1775	George	Ser.	Middlesex	Mar	83
1776	George, Esq		Cornwall	Feb	54
1790	George		Worcestershire	Aug	365
1797	George		Newcastle/Tyne	Jul	473
1799	George	"Porcupine", "Theseus"& Gun Vessel "Scorpion"	Pts/Dorset	Jul	474
1789	Grace		York	May	237
1783	Hannah		Middlesex	Jan	2
1784	Hannah		Middlesex	Jul	372
1795	Henrietta		Cornwall	Sep	534
1757	Henry		York	Dec	349
1767	Henry		Newcastle/Tyne	Nov	404
1784	Henry		Middlesex	Apr	189
1794	Henry	Ser. His Majesty's Yacht "Prss. Augusta"	Kent	Jan	5
1778	Henry Saint John		Buckinghamshire	May	184
1766	Hugh Barker, Esq		Buckinghamshire	Oct	362
1757	Humphrey		London	Sep	266
1757	Humphrey	Double Probate Will regd this month	London	Sep	
1780	Hyde		Essex	Apr	198
1756	Jacob		London	Aug	216
1756	James		Surrey	Mar	60
1763	James		London	May	213
1775	James		Pts	Jun	222
1777	James		Surrey	Aug	340
1782	James		Middlesex	Nov	528
1784	James		Surrey	Dec	629
1787	James	No Ship. A with W	Pts	Aug	358
1793	James, Esq		Devon	Jul	352
1795	James		Hertfordshire	Jun	370
1797	James		London	Apr	226
1799	James		London	Jun	417
1800	James	Ser."Defiance"	Devon	Apr	257
1758	Jane		Middlesex	Feb	29
1771	Jane		Middlesex	Nov	430

BELL (Contd)

Year	Name	Note	Place	Month	Page
1788	Jane	A with W	Kent	May	227
1798	Jane		Norwich	Feb	83
1752	John		London	Aug	204
1753	John		Middlesex	Jan	4
1753	John	A with W	Pts	Jul	197
1755	John		Middlesex	Jan	2
1755	John	A with W unad Will regd Jan 1753	Middlesex	Jan	
1755	John		Middlesex	Jun	154
1756	John		Kent	May	130
1757	John, Esq		Lincoln	Jan	3
1758	John		Pts	Feb	32
1759	John		London	Nov	348
1761	John	Ser.	Pts	Jan	2
1761	John		Middlesex	Feb	45
1761	John		Middlesex	Mar	84
1761	John		Pts/Southampton	Jun	204
1763	John		Kent	Oct	459
1766	John		Middlesex	Jan	4
1768	John		Middlesex	Oct	368
1770	John		London	Jul	254
1770	John	Double Probate Will regd 4 Tyndall	Middlesex	Jul	
1771	John		Pts	Jul	286
1772	John		London	Jun	206
1772	John		Pts	Jun	206
1773	John		Dorset	Feb	43
1774	John		Kent	Jan	5
1774	John, Esq		Nottingham	Sep	328
1775	John		Middlesex	Jan	3
1778	John	Ser.	Pts	May	187
1780	John	A with W	Pts	Feb	55
1780	John		Pts	Dec	
1781	John, Esq		Denbighshire	May	229
1782	John	A with W "Burford"	Pts	Jul	335
1783	John	A with W. "Centurion"	Pts	Dec	602
1784	John, The Reverend		Suffolk	Sep	494
1785	John	A with W Ser "Prince George,""Arrogant," "Victory,""Pheasant,""Cutter"	Pts	Jun	292
1785	John, Esq		Pts	Oct	491
1786	John		Pts/Worcester	Apr	204
1786	John		Middlesex	Jul	362
1790	John	Ser.	Kent	Sep	410
1790	John		Kent	Nov	494
1791	John		London	May	213
1792	John	A with W	Durham	Dec	596
1794	John, The Reverend		Cumberland	Jan	3
1794	John		Middlesex	Jun	300
1795	John		Middlesex	Jun	364

BELL (Contd)

Year	Name	Notes	Place	Month	No.
1796	John, Esq		Middlesex	Aug	399
1797	John, Esq		Carlisle	Oct	630
	Lt. Gen. of His Maj.				
	Forces & Col. of				
	Marines.				
1800	John, Esq		Middlesex	Aug	583
1780	John Alderman	By Int Decree	Middlesex	Mar	122
		Another Grant Dec 1778			
1760	John George		Pts	May	186
1791	Jonathan		Hertfordshire	May	210
1759	Joseph		Hertfordshire	Feb	46
1759	Joseph, Esq		London	Sep	288
1760	Joseph, Esq		Kent	Feb	46
1763	Joseph		Pts/Middlesex	Oct	461
1773	Joseph, The Reverend		Buckinghamshire	Jul	281
1783	Joseph, Esq		York	Apr	161
1800	Joseph		Middlesex	Jan	7
1764	Joshua		London	Nov	416
1767	Joyce		Middlesex	Nov	401
1777	Joyce	A with W of Goods unad	Pts	Oct	
		Will regd 401 Legard			
1787	Joyce	A with W of Goods twice	Middlesex	Jun	
		unad. Will regd 401			
		Legard last Grant Oct 1777			
1796	Lancelot, The		Norfolk	Jan	7
	Reverend				
1761	Lawrence		Pts/Devon	Sep	309
1763	Luke		London	Aug	371
1780	Luke		Warwickshire	Nov	506
1792	Luke	A with W	Middlesex	Aug	417
1790	Mark, Esq		Surrey	Feb	59
1759	Margaret	Limited Probate	Middlesex	May	161
1776	Margaret		Northumberland	Aug	344
1777	Margaret		Middlesex	Apr	148
1787	Margaret		London	Nov	484
1791	Margaret		Middlesex	May	215
1751	Margret		London	Oct	275
1778	Martha		Lincoln	Jan	6
1781	Martha	A with W unad	Lincoln	Sep	
		Will regd Jan 1778			
1754	Mary		Bedford	Jan	4
1755	Mary		Surrey	Feb	31
1764	Mary		Surrey	Jul	249
1769	Mary		Middlesex	Apr	112
1770	Mary		Surrey	Apr	130
1771	Mary		Middlesex	Jan	3
1773	Mary		Surrey	May	191
1775	Mary		Gloucestershire	Apr	127
1778	Mary		Surrey	Nov	434
1780	Mary	Double Probate	Surrey	May	
		Will regd Nov. 1778			

BELL (Contd)

1782	Mary		Bedford	Nov	531
1784	Mary		Middlesex	Nov	588
1797	Mary		Hertford	Jan	4
1779	Mary Ann		London	Oct	402
1760	Matthew		Middlesex	Feb	46
1772	Matthew		London	Jun	208
1773	Matthew	Double Probate Will regd June last	London	Feb	
1792	Matthew, Esq	A with W	Newcastle	Mar	134
1792	Matthew		Middlesex	Jun	317
1800	Matthew		Middlesex	Aug	581
1780	Melecent		Middlesex	Feb	24
1774	Mercy		London	Jun	217
1752	Michael		Middlesex	Oct	241
1800	Michael	"La Lutine"	Pts	Apr	254
1797	Miriam alias JANSON		Durham	Dec	749
1775	Nathaniel		London	Oct	368
1757	Nicholas		Pts	Apr	112
1784	Patrick	Ser "Exeter"	Pts	Aug	426
1760	Peter		Middlesex	Jan	3
1786	Philip, Esq		London	Jun	319
1764	Ralph		Surrey	Jan	1
1778	Ralph		York	Oct	390
1783	Ralph		Middlesex	Feb	57
1784	Rebecca		London	Feb	64
1751	Richard, Esq		Bedford	Oct	276
1761	Richard		Kent	Nov	379
1771	Richard		Middlesex	Aug	331
1774	Richard		Middlesex	Apr	128
1792	Richard	E.I.S. "Alfred"	Pts	Apr	198
1795	Richard		Surrey	Apr	239
1797	Richard	"London"	Pts/Cornwall	May	292
1798	Richard		Middlesex	Feb	81
1800	Richard	"Reasonable"	Pts	Feb	84
1766	Richardson	A with W	Pts	Aug	292
1751	Robert	A with W	Pts	Apr	102
1756	Robert		Pts	Dec	320
1761	Robert		Lincoln	Jan	3
1773	Robert		London	Jan	4
1776	Robert		Middlesex	Apr	166
1781	Robert	Ser.	Devon	May	228
1786	Robert	"Terrible"	Pts	Sep	464
1793	Ruth alias JENNISON		York	Jan	6
1779	Samuel		Middlesex	Apr	142
1782	Samuel	A with W	Pts	Sep	440
1792	Samuel		Essex	Feb	55
1792	Samuel	Double Probate Will regd Feb. last	Essex	Apr	

BELL (Contd)

Year	Name	Note	Place	Month	No.
1795	Samuel		York	Jul	429
1765	Sarah		Surrey	Jul	248
1790	Sarah		Kent	Jan	4
1793	Sarah		Middlesex	Apr	184
1776	Spencer		Middlesex	Apr	162
1750	Susan		Middlesex	Dec	378
1751	Susan	Will regd Dec. last	Middlesex	Jan	
	alias Susanna				
	alias Susannah				
1763	Susanna		Middlesex	Sep	420
1753	Thomas		Salop	May	130
1757	Thomas		Pts	Apr	111
1763	Thomas	A with W	Pts	Jul	322
1769	Thomas		London	Mar	77
1776	Thomas		York	May	213
1782	Thomas		Kent	Jul	337
1783	Thomas	Ser.	Pts	Mar	114
1783	Thomas	A with W "Magnanime"	Durham	Sep	443
1784	Thomas	"Minorca"	Pts	Jun	311
1785	Thomas		Staffordshire	Sep	456
1786	Thomas, 2nd	"Eagle"	Pts	Feb	66
1789	Thomas		Kent	Jul	340
1791	Thomas		Surrey	Mar	116
1791	Thomas		Middlesex	May	210
1791	Thomas, Esq	A with W of Goods unad Will regd March 1791	Surrey	Nov	
1792	Thomas		London	Dec	596
1795	Thomas, Esq		Middlesex	May	297
1798	Thomas		Kent	Jan	8
1798	Thomas	E.I.S. "Hillsborough"	Pts	Aug	525
1751	Villers		Middlesex	Mar	73
1751	William		Middlesex	May	132
1754	William		Pts	Dec	320
1757	William	A with W	Pts/Southampton	Nov	320
1758	William	Ser	Pts	Nov	321
1763	William		Surrey	Aug	369
1764	William		London	Jun	213
1767	William		Pts	Jan	3
1767	William		Buckinghamshire	May	166
1768	William, Esq		Gloucester	Feb	49
1768	William		London	May	188
1768	William		London	Dec	438
1768	William	Another Grant this month	London	Dec	438
1769	William, Esq		Kent	Jan	3
1777	William, The Reverend		Gloucester	Feb	53
1777	William		Cambridge	Oct	407
1778	William, The Reverend		Kent	Sep	363

	BELL (Contd)				
1779	William		Pts	Oct	405
1783	William		Pts/Devon	May	218
1783	William		Norfolk	May	218
1785	William	"Hannibal"	N. Britain	Jun	291
1785	William		Buckinghamshire	Aug	405
1786	William		Rutland	Mar	138
1786	William	By Sent (regd Oct 645)	Bath	Oct	503
1787	William Greaves Beaupre, Esq		Cambridge	Mar	108
1791	William	A with W	Norfolk	Nov	498
1792	William		Middlesex	Aug	417
1793	William		Surrey	Feb	69
1793	William	Will regd this month	Surrey	Feb	69
1794	William		London	Apr	186
1794	William	"Lion"	Pts	Dec	595
1795	William	No Ship	Pts	Mar	144
1796	William		Gloucester	Apr	166
1797	William		Hertford	Apr	222
1797	William		London	Nov	677
1798	William		York	Apr	240
1799	William		Middlesex	Sep	644
1800	William	"Medea" "Hector"& "Northumberland"	Pts	Nov	764
1754	Winefrede		Bristol	Jan	4
1785	BELLAARD, Gerard Paulus alias BELLAARDT	Limited Probate	Pts	Mar	113
1751	BELLACHE, Stephen alias BALLASH	By Int. Decree	Pts	Feb	34
1794	BELLAERS, Ann		Warwick	Dec	596
1788	Catherine		Leicester	Sep	429
1799	James		Ireland	Jan	10
1800	James, Esq		Lincoln	Feb	83
1772	John	A with W	Warwick	Oct	352
1755	Margery		Warwick	Nov	275
1796	BELLAMEY, John alias BELLAMY		Middlesex	Jan	7
1784	BELLAMY, Abraham alias BALLAMY	A with W	Surrey	Jul	369
1769	Alice		Middlesex	Oct	333
1780	Ann		Warwick	Jun	301
1771	Clement	A with W unad Will regd 200 Strahan	London	Jul	
1764	Daniel		Kent	Jan	5
1774	Daniel		Surrey	Jan	1
1788	Daniel, The Reverend		Surrey	Mar	120
1770	Edward, Esq		Dorset	Oct	352
1768	Edward		Middlesex	Mar	96
1791	Edward, Esq		Dorset	Oct	451
1758	Elizabeth alias HARRIS	A with W limited	Middlesex	Jun	178

BELLAMY (Contd)

Year	Name	Note	County	Month	No.
1779	Elizabeth		Hereford	May	190
1793	Frances		Surrey	Mar	126
1750	Francis	Will regd 218 Abbot	Pts	Sep	
1767	Humphrey		Berkshire	Sep	332
1750	James	A with W	Pts	May	137
1757	James		Pts	Mar	74
1750	Jane		Middlesex	Mar	69
1762	Jane		Warwick	Jun	237
1756	John		Pts/Surrey	Nov	289
1764	John		Middlesex	Feb	37
1765	John		Cambridge	Apr	132
1771	John		Dorset	Jul	285
1780	John		Kent	Jan	3
1781	John		Middlesex	Aug	376
1794	John		Middlesex	Oct	488
1796	John alias BELLAMEY		Middlesex	Jan	7
1799	John		Worcester	Jan	7
1771	Joseph		Hertford	Mar	94
1775	Joseph		Hertford	Nov	405
1795	Joshua		London	Feb	65
1755	Mary		Middlesex	Aug	209
1758	Mary		Dorset	Feb	29
1759	Mary		Kent	Feb	45
1761	Mary		Surrey	Nov	282
1774	Mary		Pts	May	167
1793	Mary		Middlesex	Oct	490
1796	Mary		Surrey	Dec	591
1754	Moses		Middlesex	Mar	69
1762	Paul		Middlesex	Feb	39
1787	Peter		London	Dec	530
1753	Richard		Monmouth	Apr	102
1759	Richard		Dorset	Aug	258
1769	Richard		Pts	Aug	273
1772	Richard, The Reverend		Monmouth	Jul	245
1776	Richard		Middlesex	May	210
1759	Ruth		Middlesex	May	158
1771	Samuel		Dorset	Mar	96
1782	Sarah		Kent	Feb	59
1776	Thomas	Int. Decree	Warwick	Apr	161
1782	Thomas		London	Oct	480
1787	Thomas		Nottingham	Aug	356
1790	Thomas		Hereford	Dec	540
1792	Thomas		Warwick	Aug	418
1796	Thomas, Esq		Monmouth	May	238
1799	Thomas		Somerset	Sep	645
1763	William		Pts	Jul	322
1771	William		Devon	May	193
1785	William		Surrey	Jan	6
1798	William		Middlesex	Nov	693

1791	BELLANGE, Michael		Middlesex	Jan	5
1776	BELLANGER, Maria	Limited Probate	Pts	Oct	414
	Margaretha				
	alias Maria Margareta				
1784	Maria Martha		Pts	Feb	64
	alias Maria Marte				
1785	BELLARDT, Gerard Paulus	Limited Probate	Pts	Mar	113
	alias BELLAARD				
1792	BELLARS, John, Esq		Rutland	May	263
1757	BELLAS, Joseph		Pts	Sep	267
1799	Robert, Esq		Kent	Dec	824
1800	BELLASS, Hannah		Middlesex	Mar	178
1762	BELLASAS, Samuel		Pts	May	187
1780	BELLCHAMBER, Ann		Cambridge	Jul	346
1759	Nathaniel		London	Jan	4
1762	BELLE, Van, Jacob	Limited Probate	Pts	Jul	325
1798	Van, Jacoba	Limited Probate	Pts	Nov	747
	Catharina				
1795	BELLEFONTAIN, Louise		Middlesex	Mar	140
1772	BELLEFONTAINE,		Middlesex	Oct	350
	Marguerite				
1791	BELLEGARDE, Eugene,	Lord	Pts	Jun	265
	Marquis of				
1798	BELLENDEN, The Right		Southampton	Feb	82
	Honourable Lady				
	Elizabeth				
1761	Henry, The Honourable		Middlesex	May	159
	Sir				
1763	James, Esq		Middlesex	Jan	8
1794	BELLENGER, Adam		Oxford	Jul	352
1767	John		Oxford	Oct	362
1769	BELLENIE, John		Middlesex	Oct	334
1789	Mary		Surrey	Dec	573
1761	Robert		London	May	158
1784	BELLERIVE, De, Nicolas		Pts	Feb	73
	Jean Daniel				
	alias DE BELLERIVE,				
	Nicolas				
1796	BELLESTRE, De, Francois	A with W	Pts	Nov	
	Marie Picote, Hon				
1764	BELLETIE, Augustine		Pts	Sep	339
	alias BELLITE				
	alias BILLITE				
1771	BELLEW, Frances	A with W	Dublin	Dec	470
1759	James		Pts	Mar	83
1770	The Right Honourable		Pts	Oct	349
	John, Lord Bellew in the				
	Kingdom of Ireland				
1775	Michael Barnwall		Pts	Jan	2
1764	Nicholas		Middlesex	Aug	299
1799	Patrick, Esq		Middlesex	Jul	478

1772	BELLEY, Samuel alias BELEY alias BAYLEY		Pts	Oct	352
1763	BELLFIELD, Elizabeth		London	May	216
1752	BELLFOUR, Alexander		Pts	Jun	147
1798	BELLIARD, Charles		Middlesex	Apr	232
1766	BELLIE, Philip		Middlesex	Apr	127
1766	Sarah Magdalen		Middlesex	Jun	212
1796	BELLIN, Benjamin	"Hebe"	Pts	Nov	542
1772	BELLINGER, James		Middlesex	Oct	350
1787	Thomas		Surrey	Dec	533
1785	Walter		Middlesex	Oct	494
1771	BELLINGHAM, Ann		Middlesex	Mar	95
1781	Edmund Baldwin		Middlesex	May	225
1762	Elizabeth		Middlesex	Jan	2
1777	James alias BELLINGHM		Middlesex	Jun	255
1775	John		Bristol	Jan	1
1797	Mary		Kent	Apr	226
1788	Nathaniel	"Eleanor""Ajax""Sulphur" "Heart of Oak""Arrogant" Ser.	Pts	Mar	120
1759	Sampson		Pts	Jun	194
1762	William		Middlesex	Apr	139
1765	BELLINGS, Richard, Sir	A with W of Goods unad Last Grant December 1737	Middlesex	Nov	
1750	BELLINGTON, George alias BALLENTINE	A with W by Int. Decree	Pts	Jan	2
1766	BELLIS, Ann		Middlesex	May	168
1769	Edward		Middlesex	Mar	76
1757	Edmund		Middlesex	Nov	322
1767	George		Middlesex	Aug	298
1788	James, Esq		Hertford	Nov	521
1787	John		Hertford	Jun	253
1776	Margaret		Middlesex	Jun	257
1783	Martha		Middlesex	Nov	554
1768	Mary		London	Nov	402
1774	Nathaniel		Middlesex	Oct	358
1750	Susanna		Middlesex	Nov	348
1773	Theophilus		Middlesex	Feb	44
1772	Thomas		Hertford	May	157
1757	William		Hertford	Aug	239
1761	William	Ser.	Middlesex	Jan	4
1796	William		Hertford	Jun	295
1798	William		Middlesex	May	308
1782	BELLISS, Hannah		Salop	Jan	5
1800	BELLISSON, Thomas		Warwick	Nov	769
1764	BELLITE, Augustine alias BELLETIE alias BILLITE		Pts	Sep	339
1758	BELLMAN, Charles		Pts	Mar	65

1797	BELLMAN, Charles alias BELMAN		Devon	Feb	72
1800	Elizabeth	A with W	Nottingham	Oct	700
1768	Hans		London	Oct	371
1788	Jane		Norfolk	Jul	337
1762	BELLNAP, Daniel		Middlesex	Apr	142
1768	BELLOMONT, The Right Honourable Richard, Earl of, in the Kingdom of Ireland		Worcester	Sep	337
1798	BELLON, Arthur		Middlesex	Oct	632
1751	William, Esq		Pts	Aug	230
1787	BELLONCLE, William		Middlesex	Oct	437
1762	BELLOON, Joseph alias BALLOW, Jose		Pts	Jul	284
1791	BELLOW, Henry, Esq		Exeter	May	213
1799	BELLOWS, Samuel		Dorset	Jan	12
1789	BELLSHAM, Thomas		Kent	Jun	299
1777	BELLWOOD, Eleanor		Middlesex	Feb	55
1754	John		London	Oct	265
1760	Richard		Middlesex	Feb	49
1760	Richard	Double Probate Will regd Feb. last	Middlesex	Mar	
1777	Richard	A with W of Goods twice unad. Will regd 49 Lynch Last Grant 1760 Ser.	Middlesex	Jul	
1780	BELLY, Gabriel		Durham	May	235
1797	BELMAN, Charles alias BELLMAN		Devon	Feb	72
1782	BELMER, Henry		London	Feb	60
1765	BELMONTE, Benjamin		London	Dec	441
1786	Jacob Abendana		Pts	Nov	557
1772	DA COSTA, Rachel alias DA COSTA, Rachel		Pts	May	164
1789	Ribca		Pts	Apr	188
1793	Ribca alias Ribca Fernandez Nunez		Pts	Jul	352
1766	BELNOT, Elizabeth		Middlesex	Jan	4
1750	BELO, Elizabeth		London	Sep	285
1788	BELOE, Stephen		Norfolk	Jun	291
1770	BELOYS, Adriaen Boogaert van	Limited Probate	Pts	Apr	
1764	BELS, Van der, Abraham, Dr.	Dr. of Law	Pts	Jul	289
1768	BELSCHES, Alexander		Middlesex	Aug	308
1795	BELSEY, Edward		Kent	Feb	68
1793	John		Lancashire	Jun	302
1763	William		Pts	May	212

1781	BELSHAM, Anne		Bedford	May	228
1771	James		Bedford	Apr	142
1790	BELSHAW, William		Middlesex	Dec	541
1783	BELSHER, William		Pts	Aug	401
1783	William	By Int. Decree. A will of a former date Proved last month	Pts	Sep	443
1792	William		Southampton	Feb	62
1750	BELSON, James		London	Oct	316
1755	James		Kent	Jun	155
1772	John, Esq		Pts/Buckingham	May	157
1783	John		Surrey	Feb	59
1799	Joseph		Middlesex	Jan	9
1770	The Honourable Lady Maria alias GOTT alias CLAVATT alias CLIFFORD		Pts	Mar	89
1800	Mary	A with W	Surrey	Aug	575
1772	Richard		Surrey	Jan	2
1795	Richard		Surrey	Oct	579
1786	William		Surrey	May	262
1799	BELSY, Nathaniel		Kent	Sep	643
1788	BELT, Daniel	No Ship Pts	York	Feb	57
1791	BELTGENS, Fredrik	Limited Probate	Pts	Dec	561
1768	BELTON, Ann		Middlesex	Aug	306
1776	Ann		Middlesex	Oct	411
1791	Ann	A with W of Goods unad Will regd 306 Secker	Middlesex	Apr	
1750	Joseph		London	May	140
1797	Mary		Middlesex	Oct	627
1758	Richard		Pts	Apr	104
1755	Stephen	A with W	Carlisle	Sep	234
1796	Thomas		Devon	Mar	108
1764	BELTY, Thomas		Kent	Mar	82
1760	BELUTEAU, Susanna		Middlesex	Jul	274
1764	BELVRIDGE, John alias BELFRIDGE		Kent	Dec	455
1754	BELWARD, Hannah		Middlesex	Apr	100
1788	Richard		Essex	Jun	290
1791	BELWOOD, William		York	Jul	318
1777	BEMAN, Betty		Southampton	May	95
1795	Mary		Middlesex	Mar	143
1771	Richard		Southampton	Jan	5
1791	Thomas	A with W No Ship	Pts	Jun	267
1783	BEMBO, Edmond alias BEMBOW, Edward	Ser.	Pts	Oct	496
1763	BEMBRICK, John		Surrey	Oct	460
1794	BEMBRIDGE, Charles		Middlesex	May	244

1780	BEMBRIDGE, Mary		Middlesex	May	242
1756	BEMEN, Richard	Ser.	Middlesex	Sep	239
	alias BEAUMONT				
1792	BEMISTER, Ann		Dorset	Jan	6
1763	Catherine		Southampton	Nov	496
1800	BEMMEL, Van, Jan	No Ship	Pts	Aug	567
	Adriaen, Esq.				
1759	BEMMISH, Elizabeth		Kent	Nov	347
1759	BEMNANT, John		Pts	Jul	225
1770	BEMONT, Robert		Middlesex	Sep	321
1792	BEMPDE, John Warden	A with W of Goods unad	Middlesex	May	
		Will regd 137 Plymouth			
1773	BEMPDEN, Van Den,	Limited Probate	Pts	Oct	409
	Lady Anna Elisabeth				
1769	Van Den, The Lady		Pts	Mar	85
	Esther Aajen				
	alias DEUTZ				
1762	BEMROSE, Robert		Middlesex	Jul	284
1750	BENALICK, John		Pts	Jun	188
1760	BENALLACK, Honour		Middlesex	Dec	451
1796	BENAMOR, James, The		Northampton	Sep	444
	Reverend				
1780	BENAZECH, Marie Esther	A with W	Middlesex	Nov	503
1798	Peter		Exeter	Dec	757
1759	BENBOW, Anne		Salop	Apr	118
1766	Charles		Middlesex	Sep	329
1785	James		Salop	Apr	173
1773	Mary		Montgomery	May	193
1761	Samuel	A with W or Testamentary	Hertford	Aug	277
		Schedules			
1759	Sarah		Surrey	Oct	317
1758	BENBRICK, Elizabeth		Surrey	Oct	283
1763	BENBURY, George		Pts	Jun	269
	alias BANBURY				
1759	BENCE, Isaac		Poole	Aug	257
1797	Isaac		Bristol	Jul	471
1750	Robert	A with W of Goods unad	Suffolk	Aug	
		Will regd 173 Edmunds			
1798	Susanna		London	Jan	8
1800	BENCKEN, Christopher		Surrey	Jul	505
	Godfrey				
1765	BENCKENDORFF, Van,	Limited Probate	Pts	Feb	46
	Joshua				
	alias CROMMELIN				
1765	BENCRAFT, James		Middlesex	Jan	5
1798	BEND, John		Hereford	Jun	381
1781	BENDALL, John	A with W	Wells	Nov	514
1800	Lucy		Middlesex	Apr	255
1799	Mary		Southampton	Jul	482
1781	Rebecca		Wells	Oct	463
1792	Robert		Middlesex	Mar	130

BENDALL (Contd)

Year	Name	Notes	Place	Month	No.
1791	Samuel		Gloucester	Apr	165
1755	Sarah		Southampton	Sep	233
1777	William		Kent	Jan	7
1785	William		London	Oct	496
1766	BENDBOW, Frances		Middlesex	May	171
1761	James		Middlesex	May	158
1761	Mary		Middlesex	Jun	202
1750	Samuel		Middlesex	Dec	378
1778	BENDELL, Thomas		Middlesex	Jan	2
1792	BENDER, Mary		Middlesex	Dec	596
1798	Robert	A with W	London	Apr	233
1775	BENDICKSON, Bendix alias BENDIXSON		Southampton	Aug	300
1766	BENDING, Joseph		Berkshire	Nov	396
1759	Richard		Pts	Jul	225
1766	BENDISH, Cecilia		Middlesex	Apr	128
1775	BENDIXSON, Bendix alias BENDICKSON	Ser.	Southampton	Aug	300
1763	BENDLEY, John		Pts	Nov	494
1788	Mary		Surrey	Jun	288
1769	BENDLOWES, Philip, Esq		York	Jun	193
1778	BENDRY, Elizabeth		Hertford	May	188
1787	James		London	May	196
1763	John		Pts	Dec	542
1760	BENDSON, Christian		Pts	Jul	273
1767	BENDT, Catharina	Limited Probate	Pts	Feb	36
1770	Francois	Limited Probate	Pts	Aug	285
1777	Gysbert, Dr	Dr in Physic Limited Probate	Pts	Oct	408
1767	Johan	A with W		Apr	124
1780	Johanna Apolonia	Limited Probate	Pts	Jun	303
1800	BENDY, Dorothy		Surrey	Dec	836
1800	James		Wiltshire	Apr	253
1758	Mary		Stafford	Apr	103
1785	Richard, Esq	E.I. Packet "Swallow"	London	Mar	111
1758	Thomas		Stafford	Apr	103
1753	BENDYSH, Henry, Esq	A with W	Suffolk	Sep	245
1754	Henry	Second Limited A with W unad. Last Grant Feb 1741/2. Will regd 133 Brown	Middlesex	Dec	
1758	Henry, Esq	A with W unad., saving etc. Will regd 133 Brown	Middlesex	Feb	
1790	William		Middlesex	May	223
1750	BENDYSHE, Katherine		Cambridge	Nov	347
1780	Margaret		Middlesex	Sep	427
1785	Martha		Middlesex	Oct	493
1777	Richard, Esq Major General of His Majesty's Forces		Middlesex	Jul	299

	BENDYSHE (Contd)				
1777	Richard, Esq		Middlesex	Jul	299
	Major General of				
	His Majesty's Forces				
1783	Robert, The Reverend	A with W	Norfolk	Apr	160
1770	BENEDICK, Elizabeth		London	Feb	41
	alias BENEDIX				
1778	BENEDICTUS, Jacob		Pts	Sep	346
1770	BENEDIX, Elizabeth		London	Feb	41
	alias BENEDICK				
1765	BENEFOLD, John		Middlesex	Sep	322
1793	John, Esq		Middlesex	Sep	455
1762	BENESON, Thomas		Essex	May	183
1760	BENEST, John	Limited A with W	Jersey	Jul	274
1765	Philip		Jersey	Apr	128
1798	BENET, Catharine		Wiltshire	Dec	760
1781	Catherine		Wiltshire	May	224
1754	Elizabeth		Middlesex	Dec	320
1783	James		Middlesex	Apr	160
1792	James, The Reverend		Suffolk	Feb	56
1763	John		Pts	Oct	458
	alias BENNETT				
1796	Joseph, The Reverend		Berkshire	Apr	161
1759	Nicholas		Devon	Jul	223
	alias BENNETT				
1752	Richard		Southampton	Aug	206
1754	Thomas, Esq		Wiltshire	Dec	318
1797	Thomas, Esq		Wiltshire	Aug	539
1763	BENETT, Ann		Southampton	Jun	265
1787	Ann		Leicester	Aug	356
	alias BENNETT				
1778	Etheldred		Bath	Nov	429
1763	BENEY, John		Middlesex	Oct	459
	alias BEANEY				
1756	BENEZET, James		London	Jun	160
1757	BENFIELD, John		Dorset	Oct	293
1779	John		Pts	Jul	288
	alias BENFOLD				
1776	Robert		Middlesex	Oct	411
1779	BENFOLD, John		Pts	Jul	288
	alias BENFIELD				
1751	William		Middlesex	Dec	326
1789	BENFORD, Elizabeth		Middlesex	Mar	134
1763	BENGALL, Henry		Pts/Southampton	Dec	539
1760	BENGE, Benjamin	A with W	Surrey	Apr	138
1788	Benjamin	A with W of Goods unad Will regd 138 Lynch	Surrey	Dec	
1774	Dinah		Sussex	Apr	130
1771	Elizabeth		Sussex	Oct	398
1783	Philip	A with W	Kent	Jun	279
1771	Samuel		Kent	Jul	284

Year	Name	Notes	Place	Month	No.
	BENGE (Contd)				
1778	Thomas		Canterbury	Jan	4
1790	William Henry		Sussex	May	222
1765	BENGEFIELD, Elizabeth		Somerset	Aug	284
1772	BENGER, Jane		Surrey	Nov	394
1765	John		London	Mar	84
1778	John		Pts	Jun	231
1793	John, Esq	Special Probate	Pts	Jan	9
1796	John		Surrey	Jan	6
1797	John	"Monarch"	Middlesex	Jul	473
1784	Jonathan	M.S. "George"	Pts/Devon	Jul	369
1786	Philip		Pts/Surrey	Jun	323
1778	Sarah		Gloucester	May	186
1779	William		Pts	Nov	443
1790	BENGOUGH, Edmund, Dr	Dr. of Physic	Pts	Oct	454
1753	George		Gloucester	Jan	4
1795	Joseph		Middlesex	Jul	432
1761	BENHAM, Dinah alias DUNCOMBE, Charlotte		Hertford	Jan	7
1782	James		Pts	Sep	443
1771	John		Surrey	Jul	284
1785	John	"Thames" "Africa" & "Worcester"	Pts	Dec	589
1763	Mary		Surrey	May	216
1774	Mary		Surrey	Mar	81
1774	Mary		Surrey	Dec	421
1796	Mary	A with W	Middlesex	Jun	292
1751	William alias BANHAM	A with W	Pts	Nov	300
1753	William		Surrey	Sep	244
1761	William		Pts	Aug	279
1798	William		Oxford	Sep	584
1799	Robert		Surrey	Dec	825
1800	Robert		Southampton	May	346
1751	Theophilus	A with W	Surrey	Apr	104
1763	Thomas		Southampton	Dec	539
1777	Thomas		Middlesex	Oct	410
1783	Thomas		Pts	Oct	495
1788	Thomas		Oxford	Jul	336
1762	BENIFOLD, Frances		Surrey	Mar	92
1764	BENING, Elizabeth	By Sentence	Cambridge	May	162
1778	Mariabella		Cambridge	Apr	145
1770	Susanna alias HOWLAND		Essex	Jan	6
1792	William, The Reverend		Cambridge	Jul	366
1800	BENINGFIELD, Cornel		Middlesex	Jun	439
1797	BENINGTON, James alias BENNINGTON, William	Ser. 'Dido'	Middlesex	Sep	587
1775	BENION, Jaques Louis, The Reverend		Pts	Dec	459

Year	Name	Notes	County	Month	No.
	BENION (Contd)				
1784	The Honourable		Pts	Aug	427
	Margareta Wilhelmina				
1798	Petronille		Pts	Jul	458
	alias MADION,				
	Petronella				
1788	BENISON, Thomas		Middlesex	Apr	173
1763	BENJAFIELD, Ambrose		Dorset	May	218
1785	Benjamin	"Superb"	Pts	Feb	67
1800	Isabella		Dorset	Jan	11
1777	John		Dorset	May	199
1778	Mary		Dorset	Mar	98
1758	Thomas		Dorset	Oct	286
1772	Thomas	A with W unad	Dorset	Mar	
		Will regd 286 Hutton			
1774	BENJAMIN, Levy		London	Feb	39
	alias PHILLIPS				
1795	BENKEN, John		Middlesex	May	303
1777	BENN, Ann		Middlesex	Nov	446
1764	Anthony		London	Sep	338
1770	Calvert, Esq		Hertford	Oct	348
1780	Calvert, Esq	Special Probate	Hertford	Apr	
		Will regd 348 Jenner			
1752	John		London	Mar	58
1788	John		London	Jun	285
1797	John		Middlesex	Feb	71
1786	Mary		Middlesex	Nov	553
1755	Richard		Hertford	Feb	33
1752	Robert, The	Dr. in Divinity	Oxford	Dec	294
	Reverend Dr.				
1763	Susannah		Surrey	Sep	417
1769	Thomas		London	Sep	305
1788	Thomas		Warwick	Aug	384
1790	Thomas		Middlesex	Jan	5
1755	William, Esq		London	Aug	211
1783	William, Esq		Middlesex	Dec	601
1798	William		Surrey	Jul	460
1759	BENNALLACK, John		Cornwall	Apr	118
1750	BENNATT, Paul		Surrey	Apr	102
1753	BENNE, Luke, Esq		London	Jan	3
1777	BENNEBROCK, The	Limited Probate	Pts	Dec	520
	Noble Lord Johannes				
	Nutjes Lord of				
1752	BENNEFIELD, William		Pts	Feb	29
1754	BENNELL, George		Northampton	Sep	244
1766	Mary		London	Feb	46
1756	Thomas		Middlesex	Dec	319
1770	BENNESS, John		Southampton	Jun	222
1759	Samuel		Sussex	Sep	288
1781	BENNET, Alexander	Ser.	Pts	Apr	180
1787	Alexander	A with W. "Alexander" & "Falcon"	Pts	Nov	483

BENNET (Contd)

Year	Name	Note	Place	Month	No.
1751	Ann		Middlesex	Jul	200
1761	Ann		London	Dec	422
1774	Ann		Essex	Apr	130
1776	Ann alias BENNETT	A with W	Middlesex	Jan	3
1786	Ann		Suffolk	Dec	603
1790	Ann		Bath	Nov	492
1768	Anthony		Middlesex	Oct	369
1786	Charles		Cornwall	Sep	462
1776	Christopher		Pts	May	215
1773	Claude		Middlesex	Sep	353
1780	Daniel alias BENNETT		Wiltshire	Jan	1
1784	Daniel alias BENNETT		Lancashire	Jul	367
1780	Dorothy		Middlesex	Feb	55
1750	Edward alias BENNETT		Pts/Devon	May	137
1770	Edward		Middlesex	Jun	221
1788	Edward		York	Dec	578
1754	Elizabeth	A with W	Oxford	Dec	319
1765	Elizabeth		London	Oct	361
1771	Elizabeth alias BENNETT		London	Aug	332
1783	Elizabeth		Kent	Jul	335
1766	Etheldred		Wiltshire	May	172
1789	Hannah		Surrey	Jan	6
1773	Henry		Hertford	Apr	145
1781	Henry		London	Feb	81
1785	Henry	A with W	Surrey	Jan	3
1760	James	A with W	Pts	Jun	229
1761	James		Pts	Apr	117
1766	James		Middlesex	Jun	214
1771	James		Hertford	Jul	284
1773	James		Pts	Oct	382
1784	James	Ser. "Jamaica" "Merlin" "Scarbro"	Pts	Aug	432
1785	James alias BENNETT		Middlesex	Dec	587
1793	James		Middlesex	Feb	68
1751	John	Double Probate Will regd Jan.1749/50	Hertford	May	
1752	John, Sir	Baronet. A with W	N. Britain	Apr	85
1761	John	Ser. A with W	Pts	Jan	3
1765	John		Middlesex	Oct	364
1777	John		Middlesex	Nov	448
1782	John, Esq		Bath	May	214
1783	John	"Chatham" & "Cornwallis"	Pts	Feb	60
1783	John, Esq		Hertford	Sep	446
1784	John	"Edgar"	Pts	Dec	628

BENNET (Contd)

1786	John		London	Mar	143
	alias BENNETT				
1786	John		Somerset	May	263
1755	Jonathan		Pts	Dec	304
1773	Joseph		Middlesex	Jul	278
1752	Mary		London	Mar	58
1786	Mary		Middlesex	Oct	505
1789	Mary		Buckinghamshire	Jan	8
1795	Mary	A with W	Glamorgan	Jan	7
1790	Michael		Northumberland	Feb	58
	alias BENNETT				
1763	Moses		Kent	Sep	419
1787	Olive		Hereford	May	200
1787	Patrick	Ser."Defence"	Pts	Jan	6
1767	Peter		Surrey	Dec	436
1761	Philip, Esq		Essex	Dec	421
1774	Philip		Somerset	Mar	81
1789	Philip		Hereford	Jun	301
	alias BENNETT				
1785	Richard		Wiltshire	May	231
1764	Robert		Pts	Feb	38
1770	Robert		Devon	Nov	390
1774	Robert, Esq		Kent	Feb	38
1777	Robert		Pts	Apr	148
1783	Robert		Middlesex	Apr	161
1783	Robert, Esq	A with W unad Will regd 38 Bargrave	Kent	Jul	
1780	Ruth		Essex	Oct	462
	alias BENNETT				
1781	Ruth	Will regd Oct. last	Essex	Sep	
	alias BENNETT				
1769	Samuel		Middlesex	May	154
1773	Samuel		Surrey	Jan	4
1786	Samuel		Middlesex	Oct	502
1785	Sarah		Somerset	Apr	174
1783	Susanna		Bath	Jul	336
1754	Thomas, Esq late surviving Principal Register in the Prerogative Court of Canterbury		Wiltshire	Feb	31
1761	Thomas		Buckinghamshire	Mar	83
1766	Thomas	A with W	Wiltshire	May	172
1770	Thomas		Middlesex	Jun	219
1770	Thomas		Cambridge	Jul	252
1772	Thomas, Esq		Glamorgan	Jun	203
1795	Thomas		London	Mar	144
1752	William		Surrey	Jul	178
1760	William		Gloucester	Aug	317
1760	William		Pts/Devon	Dec	453
1763	William		Pts	Jul	321
1763	William		Pts	Dec	542

BENNET (Contd)

1765	William		Nottingham	Sep	321
1765	William		Kent	Dec	442
1775	William		Southampton	May	172
1775	William	Ser	Pts	Jun	220
1782	William, Esq.	by Sent.	Wiltshire	Feb	62
1795	William		Gloucester	Jul	430
	alias BENNETT				
1796	William		Middlesex	Jun	293
1767	BENNETT, Abigail	Limited Probate	Somerset	Nov	403
	alias BURGES				
1782	Adam		Middlesex	Apr	163
1759	Alexander		Middlesex	Nov	351
1783	Andrew		Pts	Aug	399
1771	Ann		Essex	Feb	45
1773	Ann		Middlesex	Jan	4
1773	Ann		Middlesex	Nov	417
1776	Ann	A with W	Middlesex	Jan	3
	alias BENNET				
1778	Ann		Middlesex	May	184
1779	Ann		Middlesex	Jun	234
1787	Ann		Leicester	Aug	356
	alias BENETT				
1792	Ann		London	Aug	418
1796	Ann		Middlesex	Oct	489
1789	Anne	A with W	Sussex	Jul	346
1750	Barbara		Middlesex	Jul	221
1795	Bartholomew		Kent	Dec	671
1776	Benjamin		London	Jul	298
1785	Bentley, Esq		Lincoln	Sep	456
1775	Boyle		Middlesex	Sep	335
1791	Catherine		Middlesex	Mar	112
	alias Cathern				
1788	Champion		Surrey	Jan	3
1759	Charles		Pts	Apr	120
1787	Charles		Wells	Oct -	439
1790	Charles		London	Apr	171
1770	Christopher		Middlesex	Jan	6
1792	Clara		Middlesex	Jun	315
1780	Daniel		Wiltshire	Jan	1
	alias BENNET				
1784	Daniel		Lancashire	Jul	367
1799	Daniel		Gloucester	Oct	699
1791	Dinah		Kent	Oct	454
1757	Dorothy		Wiltshire	Apr	110
1794	Dorothy		Derby	Mar	124
1775	Easter		Middlesex	Jun	225
1768	Edmund		Cornwall	May	187
1772	Edward, The Reverend	A with W	Wiltshire	Jun	208
1774	Edward		Sussex	Jul	254
1776	Edward		Essex	Oct	413

BENNETT (Contd)

1778	Edward		London	Dec	478
1781	Edward		Chester	Sep	418
1782	Edward		Middlesex	Aug	391
1783	Edward		Pts	Nov	531
1798	Edward		Surrey	May	308
1795	Eleanor		Middlesex	Mar	148
1753	Elizabeth		Denbigh	Jun	164
1759	Elizabeth		Essex	Oct	317
1762	Elizabeth		Middlesex	Nov	445
1764	Elizabeth		Hertford	Jun	211
1768	Elizabeth		Hertford	Jun	228
1770	Elizabeth		Dorset	Jun	219
1771	Elizabeth		London	Aug	332
	alias BENNET				
1772	Elizabeth		Surrey	Aug	283
1773	Elizabeth		Middlesex	Apr	147
1778	Elizabeth		Middlesex	Jan	5
1779	Elizabeth		Kent	Jun	231
1783	Elizabeth		Cambridge	Feb	58
1784	Elizabeth		Sussex	Dec	628
1785	Elizabeth		Buckinghamshire	Jun	293
1788	Elizabeth		Bristol	Dec	
1791	Elizabeth		Middlesex	Sep	418
1795	Elizabeth		Sussex	Jan	6
1795	Elizabeth		Dorset	Jul	434
1799	Elizabeth		Essex	Mar	169
1779	Fanny	A with W	Middlesex	Oct	402
1789	Fargus		Surrey	May	234
1794	Fargus	A with W of Goods unad Will regd May 1789	Surrey	Nov	
1792	Frances		Kent	Oct	499
1767	Francis		Dorset	May	167
1779	Francis		Bristol	Jul	285
1786	Francis	A with W	London	Jan	5
1786	Francis	A with W Will regd Jan last	London	Mar	
1790	Francis, Esq		Bath	May	224
1799	Francis	A with W	Wiltshire	Dec	827
1800	Francis	"Cyclops"&"Nassau"	Pts	Jan	8
1776	George		Gloucester	Jun	257
1782	George		Pts	Oct	482
1793	George		Middlesex	May	242
1793	George		Sussex	Oct	490
1797	George		Hertford	May	298
1799	George		Hereford	Sep	643
1787	George Augustus, Esq		Southampton	Dec	532
1750	Hannah		Wiltshire	Jun	186
1793	Hellen		London	Sep	452
1763	Henry		Middlesex	Aug	369
1770	Henry	A with W unad Will regd 369 Caesar	Middlesex	Nov	

BENNETT (Contd

1776	Henry, Esq		Chester	Apr	164
1778	Henry	A with W	Middlesex	Jan	5
1756	Henry	"Bellona"	Pts	Feb	65
1794	Henry		Middlesex	Jul	352
1797	Henry	Native Infantry E. I. C. S.	Pts	Nov	678
1795	Hester		Middlesex	Mar	144
1792	Hugh		Kent	Feb	58
1797	Hugh, The Reverend		Devon	Sep	588
1764	Isaac		Surrey	Aug	296
1764	Jacob		Pts	Aug	296
	alias BRITTON, John				
1758	James		Essex	Nov	322
1759	James		Pts	Sep	287
1772	James		Middlesex	Feb	39
1772	James		Middlesex	Oct	351
1778	James	Ser	Pts	Sep	345
1782	James	"Guadeloupe"	Pts	Feb	59
	alias BENNITT				
1785	James	"Hannibal"	Pts	Sep	455
1785	James		Middlesex	Dec	587
	alias BENNET				
1791	James, Esq	Special A with W	Essex	Oct	451
1794	James		Winchester	Dec	595
1797	James		Middlesex	Jan	33
1797	James		Cambridge	Feb	69
1798	James		Dorset	Sep	585
1761	Jane		Middlesex	Feb	46
1761	Jane	Will regd in Feb last	Middlesex	Apr	
1766	Jane	A with W unad	Middlesex	Oct	
		Will regd 46 Cheslyn			
		Last Grant in April 1761			
1785	Jane		Middlesex	Oct	495
1786	Jane		Surrey	Mar	145
1796	Jane		Bath	Mar	108
1796	Jane		Kent	Apr	167
1800	Jane		Chester	Jun	432
1800	Jane	Will regd June last	Chester	Aug	
1786	Jenny		Devon	Feb	65
1772	Jeremiah		Hertford	Apr	121
1750	John		Hertford	Jan	4
1751	John		Essex	Aug	230
1753	John		Essex	May	129
	alias BENNITT				
1753	John		Wiltshire	Jul	195
1758	John		Exeter	Jan	2
1760	John		London	Jul	273
1761	John	Ser.	Devon	Sep	309
1763	John		Pts	Oct	458
	alias BENET				
1764	John	A with W	Salop	Mar	80
1765	John		Oxford	Mar	87

1765	John		London	Jun	210
1765	John		Surrey	Dec	440
1769	John		Surrey	Nov	367
1770	John		Surrey	May	173
1772	John	A with W unad Will regd 80 Simpson	Salop	Feb	
1773	John		Bristol	Feb	43
1774	John	Ser	Devon	Mar	80
1775	John		London	Apr	128
1776	John		Middlesex	Aug	348
1777	John		Middlesex	Nov	449
1778	John		Pts	Jan	3
1778	John		Dorset	Apr	143
1780	John		Pts	Sep	427
1780	John		Surrey	Dec	552
1781	John		Kent	Apr	183
1782	John		Salop	Feb	64
1782	John		Cornwall	May	212
1782	John		Middlesex	May	216
1783	John		Middlesex	Jan	5
1783	John		Pts	Mar	112
1783	John		Essex	Sep	445
1786	John		London	Mar	143
	alias BENNET				
1787	John	A with W of Goods unad Will regd 231 Busby	Essex	Feb	
1787	John	Double Probate Will regd 64 Gostling	Salop	Oct	
1787	John		Middlesex	Dec	534
1791	John		Oxford	Feb	57
1791	John		Middlesex	Nov	499
1792	John		Surrey	Apr	199
1798	John		Hereford	Oct	636
1798	John	Ser. "Suffolk"	Pts	Nov	699
1799	John		Norwich	Mar	169
1799	John		Devon	Dec	824
1762	Joseph		Middlesex	Dec	494
1765	Joseph		Surrey	Jan	5
1767	Joseph		Buckinghamshire	Apr	125
1775	Joseph		Middlesex	Oct	368
1776	Joseph		Essex	Jan	5
1783	Joseph		Somerset	Apr	164
1785	Joseph	Ser."Lionness"&"Hannibal"	Pts	Oct	495
1787	Joseph	A With W	Pts	Dec	532
1774	Katherine		Wiltshire	Mar	80
1798	Lacon		Salop	Jun	380
1795	Letitia		Surrey	Jan	4
1791	Lydia		Lichfield	Dec	561
1774	Mace		Middlesex	Jun	218
1780	Margaret		Southampton	Apr	170
1792	Maria		Surrey	Apr	197

BENNETT (Contd)

Year	Name	Note	Place	Month	Page
1795	Maria		Gloucester	Jul	434
1791	Mark	A with W	Kent	Feb	58
1784	Martha		Bedford	May	249
1797	Martha Light		Dorset	Oct	625
1750	Martin, Esq	A with W	Pts	Dec	377
1751	Mary		Montgomery	Dec	328
1756	Mary		Middlesex	Jun	160
1759	Mary		Surrey	Apr	118
1759	Mary	A with W	Surrey	Jul	224
1763	Mary		Hertford	Oct	460
1765	Mary		Middlesex	Jun	206
1774	Mary		Surrey	Jul	256
1779	Mary		Middlesex	Dec	483
1782	Mary		Middlesex	Jun	265
1784	Mary alias BENTT	A with W	Middlesex	Jun	308
1785	Mary		Surrey	Aug	406
1787	Mary		Middlesex	Dec	530
1789	Mary		Surrey	Jun	302
1790	Mary		Middlesex	Dec	537
1791	Mary		Dorset	Apr	168
1792	Mary		Middlesex	Apr	200
1793	Mary		Dorset	Aug	398
1794	Mary		Essex	Mar	125
1794	Mary		Wiltshire	Sep	446
1796	Mary		Middlesex	Jan	7
1790	Michael alias BENNET		Northumberland	Feb	58
1792	Michael		Middlesex	Feb	54
1756	Maurice		Wiltshire	Dec	318
1778	Maurice	A with W	Wiltshire	Sep	345
1751	Newsom		Surrey	Jun	167
1759	Nicholas alias BENET		Devon	Jul	223
1767	Nicholas	A with W	Cornwall	Dec	435
1757	Patrick alias Peter		Southampton	Dec	349
1774	Peter, Esq	A with W	Middlesex	May	171
1780	Peter		Middlesex	Jan	2
1793	Peter James		Surrey	Mar	127
1768	Philip		Middlesex	Mar	95
1789	Philip alias BENNET		Hereford	Jun	301
1750	Richard		Wiltshire	Jan	3
1750	Richard	A with W	Pts	Aug	253
1750	Richard		Surrey	Dec	376
1752	Richard		Pts/Middlesex	Aug	206
1762	Richard		Southampton	Apr	141
1763	Richard		Pts/Southampton	Jul	324
1767	Richard		Surrey	Jun	207

BENNETT (Contd)

1775	Richard	A with W	Middlesex	Sep	336
1776	Richard	Will regd Sept. 1775	Middlesex	Sep	
1777	Richard		Somerset	Oct	408
1779	Richard		Cornwall	Jul	287
1781	Richard (1st)	A with W	Pts	Mar	121
1784	Richard	Ser. "Cumberland"	Pts	Oct	539
1789	Richard		Kent	Oct	482
1790	Richard		Middlesex	Dec	540
1793	Richard		Gloucester	Dec	579
1794	Richard		Wiltshire	Mar	121
1795	Richard, Esq		Salop	Mar	145
1778	Richard Hannot, The Reverend		Surrey	Feb	49
1759	Robert		Surrey	May	157
1761	Robert		Essex	May	158
1763	Robert		Pts	Jul	325
1771	Robert		Berkshire	May	194
1771	Robert	Ser.	Surrey	Aug	330
1771	Robert		London	Nov	431
1779	Robert		Middlesex	Jun	233
1794	Robert, Esq		N. Britain	Oct	492
1780	Ruth alias BENNET		Essex	Oct	462
1781	Ruth alias BENNET	Will regd Oct last	Essex	Sep	
1763	Sampson		Middlesex	Jul	320
1766	Sampson		Cornwall	May	171
1774	Samuel		Bristol	Mar	84
1792	Samuel		Middlesex	May	260
1780	Sarah		Middlesex	Apr	170
1789	Sarah		Chester	Sep	451
1792	Sarah alias GEARY	Limited Probate	Middlesex	Mar	151
1796	Sarah		Coventry	Jun	293
1775	Susanna	Limited Probate	Middlesex	Sep	334
1795	Susannah		Middlesex	Apr	236
1751	Thomas		Essex	Sep	251
1754	Thomas	By Decree	London	Dec	318
1757	Thomas		Sussex	Apr	111
1757	Thomas		Middlesex	Dec	350
1760	Thomas		Essex	Nov	414
1762	Thomas		Pts	Jun	231
1764	Thomas, Esq. One of the Masters of H.M. High Court of Chancery		Middlesex	Jun	213
1764	Thomas		Pts	Jul	250
1768	Thomas		Middlesex	Feb	44
1769	Thomas		Surrey	Feb	35
1773	Thomas	Limited A with W unad Will regd 213 Simpson	Middlesex	Jun	

BENNETT (Contd)

Year	Name	Note	County	Month	No.
1779	Thomas		Middlesex	Oct	402
1783	Thomas		Middlesex	Sep	443
1783	Thomas		Oxford	Oct	500
1786	Thomas		Middlesex	Dec	602
1790	Thomas		Warwickshire	Mar	120
1790	Thomas		Surrey	Nov	494
1791	Thomas		Middlesex	Apr	169
1792	Thomas		Chester	Feb	54
1793	Thomas		London	Jan	7
1793	Thomas	Limited A with W of Goods unad. Will regd 213 Simpson Last Grant June 1773	Middlesex	Mar	
1797	Thomas, Esq	Special A with W of the rest of the Goods unad Will regd 213 Simpson Last Grant March 1793	Middlesex	Aug	
1798	Thomas		London	May	311
1798	Thomas		Worcester	Jun	377
1800	Thomas		Essex	Jul	510
1800	Thomas, The Reverend		Middlesex	Oct	702
1797	Thomas Leigh, The Reverend		Middlesex	Jun	400
1782	Thomas Stanhope		Devon	Jun	264
1756	Timothy		Middlesex	Jun	160
1754	Turgiss, Esq		Surrey	Dec	317
1776	Turner		London	Feb	51
1765	Wells		Middlesex	May	170
1755	William		Middlesex	Nov	276
1756	William		Middlesex	Jul	187
1757	William		Oxford	May	145
1762	William		Stafford	Nov	446
1765	William		Essex	Jan	4
1765	William	Double Probate Will regd this month	Essex	Jan	
1766	William		Pts	Oct	362
1767	William		Middlesex	Nov	400
1770	William		London	Jul	253
1773	William		Bristol	May	191
1774	William		Berkshire	Apr	128
1775	William	Ser.	Pts	Jun	220
	alias BENNET				
1775	William		Hereford	Dec	459
1776	William		Kent	Oct	411
1777	William	A with W	Middlesex	Jul	297
1778	William	A with W unad Will regd 253 Jenner	London	Jun	
1781	William		Kent	Jan	6
1782	William, Esq		Salop	Jan	3
1783	William		Surrey	Apr	163

BENNETT (Contd)

Year	Name	Notes	Place	Month	Page
1784	William		Surrey	Feb	66
1784	William	A with W."Exeter"	Pts	Jul	368
1784	William		Berkshire	Sep	490
1787	William		Bristol	Mar	102
1787	William		Berkshire	Apr	156
1788	William		Middlesex	Oct	470
1789	William		London	May	233
1789	William, Esq. Rear Admiral in His Majesty's Fleet	Special Probate	Devon	Dec	573
1790	William	A with W	Surrey	Aug	368
1792	William		Dorset	Apr	198
1792	William	A with W of Goods unad Will regd 102 Major	Bristol	Jun	
1793	William		Middlesex	Feb	64
1795	William alias BENNET		Gloucester	Jul	430
1796	William		Somerset	Aug	402
1797	William, Esq		Kent	Nov	677
1800	William		Buckinghamshire	Dec	835
1779	William Perce		Pts	Oct	404
1756	BENNETTA, William	A with W	Pts	Feb	29
1760	BENNETTS, James		Pts	Feb	48
1763	BENNEY, John alias BINNEY		Pts	Aug	369
1764	BENNICUTT, William alias BARNICOTT	A with W Pts	Middlesex	Jul	252
1799	BENNICK, Nicholas	Ser."Blonde" "Hannibal" & "Hindostan"	Cornwall	Jan	6
1766	BENNICKE, Hannah		Devon	Mar	90
1750	BENNING, Ambrose	Double Probate Will regd 2 Isham	Cambridge	Oct	
1778	Christian alias BENNINGH	Limited Probate	Pts	May	183
1784	Dorothy		Berkshire	Jan	3
1762	Hercules		Middlesex	Jul	287
1785	James		Durham	Feb	68
1789	James	A with W of Goods unad Will regd Feb. 1785	Durham	Sep	
1757	John		Berkshire	Sep	267
1783	John		Berkshire	May	214
1750	Nathaniel		Pts	May	139
1797	Richard		Berkshire	Apr	223
1756	William	A with W	London	Oct	266
1767	William		London	Oct	365
1768	William		Middlesex	Feb	48
1788	William		Berkshire	Oct	470
1757	BENNINGEN, Van, Maria Elizabeth alias RULAND	Limited Probate	Pts	May	175

1763	BENNINGTON, John		Pts	Jan	4
1753	Mary		Middlesex	Jun	165
1797	William	Ser."Dido"	Middlesex	Sep	587
	alias James				
	alias BENINGTON				
1762	BENNION, Mary		Middlesex	Feb	42
1794	BENNISON, Dorothy		Southampton	Jul	346
1782	John		Southampton	Mar	112
1783	William	Ser	Pts	Apr	160
1782	BENNITT, James	"Guadeloupe"	Pts	Feb	59
	alias BENNETT				
1753	John		Pts/Middlesex	Jan	3
1753	John		Essex	May	129
	alias BENNETT				
1764	John		Middlesex	Dec	458
1774	John		Pts/Kent	Dec	422
1792	Joseph		Bristol	Jun	318
1792	BENNIWORTH, Elizabeth		Middlesex	Jun	315
1785	Thomas		Hertford	Jul	353
1750	BENNOTT, Bartholomew		Southampton	May	140
1791	BENNS, Eleanor		Suffolk	Jun	268
1775	BENNY, Elizabeth		Bristol	Apr	130
1775	Elizabeth	Double Probate Will regd April last	Bristol	May	
1781	John	Ser.	Hampshire	Sep	420
	alias BINNEY				
1760	BENOIMONT, Victor		Middlesex	May	184
1763	BENOIST, Anne	A with W	Middlesex	Nov	498
1770	Anthony		Middlesex	Sep	323
1759	Hannah		Middlesex	Nov	351
1781	Mary Magdalen	A with W	Middlesex	Nov	511
1783	Mary Magdalen	A with W of Goods unad Will regd Nov. 1781	Middlesex	Sep	
1792	Peter		London	Jun	317
1800	BENOIT, James		Essex	Dec	837
1752	Mary		Middlesex	Jun	159
	alias JULIEN				
1756	BENSCHOP, Elizabeth		London	Jan	2
1754	Pleun		Middlesex	Mar	68
1753	BENSE, Daniel		Middlesex	Oct	263
1786	BENSER, John Daniel		Middlesex	Feb	68
1753	BENSKIN, Jonathan		Surrey	Mar	69
1774	BENSKYN, John		Middlesex	Aug	292
1762	Thomas		Leicester	May	183
1795	BENSLEY, Thomas		Norwich	Apr	240
1760	BENSON, Andrew		Pts	Sep	348
	alias BARNSON				
	alias BARNS				
1786	Ann		Westmorland	Jun	323
1751	Anthony		Cumberland	Apr	102
1791	Anthony		Middlesex	Jan	1
1759	Barnard		London	Mar	82

BENSON (Contd)

Year	Name	Notes	Place	Month	No.
1759	Benjamin, Esq	A with W	Suffolk	Sep	289
1761	Bernard	Ser. A with W	Pts	Sep	308
1758	Bryan, Esq		Middlesex	Oct	285
1764	Bryan		Middlesex	Apr	130
1754	Charles		Middlesex	Feb	31
1781	Dorothy		York	Apr	180
1754	Earle, Esq	Will regd 219 Wake	Wiltshire	Jun	
1750	Edward		London	Sep	286
1751	Edward		Middlesex	Apr	103
1754	Edward	A with W unad. Will regd 286 Greenly	London	Oct	
1756	Edward		Pts	Jan	3
1756	Edward		Surrey	May	130
1798	Edward		Surrey	Dec	758
1795	Edward Beckingham The Reverend		Kent	Aug	495
			Kent	Aug	495
1783	Elizabeth		London	Oct	500
1786	Elizabeth		Bedford	Sep	464
1753	Ellin		Middlesex	Jan	5
1760	Frances		Southampton	Nov	415
1786	Francis		Middlesex	Apr	204
1762	George, Dr	Dr. in Divinity	Middlesex	Apr	137
1797	George		Middlesex	Jun	399
1759	Godfrey		Pts/Middlesex	Mar	83
1786	Hannah		Southampton	Sep	462
1756	Henry		Middlesex	Aug	216
1753	James		Huntingdon	Mar	71
1773	James		Pts	Apr	145
1784	James		Middlesex	Sep	492
1785	James, The Reverend, Dr	Dr. of Law	Gloucester	Oct	491
1790	James, Esq		York	Jun	279
1781	Jane		Middlesex	Jan	4
1760	John		Surrey	Jan	2
1762	John		Middlesex	Apr	140
1764	John		York	Oct	378
1771	John		Middlesex	Mar	95
1773	John		Middlesex	Mar	95
1781	John		Westmoreland	Oct	466
1782	John		London	Jan	7
1783	John The Reverend		Bath	Feb	59
1785	John		Middlesex	Jan	4
1798	John alias Isaac	Ser. "St. George"	Pts	Apr	236
1787	John Aislabie		Middlesex	Oct	439
1757	Leticia alias Letitia		Worcester	Jul	213
1792	Margaret		Middlesex	Apr	194
1797	Margaret	A with W	Middlesex	Feb	68
1799	Margaret		York	Dec	822

BENSON (Contd)

Year	Name	Notes	County	Month	No.
1784	Margaret		Middlesex	Aug	429
1752	Martin, The Right Reverend Father in God by Divine Permission late Lord Bishop of Gloucester		Gloucester	Oct	249
1756	Mary		Middlesex	Dec	318
1763	Mary		London	May	216
1769	Mary		Middlesex	Sep	302
1775	Mary		Middlesex	Oct	369
1793	Mary		Surrey	Jan	5
1752	Matthew		Cambridge	May	118
1772	Miles	A with W	Sussex	Jun	206
1752	Peter		Pts	May	118
1759	Phebe		Middlesex	May	158
1779	Rant		Canterbury	Apr	140
1793	Rhuben		Sussex	Aug	398
1772	Robert, Esq	A with W	Middlesex	Jan	6
1778	Robert		London	Jun	233
1790	Robert		London	Jun	277
1761	Samuel		Middlesex	Feb	47
1783	Samuel	Ser.	Pts	May	215
1787	Sarah		Westmorland	Jul	312
1760	Thomas		Pts	Aug	316
1767	Thomas		Middlesex	Jun	209
1782	Thomas		York	Oct	482
1788	Thomas		York	Oct	388
1792	Thomas, Esq	A with W of Goods unad Will regd 209 Legard	Middlesex	Jun	
1794	Thomas		Middlesex	Feb	63
1754	William, Esq	By Sentence A with W	Middlesex	Dec	348
1770	William		Middlesex	Apr	132
1773	William		Essex	Oct	381
1780	William		Middlesex	Jul	347
1791	William		Surrey	Feb	55
1794	William		York	Jul	353
1797	William		Middlesex	Sep	584
1762	William Earle, Esq		Middlesex	Feb	38
1800	William Earle, Esq	A with W of Goods unad Will regd 38 St. Eloy	Middlesex	Jan	
1750	BENSTABLE, Benjamin	Serv	Pts/Surrey	May	137
1795	BENSTEAD, John	A with W	Cambridge	Oct	583
1782	Thomas alias BENSTED		Kent	Jun	267
1763	BENSTED, James		Pts	Nov	494
1769	Mary		Kent	May	151
1786	Mary		Kent	Sep	463
1790	Mary	Double Probate Will regd 463 Norfolk	Kent	May	
1775	Richard		London	Dec	458
1782	Thomas alias BENSTEAD		Kent	Jun	267

	BENSTED (Contd)				
1791	William		Kent	May	215
1767	BENT, Joseph		Berkshire	Jun	206
1789	Joseph		Middlesex	Mar	134
1750	Mary		Middlesex	Sep	285
1772	Rose		Hertford	Feb	42
1772	Thomas		London	Dec	430
1778	BENTALL, Anthony		Essex	Apr	144
1779	Arthur		Essex	Jan	4
1781	John		Essex	Oct	461
1757	Richard		Surrey	Aug	239
1784	William		Essex	Nov	587
1758	BENTAM, Charles	A with W	Pts	Jul	208
1781	BENTELY, George		Devon	Apr	183
1781	BENTHAM, Ann		Cambridge	Oct	463
1768	Bryan		Kent	Apr	140
1774	Edward, Esq		London	May	171
1774	Edward, Esq	Double Probate Will regd this month	London	May	
1776	Edward, Dr, The Reverend	Dr. in Divinity	Oxford	Sep	380
1785	Edward William	A with W	Surrey	Jul	352
1791	Elizabeth		Oxford	Mar	113
1774	Gregory		Kent	Apr	126
1792	Jeffery, The Reverend		Cambridge	Jul	365
1792	Jeremiah, Esq		Middlesex	Apr	192
1782	Joseph		Derby	May	214
1785	Mary		Kent	Mar	111
1794	Matthew		Devon	Mar	121
1782	Sarah		Kent	Jul	336
1790	Thomas, The Reverend		Chester	Dec	538
1759	William		Pts/Middlesex	May	157
1754	William Christian	A with W	Pts	Jul	123
1774	BENTHEM, Van, Anna Jacoba alias VAN DAM	Limited Probate	Pts	Sep	352
1780	BENTIMAN, John		Hertford	Feb	60
1775	BENTINCK, Agatha, Lady alias VAN SLINGELANDT	Limited Probate	Pts	Mar	85
1756	The Right Honourable Lady Amilia Catharina Baroness of Wassenaer	Limited Probate	Pts	Mar	88
1763	The Right Honourable Anne Margaret Dowager Van Wassenaer Duvenvoirde	Limited Probate	Pts	Jun	266
1779	Charles John, The Honourable		Pts	Apr	143
1792	Lady Elizabeth, Baroness alias SLOET		Pts	Nov	546

BENTINCK (Contd)

1759	The Right Honourable George commonly called Lord George	Hon.	Middlesex	Mar	81
1775	John Albert, Esq		Norfolk	Sep	336
1782	Margareta, The Right Honourable	Limited Probate	Pts	Dec	570
1778	Lady Mary George, alias The Right Honourable Mary GRIFFITH		Middlesex	Oct	401
1786	Lady Mary George, alias The Right Honourable Mary GRIFFITH	A with W unad Will regd Oct 1778	Middlesex	Jul	
1792	Renira		Middlesex	Jul	365
1784	Willem, Baron The Right Honourable	Limited Probate	Pts	Aug	425
1775	William, The Honourable	Limited A with W annexed	Pts	Jan	3
1790	BENTLE, Catharina Johanna	Limited Probate	Pts	Sep	410
1779	BENTLEY, Alce alias BENTLY	A with W annexed	Hertford	Aug	336
1770	Ann alias CAPENHURST		Middlesex	Mar	90
1773	Ann		Bedford	Jun	235
1784	Ann		Surrey	Dec	629
1750	Benjamin		Pts	Oct	315
1771	Benjamin	A with W	London	May	193
1765	Charlotte		Warwick	Nov	401
1771	David		Middlesex	Nov	430
1752	Edward		Stafford	Jul	179
1759	Edward		Pts	Mar	83
1773	Edward		Surrey	Jan	4
1762	Elizabeth		Middlesex	Nov	445
1763	Elizabeth		Kent	Jul	321
1767	Elizabeth	A with W	Middlesex	Jun	208
1777	Elizabeth		Middlesex	Dec	498
1757	George	A with W	Devon	Sep	266
1776	George		London	Apr	163
1793	George		Kent	Jul	353
1799	George		London	Jun	416
1799	George	Will regd June last	London	Dec	416
1763	Henry		Middlesex	Jan	4
1767	Henry		Lincoln	Jun	206
1799	Henry		Surrey	Feb	96
1752	Isaac		Pts	Aug	204
1769	James		Pts/Middlesex	Nov	368
1771	James		London	Oct	397
1772	Jane		Middlesex	Jan	4
1763	John		Middlesex	Dec	539
1767	John		Middlesex	Mar	86

	BENTLEY (Contd)				
1769	John		Surrey	Dec	404
1770	John		Kent	Jul	256
1772	Sir John, Vice Admiral of the White		Kent	Feb	40
1776	John		Bedford	Feb	51
1784	John		London	Jan	4
1800	John	A with W of Goods unad Will regd 51 Bellas	Bedford	Apr	
1750	Joseph		Middlesex	Oct	316
1756	Joseph		Pts	Jun	158
1761	Mary	A with W	Middlesex	Nov	382
1765	Mary		Middlesex	Jul	247
1776	Mary	A with W unad Will regd 247 Rushworth	Middlesex	Feb	
1778	Mary		Middlesex	Jan	6
1782	Mary		Kent	Jul	338
1793	Mary		Bedford	Jan	9
1794	Mary		Hertford	Jul	349
1797	Mary		Middlesex	Nov	134
1797	Mary		Kent	Jul	473
1788	Michael		Devon	Jun	288
1768	Nathaniel, Esq		Middlesex	Sep	338
1789	Nathaniel	Ser.	Devon	Feb	74
1784	Nicholas Rothwell alias GARRARD, John alias GERRAD, John	A with W "Africa" "La Naiade"	Pts	Jun	308
1800	Percival		Middlesex	Feb	85
1764	Peter		Pts	Aug	299
1757	Rachel		Devon	May	146
1760	Richard		Middlesex	Apr	135
1782	Richard		Middlesex	Mar	110
1786	Richard, Dr The Reverend	Dr. in Divinity	Leicester	Mar	145
1795	Roger, The Reverend		Surrey	Nov	623
1771	Sarah		Surrey	Oct	397
1760	Stephen		Pts/Surrey	Oct	379
1754	Thomas		London	Aug	219
1765	Thomas		London	May	171
1774	Thomas		Derby	May	167
1779	Thomas		Cambridge	Feb	39
1781	Thomas		Middlesex	Jan	3
1798	Thomas		Middlesex	Oct	632
1781	Timothy		York	May	224
1750	William	A with W unad Will regd 2 Plymouth	Middlesex	Oct	318
1764	William		Surrey	Jul	252
1777	William		Pts	Dec	496
1782	William		Stafford	Jul	336
1789	William, Esq		Middlesex	Sep	448
1798	William		Surrey	Feb	83

1800	BENTLEY, William		Leicester	Jun	431
1779	BENTLY, Alce	A with W annexed	Hertford	Aug	336
	alias BENTLEY				
1798	John		Dorset	Oct	632
1758	BENTON, Aaron		Essex	Jun	176
1789	Ann		Monmouth	Jun	300
1798	Ann		Middlesex	Aug	524
1772	Edward		Middlesex	Dec	433
1795	Edward, Esq		Middlesex	Mar	147
1788	Elizabeth		Middlesex	Mar	120
1784	Henry	"Torbay"	Pts	Mar	122
1750	Jacob		Pts	Jul	223
1780	Jane		London	Jan	2
1754	John		Pts	Aug	218
1780	John		Middlesex		236
1782	John		Surrey	Apr	164
1789	John		Leicester	Jul	350
1800	Joseph	A with W	Warwick	Oct	698
		Serg.Major 64 Regt Foot			
1777	Samuel		Worcester	Oct	409
1795	Sarah		Surrey	Apr	240
1769	Tobias		London	Nov	366
1761	William		Middlesex	Mar	83
1762	William	Double Probate	Middlesex	Feb	
		Will regd March 1761			
1784	BENTT, Mary	A with W	Middlesex	Jun	308
	alias BENNETT				
1799	BENTZ, Christopher	No Ship	Pts	Sep	643
	alias Christofer				
1788	BENWEL, Rachel		Middlesex	May	232
1758	BENWELL, Ann		Cambridge	Jul	209
1784	Ann		Buckinghamshire	Jan	3
1784	Ann		Berkshire	Dec	629
	alias Anne				
1787	Ann		Buckinghamshire	Mar	106
1789	Bethia		Surrey	Oct	486
1793	Dinah	A with W	Wiltshire	Jan	5
	alias BANNING				
1785	Hannah		Berkshire	Aug	406
1763	Henry		Oxford	Mar	111
1770	Henry		Berkshire	May	176
1784	Henry		Surrey	Aug	425
1797	James		Middlesex	Aug	543
1782	John		London	Jul	337
1789	John		Berkshire	Aug	418
1800	John		Oxford	Jan	6
1773	Joseph		Buckinghamshire	Apr	149
1798	Joseph		Surrey	Sep	584
1800	Lucy		Middlesex	Aug	580
1781	Martha		Berkshire	Oct	464
1797	Martha		Middlesex	Oct	630

BENWELL (Contd)

Year	Name	Note	Place	Month	No.
1775	Mary		Hereford	Oct	367
1780	Mary		Berkshire	Apr	172
1782	Mary		Oxford	Sep	441
1791	Mary		Berkshire	Aug	373
1792	Mary		Lincoln	Dec	594
1777	Samuel		Oxford	Mar	95
1750	William		Oxford	Feb	36
1780	William		Pts	Nov	505
1775	William Sarney		Middlesex	Oct	336
1773	BENYON, Ann		Middlesex	Dec	460
1769	Anna		Salop	Oct	333
1780	Anna	Double Probate Will regd 333 Bogg	Salop	May	
1771	Benjamin		London	Aug	329
1751	Charles, Esq		Middlesex	Dec	329
1768	George, The Reverend		Suffolk	Feb	42
1798	Harriet		Middlesex	Mar	158
1780	James		Middlesex	Sep	428
1780	John		Salop	Mar	122
1766	Mary	A with W annexed	Salop	May	167
1777	Mary		Middlesex	Oct	407
1770	Phillipa		Middlesex	Oct	351
1774	Richard, Esq		Middlesex	Oct	359
1796	Richard, Esq		Berkshire	Sep	442
1757	BER, Louin Louise		Canterbury	Feb	39
1752	BERANGER DE BOISLIN, Elizabeth		Middlesex	Aug	204
1793	BERANGER, James alias BERENGER, John James	A with W Will regd 196 Collier	Pts	Apr	
1768	BERAUD, William		Surrey	Jun	228
1762	BERCHEM, Van, Maximilian, The Right Honourable		Pts	May	
1786	Van, Sara Elizabeth	Limited Probate	Pts	Jan	
1753	BERCHERE, James Lewis		London	May	129
1766	BERCHIER, The Noble David de Saussure, Baron de		Pts	May	176
1768	BERCKEL, The Honourable Engebertran	Limited Probate	Pts	Sep	364
1797	Van, Engelbert Francoise	Limited Probate	Pts	Apr	281
1780	Van, The Right Honourable Lady Petronella Geertruid		Pts	Oct	460
1758	BERCKHOFF, Maria	Limited Probate	Pts	Apr	100
1797	BERCKLEY, John alias John Godfrey		Middlesex	Mar	132
1799	BERCLAY, George, Esq		Middlesex	Oct	700

1778	BERCY, Joan alias John Claude Simon		Middlesex	Aug	312
1787	BERDENIS, Cornelia	Limited Probate	Pts	Oct	440
1769	BERDMORE, Edward, The Reverend	Dr. of Laws	Northampton	Sep	305
1772	Genevova		Nottingham	May	159
1754	Martha		Nottingham	Feb	33
1776	Rebecca		Suffolk	May	212
1786	Sarah		Northampton	Mar	135
1772	Scrope, Dr	Dr. in Divinity A with W	Nottingham	Jul	247
1779	Scrope, The Reverend	A with W. Will regd 247 Taverner. Dr. in Divinity	Nottingham	Jul	
1774	Thomas, Dr, The Reverend	Dr. in Divinity	Northampton	Apr	131
1785	Thomas		London	Nov	539
1788	William, The Reverend		York	Jun	285
1789	William		Surrey	Mar	132
1775	BERDOE, John		Surrey	Mar	85
1770	BERDT, Dennys de		Middlesex	Aug	284
1774	BERE, Davy, Esq		Devon	Jun	213
1790	George		Middlesex	Jun	278
1793	de la, John, Esq		Gloucester	Jun	306
1799	John		Devon	Jul	481
1790	Julian	A with W	Middlesex	Oct	455
1795	Julian	A with W of Goods unad Will regd October 1790	Middlesex	Jan	
1763	Margaret		Middlesex	Jan	8
1764	BEREG, Easter alias OSTERBERG, Andreas		Pts	Aug	298
1777	BERENGER DE BEAUFAIN, Claire de alias DE BEAUFAIN, Claire		Pts	Oct	409
1753	de BOISLIN, Isaac	Limited A with W of Goods unad. Will regd 279 Lone	Pts	Jun	
1777	John James alias BERANGER, James	A with W	Pts	May	196
1793	John James alias BERANGER, James	A with W Will regd 196 Collier	Pts	Apr	
1757	BERENS, Andris alias BERNES, Andrew alias BERENS, Andrew	Will regd December last	Middlesex	Jun	
1757	BERENS, Andrew alias BERENS, Andris alias BERNES, Andrew	Will regd December last	Middlesex	Jun	
1795	Herman, Esq		Kent	Jan	5

Year	Name	Notes	Place	Month	No.
	BERENS (Contd)				
1788	John, Esq		Middlesex	Jan	4
1800	Magdalen		Middlesex	Jun	439
1760	BERENT, Anderas		Pts	Oct	380
1761	Joachim		Pts	Mar	82
	alias BERENTZ				
1761	BERENTZ, Joachim		Pts	Mar	82
	alias BERENT				
1767	BERESFORD, Ann		Surrey	Apr	125
1788	Edward, The Reverend	A with W	Nottingham	Jan	6
1775	Elizabeth		Middlesex	Aug	302
1784	Francis	"Sandwich" "Golden Rule"	Pts	Dec	629
1771	Gilbert		Chester	Mar	92
1797	James		Worcester	Apr	221
1772	Jane		Lincoln	Feb	38
1760	John		Middlesex	May	184
1778	Mary	A with W	Middlesex	Nov	433
1796	Sarah		Surrey	Jul	344
1797	Thomas		Middlesex	Apr	222
1785	William	By Sent (regd Feb 632)	Middlesex	Feb	67
1794	William	A with W	Middlesex		125
1758	BERESTEYN, VAN, The Right Honourable Christiaan Paulus	A with W Lord of Maurik	Pts	Jun	204
1787	BERETON, Barbara	A with W	Gloucester	Oct	439
1779	BEREWOUT, Aaghje		Pts	Jan	2
1772	Adriana		Pts	Apr	120
	alias BROUWER				
1771	The Right Noble Lord Evert		Pts	Feb	46
1778	Jan Ffredrik, The Honourable	Limited Probate	Pts	Mar	95
1800	Margaretha Clara	Limited Probate	Pts	Apr	254
1773	The Honourable Maria Catharina		Pts	Nov	452
	alias TRIP				
1762	BEREY, John	A with W	Pts	Nov	449
1764	BERFORD, Goerge		Pts	Mar	81
1776	BERG, VAN DEN, Adriana	Limited Probate	Pts	Feb	58
	alias CAAN				
1784	Elizabeth		Middlesex	May	248
1775	George		Bristol	May	169
1763	Hendrick		Pts	Mar	167
	alias BARRACK				
	alias BARRETT				
1800	Hester	A with W	Middlesex	Oct	698
1755	VAN DEN, Johan	Limited Probate	Pts	Nov	300
1765	Peter		Middlesex	Dec	443
1766	VAN, Wyntje		Pts	Feb	81
	alias VEEN				

1767	BERGEN, VAN, Agatha Francica alias Francisca alias VAN LINTELO	Limited Probate		Oct	393
1761	VAN DEN, Anna Maria alias STEYN alias WYBO	Limited Probate	Pts	May	191
1766	VAN, Apolonia	Limited Probate	Pts	Apr	162
1750	VAN, Francois	Limited Probate	Pts	Jan	30
1757	VAN, Hille Gouda Gertruyd alias DE CASEMBROOT alias DE CASEMBROOD	Limited Probate	Pts	Feb	68
1753	VAN DEN, Jan	Limited Probate	Pts	Jul	193
1781	VAN, John Frederick		Middlesex	Jan	48
1750	VAN DEN, Maria	Limited Probate	Pts	Apr	131
1774	Lord in Neunemerland CORTGEEN etc. etc. The Right Honourable Willem Adriaen Count of Nassau Baron of		Pts	Nov	403
1798	BERGENTHEIM, Dirk Fredrik alias VAN VOERST alias VAN ALDERNICK		Pts	Sep	622
1794	BERGER, Albert	Limited Probate	London	Oct	486
1754	Anna Sybella alias HOOFT	Limited Probate	Pts	Oct	266
1796	Catharina, Lady	Limited Probate	Pts	Oct	491
1786	Cypriaan, The Honour- able	Limited Probate	Pts	Jul	362
1790	Elisabeth Beatrix	Limited Probate	Pts	Jan	4
1778	Ffrancois alias Ffrancis		London	Dec	478
1778	Ffrancoise Hendrina The Right Honourable Lady	Limited Probate	Pts	Mar	97
1795	Gerarda Deliana	Limited Probate	Pts	Aug	495
1788	Sarah		Surrey	Mar	120
1778	Sophia Gysberta	Limited Probate	Pts	Nov	431
1767	BERGEYCK, Count of, BROUCHOVEN, Nicolaus Josephus		Pts	Nov	402
1783	BERGH, Anthony	Limited Probate	Pts	Mar	
1781	VAN DEN, Carel	Limited Probate	Pts	Jan	
1778	VAN DEN, Catharina		Pts	Aug	340
1780	VAN DEN, Catharina	Limited Probate	Pts	Apr	170
1788	VAN DEN, Egbert	Limited Probate	Pts	Mar	164
1764	DE, Johanna	Limited Probate	Pts	Oct	378
1763	DE, Maria		Pts	Dec	542
1761	Petter alias Peter		Pts	May	161

Year	Name	Note	Place	Month	No.
1756	BERGIER, Catherina Elizabeth alias HAUSMANS	A with W	Pts	Apr	95
1754	John Peter	Limited Probate	Pts	Mar	68
1756	DE, d'ALANCON, Margaret alias Margurite		Pts	Dec	317
1779	Maria Sophia alias BOUQUET, Marie Sophie	Limited Probate	Pts	Apr	
1784	BERGIN, Dennis	"Burford"	Pts	Jul	370
1756	John alias BURGON		Pts	Nov	288
1751	BERGMAN, Casper		Middlesex	Apr	104
1799	Daniel		Middlesex	Nov	758
1766	David		Middlesex	May	168
1783	John George	Ser	Pts	Jul	336
1778	Olof		Pts	Jul	274
1795	BERGNE, Jean		Middlesex	Nov	624
1784	BERGOIN, Francis		Chichester	Apr	189
1780	BERGSMA, The Honourable Adrianus, Esq	Limited Probate	Pts	Nov	505
1792	BERGSTROOM, Ffredrick alias BERGSTS, Carls Friedrick	M.S. "Commorco"	Pts	Oct	497
1750	BERIDGE, Bridget		Middlesex	Dec	376
1788	John		Derby	Dec	577
1779	Lettice		Lincoln	Mar	88
1799	William alias BERRIDGE	Ser. "Arrogant"	Pts	Feb	93
1799	BERIMAN, Isabella alias BERRIMAN		Middlesex	Feb	96
1767	BERINGER de BEAUFAIN, Hector, Esq	Limited Probate	Pts	Feb	36
1791	BERINGTON, Agatha		Worcester	Jun	
1765	Ann		Hereford	May	170
1760	John		Salop	Oct	379
1763	Joseph, Dr.	Dr. of Physick	Salop	May	216
1750	Mary		Middlesex	Sep	286
1755	Thomas		Middlesex	Dec	305
1777	Thomas		Salop	Oct	410
1791	William, Esq		Essex	Jan	4
1751	BERINGHEN, De, Elizabeth alias LE COQ DE GERMAIN	Limited Probate	Pts	Feb	42
1780	BERISFORD, Joseph		Warwick	Jul	347
1782	BERJEW, Thomas		Bristol	Nov	532
1773	BERK, Elizabeth		Buckinghamshire	Nov	414
1765	Rachel Antonia		Essex	Mar	85
1788	Rebecca		Buckinghamshire	Jan	4
1792	Sarah		Buckinghamshire	Aug	419
1765	William		Surrey	Mar	87

1782	BERKEL, Jacob		Pts	Jan	2
	alias Jacob Rokusz				
	alias Rocusz				
1783	Jacomina	Limited Probate	Pts	Apr	164
1768	Jannetje	Limited Probate	Pts	Apr	139
1786	BERKELEY, Ann De		Middlesex	Dec	600
	Champdevaux				
1786	Anne		Kent	Jul	364
1755	The Right Honourable		Middlesex	Feb	31
	Augustus, late Earl				
1765	Charles, The Honourable		Somerset	Sep	323
1776	Edward, Esq		Dorset	Aug	347
1752	Elizabeth		Middlesex	Mar	57
1792	Lady, The Right		Middlesex	Jul	363
	Honourable Elizabeth				
	Countess Dowager of				
1757	The Right Honourable		York	Nov	322
	Frances, Lady,Baroness				
	Dowager of Rochdale				
	alias Lady BYRON				
1785	Frances, The Honourable		Middlesex	Aug	403
1795	George, Dr	Dr. of Laws	Oxford	May	299
1796	George, Dr	Dr. of Laws. By Int.	Oxford	Dec	
	The Reverend	Decree. Will regd			
		May 1795			
1800	Henry, Esq	No Ship	Pts	Jul	505
1760	Isabella Bernardina		Middlesex	Jan	5
1767	James		London	Jan	4
1795	James		Middlesex	Jan	5
1780	Jane		Worcester	Apr	171
1773	The Right Honourable		Somerset	May	192
	John, Baron of Stratton				
	in the County of				
	Cornwall				
1778	John, Esq		Worcester	Jul	273
1784	John	Ser. "Sceptre"	Pts	Jul	366
1752	Judith		Middlesex	Jan	3
1774	Lionel Spencer, Esq		York	Apr	130
1769	Lucy		Worcester	Jul	233
1793	Lucy, The Reverend		Worcester	Jul	354
1768	Mary		Middlesex	Sep	337
1780	Maurice	Ser	Pts	Mar	119
	alias BERTLEY,				
	Morrice				
1788	Miles		Northampton	Nov	524
1754	Robert		Middlesex	May	123
1767	Robert	A with W unad	London	Dec	
		Will regd 123 Pinfold			
1776	Robert	A with W unad	Middlesex	Mar	
		Will regd 123 Pinfold			
1766	Thomas		Worcester	May	170
1753	BERKENHEAD, John	A with W	Middlesex	Sep	244

1794	BERKENHOUT, Charles William	"Vengence"	Pts	Nov	540
1791	John, Dr	Dr. of Physic	Oxford	Jun	268
1762	BERKER, George alias BARKER		Pts/Middlesex	Jun	234
1792	BERKHOFF, Gerrit, The Reverend	Limited Probate	Pts	Sep	460
1780	Hendrik	Limited Probate	Pts	Feb	57
1767	BERKHOUT, TEDING VAN, The Noble Born Lady Cornelia Hillegonda alias VAN SCHUYLENBURCH	Special A with W	Pts	May	
1767	TEDING VAN, Johan	A with W	Pts	Oct	
1790	TEDING VAN, Pieter Jacob	Limited Probate	Pts	Jun	
1796	BERKIN, William, Esq	Special A with W	Gloucester	Oct	489
1765	BERKINGTON, Thomas		Middlesex	Jan	4
1774	BERKLEY, Ann		Middlesex	Dec	422
1775	Beaumont Marriana	A with W	Middlesex	Nov	403
1760	Cuthbert		Middlesex	Apr	135
1799	David	Ser."Arrogant" A with W	Pts	Jan	13
1761	George		Pts	Jun	200
1751	Henry		Surrey	Aug	228
1768	John		Middlesex	Nov	403
1773	Mary alias FELLOWS		Berkshire	Aug	322
1783	Mary		Devon	May	217
1764	Samuel, Esq	A with W	Middlesex	Mar	81
1764	Samuel		Middlesex	Aug	297
1774	Samuel, Esq	Limited A with W unad Will regd 81 Simpson	Middlesex	Apr	
1790	William, Esq		Middlesex	May	225
1765	BERKOM, VAN, John	Limited Probate	Pts	Dec	470
1786	BERKS, John		Middlesex	Nov	553
1798	Joseph		Middlesex	Dec	760
1799	Samuel		Middlesex	Mar	164
1762	BERKSHIRE, Lady Catherine, The Right Honourable Countess Dowager of Suffolk and		Middlesex	Mar	
1760	Lord, The Right Honourable Henry BOWES, Earl of Suffolk and			May	216
1779	Lord Henry, The Right Honourable Earl of Suffolk and		Middlesex	Mar	130
1759	BERLAND, John		Pts/Middlesex	Nov	350
1755	Paul		Middlesex	Oct	253

1751	BERLER, Elizabeth alias BRILLER		Middlesex	Nov	300
1793	BERLEPSCH, Von, Charles Frederic alias DE BERLEPSCH, Carl Friederick		Pts	May	251
1762	BERLIGUM, Lord David, The Right Honourable Le Lende Wilhem Lord of Waelwyck	Limited Probate	Pts	Jul	308
1771	BERLIE, John Daniel		Middlesex	Apr	146
1763	BERLIN, Erik alias BERLINE, Alexander		Pts	Jul	322
1771	BERMEN, DE, John Baptiste, Lord de la Martinier	A with W	Pts	Nov	431
1781	BERMETT, Henry		Pts/Kent	Sep	420
1781	John	Ser	Pts	Jan	5
1799	BERMINGHAM, Andrew alias BIRMINGHAM	Ser."Excellent"	Pts	Jan	5
1761	Elizabeth		Middlesex	Nov	381
1761	Walter		Middlesex	Apr	117
1762	Walter	Double Probate Will regd April 1761	Middlesex	May	
1797	Walter, Esq		Galway	Nov	675
1790	BERNAL, Abraham	No Ship	Pts	Jan	5
1766	Jacob Israel alias BERNAL, Jacob		London	Jan	3
1752	GOMES, Sara alias GOMES BERNAL		Pts	Mar	64
1752	GOMES, Sara alias BERNAL GOMES, Sara		Pts	Mar	64
1788	BERNARD, Abraham		Middlesex	Jan	5
1795	Abraham		Bristol	Jun	367
1798	Albert Christopher alias John		Pts	Nov	
1757	Ann	A with W of Goods unad Will regd 3 Buckingham	London	Jul	
1765	Ann		Middlesex	Nov	402
1783	Ann		Essex	Mar	107
1790	Ann		Hertford	Jul	319
1792	Ann alias BARNARD, Anna		Surrey	Nov	544
1750	Anna Catharina	A with W	Pts	Apr	103
1776	Antoinette	Limited Probate	Pts	Oct	414
1767	Arthur, Esq		London	Aug	295
1755	Baltina alias VAN HEMERT		Pts	Apr	95
1752	Bartholomew		Middlesex	Jul	179

BERNARD (Contd)

1798	Benjamin		Devon	Mar	160
1800	Bridget		Middlesex	Dec	835
1756	Catherine		London	Oct	267
1750	Charles		Essex	Feb	36
1754	Charles	A with W unad	Essex	Nov	
		Will regd 36 Greenly			
1776	Charles	Limited A with W unad	London	Jul	
		Will regd 62 Browne			
1778	Charles		Salop	May	187
1797	Charles, Esq		Bristol	Nov	676
1797	Christian		Southampton	Apr	225
1772	Edward		Pts	Nov	390
	alias BARNARD				
1758	Elizabeth		Southampton	Nov	321
1757	Elizabeth	A with W	Middlesex	Mar	75
1765	Elizabeth		Middlesex	Dec	441
1767	Elizabeth		Middlesex	Sep	334
1761	Erasmus		Norfolk	Nov	379
1756	Frances		Middlesex	Dec	318
1779	Francis	Ser.	Buckinghamshire	Jul	287
1783	Francis, Esq	A with W	Essex	Apr	159
1761	Guiljamsz, Lord of	Limited Probate	Pts	Nov	379
	New Hellevoet and				
	The Quack				
1758	Henry		Lancaster	Jan	2
1769	Henry		London	Jun	194
1766	Herman, Dr	Dr. of Physick	London	Jul	257
1759	James, Esq		London	Jun	194
1768	James, Esq	A with W unad	London	Feb	
		Will regd 194 Arran			
1780	James		Surrey	Mar	122
1792	James		Middlesex	Apr	198
1763	Jane		Middlesex	May	215
	alias BARNARD				
1793	Johan Stephanus, Dr	Dr. of Physick	Pts	Nov	539
	alias Stephen				
1752	John		Essex	Feb	30
1753	John		Middlesex	Feb	38
1754	John		Wiltshire	Oct	267
1766	John, Sir		Huntingdon	Dec	444
1791	John, Esq		Ireland	Oct	454
1782	Magdalen		Middlesex	Feb	60
1770	Lady Maria, free		Pts	Jan	
	Lady of Cattenbroek				
	and Utterdyken Van				
	Mastwyk				
1785	Mary		Middlesex	Mar	118
1787	Mary	A with W	Pts	May	196
	alias BAILLY, Marie				
1793	Mary		Sussex	Apr	188

	BERNARD (Contd)				
1793	Dame Mary	A with W	Middlesex	Oct	495
1795	Dame Mary	A with W	Middlesex	Apr	
		Will Regd October 1793			
1799	Mary		Wiltshire	Jun	418
1768	Melchior,	Limited Probate	Pts	Feb	42
	The Honourable				
1761	Peter, Esq		Pts	Jan	5
	alias BESNARD				
1789	Sir Robert, Baronet		Huntingdon	Jan	10
1750	Sir Samuel	A with W	Pts	Apr	103
1791	Sarah		Essex	Mar	116
1760	Simeon		Middlesex	Feb	46
1755	Thomas, The Reverend		Essex	Nov	276
1762	Thomas		Kent	Oct	411
1766	Thomas, Esq		Middlesex	Jan	4
1773	Thomas, The Reverend		Essex	Nov	418
1775	William, Esq	A with W	London	May	173
1781	William Henry		Middlesex	May	229
1766	BERNARDEAU, Ann		Middlesex	Dec	442
1753	James		Middlesex	Jan	6
1773	BERNARDEIN, Judith		Middlesex	May	194
	alias BERNARDINE				
1796	BERNARDI, Christopfer		Middlesex	Mar	108
	alias Christopher				
1764	BERNARDIN, Charles		Middlesex	Mar	80
1773	BERNADINE, Judith		Middlesex	May	194
	alias BERNARDEIN				
1767	BERNARDT, Maria	Limited Probate	Pts	May	
	alias ENGELS				
1751	BERND, Bicker John, Esq	Limited Probate	Pts	Apr	102
1761	BERNDT, Peter		Pts	May	161
	alias BARNET				
1762	BERNEGE, John		Middlesex	Apr	
1798	BERNERS, Lord	A with W	N. Britain	Feb	90
	alias CAMPBELL,				
	Colin, Esq				
1782	Henry, Esq		Middlesex	Jan	5
1800	Henry, The Reverend		Middlesex	Apr	252
1782	Mary		Middlesex	Jan	5
1783	William, Esq		Middlesex	Sep	444
1756	BERNES, Andrew		Middlesex	Dec	320
1757	Andrew	Will regd December last	Middlesex	Jun	
	alias BERENS, Andrew				
	alias BERENS, Andris				
1754	BERNETT, John		Pts	Jun	160
1792	BERNEY, Dame Catherine	A with W	Kent	Jul	366
1772	Dorothy		Norfolk	Sep	319
1783	Elizabeth		Norwich	Jun	280
1782	John, Dr. The Reverend	Dr. in Divinity	Norfolk	Jul	337
1800	John		Norfolk	Dec	837

BERNEY (Contd)

Year	Name	Note	Place	Month	No.
1797	Martha		Middlesex	Jun	397
1787	Richard, The Reverend		Norfolk	Jun	257
1788	Richard		Norfolk	May	232
1795	Richard, The Reverend		Norwich	Jan	5
1767	Robert		Norwich	May	162
1786	Thomas, Esq		Norfolk	Dec	604
1762	William		Middlesex	Jun	237
1763	William, The Reverend		Norfolk	May	212
1775	William	Double Probate Will regd 237 St. Eloy	Middlesex	Aug	
1784	William		Middlesex	Aug	430
1785	William	A with W of Goods unad Will regd August 1784	Middlesex	Jul	
1785	William	E.I.S."Nassau"	Pts	Oct	492
1764	BERNIE, Robert		Surrey	Nov	416
1765	BERNIER, Ann	Limited Probate	Pts	Oct	364
1799	Joseph	"Blenheim" "Marlborough"	Pts	Oct	700
1765	BERNIN, Mary		Middlesex	Dec	442
1758	Peter		Middlesex	Oct	285
1758	BERNON, James		Middlesex	Dec	355
1769	BERNONVILLE, John The Reverend		Middlesex	Oct	332
1777	Thomas		Middlesex	Feb	52
1796	BERRECLOTH, Robert		Essex	Aug	399
1792	BERRELL, Mary	Poor	Surrey	Oct	500
1752	BERRETTS, Felice alias BARRETA, Fillece		Pts	Jun	148
1790	BERREY, Arther alias BERRY		Middlesex	Oct	455
1770	Elizabeth		Kent	Apr	132
1764	Francis alias BERRY	A with W	Pts	Dec	456
1769	Richard alias BERRY		Middlesex	Jul	236
1763	Thomas		Pts	Mar	110
1799	William, Esq		Middlesex	Dec	826
1782	BERRICK, William		Pts	May	215
1766	BERRIDGE, Isaac		Surrey	Apr	126
1790	John		Rutland	May	225
1752	Mary		Rutland	Mar	59
1777	Mary		Rutland	Nov	446
1782	Thomas		Middlesex	Jun	264
1785	Thomas		Middlesex	Feb	66
1775	Vertue		Rutland	Jul	262
1799	William alias BERIDGE	Ser. "Arrogant"	Pts	Feb	93
1795	BERRIE, Adam Govan		London	Jul	430
1771	James		London	Nov	432
1772	John		London	Jan	3
1788	John Samuel		Middlesex	Nov	523

	BERRIE (Contd)				
1769	Margaret		London	Jun	195
1761	BERRIER, William		Cambridge	Jun	200
1776	BERRIFF, John		Essex	Sep	381
1799	BERRIMAN, Isabella		Middlesex	Feb	96
	alias BERIMAN				
1768	John, The Reverend		Middlesex	Dec	438
1769	Katherine		Middlesex	Nov	367
1761	Mary		London	Sep	310
1774	Mary	A with W	Wiltshire	Dec	420
1787	Mary		Berkshire	Jul	310
1758	Richard		Pts	Feb	28
	alias BERRYMAN				
1754	Samuel		Pts	Jul	189
1750	William, The	Dr. in Divinity	London	Feb	38
	Reverend Dr.				
1762	BERRINGTON, Francis		Kent	Nov	447
1783	French		Kent	Jul	335
1769	Martha		Berkshire	Jul	235
1758	BERRISFORD, John		London	Oct	286
1759	John		Pts	Mar	82
1778	Robert		Middlesex	May	187
1751	BERROW, Capel, The		Bedford	Dec	327
	Reverend				
1756	Charles		Hereford	Dec	356
1778	Edward		Pts	May	184
1768	Elizabeth		Middlesex	Dec	438
1780	Harvey		Pts	Feb	60
1799	Hester		Bristol	Jan	4
1754	John	A with W	Middlesex	Apr	99
1755	John, Esq		Bristol	Mar	67
1757	John		Bristol	May	147
1788	John, Esq		Middlesex	Apr	178
1794	John		Middlesex	Feb	62
1773	Mary		Hertford	Jun	234
1765	Sarah		Bristol	Mar	87
1790	Sarah		Middlesex	Aug	368
1781	Thomas		Middlesex	Dec	570
1765	William		Bristol	Jul	244
1760	BERRY, Abraham	A with W	Pts	Jan	2
1795	Alley		Southampton	Aug	493
1792	Allis		York	Apr	198
1763	Ann		Middlesex	Jan	8
1772	Ann		Middlesex	Apr	123
1778	Ann		Middlesex	Feb	50
1790	Arther		Middlesex	Oct	455
	alias BERREY				
1750	Barratt		Pts	Sep	286
	alias BARRY				
1779	Bathiah		Middlesex	Apr	144
1753	Benjamin		Surrey	Aug	224

	BERRY (Contd)				
1773	Catherine		Surrey	Nov	417
1764	Charles		Kent	Jul	251
1784	Charles	"Superb"	Pts	Sep	489
	alias BURRY				
1789	Charles	A with W	Oxford	Nov	529
1758	David		Pts	Nov	319
1799	Denham		Middlesex	Mar	163
1760	Edward	A with W	Middlesex	Jan	5
1782	Edward		London	Oct	482
1787	Edward		Northampton	Dec	533
1798	Edward		Northampton	Nov	693
1757	Francis		Middlesex	Apr	239
1764	Francis	A with W	Pts	Dec	456
	alias BERREY				
1765	George		Pts	Jul	248
1784	George	Ser. "General Monk" "St. Margaretta"	Pts	Dec	628
1793	George		Middlesex	Aug	398
1776	Grace		Surrey	Feb	54
1794	Grace		Surrey	Sep	444
1763	Hanse Amerson		Pts	Feb	43
	alias BERY, Hans Amin				
1758	Henry		Surrey	Aug	238
1764	Henry	A with W	Pts	Jul	252
1753	James		Kent	Aug	223
1758	James	A with W	Pts	Aug	237
	alias BARRY				
1768	James		Pts/Kent	Feb	45
1775	James		Pts	Oct	368
1786	Jane		Middlesex	Jun	321
	alias COWAN				
1758	Jeremiah		London	May	142
1768	Jeremiah		Norwich	Jan	4
1750	John		Middlesex	Jun	189
1752	John		Pts	Jul	178
1758	John		London	Dec	356
1761	John	A with W	Surrey	Jul	241
1763	John	A with W	London··	Nov	496
1767	John		Surrey	Nov	402
1771	John		Middlesex	Apr	146
1773	John		Hertford	Dec	458
1775	John	A with W	Exeter	May	171
1778	John		Middlesex	Aug	312
1781	John		Canterbury	Jan	8
1782	John		Kent	Aug	394
1785	John		Middlesex	Jun	289
1787	John	.	Middlesex	Aug	358
1789	John		Middlesex	Mar	133
1795	John	No Ship	Pts	Jun	363

BERRY (Contd)

Year	Name	Note	Place	Month	Page
1800	John		Middlesex	Feb	81
1800	John		Sussex	Sep	645
1772	Joseph		London	Apr	121
1799	Joseph		Surrey	Aug	568
1757	Mary		Middlesex	Feb	40
1758	Mary	A with W Limited	Middlesex	May	142
	alias OAKER				
1779	Mary		Surrey	Feb	40
1785	Mary		London	Jan	8
1789	Mary	A with W	York	Oct	484
1791	Nathaniel		Middlesex	Oct	453
1784	Patrick	"Martin"	Pts	Oct	537
	alias BARRY				
1792	Peter		Kent	Feb	58
1796	Peter	A with W of Goods unad	Canterbury	Apr	
		Will regd February 1792			
1753	Peter		Pts	May	130
	alias BAREY, Pietar				
1763	Rebecca		London	May	217
1750	Richard		Ireland	Mar	68
1758	Richard	Ser.	Surrey	Jan	4
1758	Richard		Pts/London	Sep	258
1762	Richard		Kent	Aug	332
1769	Richard		Middlesex	Jul	236
	alias BERREY				
1775	Richard		Surrey	Sep	335
1784	Richard		York	Oct	538
1787	Richard	A with W	Middlesex	Apr	157
1788	Richard		Surrey	May	230
1778	Richard Curson Mears		Surrey	May	184
1759	Robert		Pts	Jun	193
	alias BARRY				
1762	Robert		Middlesex	Jun	232
1764	Robert		Somerset	Jul	254
1764	Robert		Hertford	Oct	378
1766	Robert		Oxford	Jul	257
1783	Robert		Pts	Sep	446
1788	Roseannah		Southampton	Nov	522
1752	Samuel		Middlesex	Mar	57
1795	Samuel		Southampton	Jun	367
1765	Sarah		Middlesex	Mar	88
1770	Sarah		Hertford	Apr	129
1799	Sibyl Dare		Middlesex	Sep	643
1771	Stephen		Middlesex	Jun	242
1771	Stephen		Pts	Aug	332
1750	Thomas		Bedford	Feb	38
1752	Thomas	A with W	Pts	Aug	206
1755	Thomas		London	Apr	92
1764	Thomas		Middlesex	Feb	39
1764	Thomas	A with W of Goods unad	Bedford	Mar	
		Will regd 38 Greenly			

BERRY (Contd)

1764	Thomas		Pts	Aug	298
1765	Thomas		Middlesex	Jul	245
1771	Thomas		Middlesex	Aug	329
1779	Thomas		Middlesex	Jul	289
1782	Thomas		Middlesex	Feb	61
1784	Thomas		Pts	Jan	6
1791	Thomas		Berkshire	May	209
1797	Thomas	"Crown". A with W	Pts	May	292
1800	Thomas		Northampton	Jun	433
1752	Walter		Middlesex	Mar	57
1750	William		Pts	Jun	189
1759	William		Surrey	May	159
1761	William		Pts	Mar	84
1762	William		Pts	Mar	91
1762	William alias BARRY		Pts	Apr	140
1766	William		Surrey	Aug	295
1768	William		Kent	Jul	270
1769	William	A with W	Middlesex	Apr	111
1774	William		Surrey	Feb	37
1774	William		Middlesex	Jul	258
1779	William		Warwick	Apr	144
1779	William		Pts	Jun	236
1781	William		Berkshire	Jan	8
1781	William		Gloucester	Apr	179
1784	William	"Vanguard"	Pts/Kent	Mar	122
1788	William		Oxford	Jan	4
1789	William	Special A with W	Devon	Mar	138
1777	BERRYMAN, Ann		Surrey	Feb	56
1795	Ann		Surrey	Oct	581
1766	Anne alias BURRYMAN		Surrey	Jan	2
1773	Christian		Devon	Dec	459
1771	Elizabeth alias ALLIN alias ALLEN		Surrey	Sep	366
1751	Elizabeth	A with W	Surrey	Sep	252
1761	James		Surrey	Dec	418
1753	John		Pts	Apr	101
1759	John		Middlesex	Feb	45
1771	John		Surrey	Dec	469
1758	Richard alias BERRIMAN		Pts	Feb	28
1758	Sarah		London	Nov	321
1757	Susanna		Middlesex	Oct	294
1776	Thomas		Surrey	Oct	413
1750	William		London	Feb	36
1780	BERSET, Marie Dorothie alias LENTULUS, Maria Dorothy		Pts	May	240

Year	Name	Notes	Place	Month	No.
1759	BERT, DE, Elizabeth		Surrey	Jul	230
1770	BERTAUCHE, De La, Peter alias DELABLERTAUCHE	A with W	Kent	Feb	50
1759	BERTELS, Jan		Pts	Dec	382
1793	Josephus		Middlesex	Jan	4
1763	BERTH, James		Pts	Jun	270
1750	BERTHE, John Augustus		Pts	Jul	224
1754	Magdalen alias DERSIGNY		Pts	May	124
1781	BERTHOL, Grace alias BERTHOLD alias BARTHOLD		Middlesex	Aug	377
1781	BERTHOLD, Grace alias BARTHOLD alias BERTHOL		Middlesex	Aug	377
1788	BERTHOLDT, Nicholas		Middlesex	Mar	116
1763	BERTHON, Anne		Pts	May	214
1791	Amphillis		Middlesex	Jul	314
1793	Daniel		Middlesex	Aug	400
1795	Daniel	A with W of Goods unad Will regd August 1793	Middlesex	May	
1753	Elie	By Sentence	Middlesex	Feb	40
1767	Jacob	A with W	Pts	May	165
1777	Jane		Middlesex	Nov	451
1793	Jane		Middlesex	Dec	580
1789	John		Middlesex	Jan	11
1753	Martha alias MARTINEAU	A with W	Middlesex	May	130
1756	Michael		Middlesex	Dec	320
1765	Paul		London	Jul	248
1792	BERTHONI, Joan Paul		Middlesex	Aug	417
1755	BERTHONNEUX, Marie alias DESMONTIS, Mary alias BARTHONNEAU	Will regd April last	Hertford	May	
1784	BERTHWELL, Charles	Ser."Monarca"	Middlesex	Jun	306
1784	Charles alias BURTWELL	"Coventry" "Monarca" "Superb". Another Grant last June	Pts/Middlesex	Aug	
1765	BERTIE, The Right Honourable Albemarle alias Lord Albermarle BERTIE		Lincoln	Sep	322
1778	Anne, The Honourable		Flintshire	Mar	97
1778	Anne alias Lady Vere BERTIE		Lincoln	Dec	475
1759	Bridget	A with Testamony Schedule annexed	Northampton	Jul	225
1754	Charles, Esq		Middlesex	May	123
1780	Charles, Esq		Lincoln	Mar	119
1788	Charles, The Reverend		Devon	Dec	579
1785	David		Rochester	Feb	68
1757	Elizabeth		Devon	Jan	5

	BERTIE (Contd)				
1759	The Honourable Elizabeth		Exeter	Aug	258
1782	The Right Honourable Lady Elizabeth Mountague	A with W	Somerset	Sep	443
1757	Ernle, Esq		Northampton	May	146
1771	Frances		Somerset	Feb	46
1783	Frances	A with W unad Will regd 46 Trevor	Somerset	May	
1764	Isaiah		Middlesex	Dec	456
1759	James		Middlesex	May	156
1782	Laurence alias Laurance		Pts	Jun	267
1797	Lucy		Devon	Mar	134
1753	Montague, Esq alias Lord Montague BERTIE		Southampton	Sep	246
1779	Norborne, The Reverend		Middlesex	Jul	290
1766	Norreys, Esq		Pts	Nov	398
1782	Peregrine, Esq		Buckinghamshire	Oct	482
1787	Peregrine, Esq		Essex	Jan	5
1790	The Honourable Peregrine		Oxford	Sep	413
1799	Richard, Esq		Denbigh	Jan	9
1782	The Right Honourable Robert, commonly called Lord Robert BERTIE		Middlesex	Mar	114
1772	Sophia		Middlesex	Feb	37
1751	Thomas		Norwich	Mar	71
1769	Vere, Esq. The Right Honourable, commonly called Lord Vere BERTIE		Lincoln	Feb	33
1767	William, The Reverend Dr.	Dr. in Divinity	Oxford	Mar	86
1800	Willoughby, The Right Honourable Lord BERTIE Earl of Abingdon		Middlesex	May	
1759	BERTIN, Barbara		Middlesex	Feb	47
1761	Jacob		Pts	Dec	419
1782	BERTLES, William Beckett, Dr.	Dr. of Physic	Salop	Sep	439
1780	BERTLEY, Morrice alias BERKELEY Maurice	Ser.	Pts	Mar	119
1778	BERTLING, Johannes, The Reverend	Limited Probate	Pts	Nov	431
1797	Maria Alida	Limited Probate	Pts	Jul	477
1797	BERTOEN, Claasje	Limited Probate	Pts	Jul	476
1776	BERTON, Jonathan		Monmouth	May	210

1759	BERTRAM, Charles		Middlesex	Nov	349
1792	Charles		Jersey	Jan	6
1776	Gilbert		Middlesex	Dec	489
1777	Gilbert	Double Probate Will regd in December last	Middlesex	Apr	
1782	James		Pts/Southampton	Oct	479
1784	Philip		Jersey	Sep	492
1767	BERTRAND, Bartholomew		Pts	Feb	33
1760	Isaac		Middlesex	Jan	4
1789	Louise		Middlesex	Oct	483
1774	Mary		Middlesex	Jul	257
1780	Mary	Special A with W	Pts	Jul	348
1784	Mary		Bath	Apr	190
1755	Paul		Bath	Oct	254
1751	Peter	Limited Probate	Pts	Apr	105
1760	Peter		Pts	Sep	346
1791	Robert		London	Nov	493
1782	William		Pts	Aug	391
1763	BERTWISLE, Mathew		Flintshire	Jan	7
1782	BERUSE, Peter alias BERUSO, Piter		Pts	Mar	109
1782	BERUSO, Piter alias BERUSE, Peter		Pts	Mar	109
1764	BERVIE, John		Pts	Aug	298
1788	BERWICK, Alexander	"Exeter"	Middlesex	May	227
1798	The Right Honourable Lady Anne, Baroness-Dowager		Pts	Feb	82
1778	Benjamin, Esq		Surrey	Jan	5
1760	James		Pts	Jun	229
1774	John		Worcester	Dec	424
1798	Joseph, Esq	By Int. Decree	Worcester	Dec	761
1789	The Right Honourable Lord Noel, Baron Berwick		Salop	Feb	77
1789	Peter		Bath	May	239
1755	Rachael		Middlesex	Oct	254
1792	Thomas alias BARWICK		London	Apr	200
1798	Thomas, Esq		Gloucester	Aug	525
1762	William		Pts/Montgomery	Feb	41
1763	BERY, Hans Amin alias BERRY, Hanse Amerson		Pts	Feb	43
1762	BESANT, Henry		Middlesex	Oct	412
1791	John		Middlesex	Dec	559
1769	Mary		Middlesex	Nov	364
1765	BESBEECH, Mary		London	Oct	361
1753	BESCHEFER, James		Middlesex	Nov	284
1788	BESCHEY, Jean Francois	A with W	Pts	Nov	526
1772	BESEMAKER, The Honourable Christian	Limited Probate	Pts	May	156

Year	Name	Notes	Place	Month	Page
1775	BESFORD, Thomas		Middlesex	Sep	335
1769	BESKAMP, Maria Gertruda		Pts	Jul	234
1797	BESLEY, Agness		Devon	Jul	470
1783	James		Devon	May	214
1758	Mary		Somerset	Jun	
1795	Thomas		Devon	Dec	668
1763	Sarah		Devon	Jan	7
1793	BESLY, John		Devon	Apr	189
1779	Oliver		Devon	Mar	90
1786	William		Devon	Nov	553
1761	BESNARD, Peter, Esq alias BERNARD		Pts	Jan	5
1778	Susanna		Dublin	Aug	309
1782	Susanna	A with W unad Will regd August 1778	Ireland	Jan	
1789	Susanna	Special A with W of Goods unad. Will regd 309 Hay	Dublin	Jan	
1772	BESOUTH, Lucy		Suffolk	Feb	37
1767	BESOYEN, Daniel Adriaan Le Leude Wilhelm, Lord of	Limited Probate	Pts	Jan	3
1760	Paul Sebastian Le Leudel Wilhem, Lord of	Limited Probate	Pts	Feb	65
1751	BESQUOIRT, Thomas	Limited Probate	London	Feb	34
1758	BESS, John		Pts/Devon	Oct	286
1781	BESSANT, Joshua		Middlesex	Oct	461
1763	Robert		Pts	Dec	540
1793	BESSBOROUGH, Lord William, The Right Honourable, Earl of, in the Kingdom of Ireland and Baron PONSONBY		Middlesex	May	243
1758	BESSE, Joseph		Middlesex	Aug	237
1762	Otto Frederic		Pts	Dec	495
1779	BESSELL, Mary	A with W	Essex	Nov	442
1791	William		Gloucester	Aug	370
1786	BESSFORD, Mary		Middlesex	Oct	502
1776	BESSINGE, De, James Prevost, Esq. alias The Right Honourable James MacKay de SCOWRY		Pts	Mar	131
1789	BESSLEY, William		London	Dec	572
1794	BESSON, William		Middlesex	May	246
1784	BEST, Ann		Middlesex	Jan	9
1774	Anna Maria		London	Jun	215
1799	Anthony	Limited A with W of Goods unad. Will regd 112 Foot	Middlesex	Nov	
1798	Bartholomew		Bedford	Jan	4
1751	Benjamin		Worcester	Jul	199

BEST (Contd)

Year	Name	Note	County	Month	No.
1784	Benjamin		Surrey	Aug	430
1794	Betty		Somerset	Jan	7
1791	Charlotte		Kent	Aug	374
1780	Daniel		Surrey	Feb	60
1786	Edward		Kent	Jun	319
1795	Edward, The Reverend		Stafford	Jul	429
1795	Eleanor alias Elener		Surrey	Nov	622
1753	Elizabeth		Kent	Mar	72
1778	Elizabeth		Essex	Feb	49
1779	Elizabeth		Gloucester	May	189
1792	Elizabeth		Middlesex	Oct	499
1753	Francis		Middlesex	Jan	4
1795	Francis		Worcester	Jul	432
1751	George		Devon	Jan	4
1756	George		Middlesex	Nov	288
1770	George		Pts	Jan	2
1770	George		Poole	Nov	388
1788	George		Surrey	Oct	472
1799	George		Middlesex	Sep	645
1782	Henry, The Reverend	Dr. in Divinity	Lincoln	Sep	439
1764	James		Middlesex	Dec	457
1782	James, Esq		Kent	Mar	113
1784	James, Esq	Double Probate Will regd March 1782		Oct	
1786	James		Middlesex	Sep	465
1759	John		Hertford	Mar	83
1760	John	A with W	Pts	May	186
1763	John		Southampton	Feb	46
1763	John		Pts	Jul	324
1764	John		Devon	Jun	211
1771	John	Limited Probate	Pts	Jun	244
1773	John		Wiltshire	Apr	148
1790	John		Worcester	Nov	493
1794	John		Surrey	Aug	403
1800	John		Hertford	May	345
1753	Joseph		Worcester	Feb	38
1764	Joseph		Pts	Mar	81
1782	Joseph		Middlesex	Oct	479
1789	Luke		Worcester	Apr	190
1754	Major		Surrey	May	124
1769	Margaret		Somerset	Jan	4
1792	Marmaduke, Esq		Middlesex	Feb	54
1753	Mary		Kent	May	127
1759	Mary		Hertford	Aug	259
1766	Mary		Surrey	Sep	329
1770	Mary		London	Jul	252
1782	Mary		Surrey	Sep	442
1795	Mary		Stafford	Jul	429

	BEST (Contd)				
1773	Matthew		London	Oct	381
1750	Philip		Pts	Oct	315
1771	Richard		Devon	May	193
1783	Richard	Pts	Gloucester	Mar	110
1800	Richard		Worcester	Feb	87
1763	Robert		Pts	Feb	46
1780	Robert	Ser	Southampton	May	241
1788	Robert		Surrey	Jan	4
1794	Robert	"Lion"	Pts	Oct	489
1781	Samuel		York	Jul	328
1784	Samuel	"Exeter" Ser	Pts	Jun	305
1784	Samuel	A with W	Dorset	Aug	429
1751	Sarah		Surrey	Dec	329
1773	Sarah		Middlesex	Oct	382
1780	Sarah		Kent	Jun	304
1764	Susanna		Worcester	Jan	5
1759	Thomas		Pts/Devon	Nov	350
1761	Thomas		Wiltshire	Feb	45
1768	Thomas		Wiltshire	Jun	224
1768	Thomas		Sussex	Sep	340
1775	Thomas		Essex	Feb	41
1779	Thomas		Middlesex	Mar	88
1784	Thomas	"Albany"	Pts	Sep	489
1794	Thomas		Surrey	Jan	5
1795	Thomas, Esq		Kent	Mar	148
1797	Thomas		Hertford	Jul	477
1798	Thomas		Worcester	Apr	234
1778	Ursula		Devon	Jun	230
1769	Whittingham, The Reverend		Middlesex	Apr	114
1761	William, The Reverend, Dr	Dr. in Divinity	London	Aug	278
1774	William		Southampton	Feb	39
1778	William		Worcester	Feb	49
1781	William		Pts	Apr	179
1787	William		Surrey	Jun	257
1788	William		Dorset	Mar	115
1793	William		Hertford	Dec	580
1754	William Beson		Kent	Jun	161
1777	BESTER, John		Middlesex	Mar	100
1799	BESTLAND, Lucy		Somerset	Jun	421
1765	BESTMAN, Elizabeth	A with W of Goods unad twice. Will regd 199 Edmunds	Middlesex	Mar	
1792	BESTOE, Richard, Esq		Lincoln	Jul	366
1782	BESUCHET, Louis		Middlesex	Oct	481
1784	BESWELL, Edward	A with W	Surrey	Jan	9
1787	BESWICK, Ann		Middlesex	Jan	5
1797	George		Gloucester	Apr	225
1752	John		Hereford	Mar	58

BESWICK (Contd)

1762	Sarah		Middlesex	Feb	39
1784	Thomas		Middlesex	Jan	5
1790	Thomas		Hertford	Jul	322
1776	BESWICKE, Edmund, Esq	A with W	Southampton	Apr	166
1764	John, Esq		Middlesex	Aug	297
1788	Robert	"Contractor"	Pts	Feb	55
1775	BESZANT, Britannia	A with W	Surrey	Nov	405
1763	BETCHAM, Joseph alias BEACHAM		Middlesex	Jun	265
1762	BETENSON, Edward, Sir		Kent	Dec	495
1788	Helen		Kent	Nov	544
1758	Ucretia	A with W	Middlesex	Jun	178
1774	BETEW, Esther		Middlesex	Oct	360
1799	Panton		Middlesex	Jul	479
1784	BETH, Mc, Robert	Ser. "Isis"	Pts	Jul	401
1793	BETHAM, Ann		Middlesex	Jan	8
1783	Edward, The Reverend		Middlesex	Dec	598
1795	John		Hereford	Dec	671
1789	Richard, Esq		Isle of Man	Sep	450
1757	Sarah		London	Nov	321
1783	BETHEL, Jabez		Suffolk	Oct	500
1792	Prudence		Suffolk	Dec	597
1773	Robert		Middlesex	May	195
1756	Thomas		Wiltshire	Jan	4
1767	William		Somerset	May	167
1795	William	Pts. "Sheerness"	Southampton	Feb	67
1769	BETHELL, Ann, The Honourable	A with W	Middlesex	Jul	
1778	Ann		Kent	Jul	274
1797	Ann, The Honourable	A with W of Goods unad Will regd July last	Middlesex	Sep	
1778	Bridget		Bath	Jul	272
1778	Bridget	Double Probate Regd last month	Bath	Aug	
1797	Christopher, Esq		Middlesex	Sep	586
1777	Dorothea	A with W	York	Oct	411
1768	Dorothy		Wiltshire	Oct	368
1776	Dorothy		Hereford	Sep	382
1788	George		London	Dec	577
1795	George, Esq		Wiltshire	May	300
1780	Hannah		Wiltshire	Jul	346
1795	Jane		Surrey	Sep	534
1751	Mary		Middlesex	Aug	229
1768	Mary		Surrey	Mar	97
1773	Mary		Middlesex	Sep	351
1784	Mary		Somerset	Nov	585
1784	Mary	Double Probate Will regd 97 Secker	Surrey	Nov	
1789	Mary		Middlesex	Apr	187

	BETHELL (Contd)				
1759	Matthew		Southampton	Feb	47
1768	Priscilla		Bath	Feb	42
1768	Priscilla	Double Probate Will regd this month	Bath	Feb	
1766	Samuel		Hereford	Dec	444
1766	Sarah		Middlesex	Oct	365
1758	Slingsby, Esq late one of the Aldermen of the City of London		London	Nov	320
1758	Slingsby, Esq late one of the Aldermen of the City of London	Double Probate Will regd this month	London	Nov	
1753	Thomas		Middlesex	Jun	161
1758	Thomas	A with W unad Will regd 161 Searle	Middlesex	Nov	
1762	Thomas	A with W of Goods unad Will regd 161 Searle. Last Grant November 1758	Middlesex	Jul	
1772	Thomas	A with W unad. Will regd 161 Searle Last Grant July 1762	Middlesex	Nov	
1781	Thomas		Somerset	Oct	464
1751	William		London	Apr	102
1753	William		Surrey	Jun	165
1770	William		Middlesex	Jun	220
1772	William		Middlesex	Jun	206
1772	William	Double Probate Will regd June last	Middlesex	Nov	
1784	William		London	Sep	490
1800	William, Esq		York	Feb	86
1768	BETHUNE, George	A with W	Pts	Nov	97
1785	George, Esq		Pts	Jul	355
1767	James		Middlesex	Oct	361
1767	James	Double Probate Will regd this month	Middlesex	Oct	
1771	John		Kent	Jun	242
1775	John		Sussex	Sep	336
1782	John	A with W unad Will regd 336 Alexander	Sussex	Nov	
1798	BETHWIN, Henry		Surrey	Jan	10
1773	BETHWIND, John		London	Jan	4
1764	BETKE, Charles		Surrey	Jul	252
1750	BETLEY, Edward alias BOTLEY		Pts	Jun	189
1791	BETMER, Dirk Jan	A with W	Pts	Jun	265
1766	BETNEY, Elizabeth		Surrey	Nov	396
1769	George		Surrey	Mar	77
1781	BETON, Augustin		Middlesex	Dec	572

Year	Name	Notes	Place	Month	No.
1769	BETOUZET, Mary		Middlesex	Mar	75
1751	BETSON, Thomas		Middlesex	May	132
1796	BETSWORTH, Emblem		Middlesex	Nov	542
1798	Joseph		Middlesex	May	314
1763	Washer		Middlesex	Jun	270
1764	BETT, David		Pts	Jun	213
1786	David	"Venus"	Pts	Dec	599
1789	George		Surrey	Dec	572
	alias BEETT				
1759	John		Essex	Nov	350
1796	Mary		Middlesex	Dec	592
	alias BETTS				
1756	Robert		Pts	Dec	319
1778	Thomasin		Middlesex	Feb	50
	alias BETTS, Thomasine				
1778	Thomasin	Double Probate	Middlesex	Feb	
	alias BETTS, Thomasine	Will regd this month			
1796	William	A with W	N. Britain	Jun	293
1798	William	A with W	Guernsey	Mar	153
1783	BETTALL, Stephen	Poor	Middlesex	May	213
1786	BETTEL, William	"Hussar" "Goliath"	Pts	Jun	324
	alias BETTLE				
1768	BETTELAY, Thomas	A with W	Chester	Apr	140
1770	BETTELEY, Mary		Middlesex	Feb	44
1785	BETTELLEY, Mary		Stafford	Apr	172
1757	BETTEKEN, Hacke		Westmorland	Jun	181
1785	BETTERESS, Mary		Middlesex	Jan	7
1750	Samuel		London	Jul	222
1752	BETTERIDGE, Jane		Surrey	Jul	177
1763	BETTERLEY, Elizabeth		Middlesex	Jan	5
1779	BETTERLEY, Elizabeth	A with W unad	Middlesex	Jun	
		Will regd 5 Stevens			
1800	Martha		Middlesex	Oct	700
1762	Richard		Worcester	Feb	41
1772	Thomas		Middlesex	Mar	82
	alias BATTERLEY				
1789	BETTERTON, Alexander		Gloucester	Jan	10
1798	Joseph		London	May	311
1781	Thomas	A with W. Ser.	Middlesex	Sep	422
1795	BETTESWORTH, Charles		Southampton	Feb	67
1759	Elizabeth		Middlesex	Apr	121
1752	The Right Worshipful Dr. John, Doctor of Laws. Dean & Official Principal of the Arches Court of Canterbury & Master Keeper or Commissary of the Prerogative Court of Canterbury		Middlesex	Jan	2
1762	John		Southampton	Dec	493
1779	John, Dr	Dr. of Laws	Bedford	Oct	404

	BETTESWORTH (Contd)				
1789	John, Esq		Cornwall	Feb	71
1754	-BILSON, Thomas		Sussex	Apr	97
1760	Thomas, Esq		Essex	May	185
1794	Thomas		Middlesex	Mar	125
	alias BETTSWORTH				
1795	Thomas		Sussex	Dec	667
1769	BETTEY, George		London	Apr	111
1785	Robert	E. I.S."Ganges"	Pts	Feb	67
	alias BETTIE				
1785	Robert	"Ganges". Will regd last February	Pts	Apr	
1759	Thomas		Pts/Devon	Feb	45
1797	BETTGER, Henry		Surrey	Mar	132
1796	BETTIE, John	Ser."St. Albans"	Pts	Apr	160
1785	Robert	E.I.S."Ganges"	Pts	Feb	67
	alias BETTEY				
1785	Robert	"Ganges".Will regd Feb. last	Pts	Apr	
	alias BETTEY				
1783	BETTKER, Christian		Pts	Aug	402
	alias Christian Hanson				
	alias HANSON, Christian				
1800	BETTLE, Jonathan, Esq		Northampton	Oct	700
1780	William		Pts	Dec	553
1786	BETTLE, William	"Hussar" "Goliath"	Pts	Jun	324
	alias BETTEL				
1762	BETTON, Giles		Pts	Feb	41
1774	Mary		Salop	Jul	256
1767	Richard		Salop	Jul	254
1755	BETTRIDGE, Charles		Middlesex	Mar	67
1764	William		Pts	Oct	377
	alias BRETTRIDGE				
1782	BETTS, Ann		Surrey	Feb	64
1784	Anne,		Cambridge	Jul	365
	alias Ann				
1787	Anne		Middlesex	Feb	52
1771	Avice		Middlesex	Apr	143
1769	Charles		Norfolk	Dec	406
1800	Charles, the Elder		Surrey	Mar	174
1768	Francis		Middlesex	Jul	268
1775	George		Surrey	Dec	455
1768	Hannah	Limited Probate	Middlesex	Nov	401
1772	Isaac		Middlesex	Feb	36
1800	James		Surrey	Aug	575
1769	Jane		Middlesex	Dec	404
1769	Jane	Double Probate Will regd this month	Middlesex	Dec	
1759	John		Pts	Jan	6
1761	John		Pts	Mar	83
1770	John		Middlesex	Apr	130
1793	John		Middlesex	Dec	581

BETTS (Contd)

Year	Name	Notes	County	Month	No.
1796	John	A with W of Goods unad Will regd December 1793	Middlesex	Jan	
1751	Joseph		Suffolk	Jun	167
1789	Joseph		Gloucester	Jun	297
1764	Margaret		Middlesex	Mar	80
1785	Margaret		Kent	Feb	64
1759	Martha		Middlesex	Oct	319
1796	Mary alias BETT		Middlesex	Dec	592
1754	Maurice		Essex	Dec	320
1792	Nathaniel		Middlesex	Feb	58
1767	Nicholas	A with W	Essex	Apr	123
1764	Patience		Middlesex	Mar	80
1774	Peter		Middlesex	Jan	3
1750	Sarah		Surrey	Jan	3
1773	Sarah		Norfolk	Jul	279
1762	Thomas		Kent	May	185
1769	Thomas		Middlesex	Jun	196
1794	Thomas		Kent	Mar	122
1778	Thomasine alias BETT, Thomasin		Middlesex	Feb	50
1778	Thomasine alias BETT, Thomasin	Double Probate Will regd this month	Middlesex	Feb	
1788	William	A with W	Kent	May	232
1798	William		Surrey	Jan	3
1776	BETTSON, Robert		Pts	Dec	486
1794	BETTSWORTH, Thomas alias BETTESWORTH		Middlesex	Mar	125
1762	William		London	Jan	5
1775	BETTY, Elizabeth		Middlesex	Oct	366
1760	John		Pts	Jan	2
1757	Richard		Pts	Jul	214
1770	William		Pts/Kent	May	173
1790	BEUERO, Isabella Francoise de	Limited Probate	Pts	Oct	
1780	BEUGHEM, VAN, The Honourable Jean Dominicque Hyacint		Pts	May	235
1751	BEUKELAAR, Lady Maria		Pts	Feb	37
1797	BEULWITZ, DE, Baron Ludewig Friederich	A with W	Pts	Aug	546
1758	BEUMER, Gerard	A with W	Pts	Jun	178
1764	BEUSCKOM, VAN, Elisabeth	Limited Probate	Pts	Aug	331
1767	BEUSECHUM VAN DER LINDEN, Hendrick alias Hendrik	Limited Probate	Pts	May	163
1756	BEUSECOM, VAN, Huybert		Pts	Jul	211
1787	BEUTZLER, Henry		Middlesex	Apr	156
1785	BEUZEVILLE, Elizabeth		Middlesex	Nov	543

1763	BEUZEVILLE, James		Middlesex	Jul	322
1799	James		Essex	Jan	8
1767	Peter		London	Aug	296
1782	Samuel, The Reverend		Middlesex	Jan	4
1776	Stephen		London	Jan	3
1784	Susannah		Middlesex	May	248
1766	BEVAN, Albertus		Essex	Dec	442
1764	Benjamin		Bedford	May	165
1780	Bridget		Carmarthen	May	237
1780	Bridget	Double Probate Will regd May last	Carmarthen	Dec	
1781	Charles		London	Jul	328
1784	Edward		Middlesex	Jan	4
1759	Francis	By Int. A with W	Pts	Jun	192
1763	Hannah		Middlesex	Mar	109
1791	Henry	Limited A with W	Essex	Jan	7
1777	Henry Ennew		Essex	Mar	99
1772	Isaac, Esq		Essex	Jan	3
1770	James		Bath	Jan	6
1794	Jane		Bristol	Jan	6
1751	Jarvis alias BIFFIN		Southampton	Dec	329
1755	John		Middlesex	Aug	210
1761	John		Bath	Jun	200
1776	John		Surrey	Apr	166
1779	John		Wiltshire	May	188
1786	John		Surrey	Feb	69
1796	John, Esq		Derby	May	240
1797	John, Esq	A with W	Glamorgan	Sep	584
1799	John		Bristol	Nov	760
1787	Joseph alias BEAVEAN		Brecon	Apr	159
1775	Mary		Bedford	Mar	84
1767	Paul		Glamorgan	Jul	255
1790	Paul		Kingston upon Hull	Feb	62
1778	Richard		Salop	Oct	388
1760	Rowland, Esq		Glamorgan	May	186
1773	Rowland		Surrey	Dec	459
1774	Sarah		Essex	Mar	81
1765	Silvanus		Middlesex	Jun	207
1783	Silvanus		Glamorgan	Sep	445
1762	Susanna		Surrey	Feb	42
1784	Susanna		Middlesex	Jun	308
1796	Susanna		Monmouth	Oct	489
1776	Thomas alias BEAVAN		London	Feb	55
1777	Thomas		Gloucester	Oct	406
1782	Thomas		Middlesex	Dec	572
1783	Thomas		London	Jun	284
1788	Thomas		Middlesex	Mar	114

	BEVAN (Contd)				
1796	Thomas		London	Aug	395
1773	Timothy		London	Apr	148
1786	Timothy		Middlesex	Jun	323
1761	William		Monmouth	Feb	45
1767	William	A with W	London	Sep	333
1774	William	A with W unad	London	Feb	
		Will regd 333 Legard			
1775	William		Middlesex	Nov	403
1783	William	A with W of Goods unad	London	Mar	
		Will regd 333 Legard			
		Last Grant February 1774			
1783	William	Ser	Pts	Aug	402
1786	William	A with W	Pembroke	Sep	464
1795	William		Middlesex	Oct	582
1800	William		Bristol	Dec	842
1794	William Hibbs, Esq		Middlesex	Nov	538
1790	Zacharias		Carmarthen	Jun	278
1759	BEVANS, Benjamin		Pts	Jan	4
1780	Charles	A with W	Pts	Aug	385
1776	David		Kent	Mar	112
	alias BEVENS				
1774	James		Middlesex	Apr	127
1766	John (2d)		Devon	Sep	329
	alias BEAVIN				
	alias BEAVEN				
	alias BEVIN				
1780	John		Pts	Jan	4
1761	Margaret		Middlesex	May	158
1770	William		Middlesex	Jan	6
1782	William		Pts	Feb	65
1792	BEVARN, Robert		Middlesex	Mar	129
1780	BEVELL, Samuel		Somerset	Jun	304
	alias BEVIL				
1761	BEVEN, Henry		Pts	Apr	117
1762	Jenkin		Pts	Jul	286
1769	John	Ser	Pts	Sep	301
	alias BEVIN				
1787	John		Middlesex	Apr	157
1795	John		Essex	Jan	4
1774	Richard		Sussex	Apr	128
1762	Thomas		Middlesex	Dec	493
1761	William	Ser	Pts	Jun	202
1750	BEVENAGE, VAN,	A with W	Pts	Dec	405
	Christiaan				
1756	BEVENINGTON, John		Pts	Oct	267
1776	BEVENS, David		Kent	Mar	112
	alias BEVANS				
1782	BEVER, Elizabeth		Surrey	Jan	6
1773	James		Middlesex	Nov	416
1771	Mary		Berkshire	Apr	144

	BEVER (Contd)				
1771	Mary		Surrey	Nov	431
1772	Mary	A with W of Goods unad Will regd November 1771	Surrey	May	
1773	Mary		Berkshire	Oct	382
1783	Nathaniel, Esq		Southampton	Nov	551
1792	Nathaniel, Esq	Double Probate Will regd 551 Cornwallis	Southampton	Mar	
1762	Samuel		Middlesex	Jun	234
1750	Sarah	A with W	York	Mar	67
1791	Thomas, Dr The Worshipful, late one of the Advocates of the Arches Court of Canterbury	Doctor of Laws	London	Nov	497
1795	BEVERAGE, Henry	"Carnatic" & "Europa". Ser	Pts	Mar	146
1768	BEVEREN, The Honourable Lord Theodorus Feltmande	Limited Probate	Pts	Aug	313
1774	BEVERIDGE, George	Ser	Middlesex	Jun	216
1778	James	Ser	N. Britain	Apr	145
1784	Richard	Store Ship"York"&"Burford"	Pts	Sep	193
1769	BEVERLEY, Ann		Southampton	Nov	368
1770	Gregory		Surrey	Aug	286
1754	Philadelphia		Essex	Apr	97
1764	Samuel		Pts	Apr	131
1785	Thomas		Middlesex	May	234
1773	BEVERLY, Elizabeth		Surrey	Jun	235
1797	John		Essex	Oct	627
1774	Sibella		Middlesex	Jul	256
1772	Vincent		Middlesex	Jun	208
1772	William		Middlesex	Oct	350
1795	William	A with W of Goods unad Will regd 350 Taverner	Middlesex	Dec	
1774	BEVERMEYER, Frans Herman, Esq alias Francis Herme	A with W	Pts	Dec	421
1788	BEVERS, Anthony		Pts	Mar	115
1770	The Right Honourable Galenus Trezel, Esq	Limited Probate	Pts	Dec	424
1774	Levina Pieternella alias VERWENT NOIRET	Limited Probate	Pts	May	208
1763	BEVERSTOCK, Daniel		Pts	Apr	166
1773	BEVERSTONE, Richard		Bristol	Feb	44
1791	BEVES, Benjamin		Exeter	Feb	53
1791	Benjamin		Southampton	Jun	265
1756	Richard		Pts/Southampton	May	128
1781	Samuel		Dorset	Oct	460
1796	Thomas		Surrey	Sep	446
1784	BEVIANS, John alias YAUXHALL	Ser	Pts	Mar	120

Year	Name	Will	Place	Month	Page
1780	BEVIL, Samuel alias BEVELL	Ser	Somerset	Jun	304
1790	BEVILL, Francis	A with W	Surrey	Mar	119
1766	Joan		Devon	May	171
1796	Thomas		Middlesex	Jul	347
1752	BEVIN, Arabella		Middlesex	Nov	268
1766	John (2d) alias BEAVIN alias BEAVEN alias BEVANS		Devon	Sep	329
1769	John alias BEVEN	Ser	Pts	Sep	301
1773	BEVINGTON, John		Warwick	Jun	235
1789	BEVINS, Henry		Middlesex	Mar	136
1787	Sarah		Middlesex	Mar	107
1769	BEVIS, Edward		Essex	Jun	195
1793	Emanuel	"Alfred"	Pts	May	244
1788	George	"Europe"	Pts	May	227
1784	James		Pts	Jan	7
1786	James		Dorset	May	263
1769	Joanna		Middlesex	Apr	114
1758	John		Pts	Dec	357
1759	John		Pts	Dec	384
1761	John	Ser	Southampton	Dec	422
1791	John		Dorset	May	211
1783	Judith		Devon	Jan	2
1759	Margaret		Devon	Nov	350
1750	Miles		Peterborough	May	140
1785	Samuel	A with W and Codicil of Goods unad Will regd 234 St. Eloy	Middlesex	Jan	
1788	Thomas		Wiltshire	Mar	119
1750	William		Pts	May	139
1757	William		Southampton	Nov	322
1758	BEVOIS, Thomas, Esq		Bath	May	139
1791	BEVOR, Thomas, Dr	Doctor of Laws	London	Nov	497
1769	BEW, John		Oxford	Aug	274
1795	Lucy		Berkshire	Feb	66
1787	Richard		Berkshire	Apr	160
1794	Timothy		London	Mar	125
1792	BEWES, Daniel alias BAWES		Middlesex	Oct	498
1793	Harry, Esq		Devon	Jun	299
1768	Thomas, Esq		Devon	Mar	94
1753	BEWICK, Robert		Newcastle/Tyne	Dec	308
1775	BEWICKE, Alice		Surrey	Nov	404
1774	Calverley		Surrey	Feb	40
1794	Dorothy		Surrey	May	241
1762	Elizabeth	A with W	Surrey	Oct	413
1799	Wilson, The Reverend	Dr. in Divinity	Hereford	Mar	168
1774	BEWLAY, Edward		London	Aug	291

	BEWLAY (Contd)				
1784	Elizabeth		York	Oct	540
	alias JUDSON				
1773	Robert		York	Sep	352
1784	Robert, Esq		York	Sep	490
1798	BEWLEY, Barbara		Norfolk	Apr	236
	alias BEWLY				
1776	Charles		London	Oct	413
1767	Christopher		Hertford	Nov	400
1791	Christopher	A with W of Goods unad	Hertford	Nov	
		Will regd 400 Legard			
1771	Elizabeth		Kent	Jun	241
	alias Elizbeth				
1783	Herbert	Ser.	Pts	Jul	338
1756	Jonathan		Middlesex	Jul	187
1763	Joshua		Middlesex	Apr	164
1774	Mary		Kent	Apr	130
1758	Richard		Pts	Nov	322
1754	Thomas		Coventry	Jul	189
1753	BEWLY, Ann		Surrey	Feb	39
1798	Barbara		Norfolk	Apr	236
	alias BEWLEY				
1783	William		Norfolk	Oct	495
1775	BEWSEY, Abell		Somerset	Sep	334
1778	Lazarus		Somerset	Aug	311
1785	Mary		Bristol	Dec	588
1784	Peter		Surrey	Aug	427
1772	BEWSHER, Joseph		Cumberland	Aug	284
1754	BEX, Anna Maria		Pts	Oct	266
1758	Christina Charlotta		Pts	Feb	30
1789	Josephus Carolus	Limited Probate	Pts	May	236
1797	Mary		Surrey	May	295
	alias BEXOE				
1795	BEXHILL, Thomas		Kent	Jan	5
1750	BEXLEY, Dudley		Kent	Oct	318
1797	BEXWELL, Robert	M.S."Sarah"	Pts	Dec	724
1751	BEY, Thomas		London	Apr	102
1794	BEYAART, Geertje	Limited Probate	Pts	Apr	184
1783	BEYARS, Thomas	Ser	Southampton	Jul	337
1762	BEYCHLINGEN, Marie		Pts	Aug	362
	Elizabeth Vanden				
	Heuvel Tot Said				
	Bartolotti, The Right				
	Honourable Madam,				
	Lady of Herivel Steyn				
1764	GESEG BARTOLOTTI.	Limited Probate	Pts	Nov	
	The Right Noble Willem				
	Hendrik. Lord of Blyeverve				
1761	BEYDE DE LOOSDRECHTEN,	Limited Probate	Pts	Oct	353
	Anna de Haze, Lady of				
	Mynden and				

1784	BEYEN, Anna Catharina	Limited Probate	Pts	Jun	309
1774	Arnolda Catharina alias VAN ESCH	Limited Probate	Pts	Jun	217
1799	BEYER, Christian Jacob		London	Apr	242
1777	Francis		London	Jan	4
1776	The Honourable Hendrick David Mispelblom	Limited Probate	Pts	Nov	448
1791	John		London	May	216
1763	Mary		Surrey	Mar	106
1757	Mispelblom Jacob, Esq, alias MISPELBLOM, Jacob		Pts		
1797	BEYHEW, Thomas	"Expedition". A with W	Pts	Aug	542
1767	BEYMOND, Samuel		Middlesex	Mar	85
1800	BEYNON, Edward		Surrey	Dec	837
1778	Francis, Esq		Northampton	May	185
1760	John		Glamorgan	Mar	87
1796	John	"Argonaut"	Pts	Feb	60
1771	Sarah		London	Sep	365
1788	William	A with W	Bristol	Oct	470
1795	William alias BYNON		Brecon	Apr	238
1783	BEYON, Phannel, Dr	Dr. in Divinity	Oxford	May	216
1761	BEZANT, Rebecca		Dorset	Nov	379
1766	BEZELEY, Elizabeth		Middlesex	Apr	126
1753	Hannah		London	Jul	194
1775	Joseph	By Int. Decree	London	Feb	41
1757	BEZELY, Anthony		Warwick	Feb	41
1773	BEZER, Leonard		Middlesex	Oct	383
1760	Mary	A with W	Surrey	Mar	89
1788	BEZLEY, Mary alias BISLEY	Another Grant this month	Middlesex	Apr	
1782	BEZOLL, William, Esq		Bath	Jan	6
1785	BHUK, Peter		Middlesex	Dec	585